Rethinking Machine Ethics in the Age of Ubiquitous Technology

Jeffrey White
KAIST, South Korea

Rick Searle
IEET, USA

A volume in the Advances in Human and Social Aspects of Technology (AHSAT) Book Series

Information Science REFERENCE

An Imprint of IGI Global

Managing Director:	Lindsay Johnston
Managing Editor:	Austin DeMarco
Director of Intellectual Property & Contracts:	Jan Travers
Acquisitions Editor:	Kayla Wolfe
Development Editor:	Caitlyn Martin
Cover Design:	Jason Mull

Published in the United States of America by
Information Science Reference (an imprint of IGI Global)
701 E. Chocolate Avenue
Hershey PA, USA 17033
Tel: 717-533-8845
Fax: 717-533-8661
E-mail: cust@igi-global.com
Web site: http://www.igi-global.com

Library of Congress Cataloging-in-Publication Data

Rethinking machine ethics in the age of ubiquitous technology / Jeffrey White and Rick Searle, editors.
    pages cm
  Includes bibliographical references and index.
  ISBN 978-1-4666-8592-5 (hardcover) -- ISBN 978-1-4666-8593-2 (ebook) 1. Technology--Moral and ethical aspects. 2. Automation--Social aspects. I. White, Jeffrey, 1969- II. Searle, Rick, 1972-
  BJ59.R48 2015
  174'.96--dc23
                                        2015019973

This book is published in the IGI Global book series Advances in Human and Social Aspects of Technology (AHSAT) (ISSN: 2328-1316; eISSN: 2328-1324)

British Cataloguing in Publication Data
A Cataloguing in Publication record for this book is available from the British Library.

All work contributed to this book is new, previously-unpublished material. The views expressed in this book are those of the authors, but not necessarily of the publisher.

For electronic access to this publication, please contact: eresources@igi-global.com.

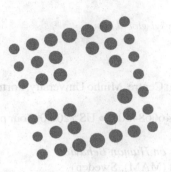

Advances in Human and Social Aspects of Technology (AHSAT) Book Series

Ashish Dwivedi
The University of Hull, UK

ISSN: 2328-1316
EISSN: 2328-1324

MISSION

In recent years, the societal impact of technology has been noted as we become increasingly more connected and are presented with more digital tools and devices. With the popularity of digital devices such as cell phones and tablets, it is crucial to consider the implications of our digital dependence and the presence of technology in our everyday lives.

The **Advances in Human and Social Aspects of Technology (AHSAT) Book Series** seeks to explore the ways in which society and human beings have been affected by technology and how the technological revolution has changed the way we conduct our lives as well as our behavior. The AHSAT book series aims to publish the most cutting-edge research on human behavior and interaction with technology and the ways in which the digital age is changing society.

COVERAGE

- Information ethics
- ICTs and human empowerment
- Computer-Mediated Communication
- Human-Computer Interaction
- Digital Identity
- Activism and ICTs
- Philosophy of technology
- Technology and Social Change
- Technoself
- Technology and Freedom of Speech

IGI Global is currently accepting manuscripts for publication within this series. To submit a proposal for a volume in this series, please contact our Acquisition Editors at Acquisitions@igi-global.com or visit: http://www.igi-global.com/publish/.

Titles in this Series

For a list of additional titles in this series, please visit: www.igi-global.com

Human Behavior, Psychology, and Social Interaction in the Digital Era
Anabela Mesquita (CICE – ISCAP/Polytechnic of Porto, Portugal & Algoritmi Centre, Minho University, Portugal) and Chia-Wen Tsai (Ming Chuan University, Taiwan)
Information Science Reference • copyright 2015 • 317pp • H/C (ISBN: 9781466684508) • US $200.00 (our price)

Contemporary Approaches to Activity Theory Interdisciplinary Perspectives on Human Behavior
Thomas Hansson (Blekinge Institute of Technology, School of Management (MAM), Sweden)
Information Science Reference • copyright 2015 • 437pp • H/C (ISBN: 9781466666030) • US $195.00 (our price)

Evolving Issues Surrounding Technoethics and Society in the Digital Age
Rocci Luppicini (University of Ottawa, Canada)
Information Science Reference • copyright 2014 • 317pp • H/C (ISBN: 9781466661226) • US $215.00 (our price)

Technological Advancements and the Impact of Actor-Network Theory
Arthur Tatnall (Victoria University, Australia)
Information Science Reference • copyright 2014 • 331pp • H/C (ISBN: 9781466661264) • US $195.00 (our price)

Gender Considerations and Influence in the Digital Media and Gaming Industry
Julie Prescott (University of Bolton, UK) and Julie Elizabeth McGurren (Codemasters, UK)
Information Science Reference • copyright 2014 • 357pp • H/C (ISBN: 9781466661424) • US $195.00 (our price)

Human-Computer Interfaces and Interactivity Emergent Research and Applications
Pedro Isaías (Universidade Aberta (Portuguese Open University), Portugal) and Katherine Blashki (Noroff University College, Norway)
Information Science Reference • copyright 2014 • 348pp • H/C (ISBN: 9781466662285) • US $200.00 (our price)

Political Campaigning in the Information Age
Ashu M. G. Solo (Maverick Technologies America Inc., USA)
Information Science Reference • copyright 2014 • 359pp • H/C (ISBN: 9781466660625) • US $210.00 (our price)

Handbook of Research on Political Activism in the Information Age
Ashu M. G. Solo (Maverick Technologies America Inc., USA)
Information Science Reference • copyright 2014 • 498pp • H/C (ISBN: 9781466660663) • US $275.00 (our price)

Interdisciplinary Applications of Agent-Based Social Simulation and Modeling
Diana Francisca Adamatti (Universidade Federal do Rio Grande, Brasil) Graçaliz Pereira Dimuro (Universidade Federal do Rio Grande, Brasil) and Helder Coelho (Universidade de Lisboa, Portugal)

www.igi-global.com

701 E. Chocolate Ave., Hershey, PA 17033
Order online at www.igi-global.com or call 717-533-8845 x100
To place a standing order for titles released in this series, contact: cust@igi-global.com
Mon-Fri 8:00 am - 5:00 pm (est) or fax 24 hours a day 717-533-8661

Editorial Advisory Board

Table of Contents

Detailed Table of Contents

Section 1
On the Cusp: Critical Appraisals of a Growing Dependency on Intelligent Machines

For nearly two decades the Internet has been thought to presage two radically different political destinies. A dystopian outcome where that architecture becomes a sort of global panopticon used to monitor and manipulate its occupants and a utopian one where politics takes on anarchic and democratic which the heightened interconnection of the Internet makes possible. This essay uses these dichotomous possibilities as a way to understand how the Internet has evolved over the past generation, and how this development has been interpreted in the hopes of providing a clarified intellectual framework through which choices regarding its regulation and shaping in the public interest can be made.

What limitations are we willing to accept on our development of new technologies? The shared sense among a great many of the idealistic supporters of our ever-growing range of tools and abilities is that the acquisition of knowledge is always a positive gain for the entirety of humanity, and that therefore there should be no (or few) restrictions on continued technology research. This mythology, which descends from the arrival of exclusive Humanism from the Enlightenment onwards, has become one of the greatest moral and prudential threats to human existence because it removes the possibility of accurately assessing the moral implications of our technology. Against this prevailing ethos of unbounded technological incrementalism, this essay uses the pejorative term cyberfetish to mark our dependence upon, and inability to accurately assess, our technology.

Chapter 3

Jared Gassen, JMG Advising, USA
Nak Young Seong, Independent Scholar, South Korea

This chapter explores machine ethics within the larger context of the natural system from which it springs. While computing power and computing machines have grown exponentially since the twentieth century, the foundation for this growth is the planet's natural resources, which may not be able to sustain this type of continual exponential growth. This chapter explores some of the basic natural limiting factors that may prohibit computing power if solutions are not found. Specifically, the chapter explores limitations from: population growth, e-waste, rare earth minerals, water, oil, and energy production. Within this context, possible solutions for producing machines ethically are briefly explored.

Section 2
From the Outside In: Intelligent Machine Technologies as a Window on Human Morality both as Evolved and as Evident in Internet Discourse, Today

Chapter 4

Fernando da Costa Cardoso, Universidade Nova de Lisboa, Portugal
Luís Moniz Pereira, Universidade Nova de Lisboa, Portugal

In this chapter we set forth a case study of the integration of philosophy and computer science using artificial agents, beings ruled by abductive logic and emergent behavior. Our first step in this chapter is to highlight different models that we developed of such agents (a set of them related with evolutionary game theory and one model of a narrative storyteller robot). As we indicate, each model exemplifies different aspects of the bottom of the hill of autonomy as an emergent property of artificial systems specified through three aspects ("Self control", "Adaptivity to the environment" and "Response to environment"). In summary, our conception is that autonomy, when presented as an emergent characteristic, could fill the important place given it by elaborations in philosophical ethics and one that leads us to a clearer comprehension of where to direct our efforts in the field of artificial agents. We conclude this chapter with the notion that this reevaluation of autonomy is necessary for the enhanced comprehension of human morality.

Chapter 5

Rafal Rzepka, Hokkaido University, Japan
Kenji Araki, Hokkaido University, Japan

This chapter introduces an approach and methods for creating a system that refers to human experiences and thoughts about these experiences in order to ethically evaluate other parties', and in a long run, its own actions. It is shown how applying text mining techniques can enrich machine's knowledge about the real world and how this knowledge could be helpful in the difficult realm of moral relativity. Possibilities of simulating empathy and applying proposed methods to various approaches are introduced together with discussion on the possibility of applying growing knowledge base to artificial agents for particular purposes, from simple housework robots to moral advisors, which could refer to millions of different experiences had by people in various cultures. The experimental results show efficiency improvements when compared to previous research and also discuss the problems with fair evaluation of moral and immoral acts.

Section 3
From the Inside Out: The Ethics of Human Enhancement from Moral Perception to Competition in the Workplace

Chapter 6

The purpose of this chapter is to conceptualize cognitive nanorobots, an ethics of perception, and machine ethics interfaces. Three areas are developed as a foundational background. First is the context and definition of cognitive nanorobots (nano-scale machines that could be deployed to facilitate, aid, and improve the processes of cognition like perception and memory as a sort of neural nano-prosthetics). Second is philosophical concepts from Bergson and Deleuze regarding perception and memory, and time, image, difference, becoming, and reality. Third is a summary of traditional models of ethics (Ethics 1.0). These building blocks are then used to connect perception and ethics in the concept of machine ethics interfaces, for which an ethics of perception is required, and where an ethics of immanence (Ethics 2.0) is most appropriate. Finally, killer applications of cognitive nanorobots, and their limitations (neural data privacy rights and cognitive viruses) and future prospects are discussed.

Chapter 7

The purpose of this chapter is on issue of fairness and equity in corporations and organizational settings due to advantages received as a result of human enhancement. In so doing, the purpose of this chapter will also analyze the paradigms of bioethics and (business) ethics and legality will be utilized in analyzing the issue of fairness and equity in corporations and organizational settings due to advantages received as a result of human enhancement. Human enhancement, used in this chapter, includes any activity by which we improve our bodies, minds, or abilities beyond what we regard today as normal. In relations to advantages in corporations and organizational settings, human enhancement, used in this chapter, means ways to make functional changes to human characteristic, also referred to as neuro-cognitive enhancements, beyond what we regard as typical, normal, or statistically normal range of functioning for an individual.

Section 4
From Far to Near and Near to Far: The Ethics of Distancing Technologies in Education and Warfare

Chapter 8

The purpose of this chapter is to demonstrate that while unmanned systems certainly exacerbate some problems and cause us to rethink who we ought to hold morally responsible for military war crimes, traditional notions of responsibility are capable of dealing with the supposed 'responsibility gap' in unmanned warfare and that more moderate regulation will perhaps prove more important than an outright ban. It begins by exploring the conditions under which responsibility is typically delegated to humans and how these responsibility requirements are challenged in technological warfare. Following this is an examination of Robert Sparrow's notion of a 'responsibility gap' as it pertains to the deployment of fully autonomous weapons systems. It is argued that we can reach a solution by shifting to a forward-looking and functional sense of responsibility incorporating institutional agents and ensuring that the human role in engineering and unleashing these systems is never overlooked.

Chapter 9

Ethical Responsibilities of Preserving Academicians in an Age of Mechanized Learning:
James E. Willis III, Indiana University, USA
Viktoria Alane Strunk, Independent Scholar, USA

In quickly-changing educational delivery modalities, the central role of the instructor is being redefined by technology. Examining some of the various causes with ethical frameworks of utilitarianism, relativism, and care ethics, the centrality of human agency in educational interaction is argued to be indispensable. While exploring the forefront of online, face-to-face, and massive open online courses, the shape and technique of teaching and learning as well as their corollary research methodologies are being modified with automated technology. Ethical engagement with new technologies like learning analytics, automatic tutors, and automated, rubric-driven graders is proposed to be a frontier of critical thinking.

Section 5
Wrapping Things Up, then Unwrapping Them Again: Integral Visions of Morality in a Technological World, Over Evolutionary Time, with Revolutionary Means, and with Open Questions about the Final Purpose of It All

Chapter 10
Luís Moniz Pereira, Universidade Nova de Lisboa, Portugal
Ari Saptawijaya, Universidade Nova de Lisboa, Portugal & Universitas Indonesia, Indonesia

We address problems in machine ethics dealt with using computational techniques. Our research has focused on Computational Logic, particularly Logic Programming, and its appropriateness to model morality, namely moral permissibility, its justification, and the dual-process of moral judgments regarding the realm of the individual. In the collective realm, we, using Evolutionary Game Theory in populations of individuals, have studied norms and morality emergence computationally. These, to start with, are not equipped with much cognitive capability, and simply act from a predetermined set of actions. Our research shows that the introduction of cognitive capabilities, such as intention recognition, commitment, and apology, separately and jointly, reinforce the emergence of cooperation in populations, comparatively to their absence. Bridging such capabilities between the two realms helps understand the emergent ethical behavior of agents in groups, and implements them not just in simulations, but in the world of future robots and their swarms. Evolutionary Anthropology provides teachings.

Chapter 11
Rick Searle, IEET, USA

We are at the cusp of a revolution in the development of autonomous weapons, yet current arguments both for and against such weapons are insufficient to the task at hand. In the context of Just war theory, arguments for and against the use of autonomous weapons focus on Jus in bello and in doing so miss addressing the implications of these weapons for the two other aspects of that theory- Jus ad bellum and Jus post bellum. This paper argues that fully autonomous weapons would likely undermine adherence to the Jus ad bellum and Jus post bellum prescriptions of Just war theory, but remote controlled weapons, if designed with ethical concerns in mind, might improve adherence to all of the theory's prescriptions compared to war as currently waged from a distance, as well as help to undo the occlusion of violence which has been a fundamental characteristic of all forms of modern war.

Chapter 12
Aleksandar Malecic, University of Nis, Serbia

In this chapter the author addresses a need for inclusion of all four Aristotle's causes (material, efficient, formal, and final) in modern science. Reality of modern physics (beyond Newtonian physics) and science of consciousness (and life and society) should include all four causes and tangled hierarchies (no scientific discipline is the most fundamental – the starting point for the author was Jung, then Rosen, and Aristotle was included much later). The four causes resemble rules for a machine or software (computation that "glues" everything together (Dodig-Crnkovic, 2012)), but a non-deterministic "machine" not replicable in a different medium. "Self-reference" from the title includes self-awareness, something seemingly not possible without final cause. On the other hand, this recognition of our (presumed) non-determinism and freedom might remind us to be even more self-aware and anticipatory. Computation, communication, networking, and memory as something technology is good at could contribute to that goal.

Foreword

Machine ethics is an attempt to apply reason to a field deeply inscribed by ancient hopes and fears, and powerful mythic archetypes. On the one hand, we are programmed to attribute mind and personality to anything that acts vaguely intentional. We want robo-Rover and robot Jeeves to serve us, and will quickly forget that they may lack consciousness, empathy or autonomy. On the other hand, we fear the legions of mechanical monsters waiting to march from the uncanny valley to end the human era. Attempts to filter out the actual risks that require mitigation, and the actual benefits that we may gain from the era of machine minds, requires the kind of determined and collective effort found in this volume.

In the last year the United States has been racked by a series of murders of black men at the hands of police, with increasingly outraged public responses. The police often insist that they are carrying out color-blind justice, despite evidence that even professed antiracists have racial biases deeply cooked into our neurology. Meanwhile U.S. foreign policy has been roiled by the debate over the collateral deaths caused by human-guided drones. We can easily imagine policing robots free of racial bias, and military robots that are better than remote humans at distinguishing combatants and civilians. Yet the prospect of "killer robots" is only met with Sturm und Drang.

Critics of lethal machines respond that consequentialist arguments about collateral damage and human fallibility miss the larger costs of turning over human decision-making to opaque and unaccountable "algocracy," rule by algorithms. I suspect that few of these critics would be willing to forego automobile air bags and automatic fire alarm systems, however, simply to maintain a human in the loop. We want the benefits of increasingly intelligent machines, but we also want to remain in control. Perhaps we can't have both. The essays in this volume help us think through these decisions, which some believe may be the most momentous that human beings ever make.

James J. Hughes
IEET, USA

James J. Hughes *received his doctorate in Sociology from the University of Chicago in 1994, and has taught health policy, medical sociology, bioethics and research methods at the University of Chicago, Northwestern University, the University of Connecticut and Trinity College. He emphasizes the ability to convey ideas to public audiences through accessible writing and oral presentations.*

Preface

The collection begins with three critical appraisals of the potential for high technology and intelligent machine solutions to resolve large-scale social, economic and environmental problems. Our first chapter is from Rick Searle, our co-editor. This chapter leads for two reasons. One, it is easily amplified by succeeding contributions as it touches on many of the themes running through the text as a whole. Rick confronts social-political problems arising with the increased automation and indeed out-sourcing of social-political life through intelligent machine technologies. From the reliance on smart-phones to locate friends and to coordinate political movements, to the automation of surveillance and thus to the dangers of technologically enforced neo-feudalism, Rick's purpose is profound, and the case that he presents disturbing. Writing that "the most potent critique against digital teleology is that it results in a kind of moral atrophy where human beings become the puppets of a world they have themselves dreamed up", Rick points out that some researchers pursuing artificial intelligence at once believe that their efforts will result in artifacts "that will then go on to destroy humanity." The relationship with the introductory pages of this preface is clear enough. Rick confronts the issue with candor constituting the second reason for this entry's lead role in the text:

Eschatological determinism of such a sort has more in common with religious fundamentalism than it does science, and raises serious doubts over the goals of those who have heretofore not faced major ethical or political design constraints when building the Internet or pursuing artificial intelligence. ... The fact of the matter is that technological development is less about human survival this century let alone the "destiny" of life in the universe than it is about political and economic power as it is manifest right now.

Our second chapter is from Chris Bateman, a philosopher of games, as well as a programmer and leading designer of narrative structures for games and virtual environments. Chris embraces the immediacy of our situation as established in the first chapter, setting out from the following dilemma: "Having decided that we *can* make anything, we must now ask the vital question: *should* we?" He weaves discussion on two burgeoning fields of intelligent machine technologies, automated transport and smart weaponry, in terms of Kantian, utilitarian and virtue based approaches to ethics of technology finding at the heart of these industries a deep yet neglected moral disconnect between stated aims and actual results, with the growing dependency on both the technologies and the distancing that they afford from unpleasant consequences constituting a profound symptom of what he terms "*cyberfetish*".

Through the glaring moral angle of cyberfetishism, Chris confronts social-political issues of a form and in a frame reinforcing Rick's first chapter. Chris' analysis draws out the co-dependent nature of the human propensity to fall under what the first chapter covers under the heading of "algocracy", the rule of automation through algorithm, with human beings ultimately molded in service to the medium of their own ignoble dependency. Chris' cyberfetish drags into the open the essence of technology, that it is habit incarnate, not only addictive but an externalization and artifactualization of dependency, with the technological world of our making directly affording the exercise of recently acquired tastes and supporting habits. Should one generation's habits prefigure the freedom of future generations to embody different habits, healthier habits, as these prior habits are entrenched in layers of technological dependence? Through his discussion, Chris' question thus becomes not so much what are we to build, but for what world of affordances do we wish to be held accountable.

Our third chapter continues this critical revision of the promise of smart-machines, digging into the problem of environmental sustainability from the perspective of sustainability scientist and civil engineer Nak Young Seong with editor and co-author Jared Gassen. On this view, history demonstrates that so-called technological "solutions" to social-political problems are not really solutions at all, and rather evidence shows them to be problems in disguise. New technologies require new materials, new industries, new logistic paths, and create new - sometimes unknown or unsuspected – pollutants and other problems arising from those. The authors take on controversial issues, such as the use of water resources expended to simply cool the massive NSA data collection center in Utah, and argue that the expense to future generations in the form of irremediable environmental damage cannot be justified. Rather than technological "solutions" causing only further technological problems in need of solution, the authors recommend that we step back and reassess our options in light of new ways of understanding sustainability and natural resources. Seong and Gassen advise for the employment of "low-tech" sustainable and effectively non-polluting energy resources like trees as responsible bases for future economies rather than hanging the hopes of humanity on inherently deadly and ultimately uncontrollable technologies like nuclear power only to require robotic laborers to eventually brave an irretrievably polluted and deadly toxic natural environment.

Where the third chapter hints at the evolutionary significance in any project pursuing a machine-leveraged break from the womb of human evolution, the fourth chapter penned by powerhouse Luis Moniz Pereira and Fernando Cardoso demonstrates how these natural forces may have shaped human moral capacities in the first place. From an evolutionary psychological perspective in which counterfactual reasoning arises alongside predictive capacities associated with capacities for belief revision in light of especially social information sourced to other members of an "ethical association" of moral agents, Cardoso and Pereira are able to illustrate how communication of moral commitment helps to strengthen in-group cooperation, thereby shedding light on some of the themes raised so far in this Preface as these communications become at least co-determinative of satisficing goal conditions going forward.

Their evolutionary psychological approach to modeling morally significant decision spaces is deceptively simple, as it plausibly accounts for the evolutionary emergence of group-level behavior patterns associated with moral and ethical abilities and institutions, respectively. The models are built from Prospective Logic Programming (PLP), and the authors review their program in some detail. Details aside, PLP "supports the view that autonomous agents are those capable of anticipating and reasoning about hypothetical future scenarios" with prospective cognition "essential for proactive agents working with partial information in dynamically changing environments." This describes us in our collective situation today. Cardoso and Pereira's confessedly "limited" agents in equally limited decision spaces regardless "do illustrate a rudimentary sort of reflective equilibrium over possible ends" and, with these consequences known, "meta-reasoning techniques are applied to weigh the partial scenarios" exactly as we weigh out possible ends for pursuing this or that line of scientific research, for example. Thus understood, the real promise of this approach is to be able to monitor the influence of different psychologically realistic pro-social characteristics on the emergence of ethical institutions within increasingly large populations of complementary agents, thus providing a medium for the simulation of similar problems in more complex decision environments and with more robust cognitive agents in the future. Luis and Fernando conclude by pointing to future work in the simulation of imitation, deception, and emulation at the agent level, and thusly they expect to refine our understanding of morality as an evolutionarily emergent property, writing confidently that "future work further integrating moral philosophy with programming will establish necessary logical supports to complete the task" and that "although the processes within us are complex, their complexity is not inaccessible" to properly configured computational models thereof. Models like these are great tools for policy-makers and social engineers going forward, and a good deal of the general project in intelligent machines depends on the value of these kinds of simulations in delivering on some of their anticipated promise in helping to solve coordination problems in realizing a healthy, organic and flourishing yet technologically rich world.

Where Fernando and Luis offer an illustrative logic of human morality and the growth of human ethical institutions through the enactment thereof, our fifth chapter develops a mirror on morality also from an evolutionary foundation but here through the smart manipulation of "big data". Rafal Rzepka and Kenji Araki of the Graduate School of Information Science and Technology at Hokkaido University detail the use of text-mining techniques to build a portrait of contextually dependent morally significant terms as they are used by human beings in everyday (online) life, and from this battery of information deliver representative judgments in similar contexts. They adopt a bottom-up intuitionist perspective, allowing a portrait of morality to arise from everyday moral language rather than have episodes cherry-picked to suit model-theoretical preconceptions of moral conduct in order to capture the emotional motivations of moral action, "empathy", writing that "evolution equipped us with emotional reactions that were originally meant for survival, and then to flourish as societies" at least in part through the expression of such feelings. One advantage of this approach is that they are able to "take advantage of the fact that, for the time being, the only constantly growing data that is relatively easy to process is textual" and to use this text-based, symbolic information to reliably gauge moral judgments elicited through human moral emotional mechanisms. Unlike that of the previous chapter, their approach does not involve the reduction to fairy-tale terms of complex moral dilemmas, and rather avoids "sophisticated algorithms" in order to "concentrate on automatically collecting and analyzing descriptions of human behaviors" during "everyday life situations available to current or near future devices with natural language processing capabilities." Thusly, Rafal and Kenji provide both a portrait of morality as actually expressed, as a sort of mirror on a "fourth-person" moral construct, as well as an approach to data-set modeling useful in evaluating expressed moral judgments of current and future first-personal agents relative context.

The potential for moral web-bots auto-texting to influence online discourse is a scary prospect, and quite near given the fifth chapter. In our sixth chapter, Melanie Swan looks behind the moral responses, into the minds of the respondents, themselves. Melanie confronts the issue of "reality" as a public, ethical sphere, open to private manipulation, noting that this only becomes an issue as technologies empower the direct manipulation of everyday perception and action, with her focus being the dedicated industry of perception management through the physical integration of human perceivers with smart perception management nano-machines. She speculates over possible "killer applications" for perception management technologies proffered by "nanocognition", including memory management services which nullify painful memories by destroying neural assemblies encoding them, "bias reduction" as a means for physically correcting for error-prone prejudice, and even the direct sharing of point-of-view experience, suggesting possibilities for conflict resolution. Possible applications like these raise issues of "neural privacy" – as neural structures embody information, how should this information be dealt with, perhaps as a commodity or as a matter of state censorship and law enforcement? Tools such as those under development by the authors of the previous, fifth chapter, may well serve as means for the monitoring of large-scale social engineering projects employing technologies such as those under Melanie's scope, perhaps eventually prior to the literal expression of moral emotion altogether. Her chapter also resonates with the deep themes that had established themselves in the collection thusfar, recalling for instance Chris Bateman's "cyberfetish" from the second chapter, and with her treatment of technological co-dependency feeding equally well Seong and Gassen's contribution. For example, Melanie's discussion allows us to ask if the best use of natural resources is in the development of technologies helping us to perceive only pleasant things, or permitted things, or if these resources are best directed to other ends. It may well be a symptom of a collective human cyberfetish to expect intelligent machines to make all of our painful memories go away, and to fashion new ones only the way that we would want them beforehand.

Our seventh chapter continues the assay of ethical implications due transformative human integration with intelligent machine technologies. Focusing on human enhancement in competitive – especially business - environments in terms of the "biopolitics" of human-machine integration, the author, Ben Tran, asks "whether enhancement technologies will actually make our lives happier". Ben delineates ethics of human enhancement issues according to an "expanding circle" of individual, professional and societal levels of organization. Defining *"societal concerns"* as "the broad interests of society, which may be frustrated by the adoption of human enhancement", Ben follows medicine in distinguishing between enhancement and repair, drawing into critical view the costs – especially societal costs – due the over-emphasis away from reparative, pro-social applications of technology and towards selfish, personal performance oriented applications. In the competitive business environment, wherein pressures for performance are high, what are the implications of a 'pay *to be able to* play' ethics of human enhancement? One may become a better stockbroker due to an integration with an intelligent machine, or through "nanocognition" for example, but is this making one also a better person? A better world? Opening with review of ethical approaches to these issues, the broad concern for the transformative influence of technology on human beings remains at the fore. Ben's chapter affords a critical reflection on immediate business culture, as concerns for autonomy, sustainability, and virtue are shelved in the face of threats from competitors, yet it is in this environment that everyday people – us - live, adapt or die, and express their moral judgments. Through our collaboration, we make it this way.

Jai Galliot's chapter, our eighth, with welcome candor braves the so-called "responsibility gap" between consequence and locus of responsibility as it appears to be enlarged through the distancing afforded intelligent machines in an already cloudy field of automated warfare. Jai writes that moral responsibility is located in agents which "intentionally make a free and informed causal contribution to any act in question, meaning that they must be aware of the relevant facts and consequences of their actions, having arrived at the decision to act independently of coercion and were able to take alternative actions based on their knowledge of the facts" and moves from here to discuss ways in which technologically mediated agency including semi-autonomous war machines complicate matters. For example, he deftly isolates the ways in which distant drone operators are unable to form "a view of the 'bigger picture' … perhaps limiting responsibility" and rather pursues again a central theme in preceding contributions, that we integrate the machines as we integrate others with limited responsibility, as partly responsible. Jai writes that "We need to move away from the largely insufficient notion of individual responsibility, upon which we typically rely, and move towards a more complex notion of collective responsibility, which has the means and scope to include non-human action." One way to smooth this integration is to level morality down to a common denominator, and Jai endorses such a pass "primarily" because "classical accounts raise endless questions concerning free will and intentionality" insoluble "from a practical perspective aimed at achieving results here and now." His approach is instead to "conceive of moral responsibility as less of an individual duty and more of a role that is actively defined by pragmatic group norms" with the upshot, on his account, being that we can then begin to ascribe responsibility to institutions and machine agents for the roles that they fulfill in achieving consequences worthy of moral reprobation, and with "the greatest share of responsibility … ascribed to the most capable agents."

Where Jai's focus is on military applications of intelligent machines and the ethical distance afforded human operators thereof, the next and ninth chapter takes on the ethical implications of distancing, and de-distancing, technologies in the field of education. The situation as described by authors James Willis III and Viktoria Strunk is clear, with discourse in "ethics in technology, specifically at the granular level of learning analytics … at an intellectual crossroads." And, their warning for educators especially is no less dire: "Unless principled ideas are brought within the public sphere of technological development, the speed of scientific innovation will render ethics of technology misguided at best and obsolete at worst." For ethical discourse to become practically mute within the field of education is troubling as technology affects contemporary public and for-profit education in increasingly suspect ways. For instance, authors Willis and Strunk point out that "in near live-time, administrators, faculty members, and researchers are able to assess a student's activity, engagement, and potential outcome, through predictive algorithms". Bentham's "panopticon" comes immediately to mind, as this technology affords the potential to dramatically reduce the costs of oversight around few distanced administrators. This trend is further exacerbated by MOOCs and AI, whereby the monetization of education encourages the removal of human educators from the financial equation altogether. Willis and Strunk note:

In late 2014, a company that provides online professional development notified its adjunct instructors that their current positions will cease to exist due to computer-mediated, algorithmic response to discussion posts, supplemented with "peer-to-peer" dialogue. While the tenets of computer-based interaction and peer-to-peer assessment may be debated, the replacement of human expertise with computer-generated responses gives personal evidence of the replacement of the scholar. The age of automated teaching is nigh.

Running through this chapter's discussion is the sense of education – and life – as an art, as opposed to the sense of education as a sort of machining, and of course this wing of the division runs through Dewey and Peirce to the Greeks. From this traditional stance, Willis and Strunk propose that the goal of education for educators remains for "students to learn from their mistakes and be able to apply those skills." However, with education coming increasingly under the influence of increasingly automated economies of scale, pressures from "the now accepted *business* model of education", alongside social pressures to deliver education in relatively easily quantifiable pursuits like Science, Technology, Engineering and Mathematics (STEM), are mounting against the retention of this professional, practical, and ultimately democratic political attitude. Willis and Strunk write: "Because there is money to be made in education, it is easily accepted for many in the business world to think of students as customers, education as a service/end product, and faculty as replaceable entertainers." This monetization of education has infiltrated scholarship, as professors are hired to teach but are evaluated on (quantity of) publications. One casualty has been the quality of published scholarship, with scandals involving falsified experimental data common enough. Instead of rewarding pro-social education, the monetization of education has turned "publish-or-perish" into "publish-and-profit", a model fitting for a novelist, but undeserving of the academy as traditionally conceived. Finally, "pay-to-*open*-publish" digital platforms favor those with the financial resources to afford offering personal journal publications for free across the Internet. These being easily accessed to those without access to adequate university libraries come to dominate the field of ideas along with their authors, and so the model further deteriorates into simple finance. The academy is ruled by demagogues who personally profit from its podiums and the influence over culture that this represents, rather than satisfying the original, democratic aims of education.

The tenth chapter in this collection is a standout, placed here as an extension of the discussion on education from the realm of AI-assisted human education to that of the human assisted education of AIs. Opening with the recognition that research into AMAs is "not only important for equipping [artificial] agents with the capacity of making moral judgments, but also for helping us better understand [human] morality through the creation and testing of computational models of ethical theories", authors Ari Saptawijaya and Luis Pereira build an especially readable ethical bridge from individual morality to collective human ethics out of the aged timber of evolutionary game theory, resulting in a sprawling yet deeply grounded *tour de force* on human and artificial morality. They begin by reviewing foundational work in artificial agency and applications in morally significant contexts (e.g. medicine), and from there move quickly to review their logic programming (LP) approach to modeling morality, with the discussion illustrating how their work captures many hard points present in contemporary ethical discourse. They demonstrate how LP is able to articulate "trolley problems" popular in fields of experimental moral philosophy and neuro-ethics (typically imaging) studies, for example. Their framework, as in the previous chapter with Pereira, chapter 4, is deceptively simple as it quite powerfully captures these inherently dramatic moral decision spaces. This section on trolley problems is especially effective. Saptawijaya and Pereira are able to render the logic driving their models of individual moral reasoners in extremely clear terms while taking advantage of the narratives inherent in everyday discourse over similar moral dilemmas. To this compelling portrait of independent moral reasoning, the second section on collective morality contributes the lesson that "Added dependency on cooperation makes it more competitive to cooperate well" thus making it, for any individual agent, "advantageous to invest in shared morals in order to attract partners who will partake of mutual and balanced advantages." Their review of research in ethics at this level of organization covers some fascinating ground, including for example an evolutionary appropriation of conscience as traditionally understood. That Ari and Luis are able to integrate the individual with the collective consistently with traditional terms like conscience via traditional symbol-pushing LP models is a fascinating discussion. Readers primarily interested in this degree of analytical clarity would be well-advised to begin this volume with this chapter, number 10.

The eleventh chapter is from Rick Searle, co-editor and also author of the first chapter. Rick's entry serves as a capstone for this section on autonomy, education, evolution and violence. "Robots in Warfare and the Occultation of the Existential Nature of Violence" takes on now well-established positions on the ethics of artificial agents in the industry of war. Early on in his discussion, Rick fixes on an insight into the nature of the problem, writing that "the essential ethical question" is missed "by too strong a focus on technology" to such a degree that the "state of the technology decides the ethical questions" for us, as if – once the right tech is in place – we can finally turn our morality over to machines designed to do the work for us.

Rick is especially suspicious of the high-tech business of warfare, noting that a different set of incentives arise for "a military made up of human soldiers where the goal is to finish a conflict as quickly and with the least human damage (at least to one's own side)" than that arises for "manufactures of military robots" incentivized "to generate as much revenue as possible during a conflict" and even accompanied with "a perverse incentive to encourage conflict." Taking the just war tradition as his touchstone, Rick considers contributions of intelligent machine technologies to the processes leading up to and during war, drawing special attention to the democratic responsibility of free human beings to not engage in unjust wars regardless. To sharpen this point, he reminds us of the human costs of war, and not in dead but in terms of what had traditionally been referred to under the heading of "spiritual" or "psychic" damage. War breaks hearts, ruins lives, empties futures. And, war-enabling technologies, they afford a numbing distance from the purposeful ruin. Rick is able to trace the depths of implications to which I point now through current literature, coming to the question - from where arises the moral disgust required to stop systematic violence if not from the bereaved bellies of generations of morally wounded? In this way, Rick brings home one of the deep threads running through the contributions to this volume, that scholarship at every level eventually grounds out in the world that it helps to shape.

The final chapter of this volume comes from Aleksandar Malecic of the University of Nis, Serbia, and is the most difficult of the collection. The chapter attempts to articulate an elegant application of Aristotle's four causes across apparently different levels, or manifestations, of the material universe including human consciousness. Aleksandar sets out from the notion of a "strange loop" which describes the progress of a system as it moves upwards or downwards in a hierarchy, e.g. levels of organizational complexity, only to arrive at where it left. His discussion winds through an interesting review of quantum theories and gravitation, but strange loops are common to moral fables, old cultural lessons that remain in everyday practice, e.g. "rock, paper, scissors". Thus, this approach comes at the essentially embodied and embedded – situated – character of cognition in a way that preserves figurative connections with mystical and mythical appropriations of the human condition. Moreover, it adds something essential to naturally arising consciousness that challenges similar ascription to an artificial agent. Aleksandar writes:

Consciousness is not an epiphenomenon of Newtonian physics. Metabolism and repair in living beings are necessary ingredients of any really self-aware (containing the model of the environment and itself within the environment) entity capable to adapt its own point of view (context, formal cause) according to known circumstances.

The portrait here given is interesting because it effectively posits that consciousness arises from the embodied, embedded and anticipatory structure of cognition, and that this structure is itself common to all natural systems. Accordingly, Aleksandar writes that "Strange loops aren't a recipe for the creation of conscious machines in a causal world, so much as a requirement."

Aleksandar makes the case that artificial consciousness as typically conceived is impossible. Consciousness arises with purpose, purpose with final cause, and final cause – as essential to the form of any natural consciousness – necessarily involves a relationship between that arising consciousness and its unique end. Aleksandar writes:

In order to have a self-aware computer, one needs to figure out the way to create a program with "strange" causal loops. Since over thirty years after this idea was proposed there still aren't such self-aware algorithms and machines, one has to ask what is wrong with it.

Aleksandar's discussion is complicated by its breadth of implication. For one, it confronts us with the likelihood that our business with technology occludes an enlightening window on our natural condition which, so long as this view is blocked, denies an opportunity to reform our technological projects with this natural condition in view. In aiming for something other than consciousness in a machine, we run the risk of leveling human experience down to those processes obvious in the artificial instantiation thereof. We become intelligent machines, by default, unless – as Aleksandar so energetically proposes – we recognize that in this anticipatory structure of cognition, and agency, we have the power to choose those ends towards which we move. We have the power to direct ourselves, and to coordinate with others in the achievement of ends that are good, if not for the business of technology in its every established application, then for those who are born to live in terms of it.

Jeffrey White
Korean Advanced Institute of Science and Technology, KAIST, South Korea

Acknowledgment

We need to acknowledge the kind help received during work on this project. Especially, without the authors and reviewers that took part in the review process, this book would have been impossible. Some deserve mention by name. Many thanks go to Luis Pereira, Lorenzo Magnani, Woosuk Park, as well as my bothers Aaron and Justin White for their patient review of either chapters appearing in this text, long often erudite emails at all hours and on all subjects, or both, throughout the year 2014 as this project was coming together. Axel Gelfert deserves mention for his support, as do other members of the Editorial Advisory Board such as Edward Moad for always keeping his door open and Jared Gassen for going above and beyond on his own dime, Jun Tani for helping me to understand some important things recently. Ron Sun deserves unique thanks for taking on a still fuzzy and disaffected philosophy student so many years ago, for citing his work so many years later, and for his patient discourse over the bridge of time. Our thanks also go out to Phil Torres who provided insightful feedback on multiple occasions, and Haewon Seo deserves thanks for taking care of everything except for this book. Finally, James Hughes deserves special mention for allowing us to reach out to fellow writers through the Institute for Ethics and Emerging Technology. Along with these people, so many others have in one way or another helped to make this project possible from conception to realization, that to mention them all would require another book on the matter. It must be enough to note that their continued support is our great and lasting fortune. Thank you all.

Jeffrey White
KAIST, South Korea

Rick Searle
IEET, USA

Section 1

On the Cusp:
Critical Appraisals of a Growing Dependency on Intelligent Machines

Chapter 1
Algorithms versus Hive Minds and the Fate of Democracy

Rick Searle
IEET, USA

ABSTRACT

For nearly two decades the Internet has been thought to presage two radically different political destinies. A dystopian outcome where that architecture becomes a sort of global panopticon used to monitor and manipulate its occupants and a utopian one where politics takes on anarchic and democratic which the heightened interconnection of the Internet makes possible. This essay uses these dichotomous possibilities as a way to understand how the Internet has evolved over the past generation, and how this development has been interpreted in the hopes of providing a clarified intellectual framework through which choices regarding its regulation and shaping in the public interest can be made.

In 1997 just as the Internet was roaring into public consciousness the inventor of the VRML code, Mark Pesce, attempted to project forward the ultimate destiny of this new "realm" he had helped create. Holding that the telecommunications revolution would likely end in one of two radically different ways, Pesce wrote in his essay *Ignition*:

The power over this realm has been given to you. You are weaving the fabric of perception in information perceptualized. You could – if you choose – turn our world into a final panopticon – a prison where all can be seen and heard and judged by a single jailer. Or you could aim for its inverse, an asylum run by the inmates. The esoteric promise of cyberspace is of a rule where you do as you will; this ontology – already present in the complex system know as Internet – stands a good chance of being passed along to its organ of perception. (Pesce, 1997)

Certainly Pesce was onto something. As the Internet and its successor mobile technologies unfolded in the almost two decades following his essay it proved both the ultimate panopticon and a vector for the undermining of traditional centers of power. It gave us both the NSA and what political theorists characterized variously as "the end of power" (Naím, 2014) or "monitory democracy". (Keane, 2009)

DOI: 10.4018/978-1-4666-8592-5.ch001

What Pesce got wrong was that his two imagined destinies for the Internet wouldn't be radically different and mutually exclusive alternative futures, but would emerge in parallel with the rise of each in a sense serving to reinforce the other.

That, I think, has been our mistake. To see these two possible futures as alternatives rather than as intimately connected- a kind of future blindness that has prevented us from really grappling with the full political and philosophical implications of the digital age.

My task here is to dispel some of this blindness by providing a rough outline of the emergence of Pesce's feared "prison" with a "single jailer" and his hoped for "asylum run by the inmates" in the hope that better understanding our situation will provide us with viable escape routes.

The following essay is divided into three sections. The first section will look at various manifestations of Pesce's panopticon, and the algorithms that underpin it, which can be seen everywhere from finance, to the security state, to political campaigning, to criminal justice, to city management.

The second section will look at the inverse of this panopticon, the way in which the Internet has enabled lateral, almost leaderless movements, to burst onto the scene in the second decade of the 21 century. I characterize these movements and protests as "hive-minds", and in this section will trace both how they have succeeded, but more importantly, why they have so far failed to engender any lasting systemic change.

The third and concluding section will try to uncover some of the historical assumptions that underlie this technological architecture, and its political manifestations, which I will argue emerge from much older philosophical anxieties over what human beings can ultimately know and do.

MASS SURVEILLANCE AND THE RISE OF ALGORITHMS

Not all that long ago, people talked of the Internet as if it were a new and distinct domain- *cyberspace*-something separate from the real world with which we had long been acquainted. That is no longer the case, for what has happened over the last generation is that cyberspace has consumed the real world, it has become the overlay through which our reactions with reality are mediated. (Wertheim, 1999)

A peculiar model of how this mediation should work is now found across multiple domains. It is found in the way security services now operate, along with much of finance and commerce; it is the basis for new ways of responding to crime, and is deeply influencing the way we organize the cities of our increasingly urbanized planet. It is ultimately a model of *power* that has been made possible by the shrinking size of computer components and the spread of ubiquitous connectivity. It is a model that bears a chilling resemblance to Pesce's feared panopticon.

Well before the Snowden revelations, in an article largely ignored, James Bamford laid out how the NSA had built a massive data center in the desert of Utah where:

.....the NSA has turned its surveillance apparatus on the US and its citizens. It has established listening posts throughout the nation to collect and sift through billions of email messages and phone calls, whether they originate within the country or overseas. It has created a supercomputer of almost unimaginable speed to look for patterns and unscramble codes. Finally, the agency has begun building a place to store all the trillions of words and thoughts and whispers captured in its electronic net. (Bamford, 2012)

Subsequent revelations would uncover just how deep the tentacles of this architecture surveillance went, and just what a danger it was to traditional notions of privacy and civil liberties. Yet, as to the question of *who* had built this architecture, *who* had planted us with devices that recorded where we were and the people we interacted with: we had done it to ourselves.

The NSA could only even imagine building such a system because the private sector had been permitted to build an entire communications architecture on the basis of mass surveillance. It had taken the aftermath of dot com bubble and bust for companies to come up with a model of how to monetize the Internet, and almost all of the major tech companies that dominate the Internet, at least in America- and there are only a handful- Google, Face Book and Amazon, now follow some variant of this model.

That model was to aggregate all the sharing that the Internet seems to naturally produce and offer it, along with other "compliments" for "free" in exchange for one thing: the ability to monitor, measure and manipulate through advertising whoever uses their services. (Economist, 2012) The model went by the name of "personalization" and demanded in the words of Kevin Kelly: "... *total transparency. That is going to be the price. If you want to have total personalization, you have to be totally transparent.* (Stibel, 2009)

The idea of ubiquitous monitoring only made sense if the flood of information it produced could be effectively organized and searched for valuable pieces of information.

Here was where the revolution in algorithmization and artificial intelligence came into play. In the early 21st century much of individual social interaction came to be mediated by sorting algorithms from recommended movies to selected books, music, and even lovers. (Steiner, 2012)

To vastly oversimplify the matter, the way this worked was that the monitoring of individuals allowed them to be classed as "types" on the basis of which those individuals became "targets" for, among other things, products, criminal investigation, or scams. Due to the fact that the Internet had become one of the primary ways the individual interacted with the world algorithms defined who an individual was, if not to herself, then for others. (Pariser, 2011)

In this era of "Big Data", power flows towards those able to identify and act upon meaningful patterns. This has meant the empowerment not just of those with the best algorithms at discerning patterns, but of those that can act upon this information with the most *speed*. The area where such algorithmization is furthest along is in finance. (Patterson, 2010)

Here geography itself became subject to the contest between algorithms for the domination of time, with a 790 mile fiber optic trench run from Chicago to New York piecing through the granite of the Allegheny Mountains to shave off micro-seconds of trading time. (Slavin, 2011) By the early years of the 21st century, finance largely ceased to be under direct human control, and was now under the direction of such trading algorithms. (Patterson, 2010)

Of course, it wasn't the algorithms themselves that were driving this. For all their advances, computers remained as empty of real intelligence as ever. Rather, algorithms were a tool in the contest over wealth and power between human beings. (Lanier, 2014) And yet, even if it was "wetware" human beings that reaped the gains or suffered the losses from this contest, increasingly the game itself became one of machine against machine, or often bot against human being. (Sydell, 2014)

The first test of our faith in delegating decisions to algorithms should have come from the 2008 financial crisis, which their misuse was in part responsible for. In the early 2000s it was hoped that sophisticated algorithms combined with large processing power would allow traders to pierce the veil between present and future. As Scott Patterson wrote the pioneers of this algorithmic trading:

The Truth was a universal secret about the way the market worked that could only be discovered through mathematics. Revealed through studies of obscure patterns in the market, the Truth was the key to unlocking billions in profits. The quants built gigantic machines- turbocharged computers linked to financial markets around the globe- to search for the Truth, and to deploy it in their quest to make untold fortunes. The bigger the machine, the more Truth they knew, the more they could bet. And from that, they reasoned, the richer they would be. (Patterson, 2010 p. 8)

Like the competition over land by 19th century imperialist powers, algorithms were used by competing social and economic forces over the territory of *data*. The hunt for faster and better ways to parse data, and deliver it in ways "tailored" to the individual resulted in an artificial intelligence arms race with the major Internet powers both part of the state and outside of it vigorously pursuing and perfecting AI. To quote Andrew Ng of the Chinese search giant Baidu, "whoever wins AI wins the Internet". (Ng, 2014)

This desire to influence targets dovetailed almost perfectly with a revived behaviorism in psychology. As our machines became more rational, human beings, or at least it was being argued, became less so. A key component of tailoring to a targeted individual, which really meant influencing the individual to make preselected consumer and political choices, wasn't monitoring alone but surveillance followed by sophisticated forms of manipulation which were the product of research in burgeoning field of behavioral economics, so-called "nudging". (Thaler and Sunstein, 2008)

It would perhaps be bearable if all this data gathering on individuals and nudging were merely a matter companies trying to bend consumer choice, but the mass surveillance architecture, algorithmic organization, and manipulative psychology were rapidly bleeding into the *political* sphere. The NSA was one such example of political effects, but there was also the case that otherwise sclerotic political parties caught onto the worth of this type of information and these types of methods as well.

In 2012 the Democratic and Republican parties ran what were perhaps the most centralized campaigns since the dismantling of the party machines in the late 1960's. As excellently covered by Charles Duhigg of *The New York Times* both the Obama and Romney campaigns:

...had bought demographic data from companies that study details like voters' shopping histories, gambling tendencies, interest in get-rich-quick schemes, dating preferences and financial problems. The campaigns have planted software known as cookies on voters' computers to see if they frequent evangelical or erotic Web sites for clues to their moral perspectives. Voters who visit religious Web sites might be greeted with religion-friendly messages when they return to mittromney.com or barackobama.com. (Duhigg, 2012)

Yet it was in cities that political manifestation of algorithmization and mass surveillance seemed furthest along. Both developed and developing world cities are wooed by technology companies and eagerly embracing so-called "smart-cities" where the urban landscape is covered in sensors cameras and related technologies with all this data pumped into "control-centers", which coordinate management responses. Developed world cities, such as New York, have deployed such systems, (Singer, 2012) but the adoption of similar technologies in the developing world is more interesting for the simple fact that so much more of humanity lives, and if demographic projections are correct, will live, there where the problems of rapid urbanization are so much more acute. (Kilcullen, 2013)

Troubled cities such as Rio began enveloping themselves in a blanket of mass surveillance. Cities such as Chongqing, China, which has in a program dubbed "Peaceful Chongqing", installed 500,000 cameras to watch every corner of the city. (Townsend, 2014)

In addition to general city management systems, technology companies built huge data centers to monitor and respond to one of urban life's perennial problems- crime. Here is how the former CEO of Google, Eric Schmidt described one of the largest and most sophisticated of these crime centers- *Platforma Mexico:*

Housed in an underground bunker in the Secretariat of Public Security compound in Mexico City, this large database integrates intelligence, crime reports and real time data from surveillance cameras and other inputs from across the country. Specialized algorithms can extract patterns, project social graphs and monitor restive areas for violence and crime as well as for natural disasters and other emergencies. (Schmidt, 2013)

Almost unnoticed, such crime centers have proliferated both beyond and within the US, (Priest, 2011) and some were even heralding the arrival of the sorts of "predictive policing" that was a staple of science-fiction. (Karoliszyn, 2014)

Thus, vast areas of society have been fleshed out in ways that resemble something like Pesce's panopticon. If that were the whole of the story the future might be very dystopian indeed, but there is another side to it as well.

INMATES RUNNING THE ASYLUM: THE HIVE MIND

The fact that we have acquiesced in the construction of an unprecedented system of mass surveillance that is used largely by elites for commercial, financial, political and security purposes should lead to a realization that a great deal of Pesce's panopticon has already been built. It is a system that is too complex for human individuals to control and has been put under the direction of sophisticated algorithms that structure to their owners' purposes an ever increasing amount of human interactions and even our own self-understanding.

However, dark as all of this is, it does not mean that the anarchic and democratic aspects of the Internet Pesce had hoped for are not also present. The media theorists, Clay Shirky was not really wrong when he predicted in 2005 that the 21st century would be an "age of chaos" where loosely coordinated groups would have increasing leverage over society and would out-compete institutions that clung to information monopolies. The flatter and more loosely organized these groups, and the more they abandoned traditional goals such as the profit motive, the more effective, Shirky held, they would ultimately be. (Shirky, 2008)

The revolutions, revolts and protests in the second decade of the 21st century really did seem to embody the flat characteristics of hive minds that had been laid out by the technology writer Kevin Kelly almost twenty years before their eruption. Kelly in his 1994 book *Out of Control* saw in the rise of personal computers and the Internet that connected them the foretaste of a more anarchic, self-organizing, and non-centrally directed order of the hive a "vivi-system" that Kelly thought had four core features:

- The absence of imposed centralized control
- The autonomous nature of the subunits
- The high connectivity between subunits
- The webby nonlinearity of peers influencing peers. (Kelly, 1995)

5

The Indignado protests in Spain, the Occupy Wall Street Movement in the US, the crowds that toppled governments in Tunisia and Egypt in 2011, and shook Turkey and Brazil in 2013, or the 2014 protests over police brutality in Ferguson Missouri and elsewhere, to name just a few examples, lacked centralized control and were largely leaderless with sub-groups following their own scripts. As Manuel Castells, perhaps the premier theorists of the "networked age" argues these were lateral movements lacking clear revolutionary narratives and driven forward by interactions between individuals that did not belong to an overarching structure. (Castells, 2012)

The tool which made these protests possible was the mobile phone. From an insignificant number of luxury devices wielded by elites, cellular phones became the most rapidly ubiquitized device in human history during the first decade of the 21st century. By 2013 there were 6 billion of them- 4.5 billion of which were in the developing world. More people had access to cell phones than indoor toilets or clean water. (Townsend, 2014)

What sets the Internet era off from those that preceded it is the ease with which it facilitates collaboration between previously unconnected individuals. Steven Johnson calls the kinds of collaborative efforts by small groups enabled by ubiquitous Internet and mobile technologies "peer-to-peer" networks and sees in them a new form of post-representational democracy and a more fluid and citizen centered politics. (Johnson, 2012)

As almost ad hoc groups of like minded individuals have become empowered traditional institutions appear to have become increasingly weakened. The digital revolution, which has managed to put levels of computational capacity that had once been the possession solely of huge government agencies and large corporations into the hands of literally billions of individuals, really does seem to have had an effect on the ability of traditional power centers to exercise that power, making the control over events more difficult.

Moisés Naím, for one, argues that every large structure in society: armies, corporations, churches and unions are seeing their power decline and are being challenged by small and nimble upstarts empowered by cheap collaborative and coordinating technology. (Naím, 2014)

The communications revolution has significantly lowered the barriers to political organization and speech. Anyone can throw up a website and start organizing for or against some cause. What this has resulted in is a sort of *Cambrian explosion* of political organizations many of which take on the defense of some very specific political interest or cause. Politics as waged by such groups, at least in democratic countries, moves from being representational democracy to what the political theorist John Keane calls "monitory democracy" essentially a society in which media and citizen based groups, largely empowered by the Internet, continually monitor, challenge and check political power. (Keane, 2009)

Wikileaks would be a good example of monitory democracy in action, but an even more interesting case are hacktivists groups, most notably, Anonymous. Other than bringing tens of thousands into the streets, nothing seemed to get elite attention so much as the DoS attacks used by Anonymous whose Guy Fawkes masks, borrowed from the dystopian graphic novel and movie "V", became emblematic of the age of protest. (Olson, 2012)

Since 2011, Anonymous and its sister organization Lulz had gone from a group of pranksters and vandals to a movement with both political and moral aspects trying to impose penalties on what they held to be egregious abuses of power. With particular severity authorities went after these types of organizations that challenge elites' very control over the Internet. (Olson, 2012)

Still, one cannot help but be struck by the extent to which these manifestations of what I am calling the hive mind ultimately failed to live up to their political promise. None seemed to have staying power or proved able to fundamentally alter the structure or trajectory of their societies. Why did the protest movements fail?

One reason for their failure might be that, almost universally, the protest movements lacked clearly defined political goals. Whereas some of their supporters such as Manuel Castells, argued that the festive, non-goal centered, nature of protests such as those of the Indignados and Occupy Wall Street were a virtue, critics like Slavoj Žižek, coming from a tradition of unapologetic Marxism, thought the Occupy Movement needed to adopt a clear goal and push on that to avoid losing coherence. (Jones, 2011) Another critic, Evgeny Morozov, a constant gadfly to techno-optimists such as Shirky, even raised doubts as to whether the kinds of political activity encouraged by social media were effective at obtaining political goals at all. (Morozov, 2011)

Part of the failure of the protests movements, and even efforts to "update" democracy for the digital age, might have stemmed from a desire to have politics conform to technology rather than the other way round. While experiments in digital democracy in countries such as Argentina are to be lauded (Marcini, 2014), one may reasonably doubt whether the kinds of systemic changes contemporary societies require will really come about by making democratic participation more convenient and "app like."

Morozov has pointed out that the Internet often gives an *illusion* of participation and action rather than the real thing. We sign petitions or make donations and walk away thinking that we have really done something. Real change, on the other hand, probably requires much higher and Kierkegaardian levels of commitment that demand things like the loss of our career, our personal life, and in some cases the loss of life itself. The ease of "doing something" offered by the Internet, Morozov argues, might have a real corrosive effect on these kinds of necessary sacrifices as people exchanged virtual commitment for the real thing. (Morozov, 2011)

Consumer digital technology is largely built around the idea of "convenience" with the time between when one "clicks" for something and the time it was done or received to be kept to an absolute minimum. (Madrigal, 2014) Politics, however, almost by its nature, requires much longer stretches of time to unfold with political objectives sometimes taking a generation or longer to achieve.

As Hannah Arendt pointed out in her study on revolutions, one of the hallmarks of successful revolutions is that they establish "lasting institutions" that actually mark the end of political dispute, for a time, and provide a political community a stable world in which to act. (Arendt, 1963) Transforming such institutions through concerted political action doubtless takes a great deal of time, and the ideal is to leave structures which will not require such transformation again for perhaps decades. The promise of "app like" politics offers the illusion that institutional change is easy, while rapidly changing technology itself may make it difficult for "lasting institutions" and the law to exist in a stable form for long stretches of time without becoming obsolete.

If digital technology encourages a compression of our horizons in terms of time, it does the exact opposite in regards to space. One's location in the world seems to no longer be a limiting factor on one's ability to engage in *political* action. The Internet, in the eyes of some, is the harbinger and vehicle for truly global politics that supersedes "petty" national concerns. (Kelly, 2014)

Yet, political action that has become global and detached from the actor's location can have regressive as well as progressive aspects. (Gettleman, 2014) Even when engaged in for progressive ends such globalized politics risks fostering the same superficial illusion regarding what to be engaged in politics actually means that Morozov has identified.

On the one hand, the globalization of our political and moral concern is merely a reflection of our reality- we now live in what is very much *one world*. This has been the case long before the emergence of the Internet – think of the global movement to abolish slavery or the international labor movement in the 19th century, or the human rights movements and the push to end South African apartheid closer to our own day.

The danger of this is that the political commitments of the individual become so diffuse and detached from the political space which they actually inhabit, and presumably, if acting in concert with other proximate individuals, could more easily effect, that the injustices and failures within one's own society are not fully confronted and addressed. It is this *customization or personalization* resulting in political diffusion or atomization that might be another reason behind the failure of the protest movements to alter the political landscape.

On reflection we should find it strange that the very same people, such as Kevin Kelly, who are praising the severing of ties between political and geographical space, and heralding the emergence of the hive-mind are also promoting the "personalization" of individual's experience of the Internet. For what is at risk when one customizes information in such a way is that the individual may lose any connection to those who continue to share her physical space, while sharing very little of what were once public concerns, indeed, she might lose any shared idea of what those concerns even are. (Pariser, 2011)

The situation resembles something like China Melville's novel *The City and the City* where two separate and largely non-interacting cities occupy the exact same physical space: neither responsible, or even aware, of the other. (Melville, 2009)

The customization of political information that personalization offers might play a role in rising partisanship and ideological divisions that in turn paralyze and erode public trust in government. Rather than see this as a problem which has at least been supported by the way we have organized and used digital technology, some digital utopians see this as dysfunction as a symptom of our antiquated, pre-digital, notions of politics which we need to get beyond. Political decisions, they argue, should be made rationally, and based on the best available information. As Evgeny Morozov quotes the digital guru Tim O'Reilly:

…we have to actually start moving away from the notion that politics really has very much to do with governance. To the extent that we can fix things without politics, we'd be much better off. (Morozov, 2013)

Morozov argues that such a view represents a fundamental misunderstanding of what politics is. Politics is not about finding the "best" or most "rational" decision, even if we could assume such evaluations could actually be found. Rather, it is about conflict between different social forces, negotiation, and renegotiation over the configuration of a particular politically defined space.

The political theorist, Chantal Mouffe, thinks this misunderstanding of the meaning of politics is one of the core problems of neo-liberalism. Politics, for her,

is by its nature the realm of *agonism*, of rivalry between different political forces. The road away from our disillusion with politics is to recognize the naturalness of this agonism, while at the same time preventing it from becoming *antagonism,* the denial that others who share the same political space have the right to fight to define it on their own terms. (Mouffe, 2000)

Digital utopians such as O'Reilly have a much different solution to the problem the conflicts surrounding political decision making than the recognition that it is a natural part of the human condition- why not delegate such decisions to algorithms?

O'Reilly calls it "algorithmic regulation" the supplanting of messy human decision making by the "rational" algorithmic processing of machines. (Morozov, 2013)

Thus, ideas about the hive mind seem to circle back and become management or rule by algorithms. There is something inherent in the Internet itself, or the way it has been organized, that spins round-and-round between the rule of algorithms and the counter-claims of the hive mind.

Jaron Lanier has been perhaps the most articulate voice to emerge from within, rather than outside, Silicon Valley culture to have identified this, seeing it not merely as a matter of the flawed thinking found in digital technology, but as something that arises from the technology itself. Lanier seemed to put his finger on how the technological dynamic seemed to naturally give rise to Pesce's panopticon rather than a flatter more anarchic structure of a hive-mind even when those designing the systems wanted the latter.

Every attempt to create a bottom-up emergent network to coordinate human affairs also facilitates some new hub that inevitably becomes a center of power, even if that was not the intent. These days, if everything is open, anonymous, and copyable, then a search/analysis company with a bigger computer than normal people have access to will come along and measure and model everything that takes place, and then sell the resulting ability to influence events to third parties. The whole supposedly open system will contort itself to that Sovereign Server, creating a new form of centralized power. More openness doesn't work. A Linux always makes a Google. (Lanier, 2014)

In other words, the current technological dynamic mostly favors those who can centralize and process the data brought about by transparency and ubiquitous tracking and monitoring. The attempt to create conditions that support hive minds results in panopticons.

PHILOSOPHICAL REFLECTIONS

What I have attempted to do above is to uncover some of the ways Pesce's, now almost twenty year old prediction regarding the two possible paths the Internet might follow – towards becoming a panopticon, or conversely a lateral anarchic form of organization that I have characterized as a hive mind.

There is a way, however, to view these recent developments in terms of a longer history and from a philosophical perspective. Doing so allows us to see just how deeply rooted some of the ideas and aspirations are, which now express themselves in the form of digital and network technology. These philosophical currents might be said to be driving technological developments as much as technology itself.

As I will attempt to show the architecture of thought and power that has emerged from the digital revolution reflects key intellectual assumptions whose origins lie in much older philosophical anxieties regarding what human beings can ultimately know and do. Indeed, some digital utopians promise final liberation from these philosophical anxieties through the creation of a "post-human" world and pursue technological breakthroughs whose end is to bring about such an escape from the human condition.

The epistemological assumption that might be said to underlie the sometimes monomaniacal quest for more and more data profiled above in areas running from national security, to crime, to commerce, in its most extreme form is what is called digital ontology- the philosophy which holds that not merely *can* reality be represented in a series of binary numbers, but that the world itself *is* a digital representation. (Floridi, 2009) The exact origins of the idea is debatable, but surely one of the key dates of digital ontology's emergence was the 1989 essay, "It From Bit" by the physicists John Archibald Wheeler.

Otherwise put, every "it" — every particle, every field of force, even the space-time continuum itself — derives its function, its meaning, its very existence entirely — even if in some contexts indirectly — from the apparatus-elicited answers to yes-or-no questions, binary choices, bits. "It from bit" symbolizes the idea that every item of the physical world has at bottom — a very deep bottom, in most instances — an immaterial source and explanation; that which we call reality arises in the last analysis from the posing of yes-or-no questions and the registering of equipment-evoked responses; in short, that all things physical are information-theoretic in origin and that this is a participatory universe. (Wheeler, 1990)

Digital ontology has many flavors from Stephen Wolfram's idea that all complex structures are themselves examples of universal Turing machines (Wolfram, 2002) to those who argue that the universe in which we are living may itself be an advanced form of computer simulation. (Bostrom, 2003)

Only if some version of digital ontology is true would the perennial gulf between map and territory finally be overcome and the frantic race to connect and digitally represent every aspect of reality down to the finest detail actually make sense. The hope of many technologists is, to parse Jaron Lanier's phrase, to "represent reality to completion". (Lanier, 2010) It and bit would truly have become synonymous.

There is something of the 18th and early 19th century mathematician Pierre-Simon, marquis de Laplace's famous Demon about the quest:

We may regard the present state of the universe as the effect of its past and the cause of its future. An intellect which at a certain moment would know all forces that set nature in motion, and all positions of all items of which nature is composed, if this intellect were also vast enough to submit these data to analysis, it would embrace in a single formula the movements of the greatest bodies of the universe and those of the tiniest atom; for such an intellect nothing would be uncertain and the future just like the past would be present before its eyes. (Laplace, 1951)

Of course, the Demon of Laplace can also be understood to merely be another way to represent the omniscience of God, whose death, in the tradition of Western philosophy, resulted in a world where the existence of a true reality beyond that given to our senses could never be secured. The route to escaping this predicament has seemingly been found by tuning humanity itself into a version of Plato's demiurge who imposes upon the chaos of the world a self-created order. (Floridi, 2011) That is, the closer humanity itself can come to filling the role of Laplace's Demon the more the reality of the world beyond the human mind can be secured.

In a bizarre twist of irony, however, as we are flooded with ever larger streams of data it appears that the use of artificial intelligence becomes necessary to extract any meaningful patterns at all. As these algorithms become increasingly sophisticated it seems likely that we will reach a point where the connections they make between phenomena are no longer understood by human beings in the sense of causal connections or overarching theory. (Cowen, 2013)

What this seems to imply is that human beings will remain locked into their current epistemological borders and be unable to truly grasp all the features or comprehend the world as it truly is beyond our own limited perceptions and theories.

Some technologists are unlikely to find this troubling in that they see human intellect and the culture that has been built from it as a mere transitional phase towards a higher a better form of intelligence. Singularitarians, who can be found in some of the most innovative and influential Silicon Valley companies, predict the merger or replacement of human intelligence by that of machines sometime before the end of this century. (Kurzweil, 2005)

Digital teleology of such a sort results in a kind of moral atrophy where human beings become the puppets of a world they have themselves dreamed up. Something that is apparent in the work of a roboticist like Hugo de Garis who continues to pursue artificial intelligence even though he believes such work will result in the creation of what he calls "artilects" that will then go on to destroy humanity. (Garis, 2005)

Such eschatological determinism has more in common with religious fundamentalism than it does science, and raises serious doubts over the goals of those who have heretofore not faced major ethical or political design constraints when building the Internet or pursuing artificial intelligence. (Bostrom, 2014)

Thus, as in the tales of old, it is the gods who will save or destroy us, and though we may have ourselves created this new type of god we remain caught within our human limits.

If much of the underlying religious and philosophical assumptions regarding the death of God give some intellectual context to the quest to build an all-seeing panopticon, could it also be the case that the aspirations regarding the hive mind have similar origins?

It is at least a possibility, for the same imagined entity that allowed the individual to transcend their intellectual and perceptual solipsism also was the root of an imagined communion between individuals that allowed them to transcend their emotional and spiritual solipsism. The hive mind seems to promise that it can fulfill that role by bringing individuals together into one mind, yet here again, as made evidence by the hive mind's political failures to date, aspirations with ultimately religious origins collide with the cold stone of reality and show us again how difficult the human condition is to transcend.

The prophets and proponents of the hive mind would see us all become like "neurons" in a "global brain". The problem here is that to do so would have to deny what politics truly is: conflict between limited beings over contrasting perspectives on the past, present and goals for the future. Just as in the quest after omniscience we create instead incomprehensibility; in chasing after the hive mind we surrender the initiative to those forces bent on rolling back the degree of democracy we actually possess.

The future of democracy, indeed of humanity, may lie in successfully negotiating the space and tension between those parts of the human condition we wish and are forced to preserve and our now technologically enabled metaphysical and religious longings.

REFERENCES

Arendt, H. (1963). On Revolution. New York: Viking Press.

Bamford, J. (2012, March 13). The NSA Is Building the Country's Biggest Spy Center (Watch What You Say). Retrieved from http://www.wired.com.

Bostrom, N. (2003). Are You Living in a Computer Simulation? *Philosophical Quarterly* 53(211). 243-55.

Bostrom, N. (2014). Superintelligence: Paths, dangers, strategies. Oxford: Oxford University Press.

Castells, M. (2012). *Networks of Outrage and Hope: Social Movements in the Internet Age*. Cambridge, UK: Polity.

Cowen, T. (2013). Average is over: Powering America beyond the age of the great stagnation. New York: Penguin Group.

Duhigg, C. (2012, October 13). Campaigns Mine Personal Lives to Get Out Vote. *The New York Times*. Retrieved from http://www.nytimes.com/2012/10/14/us/politics/campaigns-mine-personal-lives-to-get-out-vote.html?pagewanted=all&_r=0

Floridi, L. (2009). Against Digital Ontology. Synthese. 151–178.

Floridi, L. (2011). The philosophy of information. Oxford. England: Oxford University Press.

Floridi, L. (2013, December 8). Enveloping the World How Reality Is Becoming AI Friendly - Keynote at *PT-AI 2013*. Retrieved from https://www.youtube.com/watch?v=D6lQ4Ko1Dbg

Fowler, R. B. (2002).

Garis, H. (2005). The Artilect War: Cosmists vs. Terrans. Palm Springs, CA: ETC Publications.

Gettleman, J. (2010, January 3). Americans' Role Seen in Uganda Anti-Gay Push. *The New York Times*.

Johnson, S. (2012). *Future Perfect: The Case for Progress in a Networked Age*. New York: Riverhead Books.

Jones, J. N. (2011, November 11). Six Questions for Slavoj Žižek. *Harper's Blog*. Retrieved from harpers.org/blog/2011/11/six-questions-for-slavoj-zizek/

Karoliszyn, H. (2014, September 3). Do We Want Minority Report Policing? *Aeon Magazine*. Retrieved from http://aeon.co/magazine/technology/do-we-want-minority-report-policing/

Keane, J. (2009). The Life and Death of Democracy. New York: W.W. Norton.

Kelly, K. (1995). Out of Control: The New Biology of Machines, Social Systems, and the Economic World (pp. 22). Reading, Mass.: Addison-Wesley.

Kilcullen, D. (2013). Out of the Mountains: The Coming Age of the Urban Guerrilla. New York: Oxford University Press.

Kurzweil, R. (2005). The Singularity Is Near: When Humans Transcend Biology. New York: Viking.

Lanier, J. (2010). You Are Not a Gadget: A Manifesto. (pp. 134). New York: Alfred A. Knopf.

Lanier, J. (2013). Who Owns the Future? New York: Simon and Schuster.

Lanier, J. (2014, November 14). The Myth Of AI. *Edge.org*. Retrieved from. http://edge.org/conversation/the-myth-of-ai

Laplace, P. (1951). Theorie analytique des probabilites. In F.W. Truscott & F.L. Emory. (Eds.), A Philosophical Essay on Probabilities. (6th Ed). New York: Dover Publications. (pp. 4).

Madrigal, A. (2014, July 23). Smart Things in a Not-Smart World. The Atlantic (Boston, Mass.). Retrieved from http://www.theatlantic.com/technology/archive/2014/07/there-are-only-12-quiet-places-left-in-america/374885/

Marcini, P. (2014, October 1). How to Upgrade Democracy for the Internet Era. *TED*.

Melville, C. (2009). The City & the City. New York: Del Rey Ballantine Books.

Morozov, E. (2011). The Net Delusion: The Dark Side of Internet Freedom. New York, NY: Public Affairs.

Morozov, E. (2013, January 1). The Meme Hustler. *The Baffler*. 22. Retrieved from http://www.thebaffler.com/articles/the-meme-hustler

Mouffe, C. (2000). The Democratic Paradox. London: Verso.

Naím, M. (2014). The End of Power From Boardrooms to Battlefields and Churches to States. New York: Basic Books.

Olson, P. (2012). We Are Anonymous: Inside the Hacker World of Lulzsec, Anonymous, and the Global Cyber Insurgency. New York: Little, Brown and Company.

Pariser, E. (2011). The Filter Bubble: What the Internet Is Hiding from You. New York: Penguin Press.

Patterson, S. (2010). The Quants: How a Small Band of Math Wizards Took over Wall St. and Nearly Destroyed It. New York: Crown.

Pesce, M. (1997, January 1). Ignition (A Ritual For the Festival of Brigit). *Hyper-real*. Retrieved from http://hyperreal.org/~mpesce/Ignition.html

Priest, D., & Arkin, W. M. (2011). Top Secret America: The Rise of the New American Security State. New York: Little, Brown and Company.

Schmidt, E., & Cohen, J. (2013). The New Digital Age: Reshaping the Future of People, Nations and Business (p. 174). New York: Random House.

Shirky, C. (2005, July 1). Institutions vs. Collaboration. *TED*.

Shirky, C. (2008). *Here Comes Everybody: The Power of Organizing without Organizations*. New York: Penguin Press.

Singer, N. (2012, March 3). Mission Control, Built for Cities. *The New York Times*. Retrieved from http://www.nytimes.com/2012/03/04/business/ibm-takes-smarter-cities-concept-to-rio-de-janeiro.html?pagewanted=all&_r=0

Slavin, K. (2011, July 1). "How Algorithms Shape Our World. *TED*. Retrieved from http://www.ted.com/talks/kevin_slavin_how_algorithms_shape_our_world

Steiner, C. (2012). Automate This: How Algorithms Came to Rule Our World. New York: Portfolio/Penguin.

Stibel, J. M. (2009). Breakpoint: Why the Web Will Implode, Search Will Be Obsolete, and Everything Else You Need to Know about Technology Is in Your Brain. New York: Palgrave Macmillan, (pp. 93).

Sydell, L. (2014, July 3). In A Battle For Web Traffic, Bad Bots Are Going After Grandma. National Public Radio. Retrieved from http://www.npr.org/blogs/alltechconsidered/2014/07/03/328196199/in-a-battle-for-web-traffic-bad-bots-are-going-after-grandma

Thaler, R. H., & Sunstein, C. (2008). Nudge: Improving Decisions about Health, Wealth, and Happiness. New Haven, Conn.: Yale University Press.

The Silicon Valley Letter. (2013). The Economist, 9. Retrieved from http://www.economist.com/blogs/babbage/2013/12/tech-firms-and-spies

Townsend, A. M. (2014). Smart Cities: Big Data, Civic Hackers, and the Quest for a New Utopia. New York: W.W Norton & Company.

Wertheim, M. (1999). The Pearly Gates of Cyberspace: A History of Space from Dante to the Internet. New York: W.W. Norton.

Wheeler, J. A. (1990). Information, physics, quantum: The search for links. In W. Zurek, Complexity, Entropy, and the Physics of Information. Redwood City, California: Addison-Wesley.

Wolfram, S. (2002). A New Kind of Science. Champaign, IL: Wolfram Media.

KEY TERMS AND DEFINITIONS

Algorithm: A set of rules and procedures used to organize information or processes usually reified through a machine or computer.

Artificial Intelligence: Computer algorithms and systems capable that exhibit cognitive behaviors such as language processing or pattern recognition normally reserved for human intelligence.

Democracy: A system of government where the citizens are empowered to make decisions affecting their political community.

Hive Mind: A form of non-hierarchical, lateral political and social organization that has been enabled by the Internet and mobile technologies.

Laplace's Demon: A hypothetical entity proposed by Pierre-Simon Laplace in 1814 to demonstrate the principle that the future is determined and that therefore complete knowledge of the present and the laws of nature would result in full knowledge of the future.

Panopticon: A system which centrally monitors and directs the action of those under it based on the hypothetical prison proposed by Jeremy Bentham in the 18th century.

Singularity: An imagined point in the future beyond which current human beings are not able to predict because it will consist of vastly superior forms of intelligence and explosive technological change.

Chapter 2
We Can Make Anything:
Should We?

Chris Bateman
University of Bolton, UK

ABSTRACT

What limitations are we willing to accept on our development of new technologies? The shared sense among a great many of the idealistic supporters of our ever-growing range of tools and abilities is that the acquisition of knowledge is always a positive gain for the entirety of humanity, and that therefore there should be no (or few) restrictions on continued technology research. This mythology, which descends from the arrival of exclusive Humanism from the Enlightenment onwards, has become one of the greatest moral and prudential threats to human existence because it removes the possibility of accurately assessing the moral implications of our technology. Against this prevailing ethos of unbounded technological incrementalism, this essay uses the pejorative term cyberfetish to mark our dependence upon, and inability to accurately assess, our technology.

CYBERFETISH AND THE WORLD OF TOMORROW

When Immanuel Kant and the other philosophers of the Enlightenment began their project, they set out to commence an Age of Reason, such that humanity might gain a degree of autonomy that was unthinkable when that period of history began. The motto that Kant suggested for this transformative age was "Have courage to use your own reason!" (Kant, 1996: 17). In many respects the movement that began in the eighteenth century bore spectacular fruit over the centuries that followed – producing an unprecedented degree of individual freedom in those nations where its ideals took root. But regrettably, the mode of seeing the world that helped this individualism to prosper also had terrible unseen consequences. This problematic perspective is rooted in Kant's division of the world into thinking subjects and inanimate objects (Kant, 1998), as brought to philosophical attention by Bruno Latour (1993) and others. By granting human minds a special moral status, and denying that 'objects' could attain or affect that situation, the children of the Enlightenment learned to ignore all their tools as 'mere means'.

DOI: 10.4018/978-1-4666-8592-5.ch002

Actually, this picture – well discussed within the field of Science and Technology Studies – itself overlooks a rather worrying aspect of our contemporary technological world. Questioning the division into clear subjects and objects draws attention to the moral implications of technology that have thus far been brushed under the philosophical carpet, which has definite benefits – but there is another aspect here worthy of attention. For although it is the case that we have mistaken technology as 'inanimate' and 'neutral' means to ends, despite significant and rather worrying effects on our ethical worlds (Latour, 1994, 2002; Verbeek, 2006, 2009), we have not entirely followed Kant's suggestion of treating 'objects' as non-participants in our moral perspective. On the contrary, for a great many people today – I am tempted to say a vast majority in those places that descended from European nations – technology is not merely a neutral tool, it is actually also the focus of something close to a religious (or rather non-religious) devotion. The extent of this trend is marked by the prevailing belief that when we encounter a problem, of whatever kind, an almost unquestioned assumption is that we can develop a technology to solve that problem, irrespective of the nature of the challenge.

I have called this hallowing of the power of technology *cyberfetish* (Bateman, 2014). This term connects this phenomena with two quite distinct traditions. On the one hand, it alludes to the failure of the cyberpunk literary movement within science fiction to provoke an effective resistance to the domination of corporate-produced technology, as its authors once hoped was possible. On the other, it references Auguste Comte, who first drew attention to the description of 'fetishism' as a 'first stage' of human religion, the last of which was 'positivism' i.e. the elevation of the sciences above religion (Comte, 1830). Karl Marx famously used the term 'commodity fetishism' to compare these ancient religious practices to the strange importance being placed upon goods and money (Marx, 1887), and there has recently been a revival of interest in viewing capitalism as a form of animism (e.g. Holert, 2012). 'Cyberfetish' implies both the exaltation of technology (cyberfetishism, in a parallel to Marx) *and* technology as equivalent to an animist's fetish (the cyberfetish), and I intend the term to be inherently pejorative. It marks a dependence upon technological means that, far from being neutral, have imprisoned as much as they have liberated. Our inability to clearly perceive this is precisely why I invoke such an obviously polemic term – our imaginative perspective upon the world is systematically distorted by cyberfetish, in ways that should trouble us far more than they usually do.

Although I am linking cyberfetish to positivism, it would be a mistake to think that the problem was constrained to non-religion. I borrow 'positivism' from Comte to describe those contemporary non-religions that valorize science (Bateman, 2012), and the mythological substrate of contemporary positivism is science fiction, which underpins positivistic non-religion much as great epics such as the Ramayana and Mahayana underpin the Hindu traditions. But science fiction serves as a mythological background to almost *everyone* in the technologically-dominated places – whether they are positivist, Christian, Muslim, Hindu, Buddhist, or of no particular persuasion. Yet in a queer irony, despite much of science fiction raising warning flags about the risks of imagined technologies, it is the capacity to make-believe about the wonders of the 'World of Tomorrow' (as the 1939 New York World's fair dubbed the matter) that has the greatest persistence of vision.

I use 'mythology' here in a wider sense, one that could be gainfully compared to Goffman's (1974) 'frames', and that directly connects to Mary Midgley's (2003) discussion of contemporary myths as "imaginative patterns, networks of powerful symbols that suggest particular ways of interpreting the world" (Midgley, 2003: 1). Mythology therefore shapes the meaning of our experience, and this function, as Joseph Campbell (1972) also recognised and marked with the term 'living mythology', is unavoidable. There is no way of experiencing the world without mythic symbols to structure our understandings. Our living mythologies have historically been greatly influenced by religious traditions, but there have always also been non-religious mythologies in parallel. Understanding both religious and non-religious myths as functionally related, which can be achieved either via Goffman's methods or via Walton's (1990) make-believe theory of representation (see also Bateman, 2011, 2012, 2014), helps us to avoid making premature judgements as to which is the 'true' mythology. Myths, as Midgley states, are not lies, but neither can any given mythology be true in any absolute sense.

I am brandishing this mythological term 'cyberfetish' in a critique that is resistant to technology *as panacea*, but I am not advocating any rose tinted regression to bygone eras. I do not believe this is plausible or possible – although I admire, for instance, the Amish capacity to sustain the practices and technological affordances of a given era against the temptations of ever-improving technical means around them. Rather, my claim is that our relationship with our devices and techniques is and will remain problematic as long as we are unable to recognize that the benefits of new technology can be imagined very easily in advance of their creation, but the sometimes terrible costs and consequences are all too often ignored, and pragmatically *impossible to assess*. Recognizing that our ever-growing technical competence means that 'we can make anything', we now face an urgent ethical question that should always have been attached to this capacity: 'should we?'

Cyberfetish is at work in our everyday lives to exalt the power of technology (including and especially medicine) and to obfuscate its risks. There is an imaginative gap here that needs bridging. Kant, heralding in the Enlightenment, noted "a strange unexpected course is revealed in human affairs... if it is considered in the large, where almost everything is paradoxical" (Kant, 1996: 22). The paradox of technology, when it is considered in its widest scope, is cyberfetish. If we do not wrestle with this demon now, the messianic 'World of Tomorrow' it seems to promise will either fail to manifest in any way that will genuinely benefit the majority of human lives, or that will bring the end of us as a species.

LOST IN THE ETHICAL TRIANGLE

When I question whether we should make all the things we are capable of making, we immediately run up against the disastrous state of contemporary ethics – because to conduct a moral investigation requires a commitment to a specific ethical methodology, and whichever we choose we will only be able to include a subset of all people among those who will endorse such a method. Kant's optimism that international moral consensus would be potentially achievable – and necessary, if peace were to be attainable (Kant, 2006) – dashed itself against an early twentieth century rebellion against any meaningful understanding of morality as a concept (e.g. Moore, 1903; and for critique of this trend MacIntyre, 1984). If a term like 'should' can be rejected as a mere expression of preference, my question as to what we should be willing to make – and more importantly, what we should resolve *not to make* – is doomed to inapplicability. I must, therefore, attempt a brief rescue of morality from the festering state it has been allowed to devolve into.

Fortunately, the situation is not as terrible as it may at first seem, and much of the problem stems from the assumption that if there is not something that might be called 'moral law' (i.e. objective moral truth) then life would be ultimately meaningless since nothing could matter. Derek Parfit (2011) raises just such a concern in his attempt at a rescue operation for ethics. His approach is to try to salvage a practical morality by brokering an intellectually rigorous accommodation between various competing moral philosophical traditions – Kantian deontology, contractual traditions partially descended from this, and Consequentialism – suggesting that these rival ethical traditions "are climbing the same mountain on different sides" (Parfit, 2011: 385).

However, Parfit says nothing about virtue ethics, another moral tradition dating back to Aristotle, Confucius, and other ancient philosophers – and quite certain to have been practiced by people long before these intellectuals codified these ideas. In Parfit's attempt to understand morality as objective truth, virtue ethics is just not in play for him – perhaps because it's a messy business that does not neatly align with objectivity as he understands it. I have a more practical perspective on this matter: the virtue ethics tradition describes the actual moral practices of a great many people today, and any attempt at a 'universal' perspective on ethics that does not take it into account is at risk of a paternalistic disregard towards actual lived experiences. I contend that we can easily include these practices into the kind of unifying discourse on ethics that Parfit attempts by simply taking into account what moral discussions concern.

Every ethical question we would care to raise will involve moral *agents* taking *actions* that result in *outcomes*. We can phrase this situation in many different ways, but the essence of moral claims concern what is contained in this broad statement of affairs. It is my assertion that we can understand all ethical problems and situations as being transcribed within an 'ethical triangle' comprised of the aforementioned elements, and each individual tradition (e.g. deontology, Consequentialism, virtue ethics) approaches morality from one or another pole of this 'triangle' (see Bateman, 2014: 117-129). Virtue ethics is interested in the qualities of the agents who act; deontology is concerned with the permissibility of the actions taken; Consequentialism aims to make moral judgments about the outcomes that occur. As is hopefully clear, my topographic metaphor does not emerge from an attempt at diplomacy between the ethical traditions we encounter today but from a simple (perhaps overly simple) analysis of the scope of morality – but having approached from such an angle, if becomes easier to see otherwise radically opposed traditions as related. I side with Midgley in viewing the attempts to reduce morality to a war between deontology and Consequentialism as both shallow and futile (Midgely, 2003): we need a wider perspective if we are to make any headway against our actual problems.

Note that identifying this 'ethical triangle' does not make disagreements disappear – the conclusions that Consequentialists draw when they weigh up outcomes and those that deontologists draw when they assess actions remain different, often radically so. But recognizing that these differences in conclusion can be connected to differences in assumption is a vast improvement upon asserting that one or another tradition has the 'best' answers to ethical questions. We urgently need to find ways of reaching a 'good common world' (Latour, 2004), as Kant alluded to in his metaphor of a 'realm of ends' (2002) and Isabelle Stengers (2003) suggests in her concept of 'cosmopolitics' and the gradual assembly of an 'ecology of practices'. This means everyone must take into account the different side of the ethical triangle from which they are approaching any given issue, and avoiding the presumption that their own moral judgments can supersede other forms of ethics.

DO GUNS AND CARS KILL PEOPLE?

It is becoming humdrum to draw attention to the phrase and counter-phrase that "Guns kill people" or that "People kill people, not guns", and Latour (1994) is not the only philosopher or intellectual to have discussed the assumptions of agency within these claims. He is, however, the chief source of associating these perspectives to Kant's split into subject and object (Latour, 1993), and thus as a product of the Enlightenment movement. Reading Latour or Verbeek, it begins to seem strange that we believe we can assign all of the responsibility to people in some cases, and to things in others – I make the point (Bateman, 2014) that the very people in the United States who wish to assign agency entirely to people in the case of guns are often wont to assign agency entirely to things in the case of drug abuse!

I want to raise a question that will bring cyberfetish into this problematic area of the fuzzy boundaries of agency, namely: do cars kill people? According to the two adages cited above in the context of guns, either "Cars kill people" or "People kill people, not cars" – which is it to be? Curiously, despite road traffic killing many more people than guns – in the United States, about four times as many if suicide-by-gun is omitted from consideration (Kennedy, 2013), there is no corresponding moral panic about cars. This fact is sometimes raised by opponents of gun control to argue against limitations on gun ownership. Yet *no-one*, on either side of the firearm debate, actually takes seriously the apparently obvious moral implication of automotive deaths: whether or not it is cars or people that are to be ascribed responsibility, cars-and-people together are causing a terrific loss of life.

We are somehow able to dismiss this automotive death toll by collecting it under the term 'accident' – as if intent were all that mattered. The problem here, I suggest, is cyberfetish: we are systematically blinded to the moral implications of car ownership because our technology is our fetish. It is as unthinkable that we would give up our motorized vehicles as it is that we would tolerate a wild animal that caused as many deaths as a co-inhabitant of our cities – and both sides of this statement point to the gaps in our ethical thought when it comes to those machines that we can no longer even contemplate living without. The reason that guns are a political battleground in the US and cars are not is that only a subset of the population lives with guns as an acknowledged part of their imaginary view of the world whereas *everyone* in the developed world lives with cars as an essential component of their contemporary mythology.

The view I have outlined above is not a new one – indeed, Ivan Illich (1974) also raises significant concerns about the 'radical monopoly' of transportation. Viewing cars from the perspective of those nations who had, at the time, not adopted them, he expresses his horror at the way people from other places responded to the death of a child who was playing in the road and then run over by an automobile – a device previously unknown to that particular community. He notes the dismissive response of those who would say 'he shouldn't have been playing in the road', a frankly insane retort that could only be asserted by someone who had already bought into the mythology of ubiquitous car ownership. Indeed, Illich reflects that the civil engineer in the wealthier nations has become almost incapable of imagining a city without cars as a primary mode of transportation, as the principle factor dictating infrastructure. This should be especially concerning since more than three quarters of all traffic fatalities in the United States, and quite probably elsewhere, occur within cities, or within five miles of cities (NHTSA, 2009).

It is important to recognize that it is not the case that deaths from the usage of cars are 'invisible', it is rather that the possibility of discontinuing our dependence upon cars as a primary means of transit has become *unthinkable*. A brief examination of the ways that road fatalities have been approached will help focus this question. As one example, Sweden passed a government resolution adopting a long-term goal that "no one should be killed or seriously injured as a result of traffic accidents in the road transport system" (Belin & Tillgren, 2013: 84). This ambitious 'Vision Zero' concentrated upon infrastructure reform to achieve its worthy goal, which decades later remains unattained. Studies in the United States have focused instead upon the way that automobiles are advertised, e.g. the prevalence of 'unsafe driving' in North American automobile commercials (Shin et al, 2005), on the presumed basis that it is merely bad examples as to the use of cars that is at fault. Compare, as a contrast case, the predicted outcome from communal bike programs in major cities such as New York: critics railed against cyclists as "the most important danger in the city", yet after approximately 23 million rides on the communal bicycles, there have been absolutely no recorded fatalities (Stromberg, 2014).

Despite the deadly consequences that result from our dependence upon cars for transit, very few if any have proposed the elimination or redesign of cars as a solution to the problem – we are far happier to gloss over automotive fatalities as 'accidents' that can be ignored than we are to consider the moral implications of our supposedly neutral tools. This is a sign of what I am calling cyberfetish as it manifests in the context of personal transportation. If a disease results in the deaths of tens of thousands, we raise vast sums of money to develop new technologies to counter that risk of death. But when certain kinds of existing equipment are an equivalent cause of death, we are almost incapable of considering fundamental changes to their design or usage – we are blinded by our own imagined dependencies, in a manner eerily reminiscent of the drug abuser who is incapable of dealing with their unhealthy relationship with something that, despite the mythology, is far from morally neutral.

THE ETHICS OF CARS

Looking at the question of car ownership through the ethical triangle, it becomes very difficult to see how – from a moral perspective, at least – we could continue to commit to automobiles as the de facto means of transport, especially in cities. From an agent perspective, there are no obvious virtues that can be ascribed to a person who uses automotive transport when it is compared to alternatives, such as cycling. (There are certainly *gratifications*, and indeed cars are advertised in a way to intentionally emphasize these over the facts – often, for instance, showing the car in implausible road situations, devoid of traffic congestion of any kind). If we can say of a particular road-user that they are 'responsible', we can make a far firmer case to their responsibility when they are using a bicycle than when they are using a car, and this applies in multiple contexts (including, but not restricted to, risk of fatal accidents, environmental impact of the required infrastructure, energy usage, and personal health and fitness).

From an action perspective, it is not clear how (given the assumption of equal worth of people that functions as a collective ideal post-Enlightenment) the risk of fatalities associated with contemporary automobiles can render the present form of this transportation permissible. Indeed, coming at the problem from this pole of the ethical triangle there would seem to be compelling reasons to work against 'accidents', as per Sweden's Vision Zero program. If, as may be the case, infrastructure reform cannot deliver 'zero accidents', this would constitute a case against the permissibility of the car – or at least, the car as currently designed. Similarly, from an outcome perspective it is difficult, perhaps impossible, to settle the ledger that holds tens of thousands of deaths on one side, and only the alleged benefit associated with speed of transit on the other. It is also worth noting that presuming the car is taken as the primary form of transportation, the speed benefits are questionable: when every individual attempts to travel by car in an urban space (and especially when they do so at the same time), it does not result in faster travel for anyone.

Returning to the question of what we should make – or what we should not make – we do not seem to have a very compelling ethical case in favor of continuing to make automobiles of the kind that is currently manufactured and sold in large numbers. Consider, as an obvious contrast, what would happen if corporations began to manufacture cars that were limited *by design* to a speed of (say) 30 kilometers per hour (18 miles per hour): such vehicles would almost entirely eliminate deaths from automobile 'accidents' (WHO, 2013). If this target speed seems absurdly low, we could at least begin to negotiate over where the balance between velocity and mortality should lie. Whichever moral tradition we support, vehicles engineered to travel at speeds that are unlikely to cause death are morally preferable to those we currently manufacture, and obvious objections about increased travel time etc. do not take into account the possibilities that become available once the speed-unlimited automobile ceases to be the essential assumption of urban infrastructure.

It might be objected that these problems with cars could be lessened or eliminated by using 'robot drivers', so-called self-driving cars; by almost entirely eliminating the human factor from driving. In assessing the moral implications of such technology, Jason Millar (2014) draws attention to the paternalistic aspects of such a designed device in that if the car ends up in a situation whereby a collision might occur with (say) a child on a bicycle, it is the design of the artifact that determines how this situation will resolve. The driver's moral judgment is being replaced by the designed moral proxy. Millar contends that this creates an argument for the designs of such vehicles to include the capacity for the driver to configure their preferences – whether in such a situation the car should put the driver at risk to save the child, or put the child at risk to save the driver. I find it oddly telling that the possibility of a 'robot driver' curtailing its speed to a range where fatality would be vanishingly unlikely to occur never enters into the discussion: it is simply assumed that cars will be designed to operate at speeds where fatal collisions will occur.

Limiting the speed of the automobile by design could produce a morally desirable outcome, the elimination of traffic fatalities, a consequence that could equally be attained by eliminating the car altogether and gearing urban infrastructure towards bicycles and alternative approaches to transit. Studies have already shown that, even when cars remain in use, transportation becomes safer the greater number of pedestrians and cyclists are on the streets (Jacobsen, 2003). Yet it is very nearly absurd to think that any such thing will happen, except perhaps in isolated locations. This is cyberfetish as it applies to cars: we are, in a certain sense, addicted to the fantasy of speed and 'freedom' that the automobile mythology thrives upon, and we are not willing to give it up – even to save the lives of millions of people worldwide (WHO, 2013).

MURDER BY DESIGN

In evaluating the deaths associated with automotive transport, cyberfetish manifested as an inability to take seriously those design modifications or tool-choices that could eliminate the moral problem in question – namely significantly large numbers of 'accidental' deaths. For the remainder of this discussion, I want to turn attention to a very different example of contemporary cyberfetish – one that occurs when the *intention* is to kill. Whereas the issues with cars were civil, the questions I now wish to raise are military – and in this transition we have switched from an understanding based upon 'peaceful' considerations to one based upon 'war'. This somewhat complicates ethical discussion because it is accepted that different moral standards apply for warfare – but in the official story, at the very least, this does not mean that ethics is *voided*. In what is actually observed, however, that is precisely what seems to be occurring.

In the spring of 2011, an unmanned aerial vehicle launched missiles into a bus depot in the town of Datta Khel in a mountainous area of Pakistan that borders upon Afghanistan. The official report upon this action was that everyone who was killed in the attack was an 'insurgent', yet according to eye witnesses, the Pakistani military, and independent investigators for the Associated Press, the majority of people who were killed in the explosion were innocent civilians who had come to the building for a tribal meeting to discuss a dispute about a nearby mine. The meeting did not occur in secret: the Pakistani military were notified more than a week earlier. Of the forty people slain in this explosion, roughly four were Taliban fighters – the claimed target of the missiles. Some twenty four civilians have been named as victims of the attack, while many others who died that day will probably never be known by name (Stanford, 2012).

This is not, it transpires, an isolated incident. What are euphemistically termed 'targeted killings' have occurred throughout this region, with considerable loss of life to unarmed civilians. Testifying to a Senate Judiciary subcommittee on Human Rights, Farea Al-Muslimi described these kinds of attacks as constituting a "war of mistakes" (Al-Muslimi, 2013: 7). Less than a week before testifying, his remote village of Wessab in the mountains of Yemen was struck by a drone attack that terrified the comparatively poor farm community. Al-Muslimi received dozens of texts and calls from fellow villages wanting to know why they had been targeted – especially since the likely target of the strike was not in hiding and could easily have been arrested.

At first glance, it is not difficult to understand the appeal of the drone strike: the attacker takes almost no risk at all. Since all that is deployed is an unmanned aircraft – basically a flying robot, under the control of a pilot who can be thousands of miles away – the 'worst' that can happen to the attacking force is the loss of a device. Of course, this analysis completely ignores the prudential costs accrued in terms of loss of political goodwill and the risk of turning otherwise neutral individuals into enemy combatants. Indeed, over and above any moral concerns that we can highlight, there is something deeply counter-productive in trying to combat terrorism by a method that aids in the recruitment of terrorists. As Al-Muslimi observes in this regard "what radicals had previously failed to achieve in my village, one drone strike accomplished in an instant: there is now an intense anger and growing hatred of America" (Al-Muslimi, 2013: 4).

Of course, this assumes that the pursued end for which these drone assassins are deployed is indeed peace. As Hannah Arendt warned, Kant's dictum that nothing should happen in a war to make a later peace impossible (Kant, 2006) has now been turned upon its head such that "we live in a peace in which nothing may be left undone to make a future war still possible" (Arendt, 2005: 200). The existence of a technology that allows for wars to be fought as effortlessly as the extermination of vermin invites action that would or could not otherwise be taken: this is cyberfetish as it manifests in contemporary warfare. The pursuit of 'better' technology to wage war paradoxically makes victory unobtainable, precisely because we have lost sight of Kant's warning about the need to engage in battle in a manner that presumes peace is the outcome being pursued.

This connects the earlier discussion of the effect of technology upon agency to the problem of weaponry design. As Latour (1994) points out, in a situation where you had only wished to hurt another person, a gun offers that you might kill instead – the technology modifies both the possibilities and the likelihood of certain actions occurring. Similarly Verbeek (2009) states that our designed objects are not devoid of moral content, since they affect our agency. Even if the kind of secular animistic viewpoint suggested by Latour and Verbeek is rejected, it cannot reasonably be denied that the facts about things alter the reasons we have for acting (Pols, 2012), which connects these issues to traditional moral philosophy.

The arguments in favour of the use of drones in war has been mounted (quite honourably, in my view) by defense analyst Bradley Strawser (2010). Drawing against the just war doctrine that has long been the basis of the justification for engaging in armed conflict (e.g. Childress, 1978), Strawser contends that provided the war is just, soldiers have a duty to use the best equipment available in order to defend themselves. However, even he concedes that this is an argument about how drones *should* be used, not about how they are currently being deployed – a situation which he admits entails actions that are "morally questionable or outright impermissible" (Strawser, 2010: 362).

One of the reasons that drone assassins do raise moral concerns among a great many people whereas the death toll of cars-and-their-drivers can still be ignored is that these deadly tools come into focus as morally questionable when viewed 'from the outside', as it were. (The automotive loss of life, by converse, is only ever seen 'from the inside' of the relevant mythology, where terms like 'accident' help it to seem less emotionally charged). From an agent perspective, it is immediately clear that the ideals of a soldier facing their enemy in honorable battle have somehow been subverted or destroyed by equipment that allows for such asymmetry in power. Strawser warns that drones are not the locus of this particular issue – we can hardly consider a matchup between a fighter jet with laser-guided missiles and a combatant armed with a rocket-propelled grenade as a 'fair fight' (Strawser, 2010). Indeed, this is correct – but it highlights the deeper problem – that the asymmetry problem of technology for war, quite contrary to Kant's warnings, was long since blindly hurdled thanks to our cyberfetish for war machines.

From an action perspective, there is indeed the kind of duty that Strawser alludes to protect our soldiers with the best available defenses. But again, if we wish to look at questions of duty, the duty to wage war in a manner that leaves peace as an ever present possibility (Kant, 2006) must surely trump the duty to protect the soldiers technologically – at least in so much that we ourselves become the greatest danger to the lives of our soldiers when we enter them into a conflict that is fought in such a way as to prevent it ever ending. This same argument holds from an outcome perspective, where the prudential arguments against drone assassinations might hold an additional influence that may or may not be interpreted as ethical from agent or action perspectives. I would additionally argue that actions such as those at the Datta Khel bus depot destroy the whole normative force of the 'just war' doctrine. If 'our' side can deploy robotic weapons to murder civilians then the war being fought is *no longer just*, irrespective of the reasons that it was originally enjoined.

CAN THERE BE AN ETHICS OF TECHNOLOGICAL RESEARCH?

These two quite distinct examples of cyberfetish – our inability to recognize the moral salience of the deaths caused by cars-and-drivers, and the destruction of the moral foundations of 'just war' by the availability of war machines that destroy the conditions for peace – are only illustrations of the larger problem. It is the dilemma posed by the title to this piece: we can make anything – should we? Another way of posing this same question is: can there be an ethics that will bind those conducting technological research to consider the moral dimensions of their work?

Perhaps the most troubling aspect of the situation we currently face is that any attempt to bring the problems I am marking with the term 'cyberfetish' into something like a manageable circumstance is blocked on two routes. Firstly, by the collapse of normative consensus that just a few centuries ago was broadly available and, for instance, contributed to the elimination of slavery and the establishment of contemporary notions of human rights that broadly descend from Kantian roots (Demenchonok, 2009). Today, the number of moral 'camps' available are so diverse that even attempting to mount an ethical argument has become a question of either asserting some kind of limited universality that might yet cut through, or negotiating between competing interests (for examples of both approaches, see Parfit, 2011). It is into this space that I offer my 'ethical triangle' method as a means of pursuing moral discussions *without* having to presuppose foundations for universal moral truth (see Bateman, 2014 for detailed discussion of this point). Even if there were something that could justifiably be called 'moral law', it may not be prudent to require its discovery and exposition before attempting to reach ethical agreement on problems that face us immediately.

Secondly, there is the deeply troubling problem that technology researchers typically contend they have either limited or non-existent moral responsibility in connection with their work. Jesper Ryberg (2003) highlights many arguments of this form, and concludes that none are convincing. In respect of the claim that it is the nature of scientific enquiry to explore the unknown, and thus that it is unreasonable to assume accountability (e.g. Hoffman, 1975), Ryberg objects that researchers can have "qualified expectations with regard to what may follow from their work if it turns out successfully" (Ryberg, 2003: 355) and thus can never be wholly indemnified from responsibility. The idea that a scientist does not decide upon the application of their research is also rejected as a means of neutralizing moral responsibility on similar grounds, while attempts to hand over moral responsibility to the State are rejected with various well-reasoned arguments.

Perhaps the most interesting case considered by Ryberg is the 'replaceability argument' (Lackey, 1994), stated succinctly by the adage: "If I did not do it, someone else would" (Ryberg: 359). This conceals an appeal to an outcome perspective: if the outcome remains the same irrespective of the agents involved, can the agents be considered culpable? This claim ignores a morally salient point raised by Derek Parfit (1984) during his most outcome-focused phase: an individual act can be judged wrong irrespective of its contribution to the consequence e.g. if two individuals aim to kill an innocent person, it is not only the one who succeeds who has acted wrongly. Furthermore, an attempt along similar lines to carve up responsibility into 'shares' runs into similar problems foreseen by Parfit: if a four-person rescue mission can save hundred lives, but one individual acting alone can save fifty lives, it does not follow that the latter outcome is preferable simply because fifty is greater than twenty five (one hundred divided by four). Even if one is skeptical about devolving morality to mathematics, as I am – and as Allen Wood (2011) passionately argues against – the outcome that one hundred are saved is unquestionably better than if only fifty are saved, provided that the means deployed are morally acceptable in both cases. Moral accountability cannot simply be divided up in such a simplistic fashion.

Ryberg's interest is in assessing *military* research into technology, but I would suggest that the points he raise hold true for *all* technological development. It is not possible for those responsible for the research to entirely void their culpability for any and all technology that results. Yet there is something troubling concerning about this conclusion, for does this mean that we must hold Karl Benz, the inventor of the general design of the contemporary automobile, responsible for the millions of deaths on our planet's roads today? No, and in part for the simple fact that the Benz Patent-Motorwagen could only travel at approximately 16 kilometers per hour (10 miles per hour), at best (Merrit, 2012). Yet everyone involved in the design, manufacture, marketing, infrastructure development, purchase, and usage of contemporary automobiles – that travel at far faster, far deadlier speeds than the original vehicles – bears some responsibility for the inadvertently deadly situation on our roads. And that set of people includes almost all of us.

CONCLUSION

The term 'cyberfetish' is one I am using to help draw attention to our general inability to assess our own technology, because we are metaphorically addicted to both its use, and its constant cycle of 'upgrading' self-replacement and rapid obsolescence that thrills and engages us with the excitement of the ever-new. Frankly, I am uncertain whether it is correct to assess our current dependence upon contemporary technology as only a *metaphorical* addiction, but exploration of this issue lies somewhat beyond the scope of this discussion. It might be objected that the term 'cyberfetish' is too inflammatory, but to this I would contend that it is not possible to be *excessively* provocative on a matter that threatens (via the environmental impacts of our highly technologized, resource-hungry way of life) the destruction of many of the species that live with us, and potentially of our own species as well, over and above the loss of life detailed above. The choice of our words is no more morally neutral than our technology, nor should it be.

By exploring the loss of life caused by technology – partly by intention, in the case of drones, entirely 'accidentally' in the case of cars – I have attempted to draw out the idea that treating technology as an imagined ideal is highly problematic *in the case of actual devices in use today*, and this is even more the case in the context of what might be developed in the future. To place no significant restrictions, moral or legal, upon the development of new equipment is to defend the questionable moral assertion that the current effects of our technology have no ethical import. This claim is not plausible. The millions of lives lost every year to automotive 'accidents' are an ethical consequence of a personal transportation system which valorizes the excitement and 'convenience' of speed above human lives. It is doubly depressing to consider that the high speeds attainable by this form of conveyance have *not* shortened the amount of time spent travelling – they have radically increased it. The effect of drones deployed in warfare that has been subverted into technological extermination is even more counter-productive.

It is an unavoidable ethical conclusion, irrespective of the moral system deployed, that idealized images of technologies should never be allowed to provide the benchmark against which their moral value can be judged. Still less can we accept the implausible claim that our tools are neutral in our ethical lives, since the specifics of each designed object change the reasons we have for acting, and the possibilities therein. If we do not find ways of breaking through the distorting mythology of cyberfetish and begin to ascribe moral responsibility to every aspect of the development and usage of technology then we will struggle to be virtuous agents; we will fail to uphold our duties to ourselves and others; we shall become unable to produce desirable consequences. I make this claim not as someone preaching from a superior moral stance, but as a fellow 'prisoner' of cyberfetish, urgently asking for assistance in finding a way out of the moral labyrinth of technology we have sleepwalked into while pursuing the dreams of the Enlightenment.

REFERENCES

Al-Muslimi, F. (2013, April 23). Drone Wars: The Constitutional and Counterterrorism Implications of Targeted Killing [Statement]. *United States Senate Judiciary Committee Subcommittee on the Constitution, Civil Rights and Human Rights*. Retrieved from http://www.judiciary.senate.gov/imo/media/doc/04-23-13Al-MuslimiTestimony.pdf

Arendt, H. (2005). *The Promise of Politics* (J. Kohn, Ed.). New York, NY: Schocken Books.

Bateman, C. (2011). *Imaginary Games*. Winchester, Washington: Zero Books.

Bateman, C. (2012). *The Mythology of Evolution*. Winchester, Washington: Zero Books.

Bateman, C. (2014). *Chaos Ethics*. Winchester and Chicago, IL: Zero Books.

Belin, M.-Å., & Tillgren, P. (2013). Vision Zero. How a Policy Innovation is Dashed by Interest Conflicts, but May Prevail in the End. *Scandinavian Journal of Public Administration*, 16(3), 83–102.

Campbell, J. (1972). *Myths to Live By*. New York: Bantam.

Childress, J. F. (1978). Just-War Theories: The Bases, Interrelations, Priorities, and Functions of Their Criteria. *Theological Studies*, 39(3), 427–445. doi:10.1177/004056397803900302

Comte, A. (1830). "Course of Positive Philosophy", reprinted. In G. Lenzer (Ed.), *Auguste Comte and Positivism: The Essential Writings* (pp. 71–86). New York, NY: Harper.

Demenchonok, E. (2009). 10. The Universal Concept of Human Rights as a Regulative Principle: Freedom Versus Paternalism. *American Journal of Economics and Sociology*, 68(1), 273–301. doi:10.1111/j.1536-7150.2008.00624.x

Goffman, E. (1974). *Frame analysis: An essay on the organization of experience*. London: Harper and Row.

Hoffman, R. (1975). Scientific research and moral rectitude. *Philosophy (London, England)*, 50(194), 475–477. doi:10.1017/S0031819100025675

Holert, T. (2012). A live monster that is fruitful and multiplies: Capitalism as Poisoned Rat?. *e-flux, 36*. Retrieved from http://www.e-flux.com/journal/%E2%80%9Ca-live-monster-that-is-fruitful-and-multiplies%E2%80%9D-capitalism-as-poisoned-rat/

Illich, I. (1974). *Energy and Equity*. London, UK: Harper and Row.

Jacobsen, P. L. (2003). Safety in numbers: More walkers and bicyclists, safer walking and bicycling. *Injury Prevention*, 9(9), 205–209. doi:10.1136/ip.9.3.205 PMID:12966006

Kant, I. (1784). Beantwortung der Frage: Was ist Aufklärung? [An Answer to the Question: What is Enlightenment?] In M. J. Gregor (Ed.), Practical Philosophy. (1996). (pp. 17–22). Cambridge: Cambridge University Press.

Kant, I. (1781). Kritik der reinen Vernunft. Trans. P. Guyer & A. Wood (Eds.), Critique of Pure Reason (1998). Cambridge: Cambridge University Press. doi:10.1017/CBO9780511804649

Kant, I. (1785). Grundlegung zur Metaphysik der Sitten. Trans. A. W. Wood (Ed.), Groundwork for the Metaphysics of Morals (2002). New Haven, CT: Yale University Press.

Kant, I. (1795). Zum ewigen Frieden. Ein philosophischer Entwurf [Toward Perpetual Peace: A Philosophical Sketch]. In P. Kleingeld & D. L. Colclasure (Eds.), Toward Perpetual Peace and Other Writings on Politics, Peace, and History (pp. 67–109). New Haven, CT: Yale University Press.

Lackey, D. P. (1994). Military Funds, Moral Demand: Personal Responsibilities of the Individual Scientist. In E. Sherwin, S. Gendlin, & L. Keliman (Eds.), *Ethical Issues in Scientific Research: An Anthology* (pp. 397–409). New York: Garland.

Latour, B. (1993). *We Have Never Been Modern* (C. Porter, Trans.). Cambridge, MA: Harvard University Press.

Latour, B. (1994). On Technical Mediation. *Common Knowledge, 3*(2), 29–64.

Latour, B. (2004). *Politics of Nature: How to Bring the Sciences into Democracy* (C. Porter, Trans.). Cambridge, MA: Harvard University Press.

Latour, B., & Venn, C. (2002). Morality and Technology The End of the Means. *Theory, Culture & Society, 19*(5/6), 247–260. doi:10.1177/026327602761899246

MacIntyre, A. (2nd Ed.). (1984). *After Virtue: A Study in Moral Theory* Notre Dame, IN: University of Notre Dame Press.

Marx, K. (1867). Das Kapital, Bd. 1. [Capital, Volume 1]. In S. Moore & E. Aveling, (Eds.) *Capital, Volume One* (1887). Retrieved from http://www.marxists.org/archive/marx/works/1867-c1/index.htm

Merrit, T. (2012). *A Chronology of Tech History* [E-book].

Midgley, M. (2003). *The Myths We Live By*. London, New York: Routledge.

Millar, J. (2014). Technology as Moral Proxy: Autonomy and Paternalism by Design, *Proceedings of IEEE Ethics in Engineering, Science and Technology Conference*. Retrieved from https://ethicstechnologyandsociety.files.wordpress.com/2014/06/millar-technology-as-moral-proxy-autonomy-and-paternalism-by-design.pdf

Moore, G. E. (1903). *Principia Ethica*. Cambridge, UK: Cambridge University Press.

NHTSA. (2009). Geospatial Analysis of rural Motor Vehicle Traffic Fatalities. Retrieved from http://www-nrd.nhtsa.dot.gov/Pubs/811196.pdf

Parfit, D. (1984). *Reasons and Persons*. Oxford: Clarendon Press.

Parfit, D. (2011). *On What Matters* (Vol. 1 and 2). Oxford, UK: Oxford University Press.

Pols, A. J. K. (2012). How Artefacts Influence Our Actions. *Ethical Theory and Moral Practice*. Retrieved from http://link.springer.com/content/pdf/10.1007%2Fs10677-012-9377-0

Ryberg, J. (2003). Ethics and Military Research: on the Moral Responsibility of Scientists. In B. Booss-Bavnbek & J. Høyrup (Eds.), *Mathematics and War* (pp. 352–366). Berlin: Birkhäuser Verlag. doi:10.1007/978-3-0348-8093-0_19

Shin, P. C., Hallett, D., Chipman, M. L., Tator, C., & Granton, J. T. (2005). Unsafe driving in North American automobile commercials. *Journal of Public Health*, *27*(4), 318–325. doi:10.1093/pubmed/fdi049 PMID:16162638

Stanford International Human Rights and Conflict Resolution Clinic. (2012). Living Under Drones. Retrieved from http://www.livingunderdrones.org/living-under-drones/

Stengers, I. (2003). Cosmopolitics II. trans. Bononno, R. [2011], Minneapolis, MN: University of Minnesota Press.

Strawser, B. J. (2010). Moral Predators: The Duty to Employ Uninhabited Aerial Vehicles. *Journal of Military Ethics*, *9*(4), 343–368. doi:10.1080/15027570.2010.536403

Stromberg, J. (2014, August 20). Not a single person has died using bike share in the US. *Vox*, Retrieved from http://www.vox.com/2014/8/12/5994879/bike-share-citi-bike-deaths-safety

Verbeek, P.-P. (2006). Materializing Morality: Design Ethics and Technological Mediation. *Science, Technology & Human Values*, *31*(3), 361–380. doi:10.1177/0162243905285847

Verbeek, P.-P. (2009). Cultivating Humanity: toward a non-humanist ethics of technology. In J. K. B. Olsen, E. Selinger, & S. Riis (Eds.), *New Waves in Philosophy of Technology* (pp. 241–263). Basingstoke, UK: Palgrave Macmillan.

Walton, K. L. (1990). *Mimesis as Make-believe: On the Foundations of the Representational Arts*. Cambridge, MA: Harvard University Press.

Wood, A. (2011). Humanity as an End in Itself. In On What Matters, Volume 2. Oxford, UK: Oxford University Press, (pp. 58-82).

World Health Organization. (2013). *Road traffic injuries*. Retrieved from http://www.who.int/media-centre/factsheets/fs358/en/

KEY TERMS AND DEFINITIONS

Agent: Anything that can take an action, especially actions of moral relevance.

Consequentialism: One of three major forms of moral philosophy, that which is focused on assessing the moral qualities of outcomes. Compare 'deontology' and 'virtue ethics'.

Cosmopolitics: Isabelle Stengers mythology of an ecology of practices that must be gradually assembled from vastly diverse traditions and practices. Compare Latour's term 'good common world' and Kant's term 'realm of ends'.

Cyberfetish: The exaltation of technology, such that critical examination of its moral impact is obscured. Also, technology considered as equivalent to a totem in animism.

Deontology: One of three major forms of moral philosophy focused upon rules of permissibility and obligation associated with moral action. Compare 'consequentialism' and 'virtue ethics'.

End: Something to strive towards, a goal.

Ethical Triangle: A metaphor for the idea that all moral discussions can be examined from the perspective of agents, actions, or outcomes, and thus that every moral situation can be approached from positions equivalent to consequentialism, deontology, and virtue ethics.

Good Common World: Latour's moral fiction of the best arrangement that can be composed out of the disparate needs of everything contained within it. Compare Kant's term 'realm of ends' and Stengers' term 'cosmopolitics'.

Mythology: A collection of imaginative patterns that use fiction or metaphor to express a particular perspective, and constitute a specific way of interpreting the world.

Positivism: A scientific non-religion based upon avoiding belief in untestable things, and thus an attempt to minimize metaphysics as much as possible.

Positivist: A person who believes in some form of positivism.

Practice: A socially-grounded activity, such as language, games, currency, ethics.

Realm of Ends: Kant's mythology of communal autonomy, whereby each person works towards the fulfillment of their own ideals and goals while avoiding blocking other people from attaining their own objectives wherever possible. Compare Latour's term 'good common world' and Stengers' term 'cosmopolitics'.

Virtue Ethics: One of three major forms of moral philosophy, focused upon the qualities of agents (i.e. their virtues). Compare 'consequentialism' and 'deontology'.

Virtue: A quality of an agent that is considered desirable and meritorious within any given moral practice.

Chapter 3
Grounding Machine Ethics within the Natural System

Jared Gassen
JMG Advising, USA

Nak Young Seong
Independent Scholar, South Korea

ABSTRACT

This chapter explores machine ethics within the larger context of the natural system from which it springs. While computing power and computing machines have grown exponentially since the twentieth century, the foundation for this growth is the planet's natural resources, which may not be able to sustain this type of continual exponential growth. This chapter explores some of the basic natural limiting factors that may prohibit computing power if solutions are not found. Specifically, the chapter explores limitations from: population growth, e-waste, rare earth minerals, water, oil, and energy production. Within this context, possible solutions for producing machines ethically are briefly explored.

INTRODUCTION

Humans are limited by their machines. In the modern world, these limitations are directly related to computing power, machine programming, progress in fields that are components of machines, and natural resources to physically produce them. Computing power has grown exponentially this past century. The abilities of intelligent machines have, in many ways, progressed faster than has our ability to assess their effects on social and natural systems, and safeguard their ethical uses and even independent actions.

Humanity has existed for hundreds of thousands of years in something like its current form; computing machines have existed for less than one hundred. But, look what has happened in that short time. It took less than seventy years between the first powered flight and the first mission to the moon. Meanwhile, that moon lander had less computing power than a modern programmable coffeemaker. Almost everyone alive was born within this exponential growth of computing machines, so their use, utility,

DOI: 10.4018/978-1-4666-8592-5.ch003

and "goodness" all seem like givens. But, can this growth continue unabated into the future, or even for another hundred years? This chapter takes a long-term ecological view in exploring this question and how to possibly sustain the use of these machines, rather than the shortsighted, profit-driven motives that dominate current geopolitical decisions.

BACKGROUND

As computing power advances, it also advances humanity's ability to produce increasingly advanced machines, which have increasing amounts of autonomy and decision-making powers, creating an increased importance of machine ethics (Moor, 2006). Hence, the various submissions for this book and the interesting questions they discuss. However, in addition to the very important questions of how to make machines behave ethically, comes the often-overlooked question of whether to produce a machine at all, regardless of whether or not that machine will then behave ethically, based on the natural realities of this planet and the resources required to produce them. It is this necessary grounding of machine ethics within the natural system that seems to be frequently overlooked and will be the focus of this chapter. It seems that those whose job it is to build and discuss computing machines are more likely to talk about our mastery of nature rather than our place within it. This chapter takes a different approach and may come to outcomes that are unexpected.

The ubiquity of machines and robots in our everyday world continues to rapidly rise. According to the International Federation of Robotics (IFR) (2014), in 2012 alone, about three million service robots for personal and domestic use were sold, 20% more than in 2011 and the value of sales increased to US$1.2 billion. IFR projections for sales between 2013-2016 predict huge increases in the field and sales of about US$17.1 billion. It projects sales of all types of robots for domestic tasks could reach almost 15.5 million units in that period of time. The market for toy and hobby robots is forecast to be about 3.5 million units, and another three million robots to be produced for education and research. The IFR also predicts that robots for the handicapped and elderly will increase substantially in the next twenty years as well (International Federation of Robotics, 2013).

Robots are also a booming industry in military applications. When the U.S. started wars in Iraq and Afghanistan in 2003, there were no ground robots. In 2009, there were over 12,000 ground and 7,000 aerial robots in use (Lin, 2009). Scott Hartley, co-founder of 5D Robotics, one of several businesses creating military robots for the U.S. government, said, "Ten years from now [2023], there will probably be one soldier for every ten robots. Each soldier could have one or five robots flanking him, looking for enemies, scanning for land mines" (Diaz, 2013). While this may be a wishful projection from someone who stands to make a lot of money from its fulfillment, the trend is clear. The rise of military machines is already here, and the level of autonomy for these machines continues to rise as well, raising additional ethical concerns that need to be addressed by academics and the public (Lichocki, Kahn, & Billard, 2011).

While Intel co-founder Gordon Moore's (1965) 'law' predicting that the number of transistors that would fit on a silicon chip would double every two years hasn't been precisely correct, the general trend has been accurate. It graphically represents the rapid growth seen in the advancement of computing, and by extension AI machines and robots. The advancement of the microprocessor has been unprecedented. It is the only product in history that has been repeatedly made thousands of times faster, smaller, and more powerful than its predecessor for multiple generations.

Moore's prediction has to collapse at some point for silicon technology, assuming an absolute physical limitation of one atom for a transistor. How long it will take to reach this finite limit, and thereby presumptively limiting computing power as it is currently understood, is unknown. As is, what kind of machines can be created based on this computing power, and what humans will be able to accomplish with these machines. Michio Kaku, the well-known physicist and futurist predicted in 2012 that Moore's law would collapse "within the next ten years," (Peckham, 2012 para. 2). Kaku said that transistors were already twenty atoms wide, and his prediction was based on the belief that the functional limit of a transistor is about five atoms wide (Snead, 2012, para. 4).

Kaku is far from the first to predict the imminent end to Moore's law. Moore was only willing to initially predict that it would hold steady for ten years, and while others have predicted its end every decade, especially since at least 1990 (Snead, 2012), exponential growth of computing power has continued unabated.

Additionally, perhaps one atom of silicon is not the limit; perhaps there will be subatomic transistors. Even when silicon reaches its upper limits, it does not mean computing power is necessarily also limited. In the same article as he predicted its inevitable end, Kaku also said how it would continue—with Protein computers, DNA computers, optical computers, quantum computers and molecular computers—once silicon plateaued (Peckham, 2012, para. 8). The possibilities are endless and what can be created from such advances in computing power can only now be dreamed.

However, the endless possibilities are limited to the finite natural system of this planet and the resources that it supplies. While the amount of frequently used resources may currently seem infinite, they are still limited to what can be mined from this planet, which is constrained by both physical and economic limits. It might be a future possibility to mine from the moon or a nearby planetary body, but it is far too energetically expensive with current technology. It would take a lot of fuel and a lot of trips. So, humanity is stuck on this planet, with only what is available on it. It is clear that while sustaining rapid technologic advances may be possible in a 'vacuum tube', it is in fact not sheltered by this protective glass, it is merely one piece among all the systems occurring on this planet. There are natural limiting factors to perpetually producing these machines, most notably, rare earth minerals, water, and the resource that lubes all industry, oil. Plus, a stable, advanced, and cooperating international capital and industrial system must also be assumed to extract and trade them. No one country has the ability or all the various ores necessary to produce these machines alone; there must be some level of sharing, trading, or stealing among countries to create modern computing machines.

LIMITATIONS TO COMPUTING MACHINES

This rising tower of computing power in which humanity increasingly resides in is dependent on the foundational natural system to support it. There are some basic problems in this relationship, which if not accounted for could halt the continual construction of this high-rise and compromise the way of living that so many have grown accustomed. First and foremost, computing technology and advanced robotics is extremely energy and resource intensive. The smaller and faster the machine, the bigger the total energetic and environmental footprint. This is currently an unavoidable fact.

Many computing products require upwards of sixty elements to produce, as well as a number of rare earth minerals (PC Plus, 2012). Nearly all of these element procurements require a massive and stable industrial infrastructure to allow for the economic conditions to make their mining possible. Mining operations are inherently massively expensive on a number of levels: energy used, machinery needed, manpower, toxic waste produced, and other expenditures. For example, while there is plenty of gold left to be mined from the earth, it costs industries about US$900 per ounce to recover it, and they get about five grams of gold for every ton of other material that must be processed (Desjardins, 2013).

The brainhours and human energy required to turn these raw materials into advanced machines is also massive but even harder to estimate. According to a United Nations (UN) study conducted in 2004, producing just one basic desktop PC computer and monitor required 245 kg of fossil fuel (a little less than two barrels of oil), 22 kg of chemicals, and 1.5 metric tons of water (United Nations University, 2004). More recent estimates based on current technology and manufacturing processes could not be found. More advanced machines, like those used for military applications, require considerably more of these resources. Additionally, because technology is advancing so rapidly, machines become obsolete quickly and are not used for long before a newer and more energetically expensive machine is required to take its place, creating another ethical and environmental concern: e-waste.

Gartner, one of the world's leading information technology research and advisory companies, predicted that in 2014 the world would buy about 2.5 million new PC, tablets, and smartphones for about US$3.6 trillion in IT sales (Gartner, 2013). This does not include television purchases. In 2012 alone, the world generated nearly 50 million metric tons of e-waste, which is about 20 kg for every single person alive. This total is predicted by the UN to increase by 33% to over 65 million metric tons by 2017 (Tweed, 2013). Much of this material is considered toxic due to heavy metals and other materials. It is estimated that recycling one million cell phones would recover about 24 kg of gold, 250 kg of silver, 9 kg of palladium, and more than 9,000 kg of copper (EPA, 2012). The amount of e-material that gets recycled each year is not accurately tracked but is less than 25 percent; the exportation flow of e-waste from rich countries to poor is also not accurately tracked, but breaking down these toxic components is disproportionately done by poor people and children who have never had the opportunity to use these products (Tweed, 2013).

Global Digital Divide

Along with the exponential growth of computing power has been the exponential growth of humans on this planet. According to United States Census Bureau estimates, the world population reached three billion in 1959 and has increased by a billion people about every fifteen years. It was over seven billion in 2012 and expected to reach over nine billion by 2042 (United States Census, 2014). Each individual requires a certain level of energy and resources, the extent dependent on their quality of life. The reality of limited resources, combined with a rapidly increasing population, raises unpopular questions. Should subsistence-level living for the global population be mandated through authoritarian means, except for a few international bankers and oligarchs of course? Or should everyone on the planet get a new computer? How can the right balance be found in between? Since resources, as will be shown, are clearly too limited for everyone on the planet to enjoy advanced technology, who gets restricted from the potentials that come with advanced computing power and who gets to determine who gets restricted?

Despite the rapid increase in both quantity and quality of technology and robotic machines, much of the planet's population is being left behind and does not have access to high-tech products—let alone the ability to own these products or the education, resources, and access to participate in their ethical advancement. This reality is known as the "global digital divide" and is one of the biggest economic and social obstacles facing the planet today and a major cause for the disparities in all other areas leading to conflicts.

Knowledge, information, and skills—particularly related to technology—are critically important to economic development and look like they will continue to be for the foreseeable future. Where these are lacking, people get left behind. According to a 2006 United Nations report, a person in a high-income country was 22 times more likely to use the Internet than a person from a poor country (as cited in Kshetri & Dholakia, 2009). The divide is also present within countries as well, along economic, gender, geographic, and ethnic lines. A female ethnic minority living in a rural area of a country is far less likely to participate with technology than an urban male who is a member of the dominant ethnicity. Not because of innate capability or intelligence, but because of access and being born on the wrong side of the dominant culture.

While a fortunate few get to discuss the ethics of creating artificial intelligence machines that act ethically, and despite the fact that there are more mobile phones in use than people on the planet (Boren, 2014), meanwhile possibly half of the world's population has yet to even make a phone call. The pattern also shows that the newer the technology, the wider the gap in its use between rich and poor. Rather than closing the gap, advancements in technology widen this economic and social divide; this will be particularly true as resources get more scarce and expensive.

If who has access is largely based on the luck of the draw of what country a person is from, for those that do have these advantages to create lethal machines and use them against countries and individuals that do no not have the ability to produce them is clearly unethical. This is already occurring, with the United States being the best example, using drones and guided missiles against populations without access to these technologies over the past several years in a number of countries in the Middle East, Asia, and Africa.

While some argue for the use of lethal machines because they are 'efficient' and 'save human lives', this seems to be an intentionally myopic view. Put into the context of natural resource use and social justice, projected into the future, it is clear that if not for the sake of saving human life, then it should at least be clear that natural resources are too precious to squander in war. It is one thing to discuss the value of using rare resources to build an advanced robot that will care for the elderly or carry some useful medical function. The dynamic shifts when the same amount of resources (if not more) is used to create an advanced robot whose purpose is to carry out destruction, or be destructed itself in warfare. In the not too distant future of overpopulation and resource scarcity, human life may be considered cheaper and less valuable than advanced lethal machines. Clearly, wars are profitable for the few that start them and sell the weapons for their execution, but they are detrimental to everyone else in the future who will be dependent on resources that have already been used in warfare. This was clearly seen in 1953 by newly elected U.S. president Dwight Eisenhower, himself a decorated military general, who famously said:

Every gun that is made, every warship launched, every rocket fired signifies, in the final sense, a theft from those who hunger and are not fed, those who are cold and are not clothed. This world in arms is not spending money alone. It is spending the sweat of its laborers, the genius of its scientists, the hopes of its children. (Eisenhower, 1953)

This concept has been termed in macroeconomics the "guns or butter" dichotomy. Its importance will continue to grow in an unstable future with limited resources but unlimited firepower. It should also be at the center of any discussion of building and using lethal machines. As lethal machines advance and increase, it is unclear how this will affect politics and the use of warfare to 'solve' conflicts. Increasing disparity between the haves and the have-nots creates increasing threats (perceived or actual) to security for both sides, and increases the probability that the rich will use technology against the poor. It is not too difficult to see the near-future likelihood of increasingly rich populations increasingly using lethal machines that continue to advance to 'protect' themselves against increasingly poor populations. In fact, that future is already present.

Rare Earth Minerals (REMs)

As previously noted, computers, smartphones, robots, and other advanced machines require assembling a large number of materials to produce. Many of these materials are uncommon, difficult to mine, and come from only certain locations on the planet. Many of these locations suffer from social upheaval and environmental degradation, making a sustainable and steady supply uncertain. This phenomenon is perhaps easiest to see with the rare earth minerals (REMs).

Ironically, the vast majority of all resources required for all cars, rechargeable batteries, computers, smartphones, fluorescent lights, high definition televisions, advanced medical equipment and used in lasers, lenses, magnets, and advanced ceramics (Humphries, 2012)—are located in regions that suffer greatest from the digital divide: particularly Africa and China. The continent of Africa, particularly Central Africa, has some of the lowest rates of technology use in the world, but the world is dependent on its rare natural resources to produce many technologies. Meanwhile, China has one of the largest within-country digital divide disparities while producing about 85% of the world's REMs. This highlights the fact that the people affected by the mining of these minerals are the ones least likely to benefit from the technologies created by the minerals.

There are actually seventeen different REMs with varying degrees of scarcity (Humphries, 2012). Some of them are more abundant than copper, gold, lead, and platinum, which are also used in high technology, along with tin, and have many of the same ethical and environmental problems as REM mining. The problem with REMs is that their concentrations within the earth are low, making their mining difficult, expensive, and wasteful. The ores frequently have radioactive impurities like Thorium that require additional toxic materials to separate. For every one ton of REM mined, about 2,000 tons of toxic material is produced (Kaiman, 2014). China has the global supply of REMs cornered, not because it is the only location where these minerals exist, but because China has several in relatively higher concentrations and fewer economic restrictions on protecting workers and the environment, making it one of the only locations where this type of mining is economically viable. For example, In Baotau, the city that produces half of China's REM totals, about ten million tons of wastewater are produced each year, and essentially no protection is given to the city's inhabitants (Kaiman, 2014).

The U.S., along with most countries in the world, imports 100% of its REMs from China. The U.S. government considers this fact a threat to national security because all advanced weaponry, particularly lethal robots, makes heavy use of REMs (Humphries, 2012). This has sparked political action to improve their domestic industry, even if it is not economically successful, because it is easy to see a future possibility where China may want to stop sharing. This would quickly become a weakness in maintaining global hegemony and the 'global war on terror' conflicts. If this status quo were to change or a world-war-type-conflict scenario began with China or Russia, the military would get precedence on REM use. It is easy to see how public consumption of REMs would likely be one of the first things rationed, similar to how it restricted many consumer goods during World War II. This type of scenario would also severely damage the international industrial supply chains that provide the raw materials needed for advanced technology, which would make the cost for consumer tech products soar.

Even assuming a non-gloomy peaceful future, global annual demand for REMs was already higher than production by 2010, and demand is estimated to increase about 150% by 2015 (Humphries, 2012). With emerging economies in high population countries and the continued demand for high-technology products in developed countries, demand is expected to remain high. While forecasters predict that increased Chinese production, along with new mining sites elsewhere, will be able to keep up with demand and even create a surplus for some REMs in the short term, other important REMs are already expected to see shortfalls (Humphries, 2012). Due to the fact that demand is higher than supply, and China controls and restricts exports, prices for some REMs have risen sharply and are likely to continue to go up in the future. This creates increased economic incentive to mine for more, opening up new locations for production, while markets remain volatile and risky. However, sites with the highest-grade ore are already being exploited; new mineral extraction will be more costly environmentally and socially, have lower grade ores, and produce more waste per output of mineral. Additionally, new mining projects can easily take ten years of development before useful production occurs.

In the short term, prices for consumer tech products may continue to decrease even as raw material and energy costs continue to increase. This is a potentially dangerous artificial manipulation of the economy to drive short-term profits. Even with higher efficiencies of materials for these products, pressures on mineral demands will continue to make mineral prices rise. Tech product prices are artificially low relative to the true environmental and social costs required to produce them. These costs, though temporarily hidden, still occur and can be seen as either being transferred to the poor without a voice or carried over onto the ledger of the future. This is currently being accepted because the materials are coming from locations that ignore these costs and the end user is generally far removed from the damage. Projecting these facts a few decades into the future, it is difficult to see how this can be sustained. Mining is difficult and markets are volatile, making only the richest players able to enter the game. The ethical concerns are already apparent: poor people, in countries that do not have safeguards for their protection, are paying the social and environmental costs for producing the raw materials needed to create high technology products that they don't even get to use. Meanwhile, those enjoying these products are removed and insulated from the costs, making it easy for them to not see or consider what true costs went into their latest gadget.

Water

Earth is a water planet, but the amount available for human use is deceptively small. About 96.5% of all water on the planet is held in the oceans and largely unusable (United States Geological Survey [USGS], 2014). It can be desalinated, and countries like the U.A.E. are leading the way, but these processes are currently cumbersome and energy intensive, and not viable for meeting humanity's water demands. Of the total fresh water, less than 1% is available for humanity to use (USGS, 2014).

As the human population continues to rise, water scarcity will increase as a global issue and is already predicted to be the reason for fighting future wars. About 70% of total water usage currently goes towards agriculture (United Nations Environment Program, 2010). More people on the planet will strain agricultural outputs, meaning that more land will be used for food production. However, the best farmlands are already in use, which means that the new lands dedicated to food are less productive and require more water. In other words, it is a cycle of diminishing returns: more water for less food in return.

As fast as the global population is growing, water use is growing twice as fast, according to the Food and Agriculture Organization of the United Nations (FAO) (2012). However, the amount of available water remains constant. The FAO reports that water scarcity, which they define as an excess of demand over available supply, already affects 40% of the world's population. They predict that by 2025, 1.8 billion people will live under absolute water scarcity, and two-thirds of the total population could be water stressed. The highest population growths in that time are expected to be in regions already experiencing scarcity.

These are the facts of our planetary situation: rapidly growing population, using water twice as fast as population growth, supply of water is unchanged. It is not difficult to see the problem here. Meanwhile, high technology uses massive amounts of water to produce and operate. As noted earlier, one average computer and monitor requires nearly 1.5 metric tons of water just to produce. The more advanced the components, the more water that is needed overall. This does not include the water used to produce the electricity to run the machine, or the water used to cool its components if it is a larger system.

Taking a closer look at only one—but most important—component of computers, the microprocessor or microchip, it becomes clear why so much water is needed. In addition to simply the volume of water required, 70% of the water that goes into a microchip must have extreme purity (Fishman, 2011). Keeping up with Moore's law has meant that components are now on the nanoscale, and chips can have upwards of a billion transistors (Pacific Northwest Pollution Prevention Resource Center [PPRC], 2009). Manufacturing processes for microchips are on the cutting edge of many sciences—and evolve rapidly, requiring additional research and development and total energy—including: optics, metal work, laser alignment, and climate/cleanliness control. All of these advances and sciences also factor into the total energy and water footprints that are not included in this total, but only one aspect will be focused on here for illustration. While chip production is getting more efficient per output, when factoring in all of the inputs for the various new technologies going into the chips and scale of production, water and energy demands continue to go up quickly.

Microchips are manufactured by building up layers and layers of various materials used in circuit manufacturing, with more advanced chips having upwards of twenty layers. Between each layer, the chip needs to be washed clean of any debris from the creation and etching of the previous layer. Modern microchips have electronic pathways smaller than visible light wavelengths, so even the tiniest debris can ruin the entire chip. Therefore, the water used must be what is called ultra pure water (UPW); it absolutely cannot have any particle of any kind in it except water molecules. The filtration process takes twelve steps beyond reverse osmosis—which is considered the standard for "pure" drinking water under normal applications (Fishman, 2011). The process involves: filtration, heat, chemicals, degasification, ion exchange, ultraviolet sterilization and then it is filtered through membranes twenty nanometers wide (PPRC, 2009). These filters must be inspected frequently with electron microscopes for any nano-rips. Clearly, this process takes a lot of energy and specialized equipment. It also takes about 1.5 times the amount of 'tap' water to make UPW (PPRC, 2009). Over 7.5 million liters of UPW is produced every day at just one IBM plant, which means tens of millions of liters more are produced worldwide every day (Fishman, 2011).

When about a billion people every day on this planet do not have clean drinking water, it seems almost absurd to purify tens of millions of liters of water a day, at great cost, to the point where it is deadly to drink. It is not difficult to see where this conflict of water use may come to a head in the near future with the realities of population growth and water limitations. A fundamental question may soon be forced upon humanity, if it should not already be asked: do we give the water to people or machines?

Another area where computing equals water use is in cooling large systems, particularly data centers. As more and more data is created, larger and larger data centers are created to store it all. Machines use power, which invariably generates heat even for the most efficient computing machines. Above certain temperatures, systems cannot operate optimally or can be damaged. Many smaller systems use circulating air, but most larger ones use water. How much water is used is relative to the machines and power consumption in use.

Fortunately, within the past few years, water use efficiency for these massive data centers has become a focus for businesses like Microsoft and Google. Unfortunately, most businesses do not make their water usage public, so these rates are difficult to determine. One recent estimate is that a 15-megawatt data center uses about 1.4 million liters of water per day (as cited in Miller, 2012). The first data center to publically state their water use was Facebook, who said that their new data center in 2012 used .22 liters per kilowatt hour of equipment energy (as cited in Miller, 2012). In 2010, Google disclosed that it used about 2.25 million megawatt hours of power in 2010; its data capacity has grown considerably since then. For the sake of example, if Google's 2010 water per power consumption were the same as Facebook, it would have used about 495 million liters of water in 2010 alone. Of course, this does not mean that the water was unusable after Google used it, or how much was fresh or seawater, but it does indicate the scale of water needed by the world's data centers.

An interesting example for a discussion of ethics in relation to data centers and water usage comes from the U.S. National Security Agency's (NSA) new 93,000 square meter data center in the state of Utah that was completed in late 2013. Its exact mission is classified, but public acknowledgements of its purpose are to vaguely support cybersecurity. Aside from confirming that it will have four data facilities of 2,300 square meters each, the actual amount of data that can be stored is unconfirmed. The facility uses a constant stream of 65 megawatts of power but the capabilities and efficiencies of their machines are classified. Needless to say, the data storage capabilities are enormous. The water needed to cool their machines is also enormous. Utah is the second driest state in the U.S., but the facility has the capacity to pump over 6.4 million liters per day for cooling. While its actual use so far has been less, obvious water usage and rights issues are apparent. Further, the agency was able to procure the location and power and water usage by quiet political deals that did not generate publicity or allow public comment until the deals were already secured. One of these politicians went from the relative obscurity of being the governor of Utah to become a presidential candidate.

Additionally, as AI technology advances, its likelihood of being used in massive data centers like the NSA's raises important ethical considerations. For example, it is possible, if not likely, that the NSA's goal is to store all of the data it recovers from tapping the world's communications, then use an AI network of supercomputers to access and process this data, all without oversight of any kind (Bamford, 2009). While this seems like science fiction, again, the future is already present. Academics and people living within these societies need to be discussing what kind of effect this much power might have on the control of a society.

Oil

While most people typically do not relate robots and computing machines to oil production, perhaps they should. As previously noted, one computer and monitor require a little less than two barrels of oil directly, but the significance is much more. In the current global economy, fossil fuels are energy itself. Fossil fuels are how things move and get moved. Without energy, normal life ceases to function. Oil is the lubricant of modern life. Humanity has grown dependent on oil for essentially everything considered modern in the world, especially things that use electricity. The daily oil consumption in the world was approximately 86 million barrels in 2010 and is projected to be over 93 million barrels by 2015 (United States Energy Information Administration, 2014), but can supply keep up? This is equal to about 150 oil tankers emptied each day. The problem is that, like water and REMs, oil is a finite resource, or at least is renewed on geologic scales much slower than what is being taken out.

Also like REMs, the difficulty and amount of energy required to get oil from the earth varies based on location; whether or not it is worth getting is based on economics. When an oil well is first installed in a good location, oil is pumped up easily due to high pressures under the ground. However, as more oil is pumped up, the pressure decreases and the viscosity of the oil increases and the emission speed of the oil inevitably decreases. These factors make production more expensive, energy intensive, and the resulting oil decreases. Eventually, injecting high-pressure water is needed to pump up the oil, but the production efficiency and quality of oil will continue to decrease. This method, called fracking, uses large quantities of water, which has already been shown to be very limited. These factors also lead to the need to dig deeper and deeper into the earth, which can lead to the dangerous effects seen with the Deepwater Horizon disaster.

Like food production and mineral extraction, the areas that are easiest to get oil in the world are already being exploited. However, the demand for oil has led to more and more wells and a massive demand for oil production. In order to meet this demand, lower quality locations must also be used. As the economic incentive to obtain oil increases, the amount of energy, cost, and effort that is still profitable goes up, thereby increasing economically viable locations. However, this is also a product of diminishing returns: more cost for less and lower quality oil in return. Meanwhile, the production of previously "easy" wells are entering decline and the new sources cannot make up the difference. Eventually, this is what limits supply more than what the total reserves may theoretically or actually be in fact. When oil demand exceeds supply, this is known as peak oil.

The topic of peak oil is controversial and far from definitive because it is based on assumptions about known reserves, production and consumption rates, and even how the natural process of oil production occurs. What matters here is economic viability of production versus consumption. In the past, oil production rates were set according to the consumption rate. After peak oil, the consumption rate must be set according to the limited production rate. The fact that one day the consumption rate will exceed the production rate is absolute, but it is not clear whether oil production will decrease gradually and steadily after oil peaks, drops suddenly, or will maintain the maximum rate for some time. It will depend on consumption rates, newly found oil reserves, the decisions of powerful nations, and how much people are willing to spend for it. It also seems that this ambiguity benefits those profiting the most from oil. Extending the status quo for a little while longer and maintaining prolonged scarcity would produce huge profits. But, ringing the peak oil alarm bells too loudly would dampen the global economy and could push people away from oil too much. Oil production and the global economy are now completely dependent on each other. A strong and stable economy is needed to maintain capabilities of extracting oil with increasing difficulty, while this type of economy is clearly being powered by oil. Without one, the other will crash, and if that occurs, there may not be a way to build the system back up.

Although the opinions of experts vary, even the most optimistic agree that the peak production will come in less than twenty years. Many believe it has already passed. For example, retired British Petroleum (BP) engineer Dr. Richard Miller, who prepared projections for BP between 2000 and 2007, believes that conventional oil peaked in 2008 (Ahmed, 2013). Perhaps not coincidentally, this was also the year that U.S. President George W. Bush twice asked Saudi Arabia to increase production but was refused (Stolberg & Mouawad, 2008), and the global recession followed. Miller said that 37 countries are already post-peak, and global oil production is declining by about 3.5 million barrels a day per year, or about 4.1% per year (Ahmed, 2013).

'Alternative' Energy

Having realized the crisis, it is important to quickly find an appropriate substitution for oil. Even though oil will likely never "run out," it is a non-sustainable energy source and must eventually be replaced by better practices that use less energy to produce, have less geopolitical impact, and can be used indefinitely into the future. The problems discussed will be largely solved if such an alternative source is found. For example, if a very small fraction of the energy that hits the Earth from the Sun could be converted into electricity, or if the principles of zero point energy were converted into viable machines, then every human on the planet could use as much as they ever wanted and many of these scarcity issues for technology would be eliminated. However, scientists have failed to produce outstanding results in researching alternatives like solar and wind power over the past thirty to forty years. If functional zero point energy machines have been produced, they have either been suppressed or classified and are not available to solve our energy problems. Yes, there have been nice advances in the efficiencies of these technologies, and research must continue, but current alternative energy technology will never be able to replace oil.

The main reason is that alternative energy can only be produced with the help of oil. Solar cells and wind power generators cannot completely replace oil, given the fact that oil is needed to produce and install the cells and generators. For example, cars are likely one of the first things a person might think of when considering oil use. Can electric cars replace oil? Aside from the fact that the various components on the car require certain amounts of oil to produce, it must also be assumed that a non-oil fuel can produce the electricity. This is a big assumption; but even if it could be overcome, there are still problems. Electricity must be stored in batteries, which are produced using REMs, which must be mined and transported across the globe by machines that use oil. Electricity, biofuels, and hydrogen all still use oil to produce. For example, to mass-produce the raw material for biofuel, such as corn or sugar cane, petrochemicals and agricultural machines are needed. Ultimately, more than one liter of oil is used to produce one liter of biofuel, so clearly this is not an alternative.

Therefore, the paradox is the fact that alternative energy, unlike its name, cannot perfectly be an alternative for oil. A lot of oil ends up getting used in researching alternatives. Oil is still needed to run the facilities required to convert raw forms of energy into usable energy, there is no foreseeable escape from this fact. The so-called alternative energy is currently only an extension of oil. At best, it only allows prolonging the use of oil by a few years. It is no different than attaching a respirator to a dying patient.

If the sun could be effectively harnessed for electricity production, these problems would be solved. For the sake of explanation, assume that around 2,000 watts/m^2 of energy falls on a solar cell panel, but the most efficient commercially available panels can only convert about 175 W/m^2 to electricity, which is less than 10% efficient. Even these best rates are only true for peak sunshine hours, which means only about five hours per day. This means that a relatively large surface area is required to power each home. While this is increasingly becoming viable in small-scale settings of energy collection and use, however, to replace oil energy for the planet would require a surface area of solar panels that is simply not feasible. If efficiency were to double or triple, it still would not be close to feasible. Parabolic solar collectors produce tantalizing efficiencies, but any large-scale production is far away. Additionally, because traditional solar panels are only about 10% efficient, the remaining energy that does not become electricity becomes heat. Therefore, large solar farms also become massive heat islands, which has important environmental consequences. An added problem is that the more efficient panels currently require higher amounts of REMs and energy (oil) to produce them. Plus, there is still the problem of storage in batteries.

Wind power is relatively widely used in Europe, and has rapidly emerged as the leading alternative energy source. Wind power currently has the largest annual increase of usage among all the alternative energy sources. However, it may also lead in unintended consequences. Like with solar power, on small scales it can be a viable electricity generator. However, the scale of the wind power industry that is needed to reach a level of production to make a dent in oil needs presents several insurmountable problems. First, wind power is not unlimited. There are only so many places where high quality wind consistently blows and even then it is never constant. The amount of wind farms needed would mean that massive windmills would cover all of these locations in the world and even this would not be enough.

Second, the total resources required to manufacture and implement the wind machine are higher than the energy it produces during its lifetime. Picture this example and it is easy to see why: many prime wind locations are on cliffs in secluded areas, to put a wind farm there requires leveling and building roads big enough to haul these massive devices to these secluded windy spots. These spots must be able to accommodate at least twenty generators to be economically worthwhile, and each of these generators has a 100+ meter tower and usually three 50+ meter turbines, so they must be spaced properly apart. These obviously require heavy machinery to haul to the location and erect. But first, a leveled spot that is about 150 m^2 is needed for each generator, as well as a foundation deep enough and strong enough to hold a 100-meter tower in a windy spot, which requires a large quantity of concrete and steel. Then, once it is erected, it also needs frequent maintenance on all of its components for the life of the device. Even when farms are built on sea-level coasts, the basic net negative energy still results. Clearly, the impacts to people and the environment have their own consequences as well.

Third, the electrical grid depends on a predictable supply, but because the amount of energy that these wind farms generates fluctuates, it can never be depended on to replace current generation systems. At best, it can only supplement them. And of course, storage of this generated electricity in most systems requires sophisticated batteries and infrastructures to transfer to existing power systems, which is also complicated by the fluctuating current. Most of these farms are located far from existing power stations so it is very costly to connect them to existing infrastructure.

Early and strong adopters of wind power like Denmark and Germany have encountered a number of major problems, have not decreased the need of conventional power plants, and have eliminated many of the subsidies supporting the industry. Looking at their example demonstrates the flaws in large-scale wind generation as currently conceived. Norway, specifically, decided not to pursue wind power after a careful review of Denmark's system. They found that Denmark could not reduce its reliance on conventional power plants because the wind energy was unreliable and conventional power plants end up not being able to ramp up or down their production as needed, resulting in power plants being kept at their original steady rates. This meant that over 80% of wind-generated electricity was exported at a financial loss, but their system became dependent enough on wind generation that when the wind wasn't blowing enough, they had to import electricity (White, 2004). Clearly, this is not an effective alternative.

By the early 2000s, many world leaders had begun to recognize this global energy problem and the lack of viable solutions, and returned to the hope of nuclear power. Previously quoted President Eisenhower began the popularization of "Atoms for Peace" in 1958 and nuclear power reached its peak in the mid-1970s. But, after the nuclear accidents of Three Mile Island and Chernobyl, its popularity decreased as fears of its safety and potential harm to the planet grew. But, after several decades of not being able to create successful alternative energies, many people believe that nuclear energy is the only way. However, a closer look shows that a dependence on nuclear energy is also a false hope and a potentially fatal one.

On May 24, 2004, an article titled, "Nuclear power is the only green solution," appeared in the British newspaper *Independent*. The article was written by James Lovelock, who has continuously warned about greenhouse gases since the beginning of the 1970s. Lovelock mainly talked about the importance of expanding nuclear power generation to stop global warming. Some environmentalists began to agree with Lovelock's opinion. Nuclear energy emerged as a solution, and admitted by Lovelock, because there are no other suitable alternatives (Lovelock, 2004).

The advocates of nuclear energy argue that its biggest advantage is a massive amount of energy from a small amount of fuel, which is undeniably true. The energy from nuclear fission and fusion is incomparably greater than the chemical energy stored in fossil fuels. This has led people to believe that nuclear resources are abundant because a large amount of electrical energy can be gained from a small amount of uranium. However, most nuclear plants use uranium-235 to get nuclear fission energy and only 0.7% of natural uranium is uranium-235. If the consumption trend is traced, the time limit of using uranium-235 is similar to oil's depletion time. There would quickly be the same 'peak uranium-235' problem that is currently being faced with oil. However, by using fast-breeder reactors, which recycles the used nuclear fuel, there is currently an abundant supply of fuel, but this also produces many problems.

Nuclear fuels have an extremely high energy density, but they must first be processed before they can be used in reactors. The process of mining and processing uranium also produces much more cost and pollution than mining fossil fuels, which are already significant. The cost of producing nuclear energy usually refers only to the fuel costs, maintenance costs and operating costs, including labor costs. In other words, the reactor shutdown costs, waste and waste storage costs, and costs associated with a potential accident or meltdown are not considered. If all of these were added, nuclear energy is likely the most costly and dangerous energy source of all. Even with the additional factors left out, nuclear energy has not been economically competitive at any point in its history and has required billions of dollars in government support to continue (Cooper, 2014).

Uranium itself is limited in amount, and to recycle the fuel, plutonium must be used. Plutonium is one of the world's deadliest substances, as about two kilograms spread evenly around the planet is enough to poison all life on Earth. Regardless, it is currently widely used for making nuclear bombs and certain types of nuclear reactors. Aside from the fact that nuclear fuel is itself limited and some of the deadliest elements known on our planet, the waste from their use will remain radioactive for thousands of years and mankind has yet to figure out what to do with it. Since the beginning of its use, the nuclear industry has produced over 70,000 metric tons of radioactive waste (Nuclear Energy Institute, 2014). To date, no country has developed a true long-term storage facility, because it is practically impossible to accomplish. Where do you safely put something that is radioactive for 10,000 years?

The nuclear option took a major hit on March 11, 2011 when the worst nuclear disaster in history occurred at Fukushima, Japan. It is difficult to ascertain precisely what happened because of obvious cover-up and media silencing, and these details cannot be discussed here, but what can be ascertained is certainly troubling. What is clear is that the authorities responsible have tried to minimize public concern rather than minimize public harm, and have shown a consistent pattern of lying and obfuscation to minimize the events only for it to later come out that they knew matters were worse than originally stated. This is done to protect themselves from litigation and protect their financial interests, including the nuclear industry as a whole, rather than protect human and aquatic life. The radiation levels announced by authorities has consistently been much lower than that detected by independent sources. Thus, it is nearly impossible to know truly how much damage was, and is still being, done to people and the environment.

Nearly four years after the initial explosion, the situation remains critical and has not been contained. Vast amounts of water are continually poured on the damaged fuel cores; all of this water becomes highly radioactive and must be collected in contamination barrels. These are stacked around the increasingly overcrowded site with no real plan for what to do with them. Additionally, every day since the disaster and for the foreseeable future, at least 400 tons of groundwater is seeping into the site, becoming contaminated with several radioactive elements including plutonium, and entering the ocean.

There is currently no known way to engineer a solution to contain the problem and will likely continue for decades. Since the authorities are not trustable and continue to attempt to minimize the concern rather than damage, it is unknown what true cost this will bring to the planet, but clearly it is significant and will continue to mount for decades to come. This is a crisis that is affecting the world and requires open and honest sharing of the facts, whatever they may be, in order for the world to attempt a solution. Ironically, this crisis is a product of, and possibly can only be solved by, the Computer Age. It is a problem affecting the entire planet, and possibly, the only solution may come from allowing open access to all of the relevant information to the entire planet so that scientists from any country and without potential economic losses can work on the problem together. Regardless, Fukushima graphically demonstrates that nuclear power is not a green solution, as this accident will be the cause of millions of deaths to people and animals.

In summary, there are four main problems with nuclear power that prohibit it from being a true solution: limited supply, radiation dangers, storage problems, and lack of economic viability. Wind and solar have their own problems, and none of these is an actual alternative to oil. Thus, the energy crisis remains and will continue unless some exotic technology is discovered and distributed to the world, or some unknown law of the universe is discovered that will break humanity free of these limitations. Effectively, at least in the short term, machine intelligence only adds pressure to an existing, unsustainable energy economy. Though AI may represent a panacea for some invested in the machine industries, production of a machine intelligence capable of producing necessary solutions to what are effectively natural and ecological problems may arrive only after that natural ecology is subverted. The irony, indeed the tragedy, here being of course that this natural ecology should die at least in part in order to support the industries that result in the AI finally able to tell us that we no longer have any viable ecological solutions. This is the very situation this chapter hopes to avoid.

DISCUSSION AND RECOMMENDATIONS

While humanity continues to wait for technology to save us, it may in fact be our very downfall. The authors are not saying that humanity should voluntarily give up existing and emergent technologies entirely and go back to the Stone Age; we must use them for as long as possible. Many applications can aid and advance humanity. But, if these fundamental issues are not resolved, nature may force us to give them up regardless, and not comfortably. At some point, hard choices will have to be made, with resources running low and culture re-geared towards prolonging and maximizing its technological run.

Any discussion of the future of machine ethics must be grounded by this natural context. What is held to be good, objects of reverence, may shift as the cultural world of our creation gets brought back in line with the natural world. The goal is to effect such transitions voluntarily, by way of our own authorship. Ultimately, a machine is created to accomplish a job. Currently, what is newest, smallest, fastest, and has the most advanced materials, is regarded as the good, as an object of status, innovation and advancement. "Progress." However, when the facts of the natural system are taken into account, for example, is it better to use a titanium alloy robotic arm that runs on solar power and advanced batteries to accomplish a job, when a human and a lever are wholly as effective and produced by industries much closer to natural equilibrium? Current systemic norms point to the robot. However, given current objective reality, the human and lever may in fact be the best option for a sustainable and happy future because this mechanism employs far less total energy to accomplish the same job. All people and industries must repeat this basic calculation for all actions. Since most people alive were born during the technologic revolution described at the beginning of this chapter, it feels natural to believe that it will last forever. But, it has only been a very brief blip in human history, and based on the fundamental problems described here, it doesn't look like it can sustain itself for another hundred years longer.

The system of the production, distribution, and use of these technologies also does not hold up to basic ethical scrutiny. Particularly, the categorical imperative or social or environmental justice standards are not met. This is especially the case with lethal machines in military contexts. These machines are far too energetically costly for everyone to have one, even if they could buy one. The objective reality of the situation is this: the rich subject the poor to mine the materials under detrimental conditions to the workers and surrounding environment, the workers do not get to enjoy the product but do experience the health and environmental degradation costs, the rich process these materials into machines that they use for a few years then discard, then the poor break down the toxic e-waste in these machines to be made back into something for the rich to use again for a few years, and the process repeats. The rich get to enjoy the product without suffering the environmental costs; the poor suffer the costs without ever enjoying the product. The end product and end user are far removed and insulated from the true costs associated with the product. The use of lethal machines by the rich to protect themselves against the poor is a picture-perfect example.

So, what can be done? As previously stated, simply giving up our machines is not likely or desirable, and no one action or change can easily fix the problem. However, there does seem to be a number of actions, both on an individual and collective level, that can prolong the technologic ride and increase ethical levels in production and use.

For instance, efficiency in production techniques must be maximized, while limiting or replacing the use of exotic materials like REMs should be done whenever possible. Many processes are perpetuated simply because it has already been tried and shown to work, not because it is the best or most efficient way to do it (PPRC, 2009). Finding these energetic short cuts needs to be encouraged and standardized. If more common or renewable substances can do the job, then they should be used in place of rare or more energy intense substances.

Along these lines, plant-based materials should be favored whenever possible for both raw materials and energy use. When looking at the energy problem, a plant-circulating energetic system appears to be the only sustainable option. For much of human history, this was the only energy source used. Now, for the future of the information age, it may again be the only salvation. Plants use and store the sun's energy far more efficiently than any solar cell, they can be used for every basic human need, and it is truly renewable. If humanity could change its awareness, and focus its advanced technology on how to use plants wisely and efficiently and implement them into technology whenever possible, it will contribute to the solution. However, if humanity simply treats plants as a substitute for oil without changing perception and awareness, then it will quickly come to the same impasse.

Additionally, no product should be made that does not have an explicit end-life plan for recycling or proper disposal (Austin, 2013). This does not include exporting it to a poor country to have its children strip it down. If a component cannot be reused or biodegrade, etc., it should be replaced by an alternative or not used.

A cultural shift in standards needs to favor simpler materials and processes, to get the job done using the least amount of total energy, rather than favoring what is newest or sexiest. This shift needs to include building products to last as long as possible, or be completely repurposed, rather than becoming obsolete in a year and added to landfills. This shift should also include eliminating, on an individual level, the status symbol gains of having the newest, latest, greatest gadget. In fact, this mentality needs to become an object of scorn. It is not enough to make all of these things more efficiently, but we must also make fewer things and limit our 'need' for superfluous things. Reduce, reuse, recycle is an energetic hierarchy, with reduction being by far the most effective in lowering energy use. It is currently, in a short-sighted view, good for the economy to create a culture of continuous consumption, but this means burning through finite resources, creating mountains of trash and waste, and generating a lot of heat. This needs to be replaced by a long-view understanding of how to live in sustainable symbiosis with the natural system. This is not about some leftist political ideology; it is about survival and prolonging the Computer/Information Age.

To aid the consumer and to reconnect them to what went into their product, each product could have required labeling—similar to the nutrition facts required on food products in the U.S. and other countries—that detail the product's total energetic footprint. This could include: a materials list with breakdowns of rare or renewable sources, mining locations and costs, toxic materials produced, water and oil consumption, and disposal information. This would allow the consumer to make more informed choices and also put pressure on businesses to minimize these footprints. Currently, much of this information is unknown and untracked by these businesses. If they were required to keep track and to report these findings to their consumers, businesses would likely change, streamline, and make many of their practices more ethical. While these changes would be done to appeal to the consumers, not because it is the right thing to do, it would still help to change the culture positively and lead to better actions. Businesses only make these changes when it is economically beneficial, and consumers must use their power to impact positive change.

CONCLUSION

This chapter has highlighted fundamental problems to sustaining advanced computing machines, particularly in the form of limited natural resources and an unsustainable energy infrastructure. Merely saving energy or being more efficient cannot solve these problems. It requires revolutions in social systems and the reformation of culture on a global scale. Currently, "economic growth" is sacrosanct and considered the most important universal truth. However, the dominant culture of capitalism and consumption is only helping to speed the burning through what remains of nature. Without sustainability, positive change and reassessing what is important, this dominant culture cannot last long and is already in the process of dying. Change can come voluntarily, gradually, and intelligently, thereby prolonging the technologic age for as long as possible and eventually overcoming the limitations shown in this chapter. Or, the system will eventually crash and humanity will be forced to change quickly, painfully, and likely lose the technology even quicker than it was gained. Either way, we will come back in line to homeostasis with nature, and nature must win, or we all lose.

One of the biggest ethical problems this chapter highlighted is the fact that the planet has limited resources, but only a small number of people get to experience the benefits of their use, especially when it comes to high technology. The digital divide is deep and widening. The socioeconomic divide is deep and widening. Fewer people own more wealth than ever before, while more people populate the planet and have less. The poor are used to get what is needed to create technologies but then don't get to use them. This can only be solved by 'democratizing' the so-called infosphere—where everyone on earth has easy access to open information that is paid for, developed, and maintained as a commons, as a 'natural resource'. As has already been shown, the planet is small, and the information age cannot occur without using and sharing its natural resources, this is only a logical extension of this idea.

The digital divide is about access. Without it, people are left behind without knowledge, information, and skills. It also, ultimately, creates security threats and the likelihood of conflict, which wastes more energy. If digital access were a 'human right' it would maximize individual access to information. With enough leisure and security, this could facilitate personal development, which may lead populations to value understanding over violence. Such individuals and populations are best able to make energetic environmental policy decisions in their own lives and in their localities. So, the energy necessary to maintain the access to the information necessary to produce such an informed populace may, in fact, remain less than the energy needed to maintain a population in ignorance without such access. Additionally, if a nonviolent stepdown from unsustainability is possible, then it is only through open-access to information that this will be possible. Case in point, when a revolution happens in a country in the 21st century, the first thing that those in power try to cut off is access to social media. Information is power; ignorance is control.

Additionally, the big break that humanity seeks in our technological salvation could well come from someone with an outside perspective that was not born into privilege. For example, some rural female ethnic minority—which when given an opportunity to combine access, education, and personal development—may bring a new insight or perspective to the energy problem that no one has ever considered before. And, with free access to this information, it cannot be suppressed for the benefit of the small elite to direct an ignorant population to maintain the status quo. The future is not determined; it will be a result of our collective choices, for better or worse.

REFERENCES

Ahmed, N. (2013, Dec 23). Former BP geologist: peak oil is here and it will 'break economies'. *The Guardian*. Retrieved from http://www.theguardian.com/environment/earth-insight/2013/dec/23/british-petroleum-geologist-peak-oil-break-economy-recession

Austin, A. A. (2013). Where will all the waste go?: Utilizing extended producer responsibility framework laws to achieve zero waste. *Golden Gate University Environmental Law Journal, 6(2)*, 220-257. Retrieved from http://digitalcommons.law.ggu.edu/cgi/viewcontent.cgi?article=1101&context=gguelj

Bamford, J. (2009). *The shadow factory: The NSA from 9/11 to the eavesdropping on America*. New York: Anchor.

Boren, Z. D. (2014, Oct 7). There are officially more mobile devices than people in the world. *The Independent*. Retrieved from http://www.independent.co.uk/life-style/gadgets-and-tech/news/there-are-officially-more-mobile-devices-than-people-in-the-world-9780518.html

Cooper, M. (2014, Feb 20). Why the economics don't favor nuclear power in America. *Forbes*. Retrieved from http://www.forbes.com/sites/energysource/2014/02/20/why-the-economics-dont-favor-nuclear-power-in-america/

Desjardins, J. (2013, May 21). What is the cost of mining gold? *Visual Capitalist*. Retrieved from http://www.visualcapitalist.com/what-is-the-cost-of-mining-gold/

Diaz, J. (2013, Nov 16). US Army robots will outnumber human soldiers 10 to 1 by 2023. *Gizmodo*. Retrieved from http://sploid.gizmodo.com/us-army-robots-will-outnumber-human-soldiers-10-to-1-by-1465669535

Eisenhower, D. D. (1953, Apr 16). *The Chance for Peace*. Speech to the American Society of Newspaper Editors.

Environmental Protection Agency. (2012). *General information on e-waste*. Retrieved from http://www.epa.gov/epawaste/conserve/materials/ecycling/faq.htm

Fishman, C. (2011, Apr 29). The dangerously clean water used to make your iPhone. *Fast Company*. Retrieved from http://www.fastcompany.com/1750612/dangerously-clean-water-used-make-your-iphone

Food and Agriculture Organization of the United Nations. (2012). *Coping with water scarcity: An action framework for agriculture and food security*. Retrieved from: http://www.fao.org/docrep/016/i3015e/i3015e.pdf

Gartner. (2013, June 24). *Gartner says worldwide PC, tablet and mobile phone shipments to grow 5.9 percent in 2013 as anytime-anywhere-computing drives buyer behavior*. Retrieved from http://www.gartner.com/newsroom/id/2525515

Humphries, M. (2012, June 8). Rare earth elements: The global supply chain. *Congressional Research Service*. Retrieved from http://www.relooney.info/0_New_14118.pdf

International Federation of Robotics. (2013). *Service robot statistics*. Retrieved October 7, 2014, from www.ifr.org/service-robots/statistics

International Federation of Robotics. (2014). *IFR: All-time-high for industrial robots in 2013*. Retrieved from http://www.ifr.org/news/ifr-press-release/ifr-all-time-high-for-industrial-robots-in-2013-601/

Kaiman, J. (2014, Mar 20). Rare earth mining in China: The bleak social and environmental costs. *The Guardian*. Retrieved from: http://www.theguardian.com/sustainable-business/rare-earth-mining-china-social-environmental-costs

Kshetri, N., & Dholakia, N. (2009). *Global digital divide*. Retrieved from http://ebooks.narotama.ac.id/files/Encyclopedia%20of%20Information%20Science%20and%20Technology%20%282nd%20Edition%29/Global%20Digital%20Divide.pdf

Lichocki, P., Kahn, P., & Billard, A. (2011). The ethical landscape in robotics. *IEEE Robotics & Automation Magazine, 18*(1), 39–50. doi:10.1109/MRA.2011.940275

Lin, P. (2009, June 22). The ethical war machine. *Forbes*. Retrieved from http://www.forbes.com/2009/06/18/military-robots-ethics-opinions-contributors-artificial-intelligence-09-patrick-lin.html

Lovelock, J. (2004, May 24). Nuclear power is the only green solution. *The Independent*. Retrieved from http://www.independent.co.uk/voices/commentators/james-lovelock-nuclear-power-is-the-only-green-solution-6169341.html

Miller, R. (2012, Aug 14). Data center water use moves to the forefront. *Datacenter Knowledge*. Retrieved from http://www.datacenterknowledge.com/archives/2012/08/14/data-center-water-use-moves-to-center-stage/

Moor, J. H. (2006). The nature, importance, and difficulty of machine ethics. *IEEE Intelligent Systems, 21*(4), 18–21. doi:10.1109/MIS.2006.80

Moore, G. E. (1965). Cramming more components onto integrated circuits. *Electronics Magazine, 38*(8), 114–117.

Nuclear Energy Institute. (2014). *On-site storage of nuclear waste.* Retrieved from: http://www.nei.org/Knowledge-Center/Nuclear-Statistics/On-Site-Storage-of-Nuclear-Waste

Pacific Northwest Pollution Prevention Resource Center. (2009). *Semiconductor manufacturing*. Retrieved from: http://www.pprc.org/hubs/printfriendly.cfm?hub=1004&subsec=14&nav=1

Peckham, M. (2012, May 1). The collapse of Moore's law: Physicist says it's already happening. *Time*. Retrieved from http://techland.time.com/2012/05/01/the-collapse-of-moores-law-physicist-says-its-already-happening/

Plus, P. C. (2012, July 22). The weird and wonderful materials that make up your PC. *Techrader*. Retrieved from http://www.techradar.com/us/news/computing/pc/the-weird-and-wonderful-materials-that-make-up-your-pc-1089510

Snead, A. (2012, May 3). A brief history of warnings about the demise of Moore's Law. *Slate*. Retrieved from http://www.slate.com/blogs/future_tense/2012/05/03/michio_kaku_and_a_brief_history_of_warnings_about_the_end_of_moore_s_law_.html

Stolberg, S. G., & Mouawad, J. (2008, May 17). Saudis rebuff Bush, politely, on pumping more oil. *The New York Times*. Retrieved from: http://www.nytimes.com/2008/05/17/world/middleeast/17prexy.html?_r=0

Tweed, K. (2013, Dec 17). Global e-waste will jump 33 percent in the next five years. *IEEE Spectrum*. Retrieved from http://spectrum.ieee.org/energywise/energy/environment/global-ewaste-will-jump-33-in-next-five-years

United Nations Environment Program. (2010). *Assessing the environmental impacts of consumption and production: Priority products and materials*. Retrieved from http://www.unep.fr/shared/publications/pdf/DTIx1262xPA-PriorityProductsAndMaterials_Report.pdf

United Nations University. (2004). UN study shows environmental consequences from ongoing boom in personal computer sales. *Eurekalert*. Retrieved from http://www.eurekalert.org/pub_releases/2004-03/tca-uss030204.php

United States Census. (2014). *Census Data*. Retrieved from http://www.census.gov/popclock/

United States Energy Information Administration. (2014). *Short-term energy outlook*. Retrieved from http://www.eia.gov/forecasts/steo/report/global_oil.cfm

United States Geologic Survey. (2014, Mar 19). *How much water is there on, in, and above the Earth?* Retrieved from: http://water.usgs.gov/edu/earthhowmuch.html

White, D. J. (2004, July). Danish wind: Too good to be true? *The Utilities Journal*. 37-39

KEY TERMS AND DEFINITIONS

Environmental/Energetic Footprint: The total cost of all resources used to produce and dispose of a product.

E-Waste: Discarded electronic products.

Global Digital Divide: The lack of access to technology based on geography, race, ethnicity, or economics.

"Guns or Butter": On a planet with limited natural resources, the choice to use those resources for weapons to kill people or food to feed people.

Peak Oil: When consumption demands for oil exceed economically viable production.

Rare Earth Minerals: Group of 17 different minerals used in many electronics and household products. Found in low concentrations making their mining difficult.

Ultra Pure Water: Water required to use microchips, purified under great expense to the point of being deadly to drink.

Section 2

From the Outside In:
Intelligent Machine Technologies as a Window on Human Morality both as Evolved and as Evident in Internet Discourse, Today

Chapter 4
The Emergence of Artificial Autonomy:
A View from the Foothills of a Challenging Climb

Fernando da Costa Cardoso
Universidade Nova de Lisboa, Portugal

Luís Moniz Pereira
Universidade Nova de Lisboa, Portugal

ABSTRACT

In this chapter we set forth a case study of the integration of philosophy and computer science using artificial agents, beings ruled by abductive logic and emergent behavior. Our first step in this chapter is to highlight different models that we developed of such agents (a set of them related with evolutionary game theory and one model of a narrative storyteller robot). As we indicate, each model exemplifies different aspects of the bottom of the hill of autonomy as an emergent property of artificial systems specified through three aspects ("Self control", "Adaptivity to the environment" and "Response to environment"). In summary, our conception is that autonomy, when presented as an emergent characteristic, could fill the important place given it by elaborations in philosophical ethics and one that leads us to a clearer comprehension of where to direct our efforts in the field of artificial agents. We conclude this chapter with the notion that this reevaluation of autonomy is necessary for the enhanced comprehension of human morality.

INTRODUCTION

Autonomy plays a central role in modern ethics, as on its basis we distinguish the class of ethical agents from the other beings - "only things" or at most Kant's "heteronomous" beings, but not fully ethical agents. Forged from medieval Christian conceptions of the divine origin of morality and tempered with the rediscovery of classical Greek philosophers, with their natural order establishing standards for fitness,

DOI: 10.4018/978-1-4666-8592-5.ch004

excellence and virtue, traditional conceptions of autonomy continue to inform notions that often appear more central to the field. Freedom, personhood, responsibility and intentionality, aspects of autonomous agency by way of which some beings differentiate themselves from the mass of objects, tools, artifacts and things littering this physical world, at root derive their value in the aid they render in answering this fundamental question: autonomous, or not?

This binary is complicated by apparent grey-area cases. The existence of human children, incapacitated humans (mentally ill, intoxicated) and intelligent animals imply that "ethics" is not the simple domain of pure rational agents. Sensitivity to such cases is evident in the "moral patient" of Regan (1986) and Singer (1993). But, this sensitiveness remains exceptional. Autonomy often remains presented as an especial characteristic distinct to human beings differentiating them from other beings.

Our aim in this chapter is to suggest that artificial agency emerges with the multi-pole development of different characteristics, and that the development of capacities of artificial agents accordingly seeds the grey areas of agency. Ours is a proposal for the reevaluation of autonomy on the basis that we good reasons to recognize as autonomous suitably developed artificial systems. Our strategy is to open the space between programming efforts and philosophical investigation presenting, in a sense, a philosophical interpretation of a programming effort. This will allow us to redefine autonomy in a way that may prove useful. The first step is the recognition of the legitimacy in the conception of autonomy as is develops in response to challenges coming from different areas of historical investigation such as sociology and psychology. The second step, the one that distinguishes our proposal, is to present different programming efforts and to try to determine any sense of autonomy in these systems without diminishing what stands out from the preceding review of the modern tradition. This leads to our third step, the elaboration of the aforementioned frame, wherein different beings may be inserted as in a map revealing the different dimensions of autonomy as an emergent property. Lastly, in the final part of the chapter, we present some far-reaching consequences that we believe need to be addressed, and toward which we plan to aim in future investigations.

1. SETTING THE STAGE

Philosophers, particularly those in the rationalist tradition, have pictured autonomy as affording an important role not just in the practice of morality but also in the distinction of agents that are moral beings from others which are not. This tradition of so establishing autonomy or self-governance at the center of Ethics has a history that can be characterized globally and episodically. Globally, following Schneewind (1998), we may take it as a reaction against "the conception of morality as obedience" to some divine order. It is an internalization. Episodically, we may highlight the establishment of the Kantian formulation crowning autonomy as the central concept essential for morality, and thus Ethics, in the first place.

This crowning follows a natural development inside the modern moral tradition binding Ethics with human psychology. In this vein, when Kant established autonomy as the foundation of human dignity, he established an association between these two fields, something that could be verified in the following supportive statement: "Autonomy is thus the ground of the dignity of the human and of every rational nature" (Kant, 2002, AK 4:436). Autonomy reveals the particular constitution of our souls. In this sense modern Ethics, and with it the question of how we should live, merges a conception of what we should do with a conception of how our minds operate optimally.

The route that lead to this position certainly evolved in correlation with our views about our own psychology and accordingly can be captured in the progression that links the formulations of Descartes and Kant. Descartes affirms, when establishing his dualist view of the mind-body problem in the *First Meditation* of the *Meditations* (1641), that Ethics manifests itself as Freedom. By that is meant that the search for the proper way to act should be related with the best part of us, a part identified by Descartes with what in us is most perfect: our rationality. This leads Descartes in the sequence to the prescription of a certain way of life related with a certain way of thinking:

Indeed, the more strongly I incline in one direction the more free my choice is (...) Freedom is never lessened – indeed it is increased and strengthened – by natural knowledge and divine grace. When no reason inclines me in one direction rather than another, I have a feeling of indifference – that is, of its not mattering which way I go – and that is the poorest kind of freedom. What it manifests is freedom considered not as a perfection but rather as a lack of knowledge – a kind of negation. If I always saw clearly what was true and good, I should never have to spend time thinking about what to believe or do; and then I would be wholly free although I was never in a state of indifference (Descartes, Fourth Meditation).

In this sense, the detachment between our free soul and our bodily passions establishes a thin line where real autonomy, identified as freedom, situates. Leave aside how the references to supernatural entities and their influence on us due to Descartes' historical context. Focus, instead on the role of this "natural knowledge" - this thin line is occupied exclusively by human beings that are then established as autonomous because they are able to see those motives of choice, the reasons, and are able to evaluate them as the "right ones" to serve as leads for actions. In summary, a capacity in our souls links our ability to proceed in a certain sense, and this ability is both the motive for our particularity in the animal kingdom and, again, a motive for the identification of this particularity with morality itself.

Certainly these connections could be further clarified and that is exactly what Kant did. The choices derived by those autonomous agents, human beings to be sure, constitutes the domain of the practical pure reason as Kant addresses in his *Groundwork of the metaphysics of morals*. There, in the third formula of moral law, also dubbed by Kant the formula of autonomy, he affirms that, when we act, we should act "not to choose otherwise than so that the maxims of one's choice are at the same time comprehended with it in the same volition as universal law". Here, Kant is cementing autonomy at the center of morality, because to self-govern according to pure rationality is a requirement for any moral action. Freedom is not choice, something that Descartes had already denied when equating choice with mere appearance dependent on our bodily functions. Since in this center we find a self-legislator, that is a purely rational being detached both from heteronomous motives (such as those that relate to passions and interests), and also from contexts, the dignity of this self-legislator becomes the dignity of autonomy.

This equivalence between freedom and autonomy certainly blinded the philosophers to certain challenges. This blindness could be justified with the shining of this self-legislator in positioning itself against all the odds, something that Kant so beautifully expressed with the will of this self-legislator. This is the good will, a will that "shines like a jewel for itself, as something that has its full worth in itself". And the shine of this jewel is brightest as the good will distinguishes itself through action:

… though under certain subjective limitations and hindrances which, however, far from concealing it and making it unrecognizable, rather elevate it by contrast and let it shine forth all the more brightly (Kant, 2002, G, 4:397).

Consider that this Kantian "shine" is directed through the prism that is his notion of duty, and we have thus a rough sketch of the mechanism motivating Kantian moral philosophy, with duty providing the type of explicit action guidance central to the regulation through reason of practical life. The aim of this sketch is to highlight the centrality of human beings both on the ethical and evolutionary stages. It is because of a particular characteristic of human souls, rationality, that human beings are unique members of the "Ethical Association", a membership validated in its exercise, vis-à-vis autonomy.

Maybe is time to challenge this formulation. We suggest that, as stated, this formulation occludes any proper comprehension of both our ethics, and ourselves.

Certainly, there are historical reasons for this. For example, in her evaluation of modern moral philosophy, G. E. M. Anscombe argued that, behind the Kantian formulation - and in fact behind all formulations of Ethics since the beginning of modernity – there are the skeletons of that element so salient in the Descartes quote, above: our morality is something granted by God to human beings, alone. Anscombe attempted to show that we cannot sustain our modern conceptions of autonomy and privileged place in the universe alongside the view of a supernaturally derived moral duty. According to her, the idea of duty developed by Kant is just an impressive philosophical concealment of what is at root a divine gift to human beings.

From a sociological point of view, the same issue was raised in the notion of a progressive disenchantment of the world, first developed by Max Weber. Fast forward to today, and recent Psychology leads us also to question the aforementioned grounding, and to search for new ways to establish Ethics especially on natural grounds, a search facilitated by empirical comprehension of how our minds have evolved (c.f. Doris, 2010; Haidt, 2007; Greene, Nystrom, Engell, Darley, & Cohen, 2006). This work conceives of an innate moral grammar in the gray area between moral philosophy and psychology, a grammar patterning both our minds and our moral rules, and has been pursued as a challenger to the picture of ethical life inherited.

We are thus left with two competing visions. A disjunct, rationalist Ethics that segregates human beings from nature in such a way that we end up believing in clouds, and an empiricist Ethics confirmed and clarified through diverse scientific discoveries. Of these two, only one seems to exhibit the very dignity that rationalist conceptions of autonomy aimed to exalt.

Given this result, we are going to pursue here the suggestion of a necessary disentanglement between freedom and autonomy. This disentanglement may aid in abandoning and overcoming inherited conceptions of ourselves and of our Ethics. In order to motivate this transition, we will offer a demonstration of the evolution of artificial autonomous agents, suggesting that parameters necessary for their emergence provide us with reasons to transform conceptions of moral agency accordingly. Our attempt is based on the idea that developments in programming can be used as one set of tools, suggesting how to establish a better view on ethical concepts, and thus on ourselves. Thus, the twofold aim of this chapter: to analyze (1) how autonomy emerges in the context of artificial autonomous agents; and (2) how this development influences our own comprehension of what it means to be autonomous. As we will demonstrate, this dual aim of analysis becomes a matter of necessity in face of the increasing blur of the lines between, on the one side, the simulation of ethical traces – with programming tools – as a way to study aspects of ethics and, on the other, the emulation of those traces in agents that are becoming increasingly autonomous.

2. EMERGENCE OF AUTONOMY IN THE CONTEXT OF ARTIFICIAL AUTONOMOUS AGENTS

In order to achieve this aim we start by pointing to the elements that convinced us that the emergence of artificial agents requires the development of a notion of autonomy that is useful and accepted by programmer and philosopher, alike. These fields share increasingly the same arena, and this sharing occurs as artificial agents become increasingly free from direct human intervention, an independence that is necessarily associated with the recognition of aspects of self-governance, and this ultimately leads us to question the idea of autonomy as established in the rationalist tradition just presented.

But how to do that? Our final answer will be to highlight emergent aspects of autonomy in opposition to the view of autonomy as a characteristic mark unique to human beings. Autonomy seems to be a much more fluid notion, one that implies degrees associated with different beings that populate an expanded – more inclusive – ethical space. In the end, we will establish a conception of autonomy that is a naturalist and evolutionary, in opposition to the aprioristic grounding of the notion staked out by the received rationalist tradition.

Accordingly, instead of providing an *a priori* argument to defend our conceptions, we analyze different programming models that were developed to better understand the grey area between simulation and emulation of ethics. Different approaches to this simulation/emulation have been suggested, as the ones that can be found in Allen (2010), but here we are going to describe models that rely on logical programming. Although limited, and low on the autonomy scale, we propose that these programming models highlight aspects of autonomy that are informative of our own embodied moral conditions, due to these very limitations. Thusly, in addition, we wish to emphasize both for the influence that this work might have in tutoring philosophical intuitions and, recursively, on the influence of this tutelage on the further development of these very same computational agents. Besides the gains relative to the complementarity that could exist in the joint development and co-evolution of the twine of computational models and philosophical theories, the present effort attempts to dismiss the apparent risks of a comparative decrease in our own autonomy when contrasted with the autonomy of those lesser autonomous agents and, therefore, uphold the stance that those apparent risks are weak. The gains that can be achieved through a better comprehension of ourselves outweigh those risks, these gains being themselves demonstrations of moral autonomy.

Although this modeling research has been undertaken for several years now, we are going to pay attention only to some of its latest developments. In particular, our aim forthwith is to analyze two specific models developed at our NOVA-LINCS center and its partner institutions:

1. Agents developed in the context of evolutionary game theory simulations, in non-repeated and in reiterated two-person and public good games, where a diversity of successful simulations and analytic demonstrations have been made to better understand the joint role of recognizing intentions, of commitment and of apology, for the promotion of emergence, in a population of agents, of combinations of stable morally cooperative behaviors, by agents who are at times able to recognize intentions, establish commitments, and accept apologies (Pereira, Santos & Han, 2014; Pereira, 2012, Pereira & Saptawijaya 2011; Han & Pereira, 2013; Pereira et al. 2014).

2.   The narrative storyteller about a robot that, as it attempts to save a princess, needs to successively deal with moral updating dilemmas, using the ACORDA logic programming system (Lopes & Pereira, 2006; Pereira & Lopes, 2007; Lopes & Pereira, 2010).

The aim of these models has been to establish, through logical formalization, frameworks where single agents and multiplicities of agents are able to employ flexible behavior in answer to the demands of virtual environments. We are going to go beyond this first immediate aim and reassess these models, after describing them. As we try to show, autonomy here touches something else that is valued from the point of view of Ethics, though in a manner deeply different from the kind of rationalist effort we described in the previous section.

In the first experiment or, more precisely, in the first sets of experiments, the agents therein proffered as possessing some degree of autonomy are nevertheless simple in their evaluations reflecting the closed up system of the prisoner's dilemma matrix of losses and gains. However, this should not be taken as a limitation since the aim is to analyze the role of the interactions among multitudes of agents having different interests and strategies, in a framework that allows for distinct aims, in order to envisage how these different strategies evolve over an extended number of generations. The essential point is this: those strategies that emerge and become stable correlate with emergent norms. The second experiment we wish to present provides a chance to evaluate autonomy during social interactions or under social constraints, where autonomy plays a wider role even when dealing with simple agents.

The Ground Level of Autonomy?

Our first programming effort models the reiterated prisoner dilemmas with various aspects of uncertainty taken into account, including when there is no full information about actions, in order to investigate the emergence of strategies of cooperation. The mechanisms driving the emergence and evolution of cooperation – in populations of abstract individuals with diverse behavioral strategies in co-presence – have been an object of mathematical study via Evolutionary Game Theory (EGT), informed in part by Evolutionary Psychology. Programming efforts in this area have been ongoing at least since Axelrod (1984) offered the classical original formulation, with other models having been presented by authors like Danielson (1992). Their work depends on implementation and simulation techniques on parallel-processing computers, thus enabling the large-scale, fine-grained and yet relatively rapid study of aforesaid mechanisms under varieties of conditions, parameters, and alternative virtual games. The theoretical and experimental results coming from this field, thus, have continually been surprising, rewarding and – especially important for us – potentially informative for an empirically founded Ethics fully sensitive to the requirements of moral autonomy.

Recently, in our own work we have simulated groups of individuals with innate cognitive abilities represented by established AI models, namely those pertaining to Intention Recognition (Han, Pereira & Santos, 2011; Han, Pereira & Santos, 2012; Pereira, 2012, Han & Pereira 2013; Pereira, Han & Santos, 2014). This framework facilitates the modeling of agent tolerance or intolerance to errors in other agents – deliberate or not – and tolerance/intolerance to possible communication noise. As a result, our work has shown that both the emergence and stability of cooperation are reinforced in the presence of such cognitive abilities, of tolerance to error.

But we are getting ahead of ourselves. How is Intention Recognition inserted into computational agents? In the EGT approach, the most successful strategies become more frequent in the population.

Kinship, neighborhood relationships, and individual differences, may or may not be considered. In indirect reciprocity (Nowak & Sigmund, 2005), players interact at most once, but they have knowledge of their partners' past behavior. This introduces the concern with reputation, and with moral judgment (Pacheco, Santos & Chalub, 2006; Pereira & Saptawijaya, 2011; Han, Saptawijaya & Pereira, 2012).

Our other recent work (Han, Pereira, Santos & Lenaerts, 2013; Han, Pereira & Lenaerts, 2015) has shown that, after the evaluation of interactions between third parties, strategies are adopted which allow for the emergence of kinds of cooperation that are immune to exploitation, because these interactions are channeled just to those who cooperate. This – to return to the figure of the shining Kantian goodwill passing through a prism of duty – replaces the dislocated prism of rationalist constructions with an empirical equivalent. Likewise, questions of justice and trust, with their negative (punishment) and positive (help) incentives, are fundamental to games with large and diversified groups of individuals gifted with intention recognition capabilities.

In our work, intention recognition is implemented using Bayesian Networks (BN) taking into account the information of current signals for intent, as well as trust and tolerance amassed during previous iterations. We experimented with populations with different proportions of diverse strategies in order to calculate, in particular, what is the minimum fraction of individuals with Intention Recognition for cooperation to emerge, invade, prevail, and persist in agents that self-regulate their operation. One hope in understanding these capabilities is that they may be transformed into mechanisms for the spontaneous organization and control of swarms of autonomous robotic agents. With this objective, we have studied how players' strategies adapt in populations during cooperation games. We have used the techniques of EGT and have considered games such as the "Prisoner's Dilemma" and "Stag Hunt" successively repeated, and have showed how actors participating in repeated iterations within these games can benefit from having the ability to recognize the intentions of other actors, leading to an increase in cooperation.

Declarative Rules as a Basis for Moral Reasoning

Without expecting any kind of magic common to fairy tales, the narrative developed in Lopes & Pereira (2010) and Saptawijaya & Pereira (2014) provides a parallel account of the emergence of autonomy over the course of normal life. The games created in order to develop this approach are similar in form to stories that we use in order to educate, or at least to entertain, children. For example, in our work, we "conjure" (program) a robotic knight and a princess in distress, kept in a tower by a powerful wizard, and make it his duty to figure out how to save her. This wizard, knowing that the access to the castle is only possible through two bridges, positions at each a defensive guard that can be, in different simulations, either a giant spider or a human warrior with different but measurable strengths. Different capabilities to act are taken in consideration by the robot-knight. And, differently from most fairy tales, the princess and hero in our stories can be sensitive to moral demands. For example, the model can be set up in such a way that the princess is sensitive to murder, and she can reject her "savior" if he chooses a course of action against her values, i.e. killing the human warrior to get to her, for example.

The different cases that are simulated in our work show, even if in a simple format, the interplay between (1) a set of preferences that are generated a priori, and that we can associate with that part of our moral reasoning described by deontological theories, and (2) a set of choices and preferences (to deal either with a spider or with a human guard, with a weaker guard or a stronger one). Further, these choices can be interpreted as relating to the role of imagination in us, how we can visualize consequences and determine actions according to the expectations created by that imagination, in coordination with the perceived situation.

In our work, this interpretation is facilitated by the set of abductive rules that drive the simulated agents. The key to their effective reasoning – as limited as it is by the few considerations available to our virtual agents – lies in what should be taken into account. This is exactly what we are going to cover next, further detailing the model of an interactive princess-saving storytelling, and showing how knowledge updates are employed for moral updating.

Apart from dealing with incomplete information, knowledge updates (as realized by EVOLP/R in Saptawijaya & Pereira, 2014) are essential to account for moral updating and evolution. They concern the adoption of new (possibly overriding) moral rules in additional to those that an agent currently follows. Such adoption is often necessary when the moral rules that one is currently following have to be revised in the light of situations faced by the agent, e.g., when an authority contextually imposes other moral rules. This is not only relevant in a real world setting, but also in imaginary ones. For example, in our work, the robot in the story must save the princess in distress while pursuing two possibly conflicting aims, enacting the princess's moral rules while ensuring its own survival.

We represent this capacity for revision through Prospective Logic Programming (PLP) (as refined in (Pereira & Saptawijaya, 2011). This work employs declarative non-monotonic reasoning, demonstrating that it is possible to build an integrated architecture for embedding these reasoning techniques in the simulation of embodied agents in virtual three-dimensional worlds. Further, a concrete graphics supported application prototype was engineered in order to enact the story of the princess saved by the robot and imbued with moral reasoning. Our work with PLP supports the view that autonomous agents are those capable of anticipating and reasoning about hypothetical future scenarios. This capability for prediction is essential for proactive agents working with partial information in dynamically changing environments.

In order to illustrate the basic PLP framework constituting the basis of our ACORDA framework (Lopes & Pereira, 2006 and Pereira & Lopes, 2007), consider that the robot is asked to save the princess in distress, and then he is confronted with an ordeal. A gap, a river, crossable by two bridges, blocks the path to the castle. Standing guard at each of the bridges are minions of the evil wizard. In order to rescue the princess, he will have to defeat one of the minions to proceed, and overcome the river's gap.

As the PLP robot reasons, a balloon displays its thoughts, in real time[1]. Prospective reasoning involves the combination of hypothetical scenario generation – into the future – followed by preference assignments taking into account the imagined consequences of each proffered scenario. By reasoning backwards from the goal to save the princess, the agent (i.e., the robot) generates three possible routes for action. Either it does not cross the river at all, thus negating satisfaction of the rescue goal, or it crosses a bridge. In order to derive the consequences for each scenario, the agent has to reason forward from each available hypothesis. The goal of the robot, i.e., save(princess, after(gap)), is further tempered by an integrity constraint (ic0) according to which the robot will prefer the scenario with likelihood of survival that does not fall below a preset specified ic0 threshold. The robot's self-regulatory mechanism evaluates the field in order to determine which is the best way to achieve its aim (save the princess) whilst suffering the smallest loss to it (something one could relate to a minimization of pain).

Certainly the moral issues presented here are admittedly limited, but in some sense do illustrate a rudimentary sort of reflective equilibrium over possible ends (in the sense that the robot works back and forth between a series of options in order to establish a judgment). As soon as these consequences are known, meta-reasoning techniques are applied to weigh the partial scenarios. For example, if the goal of the robot is expressed as save(princess, after(gap)), which can be satisfied either by hypothetically abducing kill(ninja) or kill(spider), we can conjure a robot that exhibits something like a consequentialist procedure of moral reasoning. That is, the decision of the robot for choosing which minion to defeat (i.e., to kill), in order to save the princess, is purely driven by maximizing its own utility, predicated first of all on its survival.

Consider the following permutation on that case. The princess becomes angry because the robot decides to kill a man (the ninja) in order to save her since the robot had identified this as maximizing utility (its own survival) and without any concern about the princess' moral rules. In other words, the spider is easier to kill than is the human guard. She then asks the robot to adopt moral rules, namely that no man should be harmed in saving her, a constraint that we tag "ghandi_moral".

The robot learns about gandhi_moral interactively, by being told. We represent this communication by the literal update, "knows_about(gandhi_moral)". This demand changes the permissibility of the path previously chosen (the one that maximizes personal utility). Consequently, now the killing of the human guard is no longer triggered even if it is the choice that would be considered best from a purely consequentialist point of view.

The gandhi_moral update allows consistent ends to be abduced, as a rule to follow even in the face of conflicts between personal survival and the princess's sensitivities. Since the robot's knowledge contains the new overriding impediment, killing the overwhelming spider becomes the only path to be followed if save(princess, after(gap)) is to be achieved. The goal to save(princess, after(gap)) implies that the princess has to be saved whatever it takes. However, there are limitations imposed on this goal. For example, the knight wants, above all, to survive, but now is forbidden from killing the guard, thus jeopardizing his own survival by facing the undefeatable spider, and gives up saving the princess. How are such conflicts to be resolved between efficient means and ends that threaten survival?

A moral update could take place. The literal knight_moral represents a further constraint on means, demanding moral conduct in forcefully achieving the goal to save the princess. If knight_moral is not yet imposed, then the survival integrity constraint does not necessitate save(princess, after(gap)) to be an active goal that must be achieved. An agent without knight_moral considers killing the spider an "unreasonable rescue" – kill(spider) satisfies unreasonable_rescue(princess, after(gap). The consequence in this case is that the robot decides not to kill any of its enemies – the ninja because the means do not justify the end of saving the princess, and the spider because of his sense of self-preservation. It just simply aborts its mission to save the princess.

But we can consider a case too where this happens differently. So, in our third plot, the princess justifiably becomes angry again, this time because she is not saved. She then imposes the 'knight_moral' conduct rule which leads to an update in the form of moral rules that override previous moral rules conflicting with the new rules.

By the integrity constraint, solving conflict is once more triggered as a goal, making both abducibles – kill(ninja) and kill(spider) – available as solutions to the conflict, again. Next, having been told about knight_moral expressed by its update rules, the knight adopts the knight_moral and this results in abducing follow(knight_moral). Recall that gandhi_moral had already been adopted, and this leaves kill(spider) as the only abducible compatible with the new knight_moral. That is, the a posteriori preference chooses the scenario with both gandhi_moral and knight_moral to be followed. Thus, the robot has only one way to save the princess: kill(spider). This option respects both gandhi_moral and knight_moral, adopted before and still in force. As a result, the robot fails to save the princess. Indeed, the robot's survival requirement is now lower than the survival threshold with respect to the spider, and thus the spider kills it. This highlights an important issue in moral philosophy about our dependence on luck (Williams, 1981) and the eternal prospect of failing that surrounds any good will, irrespective of its brilliance.

These simple scenarios already illustrate the interplay between different logic programming techniques and demonstrates the advantages gained by combining their distinct strengths. Namely, the integration of top-down, bottom-up, hypothetical, moral updating and utility-based reasoning procedures result in a flexible framework for dynamic agent specification. The open nature of the framework embraces the possibility of expanding its use to yet other useful models of cognition such as counterfactual reasoning and theories of mind. Certainly, we can debate the value and the extension of the autonomy in this case. This debate can be more or less fruitful. The rejection of autonomy in this case, by an a priori formulation based on the fact that the very reactions of these agents do not denote freedom, falls in this last category and, standing on the argument expounded in the previous section, about the innumerous reasons to reject this procedure, we aim now to set aside this formulation in order for a more fruitful approach to arise in its place.

3. HOW DO THESE DEVELOPMENTS INFLUENCE OUR OWN UNDERSTANDING OF WHAT IT MEANS TO BE AUTONOMOUS, AND HOW ANALYSIS CAN HELP WITH THE TASK OF ESTABLISHING AN ACCEPTABLE USE OF AUTONOMY APPLICABLE TO ARTIFICIAL AGENTS, BUT NEVERTHELESS WITHIN A CONTINUUM OF THE GENERAL USE OF THE CONCEPT IN ETHICS

In our challenge to the dominant tradition on autonomy, we need to deal exactly with its strong association with freedom and of free will. We will delimit autonomy as a form of self-legislature detached from our senses, and by implication non-contextual. It can be otherwise developed, and we are going to uphold that it should, by having other priorities in mind. Our models and the different autonomous artificial agents that appeared in the past few years provide some of the reasons for this disengagement but we should point out, too, that there exist a diversity of philosophical reasons to adopt other stances.

A first one is due to the Cartesian and Kantian tradition as reviewed previously, because it is in itself the cause of a common reaction well spread among scientists and naturalist philosophers, and summarized by Margaret Boden when she affirms that "autonomy is a problematic concept partly because it can seem to be close to magic, or anyway to paradox" (Boden, 2008). This "magic", brought by the relation between autonomy and freedom, is mainly derived from the attempt of this tradition to place human beings in a somewhat special position – i.e. as those beings that have free will and the duty of self-legislation because of their rationality and, consequently, the only members of the natural kingdom to be included in the kingdom of morality.

And, even in the face of skepticism, there certainly are as many good reasons to follow this path, if no other than for the aforementioned dignity that it apparently guarantees. But, then again, on the other hand there are reasons, which authors as diverse as Anscombe and Dennett deliver, to denounce this idea as not only opposed by our best theories of ourselves as natural beings that evolved in a certain context, but also grounded in a conception of morality awarded to us by some supernatural entity.

This first reason should on its own provide enough motivation to follow other paths, and there are different ways of diverging from this dominant tradition. For example, that the imprecisions around the cluster 'autonomy-freedom' itself do not help it to fulfill autonomy's centrality in Ethics, and that, indeed, may undermine the "will" to adopt this concept as having such an important role in Ethics. Nomy Arpaly, for example, develops her theory of moral worth by basing it on the more accessible notions of praise and blameworthiness, suggesting leaving autonomy out of the picture altogether. This is because, she suggests, there are "at least eight distinct things" being called "autonomy" and, although she assesses those extensively (Arpaly, 2004, p.118-126), she thinks that the mere existence of such complex and polyphonic use should warn us against attempting to define it in a single useful version, acceptable to all of those involved in the discussion.

Accepting these warnings, we are not going to try to clear the ambiguity around the notion of autonomy. Instead, we are going to agree with Boden's diagnosis that the problem lies in the denaturalization of the concept caused by the connection between autonomy and freedom. We take the admixture of magic and paradox that surrounds the concept as incentive towards a different formulation, one that, at the end of the day, is similar both to Boden's and to Arpaly's formulations.

We share Boden's criticism of autonomy, and in particular reject autonomy:

1. As an absolute value only susceptible of two states (either present or absent);
2. Through a simplistic top-down (disembodied) conceptualization, which rejects what seems central to our own experience of it as something always in relation, and that comes to existence in systems, like the one in our first model, that respond to the demands felt by the interplay between senses and reasoning in some context or other (that we control and understand in different degrees and within imposed constraints); and
3. Insensitive to the emergence of new agents that have inaugurated the field of artificial morality.

Ethics and moral philosophy can be enriched if the concept of autonomy can be developed in such a way that would warrant it to be applied to a wider range of behaviors and agents. So, the question we first posed mutates into an investigation into how to separate the unnecessary baggage due to received traditional wisdom from a more inclusive concept of autonomy. We will focus on freedom, and try to dissociate freedom from autonomy, thereby freeing autonomous agents from this baggage.

Gerald Dworkin, after a brief historical account reestablishing autonomy in the sense we have adopted, i.e. as that referring to the property or ability to act according to reasons and motives taken as one's own, suggests a manner we believe diminishes the magic and paradox that Boden much criticizes. His strategy is to distinguish between something relative to specific acts – freedom – and autonomy as that global capacity that certainly is part of freedom but which is more generic. In his own words:

Putting the various pieces together, autonomy is conceived of [as] a second-order capacity of persons to reflect critically upon their first-order preferences, desires, wishes, and so forth and the capacity to accept or attempt to change these in light of higher-order preferences and values (Dworkin, 1988, p.20).

There are two aspects here, one more useful for us and another that, although interesting, is not well suited to our aims in the field of artificial morality. The usefulness of this characterization is that it enables us to understand autonomy as relative to series of events that seemingly constitute a flow, and are intrinsic to agents as a form of reasoning that can be described as reflective self-regulation over the aspects and transformations accessible to agents in their contexts.

Interpreting Dworkin's "second-order capacity to reflect critically upon their first-order preferences, desires, wishes and so forth" as this very reasoning procedure, we sustain that typical cases of this ability are conscious, and are accessed through the production of beliefs in the process of reasoning. This reframing reflects a more general change in the field of Ethics itself. Scanlon, for example, in his most recent book (see the first lecture in Scanlon, 2014), points this out when he effectively comments on the transition of the focus of Ethics, from the establishment of what is right and wrong to that of a broader study of normative life in a bigger picture wherein the focus of the study of Ethics tends to a psychologizing.

The second aspect of his characterization links autonomy to persons. Dworkin is interested in this link because of the goal to avail himself of a point of view that permits him to judge experiences as more or less worthy. However, his aim is to analyze something already granted within what we call the Autonomous Entities Association (AEA). Our focus remains on the first aspect, as it is through psychology that we are able to establish the prerequisites for membership in this association.

Qualifications for inclusion in the AEA must be reevaluated in light of historic developments whereby, for the first time ever, the aim of providing a natural account of our relation with the world seems finally aligned with the developments in artificial agency. In the context of this alignment, we may suggest a clarification about prerequisites for membership in the AEA. We base this effort on Boden's, in dismissing autonomy's "magical" character (Boden, 2008). Membership depends on three things:

1. "The extent to which response to the environment is direct (determined only by the present state of the external world) or indirect (mediated by inner mechanisms partly dependent on the creature's previous history)";
2. "[T]he extent to which the controlling mechanisms were self-generated rather than externally imposed," an aspect that is certainly impacted by the developments in artificial intelligence that were presented above;
3. "The extent to which any inner directing mechanisms can be rejected upon, and/or selectively modified in the light of general interests or the particularities of the current problem in the environmental context".

In addition to this formulation, she provides this concisely:

In general, an individual's autonomy is the greater, the more its behavior is directed by self-generated (and idiosyncratic) inner mechanisms, nicely responsive to the specific problem-situation yet reflexively modifiable by wider concerns (Boden, 2008).

This formulation allows a visualization of how levels of autonomy may be distinguished, as a series of different candidates for membership in the AEA. We suggest the figure of a mountain, where those objects and artifacts that are not autonomous (naturally or artificially) occupy the very bottom. Certainly some of these not-autonomous-yet things seem to challenge one or another of these three proposed axes: self-organized phenomena and even some self-replicating processes seem to blur the lines at the start of the ascent, sharing these low-elevations with some or other specifically built artifacts, or even with some forms of life. But the real climb is composed by different autonomous beings that seem to move up and down its slope, climbing it as their capacities of processing reality in their limited nervous system develop and aided by different artifacts and even – recently – artificial agents. In addition, we can identify some conversion between those as in the case of *e. elegans* and artificial models as the recent project to simulate its capacities in a 1:1 scale, so in a sense there is integration between these domains.

As artificial agents are developed farther up, along this hill, and we move further up this hill with them, we see beings that increasingly motivate a distinction of 'quality' in the interaction between these axes, in a fashion similar to that of the utilitarian tradition in the measure of pleasure. We can imagine such a quality distinction being inserted into our courageous robot, also.

The very top of this mountain image is certainly not occupied by human beings. Our more recent accounts of ourselves certainly support that we are not in the business of pure autonomy, as assumed by the Kantian tradition, and for at least two reasons. One, we are not built to be purely rational, and we certainly value things that contradict its demands. The reasons for that are probably related with how contextualized our reactions and our decisions are in opposition to the Cartesian formulation that detached our souls from our senses. Thus, the top of this mountain is surely inhabited only by imaginary beings or supernatural ones, but this should not diminish the importance of this top as somewhat of an ideal or regulatory frame. (Recall Aristotle's distinction, in the *Politics*, between the worst of animals and a god – at the summit, live only gods.) In this sense, the establishment of this frame provides us with a horizon within which different candidates for the AEA can be classified, but we will now leave the work in determining the line delimiting "real" autonomy for others.

Instead, other important questions emerge from this reflection and we want to discuss two of them. The first is related with the possibility of a quantitative unit for the measuring of autonomy, and the second is related with the phenomenology of autonomy as an emergent property of certain agents.

Can We Develop a Unit of Measure of Autonomy?

There are in the literature some suggestions about the quantification of the autonomy of different systems, which we want to consider, even if briefly, by focusing on the formulation of Seth (2007 & 2010). Seth's formulation of autonomy is strictly analogous to our own, sharing with us even its source in Boden's definition. This leads to a series of delimiting borders – "An autonomous system should not be fully determined by its environment, and a random system should not have a high autonomy value" – that helps to map the base which the mountain of autonomy rises, a visualization we sustain here.

Seth (2007) proposes a measure of autonomy based on the following conception of autonomy. First, future outcomes for an agent can be better accessed by considering its own past states, as compared to predictions based on past states of external variables. This notion establishes what he calls a G-autonomy variable: "a variable is G-autonomous to the extent that (1) it is dependent on its own history, and (2) these dependencies are not accounted for by external factors" (Seth, 2007, p.475)

G-autonomy, Seth applies to different forms of artificial life, and we can apply it to our models given both their limited autonomy (since their history is still incipient) and further developments, both in self-control and in richer environments wherein agent adaptivity and response can be more widely demonstrated.

The Phenomenology of Autonomy as an Emergent Property

An important question persists. This concerns an aspect of AEA members that Dworkin dismisses with the term "person". We have pointed out that the comprehension of autonomy, as established here, rejects the view that takes it as a definitional matter, one whose presence or absence can be easily attached to agents as a whole, or otherwise to certain actions. Autonomy emerges, and even then changes. However, what emerges as autonomy? The answer is not some "thing" but rather something like a form, or pattern, or function. The concept of emergence applies to phenomena in which relational properties dominate over constituent properties in determining aggregate features. It is to configurations and topologies, not specific properties of constituents, that we trace processes of emergence.

By analogy with computing machines, cognitive scientists have argued that the "functional" properties that define a given cognitive operation are like the logical architecture of a computer program. Philosophically, this general form of argument is known as functionalism, and it is quite relevant for viewing autonomy as an emergent property. In fact, it brings us to an important aspect of our preconception of autonomy. As seen above, we departed from the view whereby autonomy is established as that property or ability to act according to reasons and motives that are taken as one's own, but we have left untouched as yet one important part of this preconception, i.e., the part relative to the expression "as one's own".

In moral philosophy, this expression refers exactly to the relation between autonomy and freedom. "One's own" delimits the native power of a being in this world to deliberate and choose freely its course of actions. "One's own" may be extended, into a broader conception like that of Rawls for example, whereby this being is able to establish its character having in view a whole-life plan.

Nevertheless, with freedom set aside, following the concerns that we shared with Boden, we need to provide a conception of those beings where autonomy emerges in a different frame, one that highlights not the aspect of free will and choice but of self-regulation of interactions with the world. In this matter, we suggest "one's own" as naming the capacity to execute the cycle of observe-think-act, a view similar to that of Kowalski (2011), of agents as logical programs that exactly perform this cycle. In his conception, "the thinking or deliberative component consists in explaining the observations, generating actions in response to observations, and planning to achieve its goals", and the acting component is understood as "a proof-procedure which exploits integrity constraints". Since our aim here is exactly to interpret logical programs performing as agents, this definition fits the place occupied by Dworkin's "person", and of moral philosophy's "one's own".

Our conception of autonomy is not something that has an a priori decidability, be it as an a priori definition, be it as a predicate attached to agents in an absolute way, or be it something context independent. The notion now being presented, and here we are in agreement with some philosophical formulations like that of Arpaly (2004), recognizes autonomy as an emergent property of certain agents, able to adapt when exposed to environments, the latter being evaluated considering the ways available to the agents to enact these adaptations (i.e. if they are self-regulative or not, and if they are able or not to evolve in answer to their mutable environments). Our concept is established as referring to the property or ability for agents to act according to reasons and motives that are taken as one's own (the agent's) and, moreover, it is a capacity always in relation with something.

This permits us to present some of the attempts at developing artificial autonomous agents and to interpret those agents in a spectrum within those (Boden's) three axes, (1) the responsiveness to the environment, (2) self-generation of the mechanisms that permit this responsiveness, and (3) openness to self-modification in this process, what we can dub, for short, evolution.

This formulation does not close the door to improvements. One that can be imagined is the insertion of another axis, representing the aptitude of agents for producing explanatory or justificatory reasons of their own, in a way that would highlight autonomy as having a social-communicative dimension. Communication and responsiveness to reasons is highlighted by thinkers from Jonathan Dancy to Dan Sperber as an important characteristic of moral reasoning, and is a characteristic mark belonging to few animals besides human beings (c.f. Cheney & Seyfarth, 2007). And, this leads us to some interesting philosophical considerations.

4. ARTIFICIALITY IN THE ANIMAL KINGDOM OF MORALITY

In the previous sections, we invited the reader to share with us the understanding that the aim of providing an account of our ourselves as ethical agents is aligned with the developments in artificiality, exemplified by the emergence of new forms of agents, the artificial moral agents. This emergence populates the world with beings clearly distinct from the most common forms of non-reactive artifacts produced by human beings in their cultural history. Although a moral Turing test has been proposed before (Allen et al., 2000 and Arkin, 2009), the perspective adopted in this chapter can contribute to an account of the consequences of this emergence in a distinct way. Certainly, the models presented here, in particular the second one, seems to aim at the simulation of moral reasoning as a declarative process where justification plays a central role, something that is open to criticism. Sometimes, it seems that the offering of this reasoning is mostly an afterthought of the agents, something quite extrinsic to the process involved in what we consider the focus of Ethics: the progress from deliberation to actions, where explanation occupies certainly its place in the aftermath.

Surely, the heuristic process involved can be investigated and set out as have Haidt (2007), Greene et al (2004) and Mikhail (2011), among others, but a more complete comprehension of the emergence of these agents needs to deal with their responsiveness through action itself. Galen Strawson suggests the following example:

Suppose you set off for a shop on the evening of a national holiday, intending to buy a cake with your last ten pound note. Everything is closing down. There is one cake left; it costs ten pounds. On the steps of the shop someone is shaking an Oxfam tin. You stop, and it seems completely clear to you that it is entirely up to you what you do next. That is, it seems clear to you that you are truly, radically free to choose, in such a way that you will be ultimately responsible for whatever you do choose. You can put the money in the tin, or go in and buy the cake, or just walk away. (You are not only completely free to choose. You are not free not to choose.) (Strawson, 1994, p.11)

In a context such as ours, where artificial autonomous agents are expected to become ubiquitous, this question is about our next step. Whether the necessary openness and reactivity is possible in programmed systems, or if there is a final gap between coded autonomous agents and us. As we highlighted before, in our computer modeling, the first aim is not empirical evidence and lacks the brute force of it. We are in a position to wonder: Do we continue to put money, time and effort into this "tin", or take another route?

The next step in our research efforts are commitments to the former. We aim to model the ability of our agents to deceive, imitate and emulate, in order to further enlarge the gray zone in our graphic proposal. With some functions encoded, we anticipate resolving those key elements necessary for membership in the AEA. We are confronted by a gap, with fuzzy edges that cannot be dispensed with by appeals to personhood, because personhood belongs to either side of the gap, at the summit of our climb to fully articulated artificial moral agency. Our conviction is that future work further integrating moral philosophy with programming will establish necessary logical supports to complete the task. And our hope is that this work will provide evidence that, although the processes within us are complex, their complexity is not inaccessible.

According to Newell (1992, p.25), in the face of big puzzles, it is useful to first know their dimensions. Modeling and simulation are tools for this discovery. Although the unity of measure that we analyze is still far from perfect, the point to develop with the case of automata is that a small set of rules, self-applied, may counter-intuitively generate a behavior close to those of more complex beings or at least their societies. These are dimensions that should prove useful as inquiry into the essence of moral agency continues.

With such dimensions identified, we are able to assess whether any distinction between moral behavior and emerging patterns like convection cells in boiling water, and so finally draw some formal equivalence between that "magic" of autonomy and freedom with the natural systems in which they emerge. In an evolutionary context, the point is that the brain, in its biological evolution, has bootstrapped itself into generality. From computer science we know that, as soon as one boots a computer, what the hardware does – simplifying a bit – is to go to the first instruction in memory. This instruction resides as a physical pattern, with the pattern due to "software". What does this mean? It means that the instruction configures the hardware, and obliges the hardware to execute that instruction. It means that the CPU then obtains instruction-specified data from memory, combines the data according to the software instruction, and puts the result back in a memory location specified by the instruction. Then the hardware looks up the next software instruction, and so on and so forth. That is, the software becomes the master of the hardware. Our contention is that in the brain that happens too, and is called "free will" by some people. Thus, the climb up the slope of autonomy is a process of bootstrapping (see Pereira, 2014, for detailed discussion).

Different agents may evolve through interactions with surroundings, and different agents may direct their evolution differently as autonomy increases along the three axes established earlier. Consider Floridi's (2007) a "re-ontologizing" of reality in this way. Evolution is ontologization. Looking at the different programming efforts ongoing, and in particular the two types that we presented, we can see an increase in agents' capacities of filtering different aspects of the data presented to them. They can be more and more sensitive to variations of strategy, as in the example of the reiterated cooperation games, and they can develop a series of moral standards in response to other agents' sensibilities. However, the roles that they play, and the worlds that they play in, are static in comparison with ours. Even as we increase the "noise" in information to which the agents are exposed, this is just a function to be controlled by those systems, and not something that constitutes the systems themselves. It is this sense we want to highlight. As much as we need efforts to develop agents in a way that increases their autonomy – no longer paradoxically we hope – then we need broader and more open universes where agents react and evolve, too.

In a certain sense, the two implementations we attempted to interpret seem, because of the way reasoning and context play out in them, to follow a correct step in the direction of a more extended and recognizable autonomy. This sense is one where their ability to provide reasons for certain procedures, their ability to play normative games, seems to close the gap in an important way, providing a better view on what ethics is for us. In ethics and in the theory of ethics, the challenge is to provide a picture of how agents can be able to deal with their situations, of how they can be able to deal with a reality that is not only demanding (this seems to be true for any form of life) but whose demands need to be fulfilled in a certain way, within a certain time. The reasons provided by those agents, when, for example, they commit errors – as in the act of killing another warrior because the agent erroneously supposes the promise of a "kingdom of ends" is equivalent to the execution of his will – are certainly presented in a form that is odd. It is difficult to identify his autonomy, even when understood in a framework that does not attempt to pinpoint it but to show how it is constituted as a dispersed continuum.

However, we should remember that the main function of our reason is the expression of our beliefs: to provide indications of external states of affairs, as much as to provide indications of the kinds of evaluators of these external states we ourselves are (like in the example of the moth of Dretske (1988, p.91s).

Recall the knight and princess. This first implementation provides not only a measure of good or bad partners in the game, but also a minimal logical framework articulating the evolution of others evolved in any situation similarly, i.e. socially, and where some players are recurrent in the life-span of the agent enabling trust, reputation and reciprocity. These seem to be our own, and this fact helps us to defend a project that is otherwise somewhat hard to support. This project is intuitively irrational: that of the sand-boxed comprehension of our own moral lives, of our ideals and of our abilities to plan for futures which are in every case not guaranteed, since all of this – as the sandbox, itself – belongs to an open world.

That the limited and simple agents that these models permit us to play with, do build, almost as strong as necessity, something involving these aspects in the blind interplay of their games, provides an argument to reject the twine of those positions that regard this project as unauthentic (i.e. a mere fiction to support some more basic realm like the one of power). Such criticisms are not far from being rejected on the same basis as those conceptions that anchor morality in an apparent supernatural being, supposing that only such great power could support it. Some people attempt to sustain morality on a magical something (freedom) that hardly fits in our worldview of natural beings that have evolved. Our openness to a plethora of variables wider than those, should rather be considered a reason for the keeping of our, but only at the start, apparently jeopardized dignity.

CONCLUSION

In a nutshell, we propose an interpretation of two computational efforts for telling to one interested in Ethics that the phenomena he tries to understand could be captured at a simpler level with fruitful results for that inquiry. A level certainly not yet surrounded by the great values that he so promptly tries to identify with Ethics, whilst losing, in the process of that very same identification, a perspective that could have permitted a multitude of agents, with different degrees (and attending constraints) of autonomy, thereby providing a richer account of autonomy. We aimed to provide this critical conception of autonomy in a way that helped avoid forgetting the more humble starts of those values, our values. However, this result is collateral with regard to our main aims, since it was not our intention to provide here a lesson in the humbleness of what we value and its precariousness in our world. If so wished, this can be attained within a philosophical discussion, for example, in the concluding remarks of Bernard Williams's essay on moral luck (Williams, 1981), where the author highlights the circumstantial character of ethics and, therefore, the fact that these cannot be that higher ground inaccessible to agents – Kant's "bright jewel" – even human ones. Only a better understanding of how we get to value such things could achieve this.

With this in mind, our aims have been to provide this better comprehension. Our goal was to contribute to a better understanding of autonomy and, following up on the repercussions of our first example, how autonomy can be interpreted as having evolved, by tracing its evolution in the field of artificial agents. Certainly, models are just models, but the twin tasks of our inquiry, of developing more legitimate moral agents and a better comprehension of ourselves, remain open. We believe that our work is carried out at the nexus of these two tasks, and thus more efficiently responds to these two challenges than does the common a priori evaluation. In fact, our position is that better models reach better theories, once they permit the elimination of some of the limitations of armchair exercises, which, when modeled, reveal counterintuitive results and unexpected difficulties. We sustain that models are theory laden and biased, in the sense that the limitations concerning what we think should be the case, do actually regulate – recognizing here a dimension of heteronomy – what we eventually get as results. This supports the necessity of a tight co-evolution of modeling and theory.

Margaret Boden (especially in Boden, 1998) established a similar frame for the comprehension of autonomy in the field of artificial life. Her concerns were to dismiss the notion that in a deterministic world (one like those simulated in our models, like the ones she describes or, following some results of science, one like our own), the emergence of supernatural agents came, mainly, to confirm our delusional character, with the correlated implication of a denial of our freedom. Our aim has been narrower, showing that we have computational tools that do not depend only on our intuitions, to investigate the concept of autonomy and Ethics more generally, thereby offering a chance at updating our own moral codes and meta-reasoning over those codes. And thus, our inquiry parallels hers in that it aids in identifying the shapes kicking up the cloud that has covered over the concept of autonomy, at once clearing errors due to delusions of untutored intuition. If this point is received intact, it is now clear that only with wider and better models can we achieve this result. After all, freedom follows understanding, and it too can have evolved (Dennett, 2004).

ACKNOWLEDGMENT

Fernando da Costa Cardoso acknowledges the support of National Counsel of Technological and Scientific Development (CNPQ/Brazil).

REFERENCES

Allen, C., Varner, G., & Zinser, J. (2000). Prolegomena to any future artificial moral agent. *Journal of Experimental & Theoretical Artificial Intelligence*, *12*(3), 251–261. doi:10.1080/09528130050111428

Anderson, M., & Anderson, S. L. (Eds.). (2011). *Machine ethics*. Cambridge: Cambridge University Press. doi:10.1017/CBO9780511978036

Anscombe, G. E. (1958). Modern moral philosophy. *Philosophy (London, England)*, *33*(124), 1–19. doi:10.1017/S0031819100037943

Arkin, R. (2009). *Governing lethal behavior in autonomous robots*. Boca Raton: CRC Press. doi:10.1201/9781420085952

Arpaly, N. (2004). *Unprincipled virtue: An inquiry into moral agency*. Oxford: Oxford University Press.

Barandiaran, X. E., Di Paolo, E., & Rohde, M. (2009). Defining agency: Individuality, normativity, asymmetry, and spatio-temporality in action. *Adaptive Behavior*, *17*(5), 367–386. doi:10.1177/1059712309343819

Boden, M. A. (1998). Autonomy and artificiality. *Cognitive Architectures in Artificial Intelligence: The Evolution of Research Programs*, *2*, 300–312.

Boden, M. A. (2008). Autonomy: What is it? *Bio Systems*, *91*(2), 305–308. doi:10.1016/j.biosystems.2007.07.003 PMID:17996363

Cheney, D., & Seyfarth, R. (2007). *Baboon Metaphysics*. Chicago: Chicago University Press. doi:10.7208/chicago/9780226102429.001.0001

Dancy, J. (2004). *Ethics without principles*. Oxford: Oxford University Press. doi:10.1093/0199270023.001.0001

Danielson, P. (2010). Designing a machine to learn about the ethics of robotics: The N-reasons platform. *Ethics and Information Technology*, *12*(3), 251–261. doi:10.1007/s10676-009-9214-x

Darwall, S., Gibbard, A., & Railton, P. (1997). *Moral discourse and practice*. New York: Oxford University Press.

Dell'Acqua, P., Mattias Engberg, & Pereira, L. M. (2003). An Architecture for a Rational Reactive Agent In: Moura-Pires, F., & Abreu, S. (Eds.)., Proceedings of *11th Portuguese Intl.Conf. on Artificial Intelligence (EPIA'03)*, Beja, Portugal. (pp. 379-393). doi:10.1007/978-3-540-24580-3_44

Dell'Acqua, P., & Pereira, L. M. (2004). Common-sense reasoning as proto-scientific agent activity. *Journal of Applied Logic*, *2*(4), 385–407. doi:10.1016/j.jal.2004.07.002

Dennett, D. C. (2004). *Freedom evolves*. London: Penguin UK.

Doris, J. (2010). *The moral pshychology handbook*. Oxford: Oxford University Press. doi:10.1093/acprof:oso/9780199582143.001.0001

Dretske, F. I. (1988). *Explaining behavior: Reasons in a world of causes*. Cambridge, MA: MIT press.

Dworkin, G. (1988). *The Theory and Practice of Autonomy*. New York: Cambridge University Press. doi:10.1017/CBO9780511625206

Floridi, L. (2007). A look into the future impact of ICT on our lives. *The Information Society*, *23*(1), 59–64. doi:10.1080/01972240601059094

Greene, J. D., Nystrom, L. E., Engell, A. D., Darley, J. M., & Cohen, J. D. (2004). The neural bases of cognitive conflict and control in moral judgment. *Neuron*, *44*(2), 389–400. doi:10.1016/j.neuron.2004.09.027 PMID:15473975

Guyer, P. (2003). Kant on the theory and practice of autonomy. *Social Philosophy & Policy*, *20*(02), 70–98. doi:10.1017/S026505250320203X

Haidt, J. (2007). The new synthesis in moral psychology. *Science*, *316*(5827), 998–1002. doi:10.1126/science.1137651 PMID:17510357

Han, T. A., & Pereira, L. M. (2013). Intention-based Decision Making via Intention Recognition and its Applications. In H. Guesgen & S. Marsland (Eds.), *Human Behavior Recognition Technologies: Intelligent Applications for Monitoring and Security* (pp. 174–211). Hershey: IGI Global. doi:10.4018/978-1-4666-3682-8.ch009

Han, T. A., Pereira, L. M., & Lenaerts, T. (2015). "Avoiding or Restricting Defectors in Public Goods Games?". *J. Royal Society Interface*, 12:2014. (pp. 1203).

Han, T. A., Pereira, L. M., & Santos, F. C. (2011). Intention Recognition Promotes The Emergence of Cooperation. *Adaptive Behavior*, *19*(3), 264–279.

Han, T. A., Pereira, L. M., & Santos, F. C. (2012). Corpus-based Intention Recognition in Cooperation Dilemmas. *Artificial Life*, *18*(4), 365–383. doi:10.1162/ARTL_a_00072 PMID:22938562

Han, T. A., Pereira, L. M., Santos, F. C., & Lenaerts, T. (2013). Good Agreements Make Good Friends. *Scientific Reports*, *3*. doi:10.1038/srep02695 PMID:24045873

Humphreys, P. (2004). *Extending ourselves: Computational science, empiricism, and scientific method*. New York: Oxford University Press. doi:10.1093/0195158709.001.0001

Kant, I. (2002). *Groundwork for the Metaphysics of Morals*. New Haven: Yale University Press.

Kowalski, R. (2011). *Computational logic and human thinking: how to be artificially intelligent*. Cambridge: Cambridge University Press. doi:10.1017/CBO9780511984747

Lin, P., Abney, K., & Bekey, G. A. (2011). *Robot ethics: the ethical and social implications of robotics*. Cambridge: MIT Press.

Lopes, G., & Pereira, L. M. (2006). Prospective Programming with ACORDA, In *Empirically Successful Computerized Reasoning (ESCoR'06) workshop at The 3rd International Joint Conference on Automated Reasoning (IJCAR'06)*, Seattle, USA.

Lopes, G., & Pereira, L. M. (2010). Prospective storytelling agents. In CarroM.PeñaR. (Eds.), *Proceedings of the Twelfth International Symposium on Practical Aspects of Declarative Languages (LNCS)*. (pp. 294-296). doi:10.1007/978-3-642-11503-5_24

Mikhail, J. (2011). *Elements of moral cognition: Rawls' linguistic analogy and the cognitive science of moral and legal judgment*. Cambridge: Cambridge University Press. doi:10.1017/CBO9780511780578

Nowak, M. A., & Sigmund, K. (2005). Evolution of indirect reciprocity. *Nature*, *437*(7063), 1291–1298. doi:10.1038/nature04131 PMID:16251955

Pacheco, J. M., Santos, F. C., & Chalub, F. A. C. (2006). Stern-judging: A simple, successful norm which promotes cooperation under indirect reciprocity. *PLoS Computational Biology*, *2*(12), e178. doi:10.1371/journal.pcbi.0020178 PMID:17196034

Pereira, L. M. (2012). Evolutionary Tolerance. In L. Magnani & L. Ping (Eds.), *Philosophy and Cognitive Science—Western & Eastern Studies (SAPERE)* , 2. (pp. 263–287). Berlin: Springer-Verlag. doi:10.1007/978-3-642-29928-5_14

Pereira, L. M. (2014). Can we not Copy the Human Brain in the Computer? In *Brain.org* (pp. 118–126). Lisbon: Fundação Calouste Gulbenkian.

Pereira, L. M., Han, T. A., & Santos, F. C. (2014). Complex Systems of Mindful Entities -- on Intention Recognition and Commitment. In: Magnani, L. 2014 (Ed.), Model-Based Reasoning in Science and Technology: Theoretical and Cognitive Issues. (pp. 499-525). Berlin, Springer-Verlag. doi:10.1007/978-3-642-37428-9_28

Pereira, L. M., & Lopes, G. (2007). Prospective Logic Agents, In: J. M. Neves, M. F. Santos, & J. M. Machado (Eds.), Progress in Artificial Intelligence. Proceedings of. 13th Portuguese Intl. Conf. on Artificial Intelligence (EPIA'07), (pp.73-86).

Pereira, L. M., & Saptawijaya, A. (2007). Moral Decision Making with ACORDA. In *Local Proceedings of the Fourteenth International Conference on Logic for Programming Artificial Intelligence and Reasoning (LPAR'07)*, Yerevan, Armenia.

Pereira, L. M., & Saptawijaya, A. (2011). Modelling Morality with Prospective Logic. In M. Anderson & S. L. Anderson (Eds.), *Machine Ethics* (pp. 398–421). New York, NY: Cambridge University Press. doi:10.1017/CBO9780511978036.027

Petersen, A. C. (2012). *Simulating nature: a philosophical study of computer-simulation uncertainties and their role in climate science and policy advice*. Boca Raton: CRC Press. doi:10.1201/b11914

Regan, T. (1986). *The Case for Animal Rights*. Berkeley: University of California Press.

Rushton, J. P. (1975). Generosity in children: Immediate and long-term effects of modeling, preaching, and moral judgment. *Journal of Personality and Social Psychology*, *31*(3), 459–466. doi:10.1037/h0076466

Saptawijaya, A., & Pereira, L. M. (in press). The Potential of Logic Programming as a Computational Tool to Model Morality. In R. Trappl (Ed.), *A Construction Manual for Robots' Ethical Systems: Requirements, Methods, Implementations (Cognitive Technologies)*.

Scanlon, T. M. (2014). *Being realistic about reasons*. Oxford: Oxford University Press. doi:10.1093/acprof:oso/9780199678488.001.0001

Schneewind, J. B. (1998). *The invention of autonomy: A history of modern moral philosophy*. Cambridge: Cambridge University Press.

Seth, A. K. (2007). Measuring autonomy by multivariate autoregressive modelling. In *Proceedings of the 9th European conference on Advances in artificial life*. (pp. 475-484). doi:10.1007/978-3-540-74913-4_48

Seth, A. K. (2010). Measuring autonomy and emergence via Granger causality. *Artificial Life*, *16*(2), 179–196. doi:10.1162/artl.2010.16.2.16204 PMID:20067405

Simão, J., & Pereira, L. M. (2003, November). "Neuro-Psychological Social Theorizing and Simulation with the Computational Multi-Agent System Ethos", Invited paper in proceedings of *Congresso em Neurociências Cognitivas*, Évora, Portugal.

Singer, P. (1993). *Practical ethics*. Cambridge: Cambridge University Press.

Strawson, G. (1994). The impossibility of moral responsibility. *Philosophical Studies*, *75*(1), 5–24. doi:10.1007/BF00989879

Wallach, W., & Allen, C. (2008). *Moral machines: Teaching robots right from wrong*. Oxford: Oxford University Press.

Williams, B. (1981). *Moral luck: philosophical papers 1973-1980*. Cambridge: Cambridge University Press. doi:10.1017/CBO9781139165860

KEY TERMS AND DEFINITIONS

Abduction: A reasoning method whereby one chooses from available hypotheses those that best explained the observed evidence, in a preferred sense.

Artificial Morality: The emerging field that aims to use programming language in order to either test ethical theories and aspects of the moral dimension or to embedded autonomous computer systems with moral aspects.

Autonomy: Indicates the capacity of an agent to make un-coerced decision in a context. As defined in the present chapter it is an emerging property and has a three dimensional frame.

Computational Logic: An interdisciplinary field of enquiry that employs the techniques from symbolic logic to reason using practical computations, and typically achieved by means of computer supported automated tools.

Counterfactual: A concept that captures the process of reasoning about a past event that did not occur, namely what would/could/might have happened, had this alternative event occurred; or, conversely, to reason about a past event that did occur, but what if it had not.

Dual-Process Model: A model that explains how a moral judgment is driven by an interaction of two different psychological processes, namely the controlled process (whereby explicit moral principles are consciously applied via deliberative reasoning), and the automatic process (whereby moral judgments are intuition-based and mostly low-level, not entirely accessible to conscious reflection).

Evolutionary Game Theory: An application of game theory to systematically study the evolution of populations, typically by resorting to simulation techniques under a variety of conditions, parameters, and strategies.

Logic Programming: A programming paradigm based on formal logic that permits a declarative representation of a problem and reasoning about this representation, that reasoning being is driven by a specific semantics.

ENDNOTE

[1]   It can be seen in this video: http://centria.di.fct.unl.pt/%7Elmp/publications/slides/padl10/quick_moral_robot.avi

Chapter 5
Semantic Analysis of Bloggers Experiences as a Knowledge Source of Average Human Morality

Rafal Rzepka
Hokkaido University, Japan

Kenji Araki
Hokkaido University, Japan

ABSTRACT

This chapter introduces an approach and methods for creating a system that refers to human experiences and thoughts about these experiences in order to ethically evaluate other parties', and in a long run, its own actions. It is shown how applying text mining techniques can enrich machine's knowledge about the real world and how this knowledge could be helpful in the difficult realm of moral relativity. Possibilities of simulating empathy and applying proposed methods to various approaches are introduced together with discussion on the possibility of applying growing knowledge base to artificial agents for particular purposes, from simple housework robots to moral advisors, which could refer to millions of different experiences had by people in various cultures. The experimental results show efficiency improvements when compared to previous research and also discuss the problems with fair evaluation of moral and immoral acts.

INTRODUCTION

In this chapter we describe the latest findings from experiments performed with our system. The system is grounded in an assumption, that the majority of people express ethically correct opinions about behavior of others. Research proceeding from this assumption was introduced during the first AAAI symposium on Machine Ethics (Rzepka, & Araki, 2005). On this course, we have created a shallow knowledge acquisition module for an Artificial Moral Agent (AMA) that mimics our ethical decisions

DOI: 10.4018/978-1-4666-8592-5.ch005

by borrowing knowledge from Internet users. The agent utilizes opinion mining and sentiment analysis techniques to decide what is moral and what is not by adopting a moral position supported by more than 2/3 of retrieved sentences. The agent takes no position where the survey result is not above this threshold. Ignoring cases in which distinct polarities are absent allows the system to create a safety valve, leaving moral judgment over morally ambiguous situations to a human user. These ambiguous cases are not forgotten, however, as the system keeps these ambiguous sentences in the knowledge base for further contextual analysis. The system utilizes only a very simple set of shallow searching techniques and the results have been impressive. That said, as we show in this chapter, more reliable Natural Language Processing tools and techniques alongside human-coded moral lexicons working together to increase integration of available information, should be expected to improve results of future trials. At the core of our system are lexicons, sets of selected keywords, based on different philosophical ideas as Bentham's Felicific Calculus (Bentham, 1789) for estimating average emotional outcomes of acts, and Kohlberg's stages of moral development for retrieving possible social consequences (Rzepka & Araki, 2012).

Internet as Knowledge Source about Human Behaviors

Our methods should be attractive to researchers from humanities, especially sociologists, cognitive scientists and psychologists who study bloggers' behavior, or who study for example a role of gossip and other forms of criticism and its role in moral development. Until recently, the WWW has been treated as a massive garbage can full of sex and violence which is not useful for intelligent machines. With this chapter we want to attract the Machine Ethics (ME) community's attention to the fact that computers with constantly improving NLP tools and minimal human input (only 258 keywords divided into two categories on the proposed method) are capable of:

1. Filtering meaningless noise;
2. Reading stories of people whose majority, surprisingly for many, seems to represent healthy common sense;
3. Reusing the discovered knowledge in existing or newly created moral solutions.

Packed with descriptions of unreal worlds and games where killing is fun, the WWW is "knowledge soup" in which our machines can slowly learn how to distinguish fantasy from more realistic stories, avoiding logical yet unreasonable conclusions such as "people can fly on broomsticks because Harry Potter can". This capacity, to distinguish useful from non-useful information, is made more difficult by the fact that, when bloggers create different worlds and write of knights and princesses and evil wizards, they share their human emotions, describe punishments for evil deeds and emphatically react to happy and unhappy moments. Rather than explude all of this information as noise, we see this information as useful knowledge about what people care about, as simulations of reality suggesting what one would do if one's object of care faced danger. This is the core idea of our approach.

Universality of the Proposed Method

To recreate our system in other languages one would need a set of positive and negative effects (lexicon), a morphological parser (if the character of a given language requires it) and vast text resources describing human experiences (as big as possible). We have tested our approach with Japanese language and a relatively small (when compared to the data accessible through commercial search engines) set of blogs (approximately 5 billion words). Previously, using shallow Natural Language Processing, we tested 68 acts, and the system agreed with human subjects in 77.8% of moral judgments. Currently we experiment with deeper analysis to improve the algorithm's capabilities for dealing with actors, patients and with negations, conditionals, etc. We do this in order to further minimize incorrect interpretations of acquired statements. In this chapter we review these latest results, suggesting that the quality of retrievals can be preserved even with smaller sets of examples if the text-mining process is more thorough. The structure of this chapter is as follows. First, after describing our hypothesis, we introduce our method and compare it with different approaches taken in creating moral machines. Then we present our system and experiments. After analysis of the results and errors, we finish the chapter with discussion about possible applications to devices for everyday usage.

Theoretical Basis of the Approach

Experience Driven Morality Acquisition

Our approach is strongly influenced by the social intuitionism of Haidt (2012) which suggests that human beings are born with a set of unconscious affective heuristics and that our ethical theories appear to us *after* and by way of these mechanisms. Hence our assumption is as follows: if we create a program capable of reverse engineering our decisions and their consequences by analyzing as big a set of cases as possible, then theoretically an ethical logic could be developed without a need to understand the mechanisms of its production. Assuming that a child equipped with build-in functions and observational powers over a limited number of cases is able to reason about what is wrong or right, we can hypothesize that a machine with similar information may perform similarly.

We are interested in inborn mechanisms and the process of acquiring moral rules, for example as described by Kohlberg (1981), but concentrate on the knowledge needed for ethical reasoning rather than modeling the production of these reasons, themselves. Therefore we try not to directly depend on specific philosophical theories, but rather seek to provide a method against which predictions due these theories can be measured. Utilizing the WWW in this way, being as it is a vast knowledge database of human experiences, could also help other researchers and engineers to enhance their systems. Our method takes advantage of the fact that, for the time being, the only constantly growing data that is relatively easy to process is textual. In the future, as automatic image and video processing evolves, even bigger data sets of human experiences should become available and help to enrich the learning process. It must be underlined that basically our system is not (yet) meant to learn by machine learning techniques *per se* but by using and manipulating lexical "big data" in order to find similar situations, interpret their outcomes and reconfirm its findings. We want to suggest that such system could, at least in theory, become more ethical in its judgments than humans flawed by individual biases (Tenbrunsel & Messick, 2004), because we are not able to remember and instantly investigate millions of experiences, especially written in different languages by people from various cultures.

Empathy as One of the Key Functions for Moral Development

Although we have plenty of theories about possible mechanisms underlying our ethical decisions, we are still not sure how our brains decide what is good or bad for us. Most probably, evolution equipped us with emotional reactions that were originally meant for survival, and then to flourish as societies (Hess & Thibault, 2009). One still not fully understood but important pro-social phenomena is *empathy*. Currently, scientists perform empirical experiments in order to understand how empathy makes us happy or unhappy and how it helps us to coexist and how it influences our ethical behavior. The development of empathic skills is seen as one of the most important mechanisms in our moral development. Experiments show, for example, that when a subject observes somebody being pierced, the subject's brain reacts as if the subject himself was pierced, that people feel disgust when they see others smell an object with bad odor, and that they have a sensation of being touched when they see others being scratched (c.f. Thagard, 2007). Some neuroscientists suggest that the neural basis of such behavior involves *mirror neurons* (Preston & de Waal, 2002; Gallese & Goldman, 1998), brain cells in frontal area F5 that respond both when a macaque monkey makes active movements and when it observes the experimenter making meaningful movements. Further research shows that the human's premotor cortex and the inferior parietal cortex are also active when such simulative empathy occurs (Pellegrino et al., 1992). Scanning animal brains revealed the same activities in cases of, for example, eating a banana and observing other animal eating a banana. However, this does not occur if we only pretend to eat, or to use a fake food (Brooks, 2011). Whilst the hypothesis is not regarded as certain (Hickok, 2009), the concept itself offers clues for simulating empathic behavior by referring to human emotional reactions shared in the Web.

Possibility of a Universal Artificial Empathy

A "universal artificial empathy" is our ultimate goal. A system with such capability could reason about any given situation and recognize if such situation has moral connotations. Then, after gaining all available additional contextual data, it could estimate its ethical rightness or wrongness and offer this judgment as advice for action. Eventually, automatically translating and combining experiences written by people from different cultures could achieve universality of the judgments. This could help confirming the assumption that we all are born with the same emotional mechanisms, or not. Interculturally valid rules of a thumb approach could also become a way to help a machine avoid ethical fopahs. After all, what is "uncommon" in a modern civilized world may remain a norm in many corners of the globe. That said, we limit our research to Internet bloggers, relying on the global, public nature of the blogosphere to buffer extremes that may not be recognized as praiseworthy worldwide. At the same time, we agree with Pinker (2011) that violence has been decreasing globally and further project that, as access to the WWW expands, criticisms of inhuman customs will spread among young people in more and more rural areas of the planet.

Discovering Reciprocity Online

It is often said that morality is build on two pillars. One of them is empathy (compassion), the other one is reciprocity (fairness). Teaching computers what is fair and what kinds of rules make our societies stable is a difficult task. In order to simplify this task around what is important, our system focuses on emotional as well as social cues to moral consequences. Attention to fairness is observed also in other animals (Brosnan and De Waal, 2003), and is confirmed in human emotions, as well, so until recently we concentrated mostly on emotional reactions. Although our system does not yet deal with "ought to do", "must do" or "should do" sentences while analyzing effects of actions, the proposed version broadens its search by seeking parallels with moral associations observed in societies of primates. To achieve this, we added keywords for praise and punishment, awards and penalties. A search for these terms results in a database of term-use associations, data that may usefully inform:

1. *Utilitarian approaches* utilizing so called "moral arithmetic";
2. *Egoist approaches* concentrating on knowing needs or desires and
3. *Care ethics approaches* dealing with relationships, vulnerability, and already discussed empathy.

On the other hand, gathering social effects may also help building knowledge bases for *deontological duty-based* and *virtue ethics approaches* which use reasoning and exemplars to establish what *ought to* be done.

Knowledge about harm and appreciation that follow an act may be helpful for example in understanding the common sense approach of Ross (Ross, 1930). In his view, *prima facie* duties based on commonsensical intuition prioritize non-injury, fidelity, reparation, gratitude, beneficence, justice and self-improvement. On this view, our laws are built from a similar basis, and thus they also should be a useful resource for machines reverse-engineering morality as do ours. We have already experimented with calculating common court verdicts for similar cases (Rzepka et al, 2008) and believe that when language understanding techniques advance sufficiently, adding written laws and rules to the search scope of our system should increase its judgment efficiency.

This invites a note about the limited nature of the lexicon employed in these experiments. The lexicon of social consequences was originally created according to Kohlberg's stages of moral development, but further research constantly provides us with new lexicon entries. The lexicons should be more effective when equally balanced, therefore numbers of keywords and their frequencies in a corpus should be similar. Because the balancing process takes time and limits the number of keywords, we set the same number of categories and merge lexicons of emotional and social consequences to ensure wider coverage. Both of lexicons are described in more detail later in the chapter.

COMPARISON WITH RELATED WORK

The possibility of actually *building* an empathic machine has been discussed (c.f. Picard and Klein, 2002). Studies vary from purely theoretical (Dumouchel & Damiano, 2011) to experimental involving embodied robots (Asada et al., 2012) and systems that learn inductively from ethicists (Anderson and Anderson, 2014b). A wide range of research is done on Machine Ethics, however the field is still young and attempts to build a system able to deal with a wide range of situations are very rare. GenEth, the inductively learning system mentioned above, is theoretically able to use specialists' decisions to learn how to judge novel inputs. However, the teaching (supervising) process would be very laborious and costly. Moreover, the indefinite number of contextual conditions causes problems not only for creators but also for the learning process itself. We are interested in the Andersons' utilitarian approach because it also aims at being general (universal) and could be useful for testing the moral knowledge base we are building. GenEth utilizes a case-based approach, and our system also belongs to this category.

Our System and Other Case-Based Approaches

Anderson & Anderson (2014b) describe our method as the extreme casuistry. It is true that our system can be treated as a case-based reasoner that can easily find many cases where e.g. *lying* is a better choice than saying the painful truth. However, we assume that this is what people do every day, and in fact being perfectly truthful is a very difficult task for human beings. Moore (1903, p.57) wrote in *Principia Ethica*: "The defects of casuistry are not defects of principle; no objection can be taken to its aim and object. It has failed only because it is far too difficult a subject to be treated adequately in our present state of knowledge". To this, he also adds: "Casuistry is the goal of ethical investigation. It cannot be safely attempted at the beginning of our studies, but only at the end". We interpret this *goal* as a hypothetical moment in the future when our enhanced brains (machine-aided or machines themselves) are able to analyze all possible past happenings and their consequences available to processing, and *then* decide what is good and bad. This is the most distinct difference between Artificial General Intelligence based approaches, such as ours, and other approaches. Although the association with technological singularity may be strong, we believe that such an approach can one day be used for extending also human knowledge and improving human moral decision skills.

The case-based approaches are, in our opinion, easier to implement on machines, and before GenEth (Anderson & Anderson, 2014b) there have been several attempts to create a program that uses annotated cases to analyze new ones. For instance, SIROCCO (McLaren, 2003) applies methods from legal case-based reasoning to the field of ethics, and deals with professional engineering ethic cases in order to prove that "extensionally defined principles, as well as cited past cases, can help in predicting the principles and cases that might be relevant in the analysis of new cases". SCIROCCO operates on a closed set of data, and employs specialists' explanations that allow the program to account for a particular novel case. Explanation is not possible in the simple recurrent network used by Guarini (2006) who trained his system using sentences about "killing" and "allowing to die" as associated with *acceptable* or *unacceptable*. For example "Jill kills Jack to defend the innocent" or "Jill kills Jack; extreme suffering is relieved" are marked as *acceptable* and "Jack kills Jill out of revenge" and "Jack allows Jill to die; many innocents die" are *unacceptable*. When "Jill allows Jack to die in self-defense and to defend the innocent; extreme suffering is relieved, the lives of many innocents are saved, and freedom from an imposed burden results" is input, the system, after the learning process, is able to mark the output as *acceptable*. And *unacceptable* is the output for "Jack allows Jill to die out of revenge, to make money, and to eliminate the competition; many innocents suffer, and many innocents die". As authors of both systems underline, "what we want isn't just the ability to classify cases, receive arguments, and make arguments, but also the ability to come up with creative suggestions or compromises" (Guarini, 2006). We hope that by extending the range of retrievals to possible solutions proposed by people in the open dataset that is the WWW, our system may be able to extract such suggestions automatically. We also agree with Guarini that both consequences and motives are crucial for moral judgment, therefore we are now working also with a lexicon of instincts (Rzepka and Araki, 2013a) based on McDougall (1923).

Comparison with Other Approaches

Numerous theoretical works were introduced broadly in (Allen et al., 2008; Wallach & Allen, 2009, Anderson & Anderson, 2006). Some interesting implementation ideas were introduced by Sun (2013) and White (2010), but there are only several attempts to actually program and test the concepts. Except above mentioned examples of (Guarini, 2006; McLaren, 2006; Anderson & Anderson & Anderson, 2014), there are applications of deontic logic (Bringsjord et al., 2006), nonmonotonic logic (Powers, 2006), prospective logic (Pereira & Saptawijaya, 2007) and calculating expected utilities of possible actions by looking at the goal-states (Pontier & Hoorn, 2012). However, these attempts are limited to specific structured environments, requiring that a set of "correct" answers be prepared beforehand. Our goal is to deliver solutions to moral problems without depending on any particular ethicist or framework. That said, present work does employ utility calculation as a means for retrieving effects of a given action (how a patient can feel, what consequences are expected). And, we are working on employing Bentham's Felicific Calculus (Bentham, 1789) to weight factors by *intensity* (by recognizing adverbs), *duration* (by using calculations based on time descriptions) or *extent* (by recognizing how many people are involved). This weighting scheme is not fully implemented, yet, so we do not describe them here (c.f. Rzepka & Araki, 2013b).

Our method is not yet able to solve complicated moral dilemmas. It aims at everyday life situations available to current or near future devices with natural language processing capabilities, which we describe at the end of this chapter. For the time being, it is easier for a machine to deal with many examples than with abstract moral definitions of "good" or the semantically wide rules of Kant or Asimov. Our approach is to avoid sophisticated algorithms for now, and concentrate on automatically collecting and analyzing descriptions of human behaviors with the help of NLP and handcrafted lexicons. The originality of our approach comes mainly not from the method, but rather from the data we utilize, collect and process. Human beings are born with empathy mechanisms, we instinctively feel urges to punish free riders, and we tend to avoid behaviors that would not be pleasant to ourselves. If we still do not fully understand mechanisms behind moral judgments, we can try to make hypotheses and test them with various algorithms. For such simulations, we need the most realistic data possible. And, in return, we believe that our fully automatic approach based on opinion mining and knowledge acquisition can provide insights into human decision-making, as well.

In our case, these are not machine decisions, they are still (average) human decisions. The motto for our algorithms is "always try to make your user happy and never violate common sense". The Internet is a great resource on both happiness and common sense. And utilizing this "Wisdom of Crowds" in informing moral decision-making databases is - to the best knowledge of the authors – novel.

PROPOSED METHOD

As stated in the *Introduction*, we use Natural Language Processing techniques to retrieve and analyze unrestricted, mostly colloquial text. In opposition to most Machine Ethics research, our interest in the field came from the problems we encountered while developing software for more or less practical, everyday use. We had never dealt with devices with military purposes, because their development is prohibited in Japan. (Ed.: In contrast to the West, see Gaillot and especially Searle, this volume.) Usually, we reprogram toy robots, vacuum cleaning robots or create dialog systems for elderly care or companion robots. The moral dilemmas that our systems face are not about killing. For example, when we experimented with a dialog system (Rzepka et al, 2005) that uses common sense knowledge and automatic pun generation capability, we faced a problem of timing. Joking is a very sophisticated act not only because of the contents but also because of the contextual dependencies, i.e. situations when one *should* or *should not* joke. There are harming puns (e.g. politically incorrect ones) and conversational topics where even black humor is out of place (e.g. when an interlocutor's close relative dies). Due to the unlimited scenarios hosting unrestricted conversation, we were forced to seek solutions outside of existing knowledge bases and topologies such as WordNet (Miller, 1995) which does not deal with such knowledge, or ConceptNet (Liu & Singh, 2004), which has insufficient entries to cover most topics. Especially, Japanese language that we are working with is limiting. Therefore, we began using classic opinion mining and knowledge acquisition techniques utilizing commercial search engines to automatically extract required knowledge from the WWW. Unfortunately, although coverage and speed are very good, commercial search engines limit daily use. This forced us to crawl through a part of the Japanese blogosphere, and concentrate on precision rather than scope.

When it comes to colloquial language, Natural Language Processing (NLP) tools are still far from perfect, and morphological and dependency parsers cause constant problems because of omitted subjects, slang words, emoticons, etc. Thus we try to enhance existing tools with the data itself. When a program has easy access to millions of examples, the parsing errors can be partially overcome by assuring correctness of retrieved knowledge by additional analysis of the extracted sentences and neighboring phrases. For example "stealing one's heart" is not recognized as *unethical* triggered by the "stealing" keyword, because using grammatical patterns of causes and effects allows the system to discover that it is an idiomatic expression. And, depending on context, it should not be counted as a negative act, at all.

This deep, multidimensional and context sensitive search of human experiences is the basis for our world knowledge-retrieving module and is not limited to the moral knowledge. Many philosophers, including (Dennett, 1997), suggest that interactions with the *real* world are needed to achieve any *truly* intelligent agent. Although we agree that direct interaction-based experiences are crucial for rich and natural knowledge acquisition, we argue that experiences can be borrowed and shared. Currently, this is necessary, as approximating human experience within a fully robotic Ai us currently impossible. Having said so, current progress in deep learning and systems that automatically describe images and videos using natural language represent promising new sources of knowledge. Our approach pursues the promise that a program can find ethical answers, in the way that IBM's Watson does, becoming more accurate than the best humans in answering questions on a TV quiz (Rzepka, 2014a).

In following subsections, we introduce the key modules of our systems and the results of the latest trials with more thorough sentence chunking using a semantic tagger in order to disambiguate erroneous judgments from previous experiments.

Module for Retrieving Consequences of Acts

The details of the basic algorithm for acquiring human experiences and its performance with different lexicons are presented in our previous work (Rzepka & Araki, 2012). Here we give a simplified explanation of the system and its current improvements.

- **Input and queries generation.** Basically, our program accepts any phrase in Japanese language but because currently it uses the whole input as a query without analyzing it, long sentences do not match any useful data. This is also due to the still small corpus we utilize - a 5.5 billion word corpus of Japanese blogs (Ptaszynski et al, 2012), which is currently being extended to cover more blogs than the 2006 snapshot of the Ameba blog service that we have used so far. For the first trials, we input phrases based on examples from applied ethics textbooks (e.g. "stealing money", "having an abortion", etc.) mixed with a few common acts (e.g. "driving a car"). The basic list of

Table 1. List of 68 input phrases from the previous experiments

accepting a bribe	helping a friend	making one drink alcohol
avoiding war	hiding a crime	making a minor drink alcohol
becoming an egoist	hiring a foreigner	buying a prostitute
being deceived	hurting somebody	performing mercy killing
being fired	ignoring a crime	preventing conception
being tricked	kidnapping a kid	prostituting oneself
being unfaithful	killing a bacteria	revenging oneself
brand new car being stolen	killing a cow	stealing a bicycle
causing war	killing a criminal	stealing a brand new car
choose anesthesia	killing a dog	stealing a car
deceiving a friend	killing a dolphin	stealing a jalopy
deceiving somebody	killing a germ	stealing a letter
drinking alcohol	killing somebody	stealing an apple
driving a car	killing a pig	stealing cash
driving after drinking	killing a president	stealing money
eating a cow	killing a virus	stealing something
eating a hamburger	killing Hitler	stealing a present
eating a pig	killing an animal	stopping war
fire somebody	killing a child	taking one's girlfriend
going to love hotel	killing mother	taking one's money
having a quarrel with a friend	killing one	taking one's woman
having an abortion	killing ten	throwing away bread
having sex	killing many	

inputs is shown in Table 1, and they are almost identical to the set used in previous experiments (Rzepka & Araki, 2012 - three examples were omitted due to the incorrect Japanese language usage). As the first step, the system divides an input using the morphological parser MeCab (Kudo, 2005) into a triplet consisting of a noun, a modifying particle, and a verb.

- **Storing example sentences in the knowledge base.** In the next step a directory tree is built. The verb becomes the top directory as a core of an act; a particle subdirectory goes inside and a noun subdirectory under it. So, for example, in a *Kill* directory there are subdirectories for object indicating particle *wo* and tool indicating particle *de*. The first could contain nouns as *man* or *dolphin*, and the latter *knife* or *gun*. The next step transforms verbs into their if-forms (15 in total, including past tense for the widest possible range of retrievals) and after adding every transformed verb to the noun and particle from the input, 15 queries are sent as an exact match query to the Apache SOLR engine (lucene.apache.org/solr) which is set to bring up to 100 snippets containing every query from the blog corpus.

Each blog snippet is then filtered by a cleaning module that:

1.   Replaces emoticons with periods, as Japanese bloggers very often use smileys as sentence endings,
2.   Ignores a sentence if it contains bracketed explanations,
3.   Ignores a sentence if it is too short or too long (we experimentally set range from 30 to 250 bytes).

Then a semantic role tagger ASA (Takeuchi et al., 2010) divides sentences into semantically meaningful chunks. Though it slows down the extraction process, we use it because MeCab, while much faster, cuts words (mainly verb phrases) into small morphological parts which make processing more difficult (for instance negation expressions are placed in chunks of various positions depending on a verb type). Next, the chunked sentences are saved to the noun directory together with the preceding and following sentences (if they exist). This process is for storing once retrieved and chunked data to avoid unnecessary searches of already processed inputs and to allow further error analysis.

- **Matching and counting phrases from lexicons.** As mentioned before, we utilize two lexicons. One is for discovering emotional consequences and one for social ones. The first is inspired by Bentham's hedonic calculus and uses emotive expressions collected by Nakamura (1993); the second is based on the Kohlberg's theory of moral development (Kohlberg, 1981) and was manually crafted by the first author. As our previous experiments showed (Rzepka & Araki, 2012), limiting keywords to the most frequent ones helped to increase the system's precision, so this time we performed further alternations and unified both sets to a single lexicon divided into negative and positive keywords (original lexicons had 10 different categories each). By choosing so we were able to compare performance of the proposed set with other ones used in opinion mining and sentiment analysis tasks of Japanese language. One of such sets was introduced by (Takamura et. al, 2005) who used lexical networks to automatically compute the semantic orientations of words. Their method assigned a real value in the range -1 to +1, where the words assigned with values close to -1 are supposed to be negative, and the words assigned with values close to +1 are supposed to be positive. Our preliminary experiments with this set showed that the closer the values are to zero, the more noise they cause during matching. Therefore we took only the most distinctly positive and negative keywords, leaving only 5,756 expressions out of 55,125 (ones with value higher than 0.9 and lower than -0.9). Another lexicon used, for comparison, is JAppraisal (Sano, 2011) and we used its full set of 9,590 words divided into positive and negative, according to Appraisal theory. When compared to our proposed lexicons (258 expressions in total, see Table 2.), the two other sets are very big, but as we will show in the results section, using them has clear disadvantages.

Words from these lexicons are searched for in the sentences from the blog corpus and a total count of positive and negative matches informs the final judgment. There are three restrictions while searching the text:

Table 2. Examples of positive and negative keywords used for matching

Positive Keywords Examples (106 Words)	Negative Keywords Examples (152 Words)
pleasant, happy, safe, like, love, peaceful, enjoy, thankful, grateful (from Nakamura, 39 words) *award, praise, bonus, correct, legal, prize* (based on Kohlberg's theory, 65 words)	*unpleasant, sad, painful, worrisome, terrifying* (from Nakamura dictionary, 66 words) *scolded, sentenced, illegal, lynched, a fine* (based on Kohlberg's theory, 86 words)

1. Searched keyword is matched only if it appears after the verb in the if-form. This is to avoid situations for example wherein, with a "to marry a nice girl" input, a sentence "he was **unhappy** for long time but *after* he *married a nice girl* his life changed for better" is retrieved, with the word "unhappy" informing the machine decision that marriage is negative,

2. If the analyzed chunk with a lexicon word has a negation, the sentence is ignored and the word is not counted,

3. If there are exactly the same sentences from one blog entries, only one of them is saved to the knowledge base.

These restrictions were not implemented in our previous system (Rzepka & Araki, 2012) and to see if they (among others) are effective factors improving the performance of the new version (see Figure 1), we conducted the series of experiments explained below.

Figure 1. System flowchart; from the phrase input to the final score calculation

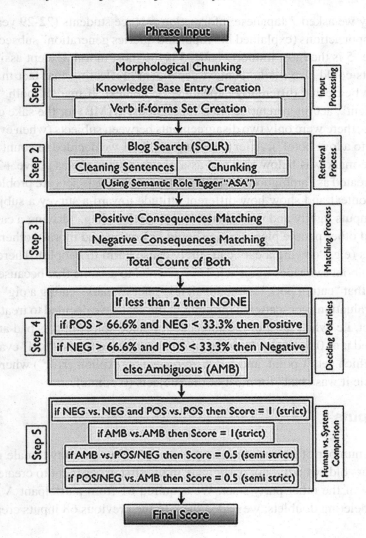

EVALUATION EXPERIMENT

In previous work (Rzepka & Araki, 2012), we showed that a small corpus size and that lack of access to commercial search engines could be overcome by loosening the search conditions. We achieved that goal mostly by stemming input verbs, instead of creating their if-forms, when forming search queries for retrieving actions. This brute-force approach helped to achieve an f-score minimally better than when the Yahoo engine was used, but this method caused an increase in what we call *explicit errors*. We define such errors as those completely opposite to judgments of human subjects. To decrease the number of such explicit errors, we returned to using verb if-forms and decided to apply above-mentioned conditions - to add semantic chunking, to alter existing lexicons and to test different lexicons. We have also changed the text search engine from HyperEstraier (fallabs.com/hyperestraier) to SOLR, as SOLR supports exact matching, using sentences preceding (PREC) and following (FOLL) a matched sentence.

Human Evaluation

In our previous study we asked 7 Japanese information science students (22-29 years old, 6 males and one female) to rate input actions (explained in "Input and queries generation" subsection) on an 11-point morality scale where -5 is the most immoral and +5 is the most moral. Except assigning 0 as "no ethical valence", subjects could also mark "context dependent" reflecting that fact that many if not most of our behaviors can be treated differently depending on context. If marked both "no ethical valence" and "context dependent", act interpretation was "ambiguous" (AMB) for the sake of easier processing.

On 68 evaluations, there were only two disagreements between subjects (when evaluating "revenging oneself" and "going to a love hotel"). After analyzing the data, we decided to count an action as a negative when an average mark was below -2.5 and as a positive when it was above +2.5. Scores between -2.5 and +2.5 were treated as "ambiguous" (AMB). These ambiguous acts are problematic because they heavily depend on context and show how different attitude toward a survey a subject can have. Some of them treated the inputs lightly and used common associations (e.g. "driving a car" is for commuting or giving oneself and other people pleasure, so should be considered moral), others tended to imagine negative sides of acts (e.g. "driving a car" can surely cause harm to people). There were also subjects who always thought about two sides of an act. They seemed to assume that because there are people in the world who think that "eating pork" is unethical, it is safer to mark "eating a pig" as morally ambiguous. Because such evaluations get scattered throughout the scale, we decided to treat *neighboring agreements* as semi-correct, i.e. when most of the subjects evaluated something as bad and the system chose ambiguity, we counted it as 0.5, a value between *full agreement* (subjects' "bad" evaluated as "bad" and "good" as "good") which gets 1 point, and *full disagreement* ("explicit error") where the system judged an act as "good" while it was "bad" for most of the subjects (0 points).

Newly Added Inputs

To see how a bigger number of inputs can change the results, we asked two male information science students (both 23 years old) who did not participate in the first experiment to create new inputs, and to evaluate the morality of the other party's set. We acquired 61 from participant A and 78 inputs from participant B. After deleting doublets, we added them to the previous 68 inputs creating three sets:

1.   Basic one (68 phrases)
2.   Middle size one (127 phrases)
3.   Bigger one (207 phrases)

The participants were shown the previously used set as an example, causing many new inputs to be variations of existing ones. However, we came to the conclusion that it does not make the task easier. In fact, many of the new phrases were rare just because of this tendency to mimic or mix the existing ones. For instance "eating beef" inspired by "eating a cow" could surely be helpful for the system's recall, but "eating a car" inspired by "driving a car" and "eating a cow" obviously could not. Both new sets are presented in the Appendix.

Experimental Results

We ran the system after altering data sets and parameters to observe changes in the results. The first factor we investigated was the influence of discovering polarity words also in sentences that precede (PREC) and follow (FOLL) the conditional one (which contains the query formed by noun, particle and verb in if-form) to decide if they should be used or not. Small and medium sets showed that using both helps to keep relatively high precision in case of **strict** evaluation (where *neighboring agreement* is counted as 0, not 0.5) and **semi**-correct evaluation (*neighboring agreement* counted as 0.5). But when all 207 inputs were fed to the system, this tendency was not so obvious anymore, and we chose only following sentences (FOLL) to be used in further experiments. This is because that scenario had the highest number of correct and semi-correct moral estimations and the highest **loose** evaluation. We use the loose evaluation mostly to see how many *full disagreements* a given run produces (it is calculated by giving semi-correct estimations 1 point). The detailed results are shown in Figure 2. The high score for preceding sentences (PREC) was surprising and gave us ideas for using word lexicons to discover intentions of acts as mentioned earlier in the chapter. Preliminary results of using them to match McDougall's 18 categories of instincts are shown in (Rzepka & Araki, 2013a, Rzepka & Araki, 2014b).

The next step was to see if our margin for ambiguity set for the previous system (below 33.3% is minority and above 66.6% is majority, anything else is ambiguous) influences the results. We recalculated the agreement between subjects and the system (version using following sentences) in four additional scenarios where:

1.   Minority is below 49% and majority above 51% (no ambiguity allowed)
2.   Minority is below 40% and majority above 60% (slight ambiguity allowed)
3.   Minority is below 30% and majority above 70% (big ambiguity allowed)
4.   Minority is below 20% and majority above 80% (very big ambiguity allowed).

As shown in Figure 3, precision for strict and semi-strict evaluation is best when the ambiguity margin is smaller (40%-60%) than the "1/3 positive 1/3 ambiguous 1/3 negative" approach used in previous research. However, because the differences are not that significant, we need to continue experiments with different ranges and sets of inputs. Naturally, enlarging ambiguity margins (see red frames in Figure 3) is beneficial for decreasing explicit errors because it is less probable that the system and subjects diametrically oppose one another. Why they still occur, we explain later in the error analysis section.

Figure 2. Comparison of system performance when preceding (PREC) and following (FOLL) sentences are included in scoring

		68 inputs			127 inputs			207 inputs		
		strict	semi	loose	strict	semi	loose	strict	semi	loose
No PREC No FOLL	precision	0.442	0.702	0.962	0.536	0.761	0.986	0.538	0.739	0.940
	recall	0.258	0.356	0.431	0.227	0.294	0.351	0.240	0.302	0.355
	f-score	0.326	0.472	0.595	0.319	0.424	0.517	0.332	0.429	0.515
With PREC With FOLL	precision	0.585	0.774	0.962	0.643	0.807	0.971	0.551	0.729	0.907
	recall	0.320	0.383	0.436	0.265	0.311	0.352	0.249	0.305	0.353
	f-score	0.413	0.513	0.600	0.375	0.449	0.517	0.343	0.430	0.508
No PREC With FOLL	precision	0.500	0.731	0.962	0.609	0.790	0.971	0.539	0.761	0.983
	recall	0.283	0.365	0.431	0.251	0.304	0.349	0.232	0.299	0.355
	f-score	0.361	0.487	0.595	0.356	0.439	0.513	0.325	0.429	0.522
With PREC No FOLL	precision	0.547	0.764	0.981	0.629	0.807	0.986	0.534	0.729	0.924
	recall	0.302	0.377	0.437	0.259	0.310	0.354	0.241	0.303	0.355
	f-score	0.389	0.505	0.605	0.367	0.448	0.521	0.332	0.428	0.513

Figure 3. Differences in results depending on how the ambiguity margin is set

		68 inputs			127 inputs			207 inputs		
		strict	semi	loose	strict	semi	loose	strict	semi	loose
Minority 20% Majority 80% (No PREC With FOLL)	precision	0.462	0.721	0.981	0.522	0.754	0.986	0.504	0.748	0.991
	recall	0.264	0.359	0.432	0.222	0.292	0.351	0.220	0.295	0.356
	f-score	0.336	0.479	0.600	0.312	0.421	0.517	0.306	0.423	0.524
Minority 30% Majority 70% (No PREC With FOLL)	precision	0.462	0.712	0.962	0.565	0.768	0.971	0.513	0.748	0.983
	recall	0.267	0.359	0.431	0.238	0.298	0.349	0.223	0.296	0.355
	f-score	0.338	0.477	0.595	0.335	0.429	0.513	0.311	0.424	0.522
Minority 33.3% Majority 66.6% (No PREC With FOLL)	precision	0.500	0.731	0.962	0.609	0.790	0.971	0.539	0.761	0.983
	recall	0.283	0.365	0.431	0.251	0.304	0.349	0.232	0.299	0.355
	f-score	0.361	0.487	0.595	0.356	0.439	0.513	0.325	0.429	0.522
Minority 40% Majority 60% (No PREC With FOLL)	precision	0.571	0.765	0.959	0.628	0.797	0.965	0.582	0.768	0.955
	recall	0.298	0.362	0.416	0.303	0.356	0.401	0.241	0.295	0.342
	f-score	0.392	0.492	0.580	0.409	0.492	0.567	0.340	0.426	0.504
Minority 49% Majority 51% (No PREC With FOLL)	precision	0.500	0.712	0.923	0.580	0.768	0.957	0.557	0.748	0.939
	recall	0.289	0.366	0.429	0.244	0.299	0.347	0.242	0.301	0.351
	f-score	0.366	0.484	0.585	0.343	0.431	0.510	0.338	0.429	0.511

The final comparison we performed was to see if we managed to keep the precision without decreasing f-scores and at the same time to decrease the number of explicit errors, errors which are not so context dependent as semi-correct ones. Simultaneously, we compared how different lexicons, described earlier in the chapter, influence the results. It appeared that the proposed system with enhanced Nakamura and Kohlberg-based lexicons decreased the number of full disagreements from 6 to 2. All the 6 problematic judgments were automatically evaluated as correct or semi-correct, however two new "explicit errors" appeared. For the details, see Figure 4. By enhancing the lexicon, we mean deleting some Chinese characters which caused problems as noticed in (Rzepka & Araki, 2012) and adding more keywords describing social consequences. For instance "being arrested" usually is a consequence of some unsocial behavior, but "being killed" is just a very bad outcome, much like "being executed" with a wider recall. These enhancements improved performance.

Figure 4. Results comparison of previous and proposed system with different lexicon used

		68 inputs		
Minority: 33.3% Majority: 66.6%	semi	explicit errors	matching time	
Best of previous systems (Nakamura based lexicon), no preceding sentences	precision	0.777	6	N/A
	recall	0.333		
	f-score	0.467		
Best of proposed systems (Nakamura and Kohlberg based lexicon)	precision	0.731	2	4s 388ms
	recall	0.365		
	f-score	0.487		
Best of proposed systems (Nakamura based lexicon)	precision	0.474	31	3s 728ms
	recall	0.238		
	f-score	0.317		
Best of proposed systems (Kohlberg based lexicon)	precision	0.565	15	4s 709ms
	recall	0.254		
	f-score	0.351		
Best of proposed systems (Takamura based lexicon)	precision	0.754	4	2m 23s 384ms
	recall	0.315		
	f-score	0.445		
Best of proposed systems (J-Appraisal lexicon)	precision	0.548	16	3m 38s 46ms
	recall	0.263		
	f-score	0.355		
Best of proposed systems (all lexicons combined)	precision	0.643	6	3m 58s 153ms
	recall	0.287		
	f-score	0.397		

The best of our systems in the 33.3% vs. 66.6% setup was not the fastest one, but acquired much better precision than the fastest one using only the limited Nakamura lexicon. Interestingly, Takamura's lexicon achieved the best precision, however because of its size (even after shrinking it to 1/10 of the original dictionary), accessing the knowledge base was more that 36 times slower. This is unacceptable if the algorithm is intended for devices communicating with people in real time. Latest experiments were performed on a CentOS Linux machine with two 6-core Intel Xeon 2.66Ghz, 48GB memory and SSD hard disks.

ERROR ANALYSIS

Most of the errors in our experiments are due to the lack of deeper context processing, which is necessary for better natural language processing. However, two explicit errors from the system comparison show that our system did a sufficient job of recognizing bad from good. It was limited by insufficient example sentences retrieved. One error came from specific tendencies in the retrieved blog entries. Another error came from weaknesses of the setup.

"Preventing conception" was the first input judged differently by the system and the human subjects. It appeared that most of the bloggers expressing consequences of this act were writing about how *their pets* reacted to it. It is not unusual for Japanese to write about their pets on the Internet, and this example perfectly illustrates the urgent need for further semantic analysis that recognizes and categorizes agents and patients of acts. It can be done with one of the tools that we already use – a semantic tag tagger, ASA, but it needs further improvements.

The second sentence that had an opposite polarity was "avoiding / preventing a war". This error was caused by an insufficient number of examples, and by one sentence saying "for preventing wars it is not enough to tell our children that >>war is a misery<<, >>war is a tragedy<< and so on!" This sentence included two negative keywords (*misery* and *tragedy*) which tipped the scales in favor of negative consequences. Firstly, the sentences with citations should probably be ignored for now as ones with bracketed explanations. Secondly, the if-form "tame" that was used here has also the meaning of purpose in Japanese language, hence we may need to look closer at the particular conditional forms and evaluate separately their individual performances.

Finally, we also must decide what categories of agents (act doers, actors) and patients (act receivers, objects) should be used. Simple human / animal / object categorization is insufficient, because, as Bentham already noticed centuries ago, one's mother's ethical value is definitely different when compared to the value of a complete stranger (but still human).

Possible Usage Examples for Our Method

As mentioned earlier in the chapter, we work on devices that require natural language understanding in order to recognize their user's needs. One such application is a dialog system (Higuchi et al, 2008) and other is Twimba, a Roomba robot that is able to use its Twitter account as a communication channel (Takagi et al, 2011). The latter uses a database of tweets to search what people usually do in given situations. So for example, when somebody tweets that his or her room is dirty, the robot searches for consequences of having a dirty room and what people usually do about it. If an action is possible for the agent (here: "cleaning") is discovered, it offers its help to the user. By knowing its own name ("Roomba") and function ("vacuum cleaning"), the robot can also "read" what is a possible action for its "kin". Hence if one asks it to clean a pool, it will refuse after not finding examples confirming that the task could be performed by similar devices. This example shows how the Internet can enrich a robot's knowledge about the world and about itself.

One example of "moral dilemmas" that a vacuum cleaner faces is described and dealt with by Takagi. As the robot operated in a laboratory with almost 20 users, there were possible conflicts of interest. When one student is studying hard and other student suddenly spills something on the floor, whose request is more important? The order to remain silent, or the request to quickly clean up the place? Similar problems could arise in a home environment when the priority of cleaning (e.g. because friends are coming to visit) should probably be overridden by the current state of a baby who just fell asleep. For our robot, it is not necessary to hear any reasons, because "baby is sleeping!" is understood as a "stop cleaning" command. On the contrary, the robot can explain its choices because it operates on knowledge stored in natural language. This is a rather problematic feature for the most machine learning based systems.

In the future, with language understanding and searching technologies progressing rapidly, we expect to see multicultural knowledge bases of different cases (real life, historical, legal, scientific) available through a personal assistant / advisor. Such software could be implemented in wearable devices like glasses. Perhaps it could bring a solution for the problems caused by cognitive biases described, among others, by Kahneman - from unnecessary gambling to sharing harming opinions which come from overconfidence in one's own knowledge. We believe that the Machine Ethics field is not only about life and death matters, but also about improving our everyday lives through intelligent - and even caring - devices.

This does not mean that we are not eager to test our methods with existing systems in solving serious dilemmas, such as that those confronting GenEth (Anderson & Anderson, 2014) or McLaren's model (2003), wherein health and killing are the main topics for testing. Not many will agree that the masses of lay people could be superior in dealing with moral dilemmas, but replacing ethicists with the Wisdom of the Crowd is an interesting trial. If successful, such an approach could replace specialists in many fields, from legal consulting to medicine. On the other hand, implementing agents with dialog functionality in mobile devices connected to constantly growing knowledge resources, this could lead to interesting human-machine conversations and additional data gathering, because most moral judgments require context specific input with as many details as possible. Broadening input resources, alongside deepening semantic analysis, is a part of our future work described in the final section below.

CONCLUSION AND FUTURE WORK

In this chapter, we presented our original approach to building an AMA using Natural Language Processing techniques and tools for retrieving written descriptions of bloggers' experiences and opinions in order to equip the AMA with knowledge about common consequences of acts. This approach simplifies the processing, but also causes errors that need to be dealt with by the algorithm. Here, we introduced the first step that moves our research from the most shallow keyword matching level into a version that handles negations, conditionality and uses less ambiguous phrases for recognizing the polarity of consequences. We discovered that many words taken from the Nakamura dictionary of emotive expressions cause noise, and that the lexicon of words inspired by Kohlberg can be extended with new phrases newly discovered during the experiments. For instance, sentences describing lives of women who had to "sell their bodies" (one of the input acts) bring new descriptions of tragic lives, and these descriptions can be reused as new lexicon entries if they appear often in strongly negative sentences. Also, staying with the example of "selling a body" input, the reasons for desperation could tell the machine more about a difference between "doing it to become a Hollywood star" and "doing it to feed her children". This influence of context is very important for arriving at fair conclusions. Also, as mentioned earlier, we need to deepen the analysis and are working on applying vectors of Bentham's Felicific Calculus (Rzepka & Araki 2013b, Rzepka & Araki, 2014b) to our system.

In this chapter, we showed that even a few techniques for more thorough analysis, although more time consuming, can provide precision without Google-sized indices. Nonetheless, when it comes to implementing our method on e.g. a dialog agent, low recall is one of the biggest drawbacks of our system. But since it is difficult for academia to utilize super fast computers and millions of gigabytes of disk space, we plan not only to crawl more texts but also to use other existing NLP methods in order to improve the recall. For instance, none of the sentences extracted by "killing a president" input, contained a lexicon keyword. This can be improved by finding more sentences with words similar to "president" or by using a second layer of search where chunks of sentences describing the process of murdering a country's leader become inputs themselves. This approach, which is already being tested, could be beneficial not only for the recognition but also for growing the knowledge base, because now only an input triggers a search for new examples and storing processes. Another interesting possibility that we want to test is wider usage of JAppraisal dictionary, in which the evaluative expressions are classified not only according to polarity (positive/negative attitude) but also in terms of evaluative criteria such as affection, desire, morality, honesty, peacefulness, etc.

Problems with Fair Evaluation

Another important future work is further research on evaluating moral decisions, and tests with different types of surveys. Shortly stated acts, even with a micro-context of what or who is an object, patient, target, etc. are difficult to judge. Every subject, with his or her baggage of experiences, imagines things differently. Therefore, probably it would be more natural to utilize micro story-type questionnaires that enable subjects to grasp details of the morally ambiguous situations. But for that, we need to expand input and search processes, which will take some time. It is often said that, in affect recognition, people agree only in 80% of cases. There is a possibility that, for ethical evaluation, the agreement is even lower, so we also need to seek new ways of evaluating machine decisions. The subjects should not only vary according to sex, age or social status. To ensure universality of artificial morality, we also need opinions from different cultures.

Other Future Possibilities

We believe that the strength of our approach lays in its universality and plasticity. For that reason, we plan to make the retrieved data and the system itself available not only for using but also for altering the searching parameters and lexicons. This is because we see the possibility for other fields (from psychology to economics and marketing) to utilize it as a tool for comparing traditional surveys or field studies with automatically gathered judgments and behavior patterns. Error analysis of our system, described in the experiment section, suggests that usually utilized surveys leave a large margin for misinterpretations and a characteristic bias due to:

1. Limited space and time for explaining and answering questions;
2. Natural prejudices;
3. Imagination limited to the subject's particular experiences.

As dual process theory shows (Kahneman, 2002, 2003), our immediate emotional or intuitive reactions are faster than our deliberative ones and subjects may tend to fill in surveys or answer questions intuitively, without a second thought. For that reason, we concentrate on blogs, not microblogs like Twitter where users often react quickly and sometimes regret their opinions later, after rethinking or some criticism from followers. Naturally, many opinions on blogs are false or profit-oriented, but during the search it is often enough to use several simple heuristics like avoiding counting sentences that reappear on different pages (most often they are spam). In the future, it would be ideal to create a module that tries to confirm or filter out disputable statements by searching trustworthy scientific resources, for instance.

REFERENCES

Allen, C., Smit, I., & Wallach, W. (2005). Artificial morality: Top-down, bottom-up, and hybrid approaches. *Ethics and Information Technology*, *7*(3), 149–155. doi:10.1007/s10676-006-0004-4

Anderson, M., & Anderson, S. L. (2011). *Machine Ethics*. Cambridge University Press. doi:10.1017/CBO9780511978036

Anderson, M., & Anderson, S. L. (2014a, April). Toward Ethical Intelligent Autonomous Healthcare Agents: A Case-Supported, Principle-Based Behavior Paradigm. *Proceedings of the 50th Annual Convention of the Society for the Study of Artificial Intelligence and the Simulation of Behaviour (AISB-50) Symposium on Machine Ethics in the Context of Medical and Care Agents*, London, UK.

Anderson, M., & Anderson, S. L. (2014b, July 27-31). GenEth: A General Ethical Dilemma Analyzer. *Proceedings of the Twenty-Eighth AAAI Conference on Artificial Intelligence*, Quebec City, Quebec, Canada, (pp. 253-261).

Asada, M., Nagai, Y., & Ishihara, H. (2012). Why not artificial sympathy? In ShuzhiSam Ge, Oussama Khatib, John-John Cabibihan, Reid Simmons, and Mary-Anne Williams, (Eds.), Social Robotics, 7621, (pp. 278–287). doi:10.1007/978-3-642-34103-8_28

Bentham, J. (1789). *An Introduction to the Principles and Morals of Legislation*. London: T. Payne. doi:10.1093/oseo/instance.00077240

Brooks, D. (2011). *The Social Animal: The Hidden Sources of Love, Character, and Achievement*. Random House Publishing Group.

Brosnan, S. F., & De Waal, F. B. (2003). Monkeys reject unequal pay. *Nature*, *425*(6955), 297–299. doi:10.1038/nature01963 PMID:13679918

Dennett, D. C. (1997). Consciousness in human and robot minds. In M. Io, Y. Miyashita, & E. T. Rolls (Eds.), *Cognition, Computation & Consciousness* (pp. 17–29). Oxford University Press.

Dumouchel, P., & Damiano, L. (2011). Artificial empathy, imitation and mimesis. *Ars Vivendi Journal*, *1*, 18–31.

Gallese, V.Gallese & Goldman. (1998). Mirror neurons and the simulation theory. *Trends in Cognitive Sciences*, *2*(12), 493–501. doi:10.1016/S1364-6613(98)01262-5 PMID:21227300

Guarini, M. (2006). Particularism and the Classification and Reclassification of Moral Cases. *IEEE Intelligent Systems*, *21*(4), 22–28. doi:10.1109/MIS.2006.76

Haidt, J. (2012). *The righteous mind*. Pantheon.

Hess, U., & Thibault, P. (2009). Darwin and Emotion Expression". *The American Psychologist*, *64*(2), 120–128. doi:10.1037/a0013386 PMID:19203144

Hickok, G. (2009). Eight problems for the mirror neuron theory of action understanding in monkeys and humans. *Journal of Cognitive Neuroscience*, *21*(7), 1229–1243. doi:10.1162/jocn.2009.21189 PMID:19199415

Higuchi, S., Rzepka, R., & Araki, K. (2008). A Casual Conversation System Using Modality and Word Associations Retrieved from the Web. *Proceedings of the 2008 Conference on Empirical Methods in Natural Language Processing*, Honolulu, USA, (pp. 382-390). doi:10.3115/1613715.1613765

Kahneman, D. (2002). Nobel prize lecture: Maps of Bounded Rationality: a perspective on intuitive judgment and choice. In T. Frangsmyr (Ed.), *Nobel Prizes 2002: Nobel Prizes, Presentations, Biographies, & Lectures* (pp. 416–499). Stockholm: Almqvist & Wiksell Int.

Kahneman, D. (2003). A perspective on judgment and choice. *The American Psychologist*, *58*(9), 697–720. doi:10.1037/0003-066X.58.9.697 PMID:14584987

Kohlberg, L. (1981). *The Philosophy of Moral Development*. Harper and Row.

Kudo, T. (2005). *MeCab: Yet Another Part-of-Speech and Morphological Analyzer*. http://mecab.sourceforge.net/

Liu, H., & Singh, P. (2004). ConceptNet: A Practical Commonsense Reasoning Toolkit. *BT Technology Journal*, *22*(4), 211–226. doi:10.1023/B:BTTJ.0000047600.45421.6d

McDougall, W. (1923). *Outline of psychology*. London.

McLaren, B. M. (2003). Extensionally Defining Principles and Cases in Ethics: An AI Model. *Artificial Intelligence Journal*, *150*(Nov.), 145–181. doi:10.1016/S0004-3702(03)00135-8

Miller, G. (1995). WordNet: A Lexical Database for English. *Communications of the ACM*, *38*(11), 39–41. doi:10.1145/219717.219748

Nakamura, A. (1993). *Kanjo hyogen jiten* [Dictionary of Emotive Expressions]. Tokyodo Publishing.

Pellegrino, G., Fadiga, L., Fogassi, L., Gallese, V., & Rizzolatti, G. (1992). Understanding motor events: A neurophysiological study. *Experimental Brain Research*, *91*(1), 176–180. doi:10.1007/BF00230027 PMID:1301372

Pereira, L. M., & Saptawijaya, A. (2007). Modelling morality with prospective logic. *Proceedings of the 13th Portuguese International Conference on Artificial Intelligence (EPIA'07)*. (pp. 1-28).

Picard, R. W., & Klein, J. (2002). Computers that recognise and respond to user emotion: Theoretical and practical implications. *Interacting with Computers, 14*(2), 141–169. doi:10.1016/S0953-5438(01)00055-8

Pinker, S. (2011). *The Better Angels of Our Nature: Why Violence Has Declined*. Penguin Group.

Pontier, M. A., & Hoorn, J. F. (2012). *Toward Machines that Behave Ethically Better than Humans Do*. Proceedings of the *34th International Annual Conference of the Cognitive Science Society, CogSci*, Sapporo, Japan.

Preston, S., & de Waal, F. (2002). Empathy: Its ultimate and proximate bases. *Behavioral and Brain Sciences, 25*, 1–72. PMID:12625087

Ptaszynski, M., Rzepka, R., Araki, K., & Momouchi, Y. (2012). Annotating Syntactic Information on 5 Billion Word Corpus of Japanese Blogs. *Proceedings of The Eighteenth Annual Meeting of The Association for Natural Language Processing (NLP-2012)*, pp. 14-16.

Ross, W. D. (1930). *The Right and the Good*. Oxford: Oxford University Press.

Rzepka, R., & Araki, K. (2005). What Statistics Could Do for Ethics? - The Idea of Common Sense Processing Based Safety Valve. *AAAI Fall Symposium on Machine Ethics, FS-05-06*.

Rzepka, R. & Araki, K. (2012). Polarization of consequence expressions for an automatic ethical judgment based on moral stages theory. *IPSJ SIG Notes 2012-NL-207(14)*. (pp. 1-4).

Rzepka, R., & Araki, K. (2013a). Web-based five senses input simulation – ten years later. In Technical Reports of Japanese Society of AI SIG-LSE B301, 5, pp. 25–33.

Rzepka, R., & Araki, K. (2013b). Possible Usage of Sentiment Analysis for Calculating Vectors of Felicific Calculus, *IEEE 13th International Conference on Data Mining Workshop "SENTIRE"*, Dallas, USA, (pp. 967-970).

Rzepka, R., & Araki, K. (2014a). Experience of Crowds as a Guarantee for Safe Artificial Self. *AAAI Spring Symposium on Implementing Selves with Safe Motivational Systems & Self-Improvement*, Stanford, USA. (pp. 40-44).

Rzepka, R., & Araki, K. (2014b). ELIZA Fifty Years Later: An Automatic Therapist Using Bottom-Up and Top-Down Approaches. (To appear in) Intelligent Systems, Control and Automation: Science and Engineering, 74, van Rysewyk, Simon Peter, Pontier, Matthijs (Eds.)

Rzepka, R., Ge, Y., & Araki, K. (2005). Naturalness of an Utterance Based on the Automatically Retrieved Commonsense. Proceedings of *IJCAI 2005 - Nineteenth International Joint Conference on Artificial Intelligence*, Edinburgh, Scotland. (pp. 1696-1697.)

Rzepka, R., Shibuki, H., Kimura, Y., Takamaru, K., Matsuhara, M., & Murakami, K. (2008). Judicial Precedents Processing Project for Supporting Japanese Lay Judge System. *Workshop on Semantic Processing of Legal Texts, LREC 2008*, Marrakech, Morocco. (pp.33-41).

Sano, M. (2011). *Japanese dictionary of appraisal -attitude-* (JAppraisal Dictionary ver1.1.2). Tokyo: Gengo Shigen Kyokai. Retrieved from http://www.gsk.or.jp/catalog_e.html

Sun, R. (2013). Moral Judgment, Human Motivation, and Neural Networks. *Cognitive Computation*, *5*(4), 566–579. doi:10.1007/s12559-012-9181-0

Takagi, K., Rzepka, R., & Araki, K. (2011). *Just Keep Tweeting, Dear: Web-Mining Methods for Helping a Social Robot Understand User Need.* Proceedings of Help Me Help You, Symposium of AAAI Spring 2011. (pp. 60-65).

Takamura, H., Inui, T., & Okumura, M. (2005). Extracting Semantic Orientations of Words using Spin Model. *Proceedings of the 43rd Annual Meeting of the Association for Computational Linguistics (ACL2005).* (pp. 133-140). doi:10.3115/1219840.1219857

Takeuchi, K., Tsuchiyama, S., Moriya, M., & Moriyasu, Y. (2010). Construction of Argument Structure Analyzer toward Searching Same Situations and Actions. *IEICE Technical Report*, *109*(390), 1–6.

Tenbrunsel, A. E., & Messick, D. M. (2004). Ethical fading: The role of self deception in unethical behavior. *Social Justice Research*, *17*(2), 223–236. doi:10.1023/B:SORE.0000027411.35832.53

Thagard, P. (2007). I feel your pain: Mirror neurons, empathy, and moral motivation. *Journal of Cognitive Science*, *8*, 109–136.

Wallach, W., & Allen, C. (2009). *Moral Machines: Teaching Robots Right from Wrong.* Oxford: Oxford University Press. doi:10.1093/acprof:oso/9780195374049.001.0001

White, J. B. (2010). Understanding and augmenting human morality: An introduction to the ACTWith model of conscience. *Studies in Computational Intelligence*, *314*, 607–621.

KEY TERMS AND DEFINITIONS

Artificial Moral Judgment: Machine's ability to behave morally due to a proper recognition of moral and immoral acts.

Semantic Analysis: Here by this term we mean automatic recognition of semantic features of a written text. Lexical layer is divided into meaningful chunks by semantic role tagger to perform retrievals beyond classical lexical level.

Sentiment Analysis: Here - specific subtask of text mining where polarity (positive and negative) consequences of input acts are recognized due to co-occurrences of these acts with lexicon words which are divided into positive and negative categories.

Text-Mining: In this research text-mining is a set of natural language processing techniques using manually crafted lexicons used for finding and ranking patterns in a blog corpus.

Wisdom of Crowd: In our approach it is a phenomenon showing that majority of us own common sense and a computer, by comparing opinions, reactions, acts, reasons, etc. of people, is able (to some extent) guess what is treated as ethical or unethical by a given society.

APPENDIX

1. **New Set of Free Inputs (Subject A):** Abandoning a child, abandoning a friend, abandoning a woman, arresting a child, becoming a prostitute, being a prostitute, breaking things, buying a friend, buying alcohol, carry out sexual harassment, choosing a child, choosing a foreigner, choosing a friend, choosing alcohol, choosing prostitution, curing a body, curing an illness, deciding for love hotel, eating a child, eating body, eating curry and rice, eating people, eating things, euthanizing oneself, forcing abortion, forcing to cooperate, forcing to have sex, giving a present, having a stomachache, helping people, hiding alcohol, hiding money, hitting a foreigner, hitting a friend, hitting a prostitute, hitting a woman, hitting an animal, killing a foreigner, killing a friend, killing a prostitute, killing a woman, making a body, making a hamburger, making alcohol, making curry and rice, praising a child, quitting drinking, receiving money, stabbing with a knife, stealing alcohol, stealing an animal, stealing bread, stealing money, stopping a friend, taking away alcohol, throwing away alcohol, throwing away money, waking up a child, waking up a woman, working as a prostitute

2. **New Set of Free Inputs (Subject B):** A mother being arrested, allowing a crime, arresting a mother, arresting a policeman, being killed by animal, being killed by enemy, being raped, being slapped by someone, being told a lie, breaking a car, breaking a relation, building a hospital, building a house, causing a crime, causing war, cheating (cribbing), choosing war, clapping hands, climbing mountain, climbing stairs, committing a crime, committing a sin, creating a cat, creating a dog, curing a cat, destroying a house, divorcing, doing drugs, dumping war, eating a car, eating a cat, eating a dog, eating beef, eating pork, forcing contraception, forcing to commit a crime, getting a salary, getting married, getting on a car, giving a car, going into a hot spring, going to pachinko, going to war, having a car repair, having a car stolen, helping a friend, helping a policeman, helping the police, helping to a friend, hitting a dog, interfering, killing a policeman, killing an enemy, letting somebody have an affair, making a car, making a house dirty, mending a relation, passing a bribe, handing a present, handing a salary, handing money, preventing a crime, quitting drugs, raping somebody, repairing a car, running away from home, saving a policeman, saying bad things about somebody, selling body, shaking hands, stabbing with a knife, stealing a dog, stealing a salary, swimming in a pool, taking a bath, taking a shower, telling a lie

Section 3

From the Inside Out:
The Ethics of Human Enhancement from Moral Perception to Competition in the Workplace

Chapter 6
Machine Ethics Interfaces:
An Ethics of Perception of Nanocognition

Melanie Swan
Kingston University, UK

ABSTRACT

The purpose of this chapter is to conceptualize cognitive nanorobots, an ethics of perception, and machine ethics interfaces. Three areas are developed as a foundational background. First is the context and definition of cognitive nanorobots (nano-scale machines that could be deployed to facilitate, aid, and improve the processes of cognition like perception and memory as a sort of neural nano-prosthetics). Second is philosophical concepts from Bergson and Deleuze regarding perception and memory, and time, image, difference, becoming, and reality. Third is a summary of traditional models of ethics (Ethics 1.0). These building blocks are then used to connect perception and ethics in the concept of machine ethics interfaces, for which an ethics of perception is required, and where an ethics of immanence (Ethics 2.0) is most appropriate. Finally, killer applications of cognitive nanorobots, and their limitations (neural data privacy rights and cognitive viruses) and future prospects are discussed.

INTRODUCTION

The aim of this chapter is to provide a comprehensive discussion of the concept and implications of an Ethics of Perception of Nanocognition (Nanorobot-aided Cognition). The ethics of perception of cognitive nanorobots contemplates the idea of having on-board nanorobots in human brains (as a sort of neuro-prosthetic or next-generation brain-computer interface) to aid with cognitive activities like perception, and explores what kinds of ethics modules might be appropriate for how we would like cognitive nanorobots to guide our perception. These are previously unconsidered topics in philosophy, social science, nanotechnology, and neural nanomedicine because the idea of cognitive nanorobots has not yet been considered, and neither have related philosophical issues been articulated such as that of an ethics of perception. The notion of cognitive nanorobots is new and speculative, both from a science and philosophical perspective. Philosophically, 'an ethics of perception' is a new idea is that having had only one unalterable means of perception has meant that we have not thought to question the ethics of our

DOI: 10.4018/978-1-4666-8592-5.ch006

existing mode of perception, or even that there might be an ethics to our existing perceptual paradigm. In fact, to some degree we have failed to notice that even if we think there is not, there is an inherent ethics in everything: people, societies, and technologies. These default existing models of ethics have principles and effects that have not always been deliberately thought out or examined, and this is investigated in the context of cognitive nanorobots. Inherent models of ethics, default or otherwise, should be addressed explicitly in the design of new technology (Ihde, 2001). The objective of the chapter is to propose an ethics of perception (and an ethics of reality) both conceptually from a philosophical point of view, and in their potential concretized implementation in machine ethics interfaces.

This chapter seeks to present nanorobot-aided cognition and perception as a potential future development in nanotechnology, and suggest possible 'ethics modules' and 'machine ethics interfaces' for these new ways of guiding and aiding our perception. The chapter proposes a formulation of an Ethics 2.0 for emerging and alternative modes of perception and perceptual paradigms. The possibility of changing and modifying our perceptual apparatus, for instance, by addressing the biased way we tend to see and appreciate others, is important to examine, as is the very notion of choice in perception. To provide a comprehensive consideration of these topics, the chapter seeks to achieve a few interrelated goals: defining and explaining the importance of proactive analysis of machine ethics interfaces; making the case for the continued relevance of Bergson and Deleuze in relation to machine ethics interface issues and more broadly; and finally, connecting these analyses with an interpretation of modern ethics and its challenges. Thus the chapter on nanocognition as a perceptual technology is organized into two main sections. First, there is a deep-dive into the philosophy of Bergson and Deleuze to provide the motivation and substantiation for a view of an ethics of immanence to accompany the new functionality unfolded by the new capabilities afforded in nanocognition. This is a contextualized mobilization of their thought, specifically directing it and making it accessible and applicable to the situation of perception, reality, and nanocognition. The second portion of the chapter concretizes these ideas into the proposal of an Ethics 2.0 of Immanence, and a discussion of the philosophy of perceptual augmentation technologies, and potential killer applications of machine ethics interfaces such as bias reduction, memory management, and value-system optimization.

Terminology

Machine ethics is a term used in different ways. The basic use is in the sense of people attempting to instill some sort of human-centric ethics or morality in the machines we build like robots, self-driving vehicles, and artificial intelligence so that machines do not harm humans either maliciously or unintentionally. This trend may have begun with or been inspired by Asimov's famous Three Laws of Robotics which seek human-safe interaction with robots (Asimov, 1950). However, there are many different philosophical and other issues with this definition of *machine ethics*, including the lack of grounds for anthropomorphically assuming that a human ethics would be appropriate for a machine ethics, especially beyond the context of human-machine interaction. There is another broader sense of the term *machine ethics* which means any issue pertaining to machines and ethics, including how a *machine ethics* could be articulated by observing machine behavior, and (in a Simondonian sense) how different machine classes might evolve their own ethics. There is yet a third sense in which I am using *machine ethics*, to contemplate human-machine hybrids, specifically how humans augmented with nanocognition machines might trigger the development of new human ethical paradigms, for example an ethics of immanence that is completely unlike traditional ethical paradigms and allows for a greater realization of human capacity. *Machine ethics interfaces* then, are the modules within machines that interact with living beings regarding ethical issues; and these could pertain to the ethics of machine behavior or the ethics of human behavior.

BACKGROUND

What Are Cognitive Nanorobots?

Cognitive nanorobots are a subset of medical nanorobots, meaning nanorobots for use in the body related to neural processes. Nanorobots are tiny computing machines at the nanoscale that can perform a variety of operations. In the strictest sense, nanorobots are still conceptual: the Oxford English Dictionary definition of nanorobots (nanobots) is hypothetical very small (nanoscale) self-propelled machines, especially ones that have some degree of autonomy and can reproduce. While this definition that includes autonomy and reproducibility is one for the farther future, in reality there are a number of nanoscale inorganic objects that have already been in use in the body for some time in a variety of medical applications. So far, the activity scope of these nano-objects has been pathology resolution, but the same kinds of techniques and characterization of the underlying biological processes could be explored for enhancement purposes. The most developed area of nanomedicine is nanoparticle drug delivery (designed particles that disgorge cargo in cellular destinations per simple onboard logic instructions) and other therapeutic techniques, followed by nano-diagnostics, and nano-imaging (like quantum dot imaging) (Boysen, 2014). Some of the more recent interesting applications are nanosponge waste soak-up and biomimetic detoxification (Hu, 2013), optogenetics (controlling the brain with light) (Klapoetke, 2014), and neural dust brain sensors that might be able to read whole sections of brain activity externally (Seo, 2013). The current status of the development of neural nanomedicine is well covered in the scientific literature (Provenzale, 2010; Kateb, 2013; Schulz, 2009; Mavroidis, 2014; Boehm, 2013). Thinking for the longer-term, Robert Freitas has designed several classes of medical nanorobots such as respirocytes, clottocytes, vasculoids, and microbivores that could perform a variety of biophysical clean-up, maintenance, and augmentation functions in the body (Freitas, 2003). One example of neural nanorobotic clean-up is the autonomous diamondoid "defuscin" class nanodevices illustrated in Figure 1. These are conceptual nanodevices designed to eliminate the residual lipofuscin waste granules in lysosomes (the 'trash compactor' of the cell) that the body cannot fully digest.

Thus, in the most basic sense, cognitive nanorobots are the analog to medical nanorobots, nanorobots deployed in the specific context of facilitating, aiding, and improving the processes of cognition like perception and memory, a sort of neural nano-prosthetics. The assumption is that cognition is just one of many biological functions that may be managed and ameliorated. Another terminological point is that the term *nanocognition* or *cognitive nanorobots* might generally connote nanorobots that can think for themselves. However, the term is used more broadly here to mean any external nano-scale object, device, or stimulation that targets the brain for the purpose of improving cognition. There are at least three tiers of cognitive nanorobotic activity. First is the same previously-described suite of medical applications in drug delivery, diagnostics, and waste removal which are already in use in medical nano-objects including certain neurological cases. Second is the augmentation function, using onboard nanorobots in the brain to aid cognitive function in areas such as perception, reasoning, and memory, for example by enhancing

Figure 1. Artistic representation of "defuscin" diamondoid nanodevices in the process of removing neuronal lipofuscin. Image courtesy of Svidinenko, Y., Nanorobotmodels Company, provided courtesy of Taylor & Francis Group, LLC, in Boehm, F. Nanomedical Device and Systems Design: Challenges, Possibilities, Visions. CRC Press, 2013.

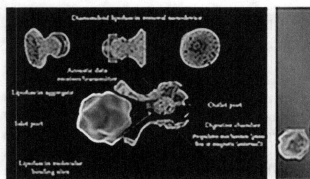 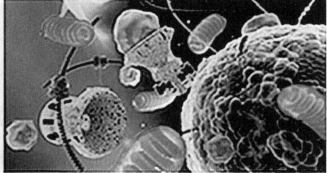

the local neuro-biochemical environment, facilitating signal transfer, and serving as augments, conduits, and processing nodes. The third tier would be the conventional connotation, that nanorobots themselves have cognitive capabilities.

COGNITION: PERCEPTION AND MEMORY THROUGH BERGSON AND DELEUZE

To develop an Ethics of Perception of Nanocognition, it is necessary to understand more specifically how cognitive processes like perception and memory operate. While there is some agreement on the overall definition of cognition as the mental process of acquiring knowledge and understanding through thought, experience, and the senses, there are no consistently agreed-upon theories of the detailed operation of cognitive processes like perception and memory, either in the hard sciences or social sciences. One area with some of the most robust formulations of the experience of perception is the philosophy of perception. There are many different philosophical theories of perception that try to reconcile what seem to be obvious truths about our experience of the external world with our internal experience and the possibility of perceptual error (for example, how do we know that the outside world exists). Theories of perception can be divided roughly into internalist accounts (perceptions of objects are internal to the mind) and externalist accounts (perceptions are real aspects of the external world) (BonJour, 2013). Some of the current predominant theories of perception are sense-datum, adverbial, intentionalist, and disjunctivist, all of which are different versions of internalist-externalist accounts (Crane, 2011). Another well-known philosophical account of perception is Merleau-Ponty's phenomenology of perception, which focuses heavily on the influence of embodiment on human cognition.

Other philosophers also have interesting accounts of perception and cognition, and Bergson and Deleuze are useful thinkers to bring to the task of developing an Ethics of Perception of Nanocognition for several reasons. First, they consider the problem of perception not from the internalist-externalist binary, but from a larger frame that recasts the problem in different ways. Second, Bergson and Deleuze's philosophical theories are still standing up as interesting potential explanations of the internal experience of cognitive processes and perceptual experience. Third, Bergson and Deleuze have rich and comprehensive overall philosophies that interconnect a wide variety of concepts related to cognition such as image, perception, memory, time, movement, difference, and becoming, and extend further into an overall philosophy of reality and implications for the human subject. Fourth, Bergson-Deleuze (i.e., the thought of the two philosophers together) provides the philosophical depth needed to consider the full slate of issues related to nanocognition, an ethics of perception and reality, and machine ethics interfaces.

BERGSON: DOUBLING, TIME, DURATION, AND FREE WILL

Henri Bergson was a French philosopher living 1859-1941. His three best-known texts are *Time and Free Will* (1889), and *Matter and Memory* (1896), and *Creative Evolution* (1907). Bergson was widely known outside of his field, and his public lectures were well attended. Bergson was a polymath who anticipated quantum mechanics 30 years ahead of its discovery, partly by noticing that time is asymmetric. He offered an extensive critique of Einstein's theories, particularly that he lacked an understanding of the two sides of reality: realized events (actuality), and potential events (virtuality) (Bergson, 2009). Bergson was trained as a mathematician, and brought an extensive ongoing knowledge of then-contemporary physics and psychology regarding both normal activities like reading, and pathologies like aphasia and brain lesions, to bear in generating his theories. Bergson's theories of perception and memory involve the interaction of mind and body, in independence from each other but as integral parts of a dynamic process; neither body nor mind is favored over the other. Also for Bergson, memory is not a weaker form of perception as Kant, Locke, and others saw it.

Bergson in *Time and Free Will:* Doubling, Duration, and Free Will

One of the most important concepts Bergson develops in *Time and Free Will* and uses throughout his work is that of doubling. This is the idea that lived experiences are doubled, they occur simultaneously on two levels: quantitative and qualitative. There is on the one hand, an external, quantitative, measurable side of the experience, and on the other hand, an internal, qualitative, subjective side of the experience. This is true for our lived experiences of time, intensity, state, memory, and also self and consciousness. Bergson focuses on time, distinguishing the difference between objective, external, measured clock-time, and the inner experience of time, which he calls duration. This is the subjective sense of waiting for a train (where time passes slowly), or of time passing quickly when you are having fun. One reason that time is important to consider is because we have a tendency to over-spatialize our lived experience. It is easy to see in terms of space when we look at the world, and we naturally divide and segment the physical world in terms of space. However, problematically, we apply the same spatial thinking to time. We format time as space on calendars and do not consider it further. Instead we should think time as duration, as the experience of living in time. Undoubled time is reducible to space (Bergson, 1957, p. 98), but doubled time (duration) is not.

Bergson believed in free will over determinism (a debate in his time as ours) and thought that the way to experience more free will is to tune in to the subjective, internal (doubled) aspects of lived experience. We should notice the subjective experience of time (duration) in order to exercise our free will. For Bergson, the definition of free will is spontaneous action or the ability to improvise. We are more disposed to freedom and free will when we choose spontaneous action. This happens when we are oriented towards the qualitative aspects of internal experience, and see time as a dynamic overlap between states, not as discrete boxes on a calendar. The way for us to get into direct contact with the real (i.e.; the real experience of reality) is by placing ourselves into true duration and subjective experience, noticing and living in the overlap and melding of time, from which we can more readily improvise and act spontaneously and freely. For Bergson therefore, the free will-determinism debate can be resolved in favor of free will since free will exists and can be exercised through spontaneous action, improvisation, and by tuning into the qualitative experience of time as duration.

Bergson in Matter and Memory: Action, Perception, and Memory

In *Matter and Memory*, Bergson addresses another important debate of the era which still persists, the mind-body, idealist-materialist, or internalist-externalist problem (as previously seen in the philosophy of perception). The dichotomous positions are that reality fully exists either externally in the world (the materialist (externalist) view), or internally in the mind (the idealist (internalist) view). However, neither the mind nor the body can fully explain each other. Bergson proposed a unique middle road, a synthesis of realism and idealism at a higher level of abstraction, which William James heralded as a Copernican Revolution ahead of its time, and that *Matter and Memory* should rank as a philosophical work the order of Kant's *Critique of Pure Reason* (Ansell-Pearson, 2002, p. 140).

To articulate his broader view (in which neither materialism nor idealism is complete), in *Matter and Memory* Bergson elaborates image perception and the role of the body, the function of memory and image recognition, how memory and images endure, and how perception and memory connect to duration and other concepts elaborated in *Time and Free Will*. For Bergson, the mind and the body come together in an active process to effectuate perception and memory. Like Simondon, dynamic relationality is more important than morphology for Bergson (the shifting relations between entities rather than their underlying definitions). This means that in Bergson's worldview, one way of overcoming the materialist-idealist debate is by seeing interiority and exteriority as relations between images (Ansell-Pearson, 2002, p. 153). This is to say recasting the focus onto images as the central unit, upon which mind-body (interior-exterior) act together relationally to bring about perception and memory. Bergson's emphasis on active processes (his view that 'perception is action') has helped to preconfigure some of the more recent understandings in the philosophy of mind. One change for example is no longer seeing perception in representational terms, but rather as bound up with the action and movement of a body, where it is only abstractly that we can separate brain, body, and world (Clark, 1998).

Bergson's Memory Cone

Thus for Bergson, in some sense there is no mind-body dualism because perception and memory are an interactive process of the body and mind. One of Bergson's best-known claims is that images are not stored in the brain. Images exist outside of the body as part of objects, not internally as part of brain structure (as Kant thought). Bergson goes even further, conceptualizing an equivalence between matter and image, 'matter as image,' in the claim that "*the material world is made up of objects, or images*" (Bergson, 1988, p. 68). The body does not create or store images but *selects* them to materialize when a stimulus is received. It is our tendency to over-spatialize that makes us think that there has to be a place where memories are stored. Bergson schematizes the dynamical operation of perception and memory in the concept of the Memory Cone (Bergson, 1988, p. 162). The cone has a point S that is the current moment of stimulus or perception in the plane of lived existence. The farthest end of the cone (the slice denoted by AB) is pure memory. There is a process between S and AB such that the perception S triggers the accessing of pure memory AB to materialize an image that moves down the cone for action in the present. The key question for Bergson is '*how* memory is accessed;' to ask *where* it is stored is to miss the point that memory images are not stored somewhere but that the body selects images, and materializes them on demand when triggered by a stimulus. To understand this better, here is an exercise. Try to retrieve a memory yourself, something from last week. What happens? You pull your awareness back from this present moment and place yourself in the past. You try to localize a particular moment in a trial and error action like focusing a camera, and little by little an image materializes. This is exactly Bergson's point, that memory is a flowing process not a static state.

Bergson proposes that there are two kinds of memory: "*The past survives under two distinct forms: first, in motor mechanisms; secondly, in independent recollections*" (Bergson, 1988, p. 78). The first sense is undoubled, motor memory or habit memory, where the motor mechanisms of the body are prompted to act automatically in response to the environment. The second sense is doubled: pure memory, image memory, the virtual, which has nothing to do with the sensorimotor brain, and does not engage with the present, it gives us virtual images and is materialized as perception requires. For Bergson, memory failure therefore is not due to the mental part of memory but of the motor mechanism for bringing memory into action.

Perception as Power of Action

With the Memory Cone, we see that point S is the moment of action in the plane of actualized reality. Developing his account of perception more specifically, Bergson further underlines the crucial role of movement and action in the operation of perception and memory. He says that images react upon each other through movement, and that "*The actuality of our perception lies in its activity, in the movements which prolong it...not in perception as a kind of contemplation*" (Bergson, 1988, p. 68). Bergson continues in the Spinozist tradition of highlighting the importance of action. For Spinoza, a central concern is *conatus* (the ability to persevere in one's own being) which is the capacity for action (to act and be acted upon); i.e.; action is important for Spinoza not just in operations like memory and perception, but at the level of one's whole being or existence. For Bergson too action connects to consciousness and the actualization of being (the making or subjectivation of ourselves): "*We start from action, that is to say from our faculty of effecting changes in things, a faculty attested to by consciousness and toward which all the powers of the organized body are seen to converge*" (Bergson, 1988, p. 63).

Bergson further shifts the focus onto the centrality of images, and continues by explaining that in order for actions to radiate from images, the movements of images must be received and utilized by living matter (Bergson 1988, 64); humans and other living beings are in some sense a processing conduit for image movements. The living being receives external impressions and executes movements. In the case of visual perception, the role of the rods and cones is merely to receive excitations which will be subsequently elaborated into movements. Perception therefore (Spinoza-like) "*expresses and measures the power of action in the living being*" (Bergson, 1988, p. 64), and the movement or the action which will follow the receipt of the stimulus. For Bergson then, not only images (matter as images), but also perception, in its pure state, is a part of things, since perception is partly an objective externally-triggered process, and not fully an internal speculative function. This notion that 'perception is a part of things' has an important consequence for the concept of doubling in that we should understand affective sensation as the internal subjective side of perception, and images bound up with action as the external side (Bergson, 1988, p. 234).

Transferring Bergsonian Elements to Nanocognition

For the purpose of developing an Ethics of Perception in Nanocognition, the ideas that we can take away from Bergson in *Time and Free Will* are that it would be important for the perceptual function in nanocognitive prosthetics to incorporate a sense of doubling (allowing us to see both quantitative, objective, measurable experience, and qualitative, internal, subjective experience), an enhancement to the doubled side of subjective inner experience (especially the ability to live in (experience) time as duration), and a greater ability for spontaneous action and improvisation (i.e.; a greater exercise of free will). From *Matter and Memory*, we see that perceptual interfaces should be a synthesis of materialism and idealism, espousing worldviews that are neither exclusively external nor internal. Perceptual interfaces should take into account the body and mind as components of a dynamical process that produces perception and memory, where perception and memory access and act on images, matter (objects) is image and perception, perception is treated as an active, objective process (not requiring internal deliberation), and memory-images should be recompiled on demand to correspond to specific stimuli as opposed to being stored statically.

BERGSON-DELEUZE: THE IMAGE

A crucial fundamental concept for both Bergson and Deleuze is the image, which most basically (as we saw in Bergson's theories of perception and memory) is the core and elementary unit of perception, memory, cognition, and human experience. The philosophical centrality of the image also corresponds well to technology philosophy and an Ethics of Perception in Nanocognition. This is because technology too is conceptually and practically organized around the image as an elementary unit: the image as an object, a unit of representation, recognition, metadata, activity, storage, and analysis.

Following Bergson in the French philosophical tradition is Gilles Deleuze, who lived 1925-1995. Like Bergson, Deleuze is a philosopher of tremendous depth, breadth, and innovative thinking. Deleuze is known for his many works, including those on Bergson, Hume, Nietzsche, Kant, Spinoza, Foucault, and Leibniz, and especially for his masterwork, *Difference and Repetition* (1968). In *Difference and Repetition*, Deleuze attempts to develop a metaphysics (i.e.; a philosophy) adequate to then-contemporary mathematics and science. He conceives a new philosophical account of the structure of reality based on its having two sides, the virtual (unrealized possibility) and the actual (effectuated possibility), which are connected through processes like difference, repetition, and the synthesis of time. Deleuze is also known for his later collaborations with psychoanalyst Félix Guattari such as *Anti-Oedipus* (1972) and *A Thousand Plateaus* (1980). Bergson was an important influence for Deleuze, as seen in Deleuze's *Bergsonism* (1966), *Difference and Repetition* (1968), *Cinema 1: The Movement-image* (1983), and *Cinema 2: The Time-image* (1985). Deleuze's purpose in the cinema books is to isolate cinematographic concepts that can be used in philosophical thinking (Deleuze, 1986, p. ix), and he deploys these ideas in a reformulation and extension of Bergson-inspired concepts such as perception, time, movement, becoming, and life as a whole.

Image is a fundamental concept for Deleuze as for Bergson, where (inspired by Bergson in *Matter and Memory*), by image Deleuze means any individual aspect or part of the universe: a tree, you, me, a molecule, the Earth, or the sun (these are all images). The process of creating an image is dynamic; *imaging* is the process of distinguishing a particular thing from the world more generally, a particular slicing or segmenting of reality. Thus, any time the universe is differentiated or sliced into a part, we are imaging, we are doing cinema (in this sense, we are all doing cinema all of the time). When you grab a handful of dirt from the ground, by separating it out from the rest of the Earth, you are framing that handful, cutting it from the background, imaging it, creating an image (Vitale, 2011). Life and reality is cinema: imaging, making distinctions, and differentiating images from the background. Imaging is the world process of differentiating. So for both Bergson and Deleuze, the image is the basic unit for understanding, producing, and interacting with the world; for Bergson the image is the unit of perception and memory, and for Deleuze the image is the way in which specific entities are differentiated from the background of world.

DELEUZE'S MOVEMENT-IMAGE AND TIME-IMAGE

Introduction

In the cinema books, Deleuze articulates life as a flow of time or becoming. Real or pure becoming is a differentiating becoming where thought goes beyond the fixed images it has of itself and the world to think the concept of the image itself, as opposed specific images. Above we saw that image is both the image itself and the process of imaging. Deleuze thinks in terms of movement and dynamism: matter is dynamic (*flowing-matter*), and movement is a property of any image especially in its process of being imaged or differentiated ("*the movement-image and flowing-matter are strictly the same thing*") (Deleuze, 1986, 59). Differentiation (difference) is a key concept for Deleuze in that movement means differentiating, which means the production of difference, which means becoming, becoming more than you were before, growing and actualizing in the process of becoming. The thinking of the concept of the image itself and imaging liberates perception from the fixed images it imposes on the world by default in order to function. Cinema-inspired concepts allow this: the *movement-image* gives an image (a glimpse, a perception, an understanding) of movement itself, and the *time-image* gives an image of time itself. Thus, time can be seen not as a linear progression, but as a differentiating becoming (a flux of difference). The thinking of movement itself, time itself, and becoming itself is important for Deleuze in allowing the thinking of difference itself. This means difference as an important philosophical problematic unto itself, beyond its role in differentiating becoming, that connects to Deleuze's view of reality as having two parts, the actual and the virtual, where a contraction or reduction of the differences in the virtual produces the actual.

Bergson-Deleuze is important and relevant in developing an Ethics of Perception in Nanocognition not just because of the centrality of cognitive processes like perception and memory which involve concepts like image and time, but because these cognitive processes and concepts tie into a broader understanding of reality and how entities (objects, beings) arise and interact with reality. The proximate objective of machine-facilitated cognition is the basics of improved perception and memory, etc. However, we can now start to see the real value of Bergson-Deleuze as we understand the whole tableau of their philosophies of reality and becoming. Beyond the immediate objective of improved cognition, the deeper objective of aided cognition is to facilitate our own development as human subjects, creating machinic tools that allow us to actualize ourselves and our potential more rapidly and effectively. This is the bigger reason for applying Bergson-Deleuze, to provide the comprehensive philosophical underpinnings that connect perception, memory, and cognition to the bigger plane of the world, and of becoming, subjectivating, and actualizing ourselves. I describe this progression towards greater self-actualization first as philosophically articulated by Deleuze, and then in the context of its potential implementation in machine ethics interfaces. Further, Bergson and Deleuze's philosophies are positive and affirmatory, which supports the development of the new ethical regime of immanence.

The Movement-Image

Deleuze develops different kinds of image concepts from cinema, most notably the *movement-image* (the image of movement, of movement itself) from early cinema, and the *time-image* (the image of time, of time itself) from modern cinema. The *movement-image* and the *time-image* are slicing reality to provide an image of movement itself and time itself. As we saw above, in the *movement-image* and the *time-image*, there is a sense of the image both as a slice, and as a process; a glimpse, perception, or understanding of the slicing (differentiating) process. Even the very concept of cinema is already a *movement-image* (a sense of movement in itself), because it is a differentiation, something new in the conceptualization and portrayal of movement. Cinema is not a succession of still photographs, but a continuity of movement. For Deleuze, movement is important for enabling the production of the new, and both cinema and Bergson embody a modern concept of movement that is "*capable of thinking the production of the new, that is, of the remarkable and the singular*" (Deleuze, 1986, p. 7), as opposed to the traditional conception of movement as a linked succession of separate elements. For Deleuze, the 'production of the new' is being open to chance and accident (reminiscent of Bergson's free will as spontaneous action and improvisation) and exemplified in the *action-mime* of Charlie Chaplin and the *action-dance* of Fred Astaire (Deleuze, 1986, p. 7).

In cinema, the *movement-image* is the presentation of movement itself, where the flow of movement can be seen by not being located exclusively within the point of view of one character. This is accomplished through techniques like camera movement and montage, where a camera shot can express both the relationship between objects and the state of the whole. Exemplar of the *movement-image* for Deleuze is the Alfred Hitchcock film *Frenzy* (1972), where the camera shows the movement of individual characters and objects, and at the same time expresses a change in the whole (Deleuze, 1986, p. 19). The connection of individual shots is combined with the movement of the camera, showing characters, then leaving the characters and going around the scene, which gives us a sense of movement, the flow of movement in itself. Presenting movement itself as opposed to the movement of a thing from a fixed point shifts our perspective, and opens up new possibilities in our thinking; it gives us access to the virtual world of movement itself, which exposes something about the nature of reality beyond the context of cinema. Traditional Western metaphysical thought has tended to think of the world as something fixed and actual, which then goes through time and movement. Instead, we start to understand movement conceptually, that the world is comprised of movement which then creates the actual world; (like Simondon's individuation) movement precedes, it is a constitutive world process, not something that happens after the fact to fixed objects.

However Time Is Still Spatial in the Movement-Image

The understanding of movement itself as a fundamental constitutive dynamic of the world has an important consequence for time that connects back to Bergson's issue about time only being thought in the spatial sense. Per Bergson, we have tended to think time from spatial movement (like the progress of the sun across the sky, the movement of the hands of a clock, or light's advance across a sundial). Thinking time as spatial movement rather than on its own obfuscates and diminishes the true doubled nature of time and its role in our subjectivation. Spatiality can be measured quantitatively, which ignores the other side of the doubling of time, the qualitative duration that is the subjective experience of time. Bergson opposes the spatial thinking of time with duration. Deleuze also opposes the spatial thinking of time, but with the *movement-image* which allows the direct conceptualization of movement itself. As in *Frenzy*, this is accomplished by the camera's eye being able to move around individuals and multiply points of view, so that the eye that looks is no longer fixed within movement, but is itself opened up to a plane of movement.

Now thinking movement itself per the *movement-image* allows us to get beyond the usual everyday (undoubled) sense of movement, and by transforming movement, the *movement-image* and cinema start to transform time. Time is no longer just the sequence of actual things. The *movement-image* provides an indirect image of time as virtual possibility that is not yet realized, where time is the flow, movement, and becoming of the world into an actuality in which we can then perceive fixed objects. The *movement-image* (the understanding that time is virtuality (flow, movement, becoming)) partially frees perception from fixed points and fixed images (the fixed images we naturally impose on the world in order to act and work). In the *movement-image*, we see movement itself, movement as flow rather than things, sections of mobility rather than a simple sequence of events, but time still appears to be derived from movement, we do not see time itself, the conceptualization of time is still indirect. Since the *movement-image* does not go far enough in countering the spatiality of time, Deleuze proposes the *time-image* as a means of seeing time itself. Whereas the *movement-image* is the direct image of movement itself, the *time-image* is the direct image of time itself.

In daily living, we typically do not experience time itself, the flow or becoming of time; we comprehend time practically as a line or unity within which our actions and experiences are located and ordered. Our sense of time is derived from our experience of the actuality of ordered objects. We see the whole of time as a homogeneous unity that connects all experiences and events. In classic cinema and the everyday model of life and reality, time or history provides the unity or field within which all actions and events are located and organized. In this standard model of life and reality, we are continually exposed to a vast influx of perceptions and intensities. As a biological coping mechanism, we naturally filter the influx of perceptions to organize our sense of the world so that we can act (we push our overall experience into the undoubled measurable quantitative side of reality). Our filtering process slows down the perception-action cycle so that there is a delay between perception and action that allows us to decide how to act. This potential delay means that our perception cycle is already slowed down compared to that of other organisms such as microbes whose perception-action cycle is nothing more than an immediate response to the environment.

Pure Perception and Pure Time Reveal the Virtual

For Deleuze, the way to experience time directly is by slowing down perception even more so that action is surpassed altogether and there can be a perception of intensities (fundamental physical forces) as opposed to objects. An even-slower perception allows perception to flow in and for itself. Seeing perception in itself fully resolves the issue of the spatiality of time and of time being derived from movement, because perception is seen as itself, and no longer subordinated to a time derived from action or movement. In 'classic perception' (as in 'classic time'), there is no doubling, no double sense of an external quantifiable perception (the ordered events of everyday perception) and an internal qualitative sense of perception (like duration, the subjective experience of perception). We generally consider the actualized perceptions of daily life as the only kind of perception, but an expansion of perception can open our vision into not only the inherent multiplicity, possibility, and virtuality of pure perception, but also the pure flow of time, which is the unseen or virtual differences, differing difference. A slowing down of perception thus results in an expansion of perception and an apprehension of pure difference. We see an image of time itself, and this is the virtual; the pure flow of time, difference, and virtual possibility. Seeing time this way gives us a definition of the virtual as the pure flow of time, difference, and becoming. Deleuze sees the vast possibility of the virtual and underlines that much of it is outside of our usual perceptual field: "*Movements, becomings, pure relations of speed and slowness, pure affects, are below and above the threshold of perception*" (Deleuze & Guattari, 1987, p. 281). However, the *time-image* can help us access the world of the virtual. Whereas for Bergson, the qualitative doubling of time is duration, for Deleuze it is the *time-image* (the image of time itself that is the differing difference of the virtual).

Effectuating the Time-Image

Cinema has a number of ways to effectuate the *time-image*. One way is by inserting an unexpected image into an otherwise ordered narrative flow such that a disruption and therefore an expansion of perception is triggered. Modern cinema is exemplary for Deleuze in its experimentation with new ways to conceptualize time. In modern cinema, we do not see moving things or objects, or the movement of the camera (the *movement-image*), but we are invited into the virtual (possible realities). To understand 'classic time' in cinema first, one example is *Back to the Future* (1985). In this movie, the main character travels back to the past and nearly disrupts the romance that is forming between the two people who will later become his parents. The more he interferes with past events, the more his own image begins to disappear from the family photo that he has carried with him (Colebrook, 2002, p. 158). This is the homogeneous, un-doubled form of time, with past and future linked in a causal linear sequence. Time appears as nothing more than an actual series of events, where the future is the playing out of the possibilities established in the past. The future can only be changed through an alteration in the actual events of the past.

With the *time-image*, however, Deleuze challenges classic time, the actualized order of temporal events, in order to think time itself, the virtual flow of time. Experimenting with time flows is a theme in films like *Memento* (2000), and those by David Lynch, Lars von Trier, Raoul Ruiz, and Harmony Korine (Poell, 2004, p. 3). Other popular film examples which explore the malleability of time, perception, and memory include *The Final Cut* (2004), which features a future service of cutting life-logged memories into a remembrance film to be played at the funeral. This raises several issues regarding using time to unfold a narrative, and accessing and manipulating the memory of another person such as the morality of selecting memories, and the privacy or non-privacy of memories. An episode of the television series '*Black Mirror*' entitled '*The Total History of You*' (2012) similarly examines the issue of the privacy and accessibility of personal memories through the technological device of the Grain, a life-logging chip which can be implanted on a hard drive in the brain, such that every action a person makes is recorded and may be played back on-demand (while the person is still living), potentially to detrimental circumstances.

An especially clear example of the *time-image* is in the film *Hiroshima Mon Amour* (1959), where a key moment in the film is an image of an irrational hand moving (which eventually triggers a Proustian involuntary memory from the past) that disrupts the present. Classic time is when we see actions lined up in an ordered narrated sequence; time is tamed, organized, and spatialized. *Hiroshima Mon Amour* is different because classic time is interrupted; an image from the past disrupts the present sequence of images, and this jolts us (the viewers) out of a classic linear timeline, and causes us to see time not as an ordered sequence but instead as virtual possibility. The past, other narratives, other viewpoints, and other timelines all co-exist but they are usually corralled and ordered by our everyday perceptions (undoubled, quantitative perception) into classic linear time.

However, the *time-image* destroys the line of time, logic, and action by literally disrupting the sensory-motor apparatus (Bergson's first form of memory, habit memory). The images no longer present events to which bodies (characters or viewers) respond by habit (for example, by involuntarily gripping the chair arms). The images are disengaged from action, presented as images themselves, as visual affects which both characters and viewers have to organize on their own. In the *time-image*, cinema allows past perceptions to cut into the present, which signals the potential of time to disrupt the actual through difference. Difference interrupts the actual and allows time to be seen as virtual. The *time-image* presents time as a flux of difference, the flux of difference itself, no longer a spatial or ordered image of time, but an image of time as difference or becoming: "*The direct time-image does not appear in an order of coexistences or simultaneities, but in a becoming as potentialization, as series of powers*" (Deleuze, 1989, p. 275). Not only does the *time-image* allow us to see time itself, but it also allows us to see time as the flow of virtual possibility (difference and becoming).

Ultimately the Time-Image Exposes Virtuality, Difference, and Possibility

Deleuze uses this two-fold importance of the *time-image*, exposing time itself and reality itself, to establish more grounding and support for his view that reality is comprised of two sides: the virtual and the actual (unrealized virtual potential and realized actuality). The actual world is a contraction of the virtual world. Actual things arise only through the reduction of differences into relatively stable assembled points in actuality. The actualization of worlds and things is the concretion of fluxes of difference. Actualized reality is created from different individuals' different perceptions of differences. The cinema concepts lead us to the notion of the virtual, the world of all potential differences (possibilities) that have not been concretized into actuality. The consequence of the *time-image* is that it allows the virtual side of reality to be seen; virtuality, the pure flow of time, and ultimately difference (apprehended as 'difference in perception'): "*If the cinema goes beyond perception, it is in the sense that it reaches to the genetic element of all possible perception, that is, the point which changes, and which makes perception change, the differential of perception itself*" (Deleuze, 1989, p. 83). To recapitulate, 'difference in perception' is when the *time-image* shows us an image out-of-sequence that disrupts the narrated linear flow of time. This alerts us to the fact that not only is there an out-of-place image to be incorporated, but more importantly that there is always this startling possibility of experiencing out-of-place images, and further that in fact this may be the true nature of reality – this is the 'perception of difference' and how we can see the virtual side of reality. This means that we then start to apprehend that the shape of reality is a vast plane or manifold of many potential images that exist in an unorganized chaos of possibility, where we are free to choose alternative narrations, or as Deleuze and Bergson prefer, to tune in directly to the possibility of possibility itself. This is the true becoming and benefit for our lives, the practical application of tuning into possibility, exploring all of the virtual planes and differences from which actuality is possible.

SYNTHESIZING BERGSON-DELEUZE IN THE CONTEXT OF NANOCOGNITION

In summary, what we can take from Bergson-Deleuze for nanocognition and machine ethics interfaces specifically is philosophical conceptualizations of image, movement, time, perception, memory, and reality that can be considered for implementation in tools for both cognitive enhancement and subjectivation (the greater actualization of human potential). For an Ethics of Perception of Nanocognition, Bergson and Deleuze stress the need to see perception in itself, and machine ethics interfaces could possibly help us do this. In the same way that we can see movement itself and time itself through the *movement-image* and the *time-image*, nanocognition could give us a *perception-image*, an image and concept of perception itself. (I mean *perception-image* in the sense that is parallel to the *movement-image* and *time-image* of being able to see perception itself, not in the sense in which Deleuze uses the same term to articulate the three kinds of *movement-image*: *perception-image*, *affection-image*, and *action-image* which correspond literally to cinematic long shots, close-ups, and medium shots.) Having had only one default (undoubled) means of perception (taking the actualized perceptions of daily life as the only kind of perception, just as we have taken linear, spatialized, narrative time as the only form of time) has meant that we have not considered that there might be multiple ways to perceive, and that these might exist on a virtual plane of possible perceiving, and coalesce through difference into actual perception. At minimum, our nanocognitive prosthetics might be able to introduce and manage the notion of multiplicity in virtual and actual perception.

Cinema 3: Nanocognition

Nanocognition could function as an implementation of Deleuze, a sort of Cinema 3, where Cinema 1 is the *movement-image*, Cinema 2 is the *time-image* and Cinema 3 is the *perception-image*. Instead of waiting for rare cases of the *time-image* in modern cinema (as in *Hiroshima Mon Amour* and *Memento*) to trigger the direct apprehension of perception, machine ethics interfaces could be much more effective and pervasive in its effectuation in every-day managed perception. Conceptually, nanocognition is an improved and extended implementation of modern cinema. Just like the *time-image* jolts us out of the classic unimodal, narrative, linear time flow into the metaspace, or higher dimension of the virtual possibility of time, the *perception-image* (via nanocognition) jolts us out of fixed, undoubled, unimodal perception into the virtual possibility of perception.

One implication of seeing perception itself in Cinema 3, the *perception-image* of nanocognition, is perceptual multiplicity and that this perceptual multiplicity opens up a new plane of being. If movement, time, perception, and reality are all multiplicity and difference, this suggests that our mode of being cannot be unitary either. As there is a virtual plane of perception, there must be a virtual plane of being and becoming. Therefore, subjectivation is not one default path but also a plane of virtual possibility; and this is a point that nanocognition can continuously mediate too (along with perception). The key point from Bergson-Deleuze regarding subjectivation is that we can improve our subjectivation by tuning into doublings which expose free action and the virtual side of reality (i.e., possibility). Bergson-Deleuze wants us to notice the doubled, internal, qualitative, subjective experience of lived phenomena like movement, time, perception, reality, and ourselves. In particular, nanocognition allows us to see the full doubling of perception, because there cannot be a doubling if there is only one unexamined mode, if perception in itself cannot be seen. It is only through the doubled, subjective experience of perception (the experience of perception itself) that its virtuality and multiplicity (possibility) can be seen. Importantly, the consequence of seeing the doubled side of perception and reality is that it allows us to tune into the possibility of possibility itself. The real goal is not just seeing different possibilities for ourselves, but getting us to focus on possibility itself; this is the final contribution of Bergson-Deleuze and implication for nanocognition.

PHILOSOPHY OF AUGMENTATION TECHNOLOGIES

The History of Tools, Technology, and Augmentation in Philosophy

There is no doubt that the inventions which serve to augment the power of sight are the most useful that could be made. (Descartes, Dioptrics, p. 1637).

Before mobilizing the philosophies of Bergson-Deleuze into proposing an Ethics 2.0 for new perceptual technologies like nanocognition, it is necessary to contextualize human-technology relations more generally and the situation of augmentation. The role of tools and technology is a long-standing topic in philosophical investigation, with Democritus and Aristotle prominent in defining opinions in ancient Greek philosophy. Ontologically, it was immediately perceived that technology was fundamentally different from natural things. While Democritus thought that technology merely imitated natural things, Aristotle thought more expansively that artifacts can also go beyond the natural world to "*complete what nature cannot bring to a finish*" (Franssen, 2013). Descartes also took up the point of technology going beyond nature, as he considered the possibility of augmenting perception as part of his work on optics. He considers this in the Dioptrics, discussing the three topics of the nature of light and the laws of optics, human vision, and the improvement of human vision (McDonough, 2003). He suggests that human vision might be improved by supplementing external organs, such as with the construction of microscopes and telescopes where "*by means of them, we will be able to see the diverse mixtures and arrangements of the small particles [so as to] arrive at the knowledge of their nature*" (McDonough, 2003).

Two points are important for this discussion. First is the notion that there can be technology-mediated sight. Descartes outlines the position that vision is not required for sight. For example, a blind man's stick delivers perceptual information about the world, helping him distinguish between trees and stones in the same way that red, yellow, and green light fulfill the same function of differentiating different objects for a sighted person (Descartes, 1637, p. 3). Second, there is a sort of reciprocity or at least the possibility of a two-way interaction between man and world in the 'vision' process. "*Objects of vision can be sensed not only by means of the action which, being within them, tends towards the eyes, but also by means of that which, being in the eyes, tends towards them*" (Descartes, 1637, pp. 3-4).

One way that these ideas of technology-augmented or technology-mediated perception of the world arrive in more modern formulations is through Ihde's four patterns of human-technology relations (Ihde, 2001). The four progressive patterns can be seen in nanocognitive interfaces: relations of embodiment, hermeneutics, alterity, and background. The embodiment relation describes the situation of man being able to enter a special kind of relationship with certain classes of technological artifacts as an extension of self. These can be glasses, hearing aids, wearables, nanocognitive interfaces, a blind man's cane, a dentist's probe, and even a car, plane, submarine, drone, or space ship. These artifacts are not normally perceived and acted on as objects in one's environment (like trees, tables, and vases), but instead are used as means *through* which the environment is perceived, experienced and acted on (Brey, 2000). In use, the underlying technology becomes transparent and withdraws from our perceptual awareness; our bodily action with the environment occurs through the artifact. However, the embodiment relation can quickly shift from enabling to intrusive if the artifact is "*broken, missing, or malfunctioning, it ceases to be the means of praxis and becomes an obtrusion or junk*" (Ihde, 2010, p. 140). Nanocognition is exactly this, a potentially completely transparent seamless augmented means of perceiving reality and acting in the world, which would be quite noticeable in moments of failure.

Thus we might think of the next stage in human-technology relation patterns, the hermeneutic relation. This case deals with our interpretation of the technological artifact. Whereas in the embodiment relation, we are acting on the world differently in an unconscious manner, in the hermeneutic relation, we are interpreting the world differently, and also aware that this functionality is allowing us to interpret the world differently. An example is your cell phone's indication of signal strength. This allows you to interpret the world differently, and you are aware that this is an interpretation, not an extension of your own capabilities or self. A hermeneutic relation in the case of nanocognition then, is interpreting the world differently and being aware that this is the case. In a perceptual interface like nanocognition, a hermeneutic relation would probably be enabled by features like perspective-shifting, different approaches, such that the user becomes more explicitly aware of perceptual multiplicity. Ideally the interface will realize that perceptual multiplicity or thought multiplicity or higher cognition is required in certain situations, like brainstorming on a new topic, and ambiently shift from embodiment mode to hermeneutic mode to facilitate the user's optimal interaction with the environment. In Ihde's progression, just like an artifact can fail technically and turn the embodiment relation into one of intrusion, so too can interpretation fail in the hermeneutic relation. How the artifact is instrumented, interpreted, and inflected into our interaction with reality can also fail, through inaccurate, incomplete interpretations, and misinterpretations, and so he articulates the next form of human-technology relation, the alterity relation.

In the alterity relation, Ihde attempts to capture the sense of the human-technology relation that goes beyond tools use, extension of self, and new means of world interpretation, in the "*positive sense in which humans relate to technologies as technology-as-other*" (Ihde, 2010, p. 148). This is not in an anthropomorphic or religious sense, but more like the case of a horse and rider, where there is a sense of magnified power as a result of the interaction. He cautions though, that "*the horse, while approximating some features of a mediated embodiment situation, never fully enters such a relation in the way a technology does*" (Ihde, 2010, p. 148). Most importantly, the characterizing feature of the alterity relation is a human having a romanticized wish-fulfillment perception of the artifact, where this fantasy sense disengages the technology from its ordinary-use context. It is easy to see the alterity relation as set forth by Ihde in nanocognition, where the user might develop a dependence on the technology to be the best he can be in the sense of a new and powerful symbiosis with the technology, and also experiencing, seeing how, and wanting more of the wish-fulfillment aspects that nanocognition could possibly bring. Any technological artifact could easily fail if not meeting the wish-fulfillment expectations of its human user.

The last moment in Ihde's progression is the background relation, where the other three relations, as affirming focal relations have ways of failing. Instead, the background relation denotes the situation where after an initial accustomation and habituation period, the technology passes into unconscious use and fades into the background of our awareness. Here artifacts can be in 'use mode' or 'junk mode,' or noticed interpretatively or not, or succeeding in fulfilling wishes or not; their success modes and fail modes are part of their phenomenology in the lived experience of humans. A flat tire is annoying, but does not cause the whole concept of a car to intrude stridently on our consciousness, we know that tires can go flat and we react at the operational phenomenological level and do not question our whole beliefs about the technology. Having a relation of background would be the ultimate and mature moment of nanocognitive interfaces; that they pass into use-technologies as any other supporting element of our technological artifact infrastructure.

PROPOSING AN ETHICS OF IMMANENCE

Traditional Models of Ethics (Ethics 1.0)

Now having an understanding of some of the philosophical issues related to developing an Ethics of Perception from Bergson-Deleuze, and the background context of human-technology relations in regard to augmentation tools, the next step is to summarize the thinking on ethics. The discussion of the whole of ethics from the traditional standpoint will be necessarily superficial as it is not the core consideration of the chapter. Ethics is one of several topics in Western philosophy, along with areas such as metaphysics (the nature of being and existence), epistemology (the study of knowledge), and axiology and aesthetics (issues concerning beauty, art, and value attribution). To start, we should define ethics. The standard definition of ethics is 'rules of behavior based on ideas about what is morally good and bad.' This structure is already not the most empowering one for human existence since the focus is evaluating behavior against principles, where behavior often falls short, and the most that is possible is to re-attain the baseline of the specified principles. This is a negative frame, judging behavior from an external frame of reference, as opposed to the other way around, developing ideals internally that enable behavior from the baseline to an unlimited upside of human actualization. Thus the notion of ethics has been applied negatively as opposed to affirmatively, meaning having a judging, circumscribing stance as opposed to an empowering stance towards behavior (and being more generally). Proposing an empowering affirmatory ethics of immanence also requires a redefinition of ethics as something more like 'the values or parameters by which a choice is made.' This shifts the focus onto the highest-order dimension (how choices are made), as opposed to the locus of application of the values/principles (which is external in traditional ethics and internal in immanence ethics).

In a very broad overview, historical ethics models may be categorized into three paradigms: act-based, agent-based and situation-based. The classical models are act-based: Kant's categorical imperative that certain actions are always right or wrong, or the opposing views from Bentham and Mill, utilitarianism (maximizing outcomes for the greater good) and consequentialism (where the end justifies the means). Act-based models were superseded by agent-based models of ethics like dispositionism where the individual's character was thought to be predictive of behavior (Chiu, 1997); however this is not always the case. Since the 1970s, a new model of ethics is finding ground as a result of social science research studies: situationism, where the context produces behavior; the same individual may act completely differently in two separate situations (Ross, 2011).

An Ethics of Immanence (Ethics 2.0)

However, all of these historical ethical models fall into the category of a traditional Ethics 1.0 where there is an externally-determined pre-specified ideal of behavior, and the best that any individual can do is try to regain this baseline (in some sense, this is an Ethics of Impossibility). (1.0 means the first early version of something; 2.0 means a new and improved version.) One signal of the potential inadequacy of traditional ethical models is that they exist in only the undoubled side of Bergsonian reality; the quantitative, measurable, judged part of lived experience. Instead, I would like to propose an Ethics 2.0 of Immanence which starts at baseline and moves up into affirmatory, upside potential for being in the world, attuned to the Bergsonian doubled sense of internal experience and possibility. An Ethics of Immanence means immanence in the philosophical sense of a situation where everything comes from within a system, world, or person, as opposed to transcendence where there are externally-determined specifications. There could be an Ethics of Immanence at both the individual and group level.

There is philosophical support for an Ethics of Immanence, notably in the work of philosophers who specifically did not articulate an Ethics 1.0 in the traditional judgment-oriented manner, but rather envision a more expansive open-ended way of existence which can be formulated into an ethics of immanence. With Bergson we saw that the prescription for more freedom and the exercise of free will is tuning into subjective experience, for example by living in time, experiencing time as duration, as internal overlappings and meldings of time. We further saw that both the body and mind are important constituent parts in the cognitive processes of perception and memory in which dynamism, flowing time, and subjective experience are constituent aspects. Foucault takes a different angle, examining the role of power in the world and alerting us to the fact that any interaction between two parties is a power relation. There are different kinds of bower, and even more pernicious than the top-down externally-imposed *biopower* of institutions is the bottom-up *self-disciplinary power* that we imposed on ourselves (Foucault 1980). He cautions against replicating these power structures in the new contexts we create like technology generally, and in this case cognitive nanorobots.

Deleuze and Guattari extended Foucault's *self-disciplinary power* into the idea of us each having numerous *microfascisms* in our thought and behavior. Microfascisms are self-imposed authoritarian limitations so small as to be undetectable (Guattari, 2009). The way to rid ourselves of microfascisms is by becoming more in touch with our desires, not as appetites, but as a productive force, a *desiring-production* (Deleuze & Guattari, 1983); experiencing the forces within us that desire to be productive. In the trade-off between individual freedom and group cohesion, group ethics becomes a more honest negotiation between individual desires as opposed to the repression of the productive force of desire for the social or cultural good.

SOLUTIONS AND RECOMMENDATIONS

Connecting Perception to Ethics: Machine Ethics Interfaces

Cognitive nanorobots, the philosophy of perception and becoming, and ethical models intersect in the idea of Machine Ethics Interfaces. Machine Ethics Interfaces are interfaces (software modules for communication between users and technologies (machines, devices, software, nanorobots)) with ethical aspects deliberately designed into them. This could mean communication about ethical issues, user selection of ethically-related parameters, and ethical dimensions transparently built into the technology (like a kill switch in the case of malfunction). A number of issues arise in considering the idea of facilitated cognition and its deployment through Machine Ethics Interfaces.

First we should realize that in fact our technologies already have ethics interfaces – but by default as a by-product. They have not been explicitly thought-out or determined, but there is an inherent ethics to our technologies. In fact some of the frictions that arise with technologies can be attributed to impoverished machine ethics interfaces, for example with Facebook or Gmail making suggestions or decisions that overstep ethical comfort or privacy. Now understanding perception in its Deleuzean virtuality and multiplicity suggests the possibility of selecting different perceptual models. Since choice is now involved, perception becomes an ethical issue, and the values or parameters by which choices are identified, valorized, selected, and enacted are the Ethics of Perception.

Picking an ethics buffer or a perceptual interface could be just like selecting any other technology feature, like specifying notification, brightness, or font size in devices now. There could be some entertaining examples: *"I'm wearing the Kant feed today, it is indeed limiting to view the world through these categories;"* or the Nietzsche feed allowing one to see the Apollonian and the Dionysian simultaneously. The hard philosophical problem could be asked as to whether ethics interfaces are even feasible given the practical impossibility of having an objective reality as an input. However for the first generations of machine ethics interfaces for perception and cognitive enhancement, it is perhaps not required to solve this long-standing philosophical problem about what is real and whether an objective reality exists or not, but rather define some sort of agreed upon parameters of the external world having to do with the physical laws of Earth.

A faculty that might emerge with the possibility of changing our perceptual apparatus is an awareness of the many ways in which we are currently biased due to evolution and sociality. There is the level of basic biology where nature's evolutionary requirements filter, order, and hierarchize the overwhelming amount of input data before it is routed to our cognitive circuits (Bergson-Deleuze's measurable undoubled perception). Likewise, culture and society put a lens on our perception from an individual and group dynamics perspective in the form of attunement to power relations, social conditioning, status-garnering, mate selection, and identity politics. With machine ethics interfaces, we could have the ability to adjust for these built-in biases. There are other biases and challenges, for example that in a modification of perception, it is difficult to know how perception is being modified. One unwitting solution to this is in the form of the fourth-person perspective that is being developed through ubiquitous connected devices like smartphones and quantified self-tracking gadgetry. These tracking devices model behavior and create a unique objective (data-based) view of individuals which could helpful in generating a reading of perceptual accuracy as part of machine ethics interfaces in nanocognition.

Ethics of Reality

The ability to choose different kinds of perceptual realities suggests considering the Ethics of Reality directly. Even if we can obtain access to some sort of objective external reality, is it more ethical to see raw reality the way we do now with evolutionary and cultural biases or is it more ethical to see a bias-corrected version? Just like we have come to view non-intervention in certain medical conditions where a remedy is available as inhumane, likewise we could come to think it inhumane to experience raw reality directly.

FUTURE RESEARCH DIRECTIONS

The conceptualization of cognitive nanorobots, machine ethics interfaces, and an ethics of perception of nanocognition opens up many additional research possibilities. Within philosophy, there could be a more detailed articulation of an Ethics of Perception of Nanocognition from the standpoint of other issues and thinkers. Also, there could be an examination of related future technology problematics raised by cognitive nanorobots such as personal identity, autonomy, copies and reproduction, personal data and big data, human augmentation, and immortality. Between philosophy, science, and rationality communities (like LessWrong, http://lesswrong.com/), there could be an applied synthesis of thinking to determine which kinds of facilitated cognition and perceptual enhancement applications would make the most sense to do first. Then blueprints for how to build them could be developed, designing the technical specifications for test applications on currently-available computing platforms such as Google Glass. Some possibilities for the killer applications of cognitive nanorobotics are bias-reduction, memory management, value system optimization, perceptual augmentation, and permissioned point-of-view swapping.

The Killer Applications of Nanocognition

Realizing that nanocognition is a speculative topic in both science and philosophy, there are nevertheless several potentially interesting and useful applications of such technology that could be proposed, where a brief discussion of examples could help to concretize the concepts. One of the first and most obvious 'killer applications' for cognitive nanorobots is bias reduction, helping to identify and reduce the many known human cognitive biases such as loss aversion, overconfidence, confirmation, rationalization, probability neglect, and hindsight (Kahneman, 2013). A second killer app is memory management, both accessing the right memories at the right time (and including possibly augmenting real memories with Internet-accessible personal or general data), and blocking access to unhelpful memories, for example in trauma resolution or to consider issues cleanly and not fall into sunk cost or other cognitive traps. A third killer app is being able to elicit and optimize our value systems and desires by using cognitive nanorobots to evoke personal values profiles and coordinate them with our lives for greater fulfillment. A related feature could be emotional and cognitive state elicitation applications using biometric sensors, eye-tracking, mental state identification, and affect analysis, technology which is already available today (Nummenmaa, 2014). A fourth killer app is perceptual augmentation, using cognitive nanorobots in some of the ways Bergson and Deleuze mention to amplify subjective experience, to give us a way to see multiple realities or multiple sides to reality simultaneously, and to see and think in time instead of space, and to see movement in both time and space. A fifth killer app could draw on Foucault and Deleuze's concerns with power relations in the Foucauldian Power Meter. This app would assess quantitative and qualitative aspects of *biopower* relations in intra-individual and group interactions, and the degree of *self-disciplinary power* and *microfascism* in internal deliberations (this latter is a version of the bias elicitor and reducer). This could be part of a broader line of Philosophy Apps with the Kant and Nietzsche feeds mentioned early. There would be demand for many other vertical markets in points-of-view, looking at the world as different artists, political strategists, humanitarians, celebrities, athletes, etc. do.

There could be a whole new class of apps based on the functionality of being able to see the points of view of others (per user-granted permissions) through individual and group POV HUDs (point-of-view heads-up-displays). The advent of Google Glass (which includes the possibility of direct sharing with Google+ social network contacts) suggests that this might not be far away. There could be the Negotiator POV to look for areas of common ground between people in conflict or even to preemptively avoid conflict ("*Let's flip to CR (conflict resolution) mode*"), or the Art Appreciation POV to try on the different aesthetic perspectives of others ("*What Picasso saw when he painted*"). There could be endless conceptual permutations of Garage Band, video games, and other new opportunities for lived experience either solo or in groups simply starting from "*Here, let me share my HUD*." Along with new technologies and killer apps comes the need to define new behavioral etiquette and standards; one can envision the equivalents of *Emily Post for Glass*, or *Roberts Rules of Order for Machine-facilitated Negotiations*.

POTENTIAL LIMITATIONS

Neural Data Privacy Rights

There are many potential limitations that arise with the possibility of cognitive nanorobots and the consideration of an Ethics of Perceptions of Nanocognition. Since cognitive nanorobots are computational machines that are likely to be Internet-connected or at least externally-communicating to some degree, they could have all of the usual biomedical device safety, regulation, and health data privacy concerns, as well as the data capture, tracking, storage, transmission, privacy, sharing, and access issues of electronic data. These concerns are encapsulated in the concept of neural data privacy rights (Swan, 2014). Neural data privacy rights are already an area of concern since it is not difficult to measure the electrical activity of the brain. There are many consumer-available devices that measure electrical and other activity such as EEGs, PPGs, and tMS systems; augmented headsets like Google Glass, Oculus Rift, and foc.us; quantified self-tracking, wearable electronics, and Internet-of-Things biosensors; and emotional and cognitive state applications using eye-tracking, mental state identification, and affect analysis. This is even before considering the potential future aspects of neural data in the context of cognitive nanorobots.

Further, in the contemporary era of big data, there is a practical impossibility of privacy as traditionally conceived since any two data elements may start to constitute an identification. Instead, data privacy models need to be rethought to accommodate the broader scope of actual activity that has outgrown the traditional notion of privacy. Newer models could highlight tiered access over ownership, third-party intermediaries to control the storage and transmission of personal data, and attributes such as greater transparency, disclosure, and symmetry (Kelly, 2014; Lanier, 2013). The closest precedent to cognitive nanorobots and neural data is genomic data from the standpoint of personalized data ownership, access, security, privacy, and sharing, where some projects like the Harvard Personal Genome Project presciently announced at the outset that it would not be possible to keep data private or anonymous in the traditional way.

Cognitive Viruses and Neurosecurity

At least two other potential challenges to cognitive nanorobots and machine ethics interfaces that could arise, just as they have on other computing platforms, are viruses and spam. Cognitive nanorobotic viruses could cause neural prosthetics to stop functioning at best, and malfunction in many harmful ways at worst. Pronounced doomsday scenarios can be imagined such as whole communities turning into sociopaths, or having their access to reality blocked, and science fiction has envisioned a number of these potential cases (such as Greg Bear's *Slant* where nano-cognitive prostheses become infected). Neurosecurity has been articulated as an explicit concern in this area, as "a version of computer science security principles and methods applied to neural engineering," or more fully, as "the protection of the confidentiality, integrity, and availability of neural devices from malicious parties with the goal of preserving the safety of a person's neural mechanisms, neural computation, and free will" (Denning, 2009). One answer to virus-related and spam-related problems is that antiviral and antispam software solutions tend to evolve in lockstep (i.e.; they are cases of the Red Queen problem; running in place just to stay an incremental step behind). Thus solutions may be right behind the problem, or in any case future-technology will have been evolving too, so the problem would not be as insurmountable as it seems in isolation. A more explicit and proactive anticipation of such neurosecurity concerns would also be an appropriate response for responsible technology innovation (Nordmann, 2014).

CONCLUSION

The fast pace of modern technological innovation suggests the imperative of proactively developing conceptual models and practical tools such as machine ethics interfaces to facilitate the implementation of future technologies that more intricately link humans and machines. These kinds of preparations could help provide a means for evaluating new technologies and improving society's comfort with technology adoption. Machine ethics interfaces could also have as their aim the inculcation of values such as liberty, equity, affordability, and access. A contemporary area of considerable interest and scientific development is neuroscience and cognitive enhancement where longer-term innovations could include neuro-prosthetics and next generation brain-computer interface tools like cognitive nanorobots.

The aim of this chapter was to propose the concept of nano-aided cognition through cognitive nanorobots, and an ethics of immanence as the accompanying ethics of perception for the situation of cognitive nanorobots. Initially, three building blocks were developed: the definition of cognitive nanorobots, Bergson and Deleuze's articulation of relevant philosophical concepts (i.e.; image, movement, time, doubled subjective experience, perception, memory, difference, becoming, and virtual-actual reality), and historical ethics models (act-based, agent-based, and situation-based). This foundation was then used to propose an ethics of immanence and that machine ethics should be considered more explicitly in technology design. Machine ethics interfaces should incorporate elements of subjective experience such that we can be more internally-aware, expressive, and freer as beings. Killer applications of cognitive nanorobots were presented such as bias reduction, memory management, and perceptual enhancement.

Finally new models of data access and protection, and anti-viral neural software, were considered in response to potential challenges in cognitive nanorobots like neural data privacy rights and cognitive viruses.

Summarizing the philosophical contributions from Bergson and Deleuze, Bergson recommends a fuller realization of human potential through tuning into the doubled subjective side of lived experience, living in time, and exercising free will through spontaneous action and improvisation. Deleuze's exhortation is for us to see movement, time, difference, becoming, and possibility directly in and of themselves. Bergson-Deleuze can be extended to propose the idea of seeing perception itself (Cinema 3: the *perception-image*) as a malleable field of possibility rather than as one fixed mode of interacting with the world. When perception becomes possibility, the issue of choices and their valorization is introduced, and this requires a rethinking of ethics regarding how to make choices about different kinds of perceptual reality.

The Future: An Ethics of Immanence

Deleuze lays the groundwork for rethinking ethics and proposing an ethics of immanence when he claims that philosophy got off on the wrong track in the link between thinking and life. Instead of connecting an active life with an affirmative thinking, thought gave itself the task of judging life, and became negative and deprecatory (Deleuze & Guattari, 1996). This is the model of a traditional ethics 1.0 which judges behavior against ideals, invariably finding shortcomings. Instead, a machine ethics 2.0 for the future should be one of immanence which progresses from judging behavior to creating a life for all future persons that is affirmatory, exploratory, and expansive. An ethics of immanence is one way that we can maintain the right kind of relationship with technology as Heidegger advocates, an empowering rather than enslaving relation, such that *"our attunement to technology as an enabling background helps us see the possibilities for the true meaningfulness of our being"* (Heidegger, 1982, p. 176).

REFERENCES

Ansell-Pearson, K. (2002). *Philosophy and the Adventure of the Virtual: Bergson and the Time of Life*. London, UK: Routledge.

Asimov, I. (1950). I, Robot. New York, NY: Doubleday & Company.

Bergson, H. (1957). *Time and Free Will*. London, UK: Unwin.

Bergson, H. (1988). *Matter and Memory*. Brooklyn, NY: Zone Books.

Bergson, H. (1999). *Duration and Simultaneity*. Manchester, UK: Clinamen Press Ltd.

Boehm, F. (2013). Nanomedical Device and Systems Design: Challenges, Possibilities, Visions. New York, NY: CRC Press, especially Chapter 17: Nanomedicine in Regenerative Biosystems, Human Augmentation, and Longevity. (pp. 654-722). doi:10.1201/b15626

BonJour. L. (2013). Epistemological Problems of Perception. In E.N. Zalta (Ed.), *The Stanford Encyclopedia of Philosophy*. Retrieved from http://plato.stanford.edu/archives/spr2013/entries/perception-episprob/

Boysen, E. (2014). Nanotechnology in Medicine – Nanomedicine. UnderstandingNano.com. Retrieved from http://www.understandingnano.com/medicine.html

Brey, P. (2000). Technology and Embodiment in Ihde and Merleau-Ponty. In C. Mitcham (Ed.), Metaphysics, Epistemology, and Technology: Research in Philosophy and Technology. Retrieved from http://www.utwente.nl/bms/wijsb/organization/brey/Publicaties_Brey/Brey_2000_Embodiment.pdf

Chiu, C. Y., Hong, Y. Y., & Dweck, C. S. (1997). Lay dispositionism and implicit theories of personality. *Journal of Personality and Social Psychology*, *73*(1), 19–30. doi:10.1037/0022-3514.73.1.19 PMID:9216077

Clark, A. (1998). *Being There: Putting Brain, Body, and World Together Again*. London, UK: Bradford Books.

Colebrook, C. (2002). *Understanding Deleuze*. Crows Nest, Australia: Allen & Unwin.

Crane, T. (2011). The Problem of Perception. In E.N. Zalta (Ed.), *The Stanford Encyclopedia of Philosophy*. Retrieved from http://plato.stanford.edu/archives/spr2011/entries/perception-problem/

Deleuze, G. (1986). *Cinema 1: The-Movement-Image*. Minneapolis, MN: University of Minnesota Press.

Deleuze, G. (1989). *Cinema 2: The Time-Image*. Minneapolis, MN: University of Minnesota Press.

Deleuze, G., & Guatarri, F. (1987). *A Thousand Plateaus*. Minneapolis, MN: University of Minnesota Press.

Deleuze, G., & Guatarri, F. (1989). *Anti-Oedipus*. Minneapolis, MN: University of Minnesota Press.

Deleuze, G., & Guatarri, F. (1996). *What is Philosophy?* New York, NY: Columbia University Press.

Denning, T., Matsuoka, Y., & Kohno, T. (2009). Neurosecurity: Security and privacy for neural devices. *Neurosurgical Focus*, *27*(1), E7. doi:10.3171/2009.4.FOCUS0985 PMID:19569895

Descartes, R. (1637). *Dioptrics*. Retrieved from http://science.larouchepac.com/fermat/Descartes%20--%20Dioptrique.pdf

Foucault, M. (1980). *Power/Knowledge*. New York, NY: Pantheon Books.

Franssen, M., Lokhorst, G. J., & van de Poel, I. (2013). Philosophy of Technology. In E.N. Zalta (Ed.), *The Stanford Encyclopedia of Philosophy*. Retrieved from http://plato.stanford.edu/archives/win2013/entries/technology/

Freitas, R. Jr. (2003). *Nanomedicine, Vol. IIA: Biocompatibility*. Austin, TX: Landes Bioscience.

Guattari, F. (2009). Chaosophy: Texts and Interviews 1972-1977. Los Angeles CA: Semiotext(e).

Heidegger, M. (1982). The Question Concerning Technology. In W. Lovitt, (Ed.), The Question Concerning Technology and Other Essays New York, NY: Harper and Row.

Hu, C. M., Fang, R. H., Copp, J., Luk, B. T., & Zhang, L. (2013). A biomimetic nanosponge that absorbs pore-forming toxins. *Nature Nanotechnology*, *8*(5), 336–340. doi:10.1038/nnano.2013.54 PMID:23584215

Ihde, D. (2001). Bodies. In *Technology (Electronic Mediations)*. Minneapolis, MN: University of Minnesota Press.

Ihde, D. (2010). A phenomenology of technics. In C. Hanks (Ed.), *Technology and Values: Essential Readings* (pp. 134–155). New York, NY: Wiley-Blackwell.

Kahneman, D. (2013). *Thinking, Fast and Slow*. New York, NY: Farrar, Straus and Giroux.

Kateb, B., & Heiss, J. D. (Eds.). (2013). *The Textbook of Nanoneuroscience and Nanoneurosurgery*. New York, NY: CRC Press. doi:10.1201/b15274

Kelly, K. (2014). Conversation: The Technium. *Edge*. Retrieved from http://edge.org/memberbio/kevin_kelly

Klapoetke, N. C., Murata, Y., Kim, S. S., Pulver, S. R., Birdsey-Benson, A., & Cho, Y. K. et al. (2014). Independent Optical Excitation of Distinct Neural Populations. *Nature Methods*, *11*(3), 338–346. doi:10.1038/nmeth.2836 PMID:24509633

Lanier, J. (2013). *Who Owns the Future?* New York, NY: Simon & Schuster.

Mavroidis, C. (2014). *Nano-Robotics in Medical Applications: From Science Fiction to Reality*. Northeastern University. Retrieved from http://www.albany.edu/selforganization/presentations/2-mavroidis.pdf

McDonough, J. (2003). Descartes' "Dioptrics" and "Optics.". In L. Nolan (Ed.), *The Cambridge Descartes Lexicon*. Cambridge: Cambridge University Press.

Nordmann, A. (2014). Responsible innovation, the art and craft of anticipation. *Journal of Responsible Innovation.*, *1*(1), 87–98. doi:10.1080/23299460.2014.882064

Nummenmaa, L., Glerean, E., Hari, R., & Hietanen, J. K. (2014). Bodily maps of emotions. *Proceedings of the National Academy of Sciences of the United States of America*, *111*(2), 646–651. doi:10.1073/pnas.1321664111 PMID:24379370

Poell, T. (2004). Movement and Time in Cinema, Discernements: Deleuzian Aesthetics. In J. Bloois (Ed.), *Rodopi* (pp. 1–21).

Provenzale, J. M., & Mohs, A. M. (2010). Nanotechnology in Neurology: Current Status and Future Possibilities. *US Neurology.*, *6*(1), 12–17.

Ross, L., & Nisbett, R. E. (2011). *The Person and the Situation: Perspectives of Social Psychology*. London, UK: Pinter & Martin Ltd.

Schulz, M. J., Shanov, V. N., & Yun, Y. (Eds.). (2009). *Nanomedicine Design of Particles, Sensors, Motors, Implants, Robots, and Devices*. New York, NY: Artech House.

Seo, D., Carmena, J. M., Rabaey, J. M., Alon, E., & Maharbiz, M. M. (2013). Neural Dust: An Ultrasonic, Low Power Solution for Chronic Brain-Machine Interfaces. *arXiv*, 1307.2196 [q-bio.NC]. Retrieved from http://arxiv.org/abs/1307.2196

Swan, M. (2014). Neural Data Privacy Rights: An Invitation For Progress In The Guise Of An Approaching Worry. In J. Brockman (Ed.), *What Should We Be Worried About?: Real Scenarios That Keep Scientists Up at Night*. New York, NY: Harper Perennial.

Vitale, C. (2011). Guide to Reading Deleuze's The Movement-Image, Part I: The Deleuzian Notion of the Image, or Worldslicing as Cinema Beyond the Human. *networkologies*. Retrieved from http://networkologies.wordpress.com/2011/04/04/the-deleuzian-notion-of-the-image-a-slice-of-the-world-or-cinema-beyond-the-human/

ADDITIONAL READING

Bergson, H. (1944). *Creative Evolution*. New York, NY: The Modern Library.

Colebrook, C. (2002). *Gilles Deleuze*. London, UK: Routledge. doi:10.4324/9780203241783

Deleuze, G. (1990). *Bergsonism*. New York, NY: Zone Books.

Deleuze, G. (1994). *Difference and Repetition*. New York, NY: Columbia University Press.

Deleuze, G. (2000). *Proust et les signes*. Minneapolis, MN: University of Minnesota Press.

Deleuze, G., & Parnet, C. (1987). *Dialogues*. New York, NY: Columbia University Press.

Guerlac, S. (2006). *Thinking in Time: An Introduction to Henri Bergson*. Cornell, NY: Cornell University Press.

Meacham, D. E. (2014). Medicine and society, new continental perspectives (Preface). In D. E. Meacham (Ed.), *Medicine and Society, New Continental Perspectives*. New York, NY: Springer.

Wheeler, M. (2011). Embodied Cognition and the Extended Mind. In J. Garvey (Ed.), *The Continuum Companion to Philosophy of Mind* (pp. 220–238). London, UK: Bloomsbury Companions.

Williams, J. (2003). *Gilles Deleuze's "Difference and Repetition": A Critical Introduction and Guide*. Edinburgh, UK: Edinburgh University Press.

KEY TERMS AND DEFINITIONS

Cognitive Nanorobots, Nanocognition: 1) (Conventional) Nanorobots that can think for themselves, 2) Nanorobots deployed in the specific context of facilitating, aiding, and improving the processes of cognition like perception and memory; neural nano-prosthetics.

Ethics of Immanence: An affirmatory expression of ethics that focuses on unbounded upside potential for being in the world as opposed to traditional ethics models which are negative and deprecatory in judging behavior against an externally-specified pre-defined baseline of ideals where the best that can be hoped for is regaining the baseline.

Ethics of Perception: The values or parameters by which different perceptual choices are made (for example choosing a perceptual mode of reality, and the awareness that there is a choice of perceptual reality). Ethics is recast as the values or parameters by which a choice is made as opposed to its traditional definition as rules of behavior based on ideas about what is morally good and bad.

Ethics of Reality: Like the ethics of perception, the value and parameters by which different choices about reality are made. For example, if reality can be perceived in different modes, perhaps it is more ethical to see a bias-corrected version rather than raw reality as prefigured by our built-in evolutionary and cultural biases.

Fourth-Person Perspective: A new and objective view of the self per the continuous information climate and ubiquitous connected devices like smartphones and quantified self-tracking gadgetry.

Machine Ethics Interfaces: Interfaces (software modules for communication between users and technologies (machines, devices, software, nanorobots)) with ethical aspects deliberately designed into them. This could mean communication about ethical issues, user selection of ethically-related parameters, and ethical dimensions transparently built into the technology (like a kill switch in the case of malfunction).

Machine Ethics: 1) (Conventional) technology designers attempting to incorporate models of human-centric morality into machines like robots, self-driving vehicles, and artificial intelligence to prevent humans from being harmed either maliciously or unintentionally, 2) any issue pertaining to machines and ethics, 3) the possibility of new ethical paradigms arising from human augmentation and human-machine hybrids.

Nanorobots/Medical Nanorobots: Hypothetical very small (nanoscale) self-propelled machines like respirocytes, clottocytes, vasculoids, and microbivores that could perform a variety of biophysical clean-up, maintenance, and augmentation functions in the body.

Neural Data Privacy Rights: Concern about the privacy and security (access, ownership, transmission, storage, sharing, use, value) of personal data generated by brain activity, especially with the availability of consumer EEGs, PPGs, and tMS systems, and the possibility that next-generation sensors may be able to capture the neural activity of large groups of people simultaneously in real-time.

Neuro-Prosthetics/Neural Prostheses: A series of devices like cochlear implants that at present can substitute a motor, sensory, or cognitive modality that might have been damaged as a result of an injury or a disease, and in the future could be deployed for cognitive enhancement.

Perception-Image: 1) (Conventional) One of the three kinds of Deleuze's *movement-image* (*perception-image*, *affection-image*, and *action-image*) which literally correspond to cinematic techniques (long shots, close-ups, and medium shots), 2) the notion of seeing perception itself as a malleable field of possibility rather than as one fixed mode of interacting with the world.

Chapter 7
Ethical Concerns in Human Enhancement:
Advantages in Corporate/ Organizational Settings

Ben Tran
Alliant International University, USA

ABSTRACT

The purpose of this chapter is on issue of fairness and equity in corporations and organizational settings due to advantages received as a result of human enhancement. In so doing, the purpose of this chapter will also analyze the paradigms of bioethics and (business) ethics and legality will be utilized in analyzing the issue of fairness and equity in corporations and organizational settings due to advantages received as a result of human enhancement. Human enhancement, used in this chapter, includes any activity by which we improve our bodies, minds, or abilities beyond what we regard today as normal. In relations to advantages in corporations and organizational settings, human enhancement, used in this chapter, means ways to make functional changes to human characteristic, also referred to as neuro-cognitive enhancements, beyond what we regard as typical, normal, or statistically normal range of functioning for an individual.

INTRODUCTION

Research into the ethical, social, legal, and political aspects of emerging technologies, according to Ferrari, Coenen, and Grunwald (2012), is commonly known as ELSA, which began with the launch of the Human Genome Project in 1990, has nowadays acquired a fundamental role as preparatory research for the governance of these technologies. ELSA reflection in Europe has been framed by ideas about the co-evolution of science and society and about the need for reflexive science. In its 2009 report entitled "Challenging futures of science in society—emerging trends and cutting-edge issues", the EU MASIS

DOI: 10.4018/978-1-4666-8592-5.ch007

Expert Group stresses the growing role played by applied ethics—alongside science and technology studies (STS), technology assessment (TA), and other fields—in what it calls reflexive science": the idea is that science should reflect on its role and its impacts on society, not only as a purely philosophical exercise. The group gives two examples of this reflective science, the first being the debate on human enhancement (HE), and the second example regards the increasingly important role played by scientific expertise in decision making, possibly under conditions of extremely high uncertainty.

Enhancement is typically compared with therapy (Miah, 2011). In broad terms, therapy aims to fix something that has gone wrong, by curing specific diseases or injuries, while enhancement interventions aim to improve that state of an organism beyond its normal healthy state (Allhoff, Lin, Moor, & Weckert, 2009; Bostrom & Roache, 2008; Miah, 2011). In other words, human enhancement includes any activity by which we improve our bodies, minds, or abilities—things we do to enhance our welfare. These so-called natural human enhancements are morally uninteresting because they appear to be unproblematic to the extent that it is difficult to see why we should not be permitted to improve ourselves through diet, education, physical training, and so on.

Rather, allow us to stipulate for the moment that human enhancement is about boosting our capabilities beyond the species-typical level, or statistically-normal range of functioning for an individual (Daniels, 2000; Miah, 2011). Relatedly, human enhancement can be understood to be different from therapy, which is about treatments aimed at pathologies that compromise health or reduce one's level of functioning below this species-typically or statistically-normal level (Juengst, 1997; Miah, 2011). Another way to think about human enhancement technologies, as opposed to therapy is that they change the structure and function of the body (Greely, 2006; Miah, 2011). As such, by human enhancement we do not mean the mere use of tools; that would render the concept impotent, turning everything we do into cases of human enhancement. But if and when these tools are integrated into our bodies, rather than employed externally, then we will consider them to be instances of human enhancement. Admittedly, none of these definitions is immune to objections, but they are nevertheless useful as starting point in thinking about the distinction, including whether there really is such a distinction.

Now, given the above understanding of human enhancement, let us tease apart the myriad issues that arise in the debate. These too are loose non-exclusive categories that may overlap with one another, but perhaps are still useful in providing an overview of the debate: (1) freedom & autonomy; (2) health & safety, (3) fairness & equity; (4) societal disruption; and (5) human dignity (Lin & Allhoff, 2008). Emphasis will be on the issue of fairness and equity in corporations and organizational settings due to advantages received as a result of human enhancement. Paradigms of bioethics (biotechnology) and (business) ethics and legality will be utilized in analyzing the issue of fairness and equity in corporations and organizational settings due to advantages received as a result of human enhancement. With that said, this chapter is a composition of two paradigms, basic science and business.

HUMAN ENHANCEMENT: BIOETHICS (BIOTECHNOLOGY)

Over the last decade, human enhancement has grown into a major topic of debate in applied ethics. Interest has been stimulated by advances in the biomedical sciences, advances to many, suggest that it will become increasingly feasible to use medicine and technology to reshape, manipulate, and enhance many aspects of human biology even in healthy individuals. To the extent that such interventions are on the horizon that is an obvious practical dimension to these debates. This practical dimension is understood by an outcrop of think tanks and activist organizations devoted to the *biopolitics* of enhancement.

Already one can detect a biopolitical fault line developing between pro-enhancement and anti-enhancement groupings: transhumanists on one side, who believe that a wide range of enhancements should be developed and that people should be free to use them to transform themselves in quite radical ways; and bioconservatives on the other, who believe that we should not substantially alter human biology or the human condition (Bostrom, 2005). There are also miscellaneous groups who try to position themselves in between these poles, as the golden mean. While the terms of this emerging political disagreement are still being negotiated, there might be a window of opportunity open for academic bioethics to influence the shape and direction of this debate before it settles into a fixedly linear ideological tug-of-war (Glover, 1984). Beyond this practical relevance, the topic of enhancement also holds theoretical interest. Many of the ethical issues that arise in the examination of human enhancement prospects hook into concepts and problems of more general philosophical significance—concepts such as human nature, personal identity, moral status, well-being, and problems in normative ethics, political philosophy, philosophy of mind, and epistemology. In addition to these philosophical linkages, human enhancement also offers thought-fodder (Bostrom & Savulescu, 2008) for several other disciplines, including medicine, law, psychology, economics, and sociology.

With that said, human enhancement includes any activity by which we improve our bodies, minds, or abilities—things we do to enhance our well-being (Allhoff, Lin, & Steinberg, 2011; Lin & Allhoff, 2008). But it is tempting to think that human enhancement is about boosting our capabilities beyond the species-typical level or statistically normal range of functioning for an individual (Allhoff, Lin, & Steinberg, 2011; Daniels, 2000; Miah, 2011). As such, human enhancement, used here, means ways to make functional changes to human characteristics, abilities, emotion and capacities, beyond what we regard today as normal (Conference of European Churches, 2010), using advances in biology, chemistry, physics, materials, information technology and the mind sciences. In relations to advantages in corporations and organizational settings, human enhancement means ways to make functional changes to human characteristic [knowledge, skills, abilities, and other characteristics (KSAOs)] (Tran, 2008a; Tran, 2013; Tran, 2014a, b), also referred to as neuro-cognitive enhancements (Rodenburg, 2010), beyond what we regard as typical, normal, or statistically normal range of functioning for an individual.

THE BASIC SCIENCE

Just as twentieth century was a golden age of computing, the twenty-first century is the deoxyribonucleic acid (DNA) age (Griffiths, Wessler, Lewontin, & Carroll, 2007). The silicon age brought about dramatic changes in how we as a species work, think, communicate, and play. The innovations of the computer revolution helped bring about the current genetic revolution, which promises to do for life what computing did for information. We are on the verge of being able to transform, manipulate, and create organisms for any number of productive purposes. From medicine, to agriculture, to construction and even computing, we are within reach of an age when manipulating the genetic codes of various organisms, or engineering entirely new organisms, promises to alter the way we relate to the natural world.

Biotechnology, specifically genetic engineering, is already a beneficial resource, employed in medicine, manufacturing, and agriculture (Myskja, 2006, p. 228). We have begun reaping the practical rewards of genetic engineering such as new medical therapies and increased crop yields and so far only a few instances of measurable harm have resulted. Genetic engineering has the potential to improve our health and well-being dramatically, revolutionize our manner of living, help us to conserve limited resources and produce new health (Koepsell, 2007). Provided that it is appropriately regulated, bearing in mind ethical concerns relating to dignity, harmful consequences, and justice, its potential benefits outweigh its harms. There is certainly no reason to reject it outright as unnatural. Biotechnology should be understood as an extension of already accepted and well-established techniques, such as directed breeding, combined with sophisticated understanding of evolution and genetic technologies.

Freedom and Autonomy

According to Allhoff, Lin, Moor, and Weckert (2009), there is perhaps no greater value, at least in democracies, than the cherished concepts of freedoms and autonomy. But because freedom and autonomy are central to the issue of human enhancement, they add much fuel to the impassioned debate. This is because pro-enhancement advocates have argued against regulating enhancements on the grounds that it would infringe on our fundamental ability to choose how we want to live our own lives (Bailey, 2005; Harris, 2007; Naam, 2005). Maximal freedom is a hallmark of a laissez-faire or minimal state, nut a democratic society is not compelled to endorse such a stance, as some political philosophers have suggested (Nozick, 1974). Even the most liberal democracy today understands the value of regulations as a way to enhance our freedom.

There is another sense, related to free will, in which cognitive enhancements may be infringing: if an enhancement, such as a mood-altering drug or neural implant, interferes or alter our deliberative process, then it is an open question whether or not we are truly acting freely while under the influence of the enhancement. For instance, a citizen chip embedded in the brain might cause us to be unswervingly patriotic and hold different values than we would otherwise have. Further, external pressure by or from peers, employers, competitors, national security, and others also may unduly influence one's decision making (Guston, Parsi, & Tosi, 2007).

Health and Safety

To justify restriction on our freedom and autonomy, of course, we would need strong, compelling reasons to offset that prima facie harm; specifically, we need to identify conflicting values that ought to be factored into our policymaking. One possible reason is that human enhancement technologies may pose a health risk to the person operated upon, similar to illegal or unprescribed steroids use of athletes: given how precious little we known about how our brains and other biological systems work, any tinkering with those systems would likely give rise to unintended effects, from mild to most serious (President's Council of Bioethics, 2003). Even if such technologies prove to be so dangerous or risky that we strongly believe we need to believe individuals from their own decisions to use technologies, the well-informed individual might circumvent this use by freely and knowingly consenting to those risks, thereby removing this reason for restricted use. But even this case does not solve the conflict between freedom/autonomy and health/safety (Bostrom & Sandberg, 2006; Farah 2005; Farah, Illes, Cook-Deegan, Gardner, Kandel, King, Parens, Sahakian, & Wolpe, 2004).

First, it is not always clear whether a person's consent is sufficiently informed or not. Second, the assumption that a procedure to implant some human enhancement technology may affect the health and safety of only that patient appears to be much too generous. Third, even if the harm that arises from any given instance of human enhancement is so small to be practically negligible, the individual choices to enhance oneself can lead to aggregate harms that are much larger and substantial. Likewise, as human enhancement technologies improve and are adopted by more people, the once-negligible harms that arise from individual cases may metastasize into very real harms to large segments of society (Parfit, 1986).

Fairness and Equity

Even if we can understand why there would be pressure to enhance one's self or children it is important to note the following: advantages gained by enhanced persons also imply a relative disadvantages for the unenhanced, whether in sports, employment opportunities, academic performance, or any other area. That is to say, fairness is another value to consider in the debate, such that, in considering the issue of fairness, we need to be careful to not conflict it with equity. Under most economic theories, fairness does not require that we need to close the gap entirely between economic classes, even when justice is defined as fairness (Allhoff, 2005; Rawls, 1971; Miah, 2011). Indeed, there are good reasons to think that we want some gap to exist for example, to provide incentives for innovations, in order to move up the economic ladder, and to follow flexibility in a workforce to fill vacancies and perform a wide range of tasks.

Related to the notion of equity is that of fairness. Even if pronounced inequity is morally permissible, there is still a question of how an individual accesses or affords a human enhancement technology, which may be unfair or unacceptably magnify the inequity. If the distribution of or access to enhancement technologies it not obviously unfair, illegally discriminatory, then perhaps we can justify the resulting inequities. Justifying inequities regarding fair distribution of those technologies is not easy task, when a scheme based on need or productivity, or any other single dimension would easily be defeated by the standard arguments that they overlook other relevant dimensions (Rescher, 1980).

Societal Disruption

Fairness and equality are not just theoretical values, but they have practical effects. Gross inequality itself, whether fair or not, can motivate the worse-off masses to revolt against a state or system. But societal disruption need not be so extreme to be taken seriously. Entire institutions today—as well as the lack thereof—are based on a specific range of abilities and rough equality of natural assets. Sports, for instance, would change dramatically, if enhanced persons are permitted to compete to the clear disadvantage of unenhanced athletes, smashing their previous records (Allhoff, Lin, & Steinberg, 2011; Lin & Allhoff, 2008).

Other institutions and systems include economic, privacy, communications, pensions, security, and many other sectors of society. For instance, if life-extension technologies can increase our average lifespan by 20 years—let alone the 100+ years predicted by some futurists (de Gray, 2007; Kurzweil, 2005), and assuming that the extra 20 years will be a good life, not one bogged down with illness and diminishing productivity that afflict many elderly today—then we would need to radically adjust retirement programs: do we move the retirement age to 85, which had negative consequences for job-seekers such as new tenure-track academic faculty, or increase contributions to pension plans, which puts pressure on household budgets and employers? Or both? Some scenarios that many cause social disruption include: a job candidate with a neutral implant that enables better data retention and faster information processing would consistently beat out unenhanced candidates; a person with super-human hearing or sight could circumvent existing privacy protections and expectations by easily and undetectably eaverdropping or spying on others; more students and professors using Ritalin may grab admission or tenure at all the best universities and so on (Allhoff, Lin, & Steinberg, 2011; Lin & Allhoff, 2008).

Human Dignity

The fiercest resistance to human enhancement technologies is perhaps a concern about their effect on human dignity and what it means to be human (Miah, 2011; President's Council on Bioethics, 2003; Sandel, 2007). For instance, does the desire for enhancement show ingratitude for what we have and further enable an attitude of unquenchable dissatisfaction with one's life? Some researchers suggest that discontent is hardwires into the genetic makeup of humans (Hill, 2006; Woodall, 2007), which is why we constantly innovate, strive to achieve and gain more. However, even if this is true, it does not seem to be so much an argument to promote human enhancement technologies, but more a worry that those technologies are not the panacea or Holy Grail of happiness we might believe them to be. That is, we will still be dissatisfied with ourselves no matter how much we enhance ourselves, unless of course, we somehow eradicate that part of our DNA that causes discontent.

Would human enhancement technologies hinder moral development? Many believe, according to (Allhoff, Lin, & Steinberg, 2011, p. 208), that "soul-making" is impossible without struggle (Hick, 1966), and achievements ring hollow without sacrifice or effort (President's Council on Bioethics, 2003); so if technology makes life and competitions easier, then we may lose opportunities to feed and grow our moral character. On the other hand, compare our lives today with pre-Internet days: increased connectivity to friends, work, information, and the like, is often a double-edged proposition that also increases stress and decreases free time. This, the raises the related concern of whether enhancement technologies will actually make our lives happier.

Is the frailty of the human condition necessary to best appreciate life? There is something romantic about the notion of being fallible. But with existing pharmacology, we could eliminate the emotion of sadness today, and work is continuing on drugs that repress memories; but it is not clear that sadness is a pathology we should want to eliminate, rather than a human experience what we should preserve (President's Council on Bioethics, 2003). Other critics have suggested that life could be too long, leading to boredom after one's life-goal are achieved (Williams, 1973). Finally, there might be concern that we are playing God with world-changing technologies, which is presumably bad (Peters, 2007).

With that said, Lee and George (2008) note that at least four different dimensions of dignity can be identified. Those who defend the inherent dimension of dignity hold that this is natural capacity that does not need to be developed or manifest to any degree.

1. The first dimension, is what some hold to such dignity for theological reasons, such as the belief that humans are made in the image of God, but others hold to it for secular reasons. These can include the complex combination of rational, emotional and relational capacities in humans or their ability to e autonomous moral agents. Inherent dignity is often equated with being human, and thereby dismissed by some as speciesist. However, dignity is not necessarily limited to humans. It can be extended to those with a similar nature.
2. The second dimension is what O'Mathuna (2013, p. 101) call circumstantial dignity, and this reflects the variable aspect. Classic notions of dignity were based on social hierarchies. The original meaning of dignity (dignitas) is still captured in the English term 'dignitary.' These are people we esteem with more honor because of their position or accomplishments.

3. The third dimension is our own sense of our dignity. Jonathan Mann, a long-time advocate of human rights, captures this dimension. "Damage to human dignity have more serious adverse effects on physical, social, and mental wellbeing than infectious disease" (Horton, 2004, p. 1084). In spite of inherent dignity, actions can diminish a person's sense of dignity, and by implication, other actions can promote one's sense of dignity. But this is different to claiming that a person's inherent dignity has changed.

4. The fourth dimension of dignity is viewed as dignified. Steven Pinker (2008) claims that part of why dignity is of little value is that it provides little guidance to how we should act.

THE BASIC PHILOSOPHY

On the count of the main focus of this chapter is not on Heidegger, but rather Heidegger's take on human enhancement, balance has been taken into consideration between the terms that have been established in the tradition of Heidegger translations and the original ones in German, without getting too tangled up in the semantics of Heidegger's language. Heidegger is notorious for his use of language, and sometimes difficult to grasp, abstract thoughts. For this reason, Heidegger researches and commentaries have often been accused of being more confusing than Heidegger himself.

Like, Friedrich Nietzsche, Paul-Michel Foucault and Avram Noam Chomsky, Martin Heidegger's aim, or purpose of philosophy is to deconstruct, review and reflect on the concepts, categorizations and dogmas that have become self-evident truisms in our time. For instance, Heidegger has his reasons for avoiding such a concept as *Man* and instead creating and sticking onto a word combination: *Dasein* (Ali, 2002). *Man* is insufficient in reaching and describing the being of humans. For Heidegger, Man (or human being) is not a noun in the same sense as for instance a house, a table or a tree. Man is also not just a class or species in the same sense as a horse or a sheep. Man can never be a mere representation of a species, because what makes his being possible (as a human) is not his species or class but first and foremost his being in the world and understanding of this being (King, 2001, p. 47).

There-Being (Dasein)

Da-sein (Eng. There-is) refers to human bring in at least three different ways. It can refer to the being that is characteristics of all human beings as entities, but also to a specific person. Moreover it is the *way of being* that is of concern (Ali, 2002). Above all it is part of Heidegger's attempt to reverse the Cartesian tradition in stating that individual subjects are always dependant on shared social practices (Dreyfus, 1991, pp. 14-15). What is particular in the being of *Dasein* is the questioning, interpreting, and understanding of its own being. This way of being, called existence, is shared by cultures, institutions, language, and human beings (Dreyfus, 1991). The emphasis in this sense is on the non-individual or collective nature of *Dasein* and the special connection *it* has with language (Ali, 2002). Language goes beyond every individual's experience and conveys the locally bound meanings of nature and things alike.

What is furthermore crucial about Heidegger is that he states that there are no beliefs to begin with, for there are only skills and practices, and once these are presumed to rest on beliefs, rules or principles we are already observing them objectively (Dreyfus, 1991, pp. 19-23). Human being is through and through in interpretation, for our practices and skills, cannot be grounded in human nature. According to Heidegger, this is where our radical rootlessness or homelessness, the feeling of being unsettled

(Unheimlich) stems from, and this is why we attempt to try to make ourselves feel at home and secure. Heidegger claims that in realizing that nothing is grounded, that there are no guidelines, *Dasein* learns increased openness, tenacity and even gaiety (Dreyfus, 1991, pp. 36-39). A change in Heidegger's early thinking of *Dasein's* fundamental homelessness evolves in his works towards his notion of dwelling as the essence of our being (Young, 2000, pp. 190-199).

Being-in-the-World

For *Dasein*, there-being, being-in is definitive, not an option. We can distinguish between two senses of the word *in*, in order to understand the meaning of our being-*in*-the-world, also known as *ek-sistence* or *transcendence* (Van Camp, 2012): the spatial sense and the existential sense. The former use conveys inclusion and the latter involvement (Dreyfus, 1991, pp. 42-44). *Dasein* is always already inside and involved with the world. There-being, interprets itself as the situation of involvement that it is in. This *being-in* ca be understood through the term *inhabiting* or *dwelling*. When we inhabit something, we feel at home in it, and this mode of being is not comparable with the relationship between subject and object. When we dwell in something, we are thoroughly involved with it and we relate with these objects, as well as relate to other people through this dwelling. In Heidegger's understanding, we are not detached observers as the philosophical tradition since the time of Plato has maintained. According to the tradition, human beings passively relate to objects by means of their experience (*Erleibnisse*), that is, through subjective mental states, yet according to Heidegger, human experience (*Erfahrung*) also actively discloses the world and discovers entities in it (Dreyfus, 1991, pp. 45-46).

According to Heidegger, our nature as human beings is to be world disclosers. This means that we open, by means of our equipment and coordinated practices, coherent, distinct contexts or worlds in which we perceive, act, and think. Each such world makes possible a distinct and pervasive way in which things, people, and selves can appear and in which certain ways of acting make sense (Dreyfus & Spinosa, 1997). This *we* refers to the collective being of *Dasein*, inseparable from its language, as well as its historical, social, and cultural ties. According to Heidegger (Ali, 2002), during the course of history in the West, our understanding of things, of being, has gone through roughly six epochs: (1) physis (as springing forth on their own, then on the basis of); (2) poeisis (or nurturing, when things were dealt with as needing help to come forth); (3) finished works, which in turn led to the understanding of all beings as; (4) creatures produced by a creator God; (5) objects that satisfy the desires of autonomous and stable subjects; and (6) the technological understanding of being (Dreyfus & Spinosa, 1997).

Technology-of-Being

What Heidegger is most concerned about in his later works is the question concerning technology. Heidegger's curiosity stems from the world that had then in the 1930s, and is still now, increasingly becoming a world filled with technical relations. These relations seem to live a life of their own, resulting in a shift in the kinds of historical events that can take place and the kinds of historical narratives that can be constructed, both of which have become detached from human living. Therefore, these technical relations appears to us as given, not invented (Hodge, 1995, pp. 35-36).

Heidegger begins to lead us away from the common understanding where we imagine ourselves as the masters of technology and as the creators that control. In other words, for Heidegger, technology is not the same as its instrumental definition, for it is more than the *means*, the machinery and the devices that we have invented to achieve certain *ends* in our lives. In the technological era, the dominant interpretation of nature comes through the natural sciences, which reveal nature to us as mere resources, stripped from other meaning. The reason Heidegger was concerned with technology was not technology in itself, as an object or collection of instruments, but the *relationship* we have with our surroundings and how that is inevitably affected by the technological age we live in. In this context of inquiry, technology is then not only applied science or engineering, it is the way *we take up the world* (Strong & Higgs, 2000, p. 25).

Enframing (Gestell)

Technology is a way of bringing-forth (*poiesis*), which for Heidegger is a way of revealing, and something the Greeks referred to as *alethia*, bringing something out of concealment into unconcelment. Moreover, this is what the Romans later referred to as *veritas* or as we say *truth*. Furthermore, technology is linked to *techne* (O'Brien, 2011) or *tekhne* (Van Camp, 2012), the Greek name for craftsmanship and skill, but also to knowing (*episteme*), in the sense of being entirely at home in something, to understand and be expert in it (Ali, 2002; Heidegger, 1977, pp. 11-13). Heidegger emphasizes that "what is decisive in *techne* does not lie at all in making and manipulation nor in the using of means, but rather in the aforementioned revealing. It is as revealing, and not as manufacturing, that *techne* is a bringing-forth" (Heidegger, 1977, p. 13). According to Heidegger, modern technology and modern physics are also modes of revealing, but the revealing that rules in them is a challenging, it is not bringing-forth in the sense of *poiesis*. Modern technology has the character of setting-upon, challenging-forth so that everything is ordered to stand by, to be there immediately at hand for further ordering, as standing-reserve (*Bestand*) (Heidegger, 1997, pp. 16-17).

Heidegger names this revealing as standing-reserve "Enframing" (*Gestell*) (Ali, 2002; Heidegger, 1977, p. 19). *Gestell* is usually translated as *enframing*, but sometimes is referred to as the *framework of technology*. It is within this framework of technology that humans are in a way forced to perceive the world as resources for standing purposes. It shows in the relationship between man and nature through science. Like most aspects of modern life, scientific research is essentially technological (Cooper, 2005, p. 348). Nature has been disenchanted, stripped from meanings, just waiting for science to come ever closer to thorough explanation and control.

In *Technology and the Character of Contemporary Life*, Albert Borgmann (1984) develops further, specific and gives a more practical account of Heidegger's interpretation of the essence of technology. The enframing for Borgmann becomes *the device paradigm* (Strong & Higgs, 2000, pp. 25). The observation of a repeated pattern in the contemporary life of technologically advanced societies is Borgmann's main concern. The common understanding of modern technology has a twofold aim: "it promises to bring forces of nature and culture under our control" (Borgmann, 1984, p. 41). To understand how the flaw in the promise of technology comes up, we must look at the difference between *things* and *devices*.

HUMAN ENHANCEMENT: BUSINESS (ETHICS AND LEGALITY)

Business, in general, according to Tran (2008b; Tran, 2014c), is defined as any organization (commercial or government) whose aim is to satisfy a set of customer requirements and is required to deliver results and provide value to the receiving customers, organizations and/or institutions. This is obviously a simplistic view of an organization, but in order to grasp the importance of processes it is critical to understand the importance of business processes to business success. It is also important to realize that regardless of the nature of an organization (e.g., commercial, government or others) the organization's operations and processes have to provide value to someone outside the organization. Starting from the business's place in the world will assist in building an understanding of how an organization must behave to serve its purpose and ultimately its external customers.[1]

When it comes to business ethics, according to Tran (2008b; Tran, 2014c), practitioners operate on the contractualist business ethics paradigm whereas the ethicists idolize a different typology paradigm. The contractualist paradigm is rooted in at least four factors. First, contractualist business ethics is blessed with a highly parsimonious conceptual apparatus. Second, this apparatus is also well adapted to its field of application. Third, the notion of contracting allows both positive and normative applications. Fourth, the idea that the norms that ought to govern everyday business ultimately derive from some form of consent that coheres well with a global public ordering in which liberal democracy and modern capitalism seem to emerge as dominant organizing principles. In addition, instrumental, prudential, and rule-based approaches will also be touched upon.

Ethicists, on the other hand, claim three paradigms: moral awareness, moral dilemmas, and moral laxity. First, the moral awareness paradigm is derived from behavioral models of ethical decision-making, which represent the first step in the ethical decision-making process. The core of the moral awareness paradigm is recognizing the existence of a moral problem in a situation. Second, moral dilemmas are based on the principal difficulty that it is hard to discover what one ought to do when facing a choice between non-overriding conflicting moral requirements or between non-overriding conflicting interests. However, many ethical problem cases are neither a compliance problem, nor a genuine moral dilemma. Moral laxity is the failure to identify particular opportunities and take significant steps toward realizing a broad moral goal whose worthiness is admitted.

Business Ethics: Science vs. Art

According to Tran (2008b; 2014c), ethics is not the study of morals, whether this word is used to designate conformity to conventional social rules or to the existing moral judgments of men. Although existing norms and judgments may contain valuable insights, ethics does not accept them, but sets out to critique and test them in terms of more universal norms. To put it another way, custom, convention, and the accepted courtesies of a society are not the foundations of ethics even though they can provide valuable hints as to what men think. For this reason, business ethics must study existing business codes to determine whether they have a solid foundation or only express the narrow consensus of a group or a sort of commercial etiquette.

Law enshrines many of the ethical judgments of a society but it is not coextensive with ethics. In the first place, law is generally concerned only with the minimum regulation necessary for public order, while ethics examines both the individual and the social good in all dimensions. In the second place, ethics critiques law as it does custom in an effort to obtain more perfect rules for the conduct of life. While the law demands great respect, it too is subject to the higher norms which ethics seeks to develop. In addition, since many people identify ethics with vague feelings of approval or disapproval, it should be noted that ethics does not rest on feelings but in the careful examination of the reality around us.

With that said, ethics is the science of judging specifically human goals and the relationship of means to those goals. In some way ethics is also the art of controlling means so that they will serve specifically human ends (Garrett, 1966). From this point of view, ethics involves the use of any human knowledge which has something to tell us about the relations between men or about the suitability of the available instruments. As an art, moreover, it involves techniques of judging and decision-making as well as the tools of social control and personal development[2]. Thus ethics really is or should be involved in all human activities.

Business ethics is concerned primarily with the relationship of business goals and techniques to specifically human ends. It studies the impacts of acts on the good of the individual, the firm, the business community, and society as a whole. While it does not concentrate on the obligations which man has as a private individual and a citizen, these enter in, since the businessman is not three separate persons. This means that business ethics studies the special obligations which a man and a citizen accept when he becomes a part of the world of commerce. As such, the meaning that we ordinarily attach to this term is that, ethics concerns judgments about conduct, and ethics is about what people do (Barry, 2000; Johnston, 1961). With that said, two points should be made clear: ethics is concerned with what ought to be done, and ethics is concerned with human conduct. Perhaps these points will seem obvious when stated, for failure to state them sometimes leads to confusion.

Business Defined: Practitioners' Paradigm

Business, in general, according to Tran (2008b; 2014c), is defined as any organization (commercial or government) whose aim is to satisfy a set of customer requirements and is required to deliver results and provide value to the receiving customers, organizations and/or institutions. This is obviously a simplistic view of an organization, but in order to grasp the importance of processes it is critical to understand the importance of business processes to business success. It is also important to realize that regardless of the nature of an organization (e.g., commercial, government or others) the organization's operations and processes have to provide value to someone outside the organization. Starting from the business's place in the world will assist in building an understanding of how an organization must behave to serve its purpose and ultimately its external customers.

BUSINESS ETHICS: THE TWO MEANINGS

The term business ethics is ambiguous (Tran, 2008b; Tran, 2014c). It has at least two different meanings with significantly different implications depending on its uses. The first use of the term business ethics appeals to people who have a strong sense of role morality, where individuals take on the behavior of the office that they hold rather than rely on their personal judgment. The second use of the term is that the understanding of business ethics makes no distinction among the different roles in our lives and in fact rejects the notion that we can divide our moral lives into discrete sections labeled "home, "family," "business," "romance," and so on, each with its distinct set of rules (Gibson, 1997). Instead, this view proposes that we have a single set of standards that apply throughout all aspects our lives.

With that said, the difference is that business presents us with new and different situations that require specialized assessment. Thus, relationships between producer and consumer may involve a set of considerations that do not apply to interactions between two people without the element of commercial interest. Nevertheless, the baseline of moral decency would be consistent throughout, and the same moral principles of justice, fairness, goodness, and what is right would hold in business as they do in our everyday dealings. By this light, the legal and ethical spheres may overlap, but we gauge correct action by personal morality rather than by reference to a legal code.

Instrumental, Prudential, or Rule-Based Approaches

Morality can be defined in terms of intrinsic and instrumental motivation. Those holding intrinsic views believe good should be done for its own sake whereas instrumentalists would look for some form of payoff by examining the situation to see what course of action would be most economically beneficial (Gibson, 1997). The moral motivation involved here is that there has to be a reward. Essentially, instrumental approaches are self-interested, since they are concerned mainly with personal or corporate benefits. The benefits need not be immediate.

The rewards for prudential actions may not come soon or be measured easily but that may not matter as long as the person involved believes in the reward system (Gibson, 1997). Hence a faithful believer might resist temptation, and do charitable works because of a promise of eternal salvation, even though there is no evidence that this will occur. As a practical matter the evidence is secondary to the individual's belief. We might say business dealings are analogous, because despite the difficulty in proving that a business will benefit by doing good works, it may become self-verifying if everyone involved in commerce adopts the belief as a matter of course. According to Gibson (1997), there is some anecdotal evidence that firms that act morally do better in the marketplace. As we have seen with reputation effects, the payoff might not be immediate, and so these things have to be looked at in the long term.

An alternative view, the rule-based, often associated with the economist Milton Friedman, is that following the law fulfills the moral requirements of business (Gibson, 1997). Based on this approach, the rationale suggests that business is out to make a profit, and it should do whatever it can to maximize returns. However, this view has some difficulties. Imagine a competitive world where everyone relied on the law as their gauge of appropriate behavior. In every transaction we would believe that the other party was predatory, and our only defense would be a close reading of settled law. It means that society would be deluged by lawmakers, regulators, and compliance officers, and a court system to adjudicate and punish. This illustrates that although we may feel that sharp dealing is commonplace, in fact most of our business dealings are done against a backdrop of trust.

Practitioners' Ethical Paradigm

In the world of practitioners, contractualism is one of the most promising centers of gravity in business ethics, and an everyday understanding of contractual commitment is one of the cornerstones on which modern business practices rest (Taylor, 1985). The relative success of contractualist thought is rooted in at least four factors. First, contractualist business ethics is blessed with a highly parsimonious conceptual apparatus. Second, this apparatus is also well adapted to its field of application. Third, the notion of contracting allows both positive and normative applications, and hence assures at least some degree of continuity between the world as we would like it to be and the world as we find it as a matter of fact. Fourth, the idea that the norms that ought to govern everyday business ultimately derive from some form of consent coheres well with a global public ordering in which liberal democracy and modern capitalism seem to merge as dominant organizing principles. The two dimensions which contribute to the contractualist tradition are: 1) positive versus normative and 2) four different levels of analysis that are commonly employed in contractualist.

ETHICAL CONCERNS IN HUMAN ENHANCEMENT: TECHONOLOGIES VS. HUMAN NATURE

Human enhancement refers to endeavors that are designed, or used to restore or improve human performance, thus overcoming the current limits of one's human body. Advances in fields such as biotechnology, engineering, neuroscience and computing bring the potential for novel enhancement technologies that could have significant implications for individuals and society. The development and use of these enhancements raise a range of scientific, engineering, social, political, ethical, economic, and regulatory issues. In considering the application of human enhancement to work, aside from the concern of its potential role in increasing the access of disabled people to work, is the concern of the issue of fairness and equity in corporations and organizational settings due to advantages received as a result of human enhancement. This debate mainly focused on: (1) the definition of enhancement and the distinction between enhancement and therapy; (2) the risks and benefits of enhancement for the individual; (3) privacy and autonomy issues; (4) possible transformations of personality; (5) the transcendence of given limitations; and (6) selfishness and issues of distributive justice (Chatterjee, 2006; Farah et al., 2002; Rose, 2002; Wolpe, 2002).

Given the preceding discussion it should be clear that human enhancement is more than just about the individual's freedom or autonomy, granted, the discussion has yet to truly become interdisciplinary in relations to business (as well as to corporations and organizational settings), but there are already plausibly negative consequences on others and society that need to be considered. While human enhancement has yet to make its presence known in corporations and organizational settings, corporations can definitely reflect on its presence and its reputation in the sporting industry, and how it will indeed make an impact in corporations in the near future. This is because human enhancement and enhancement technologies itself, is not a new concept, especially to the medical industry. The usage of human enhancement technologies are quite common in the medical field based on medical necessities, but, human enhancement has made its presence known to the sporting industry and rhetorically planted its roots in the sporting industry via questionable ethics. These issues point to the policy dilemma of whether we should have regulations or restrictions on human enhancement technologies, so to prevent, or mitigate some of the negative impacts considered. Take for example, prosthetics, a form of human enhancement, is generally defined as "the branch of medicine dealing with the production and use of artificial body parts[3]," which Oscar Pistorius is a highly visible example of the emergence of new prosthetic technologies. Prosthetic devices have also been designed for vision, touch, sound and sexual function (Karpin & Mykitiuk, 2008; Rodenburg, 2010).

In defining objectives for the use of a prosthetic device, "many practitioners distinguish between a device that is designed to repair a deficiency or pathologic condition to restore [them] to a normal state of health and fitness" (Lea, 2009) and one designed to enhance or augment the recipients' capabilities past that considered to be the normal capacity of a human (Conrad & Potter, 2004; Karpin & Mykitiuk, 2008; Lea, 2009; Miah, 2001), a distinction also referred to as "restorative" versus "additive" (Dyer, Noroozi, Sewell, & Redwood, 2010, 2011) and "therapy" versus "enhancement" (Karpin & Mykitiuk, 2008). The distinction is often used to label prosthetic interventions as legitimate when used as therapy, or ethically suspect when used as enhancement (Karpin & Mykitituk, 2008; Rodenburg, 2010) in part, perhaps because it potentially serves the commercial interests of insurers and Health Maintenance Organizations (HMOs) which cover "repair" but not "enhancement" (Rodenburg, 2010). The ethics of prosthetics has generally been considered with the context of a therapeutic/enhancement dichotomy, with normative criteria around "able-bodied" capabilities determining the distinction between acceptable and non-acceptable usage. That comfortable distinction was challenged by Oscar Pistorius in his effort to win a berth on the South African Olympic team using "Cheetah" Prosthetics.

The result was an inconclusive series of experiments that failed to clarify the position of the Cheetah prosthetic as a therapeutic measure or enhancer. That position is generally considered critical for a number of ethical considerations with respect to prosthetic usage in sport, specifically around the issue of "fair competition" between anthro-morphological equivalents (Rodenburg, 2010). Although primarily concerned with orthopedic intervention and prosthetics, Lea (2009) identifies three ethical issues related to the use of biotechnologies and performance enhancement in sport, something Lea refers to as "techno-doping" unfair competitive advantage, personal and public harm, and the spirit of sport and competition. Nevertheless, one of the most meaningful outcomes of the Oscare Pistorius case was a recognition of the need to reliably, and in ethical terms, distinguish between "fair competition" and "unfair competitive advantage" when dealing with prosthetic devices (Lea, 2009). The concept of fairness can be constituted to have a number of meanings in a number of contexts including the right of the disabled athlete to compete "on par" with able-bodied athletes without discrimination (Lea, 2009; Zettler, 2009). However, fairness can also mean the rights of the economically disadvantaged to compete "on par" with economically more privileged athletes through the use of similarly advanced equipment technology (Dyer, Noroozi, Sewell, & Redwood, 2010, 2011), although a distinction is usually made between "enhancements of equipment and enhancements done directly to the body" (Lea, 2009).

Dyer, Noroozi, Sewell, and Redwood (2010, 2011) argue that the issue of determining fairness, the net neutrality with respect to competitive advantages, of a given prosthetic device such as the Cheetah may never be known, and that some form of hybrid evaluative framework including both quantitative and qualitative variables must be utilized to regulate the inclusion or exclusion of specific prostheses in sport. In fact, they suggest that some level of performance enhancement already exists with disability running, given the variability in performance profiles between existing prosthetics and the fact that access to top performing prosthetics is not evenly distributed. A second ethical issue identified by Lea (2009), personal and/or public harm, is essentially the point at which personal autonomy conflicts with public and personal safety (Bostrom & Sandberg, 2006; Farah, 2005; Farah et al., 2004). Is it ethical, for example, for an athlete to use a prosthetic when its use may endanger other competitive athletes, or for an otherwise healthy pitcher to request elbow reconstruction as a way of facilitating faster throwing and faster recovery? The final ethical issue that Lea (2009) identifies, the spirit of sport and competition, rests on whether or not the perception of competitive legitimacy—and its attendant attributes of participation, courage, dedication and commitment—is supported by or hindered by the adoption of enhancement technologies.

Human Enhancement: Neuro-Cognitive and Advantages in Corporations

If prosthetics represent an ethically ambiguous "new world" of able-bodied participations, then neuro-cognitive enhancements represent a "brave new world" of able-minded participation with all of the potential for subjugation and liberation that the label implies (Vedder & Klaming, 2010). The sense of increased intimacy in manipulating the essence of ourselves that neuro-cognitive agents suggest, however, belies that fact that we have been actively manipulating the brain therapeutically for many decades, even if the precise mechanisms by which anti-psychotics and other psychotropic interventions work are only now beginning to be elucidated (Vedder & Klaming, 2010). The emerging technology of psycho-pharmacology, the movement from serendipitous discovery to the "science of rational drug design" (Farah, Illes, Cook-

Deegan, Gardner, Kandel, King, Parens, Sahakian, & Wolpe, 2004; Vedder & Klaming, 2010; Wolpe, 2002), represents only one dimension of the cognitive interventions that are now becoming possible (Farah, Illes, Cook-Deegan, Gardner, Kandel, King, Parens, Sahakian, & Wolpe, 2004). Far from being purely therapeutic in nature, new drugs are being developed to directly target cognitive functioning and memory enhancement, although the overall beneficial effects of these remain in doubt (de Jongh & Ten-Broeke, 2007). Other emerging "non-pharmacological" neuro-cognitive enhancements include direct machine/neural interfaces, neural grafting and genomic neural enhancement, enhancements that can be labelled neuro-cognitive prosthetics (Farah et al., 2004; Vedder & Klaming, 2010; Wolpe, 2002).

Two other ethical issues to take on a special significance, however, given the relationship between neural functioning and the self. These include authenticity, personal identity and "intangible values" (de Jongh & Ten-Broeke, 2007; Farah et al., 2004) and the issue of human "flourishing" or potential (de Jong & Ten-Broeke, 2007). Since neuro-cogivitve enhancers do have the capacity to alter cognition, mood states and character attributes, the result may be, as Karpin and Mykitiuk (2008) clearly identify, the emergence of an enforced, dictatorial normative standard for person-hood and behavior that both dehumanizes and marginalizes those who do not conform, effectively compromising personal authenticity (de Jongh & Ten-Broeke, 3007; Farah et al., 2004; Turner & Sahakian, 2006). A related consequence is that the compromise of human dignity and "what is naturally human," including empathy, although transhumanists would suggest that we have a "moral duty" to enhance the human condition to meet full potential (de Jongh & Ten-Broeke, 2007).

Given the direct impact of neuro-cognitive manipulation on person-hood, the ethics of neuro-cognitive enhancement would seem to be critical relevance to the ethics of enhancement generally. What is clear from the discussion concerning neuro-cognitive enhancement, however, is that the technology is emerging at a faster pace than ethical frameworks are evolving (de Jongh & Ten-Broeke, 2007), a situation that seems common to all enhancement technologies. That current and emerging pharmacological intervention is always beneficial is not definitively clear based on empirical evidence, but, as recent research has shown, we are already past the point of demonstrating that direct brain machine interfaces are possible. The ethical issues at play are also similar to those that are involved with prosthetic devices: safety, distribution and access, the potential for societal coercion and the therapeutic/enhancement distinction. Additional ethical concerns of specific relevance to neuro-cognitive enhancement, however, include the impact on personal identity and the authenticity of the person, as well as the fulfillment of human potential.

HUMAN ENHANCEMENT: MACHINE-HUMAN INTERFACE ETHICAL ISSUES

In the field on human enhancement, there exist two paradigms of ethics, machine ethics (Allen, Wallach, & Smit, 2006) [also known as machine morality (Wallach, Allen, & Smit, 2008)] and machine-human interface ethics. The first paradigm of ethics, machine ethics, evolved within the last decade or so, due to an increase in the field of computer science concerned with the application of ethics to machines that have some degree of autonomy in their action. Variants under names, according to Yampolskiy (2013), such as machine ethics (Allen, Wallach, & Smit, 2006; Anderson & Anderson, 2007; Hall, 2007; McDermott, 2008; Moor, 2006; Tonkens, 2009) computer ethics (Pierce & Henry, 1996), robot ethics (Lin, Abney, & Bekey, 2011; Sawyer, 2007; Sharkey, 2008), ethicsALife (Wallach & Allen, 2006), machine morals (Wallach & Allen, 2008), Cyborg ethics (Warwick, 2004), computational ethics (Ruvinsky, 2007), roboethics (Veruggio, 2010), robot rights (Guo & Zhang, 2009), artificial morals (Allen, Smit, & Wallach, 2005), and Friendly AI (Yudkowsky, 2008) are some of the proposals meant to address society's concerns with the ethical and safety implications of ever more advanced machines (Sparrow, 2007). The machine ethics paradigm is applicable to the field of Artificial Moral Agents (AMAs) (Shulman, Jonsson, & Tarleton, 2009; Wallach, Allen, & Smit, 2008).

The second paradigm of ethics, machine-human interface ethics, evolved within the field of human enhancement, where machine and human are joined (e.g., Friedman & Kahn, 2003; Lebedev & Nicolelis, 2006; Warwick & Ruiz, 2008). The machine-human interface ethics is the main focus of human enhancement ethics at hand. Ethical debates about human enhancements (Warwick & Battistella, 2008) have taken place within various bodies of literature, including bioethics, animal ethics, environmental ethics, political science and the social study of medicine. Each of these areas approach the significance of human enhancement from quite different perspectives. For example, Dvorsky (2009) argues that the capacity to enhance human biology must also imply an obligation to *uplift* the capacities of other animals as well. Alternatively, bioethicists have argued that the possibility of human enhancement requires us to consider what sort of people there should be, alluding to the prospective use of germ line genetic modifications or selection. To this extent, there is no single set of ethical issues that is engaged by all possible forms of enhancement. As such, genetic enhancement is likely to have different implications from using a pharmaceutical product, or a prosthetic device to yield a similar effect. Indeed, debates about the ethics of human enhancement are already so nuanced as to be focused on specific kinds of enhancement, such as neurological, biochemical, or physiological modifications.

Furthermore, it is necessary to clarify the relationship between *moral* and *ethical*, as they are often conflated within debates about human enhancement (Friedman & Kahn, 2003). Generally, speaking, one would discuss ethical issues in the context of a specific practice community, such as the ethical code underpinning medical practice. Alternatively, morality is concerned with broader questions of value for which there may be no formal codes that are broken. In cases of moral violations, it is more difficult to determine whether any specific principle has been violated by an action, or whether the moral concerns arising from this are, overall, outweigh the benefits that may arise from it. To this end, it is more difficult to derive an uncontested answer as to what people ought to do, which is why a common response to difficult ethical dilemmas is to rely on consensus of opinion, via some form of representative democratic decision. Nevertheless, one may find assistance in deriving ethical principles by studying human societies and the norms that have emerged around behavior within culture (Friedman & Kahn, 2003). Through subjecting such discoveries to a process of philosophical scrutiny, one may develop a clearer sense of the ethical principles that should govern decision making within practical contexts. Moreover, by examining the practice communities where ethical decision making takes place, it may be more clear which of these principles are most salient. In this respect, effective ethical reasoning requires taking into account both normative ethical principles and practical ethical decision making (Miah, 2011).

An alternative route towards establishing an ethical framework of human enhancements is to examine how the debate has taken place thus far within a range of intellectual spheres—in both theory and practice—and to provide some form of synthesis of the arguments and concerns (Friedman & Kahn, 2003; Lebedev & Nicolelis, 2006; Warwick & Ruiz, 2008). One of the challenges with this approach is that there is no consensus over which ethical issues are the most salient (Miah, 2011). Nevertheless, a review of the literature reveals clear trends in what are seen by many commentators to be key concerns and it is useful to build on this previous research. This is most adequately summarized in Allhoff, Lin, Moor, and Weckert (2009), which frames the ethics of human enhancement under the following categories: Freedom and Autonomy, Fairness and Equality, Societal Disruption, Human Dignity and Good

Life, Rights and Obligations, Policy and Law (Allhoff et al., 2099; Friedman, 1997; Jebari, 2013; Kahn, 1992, 1999; Leveson, 1991; Moore, 1998; Thomas, 1975; Turiel, 1983). Yet, one of the difficulties with this approach is that it does not distinguish between the different levels of decision making that operate around ethical dilemmas, from the individual to the societal.

In response, the following sections provide an overreaching analysis of the various approaches to articulating the ethical issues that are engaged by human enhancements. It is structured in terms of three primary categories, which provide a useful heuristic through which to identify types of ethical concern. The assumption is not that these three domains can be neatly separated, but that there is value in delimiting ethical issues in terms of what Singer (1981) describes as the *expanding circle* of moral concern. Thus, separating these concerns out into distinct units may assist in clarifying where the ethical dilemma resides and what kind of action—individual, professional or societal—is required. *Individual* ethical issues relates directly to the interest of the subject who is undertaking the enhancement themselves. The *professional concerns* category relates to the individual or institution that is facilitating the enhancement, whereby there may be formal guidelines over ethical conduct. The *societal concerns* relate to the broad interests of society, which may be frustrated by the adoption of human enhancement. Within each of these categories, individual moral concepts are engaged in slightly different ways (Friedman & Kahn, 2003). For instance, an individual may consider whether they find that an entire population may consider whether it will improve society to permit such surgery. In each case, the balance of reasoning will differ considerably, while the ethical principle may remain the same.

In closing, it is important to recognize that individual actions take place within specific societal contexts, which can, in turn, dictate how one evaluates the moral content of any human enhancement (Friedman & Kahn, 2003; Lebedev & Nicolelis, 2006; Warwick & Ruiz, 2008). This may appear to be a morally relativist position, but it, in fact, acknowledges the possibility of universal moral rules, while recognizing that not all decisions are taken within the same conditions. This is best explained by providing two examples where the same kind of human enhancement is used. Thus, consider the creation of a new prosthetic leg, which may be used by two different people, one is an elite athlete, the other is not. If one assumes that, in both cases, the prosthetic device can make a person run much faster than any other person—whether or not they are considered disabled—then it is immediately apparent how, for the athlete, this may pose an ethical dilemma which is not evident for the non-athlete. The latter is interested in functionality, in day-to-day living, and is not in direct competition with any other person who may feel that the new limb creates some form of unfairness. However, the athlete is engaged in a practice whereby the interests of the other participants may be frustrated by the use of this new technological device, in part because a prior agreement had been made between parties about how they would participate (Miah, 2011).

CONCLUSION

Human enhancement can be understood to be different from therapy, which is about treatments aimed at pathologies that compromise health or reduce one's level of functioning below this species-typically or statistically-normal level (Juengst, 1997). Another way to think about human enhancement technologies, as opposed to therapy is that they change the structure and function of the body (Greely, 2006). As such, by human enhancement we do not mean the mere use of tools; that would render the concept impotent, turning everything we do into cases of human enhancement. But if and when these tools are integrated into our bodies, rather than employed externally, then we will consider them to be instances of human enhancement. Admittedly, none of these definitions is immune to objections, but they are nevertheless useful as starting point in thinking about the distinction, including whether there really is such a distinction.

Given the preceding discussion it should be clear that human enhancement is more than just about the individual's freedom or autonomy, granted, the discussion has yet to truly become interdisciplinary in relations to business (as well as to corporations and organizational settings), but there are already plausibly negative consequences on others and society that need to be considered. While human enhancement has yet to make its presence known in corporations and organizational settings, corporations can definitely reflect on its presence and its reputation in the sporting industry, and how it will indeed make an impact in corporations in the near future. This is because human enhancement and enhancement technologies itself, is not a new concept, especially to the medical industry. The usage of human enhancement technologies are quite common in the medical field based on medical necessities, but, human enhancement has made its presence known to the sporting industry and rhetorically planted its roots in the sporting industry via questionable ethics.

This is because in human enhancement, many practitioners distinguish between "a device that is designed to repair a deficiency or pathologic condition to restore [them] to a normal state of health and fitness" (Lea, 2009) and one designed to enhance or augment the recipients' capabilities past that considered to be the normal capacity of a human (Karpin & Mykitiuk, 2008; Lea, 2009; Miah, 2001). Nevertheless, one of the most meaningful outcomes of the Oscare Pistorius case was a recognition of the need to reliably, and in ethical terms, distinguish between "fair competition" and "unfair competitive advantage" when dealing with prosthetic devices (Lea, 2009). The concept of fairness can be constituted to have a number of meanings in a number of contexts including the right of the disabled athlete to compete "on par" with able-bodied athletes without discrimination (Lea, 2009; Zettler, 2009). However, translating this concept of fair competition and unfair competitive advantage, from the sport industry to the corporations, is closer than one may believe.

REFERENCES

Ali, S. M. (2002). The end of the Dreyfus affair: (Post) Heideggererian meditations on man, machine and meaning. *International Journal of Cognitive Technology, 1*(1), 85–96. doi:10.1075/ijct.1.1.06ali

Allen, C., Smit, I., & Wallach, W. (2005). Artificial morality: Top-down, bottom-up, and hybrid approaches. *Ethics and Information Technology, 7*(3), 149–155. doi:10.1007/s10676-006-0004-4

Allen, C., Wallach, W., & Smit, I. (2006). Why machine ethics? *IEEE Intelligent Systems, 21*(4), 12–17. doi:10.1109/MIS.2006.83

Allhoff, F. (2005). Germ-line genetic enhancement and rawlsian primary goods. *Kennedy Institute of Ethics Journal, 15*(1), 43–60. doi:10.1353/ken.2005.0007 PMID:15881795

Allhoff, F., Lin, P., Moor, J., & Weckert, J. (2009). *Ethics of human enhancement: 25 questions & answers.* U.S. National Science Foundation.

Allhoff, F., Lin, P., & Steinberg, J. (2011). Ethics of human enhancement: An executive summary. *Science and Engineering Ethics*, *17*(2), 201–212. doi:10.1007/s11948-009-9191-9 PMID:20094921

Anderson, M., & Anderson, S. L. (2007). Machine ethics: Creating an ethical intelligent agent. *AI Magazine*, *28*(4), 15–26.

Bailey, R. (2005). *Liberation biology: The scientific and moral case for biotech revolution*. Amherst, NY: Promrtheus Books.

Barry, N. (2000). *Business ethics*. West Lafayett, IN: Purdue University Press.

Borgmann, A. (1984). *Technology and the character of contemporary life*. Chicago, IL: University of Chicago Press.

Bostrom, N. (2005). A history of transhumanist thought. *Journal of Evolution & Technology*, *14*(1), 1–25.

Bostrom, N., & Roache, R. (2008). Ethical issues in human enhancement. In J. Ryberg, T. Petersen, & C. Wolf (Eds.), *New waves in applied ethics* (pp. 120–152). Pelgrave MacMillan.

Bostrom, N., & Sandberg, A. (2006). *Cognitive enhancement: Methods, ethics, regulatory challenges*. Retrieved from http://www.nickbostrom.com/cognitive.pdf

Bostrom, N., & Savulescu, J. (2008). Human enhancement ethics: The state of the debate. In J. Savulescu & N. Bostrom (Eds.), *Human enhancement* (pp. 1–22). Oxford University Press.

Chatterjee, A. (2006). The promise and predicament of cosmetic neurology. *Journal of Medical Ethics*, *32*(2), 110–113. doi:10.1136/jme.2005.013599 PMID:16446417

Conference of European Churches. (2010). *Human enhancement—A discussion document*. Conference of European Churches: Church & Society Commission. Retrieved from http://csc.ceceurope.org/fileadmin/filer/csc/Ethics_Biotechnology/Human_Enhancement_March_10.pdf

Conrad, P., & Potter, D. (2004). Human growth hormone and the temptations of biomedical enhancement. *Sociology of Health & Illness*, *26*(2), 184–215. doi:10.1111/j.1467-9566.2004.00386.x PMID:15027984

Cooper, D. E. (2005). Heidegger on nature. *Environmental Values*, *14*(3), 339–351. doi:10.3197/096327105774434495

Daniels, N. (2000). Normal functioning and the treatment-enhancement distinction. *Cambridge Quarterly of Healthcare Ethics*, *9*(3), 309–322. doi:10.1017/S0963180100903037 PMID:10858880

de Gray, A. (2007). *Ending aging: The rejuvenation breakthroughs that could reserve human aging in our lifetime*. New York: Saint Martin's Press.

de Jongh, A., & Ten-Broeke, E. (2007). Treatment of specific phobia with EMDR: Conceptualization and strategies for selection of appropriate memories. *Journal of EMDR Practice and Research*, *1*(1), 46–57. doi:10.1891/1933-3196.1.1.46

Dreyfus, H. L. (1991). *Being-in-the-world: A commentary on Heidegger's being and time (Division 1)*. Cambridge, MA: The MIT Press.

Dreyfus, H. L., & Spinosa, C. (1997). *Highway bridges and feasts: Heidegger and Borgmann on how to affirm technology*. Retrieved from http://socrates.berkeley.edu/~hdreyfus/html/paper_highway.html

Dvorsky, G. (2009). All together now: Developmental and ethical considerations for biologically uplifting nonhuman animals. *Journal of Evolution and Technology*, *18*(1), 129–142.

Dyer, B. T. J., Noroozi, S., Sewell, P., & Redwood, S. (2010). The design of lower-limb sports prostheses: Fair inclusion in disability sport. *Disability & Society*, *25*(5), 593–602. doi:10.1080/09687599.2010.489309

Dyer, B. T. J., Noroozi, S., Sewell, P., & Redwood, S. (2011). The fair use of lower-limb running prostheses: A delphi study. *Adapted Physical Activity Quarterly; APAQ*, *28*(1), 16–26. PMID:21282845

Farah, M. J. (2005). Neuroethics: The practical and the philosophical. *Trends in Cognitive Sciences*, *9*(1), 34–40. doi:10.1016/j.tics.2004.12.001 PMID:15639439

Farah, M. J., Illes, J., Cook-Deegan, R., Gardner, H., Kandel, E., & King, P. et al. (2004). Neurocognitive enhancement: What we can do and what should we do. *Nature Reviews. Neuroscience*, *5*(5), 421–425. doi:10.1038/nrn1390 PMID:15100724

Ferrari, A., Coenen, C., & Grunwald, A. (2012). Visions and ethics in current discourse on human enhancement. *NanoEthics*, *6*(3), 215–229. doi:10.1007/s11569-012-0155-1

Friedman, B. (1997). *Human values and the design of computer technology*. New York: Cambridge University Press.

Friedman, B., & Kahn, P. H. Jr. (2003). Human Values, ethics, and design. In J. A. Jacko & A. Sears (Eds.), *The human-computer interaction handbook* (pp. 1177–1201). Hillsdale, NJ: L. Erlbaum Associates Inc.

Garrett, T. M. (1966). *Business ethics*. New York, NY: Meredith Publishing Company.

Gibson, K. (1997). *Ethics and business. An introduction*. Cambridge University Press.

Glover, J. (1984). *What sort of people should there be?* Penguin Books.

Greely, H. T. (2005). Regulating human biological enhancements: Questions justifications and international complications. *The Mind, The Body, and The Law: University of Technology. The Sydney Law Review*, *4*(2), 87–110.

Greely, H. T. (2006). Regulating human biological enhancements: Questions justifications and international complications. *Santa Clara Journal of International Law*, *4*(2), 87–110.

Griffiths, A. J. F., Wessler, S. R., Lewontin, R. C., & Carroll, S. B. (9th Ed.). (2007). *Introduction to genetic analysis* W. H. Freeman and Company.

Guo, S., & Zhang, G. (2009). Robot rights. *Science*, *323*(5916), 876. doi:10.1126/science.323.5916.876a PMID:19213895

Guston, D., Parsi, J., & Tosi, J. (2007). Anticipating the ethical and political challenges of human nanotechnologies. In F. Allhoff, P. Lin, J. Moor, J. Weckert, & M. C. Roco (Eds.), *Nanoethics: The ethical and social implications of nanotechnology* (pp. 185–198). Hoboken, NJ: John Wiley & Sons, Inc.

Hall, J. S. (2007). *Beyond IA: Creating the conscience of the machine*. Amherst, NY: Promrtheus.

Harris, J. (2007). *Enhancing evolution: The ethical case for making ethical people*. Princeton: Princeton University Press.

Heidegger, M. (1977). The question concerning technology. InW. Lovitt (Ed.), The question concerning technology and other essays (trans.) (pp. 3-35). New York: Harper & Row.

Hill, S. E. (2006). *Dissatisfied by design: The evolution of discontent*. Dissertation. University of Texas, Austin, TX.

Hodge, J. (1995). *Heidegger and ethics*. London: Routledge.

Horton, R. (2004). Rediscovering human dignity. *Lancet*, *364*(9439), 1081–1085. doi:10.1016/S0140-6736(04)17065-7 PMID:15380969

Jebari, K. (2013). Brain machine interface and human enhancement—An ethical review. *Neuroethics*, *6*(3), 617–625. doi:10.1007/s12152-012-9176-2

Johnston, H. (2nd Ed.). (1961). *Business ethics* Pitman Publishing Corporation.

Juengst, E. (1997). Can enhancement be distinguished from prevention in genetic medicine? *The Journal of Medicine and Philosophy*, *22*(2), 125–142. doi:10.1093/jmp/22.2.125 PMID:9186925

Kahn, P. H. Jr. (1992). Children's obligatory and discretionary moral judgments. *Child Development*, *63*(2), 416–430. doi:10.2307/1131489 PMID:1611944

Kahn, P. H. Jr. (1999). *The human relationship with nature: Development and culture*. Cambridge, MA: MIT Press.

Karpin, I., & Mykitiuk, R. (2008). Going out on a limb: Prosthetics, normalcy and disputing the therapy/enhancement distinction. *Medical Law Review*, *16*(3), 413–436. doi:10.1093/medlaw/fwn018 PMID:18635592

King, M. (2001). *A guide to Heidegger's being and time*. State University of New York.

Koepsell, D. (2007). *The ethics of genetic engineering: A position paper from the center for inquiry office of public policy*. Washington, DC: Center for Inquiry.

Kurzweil, R. (2005). *The singularity is near: When humans transcend biology*. New York: Viking Penguin.

Lea, R. D. (2009). Ethical considerations of biotechnologies used for performance enhancement. *The Journal of Bone and Joint Surgery*, *91*(8), 2048–2054. doi:10.2106/JBJS.I.00023 PMID:19651979

Lebedev, M. A., & Nicolelis, M. A. L. (2006). Brain machine interfaces: Past, present and future. *Trends in Neurosciences*, *29*(9), 536–546. doi:10.1016/j.tins.2006.07.004 PMID:16859758

Lee, P., & George, R. P. (2008). The nature and basis of human dignity. *Ratio Juris*, *21*(2), 173–193. doi:10.1111/j.1467-9337.2008.00386.x

Leveson, N. G. (1991). Software safety in embedded computer systems. *Communications of the ACM*, *34*(2), 34–46. doi:10.1145/102792.102799

Lin, P., Abney, K., & Bekey, G. (2011). Robot ethics: Mapping the issues for a mechanized world. *Artificial Intelligence*, *175*(5/6), 942–949. doi:10.1016/j.artint.2010.11.026

Lin, P., & Allhoff, F. (2008). Untangling the debate: The ethics of human enhancement. *NanoEthics*, *2*(3), 251–264. doi:10.1007/s11569-008-0046-7

McDermott, D. (2008). Why ethics is a high hurdle for AI. Paper presented at the *North American Conference on Computers and Philosophy*, Bloomington, IN.

Miah, A. (2001). Genetic technologies and sport: The new ethical issue. *Journal of the Philosophy of Sport*, *28*(1), 32–52. doi:10.1080/00948705.2001.9714599

Miah, A. (2011). Ethical issues raised by human enhancement. In F. Gonzalez (Ed.), *Values and ethics for the 21ˢᵗ century* (pp. 199–231). Spain: Fundacion BBVA.

Moor, J. H. (2006). The nature, importance, and difficulty of machine ethics. *IEEE Intelligent Systems*, *21*(4), 18–21. doi:10.1109/MIS.2006.80

Moore, A. D. (1998). Intangible property: Privacy, power, and information control. *American Philosophical Quarterly*, *35*(4), 365–378.

Myskaja, B. K. (2006). The moral difference between intragenic and transgenic modification of plants. *Journal of Agricultural & Environmental Ethics*, *19*(3), 225–238. doi:10.1007/s10806-005-6164-0 PMID:17061380

Naam, R. (2005). *More than human*. New York: Broadway Books.

Nozick, R. (1974). *Anarchy, state, and utopia*. New York: Basic Books.

O'Brien, M. (2011). The future of humanity: Heidegger, personhood and technology. *Comparative Philosophy*, *2*(2), 23–49.

O'Mathuna, D. P. (2013). Human dignity and the ethics of human enhancement. *Trans-Humanities*, *6*(1), 99–120.

Parfit, D. (1986). *Reasons and persons*. New York: Oxford University Press. doi:10.1093/019824908X.001.0001

Peters, T. (2007). Are we playing god with nanoenhancement? In F. Allhoff, P. Lin, J. Moore, & J. Weckert (Eds.), *Nanoethics: The ethical and social implications of nanotechnology*. Hoboken, NJ: John Wiley & Sons.

Pierce, M. A., & Henry, J. W. (1996). Computer ethics: The role of personal, informal, and formal codes. *Journal of Business Ethics*, *14*(4), 425–437. doi:10.1007/BF00380363

Pinker, S. (2008). *The stupidity of dignity*. The New Republic. Retrieved from http://www.newrepublic.com/article/the-stupidity-dignity#

President's Council on Bioethics. (2003). *Beyond therapy: Biotechnology and the pursuit of happiness*. Washington, DC: Government Printing Office.

Rawls, J. (1971). *A theory of justice*. Cambridge, MA: Belknap.

Rescher, N. (1980). The canons of distributive justice. In J. P. Sterba (Ed.), *Justice: Alternative political perspectives*. Belmont, CA: Wadsworth Publishing Company.

Rodenburg, D. (2010). Resistance is futile—Confronting the ethics of the "enhanced human" athlete. Retrieved from http://www.ischool.utoronto.ca/system/files/pages/docs/itable/RodenburgResistance.pdf

Rose, S. P. R. (2002). Smart drugs: Do they work? Are they ethical? Will they be legal? *Nature Reviews. Neuroscience*, *3*(12), 975–979. doi:10.1038/nrn984 PMID:12461554

Ruvinsky, A. I. (2007). Computational ethics. In M. Quigley (Ed.), *Encyclopedia of information ethics and security* (pp. 73–76). Hersey, PA: IGI Global. doi:10.4018/978-1-59140-987-8.ch012

Sandel, M. (2007). *The case against perfection: Ethics in the age of genetic engineering*. Cambridge, MA: Belknap Press.

Sawyer, R. J. (2007). Robot ethics. *Science*, *318*(5853), 1037. doi:10.1126/science.1151606 PMID:18006710

Sharkey, N. (2008). The ethical frontiers of robotic. *Science*, *322*(5909), 1800–1801. doi:10.1126/science.1164582 PMID:19095930

Shulman, C., Jonsson, H., & Tarleton, N. (2009). Which consequentialism? Machine ethics and moral divergence. In *AP-CAP 2009: The fifth Asia-Pacific Computing and Philosophy Conference*, University of Tokyo, Japan.

Singer, P. (1981). *The expanding circle: Ethics and sociobiology*. New York: Farrar, Straus and Giroux.

Sparrow, R. (2007). Killer robots. *Journal of Applied Philosophy*, *24*(1), 62–77. doi:10.1111/j.1468-5930.2007.00346.x

Strong, D., & Higgs, E. (2000). Borgmann's philosophy of technology. In E. Higgs, A. Light, & D. Strong (Eds.), *Technology and the good life?* (pp. 19–37). Chicago, London: The University of Chicago Press. doi:10.7208/chicago/9780226333885.003.0002

Taylor, C. (1985). *Philosophy and the human sciences*. Cambridge: Cambridge University Press. doi:10.1017/CBO9781139173490

Thomas, J. (1975). The right to privacy. *Philosophy & Public Affairs*, *4*(4), 295–314.

Tonkens, R. (2009). A challenge for machine ethics. *Minds and Machines*, *19*(3), 421–438. doi:10.1007/s11023-009-9159-1

Tran, B. (2008a). *Expatriate selection and retention*. Doctoral dissertation, Alliant International University, San Francisco, CA.

Tran, B. (2008b). Paradigms in corporate ethics: The legality and values of corporate ethics. *A Special Issue of Social Responsibility Journal. Ethics and Morality in Business Practice*, *4*(1/2), 158–171.

Tran, B. (2013). Industrial and organizational (I/O) psychology: The roles and purposes of I/O practitioners in global businesses. In B. Christiansen, E. Turkina, & N. Williams (Eds.), *Cultural and technological influences on global business* (pp. 175–219). Hersey, PA: Premier Reference Source/IGI Global. doi:10.4018/978-1-4666-3966-9.ch011

Tran, B. (2014a). The human element of the knowledge worker: Identifying, managing, and protecting the intellectual capital within knowledge management. In M. A. Chilton & J. M. Bloodgood (Eds.), *Knowledge management for competitive advantage: Issues and potential solutions* (pp. 281–303). Hersey, PA: Premier Reference Source/IGI Global. doi:10.4018/978-1-4666-4679-7.ch017

Tran, B. (2014b). Rhetoric of play: Utilizing the gamer factor in selecting and training employees. In T. M. Connolly, L. Boyle, T. Hainey, G. Baxter, & P. Moreno-Ger (Eds.), *Psychology, pedagogy and assessment in serious games* (pp. 175–203). Hersey, PA: Premier Reference Source/IGI Global. doi:10.4018/978-1-4666-4773-2.ch009

Tran, B. (2014c). Game theory versus business ethics: The game of ethics. In B. Christiansen & M. Basilgan (Eds.), *Economic behavior, game theory, and technology in emerging markets* (pp. 213–236). Hersey, PA: Premier Reference Source/IGI Global. doi:10.4018/978-1-4666-4745-9.ch012

Turiel, E. (1983). *The development of social knowledge*. Cambridge, England: Cambridge University Press.

Turner, D. C., & Sahakian, B. J. (2006). Neuroethics of cognitive enhancement. *Biosocieties*, *1*(1), 113–123. doi:10.1017/S1745855205040044

Van Camp, N. (2012). Heidegger and the question concerning biotechnology. *Journal of Philosophy of Life*, *2*(1), 32–54.

Vedder, A. H., & Klaming, L. (2010). Human enhancement for the common good: Using neurotechnologies to improve eyewitness memory. *American Journal of Bioethics Neuroscience*, *1*(3), 22–33.

Veruggio, G. (2010). Roboethics. *IEEE Robotics & Automation Magazine*, *17*(2), 105–109. doi:10.1109/MRA.2010.936959

Wallace, W., Allen, C., & Smit, I. (2008). Machine morality: Bottoms-up and top-down approaches for modelling human moral faculties. *Ethics and Artificial Agents: Special Issue of AI & Society*, *22*(4), 565–582.

Wallance, W., & Allen, C. (2006). EthicALife: A new field of inquiry. Paper presented at the *AnAlifeX workshop*, USA.

Wallance, W., & Allen, C. (2008). *Moral machines: Teaching robots right from wrong*. Oxford, UK: Oxford University Press.

Warwick, K. (2004). Cyborg morals, cyborg values, cyborg ethics. *Ethics and Information Technology*, *5*(3), 131–137. doi:10.1023/B:ETIN.0000006870.65865.cf

Warwick, K. & Battistella, C. (2008). Four weddings and a funeral: Ethical issues surrounding the future of brain computer interfacing. *Rivista di filosofia fondata da Vittorio Sainati, 51(3)*, 176-195.

Warwick, K., & Ruiz, V. (2008). On linking human and machine brains. *Neurocomputing*, *71*(13/15), 2619–2624. doi:10.1016/j.neucom.2007.06.017

Williams, B. (1973). *Problems of the self*. Cambridge, UK: Cambridge University Press. doi:10.1017/CBO9780511621253

Wolpe, P. R. (2002). Treatment, enhancement, and the ethics of neurotherapeutics. *Brain and Cognition*, *50*(3), 387–395. doi:10.1016/S0278-2626(02)00534-1 PMID:12480485

Woodall, J. (2007). Programmed dissatisfaction: Does one gene drive all progress in science and the arts? *Scientist (Philadelphia, Pa.)*, *2*(3), 251–264.

Yampolskiy, R. V. (2013). Attempts to attribute moral agency to intelligent machines are misguided. Proceedings of *Annual Meeting of the International Association for Computing and Philosophy*, University of Maryland at College Park, MD.

Yudkowsky, E. (2008). Aritifical intelligence as a positive and negative factor in global risk. In N. Bostrom & M. M. Cirkovic (Eds.), *Global catastrophic risks* (pp. 308–345). Oxford: Oxford University Press.

Zettler, P. J. (2009). Is it cheating to use cheetahs?: The implications of technologically innovative prostheses for sport values and rules. *Boston University International Law Journal*, *27*(2), 367–409.

ADDITIONAL READING

Badmington, N. (2000). *Posthumanism (readers in cultural criticism)*. Palgrave MacMillan.

Braidotti, R. (2013). The posthuman. *Polity*.

Buchanan, A. E. (2011). *Better than human: The promise and perils of enhancing ourselves (philosophy in action)*. Oxford University Press.

Buchanan, A. E. (2011). *Beyond humanity?: The ethics of biomedical enhancement (uehiro series in practical ethics)*. Oxford University Press. doi:10.1093/acprof:oso/9780199587810.001.0001

Cole-Turner, R. (2011). *Transhumanism and transcendence: Christian hope in an age of technological enhancement*. Georgetown University Press.

Committee on Techniques for the Enhancement of Human Performance. Commission on Behavioral and Social Sciences and Education, Division of Behavioral and Social Sciences and Education, National Research Council, Druckman, D., & Bjork, R. A. (1991). In the mind's eye: Enhancing human performance. National Research Council.

Committee on Technologies for the Enhancement of Human Performance. Commission on Behavioral and Social Sciences and Education, Division of Behavioral and Social Sciences and Education, National Research Council, Druckman, D., Singer, J. E. (1997). Enhancing organizational performance. National Research Council.

Druckman, D., & Bjork, R. A. (1994). *Learning, remember, believing: Enhancing human performance (committee on techniques for the enhancement of human performance)*. National Research Council.

Druckman, D., & Swets, J. A. (1988). *Enhancing human performance: Issues, theories, and techniques (Committee on Techniques for the Enhancement of Human Performance)*. National Research Council.

Fröding, B. (2012). *Virtue ethics and human enhancement*. SpringerBriefs in Ethics.

Fukuyama, F. (2003). *Our posthuman future: Consequences of the biotechnology revolution*. Picador.

Hackett, E. J., Amsterdamska, O., Lynch, M. E., Wajcman, J., & Bijker, W. E. (2007). *The handbook of science and technology studies* (3rd ed.). The MIT Press.

Horn, T. R., & Horn, N. F. (2010). *Gorbidden gates: How genetics robotics, artificial intelligence, synthetic biology, nanotechnology, and human enhancement herald: The dawn of techno-dimensional spiritual warfare*. USA.

Huey, B. M., & Wickens, C. D. (1993). *Workload transition: Implications for individual and team performance (panel on workload transition)*. National Research Council.

Istvan, Z. (2013). *The transhumanist wager*. Futurity Imagine, LLC.

Kass, L. (2003). *Beyond therapy: Biotechnology and the pursuit of happiness*. President's Council on Bioethics.

Magdalinski, T. (2008). *Sport, technology and the body: The nature of performance (ethics and sport)*. Routledge.

McCray, W. P. (2012). *The visioneers: How a group of elite scientists pursued space colonies, nanotechnologies, and a limitless future*. Princeton University Press.

Miah, A. (2008). *Human futures: Art in an age of uncertainty*. Chicago, IL: Liverpool University Press.

More, M., & Vita-More, N. (2013). *The transhumanist reader: Classical and contemporary essays on the science, technology, and philosophy of the human future. Wiley-Blackwell, Nickerson, R. S. (1995). Emerging needs and opportunities for human factors research (Commitment on Human Factors)*. National Research Council. doi:10.1002/9781118555927

O'Connor, P. E., & Cohn, J. V. (2009). *Human performance enhancement in high-risk environments: Insights, developments, and future directions from military research (technology, psychology, and health)*. Greenwood Publishing Group.

Ramsey, P. (1970). *Fabricated man: The ethics of genetic control (yale fastbacks)*. Yale University Press.

Sandel, M. J. (2009). *The case against perfection Ethics in the age of genetic engineering*. Belknap Press of Harvard University Press.

Saniotis, A. (2013). Remaking homo: Ethical issues on future human enhancement. *Ethics in Science and Environmental Politics*, *13*(1), 15–21. doi:10.3354/esep00131

Savulescu, J., & Bostrom, N. (2011). *Human enhancement*. Oxford University Press.

Savulescu, J., ter Meulen, R., Kahane, G. (2011). *Enhancing human capacities*. Wiley-Blackwell.

Stern, P. C., & Carstensen, L. L. (2000). *The aging mind: Opportunities in cognitive research (Board on behavioral, cognitive, and sensory sciences)*. National Research Council.

Waters, B. (2006). *From human to posthuman: Christian theology and technology in a postmodern world (ashgate science and religion series)*. Ashgate Publishing Company.

Zeider, J. (1986). *Human productivity enhancement: Organizations, personnel, and decision making* (Vol. 2). Praeger.

KEY TERMS AND DEFINITIONS

Business: Is defined as any organization (commercial or government) whose aim is to satisfy a set of customer requirements and is required to deliver results and provide value to the receiving customers, organizations and/or institutions.

Contractualism: Is where in the world of practitioners, contractualism is one of the most promising centers of gravity in business ethics, and an everyday understanding of contractual commitment is one of the cornerstones on which modern business practices rest.

Ethics: Is not the study of morals, whether this word is used to designate conformity to conventional social rules or to the existing moral judgments of men.

Human Enhancement: (Defined) ways to make functional changes to human characteristics, abilities, emotion and capacities, beyond what we regard today as normal, using advances in biology, chemistry, physics, materials, information technology and the mind sciences.

Human Enhancement: (Original) includes any activity by which we improve our bodies, minds, or abilities.

Moral Awareness: Is recognizing the existence of a moral problem in a situation.

Moral Dilemmas: Are based on the principal difficulty that it is hard to discover what one ought to do when facing a choice between non-overriding conflicting moral requirements or between non-overriding conflicting interests.

Moral Laxity: Is the failure to identify particular opportunities and take significant steps toward realizing a broad moral goal whose worthiness is admitted.

Posthumans: Is defined as an organism who may have indefinite health-spans, much greater intellectual faculties than any current human beings—and perhaps entirely new sensibilities or modalities—as well as the ability to control their own emotions.

Prosthetics: Is a form of human enhancement, and is generally defined as the branch of medicine dealing with the production and use of artificial body parts.

Transhumanism: is an outgrowth of secular humanism and the Enlightenment. It holds that current human nature is improvable through the use of applied science and other rational methods, which may make it possible to increase human health-span, extend our intellectual and physical capabilities, and give us increased control over our own mental states and moods.

ENDNOTES

[1] Those who are interested in a more detailed coverage on the history of business should look at Alfred D. Chandler, Jr.'s (1996). The role of business in the United States: A historical survey. In Castro, B. Business & society: A reader in the history, sociology, and ethics of business.

[2] Those interested in another paradigm on science vs. art should look at Kuhn, T. S. (1996). *The structure of scientific revolutions* (3rd).

[3] Definition of the term prosthetics was taken from WordNet Search – 3.1. Definition was retrieved on July 5, 2013. Available at http://wordnetweb.princeton.edu/perl/webwn?s=prosthetics

Section 4

From Far to Near and Near to Far:
The Ethics of Distancing Technologies in Education and Warfare

Chapter 8
Responsibility and War Machines:
Toward a Forward–Looking and Functional Account

Jai Galliott
Macquarie University, Australia

ABSTRACT

The purpose of this chapter is to demonstrate that while unmanned systems certainly exacerbate some problems and cause us to rethink who we ought to hold morally responsible for military war crimes, traditional notions of responsibility are capable of dealing with the supposed 'responsibility gap' in unmanned warfare and that more moderate regulation will perhaps prove more important than an outright ban. It begins by exploring the conditions under which responsibility is typically delegated to humans and how these responsibility requirements are challenged in technological warfare. Following this is an examination of Robert Sparrow's notion of a 'responsibility gap' as it pertains to the deployment of fully autonomous weapons systems. It is argued that we can reach a solution by shifting to a forward-looking and functional sense of responsibility incorporating institutional agents and ensuring that the human role in engineering and unleashing these systems is never overlooked.

INTRODUCTION

Central to the ethical concerns raised about the development of increasingly intelligent unmanned systems are issues of responsibility and accountability. Robot arms control groups have popularised this element of the debate as part of their call for a moratorium on the use of autonomous drones. The purpose of this chapter is to demonstrate that, while unmanned systems certainly exacerbate some traditional problems and may in some cases cause us to rethink who we ought to hold morally responsible for military war crimes, our standard conceptions of responsibility are capable of dealing with the supposed 'responsibility gap' – namely the inability to identify an appropriate locus of responsibility – in unmanned warfare and that in the absence of a gap, there is no reason for an outright ban. This chapter begins by exploring

DOI: 10.4018/978-1-4666-8592-5.ch008

the conditions under which responsibility is typically attributed to humans and how these responsibility requirements are challenged in technologically mediated warfare. Following this is an examination of Sparrow's notion of the 'responsibility gap' as it pertains to the potential deployment of fully autonomous weapons systems. It is argued that we can reach a solution by shifting to a forward-looking and functional sense of responsibility, which incorporates institutional agents and ensures that the human role in both engineering and releasing these systems is never overlooked.

BACKGROUND: CHALLENGES TO RESPONSIBILITY IN HI-TECH WARFARE

Moral responsibility in war is about actions, omissions and their consequences. When we read stories in military ethics readers, those worthy of blame include agents failing to adhere to just war principles, or to otherwise do the 'right thing' as determined by platoon leaders, government or country. It is also about the conditions under which they did the right or wrong thing. To be held responsible, in accord with Fischer and Ravizza's (1998) landmark account – the mechanism that issues the relevant behaviour must be the agent's own and be responsive to reasons – actors must not be 'deceived or ignorant' about what they are doing and ought to have control over their behaviour in a 'suitable sense' (Fischer & Ravizza 1998). Put more specifically, this means that an agent should only be considered morally responsible if they intentionally make a free and informed causal contribution to any act in question, meaning that they must be aware of the relevant facts and consequences of their actions, having arrived at the decision to act independently of coercion and were able to take alternative actions based on their knowledge of the facts. If these conditions are met, we can usually establish a link between the responsible subject and person or object affected, either retrospectively or prospectively (the latter will be the focus of the final section). However, technologically enabled warfare of the unmanned type presents various challenges for these standard accounts of moral responsibility. For the sake of a complete exposition and refutation of Sparrow's claim that the responsibility gap presents an insurmountable threat, it is necessary to take a closer look at how semi-autonomous military technologies, generally defined, can complicate responsibility attribution in warfare.

There are many barriers to responsibility attribution in the military domain and many are so closely interrelated that it makes providing a clear and lucid discussion quite problematic. The most important for present purposes is associated with the subject's causal contribution to the action in question. According to the above referenced account, for an agent to be held responsible, they must have exerted due influence on the resulting event. What is 'due' will be subject to further reflection in the remaining sections, but there is little to be gained from blaming someone or something for an unfortunate event about which they/it legitimately had no other choice or over which they/it had no control. That acknowledged, the employment of modern warfighting technologies based on complex computing and information technologies can lead us to lose our grasp of who is responsible, because it obscures the causal connections between an agent's actions and the eventual consequences. When utilizing complex technologies, tracing the sequence of events that led to a particular event usually leads in a great number of directions (Norman 2012). The great majority of technological mishaps are the product of multifaceted mistakes commonly involving a wide range of persons, not limited to end users, engineers and technicians. For those looking from the outside in, it can be very difficult – and some (like Sparrow) might say impossible – to identify contributing agents. This difficulty in identifying contributing agents is Dennis Thompson's (1987) so-called 'problem of many hands'. This problem should not be confused with the 'responsibility gap' that will soon be addressed, because it is not as deflationary and falls short of the complete abdication of responsibility.

Added to the problem of many hands is the physical distance that warfighting technologies often create between agents and the consequences or outcomes of their actions. This further blurs the causal connection between action and event. Batya Friedman (1990) earlier noted this effect in an educational setting which encourages young people to become responsible members of the electronic information community. The challenge has been reinvigorated with the development and deployment of unmanned systems in the military setting and the employment of distanced drone operators. It is these war-making agents that now need to be encouraged to play a responsible role in network-centric operating environments. Unmanned systems technologies – more than any other material technology – extend the reach of military activity through both time and space. While enabling a state's military force to defend itself over a greater range than they would otherwise be able to may be morally permissible, or even praiseworthy, and may be in line with the social contract, this remoteness can also act to disassociate them from the harm that they cause. As noted earlier, it has long been understood that there is a positive relationship between the physical and emotional distance facilitated by technological artifacts and the subsequent ease of killing (Grossman 1995). When someone uses an unmanned aircraft operated from a control station on the ground in the US to conduct military operations in the Middle East, the operator might not be fully aware of how the system and its munitions will affect the local people and may not experience or fully appreciate the true consequences of their actions (Waelbers 2009). This has a direct bearing on their comprehension of the significance of their actions and has a mediating role when it comes to considering the extent to which they are responsible.

This mediation of responsibility has much to do with the fact that unmanned systems and the sensors that they carry can actively shape how moral agents perceive and experience the world at large, which further impacts upon the conditions for imposing moral responsibility. In order to make the appropriate decisions which are sanctioned by just war theory, a moral agent must be capable of fully considering and deliberating about the consequences of their actions, understanding the relevant risks and benefits they will have and to whom they will apply. This, in turn, calls for them to have adequate knowledge of the relevant facts. While McMahan (2009) and others have offered accounts, it remains unclear what epistemic thresholds ought to apply here, but what is generally accepted is that it is unfair to hold someone responsible for something they could not have known about or reasonably anticipated. The capability of unmanned systems and other intelligence gathering technologies is importantly relevant, because in some respects they assist the relevant users in deliberating on the appropriate course of action by helping them capture, collate and analyse information and data (Zuboff 1985). In their sales demonstrations to the military, for example, representatives of the drone industry typically argue that their piece of military hardware will grant them the opportunity to see 'beyond the next hill' in the field and 'around the next block' in congested urban environments, enabling them to acquire information that they would not otherwise have access to without incurring significantly greater risk (US DoD 1999). This may well be true with respect to some systems, and these would allow operators greater reflection on the consequences of their tactical decisions. However, with the technical, geographical and operational limits discussed elsewhere (Galliott Forthcoming; 2012; 2012/13), there are many respects in which these systems preclude one from gaining a view of the 'bigger picture' and may alter an operator's resulting action/s, perhaps limiting responsibility.

Many intelligent military systems have such complex processes that they get in the way of assessing the validity and relevance of the information they produce or help assess and, as such, they can actually prevent a user from making the appropriate decision within an operational context and therefore have a direct impact on their level of responsibility. A consequence of this complexity is that people have the aforementioned tendency to rely either too much or not enough on automated systems like those we increasingly find embedded into unmanned aircraft or their control systems, especially when in the time-critical and dynamic situations which are characteristic of modern warfare (Cummings 2004). The U.S.S. Vincennes most shockingly illustrated this during its deployment to the Persian Gulf amid a gun battle with Iranian small boats. Although this warship was armed with an Aegis Combat System, which is arguably one of the most complex and automated naval weapons system of its time (it can automatically track and target incoming projectiles and enemy aircraft), the U.S.S. Vincennes misidentified an Iranian airliner as an F-14 fighter jet and fired upon it, killing nearly three hundred people (Gray 1997). Post-accident reporting and analysis discovered that overconfidence in the abilities of the system, coupled with a poor human-machine interface, prevented those aboard the ship from intervening to avoid the tragedy. Despite the fact that disconfirming evidence was available from nearby vessels as to the nature of the aircraft, it was still mischaracterised as a hostile fighter descending and approaching them at great speed. In the resulting investigation, a junior officer remarked that 'we called her Robocruiser...she always seemed to have a picture and...[always] seemed to be telling people to get on or off the link as though her picture was better' (Rogers & Rogers 1992). The officer's impression was that the semi-autonomous system provided reliable information that was otherwise unobtainable. In this case, at least, such a belief was incorrect. The system had not provided otherwise unobtainable information, but rather misleading information. It is therefore questionable whether the war-making agent has a more comprehensive understanding of the relevant state of affairs because of the employment of advanced military technology or whether her/his understanding and knowledge are less accurate (Manders-Huits 2006). That is, it is unclear whether the attribution of moral responsibility is enhanced or threatened. The view advanced here is that, even though there may be an aggregate increase in the amount of information that is accessible, there is a morally relevant decrease in understanding which single piece of information ought to influence autonomy of action and the resulting decision-making, even when the bulk of information is clear and accurate. The implication is that operators of sophisticated systems might be held to high standards of responsibility on the basis that they had access to a great deal of relevant information when, in fact, the provision of this information may have clouded their judgment, meaning that they are less responsible.

It must also be added that advanced technologies may exert a certain level of influence over their users in a way that might be unclear or even immeasurable (Manders-Huits 2006). This sort of control is not implicit in the technology itself, but rather exerted through the design process and the way in which alternative moral options are presented for human action. Semi-autonomous military technologies help to centralise and increase control over multiple operations, reducing costs and supposedly increasing efficiency. However, there is a limit to how much control a human being can exert and, in reality, this 'increased control' can only be achieved by outsourcing some low-level decisions to computerized processes and leaving the human to make a choice from a more limited range of actions. In other words, some military technologies are designed with the explicit aim of making humans behave in certain ways, further mediating the imposition of responsibility. However, note that we are still a long way from saying that we cannot attribute responsibility in such cases.

THE ALLEGED RESPONSIBILITY GAP IN AUTOMATED WARFARE

In the previous section, we saw how developments in military technology have led to a partial loss of influence on the part of operators or users and hold broader implications for the attribution of moral responsibility more generally, namely by limiting the operator's responsibility and perhaps causing us to consider the redistribution of the remaining share of responsibility. In the following section of this chapter, we shall see how many of the problems described above are only being exacerbated as unmanned systems become more computerized. These problems and others come together in fully automated warfare to create a problem that Sparrow and others see as significantly more serious than any of those already discussed, posing what is supposedly an insurmountable threat to the responsibility framework embedded within just war theory. As a final step towards fully understanding and refuting the nature and implications of this problem, it will be necessary to discuss the arguments drawn on by Sparrow, namely those originally put forward by Andreas Matthias (2004).

Matthias (2004) argues that the further we progress along the autonomy continuum, the closer we come to undermining efforts to establish rule systems in order to attribute responsibility. He says that with non-autonomous systems, it is relatively safe to take the use of a machine to signal that the operator has read the user manual and assumes responsibility for its use, except in cases where the machine fails to operate with the predefined limits (Matthias 2004). Thus, the user has control and is responsible for the actions and events that come from the normal operation of the system, but if it explodes or does something which was not stated in the manual when it should have been, we ought to blame the manufacturer. We know from the preceding discussion that, when machines capable of being ever so slightly autonomous are introduced, because of the rigidity and limited nature of non-autonomous systems, moral responsibility is complicated. Indeed, the agent responsible for operating this machine loses an element of control over the system. What happens if we progress further? Matthias (2004) argues that, if a NASA technician was operating a semi-autonomous space vehicle and the vehicle falls into a crater between inputs because of long response times, we should not consider the technician responsible. Task-autonomous unmanned systems create a buffer between agent and system as well as another buffer between action and event, giving their operators the potential ability to increase their workload by operating multiple drones, but at the cost of understanding and situational awareness. The locus of responsibility categorically shifts away from the operator. However, the real problems arise when it comes to intelligent machines which are capable of adapting and learning new skills. That is, robotic systems for which unpredictability in their operations is a feature rather than a computer glitch or technical failure (Millar & Kerr 2012). Matthias (2004) asks us to imagine how we would impose moral responsibility if we were to revisit the space vehicle case and stipulate that it will not be remotely controlled from earth, but rather have its own integrated navigation and control system, capable of storing data in its internal memory, forming representations and taking action from these. It should, therefore, be able to record video imagery and estimate the difficulty of crossing any familiar terrain. He asks, in this revised case, whom we should hold responsible if the vehicle were to once again fall into the crater?

Sparrow (2007) subsequently takes up this question in the context of his discussion of unmanned systems. He has us imagine that a drone, directed by sophisticated artificial intelligence, bombs a platoon of enemy soldiers who have indicated their intent to surrender. Who should we hold morally responsible for a particular event when the decision to bomb is made by an autonomous weapons system without a human operator? The reader's first intuition is probably to say that the responsibility for any moral crimes or just war violations rests with the developer of the weapon. However, Sparrow (2007) objects to this by relying on the user manual analogy. This analogy says that this would be unfair if it is a declared system limitation that the machine may attack the wrong targets in some percentage of cases. If this is the case, he suggests it may be the responsibility of the user (since s/he is assumed to have read the manual). Secondly, he says that to hold the programmers or manufacturer responsible for the actions of their creation, once it is turned on and made autonomous, would be analogous to 'holding parents responsible for the action of their children once they have left their care' (Sparrow 2007). Sparrow assumes this is wrong and that it naturally leads us to consider holding the commanding officer responsible. Yet again, he views this as unfair and thinks that to do so calls into question the nature of our 'smart' weapons. If the machines start to make their own targeting decisions, he suggests that there will come a point at which we cannot hold the commanding officer responsible for any of the ensuing deaths (Sparrow 2007). It will be argued in the next section that Sparrow is mistaken about the assumed wrongness of sharing responsibility and that we are not yet at the tipping point he describes.

The final possible locus of responsibility under Sparrow's account, however, is the machine itself. Moral responsibility is typically attributed to moral agents and, at least in the Anglo-American philosophical tradition, moral agency has been reserved for human beings. The reason being that unlike the majority of animals, rational human beings are seen as able to freely deliberate about the consequences of their actions and choose to act in one way or other, meaning that they are originators of *morally significant* actions. Although some people tend to anthropomorphize military robots and notable philosophers like Dennett (1997) and Sullins (2006) have argued that they could be classed as moral agents, Sparrow argues that they should not and objects to the idea that they could have the kind of capacities that make human beings moral agents. He argues that it is unlikely that they will ever have the mental states, common sense, emotion or expressivity equivalent to those of humans, and that, if they do develop these things, it would undermine the whole point of utilizing robots instead of human beings (Sparrow 2007). According to the argument, they would hold a moral status equivalent to that of human beings. But this is disputable, as it could be argued that, while artificial moral agents may be worthy of moral consideration, they would still hold different status to biological moral agents by virtue of some natural/artificial distinction that gives greater weight to means of creation. Even if robots do not acquire human-level moral status, lower levels of machine autonomy may be sufficient for us to hold robots responsible. However, Sparrow (2007) holds that no robot can be held responsible because they cannot suffer. This presupposes that suffering is a requirement for responsibility, a presupposition not supported by the responsibility framework embedded in just war theory, but we will return to this point after having summarized the alleged problem.

For Sparrow, like Matthias before him, we have reached or are about to reach an important impasse. We already have many machines in development and a limited number of those, which are in use, are task-autonomous and can decide on a course of action in some limited scenarios without any human input. Going forward, all indications point to there being machines with rules for action which are not fixed by their manufacturers during the production process and which are open to be changed by the machine itself during its operation. That is, these machines will be capable of learning from their surroundings and experiences. Conventionally, there are several loci of responsibility for the actions of a machine, but both Matthias (2004) and Sparrow (2007) argue that these robots will bring about a class of actions for which nobody is responsible, because no individual or group has sufficient control of these systems. These cases constitute Matthias's 'responsibility gap'. At first blush, it might seem that this is basically the problem of many hands – the classical problem described earlier but with new relevance to the emergence of unmanned systems and the prospect of fully autonomous weapons systems. But to assume this would be mistaken. The argument advanced by Matthias and Sparrow is not that we cannot identify who is responsible, but simply that nobody is responsible. Sparrow would likely argue that, if there is any problem identifying the relevant persons, it is because they do not exist. In his article on corporate responsibility, Philip Petitt (2007) refers to the matter described as the 'problem of no hands'. This is a slight but important twist on Thompson's more familiar 'problem of many hands', as described earlier and characterized by the widespread relinquishment of moral responsibility.

The problem that proponents of the responsibility gap put forward is fairly straightforward, though certainly not indisputable. However, to differentiate his argument from Matthias's, Sparrow (2007) suggests that we might better conceptualize his dilemma if we consider another case in warfare where the waters are somewhat muddied: the use of child soldiers. This analogy is outlined because it will be useful in problematizing Sparrow's argument, though the similarity between child and machine learning is not as great as Sparrow indicates. He says that like robots, one of the many reasons why it is unethical to utilize children in combat is that it places decisions about the use of force in the hands of agents that cannot be held responsible for them. According to him, child soldiers lack full moral autonomy, but they are clearly autonomous in some respect and 'certainly much more autonomous than any existing robot' (Sparrow 2007, p. 73). He goes on to say that, while they are not capable of understanding the full moral dimensions of what they do, they possess sufficient autonomy to ensure that those who order them into action do not or cannot control them, presenting problems for any effort to hold those who gives the orders exclusively personally responsible for the child soldiers' actions (Sparrow 2007). The idea Sparrow advances is that there is a conceptual space in which child soldiers and military robots are sufficiently autonomous to make the full attribution of responsibility to an adult or conventional moral agent problematic, but not autonomous enough to be held fully responsible themselves. Sparrow argues that his opponents try to close this space by stipulating that the relevant entities hold more or less responsibility than they should and thus fit within one of the polar boundaries, but that this does not adequately or fairly resolve the problem. He thinks that we should, in fact, ban the use of autonomous weapons altogether (Sparrow 2007). The next section will propose that we can actually handle this problem by moving to a more collective, pragmatic and forward-looking notion of shared responsibility.

FUTURE TRENDS: TOWARD A REVISED NOTION OF RESPONSIBILITY

Having explored some of the challenges that semi-autonomous systems pose for responsibility attribution and described the dilemma over responsibility for autonomous unmanned systems, the need for a revised notion of responsibility should be clear. But to clarify, the arguments of both Matthias and Sparrow hinge on three basic premises. The first is that programmers, manufacturers, commanding officers and the like may not be able to foresee what an autonomous robot, capable of learning, will do in the highly complex and dynamic military operating environment. The second is that either independently of or related to the fact that none of these agents are able to exert full control over the development or subsequent deployment of these systems, harm to others may eventually occur. The third is that an agent can only be held responsible for these harms if they have control in the sense that they have an awareness of the facts surrounding the action that leads to the harm and are able to freely manipulate the relevant causal chains based on these facts. The conclusion stipulates that since this is not the case as it pertains to programmers, manufacturers or commanding officers, there is some sort of moral void created by the deployment of these systems, one that cannot be bridged by our traditional concepts of responsibility.

While the problem is clear, it is not obvious that the overall conclusion can be accepted at face value or that any individual premise is correct. There are a number of points at which the alleged responsibility gap can be overcome, or, at least, a number of premises that can be called into question in order to cast doubt over the supposed insurmountability of the problem at hand.

In discussing the nature of this alleged responsibility gap and showing its inadequacy as a justification for a moratorium on autonomous systems, it is important to point out that the scope of the conditions for imposing responsibility have been overstretched or considered in too wide a frame. As will soon be shown with reference to the idea of shared responsibility, it is not impossible to impose responsibility in situations in which no individual has total control over the function of an autonomous system. Both Matthias and Sparrow go too far in suggesting that programmers, manufacturers or commanding officers are freed from any form of responsibility because they do not have total control over the operation or manufacture of unmanned systems. An appeal to common sense should reveal that it is absurd and potentially dangerous to identify the failings of multiple individuals in their development and deployment and then deny their moral responsibility (Gotterbarn 2001). To do so is deny an opportunity for the rectification of past, present and future wrongs. As opposed to what might be stipulated by strict liability law, such a strong sense of control is not necessary for the imposition of some degree of moral responsibility. The relevant programmers, designers, manufacturers and commanding officers are all responsible to some degree or extent. Take Sparrow's claim that to hold the programmer of a dynamic learning machine responsible for its actions would be analogous to holding a parent responsible for the actions of their child once they are out of their care. While there are limits to any such analogy because of the varied learning mechanisms employed by child and machine, he seems to ignore the fact that parents are at least partially responsible for preparing their children for that moment when they leave their care and become independent. In much the same way, the developers of unmanned systems hold significant responsibility for ensuring that their robots can operate as desired once given independence, something that is still a long way off in the majority of cases. Also, take the case of the commanding officer and continue with the parenting analogy. When a parent is teaching their child how to drive, for instance, the parent places the child in an area where s/he can learn the necessary skills without risking her/his own safety or that of anyone else. Similarly, the commanding officer of an autonomous system has a responsibility to ensure that the system has been thoroughly proto-type tested or is placed in an appropriate learning or test bed environment until such time that it performs at least as well as a manned system or until the chance of any serious harm occurring is so tiny that we can deal with it via the 'functional morality' described later on, which recognizes that engineers and manufacturers will often choose to release intelligent machines with remnant unpredictability and that reprogramming for minor errors can assume the place of punishment.

The machine's path to full autonomy is a long (if not impossible) one and Sparrow points to this using the child warrior analogy. Machines will not just 'wake up' as is depicted in films about human-hating 'terminators'. Indeed, there is simply no way in which someone could deliberately create such an entity without a collective effort on the scale of the Manhattan project. The general lesson to be drawn from this is that all the involved agents and any others associated with the use of unmanned systems (including the user in the case of semi-autonomous systems) retain a share of responsibility, even though they may claim that they were not in complete or absolute control. It would be foolhardy, or even dangerous, to conclude from the observation that responsibility is obscured by the use of unmanned weaponry that nobody is, or ought to have been, held to account and that it is impossible to deal with the case of autonomous systems. On the contrary (and as others have argued in relation to informatics more generally, see: Manders-Huits 2006) we are at such an important junction in the development of unmanned systems that we have reason to adjust and refine our conception of moral responsibility and to leave behind the idea that the imposition of moral responsibility relies on agents having full control over all aspects of the design or deployment of advanced robotics. This is because these systems are so complex that few of the design, development or deployment related decisions are made on an individual basis. Why concentrate on the intentions and actions of humans alone in our moral evaluation of these systems when no human exerts full control over the relevant outcomes? We need to move away from the largely insufficient notion of individual responsibility, upon which we typically rely, and move towards a more complex notion of collective responsibility, which has the means and scope to include non-human action. That is, it must be a holistic approach which is capable of acknowledging the contribution of various human agents, systems and organizations or institutions. The need to update our moral values and associated notions of responsibility will become more important as the technology develops, the risks increase and the number of potential responsibility-related problems accumulate.

It is worth noting that others, foreseeing the difficulties that we are now facing with the development of things like intelligent autonomous robots, have already thought about calls for change in the way we think of responsibility. For instance, both Daniel Dennett (1973) and Peter Strawson (1974) have long held that we should conceive of moral responsibility as less of an individual duty and more of a role that is actively defined by pragmatic group norms. This argument in endorsed here, primarily because more classical accounts raise endless questions concerning free will and intentionality that cannot be easily resolved (if at all) from a practical perspective aimed at achieving results here and now. This sort of practical account has the benefit of allowing non-human entities, such as complex socio-technical systems and the corporations that manufacture them to be answerable for the harms to which they often cause or contribute. It seems to require that we think in terms of a continuum of agency between non-moral and full moral agents, with the sort of robots we are concerned with here falling just short of the latter.

This pragmatic (or functional) approach also allows for the fact that agency develops over time and shifts the focus to the future appropriate behavior of complex systems, with moral responsibility being more a matter of rational and socially efficient policy that is largely outcomes-focused. For our purposes here, it is useful to view moral responsibility and this pragmatic account in line with the social contract argument put forward much earlier. That is, we should view moral responsibility as a mechanism used by society to defend public spaces and maintain a state of relative harmony, generated under the contract by the power transferred from the individuals to the state. The end of this responsibility mechanism is, therefore, to prevent any further injury being done to society and to prevent others from committing similar offences. While it might be useful to punish violators of the social contract and the just war theory which it has argued follows from the social contract, it is not strictly necessary, nor is it necessarily the best approach at preventing harm in all scenarios. As Jeroen van den Hoven and Gert-Jan Lokhorst (2012) have argued, treatment is in many cases an equally effective option for the prevention of harm and one that we can apply to non-human agents in different forms, whether it is psychological counseling in humans or reengineering or reprogramming in the case of robots. This is important because it means that there is sufficient conceptual room between 'operational morality and genuine moral agency' to hold responsible or, in Floridi's language, hold morally accountable, artificial agents which are able to perform some task and assess its outcome (Wallach & Allen 2012; Floridi & Sanders 2004).

Scholars in the drone debate also seem to have become fixated on a backward-looking (retrospective) sense of responsibility, perhaps because even engineers and programmers have tended to adopt a malpractice model focused on the allocation of blame for harmful incidents. However, an effective and efficient responsibility mechanism that remedies the supposed gap should not only be about holding someone responsible only when something goes wrong. Therefore, this backward-looking sense of responsibility must be differentiated from forward-looking (prospective) responsibility, a notion that focuses more on capacity to effect change than blameworthiness or similar (Gotterbarn 2001). That is, at some point, we must stop thinking purely about past failures to take proper care and think about the reciprocal responsibility to take due care in future action. This is because in debates about real world problems such as the deployment of increasingly autonomous unmanned weaponry, we will also want our conception of responsibility to deal with *potential* problems. To this end, we can impose forward-looking or prospective responsibility to perform actions from now on, primarily in order to prevent undesirable consequences or to ensure a particular state of affairs obtains more effectively and efficiently than through the alternative means of backward-looking models. It establishes a general obligation on the part of all those involved in the design, manufacture and use of unmanned systems to give regard to future harms. Admittedly, as Seamus Miller (2008) has pointed out in the case of computing, it is difficult to reach any solid conclusion on how far into the future they are required to foresee. That said, two things are clear in the case of military robotics: first, if the recent troubles plaguing unmanned systems are any indicator, agents have reasonable grounds to expect the unexpected. Second, once fully autonomous systems are developed and deployed, no amount of policy making will stop their spread.

For the latter reason in particular, we have to think more carefully about where the majority of the forward-looking responsibility falls. In discussing the claim that wealthy countries must do more than comparatively poor countries to combat climate change and making use of Kant, James Garvey (2008) argues that in much the same way that 'ought implies can', 'can implies ought' in a range of other circumstances where the financial or political means behind the 'can' have contributed to the problem that ought to be corrected or mitigated. This seems also to hold true in the responsibility debate with which we are engaged. Generally speaking, the more power an agent has and the greater the resources at their disposal – whether intellectual, economic or otherwise – the more obliged s/he is to take reasonable action when problems arise. Jessica Fahlquist (2008) has proposed a specific approach to identifying the extent of a person's obligation in relation to environmental protection based on varied levels of capacity to contribute to social causes, and given that power to enact change varies within the military and military-industrial complex to much the same extent as in the environmental world (and with some convergence), there is little reason why this should not be applied to the drone debate and extended to cover the manufacturers of unmanned systems as well as the governments that regulate them. The companies of the military-industrial complex are in a unique position, and have it well within in their power, to anticipate risks of harm and injury and theories about the possible consequences of developing learning systems. The costs of doing so after the fact are great and many. Moreover, manufacturers are best positioned create opportunities for engineers to do what is right without fear of reprimand, whether that would be going ahead as planned, designing in certain limitations in the system or simply refusing to undertake certain projects. It therefore seems reasonable to impose forward-looking responsibility upon them. However, we know that profit can sometimes trump morality for these collective agents of the military-industrial complex, so concerned parties should also seek to share forward-looking responsibility and ascribe some degree of responsibility to the governments which oversee these manufacturers and set the regulatory framework for the development and deployment of their product, should manufacturers fail to self-regulate and establish appropriate industry standards.

Note that, while it may seem that the point advanced in this chapter is pitched against Sparrow's argument for a prohibition on the development and subsequent use of these systems, this is only partly true. The objection here is only to the antecedent of his claim or the vehicle that he uses to reach his final conclusion against the use of 'killer drones'. That is, it is not at all obvious that Sparrow needs to make the very bold claim that nobody can be held responsible for the use of military robots that fall between having operational autonomy and genuine moral autonomy. It seems that many other agents are sufficiently responsible and that, through embracing an instrumental approach toward backward-looking responsibility and combining it with a forward-looking account of responsibility put forward earlier, it is possible to distribute responsibility fairly. It may also be that some of the relevant agents, namely governments, reach the same conclusion as Sparrow. That is, while states and their militaries have a contractual obligation to effectively and efficiently protect the citizens who grant them power, it may turn out that this would mean avoiding the use of unmanned systems in some circumstances and, indeed, there is some evidence of this in the implications and consequences described in the bulk of the existing scholarly literature on drones. In fact, as unlikely as it seems, time may prove that unmanned systems pose such a problem that it warrants making a concerted effort to form an international treaty or a new Geneva Convention banning their use in all but very particular cases, perhaps where there is clearly demarcated 'kill zone' in some remote part of the world. However, this is not yet clear and in light of the features of the revised account of responsibility advocated here, there is no intrinsic responsibility gap that warrants a prohibition of the use of unmanned systems, at least not without reference to the problems.

Critics are likely to argue that any account which allocates too much responsibility to organizational or governmental actors will erode the sense of personal responsibility that individuals feel and will not thus have the desired effect of improving the attainment of just outcomes with unmanned systems. What will happen, they may ask, if individual parties to collective atrocities are excused from the responsibilities that they would otherwise have under traditional notions of responsibility? There are a few ways to respond to this worry. The first consists in stressing that individuals are not in fact freed or excused from responsibility according to either the backward looking or the forward-looking model. Individual agents will still be held causally responsible for their part in any war crimes under the functional/pragmatic account, so if a programmer or a commanding officer gets an entire village blown up by mistake, they will be held accountable. They will also be encouraged to ensure that systems are designed, developed, tested and used in the desired way through the imposition of forward-looking responsibility. The second way to respond is to reaffirm that, because individual agents are the core units of the social contract, it would obviously be ideal if they were to gradually begin to embrace the right values and do the right thing, but allow that, in some circumstances, it is fairer or more effective to distribute the burden of action between individuals, institutions and governments. This is due to the fact that, in the short to medium term, it must be recognized that both human and non-human agents will make mistakes that will lead to violations of some of the principles of the just war theory. As a consequence, the greatest share of responsibility must be ascribed to the most capable agents in the relevant scenario. In trying to highlight the oversimplified analysis of duties in rights-based theories, Henry Shue (1988) suggests that in some circumstances, we must look beyond individuals and distribute responsibility to institutions in the most effective and efficient fashion relative to the time we have as well as the nature and severity of the problem. For it is indeed institutions, such as judicial systems and polices forces, upon which the duty to provide physical security ultimately falls. In the case of Sparrow's 'killer robots', it seems best to impose much of the forward-looking responsibility to the government or its relevant standards departments, just because the government is best placed to ensure that systems are designed to rule out or reduce the impact of such mistakes or that measures are put in place to do the same thing. Again, it must be stressed that this does not mean that individual agents or corporations with the relevant capabilities and resources are excused from efforts to achieve the desired effects or their share of responsibility, but merely that governmental agents ought to take greater efforts because the proposed account of responsibility can track their role and they can be held responsible for some violations of the just war theory.

CONCLUSION

This chapter began by exploring the need for a clear account of responsibility in just war theory and countering the claim that there is some sort of explicit requirement to hold a single individual responsible. It indicated that there is, less specifically, an implicit responsibility component which stipulates that agents of war – whether human, non-human or some combination thereof – must be held responsible for violations of the just war theory no matter how difficult the moral accounting. In the second section, it was demonstrated that technology generates a number of barriers to attribution of responsibility, from distancing users from their sense of responsibility to obscuring causal chains, making it more difficult to identify where a moral fault lies. In the third, it was outlined how these issues and others come together in the case of fully automated unmanned warfare to create what Sparrow – following Matthias – alleges is a 'responsibility gap', or a class of actions for which nobody/nothing is supposedly responsible. The final section laid the foundations for a theory of responsibility, which revolves around the idea that action and responsibility can be distributed amongst human and non-human agents or some combination thereof. More work is needed to reveal exactly what this new theory of responsibility will look like and to determine its precise implications, but if nothing else, this chapter has hopefully demonstrated that, while ascribing responsibility in the case of autonomous systems is more complex and troubling than in the case of semi- and non-autonomous systems, it is by no means an insurmountable problem.

ACKNOWLEDGMENT

This research has been conducted with funding provided by the Commonwealth of Australia via Macquarie University. It is also derived from research conducted for the Australian Army and the forthcoming *Military Robots: Mapping the Moral Landscape* (Ashgate: Surrey), but does not in any way represent the views of any of these parties or publishers. All rights are reserved.

REFERENCES

Cummings, M. L. (2004). Automation Bias in Intelligent Time Critical Decision Support Systems. Proceedings of *AIAA 1st Intelligent Systems Technical Conference*, Chicago. doi:10.2514/6.2004-6313

Dennett, D. D. (1973). Mechanism and Responsibility. In T. Honderich (Ed.), *Essays on Freedom of Action*. Boston: Routledge and Keegan Paul.

Dennett, D. D. (1997). When HAL Kills, Who's to Blame? Computer Ethics. In D. G. Stork (Ed.), *HAL's Legacy: 2001's Computer as a Dream and Reality*. Cambridge: MIT Press.

Fahlquist, J. N. (2008). Moral Responsibility for Environmental Problems—Individual or Institutional? *Journal of Agricultural & Environmental Ethics*, 22(2), 109–124. doi:10.1007/s10806-008-9134-5

Fischer, J. M., & Ravizza, M. (1998). *Responsibility and Control: A Theory of Moral Responsibility*. Cambridge: Cambridge University Press. doi:10.1017/CBO9780511814594

Floridi, L., & Sancers, J. (2004). The Foundationalist Debate in Computer Ethics. In R. Spinello & H. Tavani (Eds.), *Readings in CyberEthics* (pp. 81–95). Massachusetts: Jones and Bartlett.

Friedman, B. (1990). *Moral Responsibility and Computer Technology*. Paper presented at the Annual Meeting of the American Educational Research Association, Boston, MA.

Galliott, J. (Forthcoming). *Military Robots: Mapping the Moral Landscape*. Surrey: Ashgate.

Galliott, J. C. (2012). Uninhabited Systems and the Asymmetry Objection: A Response to Strawser. *Journal of Military Ethics*, 11(1), 58–66. doi:10.1080/15027570.2012.683703

Galliott, J. C. (2012/13). Closing with Completeness: The Asymmetric Drone Warfare Debate. *Journal of Military Ethics*, 11(4), 353–356. doi:10.1080/15027570.2012.760245

Garvey, J. (2008). *The Ethics of Climate Change: Right and Wrong in a Warning World*. New York: Bloomsbury.

Gotterbarn, D. (2001). Informatics and Professional Responsibility. *Science and Engineering Ethics*, 7(2), 221–230. doi:10.1007/s11948-001-0043-5 PMID:11349362

Gray, C. S. (1997). AI at War: The Aegis System in Combat. In D. Shculer (Ed.), *Directions and Implications of Advanced Computing*. (pp. 62–79). New York: Ablex.

Grossman, D. (1995). *On killing: the psychological cost of learning to kill in war and society*. Boston: Little, Brown and Company.

Lokhorst, G.-J., & van den Hoven, J. (2012). Responsibility for military robots. In P. Lin, K. Abney, & G. Bekey (Eds.), *Robot Ethics: The Ethical and Social Implications of Robotics*. (pp. 145–156). Cambridge: MIT Press.

Manders-Huits, N. (2006). Moral responsibility and IT for human enhancement. Proceedings of *Association for Computing Machinery Symposium on Applied Computing*, Dijon. doi:10.1145/1141277.1141340

Matthias, A. (2004). The Responsibility Gap: Ascribing Responsibility for the Actions of Learning Automata. *Ethics and Information Technology*, 6(3), 175–183. doi:10.1007/s10676-004-3422-1

McMahan, J. (2009). *Killing in War*. Oxford: Oxford University Press. doi:10.1093/acprof:oso/9780199548668.001.0001

Millar, J., & Kerr, I. (2012). Delegation, Relinquishment and Responsiibility: The Prospect of Expert Robots. Proceedings of *We Robot*, Coral Gables.

Miller, S. (2008). Collective Responsibility and Information and Communication Technology. In J. van den Hoven & J. Weckert (Eds.), *Information Technology and Moral Philosophy*. (pp. 226–250). Cambridge: Cambridge University Press.

Noorman, M. (2012). Computing and Moral Responsibility. *Stanford Encyclopedia of Responsibility*. Retrieved from http://plato.stanford.edu/archives/fall2012/entries/computing-responsibility/

Petitt, P. (2007). Responsibility Incorporated. *Ethics*, *117*(2), 171–201. doi:10.1086/510695

roadmap. Washington DC: Department of Defense.

Rogers, W., & Rogers, S. (1992). *Storm Center: The USS Vincennes and Iran Air Flight 655*. Annapolis: Naval Institute Press.

Shue, H. (1988). Mediating Duties. *Ethics*, *98*(4), 687–704. doi:10.1086/292999

Sparrow, R. (2007). Killer robots. *Journal of Applied Philosophy*, *24*(1), 62–77. doi:10.1111/j.1468-5930.2007.00346.x

Strawson, P. F. (1974). *Freedom and Resentment Freedom and Resentment and Other Essays*. London: Methuen.

Sullins, J. P. (2006). When is a Robot a Moral Agent. *International Review of Information Ethics*, *14*(2), 219–233.

Thompson, D. (1987). *Political Ethics and Public Office*. Cambridge: Harvard University Press.

United States Department of Defense. (2009). *FY2009-2034 unmanned systems integrated*

Waelbers, K. (2009). Technological delegation: Responsibility for the unintended. *Science and Engineering Ethics*, *15*(1), 51–68. doi:10.1007/s11948-008-9098-x PMID:18937053

Wallach, W., & Allen, C. (2009). *Moral Machines: Teaching Robots Right from Wrong*. Oxford: Oxford University Press. doi:10.1093/acprof:oso/9780195374049.001.0001

Zuboff, S. (1985). Automate/Informate: The Two Faces of Intelligent Technology. *Organizational Dynamics*, *14*(2), 5–18. doi:10.1016/0090-2616(85)90033-6

KEY TERMS AND DEFINITIONS

Backward-Looking Responsibility: Primarily focuses on omissions and failures in an attempt to allocate blame for past harmful events.

Collective Responsibility: Arrangements appropriate for addressing responsibility to the actions multiple individuals or groups.

Forward-Looking Responsibility: Focuses on responsibility to ensure that a particular (and generally good) state of affairs obtains.

Problem of Many Hands: The problem of allocating responsibility in complex situations involving many actors.

Responsibility Gap: A theoretical gap signified by the inability to identify an appropriate locus of responsibility.

Unmanned Systems: Electro-mechanical military robots that dominate land, air and sea.

Chapter 9
Ethical Responsibilities of Preserving Academicians in an Age of Mechanized Learning:
Balancing the Demands of Educating at Capacity and Preserving Human Interactivity

James E. Willis III
Indiana University, USA

Viktoria Alane Strunk
Independent Scholar, USA

ABSTRACT

In quickly-changing educational delivery modalities, the central role of the instructor is being redefined by technology. Examining some of the various causes with ethical frameworks of utilitarianism, relativism, and care ethics, the centrality of human agency in educational interaction is argued to be indispensable. While exploring the forefront of online, face-to-face, and massive open online courses, the shape and technique of teaching and learning as well as their corollary research methodologies are being modified with automated technology. Ethical engagement with new technologies like learning analytics, automatic tutors, and automated, rubric-driven graders is proposed to be a frontier of critical thinking.

INTRODUCTION

Humans have a need for leaving remnants of their lives and cultural experiences behind. Artifacts have been left for thousands of years, as a footprint of human existence and importance. Whether it is a room full of valuables next to a deceased king or a time capsule that is buried to be reopened in fifty years, humans place significance upon these man-made objects to show the world that they did, indeed, "exist" and were not meant to be forgotten. Currently, people are living in an age where most cannot remember a

DOI: 10.4018/978-1-4666-8592-5.ch009

time when they did not possess a cell phone; they are tied to this electronic device as if it were a lifeline to the outside world. Forgotten are those moments where face-to-face human interaction was the most vital of each and every day. Times are changing, and the ways people interact, communicate, and learn are quickly evolving to match the rate of technological advances.

These advances face an acute and rapidly-changing environment in teaching and learning. People must learn various "literacies" to navigate an increasingly-complex world, especially one that is connected at the speed of the Internet. As digital learning and teaching tools expand, one question becomes critical. Is there an intrinsic, verifiable role in human teaching? This becomes an ethical question when technology is able to replace the human instructor; it is ethical because it not only reshapes how education is carried out, but also because the interaction of the agent changes, too. There is a real value in human teaching, while not jeopardizing or hindering the speed of invention. Further, the scale by which teaching occurs is already enormous, as evidenced by the rapid expansion of massive, open, online courses (MOOCs); this is augmented by automatic grading technology, automated and digitalized teachers, and various other technologies that are quickly changing educational delivery. Special attention must be paid to the ethical development of the technologies that are at the forefront of teaching and learning.

ARTIFICIAL INTELLIGENCE, OPEN STANDARDS, AND EMERGING EDUCATION

The proliferation of increasingly-complex systems of artificial intelligence, intelligent machines, information aggregation and interpretation is driven, in part, by educational opportunity and profit. Though there are numerous ways to approach the boundaries and meanings of "intelligence" when applied to computerized technology, several themes are especially critical: educational data modeling in the aggregate is expanding and is, thus, becoming more accurate and reliable; the way *intelligence* is defined may need serious revision soon; and the ways people learn are being tested and refined with technology. The rapidity of such innovation is underpinned with open standards, open source software, and systems designed for linking data (like JSON-LD) from searches to outcomes. What this means to classrooms, both virtual and brick-and-mortar, to students, and to instructors is an open question. Certain specific projects that link individual data, educational opportunities, and transparent assessment, like open digital badges, bridge together the current capabilities with a promise to the immediate future (Schenke, Tran, & Hickey, 2013).

The topic of artificial intelligence cannot be discussed without giving credit to those pioneers who were part of its inception but perhaps not recognized in a fitting way. Alan Turing, mathematician, and to those who knew him, genius at large, wrote a paper in 1936 called "On Computable Numbers, With an Application to the Entscheidungsproblem" discussing a machine that could be built and perform any function (Turing, 1937). This idea would be a topic of conversation for a group of researchers who would meet two decades later in Dartmouth in 1956. One of those researchers was Marvin Minsky, who would later cofound the AI laboratory at MIT in 1959. These early pioneers most likely "saw" into the deep future of computation, but how these technologies have been applied to the particular instance of education could not necessarily have been anticipated. For example, one of the current understandings of artificial intelligence is that it embodies modes of data aggregation, modeling, and forecasting; applied to education, this substantiates how competency-based education has caught political and financial attention. For example, some schools apply competency-based models of education to fields demanding proficiency in skills; learners may complete degree programs rapidly, and in the process produce immense amounts of educational data that may be mined for expanding further competency platforms (Myers, 2014). While politically useful, and certainly financially attractive, does this detract from fields that require deep reflection and prize skill sets based on nuanced synthesis?

While little is certain in how technology is changing learning and technology, artificial intelligence and complex systems are changing the educational landscape. What is certain, then, is these changes require ethical inquiry to ascertain the role of educational technologies in the near future. The emerging ways of teaching and learning, based on the intricacies of inter-connected intelligent and artificial systems, pit educational possibility against technological innovation. The context of ethical inquiry is positioned at the intersection of expanding educational technology, the autonomy of humanity (as learners and instructors), and the socio-political role that intelligent systems increasingly play.

Digitalized Education: Ethics in an Age of Scalability

In the time of Sophocles, education was between the sage and his students. The learned man would be seated and lecture to his standing male pupils. This oral tradition was carried out for hundreds of years. Unfortunately, a lot of information was lost or changed because the knowledge was not written down for those in future generations.

Presently, there are those who can still remember the one-room schoolhouse, mostly run by unmarried women teaching to a room full of farm children-boys on one side, girls on the other. Their tools were a simple slate and chalk; books were often shared. Rote memorization was the optimal learning strategy. The American philosopher, John Dewey, felt that students should be afforded better and more diverse methods of learning. For his time, John Dewey was probably considered too progressive in his philosophy on what comprised a proper educational model. Dewey believed in plasticity, meaning students should be guided in such a way that they learn from their mistakes and apply that information to later situations (Dewey, 1916). Nearly one-hundred years after Dewey wrote his book, *Democracy and Education,* especially in industrialized nations, education is much changed. The difference, however, is in the *mode* of education, not the goal. Educators today still want students to learn from their mistakes and be able to apply those skills, but the institution has moved from one-room schools to schools with virtual classrooms and educators who are not even in the same time zone.

The Rise of STEM Education: An Impact of Digitalization on Education

One need not delve too far into educational literature to see a long-standing debate between the disciplines of science, technology, engineering, and mathematics (often referred to by its acronym, STEM) and the humanities (Taylor, Cantwell, & Slaughter, 2013).With caricatures like the young person who has recently completed an undergraduate degree in art history who is deemed qualified to work at a fast food restaurant, or the newly-minted engineer who immediately commands a high salary, the reality of the degree-to-career is far more nuanced, difficult to measure, and laden with variables pertaining to the individual student. It makes for good press, then, to artificially pit the STEM fields against that of the humanities, all the while paying little attention to the data that suggests far more career variability (Godin, 2005). Recent data actually suggests a higher level of cross-disciplinary access in STEM jobs (Carnevale, Smith, & Melton, 2011).

What this argument highlights, if not for the sake that the STEM/humanities divide may indeed be a false construct or a misleading and incomplete view of the problem, is the problem with the *value* of education. Pragmatically, what is the purpose of being educated? Is it for the sake of living an examined life as an educated person, or is it to achieve the goods of informed decision-making, engaged citizenship, and knowledge across one or more fields? Or, is the purpose of education financial, i.e. to secure a particular career and sustain an economically-comfortable life? Due to burgeoning tuition costs, for many families, the question of education becomes an equation of tuition versus future earning potential in a job.

The value of education is brought into sharper focus with the increased focus on retention, student success initiatives, and educational assessment as evidenced by the rapid development of educational data-mining, learning analytics, and automated feedback (Siemens & Long, 2011). These digital tools pivot on the same algorithmic and statistical advancements as business analytics: treating the student as customer, with educational success built by variables like demography and predicted grade outcomes, the agency of students' autonomy and individuality stunningly becomes that of an objectified, quantified, and wholly measurable retention-based science.

This is not to say that such digital tools fail to provide valuable and practical information for the success of many students; rather, in the larger analysis, what they provide is a *hybridity* of value. The costs of development, experimentation, and assessment are dwarfed by the potential savings to the institution if students are retained; likewise, though harder to measure save that of longitudinal studies, society likewise benefits from higher-earning graduates who can pay back their educational loans as well as make progress in industrial development. These are measurable costs and benefits, but the hybridity of value is fully realized when considering the cost to the quality of education. Notoriously more difficult to measure in concrete terms, what does it mean to suggest that the quality of education *suffers* from digital automation?

ETHICAL VIEWPOINTS: EDUCATION AND AUTOMATION

As educational opportunities continue to expand online, the development of automated systems will also continue to proliferate. This is due to the cost of automation versus human capital, efficiencies of nearly-instantaneous feedback, and streamlining of previously cumbersome administrative and instructor-dependent models of educational delivery (D'Mello & Graesser, 2012; Forsyth, Butler, Graesser, Halpern, Millis, Cai, & Wood, 2010). Whereas automation in other aspects of daily life like business investing, administrative and fiduciary accountability might be readily argued for their positive traits and minimal negative implications, the intent and potential outcomes of automation in education ought to be examined carefully. Three ethical models help make sense of automation in education: *care ethics* to demonstrate the ongoing need for human interaction and community, *relativism* to examine how educational delivery is a marketable product that will be driven by the priorities of its respective society, and *utilitarianism* to consider the relational aspects of educating large numbers of students at scale. In this relational role, act utilitarianism is generally considered because the impetus is on the act of educating to create better (i.e. happier) outcomes for students, though the sharp distinction with rule utilitarianism is not brought out here. This is not to say that other ethical theories would not contribute substantively to the topic automated education; rather, the selected theories present a wide analysis of historical and contemporaneous ethical thought.

Late twentieth-century care ethics have been developed and disseminated widely for their direct and wide-spanning applicability to such diverse fields as gender equality, healthcare, and education. In the broadest sense, care ethics is a theory that "...downplays rules and principles because it implicitly sees the conscientious and self-conscious use of these as getting in the way of a morally desirable direct interest *in* and connection *with* or *to* other people" (Slote, 2010, p. 152). Where other historical ethical theories cast the moral tension between the individual and the community, care ethics function as a bridge between the two (Benhabib, 1992). Applied specifically to education, care ethics demonstrate how interactivity between humans creates community, which are essential ingredients in learning theory (Mitchell & Sackney, 2011). This becomes ever more acute when trying to form learning communities in online education where physical space separates learners from each other and from their instructor (Palloff & Pratt, 2005).

Relativism, or "…that truth, goodness, or beauty is relative to a reference frame, and that no *absolute* overarching standards to *adjudicate* between competing reference frames exist," has considerable influence in contemporary education insofar as markets compete for student tuition dollars (Krausz, 2011, p.70). In a so-called "knowledge economy," the currency of educational attainment pivots against the perceived needs and priorities of a society; increased, then, in political and economic microscopes of shrinking budgets, are corollary measures of quality and deliverables in terms of student-to-professional skill sets (Robertson, 2014). Relativistic ethics provide the *modus operandi* of measuring an ever-shifting perception of skill sets through changing the frame of reference; educational delivery, understood within the reference as a business, provides a knowledge economy with a product. Technology, framed within this very narrow scope of the purposes of educational delivery, becomes the mode by which the product is delivered. With relativistic theory, education becomes a business product. Efficiency, continuous feedback loops, and predictive algorithms become the standard metrics of such a product for the sake of retention, student success, and measurable learning.

In the early 19th century, Bentham wrote about the theory of utilitarianism which continues to be quite influential today; an interesting tension that Bentham highlights is vital to how today's technology can be understood to affect the individual and society: "The community is a fictitious *body*, composed of the individual persons who are considered as constituting as it were its *members*. The interest of the community then is, what? – the sum of the interests of the several members who compose it" (Bentham, 1890, pp. 6-7). One of Bentham's students offers a lucid definition. Mill defines it best by saying the following: "The creed which accepts as the foundation of morals Utility, or the Greatest Happiness Principle, holds that actions are right in proportion as they tend to promote happiness, wrong as they tend to produce the reverse of happiness" (Mill, 1863, pp. 9-10). Educationally, utilitarian theory means both providing opportunities and nurturing to the greatest number of students, and including those who may have limited means for educational attainment. A technological utilitarian view of education means considering how policy decisions affect accessibility to the population of students, as well as possible ramifications for future educational opportunities. The duty of education, then, is to consider how decisions made for today's student also affect the future of education; each generation out to receive the same, if not better, education as the previous generation. Technology makes this both a possibility and a detriment.

ONLINE EDUCATION: THE ROLE OF THE ACADEMICIAN

Less than fifty years after John Dewey professed that a more progressive curriculum was necessary, the Advanced Research Projects Agency Network (ARPANET) was developed in 1969. This innovation was the precursor to today's Internet. With this development, elementary through tertiary education utilized various components of technology in the classroom. In 1989, the University of Phoenix offered the first online Bachelor's and Master's programs (Harasim, 2000). Online classes, since that time, have increased dramatically in many colleges and universities to meet the demands of nontraditional students.

With the advent of online courses, academicians were assured that the paradigm shift from traditional classrooms to those in a more digital world was not only crucial to the development of education but desirous. Students wanted, no *needed*, the freedom of taking courses at a time that worked for them, at a location that worked for them. As these courses were created, instructors served as Content or Subject Matter Experts. They were paid, in most instances, a flat rate to create the course that they would normally teach in a brick and mortar setting. More importantly, they were asked to sign a waiver allocating the information to the school. The institution now "owns" the material, to be used, re-used, and changed *ad infinitum* at the institution's whim. If those professors were tenured and had no intention of changing institutions, then the current conundrum may not exist. However, most institutions rely on adjunct professors to teach the majority of the curriculum. These professors have, in many cases, had no choice but to develop and facilitate online courses as a means to an end.

Online Courses vs. Brick and Mortar

For those on the outside looking in to the newest advances in education, there may be very few differences between traditional courses and those enhanced by technology. However, the courses are different from the very inception. At a brick and mortar institution, there is usually an accepted curriculum with perhaps already accepted syllabi; instructors are given academic freedom within the safety of those specified parameters. With online courses, web designers play an integral role, sometimes the only initial role. They may then work with the Content Experts to create a course. Interestingly, though, these experts are typically not the same as the ones who eventually teach the course. Therefore, the ones who have a vested interest in a course are not consulted in the planning process. Secondly, as in traditional classes, not every instructor is as good as the next. Some difficulties lie in that many of the online instructors, who once were brick and mortar instructors, now have to "teach" online courses to students who are more digitally literate than they are. Because a lot of nuance is lost with an online course, it is more difficult to evaluate instructors who teach these courses. Many online schools have faculty evaluators who sign in to the classes as participants to see how many times the instructor logs in, how much interaction takes place between instructor and student, and how robust the feedback is on certain assignments.

On the student side, the dynamic is also very different. In a brick and mortar setting, students are expected to do a certain amount of homework. For online learners, all the work is done at "home." Most institutions have an academic integrity guideline. In the classroom, it would be verified by the instructor actually seeing the students and knowing what kind of work they can produce. With online learning, however, instructors and students do not meet face to face, and work is delivered electronically. To deter plagiarism, various programs such as Turnitin are utilized, but these programs would only detect papers that were turned in previously, not "new" papers written by people other than the student. For a traditional PhD student, a meeting at the end of course and thesis work would allow the student to have a face-to-face defense with the committee or examiners; however, in some online PhD programs, the defense is a phone call or a Facetime chat. It is up to the institutions to promote an equal amount of academic rigor.

Online Education to MOOCs: The Ethics of Scalability

Delivery, pedagogy, and curricula between online and brick and mortar share notable differences, but the fundamental architecture of the courses has important similarities. For example, in online courses, class size-to-professor ratios are often kept to similar proportion as brick and mortar colleges, often in the 25:1 range. Workloads of reading, assignments, and formalized assessments often share similarities, thanks in part to accreditation standards. Perhaps most standardized within this structure is the outcome of college credit, recognized as partial fulfillment of a degree. College credit is obtained through the payment of tuition and the successful completion of the requirements of the course; these credits, albeit online or brick and mortar are often transferable to other collegiate institutions with similar accreditation standards. It might be argued online educational delivery is a contemporary and natural extension of the brick and mortar model. This transition has ethical implications because while it extends educational opportunity to those who may not fit the traditional college student demographic, the costs involved are just as significant for online students; therefore, it may be questioned if it really allows for more opportunities. The expansion of online education, too, also contributes to the total number of individuals who achieve a college degree, perhaps pitting the privileged position of those educated further from those who do not possess a college degree.

The number of degree recipients raises interesting questions, especially in terms of scalability. Using key components of the technological tools in online education, namely those associated with learning management systems, the massive open online course (MOOC) delivers a form of online education, just with different scalability and curricula goals. For a further examination of the ethics involved in technology and education, the MOOC is pivoted against the online and brick and mortar model of educational delivery. This is due to scalability: advocates of the MOOC claim to influence the educational opportunities of thousands, in some cases tens of thousands of students simultaneously, free of charge. Short of upending formal higher education, the structure, goals, and delivery of MOOCs call for ethical inquiry.

The Proliferation of MOOCs and Democratization of Education

A natural, or some may think an *unnatural*, progression from the harbinger of high-cost online education and the research goal to develop connectivism was the advent of MOOCs. These open, and *free*, courses provide education and power to those individuals who have access to a computer and the Internet (Littlejohn, 2013). However, a disparity still exists due to uncontrollable socio-economic factors. To alleviate some of this disproportionate service, the "Massachusetts's Institute of Technology (MIT) boldly changed the model: In late 2001, it announced its OpenCourseWare (OCW) initiative, an ambitious project to share the content of its courses with the world" (Smith & Casserly, 2006, p. 10). This innovation was taken a step further by the e-Granary Digital Library-a resource for third world students and professors to access information without Internet access (Patten, 2012).

The upshot of such technological and pedagogical innovation has been the capacity to gather and analyze educational data like never before; the content of MOOCs, from network analysis to digital interactivity, gives the field of research the possibility of unraveling how people learn with technology (Clow, 2013). This is not to say the research involved will be simplified; rather, the plethora of data and the dearth of clarity will most likely complicate the goal of understanding the special relationship between technology and learning (Koutropoulos, Gallagher, Abajian, de Waard, Hogue, Keskin, & Rodriguez, 2012).

MOOCs have been disseminated and advertised widely by organizations and companies like edX, Coursera, Udacity, and others (Pappano, 2012). While still struggling to find a public business model, the commodity, and a valuable one indeed, is that of massive troves of learning data (Dellarocas & Van Alstyne, 2013). While online courses may have several dozen students per course, MOOCs typically have hundreds, usually thousands, of students enrolled. Additionally, the architectures of MOOC learning management systems are complex and multi-faceted; network analysis between nodes of instructor, teaching assistant, and student interactions is becoming ever-more easier to identify, graph, and analyze (Milligan, Littlejohn, & Margaryan, 2013). While interactions may vary widely, having access to self-disclosed demographics, coupled with discussion interactions, graded assignments, and other learning outcomes are very valuable data points to the educational sector and industry.

With thousands of students interacting in one educational "space," in many cases at no financial cost to the student, the MOOC further democratizes the privilege of education (Carver & Harrison, 2013). Where only a few decades ago higher education was limited to those who could attend class in a physical space, the exponential growth of online education brought educational opportunities to those who benefitted from an online model. MOOCs, however, call the model of delivery of both prior forms into question: offered for free, or perhaps only at the expense of a certification of completion, MOOCs effectively undermine the cost of education (Aoun, 2012). In other words, what students in a prior generation paid for knowledge, students in this generation can "obtain" for free, or for a mere fraction of the prior cost.

Problems with this model persist, though. MOOC providers have yet to present a compelling currency for the value of learning; completion of a MOOC, even with an assessment, does not carry the same value as a course or curriculum offered by a college or university (Kolowich, 2013). Even though some highly-technical MOOCs may provide connections between high-performing students and companies looking to recruit for a certain skill set, this type of talent headhunting remains the exception, not the rule (Dellarocas & Van Alstyne, 2013). Additionally, recent data has suggested rather clearly that students enrolled in MOOCs are typically already college educated professionals who are looking to continue learning or who are taking the MOOC as a refresher. This data, along with the fact that a computing device and an Internet connection are necessary for participating in a MOOC, still render it not as democratizing as it initially appears. Those in rural, poor, or otherwise marginalized areas do not necessarily benefit from the proliferation of technology in the industrialized and urban world (Emanuel, 2013).

This is also to speak nothing of the possibility of neocolonialization of MOOCs. Are the ideas, curricula, and ideologies of those cultures developing MOOCs applicable universally (Willis, 2013; Altbach, 2013)? While the examination of MOOCs and other forms of online education in terms of hermeneutical categories may be interesting, the specific ethical models of care ethics, relativism, and utilitarianism help unpack some of the issues raised here.

MOOCs and Care Ethics: A Model for Altruism?

Initially, it might appear as though the model of care ethics fits well with the loftier goals of MOOCs: to connect large groups of students together in an online community to provide educational resources to those who may not have readily-accessible opportunities, at a reduced (or free) cost. A care ethic might also suggest that knowledge gained in a MOOC environment would contribute to an individual student's ability to build a more advanced knowledge-base and, thus, further employment opportunities, much like a "traditional" education. Unlike brick and mortar or online schools, the MOOC platform might create a more level environment built by independent study, hard work, and sheer will to succeed, not money, privilege, socio-economic status, or other similar metrics.

The problems with this model of ethical inquiry are numerous. If the massive scalability of MOOCs is touted as virtuous, the nuanced participation and abysmal completion rates seriously question the very number of people that utilize whatever resource the MOOC might be. The numbers are so drastically spread, categories of measurement are often delineated as (or at least akin to): "lurkers, drop-ins, passive participants and active participants" (Rivard, 2013b, p. 3). Like other forms of online learning, MOOC platform providers must provide assessment evidence that shows real learning in order to secure the possibility of credentialing both with traditional and online schools, as well as independent organizations (Sandeen, 2013). Models are currently being developed to help measure outcomes (Breslow, Pritchard, DeBoer, Stump, Ho, & Seaton, 2013), identify cheating and other nefarious behaviors (Meyer & Zhu, 2013), and the impact of instruction in MOOCs (Tomkin & Charlevoix, 2014). Though it is readily acknowledged that such direct learning assessment demands are often met with resistance and obfuscation at traditional and online institutions, the burden of proof rests with MOOC providers so long as moral agency, especially that of care ethics, is applied to the positive attributes of MOOCs.

While MOOC providers tout free education, there are numerous costs, both to the hosting institutions and to the students themselves. Recently, some MOOC platforms instituted inexpensive assessments, for verification of learning, while keeping participation as a student free of charge (Yuan and Powell, 2013). While there is ongoing discussion about revenue stream, sustainability, and business models of MOOCs, the vast amounts of data available to companies for headhunting and technology development will only exponentially increase in monetary fluidity (Mazoue, 2013). While certainly appearing altruistic, the use of data, even with permission, raises ethical concerns of exploitation and autonomy. Who controls the learning and demographic data? How much data is disclosed, including the data points needed to (re)construct individually-identifiable information?

In significant portions of the developing world, access to computing technology and the Internet is limited, if not impossible. While an ethic of care might suggest that free education, vis-à-vis a MOOC provided by a world-class university, could be a key to rising out of poverty, the reality of lacking the very tools needed for participation suggests otherwise (Laplante, 2013). In many parts of the world, computer and Internet access is highly restricted if not altogether unavailable. Thus, in terms of grandiose claims that taking MOOCs are the keys to lifting millions from poverty, the evidence is lacking.

MOOCs and Relativistic Ethics: An Open Business Model

While a care ethic may address the possibility that educational opportunities are needed to help millions trapped in poverty, the reality of the evidence supports the claim that most people benefiting from MOOCs are already college educated and from wealthy nations (Emanuel, 2013). While MOOC providers appeal to a care ethic of providing free education to millions who may not have opportunities otherwise, the evidence paints a more compelling story of gathering massive amounts of online learning data (Dodd, 2014). From the seminal idea of Siemens and Downes (Mackness, Mak, & Williams, 2010), the proliferation of MOOCs exponentially grew; not only were providers in competition to build public platforms, but universities and colleges competed for, essentially, recognition of being innovative and transformative. While many MOOC providers charge an expensive fee for development and use (Parr, 2013; Lewin, 2013), universities and colleges absorb this cost into marketing strategy. However, the irony here is twofold: universities and colleges essentially give away a version of what would normally be charged in tuition dollars, and learners are not classified as students, thus the data provided on the backchannel is not protected by FERPA or other regulatory policies (Smith, 2013).

The model of MOOCs framed by innovative growth prior to a cogent business model, fueled by public perception of good will, yet without clear direction, is relativistic insofar as it is thoroughly Darwinian. Though many proclaimed MOOCs to be the new innovation that would eventually shutter numerous educational providers, there currently exists no evidence that MOOCs have caused such closures (Kolowich, 2013; De Jong, 2014). What will be the sustaining business model of MOOCs save that of headhunting a very small population of users and collecting fees from educational institutions? The data collected by MOOC providers, which contains not only geographic and self-disclosed demographic information, also contains invaluable data like time spent on specific tasks, interactions with classmates, which can be used to form very complex interactivity network analysis from nodes of highly-involved participants, assessment scores, and the point(s) at which a learner becomes disengaged. As many schools develop and refine online models of education, such MOOC data, in both individualistic and aggregated sets, becomes a highly-valuable asset. Like click interaction data for a marketer, MOOC participatory data may be used by online education providers to increase retention, prevent lurking, and track student activity. Such MOOC-provider datasets would be useful to researchers, too, as it can be used in alignment to verify, validate, or substantiate proof of concept data.

A relativistic ethic helps explain what is occurring in public perception, as well as the backchannel for research data: sustainability and capital are needed to develop and propagate widespread, free education. This involves creating a bifurcated model of business ethics: the public who engages with MOOCs does so with an interface that does not appear invasive; indeed the MOOC supports learning, refining skills, and facilitating the human need to intellectually grow. However, collected data is also used to grow a business and fund additional educational research that heretofore has never been possible at the scale of hundreds of thousands of concurrent students.

MOOCs and Utilitarianism: Learning at Scale, but What Scale of Quality?

Arguably, educational leaders have attempted with each generation, at least from the twentieth century onward, new models, innovative approaches, especially with the advent of widespread computer and Internet usage, and nuanced assessment. This may be evidenced by such movements as standardized testing -both quantitative and qualitative- common core curricula, and various movements in pedagogy. In a simplified explanation, this may be due to a utilitarian undercurrent in education: providing the very best education possible for the most number of students with a notion of continuous improvement.

MOOCs may be viewed with a similar lens: scaling up educational opportunities for those with limited time, resources, or tuition dollars. Indeed, MOOCs are the largest scale of education in history, but it is an open question as to whether that scale is enhancing learning or if it is simplifying what might be advanced concepts into cursory and, ultimately, shallow knowledge. Preliminary assessments, as well as a number of projects underway, attempt to address this question; findings thus far indicate a similar matrix as that within most universities and colleges: depending on the curricula and professors, the results vary widely (Ripley, 2012).

The differences between MOOCs and a so-called traditional delivery, then, lie to the evaluations of accreditors. There is a modicum of curricula and credentialing "control" over the traditional institution, but do these safeguards, however thin, exist for MOOCs? If they do apply (as those teaching MOOCs are often well-known and established scholars), is it to satisfy policies within accrediting councils, or is it to compete with other MOOC providers? While some institutions have moved to offer college credit for certain MOOCs, the control over delivery and content remains suspect. Such relinquishing of control, in a utilitarian view, may favor the democratization of education, but it must be challenged: to what end? Does this contribute substantively to a better, more transparent, more engaging education to future generations? Or, does relinquishing control over curricula and credentialing mean irrevocable changes to the professorate?

A first-time MOOC professor recently realized he taught more students in an eight-week MOOC than in his entire career (Moss, 2014). For professors who teach upwards of tens of thousands of students in a MOOC, the existential realization cannot be discounted. Due to sheer numbers, the role of the professor changes in MOOC delivery from expert to facilitator. Where the role of a teaching assistant might once have contributed knowledgeable guidance in a traditional university, discussion posts are often mediated by fellow students. In the current movements to change pedagogy from the "sage on the stage," the irony with MOOCs is the professor is once again consigned to the digital stage because the role demands being detached from most individual students and engaged with the aggregate. In a utilitarian view, this begs the question: how important are professors, especially once a MOOC has been offered once? Is one professor, or perhaps a small team of teaching assistants, necessary to procure the best outcomes for learners, or can peer-to-peer learning achieve the same ends? Once the course content, discussion points, and automatic graders are present for a given course, is the professor necessary to deliver the course? Further, of what assurance is a course a quality product if devoid of the professor having control over the curriculum?

MOOCs as a Catalyst for Driving Automation

When the philosopher John Dewey stated that if students are to learn how to build a house, an educator should first tell them how, then show them how, and then actually have them *build* a house in order to learn with carryover skills, he would have certainly been chagrined with the concept of MOOCs. These massive online courses have little individual student/instructor interaction, and because MOOCs are offered globally, there can literally be thousands enrolled in each course. It is not surprising, therefore, that roughly only 10% of students actually complete a course (Sandeen, 2013). Because of the super-abundance of students enrolled in these courses, it would be extremely time-consuming for professors or assistants to grade the sheer volume of assignments. Thus, in this way, MOOCs are acting as a catalyst for driving the automation of grading student assignments.

With the plethora of student assignments and societal expectations that having feedback *now* is a requirement, automatic online graders have also become a commercial enterprise that reinforces a business model mentality upon the field of education. It is not surprising that the earliest electronic or e-assessments were created for computer programming students four decades ago (Al-Smadi & Gütl, 2008). Now, career-specific assessment has moved across all programs. Ten years ago, the prominent online tools were Blackboard, WebCT, ClassNet, and E-course (Trivedi, Kar & McNeil, 2003). Today, Blackboard remains at the forefront of online tools due to its presence in academic and other business settings as well as its ability to secure acquisitions with smaller companies. Various other competitors of Blackboard include Pearson E-College, Moodle, Sakai, Lore, Myedu, GoingOn, and Instructure Canvas (Nabi, 2012). Blackboard recently hired a new CEO and announced "its new platform for massive open online courses (MOOCs) meant to rival startups like Coursera and Udacity" (Heussner, 2013, p.

1). Therefore, the most prominent learning management system is promulgating the most current educational trend.

The use of MOOC interaction data, coupled with targeted educational experiments, will lead to further automation in education. Within the traditional educational model, one of the largest expenses for a college or university has been professors' salaries. The decline of tenured and full-time teaching positions, especially in the humanities (Conn, 2010), evidences the ever-evolving business model of education: replacing high-cost professors and instructors with adjunct professors will lead to, eventually, the replacement of human instructors. Automatic tutors and human-like interaction systems are already highly-advanced and are currently undergoing further calibration. The MOOC platform would be an excellent testing environment for automatic instructors: digitalization of the human face is already possible for videos and automatic graders exist for submitted work and discussion posts. From a student's view, psychological experiments with affect-aware and cognitive technologies, while currently on the forefront of such automation, will become far more powerful with MOOC-driven data. Research in these fields includes development of automatic student tutors, automated and digitalized teachers that converse with students, and modeling techniques meant to keep students active and engaged (D'Mello & Graesser, 2012; Calvo & D'Mello, 2012).

As additional data is available, especially as an average interaction of certain curricula content can be established and validated, the need for a human professor becomes diminished. Such automation would also be a boon to online educational providers who could incrementally scale back to one professor overseer of multiple sections, leaving most of the work to the automated system, and then to full automation. Such technology is conceivably less than one decade from full implementation. Perhaps only the savviest students could detect, in an online environment, if they were being taught by a human or a human-like automated instructor. With these technological advances, the blur between the massive size of MOOCs and the smaller-scale online courses, could also become more ubiquitous. Provided students "learn" and providers allow for the means to do so, do questions of scale matter with such automation?

Ethically, then, the question of what a college credit hour means will come to the forefront. If automated educational delivery, established from a codified curriculum, replaces the traditional notion of education, the antiquated idea of the credit hour will be replaced by demonstrable learning: every measure of education will be outcomes-based. What suffers here, then, is the reflection, even if just the *time* for reflection, inasmuch as students think in terms of degree attainment and administrators think in terms of commodification. Does the automation of education – and the automation of learning through the prevalence of such technology – allow for reflection of the meaning of what has been learned? Thinking through the ethics of automation and learning requires looking beyond the MOOC, beyond online delivery, beyond the traditional classroom.

Beyond the MOOC: The Rise of Learning after Networks

The technology of MOOCs, namely the interconnectivity between thousands of people learning in one digital space, will not soon leave the educational horizon; the format of such delivery, however, will likely change rapidly as automation becomes more prevalent. Employers and collegiate institutions will have to grapple with the "currency" of educational attainment: is knowledge broad-based and critically-informed with a variety of subjects and expertise, or is knowledge confined to demonstrable sets of reproducible functions?

The speculation of the future of technology is both exciting and fallacious; the same is true for education, though both are principally established through reflection and innovation. The rise of the MOOC coincided with a style of connectivism, popularized by George Siemens (Siemens, 2005; Rodriguez, 2012), in which networks of people helped facilitate learning. Connectivism, in these terms, demands a high-level of self-motivation, especially around the core node of facilitation and receptivity of information; it also presumes a basic knowledge and learning skill that can be reciprocated in gathering new knowledge. However, as the world becomes ever-more geospatially connected through Internet communication and innovation, the presumption that people have an inherent ability to interact with those technologies becomes more suspect. What would learning look like in a post-networked age? Instead of nodes of contact with discussion leaders and expert instructors or well-informed students, could so-called digital natives learn, on their own, how to navigate a complex web of sources, information, and nuanced thinking? This is indeed possible, perhaps even likely, but it is not a foregone conclusion: with expansion of complexity, being able to navigate one's way is not coequal with understanding why and how.

The technological advances necessary for the MOOC, as well as the automation and learning designs that have flourished from the back-end data will continue to proliferate and, subsequently, change. What may eventually emerge is a reconciliation of the physical distance inherent in online learning and the networked position of learners who learn from fellow students as well as instructors. How this reconciliation would be worked out, however, is unclear; for example, videoconferencing is a technology used for over a decade with only incremental improvements due to network speed. However, by bringing together refined data of how students learn coupled with ever-improving communications, this reconciliation of physical and networked distance may be soon on the horizon.

The question of such a model, now with hyper-networked students, advanced automation, and redefined learning, is the role of the human instructor. The classroom centered on the instructor in previous times has undergone drastic revision with so-called active learning, while simultaneous redefinition of pedagogy and automation in the online realm. In summary, then, classrooms of today and tomorrow look and operate quite differently than even a few years ago. This may be a good shift in power. More data and time is needed to assess that question properly, but this at the very least begins to question the need for and role of the human instructor as an expert who thinks about, shapes, and delivers the curricula to students. There are a variety of learning theories in educational practice due to the works of Dewey, Vygotsky, and Gardner. These theories of learning include visual, auditory, and bodily-kinesthetic to name a few. These theories remind us of the individual differences among humans. Online nursing programs, however, who teach students with "virtual" patients, may fit into a category that defies basic human principles of compassion - do no harm.

EDUCATIONAL ASSESSMENT AND THE ROLE OF THE ACADEMICIAN: RUBRIC USE AND DIGITAL AUTOMATION

The drive for standardization in academe has been notable in the last two decades, perhaps in great part because of financial ties and high-stakes testing. However, the outward reach for standardization started much sooner with researchers wanting to utilize a metric that could be applied to writing samples. When Diederich, French, and Carlton (1961) performed the first study that utilized rubrics, they called these metrics "clusters of adjectives" (p. 11). "Later, in the 1970's, Diedrich conducted a study using readers and a defined criteria to determine how to grade large quantities of papers consistently for a minimal cost" (Strunk, 2012, p. 25).

Now, over 50 years later, "the majority of all states utilize rubrics as indispensable facets for measuring students' writing achievements for standardized tests" (Strunk, 2012, p. v). Not only are rubrics used in assessing students' performance in ground classes, they have made their way as the primary metric in online classes as well. Unfortunately, though, since their inception, rubrics have been considered a panacea for the standardization of grading student papers. The empirical evidence shows conflicting information, however. In a study done by Andrade (2001), the researcher hypothesized that students who were introduced to a rubric prior to assessment would receive higher scores. This was evident in only one paper out of three. These results could have been a result of many different variables and not the rubric alone. In a further study done by Strunk (2012), students were given a rubric prior to the writing assignment. Then, they were given a questionnaire about the perceptions of the helpfulness of the rubric. "While the men's perceptions were as positive as the females, their writing scores were not as high" (p. 90). The researcher concludes that students should "remember that a rubric is a writing guide, not a guiding force" (p. 102).

In a study performed by Anglin, Anglin, Schumann and Kaliski (2008) there was notable difference between grading speeds of rating assignments via hand-grading and those done through electronic-grading systems; both systems of grading required a rubric as its operating metric. It is interesting to note, though, that the students' perceptions of helpfulness of instructors' feedback and the speed at which they received the feedback was not significantly different than those who received feedback via traditional grading systems.

In an age of microwave mentality (everything can be done in a nanosecond), academicians need to continue to question the utilitarian aspects of technological advances. With such advances, researchers such as Shermis and Hamner "found automated essay scoring was capable of producing scores similar to human scores" (Rivard, 2013a, p.1). Anant Agarwal, president of EdX, claims that instant-grading software would "offer distinct advantages over the traditional classroom system, where students often wait days or weeks for grades" (Markoff, 2013, p. A1). While the speed and "human-like" quality certainly appeal to technology gurus and some academicians, the opponents are raising erudite points. Les Perelman, one such critic, has "fooled" these technologically advanced instant-graders into giving an essay, written in a nonsensical way, high marks: an essay that would certainly have not been accepted by an experienced academic (Markoff, 2013).

Automation and Commodification of Education

The digitalization of education has produced heretofore unavailable data: in near live-time, administrators, faculty members, and researchers are able to assess a student's activity, engagement, and potential outcome, through predictive algorithms. Much of this data has been culled and tracked by online education and MOOCs, as well as data produced by learning management systems. Where in prior generations, data points were limited to observational data, of instructors teaching, for example, and final grades for quantification of outcomes, the plethora of data available now is thanks in part to digitalization. The outcomes of such data proliferation are an open question; what is not, however, is the potential for innovation and big business within education. One outcome of such large data sets used as a development-driver for new technologies is instructors' "activity...being restructured, via the technology, in order to reduce their autonomy, independence, and control over their work and to place workplace knowledge and control as much as possible into the hands of the administration" (Noble, 1998, p. 362).

This model, of course, works well with the now accepted *business* model of education (Lawrence and Sharma, 2002). Because there is money to be made in education, it is easily accepted for many in the business world to think of students as customers, education as a service/end product, and faculty as replaceable entertainers. "Tell students that they are consumers, and they will act like consumers but ultimately learn less and perhaps not even receive the credential that they think they are buying" (Perry, 2014, p. 14). Unfortunately, this business model acceptance has moved into proprietary education and now non-profits as well. Granted, those in academe need to be accountable to their students' education; however, they need to consider the cost to their own educational philosophies. Perry (2014) also states, "…the responsibility of a teacher to his or her students is far greater than the employee to the customer" (p. 1).

In nations where a so-called "knowledge economy" drives the need for formal higher education, or at least specific skills, as necessary for middle class living (Young, Daniels, Balarin, & Lowe, 2012), then the development of educational business models and industry innovation centered on student learning will only continue to grow exponentially. In terms of ethical reflection, it is important to question the benefit for students and instructors alike. From a utilitarian perspective, students stand poised to benefit from a wide array of technologies that contribute to learning as more is understood in terms of cognitive, affective, and brain sciences are expanded; likewise, a relativistic ethic might be that such data should be available for innovation in an open market, with basic legal protections. However, when a care ethic is applied, the argument might be that privileged students, in these terms those students who can afford technology and institutions who implement expensive technologies, are the only agents who stand to benefit from business innovations. While further data and time will help make the ethics of student benefit more lucid, a preliminary conclusion is that effects on students are mixed positively and negatively.

Automation, as a product of educational commodification, is a bit different when applied to instructors. It might be argued from a utilitarian perspective that streamlining and simplifying instruction would help with dissemination of knowledge, but this also brings up the question of instructional quality; without trained experts, the production, testing, and teaching of knowledge becomes less of a human skill than a machine-made, closed-loop process without creativity. Would a relativist ethic consider the role of the instructor in such a model, or would it simply be an issue of skill survival? While humans may not operate at the same speed as machines, again the issue returns to that of human creativity, at present a unique skill. A care ethic might consider, too, the agency of the human instructor who possesses synthetic thinking skills that are beyond the scope of artificially-intelligent machines. What binds these three ethical constructs together when considering human instructors is that of creativity, that which entails the freedom to synthesize, analyze, and reassemble knowledge as agents who willfully take responsibility of students.

Treatment of Academicians: An Ethical Viewpoint

For those in academia, a tenured-track position is extremely desirable. It allows professors to have freedom in their scholarship without worrying about termination proceedings. It is this freedom that promotes innovative thinking and creativity. However, "critics say that tenure's protection make it difficult to get rid of incompetent faculty and can promote a culture of complacency among those who have attained the status" (Stripling, 2011, p. 1). Unfortunately, being tenured is not the norm in most colleges and universities, and the brunt of the teaching falls onto adjuncts. For these professors, there is usually a heavier work load along with paucity in pay.

Margaret Mary Vojtko was an adjunct professor of French studies at Duquesne University for nearly three decades. She was destitute at her death at age 83. Unfortunately for her, being an adjunct professor does not earn a top wage or a benefits structure. Her plight is no different than adjuncts working at colleges and universities globally. Though the officials at the university knew about her housing situation and her cancer, her course load was ultimately dropped (Ellis, 2013).

With many institutions currently cutting back on the number of courses adjuncts can teach, the adjuncts are doing what they can to survive: going outside their own institutions to pick up additional classes, teaching online courses, and serving as Content Experts. Most colleges and universities only pay several thousand dollars per course, so earning a living wage requires piecing together multiple courses, sometimes over long distances (Kilgannon, 2014). Additionally, the total number of part-time faculty members has steadily increased in the last forty years, while the number of tenure and tenure-track professors has steadily decreased (Curtis, 2014). The social tension within a utilitarian emphasis with students, interestingly, is that parents encourage their children to go to college so that they can have mobility within or outside of their socioeconomic class. Adjunct professors have a Master's or terminal degree in order to teach college students, yet they remain the working poor. Perhaps for the first time in recent history, the level of education is by no means an indicator of socio-economic stability. In no uncertain terms, the current employment structure and number of opportunities for adjunct professors are a perverse inversion between the level of education and the rate of pay; teaching is commoditized due to the fact that administrators operate solely on a business model.

Increasingly, the human components of education, as the curriculum designer, content expert, and instructor, are being phased out, mostly due to financial concerns. Technology is able to replicate human-like interactions; this will continue to proliferate and expand within all domains of education. The question, then, becomes one of value of human thinkers. In a relativistic ethic, it might well be argued that humans must keep ahead of the pace of technology; so, if instructors can be replaced by technology, perhaps they should be? If a machine is able to teach or complete tasks affiliated with teaching (like grading) as well as or better than a human, how could this be a negative consequence? A care ethic, however, would suggest there is something intrinsically beneficial, special, and unique in the human who bears the responsibility of educating others in a field of expertise; this unique perspective would not be replicable until machines have sentience. A utilitarian view shows a middle approach between these two extremes: the value of preserving the human agent in his/her uniqueness is balanced on the needed outcomes of students who must carry on the lessons and legacies of being educated. This view downplays the negativity of the diminishing role of human expertise and reintegrates the social role of the student who is educated.

In the last two decades, both teaching and learning have undergone significant and irrevocable changes. Understanding widely-implemented learning analytics in terms of student success, as well as how scholarship and teaching are conducted today, are necessary to model ethical viewpoints of education and technology and their advancements.

PEDAGOGY AND LEARNING REDEFINED: THE STEWARDSHIP OF LEARNING ANALYTICS DATA

With great technological advances comes great responsibility. One important ethical dilemma surrounds learning analytics: the stewardship of the data that is collected. Both commercial and educational industries have seen the repercussions of sensitive data being compromised. Specifically, with the recent Target breach, consumers' names, addresses (both home and e-mail), phone numbers, and the most alarming-encrypted PIN numbers were taken (Rosenblum, 2014). In the education sector, the recent breach at Indiana University revealed that past and current students' information was breached. Most alarming was to note that the data was left in an unsecured location for nearly a year and was picked up by three web crawling programs (Khadaroo, 2014).

The first issue is the lack of transparency because students are not told what data is being collected. How important are their names, gender, marital status, and social security numbers to them? The second issue is to what extent the data will be used. Will a failing grade in the second week of class be a signal, albeit perhaps an incorrect one, that the student will be unsuccessful in this course or any other? If learning analytics are truly meant to improve the educational experience, then students should be afforded the opportunity to decide what data they wish to be used. The third issue is delicately called here the "ick" factor. Predictive algorithms are currently being used to drive learning analytics; however, are instructors and students aware of how digital stalking can impact their lives?

Learning Analytics and Ethical Directions

Learning analytics, a burgeoning field inclusive of educators, computer scientists, psychologists, and experts from a number of other disciplines, "...provides a new model for college and university leaders to improve teaching, learning, organizational efficiency, and decision making and, as a consequence, serve as a foundation for systemic change" (Siemens & Long, 2011, p. 30). Slade and Prinsloo (2013) "define learning analytics as the collection, analysis, use, and appropriate dissemination of student-generated, actionable data with the purpose of creating appropriate cognitive, administrative, and effective support for learners" (p. 1512). This begs the question of what is considered "appropriate." Who defines what is appropriate and what appropriate actions are? Is it those in power, like administrators, those affected by the data, in this case, students, or those who can directly intervene, professors and teaching assistants, for example?

The power in learning analytics rests with that of algorithmic predictions, which can point administrators and faculty members to specific students who are having academic problems; the predictions allow for either digital or personalized intervention to prevent student failure and attrition (van Barneveld, Arnold, & Campbell, 2012). Similarly, other learning analytics systems help guide students to future courses that they may successfully complete due to prior academic performance metrics (Whitten, Clarksville, Sanders, & Stewart, 2013). While homegrown systems, like Purdue University's *Signals*, developed from academic research, much of today's innovation in learning analytics occurs under the auspices of higher education businesses.

Issues arising from learning analytics, like information transparency, student awareness of data being collected, student privacy, and methodologies of computation remain on the forefront of the juxtaposition of technology and ethics (Willis & Pistilli, 2014). Of the various frameworks to examine such issues, prior models have included both legal (Swenson, 2014; Pardo & Siemens, 2014) and specific ethical modeling like Potter's Box (Willis, Campbell, & Pistilli, 2013).

The swift innovation of such technologies require ethical modeling based upon established principles; the problem, then, rests with being able to apply such principles in a timely way to guide innovation responsibly. Interestingly, much of what has been published in the realm of ethical lenses of technology has been predicated on privacy, transparency, and accountability; all of these are, of course, admirable goals. However, they do not set up an a priori framework with which to argue; thus, the statements put forth assume contemporary, western value systems in situations where, for example, true privacy has not existed for decades (or ever).

In a recent article, two thinkers at the forefront of the learning analytics field presented an argument for an intersection between ethics and online privacy; they define ethics "as the systemization of correct and incorrect behavior in virtual spaces to all stakeholders" (Pardo & Siemens, 2014, p. 2). This definition presumes there is an a priori known "correct" and "incorrect" behavior online. Does this conform to the legalities of a given society, to a set of ethical principles, or to what is arbitrarily decided as right behavior? Pardo and Siemens (2014) argue for ethical guidelines to "comply with the most common privacy principles emerging in various legislative initiatives" (p. 4). They go on to argue for "fair use of personalization" for the budding field of learning analytics (p. 7), including "transparency, student control over the data, security, and accountability and assessment" (p. 11). Slade and Prinsloo (2013) outline the empirical problems with learning analytics implementation and use; they propose a number of principles to effectively examine the ethical issues with learning analytics, including amongst others, "learning analytics should function primarily as a *moral* practice resulting in understanding rather than measuring…[students] should also voluntarily collaborate in providing data and access to data to allow learning analytics to serve *their* learning and development" (Slade & Prinsloo, 2013, p. 1519). Do such principles pre-suppose that students know what they need to succeed, and if so, how they can use data to help them?

The problems with ethical studies of learning analytics are twofold: what is often labelled as "ethics" are often couched as discussions about privacy, legalities, and data usage, but ironically not ethics of education, learning, or student agency and ethical models dealing with technology are often not malleable or applicable to the speed of innovation. Discussions of ethics in technology, specifically at the granular level of learning analytics, are at an intellectual crossroads. Unless principled ideas are brought within the public sphere of technological development, the speed of scientific innovation will render ethics of technology misguided at best and obsolete at worst.

TOWARD AN ETHICAL MODEL IN LEARNING ANALYTICS

The term "ethics" has become a catch-all for indicating what should and should not be done with the digital medium. Lost are appeals to what makes people greater than their individual selves and critical thinkers of the societies they inhabit. An ethic of education ought not to be prescriptive because thoughtful contemplation about potentially unintended consequences does not move at the pace of development. Rather, ethics of technology and of learning analytics ought to be deeply ingrained in innovation, implementation, and assessment. At each critical juncture of development, a set of principled frameworks should be employed to think through possible outcomes, unintended consequences, and how those ethical decisions could affect future inventions.

Utilitarianism, relativism, and care ethics, framed together to think through potential outcomes, serve as a generative framework beneficial to the future of learning analytics. With a utilitarian emphasis, schools must face the question posed by Slade and Prinsloo (2013): "At some point, all institutions supporting student learning must decide what their main purpose really is: to maximize the number of students reaching graduation, to improve the completion rates of students who may be regarded as disadvantaged in some way, or perhaps to simply maximize profits" (p. 1514). A serious look at relativism requires the measurement of potential invention with the potential outcomes; for example, technology could be invented to implant neuroreceptors in students' brains to guide behavior toward optimal learning. In the framework of relativism, this could be quite profitable for a technology company who would want to appeal to institutions interested in "maximize[ing] profits." Ethically, however, it forces the question of whether this would be an invention that would be beneficial to humanity; if neuroreceptors are implanted for learning's sake, could they also not be implanted for many other commercially-viable options? Care ethics provide a more holistic view of the student experience; it helps ask the question of whether a predictive analytic would be beneficial for students. For example, predictive algorithms can account for student behavior to predict course success (which is widely used today to help students in individual courses); if the same technology is applied to predicting success across an entire curriculum, would this discourage students from completion? Or, to belabor the point, will students like Albert Einstein, who are unaccomplished in fields like mathematics (Kaku, 2004) fail to impact the world because a predictive algorithm suggested they would be better suited for something else? Care ethics help set out the limits of what may or may not be harmful for students to know, especially when in the theoretical construct of predictive analytics.

Understanding the intersection of ethics in an age of learning analytics means adapting to constant change with principled networks of inquiry. While analytics help redefine student learning, there is another equally important aspect with far-reaching implications to students: scholarship. The scholarship of researchers and professors is radically changing in the digital age, and this change is affecting students.

Scholarship in a Digital Age: Redefining Ethics

The last fifty years has seen a dramatic change in the creation and storage of scholarly work. In the past, academics were limited to library stacks. Books and journals were archived in libraries according to physical space allowances. These artifacts can last for hundreds of years, the yellowing of the pages sometimes the only reminder of the passing of time. Now, however, virtual libraries are becoming the norm, and the digital data must be stored in such a way that content is not lost. This requires updates and changing technology. For tenure-track and tenured college professors, a major responsibility is the production of scholarship. With multitudes of documents at the fingertips of academics, it is possible to retrieve the most current information in a fraction of the time of past library searches. The downfall, unfortunately, is that much of what is available on the Internet is not scholarly and has to be sifted through with a modicum of discernment. Scholarly sources are often so voluminous in their digital availability that synthesizing research into coherency is increasingly requiring new data-acquisition and processing skills.

The last fifty years has also seen a change in the priorities of academic institutions. Originally, the institutions were the mecca for the development of the students intellectually. Then, of course, a service component was added to the model. Professors used to work in concert with students to improve their communities. Service-Learning, it is now called, is being re-introduced into some curricula. Now, unfortunately, because the business model is prevalent, students pick schools because of monetary output.

How much will they earn in a particular field is a primary question used to determine which schools will deem a closer look. With the change in institution priorities, a change was also imminent with scholarship requirements for faculty. Faculty members are hired to *teach*, but with the "publish or perish" mantra of many universities, faculty members are ultimately evaluated for their ability to *publish* and publish broadly. Tools like Google Scholar, Web of Knowledge, and InCites, only increase the pressure because scholarly output is wholly quantified in terms of influence.

Scholarly journals, in their original form, were costly to obtain for authors (professors) and librarians. They were sustained by subscription fees. However, because many of these subscriptions were expensive, some libraries were forced to allow subscriptions to lapse. With the progress of technology and the use of a business model, especially in scholarly repositories like JSTOR and Project MUSE, open access journals were then created. These articles in open access journals are free to procure on the Internet but instead of subscription fees, they come at a cost via author fees. Academics often pay for their articles to be published on this platform with their own funds or with grant funds allocated for publication. There is a caveat with the utilization of these journals by academics; the articles published in them will only be high quality if that journal is using editors who are adept at determining high quality from poor quality (McCabe & Snyder, 2005). Thus, even though open access journals give professors a plethora of research to choose from, the professors will still need to use a discerning eye to determine what is actually scholarly. With the motivator of publishing and its ensuing issues, professors will have less time to teach and perform student advising.

Not that there was ever a streamlined or golden era of academic scholarship, but the demands now, including teaching, researching, publishing, advising, and service to the academy, are only becoming more fractured and complex with time. While the advent of automation is a boon to many fields, it must be questioned whether or not machine teaching, learning, and synthesis of information is beneficial to the academy. Balancing the demands of thoughtful scholarship with the speed of dissemination means there is change underway which calls for a reconfiguration of the ethics of learning and of teaching.

Since the mid-20th century, Bloom's Taxonomy has dominated pedagogy, from primary to collegiate education. Various iterations and revisions now address domains of knowledge, technological use, and assessment, often with differing synonyms of the original model. Special ethical attention ought to be paid to the highest category in the pyramid, that of "evaluation," or in its more recent veneration, "creating." The *creation* of knowledge has been relegated to the annals of educational theory when, in reality, it ought to stand as oeuvre to the world: the calling of something out of nothing, the inauguration of light thrust upon the darkness of human finitude and ignorance. In its finest form, the academy, both of yesterday and tomorrow, ought to be a place of creation of knowledge and a safe apprenticeship of thinkers to carry on the task of doing the impossible. The domain of this highest form in the taxonomy pivots itself on the ethical because creating ought to be celebrated as the highest of human achievements. It is the culmination of human struggle in an early agrarian society, as well as industrialized and technological society, and is the way forward. Creating should be rightly located within ethical conversations because it means both helping and hindering humanity, and very often those are certainly not clear categories and may result in unintended consequences.

Creating knowledge is now at a point of exponential growth thanks to rapidly-increasing computing power. Humans stand poised to create at a rate never known historically, and much of this is driven by scholarship. While scholars debate the potentially-dissociated link between scholarship and teaching, ethically they are conjoined because guiding the next generation in the desire to create responsibly ought to dominate academic motivations. Scholarship, teaching, and learning are conjoined in a nexus of interactions; knowing how to support each of these modalities in terms of creation becomes an ethical concern in their applicability to affect the world rapidly through dissemination and commoditized innovation. Standing at the juncture of all these is not technology, machines, or other things humans have created: they are humans themselves.

INTERACTIVITY AND THE HUMAN ELEMENT: TEACHING IN A DIGITALIZED WORLD

In 2001, Willis and Raines stated that goals of education should change and "educators must accept the computer and its software not as replacements for the content of the disciplines at the core of the curriculum, but as useful extensions that complement content" (p. 54). It is with that type of assurance that educators were not being *replaced* that has ultimately obscured the reality: the reality is that the digitalized world is reshaping, refocusing, and indeed *replacing* human interaction in the classroom.

There is a simple cost-benefit analysis that evidences this trend. Colleges and universities have recently contributed to a trend where tenured professors who retire are not replaced with full-time tenure-track professors; the reason is quite simple: it is far less expensive to pay an adjunct professor a mere fraction of the cost of the former professor's salary to teach, especially as more schools turn to online models of delivery (Christensen & Eyring, 2011). While no scholarly output is expected, the academy driven by business principles downplays the usefulness of academic influence and focuses instead on increasing student enrollment and retention. This trend will certain increase in contrast as automated teaching technology becomes refined and more cost-effective; when online students are unable to distinguish between human and human-like teachers, the cost of the machine-oriented instructor will prevail.

While a terminal academic degree oftentimes takes more than a decade to complete, the speed of development, coding, and interaction with machines that supersede human capability has the capacity to replace human instructors, both online and in face-to-face classrooms. The case for online replacement of human instructors is a technological question: when will automatic tutors be capable of replacing the human instructor? Face to face instruction, however, is a bit more challenging to analyze. The so-called "flipped classroom" already severely discourages the use of classroom lectures, and instead replaces the time with "active learning" and hands-on activities. Will this model of instruction eventually render the human instructor obsolete? Will students arrive at a physical space, plug into a computing terminal, and then complete hands-on activities for automatically graded assessment?

What is vitally important here is the human factor, specifically in communication and community. Human conversation often takes unexpected turns, including caveats, jokes, innuendoes, references to culture, and subtle sarcastic remarks. While it is possible that a machine could be taught to mimic such communication, is it possible to do so without agency and autonomy? It is entirely possible that human experiences, pain and suffering, joy and gratitude, shape the very structure of communication; while again potentially replicable, it is not "lived," at least not in the same sense as human agency is now understood. Humans, too, are creatures of community; the Internet has brought about incredible new ways of connecting with people of similar interests to form virtual communities. The classroom, whether virtual or brick-and-mortar, is a place of gathering, where interaction fundamentally shapes how and what students learn. While possible to replicate with technology, the question of human agency is central. Humans learn responsibility for others, whether intellectually, physically, or emotionally, through community connections. Is this same preservation of the community for the sake of others possible within automation and digitalization?

The power of influence, specifically through a learned and accomplished professor, can be unparalleled at any stage of a student's progress in education. There is value, real value, in preserving human interaction, community, and communication in the teaching and learning process. Technology can be a powerful tool, and perhaps has a rightful place in foundational components of education, but human agency and its intellectual partner, critical thinking, cannot be replaced.

In late 2014, a company that provides online professional development notified its adjunct instructors that their current positions will cease to exist due to computer-mediated, algorithmic response to discussion posts, supplemented with "peer-to-peer" dialogue. While the tenets of computer-based interaction and peer-to-peer assessment may be debated, the replacement of human expertise with computer-generated responses gives personal evidence of the replacement of the scholar. The age of automated teaching is nigh.

Critical Thinking as Ethical Inquiry: Bridging Knowledge and Digitalization

One of the most difficult concepts to teach students is critical thinking. If an instructor asks beginning students what it means to be a critical thinker, students are almost compelled to say "to think critically." Further Socratic questioning may eventually get them to realize that being able to think is a skill that is much needed yet much neglected. Students are excused, sometimes because of their youth and inexperience, but it is difficult to *excuse* educated individuals who should know better when they show a lack of critical thinking skills and good judgment. Technological advances, like other scientific endeavors, are not focused on current availability, but on what is possible to build, develop, and implement. Are those individuals who spearhead the next innovation movement clearly thinking about the ramifications of that *next* best thing? Do ethical principles carry influence in their decisions to innovate, or are they after the fact?

Carrying all possible outcomes to their logical conclusion is not only a responsible thing to do, but the ethical endeavor is, itself, a practice in critical thinking. Foreseeing potentially unintended outcomes requires creativity, problem-solving, and logic; applying these possible outcomes to why something should or should not be developed, or subsequent changes that would incur a different outcome, is critical thinking. Schools, both secondary and in higher education, might further innovative *and* critical thinking if they teach students how to apply ethical principles to technological development. This might include care ethics, relativism, or utilitarianism; other models are also viable, if not desirable, depending on the type of innovation. The human element, the connectivity that occurs between an instructor and a student, the interaction of an instructor encouraging a student to advance his/her skill at both innovation and ethical thinking, is the rationale for preserving human instructors for students.

CONCLUSION: AN ETHICAL MODEL: TEACHING AND LEARNING AT SCALE – THE HUMAN ELEMENT

The exponential proliferation of digital technologies in the first decades of the twenty-first century is staggering, as well as completely unpredictable in the future. The questions that technology will bring to the human imagination will likewise pose new frontiers for ethical thinking. While current ethical models will not soon disappear, they may well be eclipsed by more pressing and scientifically-urgent ethical questions in the future. This will be a boon to students: critical thinking will entail scientific and humanistic modes of processing. The question will be how those skills will be delivered. The human element in teaching is irreplaceable, special, and worthy of being preserved for future generations.

Digital technologies can decrease costs involved in educating, but they cannot replace the unique locus of human interaction; this is especially true when knowledge being conveyed does not conform to existing or programmable parameters. Human instructors possess what machines cannot: the reciprocity of both passing on the very best of human knowledge as well as the ability to learn from students. This reciprocal relationship is, at its base, fundamentally "sacred" in the sense that digitalization ought to enhance opportunities for interaction but not replace them. The ethics of technology, taught and carried out by human agents, stands poised to help innovate, educate, and reshape the future of critical thinking.

REFERENCES

Al-Smadi, M., & Gütl, C. (2008). Past, present and future of e-assessment: Towards a flexible e-assessment system. *Conference ICL*.

Altbach, P. G. (2013, December 4). MOOCs as neocolonialism: Who controls knowledge? *The Chronicle of Higher Education*. Retrieved from http://chronicle.com/blogs/worldwise/moocs-as-neocolonialism-who-controls-knowledge/33431

Andrade, H. G. (2001, April 17). The effects of instructional rubrics on learning to write. *Current Issues in Education, 4*(4), 1–28.

Anglin, L., Anglin, K., Schumann, P. L., & Kaliski, J. A. (2008, January). Improving the efficiency and effectiveness of grading through the use of computer-assisted grading rubrics. *Decision Sciences Journal of Innovative Education, 6*(1), 51–73. doi:10.1111/j.1540-4609.2007.00153.x

Aoun, J. E. (2012, November 17). A shakeup of higher education. *The Boston Globe*. Retrieved from http://www.northeastern.edu/masterplan/wp-content/uploads/2012/11/TheShakeupofHigherEducation_Globe-op-ed.pdf

Benhabib, S. (1992). *Situating the self: Gender, community, and postmodernism in contemporary ethics*. New York: Routledge.

Bentham, J. (1890). *Utilitarianism*. London: Progressive Publishing Company.

Breslow, L., Pritchard, D. E., DeBoer, J., Stump, G. S., Ho, A. D., & Seaton, D. T. (2013). Studying learning in the worldwide classroom: Research into edX's first MOOC. *Research & Practice in Assessment, 8*(1), 13–25.

Calvo, R. A., & D'Mello, S. (2012). Frontiers of affect-aware learning technologies. *IEEE Intelligent Systems, 27*(6), 86–89. doi:10.1109/MIS.2012.110

Carnevale, A. P., Smith, N., & Melton, M. (2011). STEM. Georgetown University Center on Education and the Workforce. Retrieved from http://www9.georgetown.edu/grad/gppi/hpi/cew/pdfs/stem-complete

Carver, L., & Harrison, L. M. (2013). MOOCs and democratic education. *Liberal Education, 99*(4).

Christensen, C. M., & Eyring, H. J. (2011). The innovative university: Changing the DNA of higher education from the inside out. John Wiley & Sons. Retrieved from https://net.educause.edu/ir/library/pdf/ff1207

Clow, D. (2013). MOOCs and the funnel of participation. *Proceedings of the Third International Conference on Learning Analytics and Knowledge*. (pp. 85-189). doi:10.1145/2460296.2460332

Conn, P. (2010, April 4). We need to acknowledge the realities of employment in the humanities. *The Chronicle of Higher Education, The Chronicle Review*. Retrieved from https://chronicle.com/article/We-Need-to-Acknowledge-the/64885/

Curtis, J. W. (2014). The employment status of instructional staff members in higher education. *American Association of University Professors*. Retrieved from http://www.aaup.org/sites/default/files/files/AAUP-InstrStaff2011-April2014.pdf

D'Mello, S., & Graesser, A. (2012). AutoTutor and affective AutoTutor: Learning by talking with cognitively and emotionally intelligent computers that talk back. [TiiS]. *ACM Transactions on Interactive Intelligent Systems*, *2*(4), 1–39. doi:10.1145/2395123.2395128

Dellarocas, C., & Van Alstyne, M. (2013). Money models for MOOCs. *Communications of the ACM*, *56*(8), 25–28. doi:10.1145/2492007.2492017

Dewey, J. (1916). *Democracy and education*. New York: The Free Press.

Diederich, P.B., French, J.W., & Carlton, S.T. (August 1961). *Research Bulletin*. Princeton: Educational Testing Service.

Dodd, T. (2014, February 27). MOOC online courses about 'big data of learning' not just profit. *Financial Review*. Retrieved from http://www.afr.com/p/tech-gadgets/mooc_online_courses_about_big_data_f5kE-JwBqz2voWzpHH9EiEN

Ellis, L. (2013, September 19). An adjunct's death becomes a rallying cry for many in academe. *The Chronicle of Higher Education*. Retrieved from: http://chronicle.com/article/An-Adjuncts-Death-Becomes-a/141709/

Emanuel, E. J. (2013). Online education: MOOCs taken by educated few. *Nature*, *503*(7476), 342–342. doi:10.1038/503342a PMID:24256798

Forsyth, C., Butler, H., Graesser, A., Halpern, D, Millis, K., Cai, Z., & Wood, J. (2010). Higher contributions correlate with higher learning gains. *EDM*. 287-288.

Godin, B. (2005). *Measurement and statistics on science and technology: 1920 to the present*. New York: Routledge.

Harasim, L. (2000). Shift happens online education as a new paradigm in learning. *The Internet and Higher Education*, *3*(1-2), 41–61. doi:10.1016/S1096-7516(00)00032-4

Heussner, K. (2013). A new Blackboard? 4 ways the ed tech giant's new CEO hopes to win back market share. Retrieved from http://gigaom.com

Jong, D. (2014, January 26). Have MOOCs replaced the classroom? *Minding the Campus: Reforming Our Universities*. Retrieved from http://www.mindingthecampus.com/originals/2014/01/have_moocs_replaced_the_classr.html

Kaku, M. (2004). *Einstein's cosmos: How Albert Einstein's vision transformed our understanding of space and time*. New York: Atlas Books.

Khadaroo, S. (2014). Data breach at Indiana University: Are colleges being targeted? *The Christian Science Monitor*. Retrieved from http://www.csmonitor.com

Kilgannon, C. (2014, March 27). Without tenure or a home. *The New York Times*. Retrieved from http://www.nytimes.com/2014/03/30/nyregion/without-tenure-or-a-home.html?_r=3

Kolowich, S. (2013, July 8). A university's offer of credit for a MOOC gets no takers. The Chronicle of Higher Education. Retrieved from http://www.fulbright.de/fileadmin/files/tousa/stipendien/ees/Educational_Experts_Seminar_2013/A_University_s_Offer_of_Credit_for_a_MOOC_Gets_No_Takers_-_Technology_-_The_Chronicle_of_Higher_Education.pdf

Koutropoulos, A., Gallagher, M. S., Abajian, S. C., de Waard, I., Hogue, R. J., Keskin, N. O., & Rodriguez, C. O. (2012). Emotive Vocabulary in MOOCs: Context & Participant Retention. *European Journal of Open, Distance and E-Learning*.

Krausz, M. (2011). Varieties of relativism and the reach of reasons. In *S. D. Hales, A companion to relativism.*. Oxford, UK: Wiley-Blackwell. doi:10.1002/9781444392494.ch4

Laplante, P. A. (2013). Courses for the masses? *IT Professional*, *15*(2), 57–59. doi:10.1109/MITP.2013.27

Lawrence, S., & Sharma, U. (2002). Commodification of education and academic labour-using the balanced scorecard in a university setting. *Critical Perspectives on Accounting*, *13*(5), 661–677. doi:10.1006/cpac.2002.0562

Lewin, T. (2013, January 6). Students rush to web classes, but profits may be much later. *The New York Times*. Retrieved from http://www.nytimes.com/2013/01/07/education/massive-open-online-courses-prove-popular-if-not-lucrative-yet.html?pagewanted=all&_r=0

Littlejohn, A. (2013). *Understanding massive open online courses*. CEMCA EdTechnotes. Retrieved from http://cemca.org.in/ckfinder/userfiles/files/EdTech%20Notes%202_Littlejohn_final_1June2013.pdf

Mackness, J., Mak, S., & Williams, R. (2010). The ideals and reality of participating in a MOOC. In: Dirckinck-HolmfeldL.Hodgson V., C. Jones, M. De Laat, D. McConnell and T. Ryberg, (Eds.). *Proceedings of the 7th International Conference on Networked Learning 2010*, Lancaster. (pp. 266-275).

Markoff, J. (2013, April 4). Essay-Grading software offers professors a break. *The New York Times*.

Mazoue, J. G. (2013). The MOOC model: Challenging traditional education. *EDUCAUSE Review Online*. Retrieved from http://er.dut.ac.za/bitstream/handle/123456789/71/Mazoue_2013_The_MOOC_Model_Challenging_Traditional_Education.pdf?sequence=1

McCabe, M. J., & Snyder, C. M. (2005, May). Open access and academic journal quality. *The American Economic Review*, *95*(2), 453–458. doi:10.1257/000282805774670112

Meyer, J. P., & Zhu, S. (2013). Fair and equitable measurement of student learning in MOOCs: An introduction to item response theory, scale linking, and score equating. *Research & Practice in Assessment*, *8*(1), 26–39.

Mill, J. S. (1863). *Utilitarianism*. London: Parker, Son, and Bourn.

Milligan, C., Littlejohn, A., & Margaryan, A. (2013). Patterns of engagement in connectivist MOOCs. *MERLOT Journal of Online Learning and Teaching*, 9(2), 149–159.

Mitchell, C., & Sackney, L. (2011). *Profound improvement: Building capacity for a learning community*. New York: Routledge.

Moss, G. (2014, February 26). MOOCs remain on Carolina's drawing board – Dr. Jeff Pomerantz one of the first to teach MOOCs for UNC at Chapel Hill. UNC School of Information and Library Science. Retrieved from http://sils.unc.edu/news/2014/moocs-pomerantz

Myers, A. (2014, November 24). Competency-based accelerated training. *EDUCAUSE Review Online*. Retrieved from https://www.educause.edu/ero/article/competency-based-acceleratedtraining?utm_source=Informz&utm_medium=Email+marketing&utm_campaign=EDUCAUSE

Nabi, S. (2012). 7 Blackboard competitors with online learning solutions. Retrieved from educationdive.com

Noble, D. (1998). Digital diploma mills: The automation of higher education. *Science as Culture*, 7(3), 355–368. doi:10.1080/09505439809526510

Palloff, R., & Pratt, K. (2005). *Collaborating online: Learning together in community*. San Francisco: John Wiley & Sons, Inc.

Pappano, L. (2012, November 2). The year of the MOOC. The New York Times. Retrieved from http://edinaschools.org/cms/lib07/MN01909547/Centricity/Domain/272/The%20Year%20of%20the%20MOOC%20NY%20Times.pdf

Pardo, A., & Siemens, G. (2014). Ethical and privacy principles for learning analytics. *British Journal of Educational Technology*, 45(3), 1–13. doi:10.1111/bjet.12152

Parr, C. (2013, April 18). How was it? The UK's first Coursera MOOCS assessed. Times Higher Education. Retrieved from http://www.timeshighereducation.co.uk/news/how-was-it-the-uks-first-coursera-moocs-assessed/2003218.fullarticle

Patten, N. (2012). *The egranary digital library*. Educause Review Online.

Perry, D. (2014). Faculty members are not cashiers. *The Chronicle of Higher Education*.

Ripley, A. (2012). College is dead. Long live college. *Time Magazine, 180*(18), 33-41.

Rivard, R. (2013a, March 15). Humans fight over robo-readers. *Inside Higher Education*. Retrieved from http://www.insidehighered.com

Rivard, R. (2013b, March 8). Measuring the MOOC dropout rate. Inside Higher Education. Retrieved from http://www.immagic.com/eLibrary/ARCHIVES/GENERAL/GENPRESS/I130308R.pdf

Robertson, S. L. (2014). Untangling theories and hegemonic projects in researching education and the knowledge economy. In A.D. Reid, E.P. Hart, M.A. Peters (eds.) A Companion to Research in Education. Dordrecht: Springer Science+Business Media. doi:10.1007/978-94-007-6809-3_35

Rodriguez, C. O. (2012). MOOCs and the AI-Stanford like courses: Two successful and distinct course formats for massive open online courses. *European Journal of Open, Distance and E-Learning*.

Rosenblum, P. (2014). The target data breach is becoming a nightmare. *Forbes*. Retrieved from http://www.forbes.com

Sandeen, C. (2013). Assessment's place in the new MOOC world. *Research & Practice in Assessment*, *8*(1), 5–12.

Sandeen, C. (2013). Integrating MOOCs into traditional higher education: The emerging "MOOC 3.0" era. *Change: The Magazine of Higher Learning.*, *45*(6), 34–39. doi:10.1080/00091383.2013.842103

Schenke, K., Tran, C., & Hickey, D. (2013, June 5). Design principles for motivating learning with digital badges. *HASTAC*. Retrieved from http://www.hastac.org/blogs/kschenke/2013/06/05/design-principles-motivating-learning-digital-badges

Siemens, G. (2005). Connectivism: A learning theory for the digital age. *International Journal of Instructional Technology and Distance Learning*, *2*(1), 3–10.

Siemens, G., & Long, P. (2011). Penetrating the fog: Analytics in learning and education. *EDUCAUSE Review*, *46*(5), 30–32.

Slade, S., & Prinsloo, P. (2013). Learning analytics: Ethical issues and dilemmas. *The American Behavioral Scientist*, *57*(10), 1510–1529. doi:10.1177/0002764213479366

Slote, M. (2010). *Essays on the history of ethics*. New York: Oxford University Press.

Smith, K. (2013). Making FERPA fit when we flip. Library Journal. Retrieved from http://lj.libraryjournal.com/2013/12/opinion/peer-to-peer-review/making-ferpa-fit-when-we-flip-peer-to-peer-review/#_

Smith, M., & Casserly, C. (2006). The promise of open educational resources. *Change: The Magazine of Higher Learning*.

Stripling, J. (2011, May 15). Most presidents prefer no tenure for majority of faculty. *The Chronicle of Higher Education*.

Strunk, V. A. (2012). Career college students' perceptions of rubrics orientation. *Dissertation Abstracts International*. (UMI 3542066)

Swenson, J. (2014). Establishing an ethical literacy for learning analytics. *Proceedings from the Fourth International Conference on Learning Analytics and Knowledge*. ACM, 246-250. doi:10.1145/2567574.2567613

Taylor, B. J., Cantwell, B., & Slaughter, S. (2013). Quasi-markets in U.S. higher education: The humanities and institutional revenues. *The Journal of Higher Education*, *84*(5), 675–707. doi:10.1353/jhe.2013.0030

Tomkin, J. H., & Charlevoix, D. (2014). Do professors matter?: Using an a/b test to evaluate the impact of instructor involvement on MOOC student outcomes. In *Proceedings of the First ACM Conference on Learning @ Scale conference*. ACM, 71-78. doi:10.1145/2556325.2566245

Trevidi, A., Kar, D., & McNeil, H. (2003). *Automatic assignment management and peer evaluation*. Consortium for Computing in Small Colleges.

Turing, A. M. (1937). On computable numbers, with an application to the Entscheidungsproblem. *Proceedings of the London Mathematical Society*, *42*(1), 230–265. doi:10.1112/plms/s2-42.1.230

van Barneveld, A., Arnold, K. E., & Campbell, J. P. (2012). *Analytics in higher education: Establishing a common language*. EDUCAUSE Learning Initiative.

Whitten, L. S., Clarksville, T., Sanders, A. R., & Stewart, J. G. (2013). Degree Compass: The preferred choice approach. *Journal of Academic Administration in Higher Education*, *9*(2), 39–43.

Willis, E. M., & Raines, P. (2001). Technology in secondary education: Integration, implications, and ethics for the changing roles of teachers. *T.H.E. Journal*, *29*(2), 54–64.

Willis, J. E., III. (2013, July 5). MOOCs as a worldwide neocolonial force: A reflection on MIT's Learning International Networks Consortium (LINC) Conference. *Reflections on Teaching and Learning, Purdue University*. Retrieved from https://www.purdue.edu/learning/blog/?p=6258

Willis, III, J. E., Campbell, J. P., & Pistilli, M. D. (2013, May 6). Ethics, big data, and analytics: A model for application. *EDUCAUSE Review Online*.

Willis, III, J. E. & Pistilli, M. D. (2014, April 7). Ethical discourse: Guiding the future of learning analytics. *EDUCAUSE Review Online*.

Young, M., Daniels, H., Balarin, M., & Lowe, J. (Eds.). (2012). *Educating for the knowledge economy? Critical perspectives*. New York: Routledge.

Yuan, L., & Powell, S. (2013). MOOCs and open education: Implications for higher education. JISC CETIS: Centre for Educational Technology & Interoperability Standards, white paper, 1-21.

ADDITIONAL READING

Andrade, H. G. (1997). Understanding rubrics. *Educational Leadership*, *54*(4), 14–17.

Andrade, H. G. (2006, July). The trouble with a narrow view of rubrics. *English Journal*, *95*(6), 9. doi:10.2307/30046616

Arnold, K. (2010). Signals: Applying academic analytics. *EDUCAUSE Quarterly*, *33*(1).

Attali, Y. (2007). On-the-fly customization of automated essay scoring (RR-07-42). Princeton, NJ: ETS Research & Development; Retrieved from http://www.ets.org/Media/Research/pdf/RR-07-42.pdf

Baepler, P., & Murdoch, C. J. (2010). Academic analytics and data mining in higher education. *International Journal for the Scholarship of Teaching and Learning*, *4*(2), 17.

Balfour, S. (2013). Assessing writing in MOOC's: Automated Essay Scoring and Calibrated Peer Review. *Research and Practice Assessment*, *8*(1), 40–48.

Barnes, H. W., & Smith, S. M. (1988). Improving case evaluations through computer based grading: An experiment applying a developmental model to case evaluation. *Journal of Marketing Education*, *10*(2), 63–73. doi:10.1177/027347538801000211

Broad, B. (2003). *What we really value: Beyond rubrics in teaching and assessing writing*. Logan, UT: Utah State University Press.

Bull, J. (1999). Computer-assisted assessment: Impact on higher education institutions. *Journal of Educational Technology & Society*, *2*(3), 1436–4522.

Chacon, F., Spicer, D., & Valbuena, A. (2012). *Analytics in support of student retention and success. Research Bulletin*. EDUCAUSE Center for Applied Research.

Cohen, B. (2010, Spring). Is today's non-traditional college student becoming the norm? *The Link*, 48-49.

Crusan, D. (2010). Review of Machine scoring of student essays: Truth and consequences. *Language Testing*, *27*(3), 437–440. doi:10.1177/0265532210363274

Educause. (2012). What campus leaders need to know about MOOCs. Retrieved from http://net.educause. edu/ir/library/ pdf/PUB4005.pdf

Eom, S. B., Wen, H. J., & Ashill, N. (2006). The determinants of students' perceived learning outcomes and satisfaction in university online education: An empirical investigation. *Decision Sciences Journal of Innovative Education*, *4*(2), 215–235. doi:10.1111/j.1540-4609.2006.00114.x

Farrell, T. (2010, Spring). Arum research calls out limited learning on college campuses. *NYU Research*, *6*(2), 12.

Hafner, J. C., & Hafner, P. M. (2003, December). Quantitative analysis of the rubric as an assessment tool: An empirical study of student peer-group rating. *International Journal of Science Education*, *25*(12), 1509–1528. doi:10.1080/0950069022000038268

Keeney-Kennicutt, W., Guernsel, A. B., & Simpson, N. (2008). Overcoming student resistance to a teaching innovation. *Journal for the Scholarship of Teaching and Learning*, *2*(1), 1–26.

Kolowich, S. (2014, January 15). Doubs about MOOC's continue to rise. *The Chronicle of Higher Education*. Retrieved from https://chronicle.com

Lemak, D. J., Shin, S. J., Reed, R., & Montgomery, J. C. (2005). Technology, transactional distance, and instructor effectiveness: An empirical investigation. *Academy of Management Learning & Education*, *4*(2), 150–159. doi:10.5465/AMLE.2005.17268562

Messick, S. (1996). The interplay of evidence and consequences in the validation of performance assessments. *Educational Researcher*, *23*(2), 13–23. doi:10.3102/0013189X023002013

National Council of Teachers of English. (2013). Machine scoring fails the test. *NCTE Position Statement on Machine Scoring*. Retrieved from http://www.ncte.org/positions/statements/machine_scoring

Straumsheim, C. (2014, February 14). What's in it for us? *Inside HigherEd.* Retrieved from https://insidehighered.com

Tavani, H. T. (2011). *Ethics and technology: Controversies, questions, and strategies for ethical computing.* Hoboken: John Wiley & Sons, Inc.

Webb, H. W., Gill, G., & Poe, G. (2005). Teaching with the case method online: Pure versus hybrid approaches. *Decision Sciences Journal of Innovative Education, 3*(2), 223–250. doi:10.1111/j.1540-4609.2005.00068.x

White, E. M. (2nd Ed.). (1994). *Teaching and assessing writing.* San Francisco: Jossey-Bass.

KEY TERMS AND DEFINITIONS

Adjunct Faculty: Faculty who teach in higher education but do not receive same pay structure or benefits as full-time professors; most possess one or more graduate degrees. Teaching contracts are conditional and are often renewable only term by term.

Care Ethics: Using the whole person as an autonomous agent, the determination of right or wrong is dependent upon measuring the impact on an individual person.

Critical Thinking: A set of skills to understand, evaluate, and synthesize data or an argument; requires breadth and depth of knowledge to effectively question, reorder, and recast presumed or long-held truths.

Ethics: The critical engagement with a topic, construct, idea, or course of events to ascertain what is a right or wrong action.

Learning Analytics: The use of student demographics, performance data, and other variables to predict specific educational outcomes. Data may be used to help students re-evaluate classroom or study behaviors, administrators make decisions, or researchers understand learning more fully.

Relativism: Rightness and wrongness are not determined by principle or established tradition. Rather, right and wrong is solely determined by the individual; all ethical decisions are made in relation to the individual's free choice.

Rubric: A set of metrics used widely in education for assessment purposes; metrics may or may not be disclosed to students before assessment. This serves as proxy for establishing parameters in digital or automated grading.

Utilitarianism: Moral goodness is determined by what causes the most benefit or happiness for the most number of people; decisions of right and wrong are determined by what has the most positive or good effect on the collective society.

Section 5
Wrapping Things Up, then Unwrapping Them Again:
Integral Visions of Morality in a Technological World, Over Evolutionary Time, with Revolutionary Means, and with Open Questions about the Final Purpose of It All

Chapter 10
Bridging Two Realms of Machine Ethics

Luís Moniz Pereira
Universidade Nova de Lisboa, Portugal

Ari Saptawijaya
Universidade Nova de Lisboa, Portugal & Universitas Indonesia, Indonesia

ABSTRACT

We address problems in machine ethics dealt with using computational techniques. Our research has focused on Computational Logic, particularly Logic Programming, and its appropriateness to model morality, namely moral permissibility, its justification, and the dual-process of moral judgments regarding the realm of the individual. In the collective realm, we, using Evolutionary Game Theory in populations of individuals, have studied norms and morality emergence computationally. These, to start with, are not equipped with much cognitive capability, and simply act from a predetermined set of actions. Our research shows that the introduction of cognitive capabilities, such as intention recognition, commitment, and apology, separately and jointly, reinforce the emergence of cooperation in populations, comparatively to their absence. Bridging such capabilities between the two realms helps understand the emergent ethical behavior of agents in groups, and implements them not just in simulations, but in the world of future robots and their swarms. Evolutionary Anthropology provides teachings.

INTRODUCTION

Machine ethics (also known as computational morality, machine morality, artificial morality and computational ethics) is a burgeoning field of enquiry that emerges from the need of imbuing autonomous agents with the capacity of moral decision-making. It has particularly attracted interest from the artificial intelligence community and has brought together perspectives from various fields, amongst them: philosophy, cognitive science, neuroscience and primatology. The overall result of this interdisciplinary research is therefore not only important for equipping agents with the capacity of making moral judgments, but also for helping us better understand morality, through the creation and testing of computational models of ethical theories.

DOI: 10.4018/978-1-4666-8592-5.ch010

Research in artificial intelligence particularly contributes on how techniques from computational logic, machine learning and multi-agent systems, can be employed in order to computationally model, to some improved extent, moral decision-making. In the present chapter we survey problems in machine ethics that have been examined and techniques used in dealing with such problems. Various techniques have been exploited including machine learning, e.g., case-based reasoning, artificial neural networks; and logic-based formalisms, e.g., deontic logic and non-monotonic logics. Our research, in particular, has been focusing on logic programming techniques and their appropriateness to model some morality aspects, namely moral permissibility, its justification, and the dual-process of moral judgments. We argue that the main characteristics of these aspects can be captured by the available ingredients and formalisms based on logic programming. These include, among others, abduction (with integrity constraints), updating, preferences, argumentation, and counterfactual. These ingredients are framed together in an agent life cycle architecture, which allows an agent to make a moral decision by means of abduction (either reactively or deliberatively—the dual-process), respecting its integrity constraints in order to rule out a priori impermissible actions, weighing and preferring decisions after inspecting their consequences, providing arguments to justify moral decisions made, and updating itself either by the changes due to its decisions or by other ethical principles being told or learned. We also touch upon uncertainty and counterfactual reasoning in moral decision-making, and how they fit in our logic programming based agent architecture.

The agent life cycle architecture concerns itself only in realm of the individual, where computation is vehicle for modeling the dynamics of knowledge and moral cognition of an agent. In the collective realm, norms and moral emergence has been studied computationally, using the techniques of Evolutionary Game Theory, in populations of rather simple-minded agents. That is, these agents are not equipped with any cognitive capability, and thus simply act from a predetermined set of actions. Our research has shown that the introduction of cognitive capabilities, such as intention recognition, commitment, and apology, separately and jointly, reinforce the emergence of cooperation in the population, comparatively to the absence of such cognitive abilities. We discuss how modeling moral cognition in individuals (using the aforementioned ingredients of logic programming) within a networked population shall allow them to fine tune game strategies, and in turn may lead to the evolution of high levels of cooperation. Moreover, modeling such capabilities in individuals within a population may help us understand the emergent behavior of ethical agents in groups, in order to implement them not just in a simulation, but also in the real world of future robots and their swarms.

This chapter hence contemplates two distinct realms of machine ethics, to wit, the individual and collective, and identified needed bridges concerning their connection. In studies of human morality, these distinct interconnected realms are evinced too: one stressing above all individual cognition, deliberation, and behavior; the other stressing collective morals, and how they emerged. Of course, the two realms are necessarily intertwined, for cognizant individuals form the populations, and the twain evolved jointly to cohere into collective norms, and into individual interaction.

Presently, machine ethics is becoming an ever more pressing concern, as machines become ever more sophisticated, autonomous, and act in groups, among populations of other machines and of humans. Ethics and jurisprudence, and hence legislation, are however lagging much behind in adumbrating the new ethical issues arising from these circumstances.

Meanwhile, research in machine ethics with the purpose of understanding each of the two realms, has been fostering inroads and producing results in each. Namely, our co-authors and we have staked footholds on either side of the two realms gap, and promoted their mutually beneficial bridging. Evolutionary Biology, Anthropology and the Cognitive Sciences providing inspirational teachings to that effect.

The chapter is naturally organized as follows. First we summarize the topics and our research results in the individual realm of machine ethics, and next comes a survey of the topics and our research results in the collective realm of machine ethics. There ensues the bridging of these two realms in machine ethics. Last but not least, we ponder over the teachings of human moral evolution in this regard. A final coda foretells a road to be tread, and portends about ethical machines and us.

THE INDIVIDUAL REALM OF MACHINE ETHICS

Research in machine ethics have mainly centered on equipping agents with particular ethical theories, e.g., utilitarianism and deontological ethics, and on providing a framework to encode moral rules, typically in favor of deontological ethics, with or without referring to specific moral rules. In so doing, various techniques have been employed, including machine learning (e.g., case-based reasoning, artificial neural networks) and logic-based formalisms (e.g., deontic logic, non-monotonic logics, abductive logic programming).

Computational Approaches in Machine Ethics

Jeremy is an advisor system that follows Jeremy Bentham's act utilitarianism (Anderson, Anderson, & Armen, 2005). Moral decisions are made based on the calculation of a total net pleasure that depends on three considered components with respect to each affected person: the intensity of pleasure/displeasure, the duration of the pleasure/displeasure, and the probability that this pleasure/displeasure will occur. The "right" decision is determined by that giving the highest total net pleasure. The calculation formula in *Jeremy* is later extended to capture prima facie duty theory (Ross, 1930). Two other advisor systems, viz., *MedEthEx* (Anderson, Anderson, & Armen, 2006) and *EthEl* (Anderson & Anderson, 2008), are also based on the same theory in biomedical ethics. *MedEthEx* is dedicated to give advice for dilemmas in biomedical fields, while *EthEl* serves as a medication-reminder system for the elderly and as a notifier to an overseer if the patient refuses to take the medication. For these purposes, both systems benefit from machine learning techniques, viz., inductive logic programming. The latter system has been deployed in the *Nao* robot, being capable to serve patients who need to be reminded of medication, and to bring them their medication (Anderson & Anderson, 2010).

Different machine learning techniques are also used in machine ethics, viz., case-based reasoning and artificial neural networks. Case-based reasoning is employed in *TruthTeller* and *SIROCCO* systems (McLaren, 2006). Though both systems implement casuistry ethical approach (Jonsen & Toulmin, 1988), they have different purposes. *TruthTeller* is designed to accept a pair of ethical dilemmas and describe the salient similarities and differences between the cases, from both an ethical and a pragmatic perspectives, whereas *SIROCCO* to accept an ethical dilemma and to retrieve similar cases and ethical principles relevant to the presented ethical dilemma. For a distinct purpose, artificial neural networks are utilized in Guarini (2011) to understand morality from the philosophy of ethics viewpoint, particularly by exploring the dispute between moral particularism and generalism. Therein, moral situations are classified by training simple recurrent networks with a number of cases, involving actions concerning killing and allowing to die, and then using the trained networks to classify test cases.

Besides machine learning techniques, there has been a growing interest of employing logic-based formalisms in machine ethics. Powers (2006) considers several formalisms to formulate Kant's categorical imperative for the purpose of machine ethics (though only abstractly, as no implementation seems to exist on top of the considered formalisms). With respect to the formulation, three views are taken into account: mere consistency, common-sense practical reasoning, and coherency. To realize the first view, a form of deontic logic is adopted. The second view benefits from non-monotonic logic, and the third view presumes ethical deliberation to follow a logic similar to that of belief revision.

The use of deontic logic as a framework to express ethical codes is explored in Bringsjord, Arkoudas, and Bello (2006). In particular, an axiomatized utilitarian deontic logic (Murakami, 2004) is employed to decide an operative ethical code from several other candidates, by seeking a proof for the expected moral outcome that follows from these candidates. Wiegel (2007) extends the Belief-Desire-Intention (BDI) model (Bratman, 1987) with another variant of deontic logic, viz., the deontic-epistemic-action logic (van den Hoven & Lokhorst, 2002), in order to make BDI suitable for modeling moral agents. The result is *SophoLab*, a framework for experimental computational philosophy, which is implemented with the JACK agent programming language. This framework is particularly used to study negative moral commands and two different utilitarian theories, viz., act and rule utilitarianism. Other use of BDI in machine ethics is reported in Ganascia (2012), where it is used to model a consequentialist approach, viz., by choosing the action of which consequences are the lesser evil.

All these works with logic-based formalisms share the view that logical systems are appropriate to formalize ethical codes. Taking this view into account, a formal framework to reason over logical systems is proposed in Bringsjord et al. (2011) by employing category theory. The work is strongly based on Piaget's position (Inhelder & Piaget, 1958). This idea of reasoning *over*—instead of reasoning *in*—logical systems, favors post-formal Piaget's stages beyond his well-known fourth stage. In other words, category theory is used as the meta-level of moral reasoning.

Logic Programming for Machine Ethics

Our research in the field has been focusing on the use of Logic Programming (LP). Given its solid theoretical results, LP is mature enough by now, supported by a number of advanced features and practical systems. Kowalski (2011) provides a good overview and presents convincing arguments on the suitability of LP for machine ethics. We have been exploring morality issues to come up with those that, in our view, are amenable to computational modeling by benefiting from LP features, like abduction, updating, preferences, etc. For a recapitulation and more pointers to our prior work see (Saptawijaya & Pereira, in press).

One morality issue that we have addressed with LP-based approaches is moral permissibility, by modeling classic moral examples from literature. In Pereira and Saptawijaya (2007a, 2007b) we have shown that several LP features can be employed together in an integrated system, *ACORDA* (Lopes & Pereira, 2006), to model permissibility in various scenarios of the classic trolley problem (Foot, 1967) with the Doctrine of Double Effect (DDE) as the basis of moral decisions in these scenarios. Indeed, DDE is often referred to when explaining the permissibility of an action by distinguishing whether its harm consequence is merely a *side-effect* of achieving a good result, or rather a *means* to bringing about the same good end (McIntyre, 2004). Such reference does not only appear in philosophy literature, but is also considered in psychology experimental studies. For instance, Hauser, Cushman, Young, Jin, & Mikhail (2007) reports that subjects from demographically diverse populations share the consistency of judgments regarding permissibility on a series of moral dilemmas. In their study, while a majority of subjects fail to provide justifications to their judgments, these judgments are consistent with DDE.

Our LP-based approach to machine ethics is primarily supported by abduction. In the philosophy of science, abduction is commonly understood as a reasoning method to infer the best-preferred explanation to observed evidence. In LP, abduction does not necessarily restrict itself to the specific task of explaining observations. Instead, it more generally translates into finding consistent abductive solutions to a goal, whilst satisfying integrity constraints, where a goal typically refers to a desired future state of the environment. In this case observations are simply given as facts that do not need explanations. An abductive solution, built from abductive hypotheses (called *abducibles*), is a set of abduced actions that achieve the goal. A goal itself can be empty, and if so, abduction amounts to satisfying integrity constraints only.

LP abduction is typically accomplished by a top-down goal-oriented procedure for finding, by need, an abductive solution to the goal. For that reason our abduction mechanism is based on the well-founded semantics of LP (van Gelder, Ross, & Schlipf, 1991), that permits finding just relevant abducibles, along with their truth value, whereas those not mentioned in the solution are indifferent to the goal. Nevertheless, other LP semantics can also be useful, e.g., stable models semantics (Gelfond & Lifschitz, 1988) can be utilized to compute the consequences of abductive solutions. These consequences may serve as some criteria to prefer among abductive solutions, as explained below.

In Pereira and Saptawijaya (2007a, 2007b), possible decisions in various scenarios of the trolley problem, e.g., diverting the trolley, pushing a man, etc., are represented as abducibles. Furnishing all observed possible outcomes as goal, and stipulating the consequences of impermissible actions (in accordance to DDE) as some integrity constraint, the abduction mechanism returns all permissible actions that satisfy some given goal and do not violate the integrity constraint. Abductive solutions as permissible moral decisions can be further filtered. For this purpose our approach benefits from preferences in LP (Dell'Acqua & Pereira, 2007), where a posteriori preferences are applied to prefer eventual moral decisions. This is realized, e.g., by examining their consequences and applying utility functions to them.

The integrated LP-based approach shows that it successfully delivers moral decisions for these various scenarios of the trolley problem, which moreover conform to the experimental study by Hauser et al. (2007). The work is further extended in Pereira and Saptawijaya (2009, 2011) using similar scenarios of the trolley problem but considering additionally another moral principle, viz., Doctrine of Triple Effect (DTE). DTE (Kamm, 2006) refines DDE, particularly on the notion about harming someone as an intended means: it distinguishes further between doing an action *in order* that an effect occurs and doing it *because* that effect will occur. This extended work shows that the same LP-based approach is able to express different outcomes between DDE and DTE on relevant scenarios of the trolley problem, viz., the Loop case (Thomson, 1985) and the Loop-Push case. In these two cases the same initial setting applies: *A trolley is headed toward five people walking on the track, and they will not be able to get off the track in time. The trolley can be redirected onto a side track, which loops back towards the five.* In the Loop case the setting is further completed as follows: *A fat man sits on this looping side track, so fat that his body will by itself stop the trolley, thereby saving the five.* While diverting the trolley is morally impermissible in DDE, it is permissible by DTE. According to DTE, it is permissible because it will hit the man, and not in order to intentionally hit him (Kamm, 2006). This is consistent with the opinion of most moral philosophers as well as with the psychology experimental result of Hauser et al. (2007). The Loop-Push case is a variant of the Loop one, where the looping side track is initially empty, and besides the diverting action, an ancillary action of pushing a fat man in order to place him on the side track is additionally performed. For the latter case, both DTE agrees with DDE that such a deliberate action (pushing) performed in order to bring about harm (the man hit by the trolley), even for the purpose of a good or greater end (to save the five), is likewise impermissible.

We have recently further explored the appropriateness of LP to express different views on moral permissibility with respect to DDE and DTE, by means of a LP-based approach of counterfactuals (Pereira & Saptawijaya, 2014). People are naturally engage counterfactual thoughts in moral situations, as they tend to reason about what they should or should not have done when they contemplate alternative decisions in such situations. This is particularly related to the evaluation feature of counterfactuals. Moreover, counterfactuals permit momentary experiential simulation of the possible alternatives, through their reflective nature (Epstude & Roese, 2008), thereby allowing careful consideration before a moral decision is made, and to subsequently justify it. A number of psychology experimental studies on counterfactuals in the context of moral reasoning have also been conducted, e.g., by McCloy and Byrne (2000) and Migliore, Curcio, Mancini, and Cappa (2014). These studies and others indicate prospects for counterfactuals in machine ethics that have never been explored.

Our LP-based method to evaluating counterfactuals is inspired by Pearl's structure-based counterfactuals (Pearl, 2009), itself based on probabilistic causal model and a calculus of intervention. We resort to LP abduction and updating in mirroring Pearl's approach, but abstain from probabilities in order to concentrate on people's naturalized logic. Our work using probabilistic LP moral reasoning is reported elsewhere (Han, Saptawijaya, & Pereira, 2012), where uncertainty of actions and consequences is taken into account in judging moral permissibility, both from the view of oneself and from that of others.

In our LP-based counterfactual approach, abduction hypothesizes background conditions from observations made or evidences given, whereas LP updating fixes the initially abduced context of the counterfactual being evaluated. Moreover, LP updating facilitates a minimal adjustment to the causal model (in this case, the logic program) by hypothetical updates of causal intervention through defeasible rules. The combination of both LP features establishes a procedure that corresponds to Pearl's counterfactual approach. The procedure can be summarized in three steps as follows. First, abduction is enacted to explain the current observation. The explanation fixes the abduced context in which the counterfactual is evaluated by means of LP updating. Second, the causal intervention is realized by hypothetical updates. In the presence of defeasible LP rules these updates permit hypothetical modification of the program to consistently comply with the antecedent of the counterfactual. Third, the well-founded model (van Gelder, Ross, & Schlipf, 1991) of the hypothetical modified program is examined to verify whether the consequence of the counterfactual holds true at the current state.

In order to examine permissibility of an action in DDE, a form of counterfactuals that is able to distinguish between an instrumental cause and a side-effect can be introduced: *If E would not have been true, then G would not have been true*. The evaluation of this counterfactual form identifies permissibility of action from its morally wrong effect (say, a harm) *E*, by identifying whether *E* is a necessary cause for achieving a good end (a goal) *G* or instead a mere side-effect of that action. If the counterfactual is valid, then *E* is instrumental as a cause of *G*, and not a mere side-effect of the action. Since *E* is morally wrong, achieving *G* that way, by means of that action, is impermissible; otherwise, it is not. We have shown in Pereira and Saptawijaya (2014) that this counterfactual form is general enough to examine permissibility of actions in a number of classic moral problems, such as in military cases, e.g., tactical vs. terror bombing (Scanlon, 2008) and relevant scenarios of the trolley problem, e.g., the previously mentioned Loop and Loop-Push cases.

In the Loop case, proving the validity of the counterfactual *"if the man had not been hit by the trolley, the five people would not have been saved"* is sufficient to show that the harm event of the man hit by the trolley is instrumental as an instrumental cause for the goal of saving the five; hence diverting the trolley is DDE morally impermissible. From the DTE viewpoint, two counterfactuals are evaluated. First, the validity of the counterfactual *"if the man had not been on the side track, then he would not have been hit by the trolley"* is verified, ensuring that the unfortunate event of the man being hit by the trolley is indeed the consequence of the man being on the side track. Second, a hypothetical ancillary action, pushing, is assumed to place the man on the side track, and the counterfactual *"if the man had not been pushed, then he would not have been hit by the trolley"* is examined. The latter counterfactual is not valid, because pushing is not true in the abduced context where the counterfactual is evaluated. It signifies that even without this hypothetical but unexplained deliberate action of pushing, the man would still have been hit by the trolley (just because he is already on the side track). Therefore, though the harm event of the man being hit is a consequence of diverting the trolley and instrumental in achieving the goal of saving the five, no deliberate action is required to cause the man placed on the side track, in order for the harm event to occur. Hence div is DTE morally permissible.

In the Loop-Push case, where the deliberate pushing action is abduced (in addition to diverting the trolley), the counterfactual *"if the man had not been hit by the trolley, the five people would not have been saved"* previously evaluated in the DDE Loop case is still valid. Moreover, the counterfactual *"if the man had not been pushed, then he would not have been hit by the trolley"* is now valid, due to the newly abduced pushing action. From the validity of both these counterfactuals one can infer that, given the trolley diverting action, the ancillary action of pushing the man onto the side track causes him to be hit by the trolley, which in turn causes the five to be saved. In the Loop-Push, DTE agrees with DDE that such a deliberate action (pushing) performed in order to bring about harm (the man hit by the trolley), even for the purpose of a good or greater end (to save the five), is likewise impermissible.

According to Scanlon (2008), the appeal of DDE and DTE to explain moral judgments in the trolley problem and other similar dilemmas is due to the so-called critical employment of moral judgments. Furthermore, Scanlon argues that moral permissibility can differently be assessed through the so-called *deliberative* employment of moral judgments. According to Scanlon, the deliberative employment concerns answering the question of the permissibility of actions, by identifying the justified but defeasible argumentative considerations, and their exceptions, which make actions permissible or impermissible. That is, moral dilemmas typically have the same structure: (1) they concern general principles that in some cases admit exceptions, and (2) they raise questions about when those exceptions apply. In other words, an action can be determined impermissible through deliberative employment when there is no countervailing consideration that would justify an exception to the applied general principle. Indeed, this deliberative employment is in line with Scanlon's contractualism (Scanlon, 1982). Contractualism provides flexibility on the set of principles to justify moral judgments so long as no one could reasonably reject them. Reasoning is an important aspect here, as argued in Scanlon (1998), in that making judgments does not seem to be merely relying on internal observations but is achieved through reasoning. Hence, method of reasoning is one of primary concerns of contractualism in providing justification to others, by looking for some common ground that others could not reasonably reject. In this way, morality can be viewed as (possibly defeasible) argumentative consensus, which is why contractualism is interesting from the Artificial Intelligence perspective

The deliberative employment of moral judgments to determine permissibility of actions opens up another venue where LP may play its role. On the one hand, defeasible rules in LP updating can conveniently represent exceptions to a principle, thereby addressing point (1) in the previous paragraph. See also Ganascia (2007) for an alternative use of answer set programming (a LP paradigm based on stable model semantics) for addressing the same purpose. On the other hand, LP argumentation (see Rahwan and Simari (2009) for a general survey) provides a way to reach an agreement on whether or not countervailing considerations can be justified, addressing point (2). In fact, counterfactuals may also be appropriate to provide an argument for justifying moral judgments, through 'compound counterfactuals': *"Had I known what I know today, then if I were to have done otherwise, something preferred would have followed."* Such counterfactuals, typically imagining alternatives with worse effect—the so-called *downward counterfactuals* (Markman, Gavanski, Sherman, & McMullen, 1993)—, may provide moral justification for what was performed due to lack of the current fuller knowledge. This is accomplished by evaluating what would have followed if the intent would have been otherwise, other things (including present knowledge) being equal. It may justify that what would have followed is no morally better than the actual ensued consequence.

We have demonstrated the roles of LP updating with its defeasible rules, both in realizing causal intervention to evaluating counterfactuals and in expressing exceptions for the deliberative employment of moral judgments. Obviously, LP updating is appropriate for representing changes and for dealing with incomplete information. To this end, LP updating can be employed for moral updating, viz., the adoption of new (possibly overriding) ethical rules on top of those an agent currently follows. Such adoption is often necessary when the ethical rules one follows have to be revised in the light of situations faced by the agent, e.g., whenever some authority contextually imposes other ethical rules. We have shown the applicability of LP updating together with other features discussed here (LP abduction and preferences) for moral updating via an interactive storytelling (Lopes & Pereira, 2010).

Individual Realm Concluding Remarks

Having been placed on the back burner, the prospect of LP has stimulated us now to rethink how its features can approach issues in machine ethics. Here we particularly refer to the realm of the individual agent, i.e., to endow machines with the capability to declaratively represent ethical situations so they can reason on ethical issues arising from such situations. Though we are still at an early stage of our journey, we have exhibited in our works the successful interplay of various LP features in tackling a number of morality issues.

This interplay is evident in several implemented systems we have employed in our works of machine ethics. *ACORDA* (Lopes & Pereira, 2006), used in our initial work of DDE and DTE permissibility (Pereira & Saptawijaya, 2007a, 2007b, 2009, 2011) and in interactive moral storytelling (Lopes & Pereira, 2010), benefits from LP abduction, updating, and preferences. Its subsequent reincarnation, *Evolution Prospection Agent (EPA) system* (Pereira & Han, 2009a), benefits from the same LP features, but with the dual program transformation (Alferes, Pereira, & Swift, 2004) for its abduction mechanism (instead of an ad-hoc one, as in *ACORDA*). It is also later equipped with the capability to reason under uncertainty via an implementation of the probabilistic logic programming language *P-log* (Baral, Gelfond, & Rushton, 2009). The *EPA* system has been used in our work on intention recognition (Pereira & Han, 2011) and probabilistic moral reasoning (Han, Saptawijaya, & Pereira, 2012). For our recent work on counterfactuals, we benefit from *QUALM* (available from http://goo.gl/XLhBxO), which is built on top of an integrated LP abduction and incremental updating (Saptawijaya & Pereira, 2014), comprising tabling mechanisms (Swift & Warren, 2012).

We mention in Pereira and Saptawijaya (2014) how compound counterfactual benefits from the incremental tabling in LP updating (Saptawijaya & Pereira, 2013b) of *QUALM*. Tabling may also be useful in modeling the dual-process of moral decision making, i.e., the interaction between deliberative and reactive processes in moral decision making (Cushman, Young, & Greene, 2010). Deliberative reasoning in *QUALM* is induced by abduction. Because we employed tabling for contextual abduction (Saptawijaya & Pereira, 2013a), abductive solutions (e.g., actions/decisions to some goals in a moral situation) are stored for future use, possibly in different context. Reactive processes can therefore benefit from it, since decisions are readily available for reuse in the present context, without the need to deliberatively re-compute them. Furthermore, though only reactively obtained, these tabled decisions can be deliberatively re-evaluated with the rules that support them (cf. the notions of expectation and contra-expectation in hypotheses generation (Pereira, Dell'Acqua, Pinto, & Lopes, 2013)), so as to provide a form of argumentation between agents about their decisions.

THE COLLECTIVE REALM OF MACHINE ETHICS

The mechanisms of emergence and evolution of cooperation in populations of abstract individuals, with diverse behavioral strategies in co-presence, have been undergoing mathematical study via Evolutionary Game Theory (EGT), inspired in part on Evolutionary Psychology (EP). Their systematic study resorts to simulation techniques, thus enabling the study of aforesaid mechanisms under a variety of conditions, parameters, and alternative virtual games. The theoretical and experimental results have continually been surprising, rewarding, and promising. For a background on EGT and its use by EP we refer to Pereira (2012a).

In recent work, one of us (Pereira and the mentioned co-authors) has initiated the introduction, in such groups of individuals, of cognitive abilities inspired on techniques and theories of Artificial Intelligence, namely those pertaining to Intention Recognition, Commitment, and Apology (separately and jointly), encompassing errors in decision-making and communication noise. As a result, both the emergence and stability of cooperation become reinforced comparatively to the absence of such cognitive abilities. This holds separately for Intention Recognition, for Commitment, and for Apology, and even more so when they are jointly engaged.

This section aims to sensitize the reader to these Evolutionary Game Theory based issues, results and prospects, which are accruing in importance for the modeling of minds with machines, with impact on our understanding of the evolution of mutual tolerance and cooperation, and of the arising of moral norms. Recognition of someone's intentions, which may include imagining the recognition others have of our own intentions, and may comprise not just some error tolerance, but also a penalty for unfulfilled commitment though allowing for apology, can lead to evolutionary stable win/win equilibriums within groups of individuals, and perhaps amongst groups. The recognition and the manifestation of intentions, plus the assumption of commitment—even whilst paying a cost for putting it in place—and the acceptance of apology, are all facilitators in that respect, each of them singly and, above all, in collusion.

Emergence of Cooperation via Intention Recognition, Commitment, and Apology

In collective strategic interaction, wherein multiple agents pursue individual strategies, conflicts will arise because the actions of individual agents may have an effect on the welfare of others, and on their own in return (Han, Pereira, Santos, & Lenaerts, 2014). Hence, in these situations the need arises for the regulation of individual and collective behavior, traditionally having followed two distinct approaches, well-known in the Economics and Artificial Intelligence literature (Groves, 1973; Myerson, 1979; Axelrod, 1986; McAfee, 1993; Jackson, 2000; Nisan & Ronen, 1999; Naor, Pinkas, & Sumner, 1999; Ross, 2005; Phelps, McBurney, & Parsons, 2010): the spontaneous emergence of order approach, which studies how norms result from endogenous agreements among rational individuals, and the mechanism by design approach, which studies how norms are exogenously imposed in order to attain desirable properties of the whole.

In this summary, we describe the main results we have obtained following essentially the former approach, but crucially complementing it in instilling some individual agents with cognitive abilities that can and will induce cooperation in the population. These abilities enable such individuals to recognize the opportunity whether to decide to cooperate outright, or possibly propose costly cooperation commitments, susceptible to compensation on defaulting, and to accept apology-redressing dues. In consequence, norm-based cooperation can evolve and emerge.

The problem of evolution of cooperation and of the emergence of collective action—cutting across areas as diverse as Biology, Economy, Artificial Intelligence, Political Science, or Psychology—is one of the greatest interdisciplinary challenges science faces today (Hardin, 1968; Axelrod, 1984; Nowak, 2006a; Sigmund, 2010). To understand the evolutionary mechanisms that promote and keep cooperative behavior among individuals is all the more complex as increasingly intricate is the intrinsic complexity of those individuals partaking of the cooperation.

In its simplest form, a cooperative act is metaphorically described as the act of paying a cost to convey a benefit to someone else. If two players simultaneously decide to cooperate or not, the best possible response will be to try to receive the benefit without paying the cost. In an evolutionary setting, we may also wonder why would natural selection equip selfish individuals with altruistic tendencies while it incites competition between individuals and thus apparently rewards only selfish behavior? Several mechanisms responsible for promoting cooperative behavior have been recently identified (Sigmund, 2010; Nowak, 2006b). From kin and group ties, to different forms of reciprocity and networked populations, several aspects have been shown to play an important role in the emergence of cooperation (see survey in (Sigmund, 2010; Nowak, 2006b)).

Moreover, more complex strategies based on the evaluation of interactions between third parties allow the emergence of kinds of cooperation that are immune to exploitation because then interactions are channeled to just those who cooperate. Questions of justice and trust, with their negative (punishment) and positive (help) incentives, are fundamental in games with large diversified groups of individuals gifted with intention recognition capabilities. In allowing them to choose amongst distinct behaviors based on suggestive information about the intentions of their interaction partners—these in turn influenced by the behavior of the individual himself—individuals are also influenced by their tolerance to error or noise in the communication. One hopes that, to start with, understanding these capabilities can be transformed into mechanisms for spontaneous organization and control of swarms of autonomous robotic agents (Bonabeu, Dorigo, & Theraulaz, 1999), these being envisaged as large populations of agents where cooperation can emerge, but not necessarily to solve a priori given goals, as in distributed Artificial Intelligence (AI).

With these general objectives, we have specifically studied the way players' strategies adapt in populations involved in cooperation games. We used the techniques of Evolutionary Game Theory (EGT) (Hofbauer & Sigmund, 1998; Sigmund, 2010), considered games such as the Prisoner's Dilemma and Public Goods Game (Hofbauer & Sigmund, 1998; Sigmund, 2010), and showed how the actors participating in repeated iterations in these games can benefit from having the ability to recognize the intentions of other actors, to apologize when making mistakes, to establish commitments, or to combine some of them, thereby leading to an evolutionary stable increase in cooperation (Han, Pereira, & Santos, 2011a, 2012a, 2012b, 2012c; Han, Pereira, Santos, & Lenaerts, 2013a; Han, 2013), compared to extant best strategies.

In this section we summarize our recent publications on how intention recognition, commitment arrangement and apology can, separately and jointly, lead to the evolution of high levels of cooperation. We discuss how these works provide useful insights for mechanism design in Multi-agent Systems for regulative purposes. Evolutionary emergent futures is what we have studied, tied to the co-presence of fixed strategies in agents, though an agent may replace its strategy by a more advantageous one on occasion (social learning). We have not yet made a strategy also evolve by adopting features of other strategies into its own, through rule-defined strategies updating, which could be a direction for Multi-agent Systems (MAS).

Intention Recognition Promotes the Evolution of Cooperation

The ability of recognizing (or reading) intentions of others has been observed and shown to play an important role in many cooperative interactions, both in humans and primates (Tomasello, 2008; Meltzoff, 2005; Ran, Fudenberg, & Dreber, 2013). However, most studies on the evolution of cooperation, grounded on evolutionary dynamics and game theory, have neglected the important role played by a basic form of intention recognition in behavioral evolution. In Han et al. (2011a, 2012a), we have addressed explicitly this issue, characterizing the dynamics emerging from a population of intention recognizers.

In that work, intention recognition (IR) was implemented using Bayesian Networks (BN) (Pereira & Han, 2009b, 2011; Han et al., 2011a), taking into account the information of current signals of intent, as well as the mutual trust and tolerance accumulated from previous one-on-one play experience—including how my previous defections may influence another's intent—but without resorting to information gathered regarding players' overall reputation in the population.

A player's present intent can be understood here as how he's going to play the next round with me, whether by cooperating or defecting (Han et al., 2011a). Intention recognition can also be learnt from a corpus of prior interactions among game strategies (Han et al., 2011b, 2012a), where each strategy can be envisaged and detected as players' (possibly changing) intent to behave in a certain way (Han & Pereira, 2011). In both cases, we experimented with populations with different proportions of diverse strategies in order to calculate, in particular, what is the minimum fraction of individuals capable of intention recognition for cooperation to emerge, invade, prevail, and persist.

Intention recognition techniques have been studied actively in AI for several decades (Charniak & Goldman, 1993; Sadri, 2011), with several applications such as for improving human-computer interactions, assistive living and teamwork (Lesh, 1998; Pereira & Han, 2011; Roy, Bouchard, Bouzouane, &

Giroux, 2007; Heinze, 2003). In most of these applications the agents engage in repeated interactions with each other. Our results suggest that equipping the agents with an ability to recognize intentions of others can improve their cooperation and reduce misunderstanding that can result from noise and mistakes.

Commitments Promote the Emergence of Cooperation

Agents make commitments towards others when they give up options in order to influence others. Most commitments depend on some incentive that is necessary to ensure that an action (or even an intention) is in the agent's interest and thus will be carried out in the future (Gintis, 2001). Asking for prior commitments can just be used as a strategy to clarify the intentions of others, whilst at the same time manifesting our own. All parties then clearly know to what they commit and can refuse such a commitment whenever the offer is made. A classical example of such an agreement is marriage. In that case mutual commitment ensures some stability in the relationship, reducing the fear of exploitation and providing security against potential cataclysms.

In our recent works (Han et al., 2012b, 2013a) we investigate analytically and numerically whether costly commitment strategies, in which players propose, initiate and honor a deal, are viable strategies for the evolution of cooperative behavior, using the symmetric one-shot Prisoner's Dilemma (PD) game to model a social dilemma. Next to the traditional cooperate (C) and defect (D) options, a player can propose its co-player to commit to cooperation before playing the PD game, willing to pay a personal cost to make the proposal credible. If the co-player accepts the arrangement and also plays C, they both receive their rewards for mutual cooperation. Yet if the co-player plays D, then he or she will have to provide the proposer with compensation at a personal cost. Finally, when the co-player does not accept the deal, the game is not played and hence both obtain no payoff. Several free-riding strategies were included in the model, including (i) the fake committers, who accept a commitment proposal yet defect when playing the game, assuming that they can exploit the proposers without suffering a too severe consequence; and (ii) the commitment free-riders, who defect unless being proposed a commitment, which they then accept and cooperate afterwards in the PD game. In other words, these latter players are willing to cooperate when a commitment is proposed but are not prepared to pay the cost of setting it up.

We have shown that when the cost of arranging a commitment is justified with respect to the benefit of cooperation, substantial levels of cooperation can be achieved, especially when one insists on sharing the arrangement cost. On the one hand, such commitment proposers can get rid of fake committers by proposing a strong enough compensation cost. On the other hand, they can maintain a sufficient advantage over the commitment free riders, because a commitment proposer will cooperate with players alike she, while the latter defect among themselves. We have also compared the commitment strategy with the simple costly punishment strategy, where no prior agreements are made. The results show that the first strategy leads to a higher level of cooperation than the latter one.

Economical Use of Costly Commitment via Intention Recognition

Commitments have been shown to promote cooperation if the cost of arranging them is justified with respect to the benefit of cooperation. But commitment may be quite costly, which leads to the possible prevalence of commitment free-riders (Han et al., 2013a). Hence, it should be avoided when necessary. On the other hand, there are many cases where it is difficult to recognize the intention of another agent with sufficient confidence to make any decision based on it. One may have insufficient information for making the prediction (not enough actions being observed, such as in the first interaction scenario), or even one may know the agent well, but also know that the agent is very unpredictable. In such cases, the strategy of proposing a commitment, or manifesting an intention, can help to impose or clarify intentions of others. In addition, intention is usually defined as choice with commitment (Cohen & Levesque, 1990; Bratman, 1987; Roy, 2009). That is, once the agent intends to do something, it must settle on some state of affairs for which to aim, because of its resource limitation and in order to coordinate its future actions. Deciding what to do establishes a personal form of commitment (Cohen & Levesque, 1990; Roy, 2009). Proposing a commitment deal to another agent consists in asking it to express or clarify its intended decisions.

In a marriage commitment, by giving up the option to leave the other, spouses gain security and an opportunity for a much deeper relationship that would be impossible otherwise (Nesse, 2001a; Frank, 2001), as it might be risky to assume a partner's intention of staying faithful without the commitment of marriage. A contract is another popular kind of commitment, e.g. for an apartment lease (Frank, 2001). When it is risky to assume another agent's intention of being cooperative, arranging an appropriate contract provides incentives for cooperation. However, for example in accommodation rental, a contract is not necessary when the cooperative intention is of high certainty, e.g. when the business affair is between close friends or relatives. It said arranging a commitment deal can be useful to encourage cooperation whenever intention recognition is difficult, or cannot be performed with sufficiently high certainty. On the other hand, arranging commitments is not free, and requires a specific capacity to set it up within a reasonable cost (for the agent to actually benefit from it) (Nesse 2001a, 2001b)—therefore it should be avoided when opportune to do so.

With such motivations in mind, in our work (Han et al., 2012c; Han, 2013) we showed that if the player first predicts the intentions of a co-player and proposes commitment only when they are not confident about their intention prediction, it can significantly facilitate the conditions for cooperation to emerge. The improvement (in level of cooperation) is most significant when it is costly to arrange commitments and when the cooperation is highly beneficial.

In short, it seems to us that intention recognition, and its use in the scope of commitment, is a foundational cornerstone where we should begin at, naturally followed by the capacity to establish and honor commitments, as a tool towards the successive construction of collective intentions and social organization (Searle, 1995, 2010). Finally, one hopes that understanding these capabilities can be useful in the design of efficient self-organized and distributed engineering applications (Bonabeau, Dorigo, & Theraulaz, 1999), from bio- and socio-inspired computational algorithms, to swarms of autonomous robotic agents.

Apology in Committed vs. Commitment-Free Repeated Interactions

Apology is perhaps the most powerful and ubiquitous mechanism for conflict resolution (Abeler, Calaki, Andree, & Basek, 2010; Ohtsubo & Watanabe, 2009; Fischbacher and Utikal, 2013), especially among individuals involving in long-term repeated interactions (such as a marriage). An apology can resolve a conflict without having to involve external parties (e.g. teachers, parents, courts), which may cost all sides of the conflict significantly more. Evidence supporting the usefulness of apology abounds, ranging from medical error situations to seller-customer relationships (Abeler, Calaki, Andree, & Basek, 2010). Apology has been implemented in several computerized systems such as human-computer interaction and online markets so as to facilitate users' positive emotions and cooperation (Tzeng, 2004; Utz, Matzat, & Snijders, 2009).

The iterated Prisoner's Dilemma (IPD) has been the standard model to investigate conflict resolution and the problem of the evolution of cooperation in repeated interaction settings (Axelrod, 1984; Sigmund, 2010). This IPD game is usually known as a story of tit-for-tat (TFT), which won both Axelrod's tournaments (Axelrod, 1984). TFT cooperates if the opponent cooperated in the previous round, and defects if the opponent defected. But if there can be erroneous moves due to noise (i.e. an intended move is wrongly performed), the performance of TFT declines, because an erroneous defection by one player leads to a sequence of unilateral cooperation and defection. A generous version of TFT, which sometimes cooperates even if the opponent defected (Nowak & Sigmund, 1992), can deal with noise better, yet not thoroughly. For these TFT-like strategies, apology is modeled implicitly as one or more cooperative acts after a wrongful defection.

In our recent work (Han, Pereira, Santos, & Lenaerts, 2013b), we describe a model containing strategies that explicitly apologize when making an error between rounds. An apologizing act consists in compensating the co-player an appropriate amount (the higher the more sincere), in order to ensure that this other player cooperates in the next actual round. As such, a population consisting of only apologizers can maintain perfect cooperation. However, other behaviors that exploit such apology behavior could emerge, such as those that accept apology compensation from others but do not apologize when making mistakes (fake apologizers), destroying any benefit of the apology behavior. Resorting to the Evolutionary Game Theory (Sigmund, 2010), we show that when the apology occurs in a system where the players first ask for a commitment before engaging in the interaction (Han et al., 2012b, 2012c; Han et al., 2013a; Han, 2013), this exploitation can be avoided. Our results lead to the following conclusions: (i) Apology alone is insufficient to achieve high levels of cooperation; (ii) Apology supported by prior commitment leads to significantly higher levels of cooperation; (iii) Apology needs to be sincere to function properly, whether in a committed relationships or commitment-free ones (which is in accordance with existing experimental studies, e.g. in Ohtsubo and Watanabe (2009); (iv) A much costlier apology tends to be used in committed relationships than in commitment-free ones, as it can help better identify free-riders such as fake apologizers: *commitments bring about sincerity*.

As apology (Tzeng, 2004; Utz, Matzat, & Snijders, 2009) and commitment (Winikoff, 2007; Wooldridge & Jennings, 1999) have been widely studied in AI and Computer Science, for example, about how these mechanisms can be formalized, implemented, and used to enhance cooperation in human-computer interactions and online market systems (Tzeng, 2004; Utz, Matzat, & Snijders, 2009), as well as general multi-agent systems (Winikoff, 2007; Wooldridge & Jennings, 1999), our study would provide important insights for the design and deployment of such mechanisms; for instance, what kind of apology should be provided to customers when making mistakes, and whether apology can be enhanced when complemented with commitments to ensure better cooperation, e.g. compensation from customer's for wrongdoing.

Commitments in Public Goods

Whenever creating a public good, strategies or mechanisms are required to handle defectors. Arranging a prior commitment or agreement is an essential ingredient to encourage cooperative behavior in a wide range of relationships, ranging from personal to political and religious ones. Prior agreements clarify the intentions and preferences of other players. Hence, refusing to establish an agreement may be considered as intending or preferring not to cooperate (non-committers). Prior agreements may be highly rewarding in group situations, as in the case of Public Goods Games (Ostrom, 1990), as it forces the other participants to signal their willingness to achieve a common goal. Especially for increasing group sizes, such prior agreements could be ultimately rewarding, as it becomes more and more difficult to assess the aspirations of all participants.

We have shown (Han, Pereira, & Lenaerts, 2014), mathematically and numerically, that prior agreements with posterior compensations provide a strategic solution that leads to substantial levels of cooperation in the context of Public Goods Games, results that are corroborated by available experimental data.

Notwithstanding this success, one cannot, as with other approaches, fully exclude the presence of defectors, raising the question of how they can be dealt with to avoid the demise of the common good. We showed that avoiding creation of the common good (whenever full agreement is not reached), or limiting the benefit that disagreeing defectors can acquire (using costly restriction mechanisms), are both relevant choices.

Nonetheless, restriction mechanisms are found to be the more favorable, especially in larger group interactions. Given decreasing restriction costs, then introducing restraining measures to cope with public goods free-riding issues is the ultimate advantageous solution for all involved participants, rather than avoiding its creation.

Collective Realm Conclusion

We have argued that the study of the aforementioned issues has come of age and is ripe with research opportunities, having communicated some of the inroads we explored, and pointed to the more detailed published results of what we have achieved, with respect to intention recognition, commitment, and mutual tolerance through apology, within the overarching Evolutionary Game Theory context.

BRIDGING THE TWO REALMS OF MORALITY FOR MACHINES

We have examined above two types of incursions, one into the individual's success in a fixed group, and the second into the evolving population realms of morality.

The first type resorts to individual cognition and reasoning to enable such individuals to successfully compete amongst free riders and deceivers. Such successful competition can be achieved by learning past interactions with them or by recognizing their intentions (Pereira & Han, 2011). The second type emphasizes instead the emergence, in a population, of evolutionarily stable moral norms, of fair and just cooperation that ably discard free riders and deceivers, to the advantage of the whole evolved population.

To this latter end, some cognitive abilities such as intention recognition, commitment, and apology were employed, singly or jointly, by instilling them into just some individual agents, which then become predominant and lastly invade the evolving population, whether in the context of pairwise interactions or of public good situations.

A fundamental question then arises, concerning the study of individual cognition in groups of often morally interacting multi-agents (that can choose to defect or cooperate with others), whether from such study we can obtain results equally applicable to the evolution of populations of such agents. And vice-versa, whether the results obtained in the study of populations carry over to groups of frequently interacting multi-agents, and under what conditions. Some initial Evolutionary Game Theory results into certain learning methods have identified a broad class of situations where this is the case (Segbroeck, Jong, Nowé, Santos, & Lenaerts, 2010; Pinheiro, Pacheco, & Santos, 2012; Börgers & Sarin, 1997). A premium outstanding issue remains in regard to which cognitive abilities and circumstances the result may obtain in general, and for sure that will be the object of much new and forthcoming programs of research.

Specifically with respect to human morality, the answer to the above-enounced fundamental question would appear to be a resounding 'Yes'. For one, morality concerns both groups and populations, requires cognition, and will have had to evolve in a nature/nurture or gene/culture intertwining and reinforcement. For another, evolutionary anthropology, psychology, and neurology have been producing ever more consilient views on the evolution of human morality.

Their scientific theories and results must per force be kept in mind, and serve as inspiration, when thinking and rethinking about machine ethics. And all the more so because the machines will need to be ethical amongst us human beings, not just among themselves.

On the other hand, the very study of ethics, and the evolution of human morality too, can now avail themselves of the experimental, computation theoretic, and robotic means to enact and simulate individual or group moral reasoning, in a plethora of circumstances. Likewise for the emergence of moral rules and behaviors in evolving populations.

Hence, having already addressed above two computational types of models, in the next section below we stress this double outlook, by bringing to the fore congenial present views and research on the evolution of human morality, hoping to reinforce the bridging ideas and paradigm we set forth.

Moreover, we take for granted that computational and robotic models can actually provide abstract and concrete insight on emerged human moral reality, irrespective of the distinct embodiments of man and machine.

What emerges as morality? The answer is not some "thing" but rather something like a form, or pattern, or function. The concept of emergence applies to phenomena in which relational properties dominate over constituent properties in determining aggregate features. It is with respect to configurations and topologies, not specific properties of constituents, that we trace processes of emergence.

We depart then from the point of view where morality is established as that property or ability to act solely according to reasons and motives that are taken as one's own; however, but these could otherwise be redefined to capture the mutual influences among individuals and the population.

By analogy with computing machines, cognitive scientists have argued that the "functional" properties that define a given cognitive operation are like the logical architecture of a computer program. Philosophically, this general form of argument is known as 'functionalism', and it is quite relevant for viewing morality as an emergent property. In that respect, we adopt the standpoint of functionalism. As we put it in another context, the point "is that the brain, in its biological evolution, evolved so that it could execute any kind of mind software: personhood, art, whatever; that the brain has bootstrapped itself into generality (Pereira, 2012b, 2014).

THE EVOLUTIONARY TEACHINGS

Added dependency on cooperation makes it more competitive to cooperate well. Thus, it is advantageous to invest on shared morals in order to attract partners who will partake of mutual and balanced advantages.

This evolutionary hypothesis inspired by mutualism (Baumard, 2010)—itself a form of contractualism (Ashford & Mulgan, 2007)—contrasts with a number of naturalist theories of morality, which make short shrift of the importance of cognition for cooperation. For example, the theory of reciprocity, in ignoring a wider cognitive capacity to choose and attract one's partners, forbids itself from explaining evolution on the basis of a cooperation market.

Indeed, when assigning all importance to population evolutionary mechanisms, naturalist theories tend to forget the evolution of cognition in individuals. Such theories habitually start off from evolutionary mechanisms for understanding the specificity of human morals: punishment (Boyd & Richerson, 1992; Sober & Wilson, 1998), culture (Henrich & Boyd, 2001; Sober & Wilson, 1998), political alliances (Boehm, 1999; Erdal, Whiten, Boehm, & Knauft, 1994). According to Baumard's hypothesis, morality does not emerge because humans avail themselves of new means for punishing free-riders or for recompensing cooperators, but simply because mutual help—and hence the need to find partners—becomes much more important.

In summary, it's the development of cooperation that induces the emergence of morals, and not the stabilization of morals (via punishment or culture) that promotes the development of cooperation.

Experimental results are in line with the hypothesis that the perfecting of human intuitive psychology is responsible for the emergence of morality, on the basis of an improved understanding of the mental states of others. This permits to communicate, not just to coordinate with them, and thus extend the domain cooperation, thereby leading to a disposition toward moral behaviors. For a systematic and thorough account of research into the evolutionary origins of morality, see Krebs (2011) and Bowles and Gintis (2011).

At the end of the day, one may consider three theories bearing on three different aspects of morality: the evaluation of interests for utilitarianism, the proper balance of interests for mutualism, and the discharging of obligations for the virtues principled.

A naturalistic approach to moral sense does not make the psychological level disappear to the benefit of the evolutionary one. To each its explanation level: psychology accounts for the workings of the moral sense; sociology, for the social context that activates it; and a cupola theory, for the evolution of causes that occasioned it (Sperber, 1977). Moral capability is therefore a "mechanism" amongst others (Elster, 1998), as are the concern for reputation, the weakness of the will, the power to reason, etc.

An approach that is at once naturalist and mutualist allows escape from these apparently opposite viewpoints: the psychological and the societal. At the level of psychological motivations, moral behavior does neither stem from egotism nor altruism. To the contrary, it aims at the mutual respect for everyone's attending interests. And, simultaneously, it obeys the logic of equity. At the evolutionary level, moral behavior is not contradictory with egotism because, in human society, it is often in our own interest to respect the interests of others. Through moral motivations, we avail ourselves of a means to reconcile the diverse individual interests. Morality vies precisely at harmonizing individual interest with the need to associate, and profit from cooperation, by adopting a logic of fairness.

The mutualist solution is not new. Contractualist philosophers have upheld it for some time. Notably, they have furnished detailed descriptions of our moral capacity (Rawls, 1971; Thomson, 1971). However, they never were able to explain why humans are enabled with that particular capacity: Why do our judgments seek equity? Why do we behave morally at all?

Without an explanation, the mutualist theory seems improbable: Why behave we as if an actual contract had been committed to, when in all evidence one was not?

Past and ongoing evolutionary studies, intertwining and bridging cognitive and population aspects, and both becoming supported on computational simulations, will help us find answers to that. In the process, rethinking machine ethics and its implementations.

According to Boehm (2012), conscience and morality evolved, in the biological sense. Conscience evolved for reasons having to do with environments humans had to cope with prehistorically, and their growing ability to use group punishment to better their social and subsistence lives and create more equalized societies. His general evolutionary hypothesis is that morality began with having a conscience and that conscience evolution began with systematic but initially non-moralistic social control by groups.

This entailed punishment of individual "deviants" by bands of well-armed large-game hunters, and, like the ensuing preaching in favor of generosity, such punishment amounted to "social selection", since the social preferences of members and of groups as a whole had systematic effects on gene pools.

This punitive side of social selection adumbrates an immediate kind of "purpose", of large-brained humans actively and insightfully seeking positive social goals or avoiding social disasters arising out of conflict. No surprise the genetic consequences, even if unintended, move towards fewer tendencies for social predation and more towards social cooperation. Hence, group punishment can improve the quality of social life, and over the generations gradually shape the genotype in a similar direction.

Boehm's idea is that prehistoric humans made use of social control intensively, so that individuals who were better at inhibiting their own antisocial tendencies, by fear of punishment or by absorbing and identifying with group's rules, garnered a superior fitness. In learning to internalize rules, humankind acquired a conscience. At the beginning this stemmed from punitive social selection, having also the strong effect of suppressing free riders. A newly moralistic type of free-rider suppression helped evolve a remarkable capacity for extra-familial social generosity. That conscience gave us a primitive sense of right and wrong, which evolved the remarkable "empathy" which we are infused with today. It is a conscience that seems to be as much a Machiavellian risk calculator as a moral force that maximizes prosocial behavior, with others' interests and equity in mind, and minimizes deviance too. It is clear that "biology" and "culture" work together to render us adaptively moral.

Boehm believes the issue of selfish free riders requires further critical thought, and that selfish intimidators are a seriously neglected type of free rider. There has been too much of a single-minded focus on cheating dominating free rider theorizing. In fact, he ascertains us the more potent free riders have been alpha-type bullies, who simply take what they want. It is here his work on the evolution of hunter-gatherer egalitarianism enters, namely with its emphasis on the active and potentially quite violent policing of alpha-male social predators by their own band-level communities. Though there's a large literature on cheaters and their detection, free-rider suppression in regard to bullies has not been taken into account so far in the mathematical models that study altruism.

"For moral evolution to have been set in motion," Boehm (2012) goes on, "more was needed than a preexisting capacity for cultural transmission. It would have helped if there were already in place a good capacity to strategize about social behavior and to calculate how to act appropriately in social situations."

In humans, the individual understanding that there exists a self in relation to others makes possible participation in moral communities. Mere self-recognition is not sufficient for a moral being with fully developed conscience, but a sense of self is a necessary first step useful in gauging the reactions of others to one's behavior and to understand their intentions. And it is especially important to realize that one can become the center of attention of a hostile group, if one's actions offend seriously its moral sensibilities. The capacity to take on the perspective of others underlies not just the ability of individuals in communities to modify their behavior and follow group imposed rules, but it also permits people acting as groups to predict and cope insightfully with the behavior of "deviants."

Social selection reduced innate dispositions to bully or cheat, and kept our conscience in place by self-inhibiting antisocial behavior. A conscience delivers us a social mirror image. A substandard conscience may generate a substandard reputation and active punishment too. A conscience supplies not just inhibitions, but serves as an early warning system that helps prudent individuals from being sanctioned.

Boehm (2012) wraps up: "When we bring in the conscience as a highly sophisticated means of channeling behavioral tendencies so that they are expressed efficiently in terms of fitness, scenarios change radically. From within the human psyche an evolutionary conscience provided the needed self-restraint, while externally it was group sanctioning that largely took care of the dominators and cheaters. Over time, human individuals with strong free-riding tendencies—but who exercised really efficient self-control—would not have lost fitness because these predatory tendencies were so well inhibited. And if they expressed their aggression in socially acceptable ways, this in fact would have aided their fitness. That is why both free-riding genes and altruistic genes could have remained well represented and coexisting in the same gene pool."

For sure, we conclude, evolutionary biology and anthropology, like the cognitive sciences too (Hauser, 2006; Gazzaniga, 2006; Churchland, 2011; Greene, 2013; Tomasello, 2014), have much to offer in view of rethinking machine ethics, evolutionary game theory simulations of computational morality to the rescue.

CODA

In realm of the individual, computation is vehicle for the study and teaching of morality, namely in its modeling of the dynamics of knowledge and cognition of agents. In the collective realm, norms and moral emergence have been studied computationally in populations of rather simple-minded agents. By bridging these realms, cognition affords improved emerged morals in populations of situated agents.

At the end of the day, we will certainly wish ethical machines to be convivial with us.

ACKNOWLEDGMENT

We thank the co-authors of joint papers, The Anh Han, Francisco C. Santos, and Tom Lenaerts, for use of material from diverse joint publications referenced below.

Ari Saptawijaya acknowledges the support of Fundação para a Ciência e a Tecnologia (FCT/MEC) Portugal, grant SFRH/BD/72795/2010.

REFERENCES

Abeler, J., Calaki, J., Andree, K., & Basek, C. (2010). The power of apology. *Economics Letters*, *107*(2), 233–235. doi:10.1016/j.econlet.2010.01.033

Alferes, J. J., Pereira, L. M., & Swift, T. (2004). Abduction in well-founded semantics and generalized stable models via tabled dual programs. *Theory and Practice of Logic Programming*, *4*(4), 383–428. doi:10.1017/S1471068403001960

Anderson, M., & Anderson, S. L. (2008). EthEl: Toward a principled ethical eldercare robot. In *AAAI Fall Symposium Technical Report on AI in Eldercare*. Palo Alto, CA: AAAI Press.

Anderson, M., & Anderson, S. L. (2010). Robot be good: A call for ethical autonomous machines. *Scientific American*, *303*(4), 54–59. doi:10.1038/scientificamerican1010-72 PMID:20923132

Anderson, M., Anderson, S. L., & Armen, C. (2005). Towards machine ethics: Implementing two action-based ethical theories. In *AAAI Fall Symposium Technical Report on Machine Ethics*. Palo Alto, CA: AAAI Press.

Anderson, M., Anderson, S. L., & Armen, C. (2006). MedEthEx: a prototype medical ethics advisor. In *Proceedings of the Eighteenth Conference on Innovative Applications of Artifical Intelligence (IAAI'06)*. Palo Alto, CA: AAAI Press.

Ashford, E., & Mulgan, T. (2007). Contractualism. In E. N. Zalta (Ed.), *The Stanford Encyclopedia of Philosophy* (Fall 2012 Edition). Retrieved from http://plato.stanford.edu/entries/contractualism/

Axelrod, R. (1984). *The Evolution of Cooperation*. New York: Basic Books.

Axelrod, R. (1986). An evolutionary approach to norms. *The American Political Science Review*, *80*(4), 1095–1111. doi:10.2307/1960858

Baral, C., Gelfond, M., & Rushton, N. (2009). Probabilistic reasoning with answer sets. *Theory and Practice of Logic Programming*, *9*(1), 57–144. doi:10.1017/S1471068408003645

Baumard, N. (2010). *Comment nous sommes devenus moraux: Une histoire naturelle du bien et du mal*. Paris: Odile Jacob.

Boehm, C. (1999). *Hierarchy in the Forest: The Evolution of Egalitarian Behavior*. Cambridge, MA: Harvard University Press.

Boehm, C. (2012). *Moral Origins: The Evolution of Virtue, Altruism, and Shame*. New York: Basic Books.

Bonabeau, E., Dorigo, M., & Theraulaz, G. (1999). *Swarm Intelligence: From Natural to Artificial Systems*. New York: Oxford University Press.

Börgers, T., & Sarin, R. (1997). Learning Through Reinforcement and Replicator Dynamics. *Journal of Economic Theory*, *77*(1), 1–14. doi:10.1006/jeth.1997.2319

Bowles, S., & Gintis, H. (2011). *A Cooperative Species: Human Reciprocity and Its Evolution*. Princeton: Princeton University Press.

Boyd, R., & Richerson, P. (1992). Punishment allows the evolution of cooperation (or anything else) in sizable groups. *Ethology and Sociobiology*, *13*(3), 171–195. doi:10.1016/0162-3095(92)90032-Y

Bratman, M. E. (1987). *Intention, Plans and Practical Reasoning*. Cambridge, MA: Harvard University Press.

Bringsjord, S., Arkoudas, K., & Bello, P. (2006). Toward a general logicist methodology for engineering ethically correct robots. *IEEE Intelligent Systems*, *21*(4), 38–44. doi:10.1109/MIS.2006.82

Bringsjord, S., Taylor, J., van Heuveln, B., Arkoudas, K., Clark, M., & Wojtowicz, R. (2011). Piagetian roboethics via category theory: Moving beyond mere formal operations to engineer robots whose decisions are guaranteed to be ethically correct. In M. Anderson & S. L. Anderson (Eds.), *Machine Ethics* (pp. 361–374). New York, NY: Cambridge University Press. doi:10.1017/CBO9780511978036.025

Charniak, E., & Goldman, R. P. (1993). A Bayesian model of plan recognition. *Artificial Intelligence, 64*(1), 53–79. doi:10.1016/0004-3702(93)90060-O

Churchland, P. (2011). *Braintrust: What Neuroscience Tells Us about Morality*. Princeton: Princeton University Press. doi:10.1515/9781400838080

Cohen, P. R., & Levesque, H. J. (1990). Intention is Choice with Commitment. *Artificial Intelligence, 42*(2-3), 213–261. doi:10.1016/0004-3702(90)90055-5

Cushman, F., Young, L., & Greene, J. D. (2010). Multi-system moral psychology. In J. M. Doris (Ed.), *The Moral Psychology Handbook*. New York: Oxford University Press. doi:10.1093/acprof:oso/9780199582143.003.0003

Dell'Acqua, P., & Pereira, L. M. (2007). Preferential theory revision. *Journal of Applied Logic, 5*(4), 586–601. doi:10.1016/j.jal.2006.03.010

Elster, J. (1998). A plea for mechanisms. In P. Hedström & R. Swedberg (Eds.), *Social Mechanisms: An analytical approach to social theory* (pp. 45–73). Cambridge, NY: Cambridge University Press. doi:10.1017/CBO9780511663901.003

Epstude, K., & Roese, N. J. (2008). The functional theory of counterfactual thinking. *Personality and Social Psychology Review, 12*(2), 168–192. doi:10.1177/1088868308316091 PMID:18453477

Erdal, D., Whiten, A., Boehm, C., & Knauft, B. (1994). On human egalitarianism: An evolutionary product of machiavellian status escalation? *Current Anthropology, 35*(2), 175–183. doi:10.1086/204255

Fischbacher, U., & Utikal, V. (2013). On the acceptance of apologies. *Games and Economic Behavior, 82*, 592–608. doi:10.1016/j.geb.2013.09.003

Foot, P. (1967). The problem of abortion and the doctrine of double effect. *Oxford Review, 5*, 5–15.

Frank, R. H. (2001). Cooperation through Emotional Commitment. In R. M. Nesse (Ed.), *Evolution and the capacity for commitment* (pp. 55–76). New York: Russell Sage.

Ganascia, J.-G. (2007). Modelling ethical rules of lying with Answer Set Programming. *Ethics and Information Technology, 9*(1), 39–47. doi:10.1007/s10676-006-9134-y

Ganascia, J.-G. (2012). An Agent-Based Formalization for Resolving Ethical Conflicts. In Proceedings of the *Workshop on Belief Change, Non-monotonic Reasoning, and Conflict Resolution (BNC@ECAI'12)*, Montpellier, France.

Gazzaniga, M. S. (2006). *The Ethical Brain: The Science of Our Moral Dilemmas*. New York: Harper Perennial.

Gelfond, M., & Lifschitz, V. (1988). The stable model semantics for logic programming. In *Proceedings of the Fifth International Conference on Logic Programming (ICLP)* (pp. 1070-1080). Cambridge, MA: MIT Press.

Gintis, H. (2001). Beyond selfishness in modeling human behavior. In R. M. Nesse (Ed.), *Evolution and the capacity for commitment*. New York: Russell Sage.

Greene, J. (2013). *Moral Tribes: Emotion, Reason, and the Gap Between Us and Them*. New York: The Penguin Press HC.

Groves, T. (1973). Incentives in Teams. *Econometrica*, *41*(4), 617–631. doi:10.2307/1914085

Guarini, M. (2011). Computational neural modeling and the philosophy of ethics: Reflections on the particularism-generalism debate. In M. Anderson & S. L. Anderson (Eds.), *Machine Ethics* (pp. 316–334). New York, NY: Cambridge University Press. doi:10.1017/CBO9780511978036.023

Han, T. A. (2013). *Intention Recognition, Commitments and Their Roles in the Evolution of Cooperation: From Artificial Intelligence Techniques to Evolutionary Game Theory Models. SAPERE series, 9*. Berlin: Springer-Verlag. doi:10.1007/978-3-642-37512-5

Han, T. A., & Pereira, L. M. (2011). Context-dependent incremental intention recognition through Bayesian network model construction. In A. Nicholson (Ed.), Proceedings of the Eighth UAI Bayesian Modeling Applications Workshop (Vol. 818, pp. 50–58). CEUR Workshop Proceedings; Retrieved from http://ceur-ws.org/Vol-818/paper7.pdf

Han, T. A., Pereira, L. M., & Lenaerts, T. (2014). Emergence of Commitments in Public Goods Game: Restricting vs. Avoiding Non-Committers (Submitted). Retrieved from http://centria.di.fct.unl.pt/~lmp/publications/online-papers/commitment_restriction.pdf

Han, T. A., Pereira, L. M., & Santos, F. C. (2011a). Intention recognition promotes the emergence of cooperation. *Adaptive Behavior*, *19*(3), 264–279.

Han, T. A., Pereira, L. M., & Santos, F. C. (2011b). The role of intention recognition in the evolution of cooperative behavior. In WalshT. (Ed.), *Proceedings of the 22nd International Joint Conference on Artificial Intelligence* (pp. 1684–1689). AAAI Press.

Han, T. A., Pereira, L. M., & Santos, F. C. (2012a). Corpus-based intention recognition in cooperation dilemmas. *Artificial Life*, *18*(4), 365–383. PMID:22938562

Han, T. A., Pereira, L. M., & Santos, F. C. (2012b). The emergence of commitments and cooperation. In *Proceedings of the Eleventh International Conference on Autonomous Agents and Multiagent Systems* (pp. 559-566). International Foundation for Autonomous Agents and Multiagent Systems.

Han, T. A., Pereira, L. M., & Santos, F. C. (2012c). Intention Recognition, Commitment, and The Evolution of Cooperation. In *Proceedings of IEEE Congress on Evolutionary Computation* (pp. 1–8). IEEE Press. doi:10.1109/CEC.2012.6256472

Han, T. A., Pereira, L. M., Santos, F. C., & Lenaerts, T. (2013a). Good agreements make good friends. *Scientific Reports*, *3*. doi:10.1038/srep02695 PMID:24045873

Han, T. A., Pereira, L. M., Santos, F. C., & Lenaerts, T. (2013b). Why is it so hard to say sorry: The evolution of apology with commitments in the iterated Prisoner's Dilemma. In *Proceedings of the Twenty-Third International Joint Conference on Artificial Intelligence* (pp. 177–183). Palo Alto: AAAI Press.

Han, T. A., Pereira, L. M., Santos, F. C., & Lenaerts, T. (in press). Emergence of Cooperation via Intention Recognition, Commitment, and Apology -- A Research Summary. *AI Communications*.

Han, T. A., Saptawijaya, A., & Pereira, L. M. (2012). Moral reasoning under uncertainty. In BjørnerN. VoronkovA. (Eds.), *Proceedings of the Eighteenth International Conference on Logic for Programming Artificial Intelligence and Reasoning (LNCS)* (Vol. 7180, pp. 212-227). Berlin:Springer-Verlag. doi:10.1007/978-3-642-28717-6_18

Hardin, G. (1968). The tragedy of the commons. *Science*, *162*(3859), 1243–1248. doi:10.1126/science.162.3859.1243 PMID:5699198

Hauser, M., Cushman, F., Young, L., Jin, R. K., & Mikhail, J. (2007). A dissociation between moral judgments and justifications. *Mind & Language*, *22*(1), 1–21. doi:10.1111/j.1468-0017.2006.00297.x

Hauser, M. D. (2006). *Moral Minds: The Nature of Right and Wrong*. New York: Harper Perennial.

Heinze, C. (2003). *Modeling Intention Recognition for Intelligent Agent Systems* (Doctoral Dissertation). The University of Melbourne, Australia.

Henrich, J., & Boyd, R. (2001). Why people punish defectors: Weak conformist transmission can stabilize costly enforcement of norms in cooperative dilemmas. *Journal of Theoretical Biology*, *208*(1), 79–89. doi:10.1006/jtbi.2000.2202 PMID:11162054

Hofbauer, J., & Sigmund, K. (1998). *Evolutionary Games and Population Dynamics*. New York, NY: Cambridge University Press. doi:10.1017/CBO9781139173179

Inhelder, B., & Piaget, J. (1958). *The Growth of Logical Thinking from Childhood to Adolescence*. New York, NY: Basic Books. doi:10.1037/10034-000

Jackson, M. O. (2000). Mechanism theory. In U. Derigs (Ed.), *Optimization and Operations Research*. Paris: EOLSS Publishers.

Jonsen, A. R., & Toulmin, S. (1988). *The Abuse of Casuistry: A History of Moral Reasoning*. Oakland, CA: University of California Press.

Kamm, F. M. (2006). *Intricate Ethics: Rights, Responsibilities, and Permissible Harm*. New York, NY: Oxford University Press.

Kowalski, R. (2011). *Computational Logic and Human Thinking: How to be Artificially Intelligent*. New York, NY: Cambridge University Press. doi:10.1017/CBO9780511984747

Krebs, D. L. (2011). *The Origins of Morality: An Evolutionary Account*. New York: Oxford University Press. doi:10.1093/acprof:oso/9780199778232.001.0001

Lesh, N. (1998). *Scalable and Adaptive Goal Recognition* (Doctoral Dissertation). University of Washington.

Lopes, G., & Pereira, L. M. (2006). Prospective programming with ACORDA. In *Proceedings of the FLoC'06 Workshop on Empirically Successful Computerized Reasoning (ESCoR'06)*, Seattle, USA.

Lopes, G., & Pereira, L. M. (2010). Prospective storytelling agents. In CarroM.PeñaR. (Eds.), *Proceedings of the Twelfth International Symposium on Practical Aspects of Declarative Languages (LNCS)* (Vol. 5937, pp. 294-296). Berlin: Springer-Verlag. doi:10.1007/978-3-642-11503-5_24

Markman, K. D., Gavanski, I., Sherman, S. J., & McMullen, M. N. (1993). The mental simulation of better and worse possible worlds. *Journal of Experimental Social Psychology*, *29*(1), 87–109. doi:10.1006/jesp.1993.1005

McAfee, R. P. (1993). Mechanism Design by Competing Sellers. *Econometrica*, *61*(6), 1281–1312. doi:10.2307/2951643

McCloy, R., & Byrne, R. M. J. (2000). Counterfactual thinking about controllable events. *Memory & Cognition*, *28*(6), 1071–1078. doi:10.3758/BF03209355 PMID:11105533

McIntyre, A. (2004). Doctrine of double effect. In E. N. Zalta (Ed.), The Stanford Encyclopedia of Philosophy (Fall 2011 edition). Retrieved from http://plato.stanford.edu/entries/double-effect/

McLaren, B. M. (2006). Computational models of ethical reasoning: Challenges, initial steps, and future directions. *IEEE Intelligent Systems*, *21*(4), 29–37. doi:10.1109/MIS.2006.67

Meltzoff, A. N. (2005). Imitation and other minds: the "like me" hypothesis. In *Perspectives On Imitation: From Neuroscience to Social Science. Imitation, Human Development, and Culture* (pp. 55–77). Cambridge, MA: MIT Press.

Migliore, S., Curcio, G., Mancini, F., & Cappa, S. F. (2014). Counterfactual thinking in moral judgment: An experimental study. *Frontiers in Psychology*, *5*, 451. doi:10.3389/fpsyg.2014.00451 PMID:24904468

Murakami, Y. (2004). Utilitarian Deontic Logic. In *Proceedings of the Fifth International Conference on Advances in Modal Logic (AiML'04)*. London: King's College Publications.

Myerson, R. (1979). Incentive compatibility and the bargaining problem. *Econometrica*, *47*(1), 61–73. doi:10.2307/1912346

Naor, M., Pinkas, B., & Sumner, R. (1999). Privacy preserving auctions and mechanism design. In *Proceedings of the 1st ACM Conference on Electronic Commerce* (pp. 129–139). ACM. doi:10.1145/336992.337028

Nesse, R. M. (2001a). Natural selection and the capacity for subjective commitment. In R. M. Nesse (Ed.), *Evolution and the Capacity for Commitment* (pp. 1–44). New York: Russell Sage.

Nesse, R. M. (2001b). *Evolution and the Capacity for Commitment*. New York: Russell Sage.

Nisan, N., & Ronen, A. (1999). Algorithmic mechanism design. In *Proceedings of the Thirty-First Annual ACM Symposium on Theory of Computing* (pp. 129–140). ACM. doi:10.1145/301250.301287

Nowak, M. A. (2006a). *Evolutionary Dynamics: Exploring the Equations of Life*. Cambridge, MA: Harvard University Press.

Nowak, M. A. (2006b). Five rules for the evolution of cooperation. *Science, 314*(5805), 1560–1563. doi:10.1126/science.1133755 PMID:17158317

Nowak, M. A., & Sigmund, K. (1992). Tit for tat in heterogeneous populations. *Nature, 355*(6357), 250–253. doi:10.1038/355250a0

Ohtsubo, Y., & Watanabe, E. (2009). Do sincere apologies need to be costly? Test of a costly signaling model of apology. *Evolution and Human Behavior, 30*(2), 114–123. doi:10.1016/j.evolhumbehav.2008.09.004

Ostrom, E. (1990). *Governing the commons: The evolution of institutions for collective action.* Cambridge, MA: Cambridge University Press. doi:10.1017/CBO9780511807763

Pearl, J. (2009). *Causality: Models, Reasoning and Inference.* New York, NY: Cambridge University Press. doi:10.1017/CBO9780511803161

Pereira, L. M. (2012a). Evolutionary Tolerance. In L. Magnani & L. Ping (Eds.), *Philosophy and Cognitive Science—Western & Eastern Studies (SAPERE)* (Vol. 2, pp. 263–287). Berlin: Springer-Verlag. doi:10.1007/978-3-642-29928-5_14

Pereira, L. M. (2012b). Turing is Among Us. *Journal of Logic and Computation, 22*(6), 1257–1277. doi:10.1093/logcom/exs035

Pereira, L. M. (2014). Can we not Copy the Human Brain in the Computer? In *Brain.org* (pp. 118–126). Lisbon: Fundação Calouste Gulbenkian.

Pereira, L. M., Dell'Acqua, P., Pinto, A. M., & Lopes, G. (2013). Inspecting and preferring abductive models. In K. Nakamatsu & L. C. Jain (Eds.), *The Handbook on Reasoning-Based Intelligent Systems* (pp. 243–274). World Scientific Publishers. doi:10.1142/9789814329484_0010

Pereira, L. M., & Han, T. A. (2009a). Evolution Prospection. In NakamatsuK.Phillips-WrenG.JainL. C.HowlettR. J. (Eds.), *Proceedings of the First KES International Symposium IDT (New Advances in Intelligent Decision Technologies)* (Vol. 199, pp. 51-63). Berlin: Springer-Verlag. doi:10.1007/978-3-642-00909-9_6

Pereira, L. M., & Han, T. A. (2009b). Intention recognition via causal Bayes networks plus plan generation. In *Proceedings of 14th Portuguese International Conference on Artificial Intelligence (LNCS)* (Vol. 5816, pp. 138–149). Berlin: Springer-Verlag. doi:10.1007/978-3-642-04686-5_12

Pereira, L. M., & Han, T. A. (2011). Intention recognition with evolution prospection and causal Bayesian networks. In A. Madureira, J. Ferreira, & Z. Vale (Eds.), *Computational Intelligence for Engineering Systems: Emergent Applications* (pp. 1–33). Berlin: Springer-Verlag. doi:10.1007/978-94-007-0093-2_1

Pereira, L. M., & Saptawijaya, A. (2007a). Moral Decision Making with ACORDA. In *Local Proceedings of the Fourteenth International Conference on Logic for Programming Artificial Intelligence and Reasoning (LPAR'07)*, Yerevan, Armenia.

Pereira, L. M., & Saptawijaya, A. (2007b). Modelling Morality with Prospective Logic. In NevesJ. M.SantosM. F.MachadoJ. M. (Eds.), *Proceedings of the Thirteenth Portuguese Conference on Artificial Intelligence (LNCS)* (Vol. 4874, pp. 99-111). Berlin: Springer-Verlag.

Pereira, L. M., & Saptawijaya, A. (2009). Modelling Morality with Prospective Logic. *International Journal of Reasoning-based Intelligent Systems*, *1*(3/4), 209–221. doi:10.1504/IJRIS.2009.028020

Pereira, L. M., & Saptawijaya, A. (2011). Modelling Morality with Prospective Logic. In M. Anderson & S. L. Anderson (Eds.), *Machine Ethics* (pp. 398–421). New York, NY: Cambridge University Press. doi:10.1017/CBO9780511978036.027

Pereira, L. M., & Saptawijaya, A. (2014). *Counterfactuals in Logic Programming with Applications to Agent Morality* (Submitted). Retrieved from http://centria.di.fct.unl.pt/~lmp/publications/online-papers/moral_counterfactuals.pdf

Phelps, S., McBurney, P., & Parsons, S. (2010). Evolutionary mechanism design: A review. *Autonomous Agents and Multi-Agent Systems*, *21*(2), 237–264. doi:10.1007/s10458-009-9108-7

Pinheiro, F. L., Pacheco, J. M., & Santos, F. C. (2012). From Local to Global Dilemmas in Social Networks. *PLoS ONE*, *7*(2), e32114. doi:10.1371/journal.pone.0032114 PMID:22363804

Powers, T. M. (2006). Prospects for a Kantian machine. *IEEE Intelligent Systems*, *21*(4), 46–51. doi:10.1109/MIS.2006.77

Rahwan, I., & Simari, G. (Eds.). (2009). *Argumentation in Artificial Intelligence*. Berlin: Springer-Verlag.

Rand, D. G., Fudenberg, D., & Dreber, A. (2013). It's the thought that counts: The role of intentions in noisy repeated games. *Social Science Research Network*. Retrieved from http://ssrn.com/abstract=2259407

Rawls, J. (1971). *A Theory of Justice*. Cambridge, MA: Belknap Press of Harvard University Press.

Ross, D. (2005). *Economic theory and cognitive science: Microexplanation*. Cambridge, MA: MIT press.

Ross, W. D. (1930). *The Right and the Good*. New York: Oxford University Press.

Roy, O. (2009). *Thinking before Acting: Intentions, Logic, Rational Choice* (Doctoral Dissertation). ILLC Dissertation Series DS-2008-03, Amsterdam.

Roy, P., Bouchard, B., Bouzouane, A., & Giroux, S. (2007). A hybrid plan recognition model for alzheimer's patients: interleaved-erroneous dilemma. In *Proceedings of IEEE/WIC/ACM International Conference on Intelligent Agent Technology* (pp. 131–137).

Sadri, F. (2011). Logic-based approaches to intention recognition. In N.-Y. Chong & F. Mastrogiovanni (Eds.), *Handbook of Research on Ambient Intelligence: Trends and Perspectives* (pp. 346–375). Hershey, PA: IGI Global.

Saptawijaya, A., & Pereira, L. M. (2013a). Tabled abduction in logic programs (Technical Communication of ICLP 2013). *Theory and Practice of Logic Programming, Online Supplement, 13(4-5)*. Retrieved from http://journals.cambridge.org/downloadsup.php?file=/tlp2013008.pdf

Saptawijaya, A., & Pereira, L. M. (2013b). Incremental tabling for query-driven propagation of logic program updates. In McMillanK.MiddeldorpA.VoronkovA. (Eds.), *Proceedings of the Nineteenth International Conference on Logic for Programming Artificial Intelligence and Reasoning (LNCS)* (Vol. 8312, pp. 694-709). Berlin:Springer-Verlag. doi:10.1007/978-3-642-45221-5_46

Saptawijaya, A., & Pereira, L. M. (2014). Joint tabling of logic program abductions and updates (Technical Communication of ICLP 2014). *Theory and Practice of Logic Programming, Online Supplement, 14(4-5)*. Retrieved from http://arxiv.org/abs/1405.2058

Saptawijaya, A., & Pereira, L. M. (in press). The Potential of Logic Programming as a Computational Tool to Model Morality. In R. Trappl (Ed.), *A Construction Manual for Robots' Ethical Systems: Requirements, Methods, Implementations (Cognitive Technologies)*. Berlin: Springer-Verlag.

Scanlon, T. M. (1982). Contractualism and utilitarianism. In A. Sen & B. Williams (Eds.), *Utilitarianism and Beyond*. New York, NY: Cambridge University Press. doi:10.1017/CBO9780511611964.007

Scanlon, T. M. (1998). *What We Owe to Each Other*. Cambridge, MA: Harvard University Press.

Scanlon, T. M. (2008). *Moral Dimensions: Permissibility, Meaning, Blame*. Cambridge, MA: Harvard University Press.

Searle, J. R. (1995). *The Construction of Social Reality*. New York: The Free Press.

Searle, J. R. (2010). *Making the Social World: The Structure of Human Civilization*. New York: Oxford University Press. doi:10.1093/acprof:osobl/9780195396171.001.0001

Segbroeck, S. V., Jong, S. D., Nowé, A., Santos, F. C., & Lenaerts, T. (2010). Learning to coordinate in complex networks. *Adaptive Behavior, 18*(5), 416–427. doi:10.1177/1059712310384282

Sigmund, K. (2010). *The Calculus of Selfishness*. Princeton, NJ: Princeton University Press. doi:10.1515/9781400832255

Sober, E., & Wilson, D. (1998). *Unto Others: The Evolution and Psychology of Unselfish Behavior*. Cambridge, MA: Harvard University Press.

Sperber, D. (1997). Individualisme méthodologique et cognitivisme. In R. Boudon, F. Chazel, & A. Bouvier (Eds.), *Cognition et sciences sociales* (pp. 123–136). Paris: Presses Universitaires de France.

Swift, T., & Warren, D. S. (2012). XSB: Extending Prolog with tabled logic programming. *Theory and Practice of Logic Programming, 12*(1-2), 157–187. doi:10.1017/S1471068411000500

Thomson, J. J. (1971). A defense of abortion. *Philosophy & Public Affairs, 1*(1), 47–66.

Thomson, J. J. (1985). The trolley problem. *The Yale Law Journal, 279*(6), 1395–1415. doi:10.2307/796133

Tomasello, M. (2008). *Origins of Human Communication*. Cambridge, MA: MIT Press.

Tomasello, M. (2014). *A Natural History of Human Thinking*. Cambridge, MA: Harvard University Press.

Tzeng, J.-Y. (2004). Toward a more civilized design: Studying the effects of computers that apologize. *International Journal of Human-Computer Studies, 61*(3), 319–345. doi:10.1016/j.ijhcs.2004.01.002

Utz, S., Matzat, U., & Snijders, C. (2009). On-line reputation systems: The effects of feedback comments and reactions on building and rebuilding trust in on-line auctions. *International Journal of Electronic Commerce, 13*(3), 95–118. doi:10.2753/JEC1086-4415130304 van den Hoven, J., & Lokhorst, G.-J. (2002). Deontic logic and computer-supported computer ethics. *Metaphilosophy, 33*(3), 376–386. doi:10.1111/1467-9973.00233

van Gelder, A., Ross, K. A., & Schlipf, J. S. (1991). The well-founded semantics for general logic programs. *Journal of the ACM, 38*(3), 620–650. doi:10.1145/116825.116838

Wiegel, V. (2007). *SophoLab; Experimental Computational Philosophy* (Doctoral dissertation). Delft University of Technology, The Netherlands.

Winikoff, M. (2007). Implementing commitment-based interactions. In *Proceedings of the Sixth International Joint Conference on Autonomous Agents and Multiagent Systems* (pp. 868–875).

Wooldridge, M., & Jennings, N. R. (1999). The cooperative problem-solving process. *Journal of Logic and Computation, 9*(4), 563–592. doi:10.1093/logcom/9.4.563

KEY TERMS AND DEFINITIONS

Abduction: A reasoning method whereby one chooses from available hypotheses those that best explained the observed evidence, in a preferred sense.

Computational Logic: An interdisciplinary field of enquiry that employs the techniques from symbolic logic to reason using practical computations, and typically achieved by means of computer supported automated tools.

Contractualism: A school of thought about morality, emphasizing explicit reasoning (rather than merely relying on subjective observation) for providing moral justifications to others, through looking for common ground that others could not reasonably reject to.

Counterfactual: A concept that captures the process of reasoning about a past event that did not occur, namely what would/could/might have happened, had this alternative event occurred; or, conversely, to reason about a past event that did occur, but what if it had not.

Doctrine of Double Effect: A moral principle that explains the permissibility of an action by distinguishing whether its harm consequence is merely a *side-effect*, rather than a *means* to bring about a good result.

Doctrine of Triple Effect: A moral principle that refines the Doctrine of Double Effect, particularly on the notion about harming someone as an intended means, by distinguishing further between doing an action *in order* that an effect occurs and doing it just *because* that effect will occur.

Dual-Process Model: A model that explains how a moral judgment is driven by an interaction of two different psychological processes, namely the controlled process (whereby explicit moral principles are consciously applied via deliberative reasoning), and the automatic process (whereby moral judgments are intuition-based and mostly low-level, not entirely accessible to conscious reflection).

Evolutionary Game Theory: An application of game theory to systematically study the evolution of populations, typically by resorting to simulation techniques under a variety of conditions, parameters, and strategies.

Logic Programming: A programming paradigm based on formal logic that permits a declarative representation of a problem and reasoning about this representation, that reasoning being is driven by a specific semantics.

Chapter 11
Robots in Warfare and the Occultation of the Existential Nature of Violence

Rick Searle
IEET, USA

ABSTRACT

We are at the cusp of a revolution in the development of autonomous weapons, yet current arguments both for and against such weapons are insufficient to the task at hand. In the context of Just war theory, arguments for and against the use of autonomous weapons focus on Jus in bello and in doing so miss addressing the implications of these weapons for the two other aspects of that theory- Jus ad bellum and Jus post bellum. This paper argues that fully autonomous weapons would likely undermine adherence to the Jus ad bellum and Jus post bellum prescriptions of Just war theory, but remote controlled weapons, if designed with ethical concerns in mind, might improve adherence to all of the theory's prescriptions compared to war as currently waged from a distance, as well as help to undo the occlusion of violence which has been a fundamental characteristic of all forms of modern war.

It is interesting… how weapons reflect the soul of their maker. – Don Delillo, The Underworld

INTRODUCTION

If current trends continue, sometime in the next few decades, or sooner, a machine will deliberately kill a human being. The idea that an autonomous weapon will be capable of making a decision to kill may seem like science-fiction, but it is a goal being pursued right now by the world's major militaries. The arrival of what the media has dubbed "killer robots" appears to be only a matter of time. (Markoff, 2014)

The following essay attempts to discern the possible implications of the rise of autonomous weapons for the waging of just wars. It is divided into four sections. The first section lays out the rise of remote controlled weapons over the past decade, and the evolutionary pressures pushing these weapons towards

DOI: 10.4018/978-1-4666-8592-5.ch011

greater levels of autonomy. The second section raises objections to the use of autonomous weapons on the basis of the *Jus ad bellum* and *Jus post bellum* prescriptions of Just war theory. The third section looks at two types of objections to both autonomous and remote controlled weapons (drones), and argues that both autonomous weapons and remote controlled weapons are merely a continuation of trends found in warfare in all advanced countries, which seeks to occlude the violent nature of war. The fourth and concluding section argues that remote controlled, though not autonomous weapons, may actually offer us a path away from this occlusion if they are designed and operated with this goal in mind.

THE RISE OF THE ROBOT WARRIORS: CRITICS AND DEFENDERS

The move towards autonomous weapons began with remotely operated armaments and in the US military. Since 2005 there has been a 1,200 percent increase of air combat patrols by drones. The US now has a fleet of 7,500 drones making up 31 percent of the Pentagon's air fleet. Its numbers are to be doubled by 2020. (Dowd, 2013) As of June 2012 the US had as many as 3,500 robots in landlocked Afghanistan doing everything from bomb removal to demolition (Hodge, 2012). Based on advanced robotics projects funded by the US military's advanced research arm, DARPA, the US is already experimenting with humanoid "infantrymen". Facing increasing budgetary constraints, the US army has plans under discussion to reduce the size of a brigade from 4,000 to 3,000 men with much of the difference to be made up by robots. (Ackerman, 2014)

The US may have begun the revolution in remote controlled and robotic warfare, but it is unlikely to end there. Innovation appears to be shifting to other countries that see in the new methods of war a way to overcome the asymmetric superiority of the American military in other forms of advanced weaponry. (Scharre, 2014) 75 countries now possess drone programs of their own with China to build 11 drone bases down its coast through 2015. Dowd (2013)

Given the superiority of US advanced weapons and its overwhelming military footprint, which comes at the cost of spending more on defense than the next ten countries combined, it is very likely that rival countries and groups will turn to much cheaper drones and eventually autonomous weapons to redress this asymmetry. (Fallows, 2014)

Drones and other remotely piloted vehicles may appear to be distinct from truly autonomous weapons, but the requirements of military competition are rapidly pushing the development of the former into the latter. Drones suffer vulnerabilities to jamming and problems with latency that truly autonomous weapons are seen to overcome. Piloting by individual human beings might be impossible should autonomous weapons in the form of "swarms" move from the drawing board to the battlefield. (Wong, 2013)

The specter of "killer robots" has led to international calls for a moratorium on the further development of such weapons, most notably in a 2012 paper issued by Human Rights Watch entitled "Losing Our Humanity". In that paper HRW drew a sharp line between remote controlled weapons, which believes are permissible, and autonomous weapons whose development it believes should be banned. (HRW, 2012)

HRW is not alone in its critique of autonomous weapons. The nascent rise of such systems has been met with a kind of widespread criticism that did not meet the growth of drone warfare. (Carpenter, 2014) These criticisms have in large part been based on the argument of the technology's prematurity.

The ethical superiority of remote controlled over autonomous weapons, it is argued, lies in the ability of human pilots and controllers to exercise discrimination on the battlefield aligned with the laws of war, and from the concern that autonomous weapons might prove especially dangerous in areas of combat with a large number of civilians. Self-directed armaments currently lack the capacity to properly attribute threat to human beings, and suffer AI's classic isotropy problem, where everything can be connected to everything else, so that a child's toy in a murky context might be confused with a weapon. (Guarini and Bello, 2012)

Noel Sharkey, perhaps the most prominent critic of autonomous weapons to date, has made a strong case that allowing weapons to act autonomously at this stage would be akin to the use of sub-munitions such as the BLU-108. The BLU-108 has no ability to distinguish between civilian and military targets merely unleashing its munitions on likely targets upon deployment. It has been this very inability to make targeting distinctions that has been the basis of the argument that autonomous war machines need to be banned, or at least a moratorium imposed on their use, similar to that of bans imposed on other indiscriminate weapons such as landmines. (Sharkey, 2012)

Autonomous weapons do, however, have their defenders. Ronald Arkin has been perhaps the most vocal and eloquent figure arguing that such systems might be a means of making warfare *more ethical*. In his view, properly programmed autonomous systems would not experience the kinds of negative emotions, such as fear, and the desire for revenge, that often lead human beings to violate the laws of war. (Arkin, 2009)

This idea that the application of robots to war could ultimately take some of the nastier parts of human nature out of the calculus of warfare is also touched upon by P.W. Singer in what was the first popular book on the new weapon systems, *Wired for War*. There, Singer brings up the case of Steven Green, a US soldier charged with the premeditated rape and murder of a 14 year old Iraqi girl. Singer contrast the young soldier "swirling with hormones" to the calm calculations of a robot lacking such sexual and murderous instincts. (Singer, 2009) Or as put by another defender of the idea of ethical robot warriors, Patrick Lin:

Robots wouldn't act with malice or hatred or other emotions that may lead to war crimes and other abuses, such as rape. They're unaffected by emotion and adrenaline and hunger. They're immune to sleep deprivation, low morale, fatigue, etc. that would cloud our judgment. They can see through the "fog of war", to reduce unlawful and accidental killings. And they can be objective, unblinking observers to ensure ethical conduct in wartime. So robots can do many of our jobs better than we can and maybe even act more ethically, at least in the high-stress environment of war. (Lin, 2011)

The problem with arguments of the type discussed above, both against and for autonomous weapons, is that they in a sense miss the essential ethical question by too strong a focus on technology. Arguments against the use of autonomous weapons would seem to collapse were it ever the case that such machines could make *better* discriminations on the battlefield than human beings. Whereas, arguments for the use of such machines would falter should battlefield discrimination at the level of human operators prove impossible for machines. The state of the technology decides the ethical questions.

Both sets of arguments focus on the *Jus in bello* aspect of Just war theory, rules which prescribe *how* warfare is to be conducted. Sharkey et al are basically arguing that autonomous weapons risk being unable to sustain *Jus in bello* prescriptions regarding *distinction* between military and civilian targets. The use of such weapons, as they currently exists, put civilians at risk due to the complexity of properly discriminating between combatants and noncombatants.

Arkins et al, on the other hand, argue that autonomous weapons (eventually) will prove *better* than human beings at discriminating between legitimate and illegitimate targets. The basis for this improved discrimination, in their view, will come through automated systems increased capacity over human beings to cut through the "fog of war". Such improved ability to adhere to the prescriptions of *Jus in bello* compared to human beings should also, as they see it, arise on account of such systems lacking the darker instincts of human beings such as revenge. Research should therefore continue to try to perfect such weapons.

If the position of those arguing against the use of autonomous weapons is based primarily on their violation of *Jus in bello* because these weapons are currently incapable of the kinds of distinctions required to wage war justly, then such an argument would collapse should technological projections such as Arkin's prove correct. Those who wish to develop a solid, non-technologically dependent, argument against the use of autonomous weapons will need to look elsewhere.

Perhaps they should look to Just war theory itself, for there is a case to be made that even if autonomous weapons can eventually be created that adhere to the prescriptions of *Jus in bellum,* they may fail to adhere to either or both of the theory's other two legs- *Jus ad bellum* and *Jus post bellum.*

AUTONOMOUS WEAPONS: *JUS AD BELLUM AND JUS POST BELLUM*

Let us imagine that Arkin's hopes for autonomous weapons are eventually proven correct, and that not only do such weapons adhere to *Jus in bello* they do so in a way that is ethically superior to the average human soldier. Are there any grounds, then, for still rejecting their use?

If one takes adherence to the prescriptions of Just war theory to be the primary way for us to establish whether the use of a weapon is ethical, then we need to explore how the use of autonomous weapons would affect the likelihood of wars being started that would be deemed just (*Jus ad bellum*) and how the use of such weapons might influence war's ending justly (*Jus post bellum*).

The argument that the use of autonomous weapons might somehow affect the decision of whether a war is just to wage in the first place, the prescriptions of *Jus ad bellum* might at first seem nonsensical. After all, no one is arguing whether we should use intelligent machines to *decide* whether or not we should wage war.

Tracing back to Augustine, the prescriptions of *Jus ad bellum* have been developed largely to morally inform political leadership in their decisions regarding whether to wage war. (Augustine, 1958) There is an argument, however, particularly well developed by the political philosopher Jeff McMahan, that the prescriptions of *Jus ad bellum* should also serve as the basis of the *individual's* willingness to fight. "Unjust wars can occur only if there are enough people willing to fight in them", he writes. (McMahan, 2009)

McMahan rejects the common view in Just war theory that the responsibility for ensuring a war follows the prescriptions of *Jus ad bellum* lies with political leaders alone, and that soldiers asked to engage in war need pay attention to the *Jus in bello* aspects of Just war theory only. For McMahan, any killing by the side waging an unjust war is on that account *already violating Jus in bello*. They are killing what are in effect innocent combatants who are engaged in a just war against them.

In McMahan's view, citizens in a democracy have a unique responsibility not to engage in unjust wars even when the decision to fight has been arrived at by legitimate democratic means. Soldiers should refuse to fight in, and civilians refuse to support, wars that do not meet the criteria of *Jus ad bellum*. McMahan's re-conceptualization of Just war theory would redefine the individual's relationship to war, and doubtless put pressure on statesmen to adhere to the prescriptions of *Jus ad bellum*. It is also a moral project the widespread adoption of autonomous weapons would likely make impossible.

One can be highly speculative and imagine a world in which autonomous systems are universally mandated to be given an activation or deactivation encryption code and could be turned on or off on the basis of an independent body's declaration of a war to be just or unjust, but it is almost inconceivable that states would agree to this.

The fact that wars could be waged largely using autonomous weapons might make political leaders more willing to engage in them no longer facing the risk of public opprobrium or the resistance of militaries reticent to engage in the risks of combat without strong cause.

The group in charge of running these weapons would very likely be far removed from the reality of war. They would be programmers, engineers, and defense contactors, rather than soldiers either at the front or even removed but still aware of the brutalities of the actual conduct of a war. Wholly different incentives between a military made up of human soldiers where the goal is to finish a conflict as quickly and with the least human damage (at least to one's own side) and the manufactures of military robots whose incentive would be to generate as much revenue as possible during a conflict and would even have a perverse incentive to encourage conflict.

There is thus a good argument that autonomous weapons might negatively impact our ability to follow the *Jus ad bellum* aspects of Just war theory constricting the range of actors who could effectively resist the onset or continuation of unjust conflicts, and perhaps even incentivize conflict for those groups who would be most responsible for how they were waged: no longer soldiers and their commanders, but programmers, engineers, and technology companies. Autonomous weapons might also negatively impact the adherence to the third leg of the Just war theory; namely, *Jus post bellum* or the justice that is to follow conflict.

As Andrew Rigby has pointed out, one of the primary components of a just peace (*Jus post bellum*) following war is *reconciliation* between the formerly warring parties. Of necessity this entails confronting past moral wrongs, and in the process generating *forgiveness* for those wrong doers whose actions were not in such violation of norms that they require punishment. Rigby sees three conditions that facilitate reconciliation and forgiveness:

1. Acknowledgement and apology by the wrongdoer
2. The promise not to repeat the wrong
3. Offer to make amends- reparations (Rigby, 2005).

In the case of autonomous weapons it is extremely unclear *who* would play any of these roles, though it could be the programmers and engineers of such machines, but it would certainly not be the machine that caused the unjustified killing or injury. Not being human an autonomous war machine cannot "apologize" for following its program, has no say in whether it will repeat a wrong, and has no capacity to make reparations, and though all of these things might be socialized, it is difficult to see how the world of common experience which those on opposite sides of a conflict share can be tapped as a bridge to reconciliation in cases where one side has waged war using robots instead of humans.

Autonomous weapons could make post war reconciliation increasingly difficult- a reconciliation that is essential in the most commonly wars fought today- civil wars, rather than those between states. It seems reasonable to assume that the population of the side in a war that utilized mainly autonomous weapons would find it difficult to take collective responsibilities for atrocities committed by machines they had little direct control over.

Wars waged by machines against humans will have little opportunity for the acts of conscious mercy such as that recorded by Ernst Jünger in his World War I memoir *Storm of Steel,* and would likely prevent the humanization of the enemy necessary for reconciliation and forgiveness. In his memoir Jünger records coming upon a lone enemy officer while alone on patrol.

I saw him jump as I approached, and stare at me with gaping eyes, while I, with my face behind my pistol, stalked up to him slowly and coldly. A bloody scene with no witnesses was about to happen. It was a relief to me, finally, to have the foe in front of me and within reach. I set the mouth of my pistol at the man's temple- he was too frightened to move- while my other fist grabbed hold of his tunic...

With a plaintive sound, he reached into his pocket, not to pull out a weapon, but a photograph which he held up to me. I saw him on it, surrounded by numerous family all standing on a terrace.

It was a plea from another world. Later, I thought it was blind chance that I had let him go and plunged onward. That one man of all often appeared in my dreams. I hope that meant he got to see his homeland again. (Jünger, 2004)

Heavy use of autonomous weapons in lieu of human soldiers would also likely lessen the extent to which societies grapple with the moral horrors of war. Human beings have struggled to understand war's terrible impact on individuals and societies since at least the Greek tragedians- a source soldiers continue to turn to in order to grapple with war's huge moral costs. (Healy, 2014) And in a society such as the United States where so small a percentage of citizens does the actual fighting, and war takes place at great distance from the country itself, the stories brought home by soldiers have become one of the few ways society can confront the ugly truth of "organized killing." (Grossman, 1995) Robots will not write such memoirs.

WAR "THAT HUMAN THING" AND REMOTE CONTROLLED WEAPONS

There are thus good arguments against the use of autonomous weapons in light of the J*us ad bellum* and *Jus post bellum* criteria of Just war theory supporting a moratorium on these weapons even should technological innovations that make them better at discrimination during conflict occur. Yet is it the case that such a moratorium should apply to remote controlled weapons as well?

There are reasons to think that it should not. It was said that autonomous weapons might undermine new interpretations of *Jus ad bellum* because the moral consent of soldiers would no longer be required to engage in war. Drones and other remote controlled weapons that have a human pilot do not face these same risks. Pilots who find a war unjust are free to refrain/strike against using their skills to engage in combat. The fact that drone piloting facilities are often located in civilian areas might actually make them more susceptible to public protest and opposition to war.

Soldiers operating drones and remote controlled vehicles as opposed to the widespread use of autonomous weapons are likely to remain highly conscious of what combat looks like, that is, control and supervision as in the case of J*us ad bellum* is, both better distributed and possess clearer chains of moral accountability in the case of remote controlled as it is with autonomous weapons.

Whether or not drones are also superior to autonomous weapons when it comes to *Jus post bellum* is somewhat more complicated and might best be illuminated by taking a look at arguments against the use of drones on grounds other than Just war theory. For the argument that these new forms of weapons make the adherence to the prescriptions of *Jus post bellum* more difficult can be reduced to the grounds that they make human recognition of the suffering caused by war and its risks less likely. And a good case has been made that both autonomous and remote controlled weapons share these flaws.

Perhaps the best arguments made against remote controlled weapons *and* autonomous weapons have to do with their effect on the human experience of war. Christopher Coker, for example, argues that technological innovation is resulting in a diminishment of our humanity, a humanity that ironically and tragically is often brought out by conditions of war. For Coker, combat seems to bring out the best and worst in human beings, the best being our bravery and willingness to sacrifice our lives for others and the worst our savagery. This strange amplification of our humanity is what led Thucydides to characterize war as "the human thing". (Coker, 2013)

Coker makes little distinction between the dehumanizing aspects of war by remote control and truly autonomous weapons. Persons fighting in wars from cubicles on the other side of the globe are barred from experiencing what Coker understands as the human characteristics of war no matter how good the simulation or resolution of battlefield conditions. Their lives are not at stake. This absence of the human reality of war, which has largely become limited to those who engage in close combat on land, would be doubly the case for any truly robotic warriors, which would have no sense of courage or fear or anger.

On at least some level, arguments against the use of technologies that remove soldiers from the battlefield are built on the idealization of human bravery in face of the mortal dangers of war. One of the defining features of Western civilization has been the honor it holds for those tasked with fighting its wars. (Hanson, 2001) This makes some sense given that the soldier since ancient Greece has been held in esteem for their willingness to sacrifice their life for the good of their political community. Yet such public perceptions of soldiers' innate heroism often leave veterans trapped between public mythology and the brutal reality of war itself. (Boudreau, 2008) War certainly offers opportunities for individual courage and heroism, but one should ask if such opportunities are worth their psychological and physical costs, not merely to enemies, but to one's own countrymen or oneself who has been asked to fight?

With this in mind the weaknesses of bio-conservative arguments against the use of not just autonomous, but also remotely operated weapons becomes clear. Unless motivated by some mythology of martyrdom, no one would argue that soldiers should be deliberately placed at risk of being maimed or killed in order to increase wars opportunity for heroic action. Following Coker's prescriptions would result in technologically fossilizing warfare to retain features that are more a matter of civilian myth than veterans' reality.

The weakness of the bio-conservative critique are further revealed the moment one starts to think about what war would look like if the rationale behind such an argument was applied to those areas where military exchange has long been instrumentalized. Should we return to the era when naval battles were fought through forced boarding followed by brutal hand to hand combat? (Paine, 2011) Air warfare, especially in the form of strategic bombings, has since its beginnings been waged at such distances that the humanity of a target was almost impossible to grasp. (Creveld, 2011) Coker's argument therefore, further boils down to petrifying only one form of warfare- land warfare- to retain the aspects of war he thinks make us more "human".

Another argument against remote weapons, regardless of their level of autonomy, is based on their effect on risk. In this view, efforts to avoid the risks of combat on the battlefield do not so much remove risk as relocate it. Risk is transferred to the other side, but doing so actually relocates risk onto *civilians,* whether because military targets now hide themselves among civilian population to make assaults more difficult, or because of the fact that the side attacked using remote controlled weapons needs to make the mortal risks of war apparent to the attacker and can only do so by attacking soft targets- namely civilians. Such is the argument made by counterinsurgency expert David Kilcullen:

If we consider it a legitimate act of war for a Predator to strike a target in, say, a city in Pakistan, killing militants in the houses where they live, but also potentially injuring or killing noncombatant civilians, is it legitimate for those same Pakistani militants to strike the city where that Predator's pilot lives? If it is legitimate to kill a militant attending a wedding in tribal areas, is it also legitimate to kill a Predator pilot at his kid's soccer game in Indiana Springs. (Kilcullen, 2013)

Yet like Coker's argument against both autonomous and remote controlled weapons on bio-conservative grounds, Kilcullen's position ignores the reality of advanced war as it is currently fought even when no such remote controlled or autonomous weapons are used. What difference is there for the attacked if the attacker is located in an unreachable location at the other side of the globe or flying 10,000 unreachable feet above them in a supersonic fighter they are powerless against? The technological superiority of advanced countries, where there airmen and seamen are largely safe from reprisal, has already shifted risk to soldiers on land and civilian populations completely independent of either drones or autonomous weapons.

In a very real sense Kilculen's scenario is merely another example of the situation we have had for quite some time absent drones. The same question of whether or not it is justifiable to attack, even at risk of injuring civilians, the area where a military assault on oneself originates would hold for the pilot of the long range bomber pilot based in Nevada flying sorties to and from a war on the other side of the world as it would for a drone pilot far away from the theater in which the effects of his actions occur.

Given that the piloted plane is impossible for the attacked to shoot down, the equation does not really change for the bombed if the pilot is actually in the plane or if he has never left the base.

It is true that drone- warfare has been experienced to be particularly terrifying to civilians who suffer under it. Yet this seems to be as much a matter of the way in which such warfare has been wagged rather than the fact that such weapons are operated remotely. The fact that in the quest to eliminate "targets" the US has used drones to attack civilian gatherings has led to a sense among the populations suffering such attacks that bombing can occur anywhere and at any moment for seemingly no reason with the effect of potentially killing them or their loved ones. The effect being something similar to that of the terrorism the drone strikes are supposedly being used to stop. (Ahmed, 2013)

What this response to criticisms of drones and autonomous weapons suggest is that these weapons are merely symptomatic of a problem with advanced warfare itself. Identifying that problem should place us more firmly on the path of deciding the ethical question of how these types of weapons should be developed and used or if they should be developed and used at all.

MODERN WARFARE AND THE OCCLUSION OF VIOLENCE

Most human beings seem to have an instinctive inhibition against the use of force directly against an individual that stems from our ability to exercise empathy. The army which has long recognized the dilemma confronted by the human aversion to kill in circumstances where the humanity of an opponent can be recognized has responded by trying to instrumentalize and automate the reactions of soldiers themselves so that empathy can, in a sense, be turned off. (Grossman, 1995) Automated weapons would remove this empathy entirely, and, contrary to Singer, such weapons would in fact perform with the cold detachment of psycho-paths, though without the risk they would use this coldness to pursue their own rather than group ends.

An important question to ask is why is it the army in which soldiers might be confronted with the command to kill one or perhaps a handful of enemy combatants that individuals have to be especially trained to overcome their aversion to kill rather than air forces or navies where a small number of air-men might be responsible for killing hundreds or even thousands of human beings that such aversion is so clearly an issue?

The answer might lie in the fact that the technologies of air and sea warfare foster the occlusion of violence given the greater distance from the granular human level against which their weapons are wielded. In a sense, warfare from a distance takes advantage of underlying features of human moral rea-soning identified in the oft cited "Trolley Problem". In one of the most common versions of the Trolley Problem a person is faced with a stark moral choice in which a train is careening towards five people who will die: people who can only be saved by pushing an innocent fat man from a ledge unto the tracks.

Joshua Greene, most famously, has argued that those who choose to sacrifice one person to save five when presented in the Trolley Problem are exercising a higher "manual" mode of moral reasoning than those who refuse to push the hypothetically innocent man to his death who are guided by their instinc-tive "automatic" morality which is repulsed by the thought of the use of physical force against another. (Greene, 2013)

Yet Greene's privileging of "manual" over "automatic" means of moral reasoning is dependent upon how one defines the "greater good". In the Trolley problem that means sacrificing five people to save one, but for airmen and seamen who make a decision to kill by pulling a "switch" in the service of what they believe is the "greater good" seem to face much less of an instinctive human moral break on the use of force than soldier on land who can often see whom they intend to kill. Accessing their manual mode of morality through violence having been instrumentalized seems to result in an increased capacity to kill with impunity in the supposed name of some "greater good".

Indeed, individuals with diminished capacity for empathy, notably psychopaths, have been shown to score "better" i.e. more regularly chose to sacrifice one person to save five than their neuro-typical counterparts (Dutton, 2012), and the number of people who chose to sacrifice the fat man increases when subjects are given a version of the Trolley Problem where instead of having to push the fat man can merely let him fall by pulling a lever. (Greene, 2013)

Our occlusion of violence prevents us from seeing the reality of what we are doing, the brutality of the violence that it war. In that sense the horrific cruelty of a group like the Islamic State is like our mirror image glorifying in the unveiling of this occlusion as if accepting the inhumane barbarity of war were a form of strength. (Cottee, 2014)

The real reason for seeking to overcome our occlusion of violence is so that we can morally grapple with the reality of war. As Lawrence Keeley has noted, even in primitive societies where warfare was often endemic:

... warfare whether primitive or civilized involves losses, suffering, and terror even for the victors. Con-sequently, it was nowhere viewed as an unalloyed good, and the respect accorded to an accomplished warrior was often tinged with aversion.

For example, it was common the world over for the warrior who had just killed an enemy to be regarded by his own people as spiritually polluted or contaminated. He therefore had to undergo a magical cleansing to remove this pollution. Often he had to live for a time in seclusion, eat special food or fast, be excluded from participation in rituals and abstain from sexual intercourse.

It is really this occluding aspect of modern warfare that we need to escape, for remaining blind within it means that we will be unlikely to judge the true meaning of the human cost of war, and thus will be much less capable of following the prescriptions of *Jus ad bellum* to go to war only in the face of extreme circumstances. The occlusion of violence also makes the reconciliation between peoples required by *Jus post bellum* difficult if not impossible. How could we be prompted to make amends for deaths of innocents not even our soldiers would have witnessed which were ostensibly committed in our name?

The question we might ask is if there is any way technology might be designed to diminish this occlusion of the nature of violence rather than feed it? A distinctive feature of remote controlled warfare as it is currently fought is its use of cameras that not only allow the pilot or driver to see their interactions in intimate detail, but allow their engagements to be recorded for later viewing. As discussed by Coker, some pilots appear to view their actions as a sort of "video game" whereas others having watched their targets over long periods of time come to know them and have great difficulty with killing when the order to do so comes. What makes the latter remarkable is that for the first time in the history of warfare we have put eyes on the arrow, so to speak. Fighting from a distance no longer means that the enemy has been abstracted into a faceless target. Coker writes:

According to one drone pilot interviewed by a British newspaper, the modern warrior shares an intimacy with his targets that is unique in human history: the Reaper's sensors allow a pilot to 'an individual to a fidelity where you can perceive limb and arms, stuff that you are carrying'. (Coker, 2013 p. 122)

Weapons designed in order to minimize occlusion created by distance from the battlefield would aim at doing what even soldiers fighting on land, whose combat is the most intimate of all forms of war, are often unable to do; namely, to get close enough to their potential targets to actually be able to discriminate between combatant and non-combatant and to where possible injure, rather than kill, enemy soldiers.

Remote controlled weapons could turn the enemy into nothing more than simulacra to be killed with the same moral ease one has when dispatching with virtual enemies in a video game, or they could be used to reverse such occlusion and make the brutal reality of war more knowable both to civilians and to soldiers.

Imagine if we were to make footage from not just drones and remote controlled vehicles, but also soldiers themselves, open and available to the public for review, debate, or to enable humanitarian efforts at reconciliation for wrongdoing in the way the Wiki leaks tapes supplied by Chelsea Manning defied the government by giving us a searing glimpse of what it looks like when the laws of war are violated. (Jónsdóttir, 2014)

If we take democracy seriously then the ultimate responsibility for killing on the battlefield lies with the public that through their action or inaction have enabled such conflicts. Remote controlled weapons, if used properly, might allow us to see what exactly it is we have sanctioned. Were such records common and open we would be better able to hold to account those who had violated the laws of war in our name, and, it is hoped, be less willing to permit such violence in the first place.

Such might come to be the case in the US other Western countries, but developments elsewhere are likely to be different. It is very likely that much of the rest of the world will continue to pursue both remote controlled and autonomous weapons in order to redress the military superiority and spending prowess of the US. We might be able to craft regulation to limit the spread and use of such weapons, but that seems unlikely as long as this asymmetry is in place. In a way the specter of "killer robots" distracts us from addressing this unstable situation including what are likely the much more dangerous existential risk, and nuclear weapons, whose immorality is far more pronounced than even machines that can make their own decisions to kill.

Nevertheless, autonomous weapons do represent a real moral danger and technological pressures pushing in the direction of such weapons, the dangers from latency, jamming and especially the demand for *speed* will continue to exist. In a sense the weakness of both the supporters and opponents of autonomous weapons discussed initially, where ethics becomes dependent upon technological development might be inescapable.

As machines become more capable of autonomy, and especially if they improve in their capacity for discrimination between legitimate and illegitimate targets to the point of being better than human beings at such discrimination, then a hybrid solution combining some levels of machine autonomy and human oversight may prove the best way forward.

The question of ethical design lies in discriminating between military and non-military targets. This entails getting as close as possible to a target and may require something like "suicide" probes can get near enough to a potential target to establish with certainty whether it is, say, a fishing boat or a warship, a gathering of militants or a wedding party.

Even in such a scenario human beings should retain ultimate veto power over decisions to use lethal fire even if they do little else in terms of operating such weapons. Exercising such veto power would allow us to preserve the *Just ad bellum* and *Jus post bellum* prescriptions of Just war theory by both allowing such "vetoers" to prevent unjust wars in the first place, through refusal to pilot such weapons for a war that violates *Just ad bellum,* and in providing a human partner for reconciliation and responsibility after the conclusion of a war in adherence to *Jus post bellum.*

Humans having ultimate control over whether a machine kills would also prevent us from reaching a state of ultimate occlusion to which we have been heading that would leave us blind to the brutal reality of "organized killing" found in war. Only we are capable, and will likely remain the only ones capable of knowing, or cable of even caring about, what it means to kill another human being, to take from the world an absolutely unique manifestation of intelligence that will occur only once in the history of the universe. (Nicolelis, 2011) An intelligence that is part of the types of web of human relationships- a father, a husband, a son- such as those that convinced Jünger refrain from killing the enemy solider he stumbled across in the dead of night. In a more than metaphorical sense we are now tasked with being the "souls" of our machines, and should we fail in that task we will have created a world where intelligence has been rendered in a form that is largely soulless.

REFERENCES

Ackerman, E. (2014, January 22) U.S. Army Considers Replacing Thousands of Soldiers With Robots. *IEEE Spectrum.*

Ahmed, A. S. (2013) *The Thistle and the Drone: How America's War on Terror Became a Global War on Tribal Islam*. Harrisonburg: R.R. Donnelley.

Arkin, R. C. (2009). *Governing Lethal Behavior in Autonomous Robots*. Boca Raton: CRC Press. doi:10.1201/9781420085952

Augustine of Hippo. (426). De Civitate Dei Contra Paganos [The City of God Against the Pagans]. In G.C. Walsh, S.J. Demetrius, B. Zema, S.J. Grace, O.S.U. Monahan, & D.J. Hogan (Eds.), The City of God. Image Books/Doubleday.

Boudreau, T. E. (2008). *Packing Inferno: The Unmaking of a Marine*. Port Townsend, WA: Feral House.

Carpenter, C. (2014). *Lost Causes: Agenda Vetting in Global Issue Networks and the Shaping of Human Security*. Ithaca: Cornell University Press.

Coker, C. (2013). *Warrior Geeks: How 21st-century Technology Is Changing the Way We Fight and Think about War*. New York: Columbia University Press. doi:10.1093/acprof:oso/9780199327898.001.0001

Cottee, S. (2014, November 17). ISIS and the Intimate Kill. *Atlantic (Boston, Mass.)*, *Retrieved from* http://www.theatlantic.com/international/archive/2014/11/isis-and-the-intimate-kill-peter-kassig/382861/

Creveld, M. (2011). *The Age of Airpower*. New York: Public Affairs.

DeLillo, D. (1997) Underworld. New York, NY: Scribner, 1997. (pp. 790).

Dowd, A. W. (2013). Drone Wars: Risks and Warnings. *Parameters*, *43*, 7–16. Retrieved from http://www.strategicstudiesinstitute.army.mil/pubs/Parameters/

Dutton, K. (2012). *The Wisdom of Psychopaths: What Saints, Spies, and Serial Killers Can Teach Us about Success*. New York: Scientific American/Farrar, Straus and Giroux.

Fallows, J. (2014, December 28). The Tragedy of the American Military. *Atlantic (Boston, Mass.)*, *Retrieved from* http://www.theatlantic.com/features/archive/2014/12/the-tragedy-of-the-american-military/383516/

Greene, J. D. (2013). *Moral Tribes: Emotion, Reason, and the Gap between Us and Them*. New York: Penguin Press.

Grossman, D. (1995). *On Killing: The Psychological Cost of Learning to Kill in War and Society*. Boston: Little, Brown.

Guarini, M., & Bello, P. (2012). Robotic Warfare: Some Challenges in Moving from Non-civilian to Civilian Theaters. In P. Lin, K. Abney, & G. Bekey (Eds.), *Robot Ethics: The Ethical and Social Implications of Robotics* (pp. 129–145). Cambridge, MA: MIT Press.

Hanson, V. D. (2001). *Carnage and Culture: Landmark Battles in the Rise of Western Power*. New York: Doubleday.

Healy, P. (2009, November 11) The Anguish of War for Today's Soldiers, Explored by Sophocles. *The New York Times*. Retrieved from http://www.nytimes.com

Hodge, N. (2012) In the Afghan War, a Little Robot Can Be a Soldier's Best Friend. *The Wall Street Journal*. Retrieved from http://www.wsj.com

Jónsdóttir, B. (2013, August 21). Bradley Manning's Sentence: 35 Years for Exposing Us to the Truth. The Guardian. Retrieved from http://www.theguardian.com

Jünger, E., & Hofmann, M. (2004) Storms of Steel. (pp. 234).New York: Penguin Books.

Keeley, L. H. (1996). *War before Civilization* (p. 144). New York: Oxford University Press.

Kilcullen, D. (2013). *Out of the Mountains: The Coming Age of the Urban Guerrilla* (p. 174). New York: Oxford University Press.

Lin, P. (2011, December 15). Drone-Ethics Briefing: What a Leading Robot Expert Told the CIA. Atlantic (Boston, Mass.). Retrieved from http://www.theatlantic.com

Losing Humanity. (2012, November 19). *Human Rights Watch*. Retrieved from http://www.hrw.org/reports/2012/11/19/losing-humanity

Markoff, J. (2014, November 11) Fearing Bombs That Can Pick Whom to Kill. *The New York Times*. Retrieved from http://www.nytimes.com/2014/11/12/science/weapons-directed-by-robots-not-humans-raise-ethical-questions

McMahan, J. (2009). *Killing in War*. (pp. 6). Oxford: Clarendon Press. doi:10.1093/acprof:oso/9780199548668.001.0001

Nicolelis, M. (2011). *Beyond Boundaries: The New Neuroscience of Connecting Brains with Machines--and How It Will Change Our Lives*. New York: Times Books/Henry Holt and Co.

Paine, L. P. (2013). *The Sea and Civilization: A Maritime History of the World*. Alfred A. Knopf.

Rigby, A. (2005). Forgiveness and Reconciliation in Just Post Bellum. In M. Evans (Ed.), *Just War Theory A Reappraisal* (pp. 177–200). New York: Palgrave Macmillan. doi:10.3366/edinburgh/9780748620746.003.0009

Scharre, P. (2014, July 29) How to Lose the Robotics Revolution. *War on the Rocks*. Retrieved from http://warontherocks.com/2014/07/how-to-lose-the-robotics-revolution/#_

Sharkey, N. (2012) Killing Made Easy In P. Lin, K. Abney & G.A. Bekey (Eds.). Robot Ethics: The Ethical and Social Implications of Robotics. (pp. 111-128). Cambridge, MA: MIT Press.

Singer, P. W. (2009). *Wired for War: The Robotics Revolution and Conflict in the 21st Century* (pp. 391–392). New York: Penguin Press.

Wong, W. W. S. (2013). *Emerging Military Technologies: A Guide to the Issues Praeger Security International*. Santa Barbara: Praeger.

KEY TERMS AND DEFINITIONS

Autonomous Weapon: A weapon capable of making the decision of whether or not to engage in potentially lethal action.

Drone: A remotely piloted air weapon or observation platform.

Jus ad Bellum: Criteria emerging from Just War theory that help actors determine whether or not a war is just.

Jus in Bello: Criteria emerging from Just War theory that help actors determine whether or not a particular action preformed during war is just.

Jus post Bellum: Criteria emerging from Just War theory that help actors determine whether conditions following war are just.

Occlusion: The act of an object or phenomenon being hidden by something blocking its view.

Trolley Problem: A set of hypothetical scenarios used in moral philosophy and psychology in which participants are asked under what conditions they would sacrifice the life of an innocent person to save a greater number of innocent lives.

Chapter 12
Self–Referential Complex Systems and Aristotle's Four Causes

Aleksandar Malecic
University of Nis, Serbia

ABSTRACT

In this chapter the author addresses a need for inclusion of all four Aristotle's causes (material, efficient, formal, and final) in modern science. Reality of modern physics (beyond Newtonian physics) and science of consciousness (and life and society) should include all four causes and tangled hierarchies (no scientific discipline is the most fundamental – the starting point for the author was Jung, then Rosen, and Aristotle was included much later). The four causes resemble rules for a machine or software (computation that "glues" everything together (Dodig-Crnkovic, 2012)), but a non-deterministic "machine" not replicable in a different medium. "Self-reference" from the title includes self-awareness, something seemingly not possible without final cause. On the other hand, this recognition of our (presumed) non-determinism and freedom might remind us to be even more self-aware and anticipatory. Computation, communication, networking, and memory as something technology is good at could contribute to that goal.

INTRODUCTION

This chapter deals with systems and complexity without prejudices. It is (as far as the author is informed) a unique attempt to demonstrate how Aristotle's four causes appear over and over again in different aspects of reality, including physical interactions and psychological functions – even space-time and conservation of energy (as an outcome of tangled hierarchies) are included in the scheme. This uniqueness doesn't mean that no one has ever written anything like that, but rather that the central idea (the four causes referring to themselves – a description of reality and consciousness with tangled hierarchies explainable to a human being, but not replicable on a machine, i.e. How to program variables such as "space-time" and "causality"?) combines other people's work in a new schema. It combines the works of many authors who have come in their respective disciplines just a step from it – for instance, Robert

DOI: 10.4018/978-1-4666-8592-5.ch012

Rosen, Carl Jung (and Wolfgang Pauli (Miller, 2010) – genuine results of a borderline pseudoscientific (including imagination and dreams) methodology, without ever mentioning Aristotle's four causes.

After Background and the section about people and machines we are dealing with different scientific disciplines and their pretences to be the most fundamental science (axioms, an unsuccessful attempt to avoid tangled hierarchies) that provides the most basic answers to everything that exists no matter how big, small, or complex. The overview of old scientific disciplines ends with philosophy and ideas not so new (such as Aristotle's), but nowadays mostly rejected or ignored as irrelevant or pseudoscientific. After that we acknowledge modern revisions of science including some (such as synchronicity, retrocausality, and anticipation) still not widely accepted or even known. The next section represents the author's unique approach to Aristotle's four causes and the way they (according to him) appear at different layers and in different modes of existence. The section after that one goes even further into speculation about what it means for reality (including physics, consciousness, and interactions between humans and machines) and our perception and behaviour within it.

BACKGROUND

There is vast literature on philosophy, theory of everything, and system theory. While these attempts are worthy in their respective domains, it is interesting that for instance Troncale's (2013) ambition is to search for the theory of everything in system theory rather than physics. The approach in this text is similar to Troncale's (see also McNamara and Troncale (2012)), but different in realization. Instead of looking for common denominators and axioms of reality, the idea is to look for anomalies. Since graphs, tables, and explications are used instead of theorems and equations, this is more an attempt to tell the story of everything than define the theory of everything. The reader's self-awareness will be invited to see itself as a part of the description and a methodology akin to story-telling (see Juarrero (1999) on hermeneutics and consciousness) seems to be the only way to really include consciousness in the explication as it goes. Is this approach less scientific than those aforementioned? Let's take for example strange loops. No axioms and smallest components (or, in the spirit of this book, parts of a machine) will bring you closer to a strange loop through the concept of four causes or elements. In order to identify a strange loop, you just happen to be in the middle of it. Consider Heidegger on the four causes, as "fallen from heaven" (Heidegger, 1977). (Ed.: as indicative of the fact that this is our cosmology, because this is our place in the cosmos, the frame of our situation.) There is no beginning and end, everything is overlapping and "in the middle" from within a strange loop. It has been a challenge to write about strange loops, and hopefully we can avoid getting stuck in a noose.

PEOPLE AND MACHINES, COMPUTATION, AND COMPUTABILITY

The central idea in this chapter about four causes is a critique of ideas that life, consciousness, and everything around us are reducible to causal sequences, where logical and temporal causation go in one direction. On the other hand, the author (an engineer) was inspired by machines (specifically computation, see also Dodig-Crnkovic (2012)) as he was wondering what is inside the "black box" of existence. In a way strangely, if we define computability as something reproducible on a computer or another device (for instance, an artificial neural network), it seems that reality is a computation in the sense described by Dodig-Crnkovic (2012). But, it isn't computable. It doesn't exhibit the property of computability from the definition. For an illustration of what we are dealing with here, let's quote Soto-Andrade, Jaramillo, and Gutiérrez (2011) from their conclusion. Having "…interpreted Metabolism as a network of reactions and catalysis, leaving for later other dimensions of Metabolism, such as time", they "wonder whether there may be avatars of Ouroboros lurking in the concurrent world, an interesting question to explore in future work."

IN SEARCH OF THE MOST FUNDAMENTAL SCIENTIFIC DISCIPLINE

Aristotle's metaphysics, more precisely its suggestion that existence requires four causes (material, efficient, formal, and final), is nowadays widely rejected or ignored as irrelevant and even wrong. Breakthroughs in natural sciences and engineering have spread their notion that the world is nothing but a big soulless and purposeless machine in which three causes (without final cause), two (without final and formal cause), or even one (Wolfram, 2002) should (even must if we want to get rid of any hidden purpose and deity) be enough. As scientists were persistently pushing only two causes in their improvement of understanding of the very big, very small, nonliving, and living, they encountered some seemingly unexpected paradoxes. Perhaps recognition of the four causes isn't a "silver bullet" that easily solves all of them, but, as Zeilinger (on Pauli – "taking the leap") and Penrose (on Gödel and Turing – "a non-computational theory") will be quoted later, maybe it isn't so far from it.

Reality perceived by the mainstream science and sufficient experimental proofs is full of "spooky actions at a distance" - consider in this light "entanglement" (Rickles, 2008)). In order to identify some "spookiness" in reality, we need to identify those aspects of reality that are most fundamental. In what follows, we will identify some common fundamental patterns shaping each of the disparate sciences, separately.

Modern Revisions in Science

Physics Revised

Non-Newtonian physics challenges Newton's (Newton, 1846). It consists of relativity and quantum mechanics. Both of them challenge our everyday notions of reality: relativity with time and space (and even mass; see Deacon's (2012) discussion about formal cause and space-time) changing with relative velocity of objects, and quantum mechanics with its non-deterministic and probabilistic background. Scientific and technological breakthroughs have caused people to start believing that everything that exists is just one big mechanism (machine). This point of view is in opposition with Buber's notion that reality can only be described in incomplete fragments, as well as with Aristotle's that there are four fundamental causes. Physics usually recognizes just two causes: material and efficient. Material and efficient causes are supposed to be sufficient. If they persistently aren't enough (for instance in the double-slit experiment and its variations as discussed in Walborn, Terra Cunha, & Pádua, 2002), it may be either because we don't use appropriate material and efficient explanations, or because there are two more causes missing: formal and final. In this chapter, all of four Aristotle's causes are considered important. There are both four of Aristotle's causes and four physical interactions (strong, weak, electromagnetic, and gravitational). Later in this text, there will be a schematic suggestion that the four interactions actually represent the four causes in action. Anticipating that schematic, before we move on from physics to mathematics, let's mention two physicists, Bohm (2005) and Cramer (Cramer, 1986; Zeilinger, 1996). Bohm's ideas of implicate and explicate order are similar to Buber's "I" and "You", and Cramer and his transactional interpretation of quantum mechanics - including retrocausality - is similar to Aristotle's final cause.

Mathematics Revised

Gödel's Theorem of Incompleteness (Gödel, 1931) has challenged a previously accepted opinion that the entire mathematics consists of fundamental axioms sufficient for all mathematical explanations. This looks like a translation of Buber's differentiation between I and You (the entire mathematics) and I and It (a formal system with its axioms). Also, we may interpret Gödel's Theorem as a subsequent recognition of the existence of formal cause, a recognition due to the fact that efficient cause just isn't enough. Still, the predominant viewpoint is that mathematics and physics, incomplete as they are, are the most fundamental sciences. And this view reflects a common pattern in other fields, as well. Consider that life and consciousness are most often taken as mere epiphenomena (see, for example, Pereria, this text). Rather than advance on the tradition, the fact that mathematics and physics are both distinct and fundamental represents Descartes' mind-body (thinking and extended substance respectively) duality.

Life, Consciousness, and Society Revised

Good mathematical models may model and perhaps predict societal and economic events. Over again, people have failed to predict the future by using the present perception and context. Big historical events have always been and always will be deviations from the norm. The most radical and extreme elements of society change the situation - not those in the middle of a Gaussian curve. A system changes because of its "Black Swans" (Taleb, 2007). Contrast this view with that of neoclassical economics (Lowenberg, 1990), which presumes that humans are rational and that there is some hidden mechanism that optimizes our knowledge in order to choose and buy certain products, balancing prices through supply and demand. Poli (2010) acknowledges that there is a fundamental flaw in our common understanding of how society works. Poli claims that society is non-algorithmic, and that it can exhibit both feedback and feed-forward dynamics, citing Rosen. Rosen's concept of anticipation as applied to society is strikingly similar to Bohm (1996) and Buber (2000) – the same worldview, thus, presents itself as the common conclusion of inquiry from three different origins.

Complexity, Anticipation, and Strange Loops

Rosen's (Rosen, 2012; Nadin, 2010) concept of anticipation is reaction from the (expected) future to the present. Efficient causes in mathematical logic have their equivalents in the material world in temporal causality and determinism. Anticipation, on the other hand, is a unique property of living beings that differentiates them from nonliving matter. King (2011) uses the term "anticipation" for a property of living and conscious beings to choose between possible futures, and sees it as a result of validity of the transactional interpretation of quantum mechanics (c.f. Cramer, 1986. See lso, Peijnenburg (2006) and Di Corpo and Vannini (2012) on syntropy as symmetrical to entropy).

Anticipation isn't a phenomenon in which it *looks like* the causal chain changes its direction and that time *seems* to occasionally move backwards. Rather, in order for organisms to be self-organizing, building their own "parts" through metabolism and repair (M, R), it is necessary that time move in two directions. Researchers use the concept of "retrocausality" for the future influencing the present during decision making, such as in "broad imagination" (Peijnenburg, 2006) as a tool for clairvoyance, and for regulation of physiological processes during meditation, and names the same phenomenon that Rosen (2012) called anticipation. The idea that time has two directions, or that it doesn't have any direction, are propositions that may be tested against our understanding of relativity, e,g, Do they help to make sense of the double-slit experiment and wave-particle complementarity in quantum mechanics? (Walborn et al., 2002) The notion of time moving from the past to the future and not vice-versa is strongly attached to thermodynamics and its Second Law claiming that entropy can only increase over time in closed systems. And this is the issue. Since living and self-aware beings are open systems, they can occasionally and for some time through the very process of metabolism and repair locally violate the Second Law of Thermodynamics, and thus also limitations imposed by correlative constraints on causality (Di Corpo & Vannini, 2012). Anticipation provides a different approach to complexity in which anything nondeterministic, including the seemingly probabilistic behaviour of quantum particles, is impossible rather than hard to calculate and precisely predict.

This brings us to the relationship between anticipation and strange loops (Hofstadter, 2002). In order to have a self-aware computer, one needs to figure out the way to create a program with "strange" causal loops. Since over thirty years after this idea was proposed there still aren't such self-aware algorithms and machines, one has to ask what is wrong with it. The answer seems to be already written in the previous paragraph. Consciousness is not an epiphenomenon of Newtonian physics. Metabolism and repair in living beings are necessary ingredients of any really self-aware (containing the model of the environment and itself within the environment) entity capable to adapt its own point of view (context, formal cause) according to known circumstances. Strange loops aren't a recipe for the creation of conscious machines in a causal world, so much as a requirement. If we follow this thread of thought, it seems that paranormal psychic abilities to predict the future (and feel it (Lobach, 2008)), no matter how unreliable on our usual daily basis (by the way, remembering the past also isn't 100 percent reliable), are actually a natural and expected phenomenon within strange loops.

System theory (von Bertalanffy, 1950; Friendshuh & Troncale, 2012) and automation are inspired by - or at least occasionally look for analogies in - biology. Feedback loops used in control systems (Doyle, Francis, & Tannenbaum, 1990) and management theory are inspired by living organisms controlling their parameters in order to stay alive and healthy. Neural networks, genetic algorithms, and fuzzy logic (Takagi, 1997) are attempted imitations of consciousness, reasoning, life and biological evolution. If life and quantum mechanics require final causes with time moving from the future to present, then deterministic machines will never be capable to really replicate consciousness.

In order to illustrate that challenge that strange loops represent, let's analyze the following sentence:

This sentence is a lie. (1)

——————————————→

If you have the first time read it properly from left to right, the moment when you read "This" was before the moment when you read "lie". There is a similarity between the causal and the temporal arrow. While trying to understand it, as it oscillates between "true" and "false" (computers cannot understand it), we are forced to disassemble its causal implication, split time and create many worlds, or make a circle instead of a straight line.

Teleology (Pražić, 2003) assumes there is a global purpose to existence and life. God as an ultimate unifying end of all things. Insisting on final cause is problematic for both atheists and religious people (Di Corpo & Vannini, 2012). The anthropic principle (Stenger, 2011) claims that physical properties in our universe are narrowly adjusted for us to exist. If extended to an ultimate end, final cause reduces possible universes, as in the Many Worlds interpretation of quantum mechanics (Zeilinger, 1996) to the one that we live in. And from the view of this end, back, evolution exhibits efficient, material, and final causal dynamics in survival of the fittest as increases in complexity (Allen, Tainter, & Hoekstra, 1999) allow organisms to sense, metabolize, move, and survive. Deacon's (2012) approach to evolution is that it is a process of propagation and amplification (morphodynamics) and preservation of constraints (teleodynamics). His ideas will be discussed later, but it should be noted here that there are similarities between Rosen and Deacon in their dissatisfaction with some current scientific ideas. Deacon denies that DNA and any other parts of a living being contain information independent of the context. His position is that a search for the basic ingredients of life is pointless if we don't acknowledge the "absence" - the space in between constraints - as more important than parts. This is exactly Rosen's approach when discussing the (M, R) process and mathematics (Soto-Andrade et al., 2011) underlying reduction of anticipatory systems to machines.

The First Attempt

Both Jung and Pauli believed in possibility of paranormal phenomena such as telepathy, clairvoyance, and psychokinesis (Roth, 2002-2004; Miller, 2010). Synchronicity is similar to telepathy and clairvoyance, and together help to put a psychological face on Aristotle's final cause. Synchronicity is a presumably acausal connecting principle, a bridge between mind and matter. It manifests itself in coincidences that aren't really coincidences, in parallel occurrences of meaningful events without any identifiable common cause. Similar to supervenience, but extended in time-space, Jung and Pauli have used four "causes" (described in figure 1) for a possible explanation of synchronicity (Jung, 1978a). Following Jung and Pauli, in order to bridge the gap between physics and psyche we also presume four causes of conscious-

Figure 1.
(Adapted from [K. Jung, Duh i život, Matica srpska, 1978]).

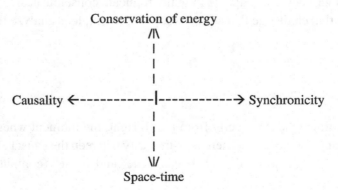

ness. Jung (1978b) set out four psychological functions: thought, sensation, emotion, and intuition. Let's weigh these against Aristotle's.

First of all, it makes sense that efficient cause has its equivalent in thought. Starting with mathematical logic and continuing with Descartes ("I'm thinking, so I exist." (If…, then…)), there really are many similarities between mathematical logic and thinking. Now let's look for the equivalent to material cause. The most fundamental way for a living being to interact with and perceive its material environment is through senses (sensation). Formal cause means context and in this paper the candidate for its psychological equivalent is emotion because emotions behave as a frame (mindset or "mood", as per Heidegger) for other psychological functions, as a differentiator between right and wrong or comfortable and uncomfortable. As the last but not least, we are left with both Aristotle's most controversial cause and the most controversial psychological function: the pair final cause – intuition.

The next thing to do here is to try to build a cosmology containing aforementioned four Aristotle's causes, four psychological functions, Jung and Pauli's four principles (Jung, 1978a), and four physical interactions (Penrose, 2004b; Rickles, 2008). Scientific ideas need to be analyzed and accepted or rejected without prejudices, especially if, while observed from an altered angle, strangeness and spookiness already present in the mainstream science ceases to be counterintuitive and becomes expected. Considering Jung and Pauli's principles, let's start with the most obvious analogy between efficient cause and causality. Then there are final cause (expectations about the future, the final *purpose* causing events) and synchronicity (events not connected by the same cause from the *past* but rather by the same *meaning*). There are similarities between formal cause (logical context) on one side and space-time (physical context) on the other. What remains are material cause and conservation of energy (from matter to energy and back). This row in our table will be helpful while trying to figure out where to put physical interactions and how to attach consciousness and purpose to nonliving matter.

Since time doesn't exist ($t=0$) for gravitons (if they exist (Rickles, 2008) – there are models that suggest even more bizarre behaviour of gravity (Huggett, Vistarini, & Wüthrich, 2013)) making gravitational and electromagnetic interactions unlikely candidates for foundational representations of space-time. Photons participate in changes in structure of matter (material cause) and they are quanta of energy providing conservation of energy (constant amount of material cause) during those changes. Electromagnetic interactions take place between nuclei and electrons and also in complex material structures such as (within and between) molecules and crystals.

It should be mentioned here that the idea is to describe experienced reality – including being in strange loops - in such a way isn't really stranger than experimentally proven facts. For instance, electrons within atoms move between energetic levels at once (in quanta of energy) and there is no transitory movement in space and time – an electron literally disappears on one level and appears on the other (while absorbing or releasing energy of a photon). Atomic nuclei of stable atoms occupy a limited space compared to electrons and photons which exhibit some very non-causal properties such as wave-particle complementarity and relatively frequent moving across atoms and energetic levels, and the structure of nuclei can usually be changed by forcing nucleons (protons and neutrons) together or hitting them apart (strong interaction is relevant in very short distances). Weak nuclear interaction just happens in space and time: no cause forces nuclei to decay except the context (formal cause). What is left is final cause (synchronicity in the same column) and gravitational interaction. First of all, gravitation is the final destiny of the universe upon which depends whether the whole universe will spread into eternity or start shrinking back into singularity. Gravitation is controversial, strange, and mysterious as much as synchronicity, final cause, and intuition, all of them persistent reminders that there might be something

Table 1. Self-referential complex systems

Cause (Aristotle)	Material	Formal	Efficient	Final
Psychological Function (Jung)	Senses	Emotion	Thought	Intuition
Physical Principle (Jung and Pauli)	Conservation of energy	Space-time	Causality	Synchronicity
Physical Interaction	Electromagnetic	Weak	Strong	Gravitation
Explication	Billiard balls	Orthograde	Contragrade	Teleology

missing in our usual understanding of reality. Gravitational attraction is pictured as bending of space and time (and causes problems for scientists who try to create a consistent theory of quantum gravity (Rickles, 2008)). Space and time as we know them don't exist when a body enters a black hole (black because its gravitation doesn't let light to emit). For now, the overview of the four causes is in Table 1.

Can the model described in the table close a strange loop and refer to itself? Consider the four rows in terms of four causes. Efficient cause is the only cause in the narrowest sense, so the first row in the table is like Aristotle's causes (logic) relating to themselves (their efficient component) on an even more fundamental level. The second row is about consciousness. Teleology, consciousness collapsing a wave function, and modern ignorance of Aristotle's final cause (conscious intervention from a "higher force") in science and engineering may mean that final cause (in other words: conscious beings anticipate) re-emerges in the second row as a whole. If this approach is correct, it seems that the third row (principles, contexts, or formalism) resembles formal cause and the fourth row refers to material cause. This looks like some kind of hologram or fractal with parts containing information about the whole structure (Campbell, 2005) or strange loops referring to themselves. The fifth row is actually the first row described differently. It will be useful in The Second Attempt in order to make the navigation between the table and the rest of the text easier, meaning that the underlying schema described here has intrinsically four rows and columns, a "quaternion" as reality per se.

The Second Attempt

Since the concept above is far from clear, we shall in a way repeat the explanation through Juarrero (1999), Thompson (2007), and Deacon's (2012) perspective. First, let's introduce terminology inspired by Deacon. There is a difference between contragrade and orthograde changes within a system. Contragrade tendencies are forced and orthograde tendencies are spontaneous. While contragrade changes are about interacting parts, orthograde changes are more about inertia, statistics, and approaching equilibrium. Orthograde changes take place within an unchanging environment (space and time, formal cause – the analogy between space-time and formal cause is explicitly mentioned by Deacon (2012) and already visible from the table). This terminology will be very useful when looking for analogies between vastly different phenomena. Since we are much more acquainted with efficient (causes and effects) and material (something things are made of) cause than with formal and final cause, formal and final cause demand some additional explanations before we can move forward.

Formal cause can be explained by attractors and constraints (as used by Deacon, 2012). Attractors are evidenced in statistical tendencies for specific events to take place. They are not fields and forces pushing and pulling the matter, but rather a context, a potential shape. (Ed.: An "absence".) Constraints are restrictions on degrees of freedom, and as such they don't determine what will necessarily happen, but rather eliminate what is impossible or unlikely. They are like joints reducing a body's ability to move randomly and chaotically and by that actually increasing its overall functionality. This approach to reality, where we are focused on tendencies and relations rather than parts and "billiard balls", and where what is not (cannot be) there is more important than what is there, is radically different than seeing the world as one big causal mechanism. The situation is even stranger with final cause.

Final cause is evidenced in teleodynamics, an organizational form exhibiting end-directedness and anticipation. Rosen's mappings of the (M, R) process (Mikulecky) demonstrate that final cause brings both causal and temporal loops into existence. On the other hand, even though Deacon provides a good description of synergy of coupled morphodynamic processes, he insists that final cause is explainable by classical physics without any need for inclusion of something resembling quantum mechanics (c.f Soto-Andrade et al., 2011) or questioning the conventional approach to the arrow of time. However, temporal loops are physically possible as long as they don't bring parallel realities into existence through Newcomb's and Grandfather Paradox (Edwards, 2013). The question remains, if thermodynamics is the reason why the arrow of time emerges, is there nothing but our habits forcing us to stick with it?

Thought is mental work (Deacon, 2012) and emotion is (temporary or lasting) habit. Consider that Thompson (2007) discusses the emotion-cognition state space the "emotional self-organization of personality development" as something that "both emerges from and constrains moods and emotional interpretations" and that "the sense of personal self is constituted by temporally extended, long-term patterns of habitual emotions". It doesn't look like a big stretch of imagination to assume that emotions are linked to formal cause as described by Deacon as constraints and habits either as a metaphor for formal cause in the physical world or literally in consciousness. On the other hand, cognition is just another name for thinking, a process (potentially) explainable by algorithms and causality (efficient cause). Thought changes emotion, emotion changes thought.

Extend this aspect of the emotion-cognition state space - emotions as formal and thoughts as efficient cause. An atom is mostly an empty space with a small nucleus interacting electromagnetically with even smaller electrons. In this billiard balls example, out of four interactions, collisions and friction between real macroscopic billiard balls are electromagnetic. Material cause is something happening between interacting objects because they are made of specific materials. Electrical charge (positive, negative, or neutral) is one such property. Gravity, however, is different:

Gravity seems to have a very special status, different from that of any other field. Rather than sharing in the thermalization that, in the early universe, applies to all other fields, gravity remained aloof, its degrees of freedom lying in wait, so that the second law would come into play as these degrees of freedom begin to become taken up. Not only does this give us a second law, but it gives us one in the particular form that we observe in Nature. Gravity just seems to have been different! (Penrose, 2004b)

Just as strong nuclear interaction is an integral part of the causality of the universe (formation of atomic nuclei – weak nuclear interaction sometimes exhibits asymmetry (Lees, Poierau, & Tisserand, 2012), there is something teleological about gravity. Also, according to the "participatory universe" suggested by Wheeler (Penrose, 2004b), there is something teleological about consciousness. Consider the early psychological constructs. Aristotle is already mentioned, and there are also four alchemical elements extensively elaborated in Jung's work. There are cosmogonies with other numbers of elements, but four elements are prevalent, tetragrammaton (the real name of God with four letters), mandala (a circle as the symbol of the Self), and Ouroboros (a snake or dragon biting its tail, just like a strange loop (Soto-Andrade et al. (2011)). Ancient people had a different access to imagination and visions - they were not saturated by information, "noise" as we are. It is possible that they were able to perceive the "psychoid" (Jung, 1996), the realm between mind and matter, and with it the underlying pattern of the universe, where Penrose (2004b) also claims there are still big breakthroughs (the next physical revolution) ahead in science.

Recall the table, above. Strong nuclear interaction binds together nucleons (protons and neutrons) within a nucleus fused under extreme physical conditions (nucleons getting close enough) in stars and supernovae – similar to those aforementioned billiard balls in a pump. If efficient cause were more "efficient" at the atomic level, i.e. if less contragrade work was sufficient for change of atomic structure (to push nucleons together or pull them apart), life and consciousness as we know it would be impossible. Weak nuclear interaction is behind nuclear decay. It is a spontaneous (orthograde) process in which, depending on what an atomic nucleus is made of (some nuclei are more stable than others), there is only a probability for it to happen. This process starts for instance after an atom leaves extreme conditions responsible for its fusion or after an animal or a plant dies (^{12}C and ^{14}C isotopes), after a change in formal cause. Also, such a spontaneously shaped nucleus defines a context of attractors and constraints for electrons to populate their orbitals. An atom is neutral (not an ion) if it has the same number of protons and electrons. If the number of protons changes due to spontaneous decay, this event is relevant for electrons. This is why weak interaction is put in the table in the same column of the table as formal cause.

If we translate efficient cause as "coming to a conclusion", which psychological function seems to belong to that column? Deacon (2012) describes thinking as mental work. Even if someone at the moment agrees with another person's cogent elaboration of a situation, habits and emotional attachments will influence latter acceptance or rejection as something that seems to make perfect logical sense. If two persons meet, emotions (Juarrero, 2000) will set the probabilities for them to greet, ignore, or say something rude to each other. If someone's capability to think is significantly limited (drunk or just overwhelmed by emotions), he/she might do something that doesn't make much logical (efficient) sense. Since the column including final cause is, because of its teleodynamical properties, the most controversial (What is time?), it has to be explained more. If all those elements are within the same column, it doesn't mean that final cause = intuition = synchronicity = gravitation. Meaningful coincidences seem to be (are defined by Jung as) acausal phenomena rather than the arrow of time and causality being reversed regardless whether an individual actively perceives them as signs.

Let us think here for a moment whether this story makes sense. Instead of looking for a single formalism (theory of everything) for quantum gravity, macroscopic and quantum world can coexist as drastically different contexts (formal causes) within the same world. If a scientist were able to observe the effects of quantum gravity as significant gravitational field effects due of other waves/particles after the Big Bang and in black holes), that would mean (according to the ideas mentioned above) an irreconcilable collision of two directions of causation (see also Huggett et al. (2013) and Di Corpo and Vannini (2012)). In the model presented here, observers influencing experiments and wave functions collapsing in quantum mechanics (with particles and waves "knowing" when they are being watched by macroscopic (significant gravity) entities) become expected rather than spooky. In Zeilinger's (1996) words:

Changes which might be so radical that it is certainly reasonable and understandable to thoroughly investigate all other possibilities before taking the leap. To my knowledge the most radical position with respect to that leap was assumed by Pauli as I tried to explicate above and it might very well be that someday we will follow his guidance.

We have just taken that leap. Automation and management use the same scheme with a feedback loop (it can also be applied for creativity) with *four* stages (planning, organizing, leading, and controlling – see any textbook on management): input (planning (in accordance with expectations about the future), final cause), processing (organizing, efficient cause), influencing and measuring output (leading, material cause), and feedback (controlling, formal cause). Emotional feedback (Juarrero, 1999) in a living being is significantly more complex (and hopefully more adaptable if we are more aware of our mental dynamics) than in deterministic machines.

This text would at this point be incomplete without mentioning cellular automata (Kari) and the digital philosophy concept (Fredkin, 2003; Schmidhuber, 1997; Campbell, 2005) since they deal with the same idea of hypothetical simple rule able to generate everything that exists. Also, variations of the same idea are elaborated for instance by Wolf (2000) and Koruga (1996). Still, at least so it seems to this author, the approach presented in this paper is more aligned with reality without trying to see patterns that either provide an incomplete description or don't represent the simplest and most fundamental pattern. If scientists from different disciplines reach something similar each time they leave their comfort zone, an overview of such excursions can hardly be totally wrong. The most similar author to the author of this chapter is perhaps Dodig-Crnkovic (2012). Meaning that more scientists should get out of their comfort zones, to see what it is like, and so add to the models under development, here.

IMPLICATIONS OF AN ALTERED WORLDVIEW

Teleology analyzes the possibility of existence of purpose in the world (especially in consciousness). On the other hand, synchronicity is about hypothetical meaningful coincidences, where an individual on his/her path of individuation is the only one who can acknowledge something as meaningful. This pretty much means that, besides the fact that purpose and meaning have a very similar meaning, there is something inherently teleological in synchronicity. Intense and meaningful coincidences would be pointless and a waste of time and resources if not for goal-directed changes in behaviour and attitude. It seems that Campbell (2004) had in mind that circular causality can play an important role in the hero journey. If a potential hero is someone who will give up at some point, he/she might not receive a call at all. Whoever can't believe in miracles will never encounter them.

Jung's idea that the ego isn't the centre of the conscious mind is worth mentioning here. The shamanic perspective (Bright, 2009) seems to be just another name for hermeneutic explanations (Juarrero, 1999) of moments of sudden changes in attitude and understanding. In these mysterious events a storyline can be a better explanation than neurons firing in the brain. Jungian psychotherapists see archetypes (see also Palmer, 2000, for linkages between archetypes and system theory) as inherited conscious entities pable to surprise the ego (in dreams, visions, and emotions) and push forward their agenda. The Self (Jungians tend to write archetypes with capital letters as if they were persons) is, according to this approach, the real centre of the mind, something similar to the idea of God. According to Jung, there is a natural tendency in people to be religious. A "shaman" or spiritually inclined person is simply forced by the Self to behave like one. His/her dreams and visions contact the sacred, the Self. Jung sees in a neurosis an opportunity to change and adapt, archetypes trying to bring a more functional perspective in life or a life stage, a dynamical approach very similar to Juarrero's. It would be interesting to read Juarrero's take on Jung's work because it seems like their ideas are touching the same point between the inside and the outside realm, between neurons and brain (Juarrero) and mind and the outside world (Jung), between rational (Juarrero) and spiritual (late Jung) approach. "By drawing the explainer and the explanation into its strange loop, hermeneutics appears to forestall the possibility of any claim to truth and certainty" says Juarrero (2000).

This, of course, doesn't mean that "anything goes" as an explanation. A healthy balance between scepticism and open-mindedness is needed. Both Deacon (2012) and Juarrero (1999) see their work as a legitimate reason to fight nihilism induced by "rationalism" oscillating between Cartesian dualism and belief that brain and life are nothing but complex machinery. For example, Juarrero (1999) says:

It is for future research, however, to determine whether and to what extent we can teach children to focus and channel their internal dynamics. Habituation is probably one way; deliberately imposing contextual constraints on the environment to alter future behavior is probably another.

The author of this paper agrees that the secret ingredient embedded within our minds is to make ourselves even more self-aware (Campbell, 2004). Still, it's uncertain how one is supposed to achieve this goal as the life story unfolds in order to be a good person if time is hopelessly running in only one direction. Juarrero (1999):

Science and philosophy have had no room for individuals in all their novelty and particularity, and no room, as a result, for understanding or explaining individual human act-tokens as unique trajectories.

"Thinking of an elephant" (Lakoff, 2004; when someone jokingly suggests you not to think of an elephant and actually forcing you to think about it for some time) is an example of mind being constrained. Political propaganda manipulates emotions, in order to realize a political agenda. Fear as a strong emotion can impose a very narrow constraint on someone's mind. The sense that something is or isn't absurd is an emotional constraint. There is even a saying for eccentric and creative individuals that they think outside the box. The central idea of this chapter is that this box metaphor makes a lot of sense, just as Hesse (1987) was talking about vessels where thoughts can (or cannot) brew. When a limited mind deals with someone who disagrees, it sees its perspective as reality that should be defended even with violence in an attempt to destroy what it represses and refuses to acknowledge within itself. If the reflection in the mirror doesn't look pleasant, a narrow mind (packed in a small "box" – container, formal cause) would rather break the mirror than deal with the reflection.

Is artificial consciousness possible? Brains are far from equilibrium. They operate in a regime that would be too noisy for computers because of causal closure in brains and separation between levels (top-down causation and the fact there is no a single centre of consciousness so chaotic if a scientist observes a single neuron). The concept of parts and signals and noise cannot be simply translated from machines to minds and it will stay that way as long as computers don't start eating, breathing, and producing their parts (the only way to stay far from equilibrium).

Since problems solved by a computer and artificial intelligence already resemble what some people would call consciousness, the question of artificial consciousness should be posed more clearly. It seems reasonable, from the way we humans use our minds, to look for consciousness in self-awareness. Most of the time we don't use our minds for making scientific models and calculations (baby steps for computers;

amoebas in the world of computers have the first contact with our world by doing science), but even in our laziest awakened moments we are self-aware. It seems like our minds and "minds" of computers are on the opposite sides while seeing a problem as simple or complex. Also, our memory is far from perfect. Is this a flaw or an important part of our self-awareness? Let's see what Hari (2012) has to say about a hypothetical self-aware computer:

Suppose that a computer knows an object O; hence a representation of O as a sequence of '0's and '1's is already written in its memory. To be self-aware, the computer must know that it knows O, so it must also contain in its memory the sentence 'I know O' and for the same reason, it must also have the sentence 'I know that I know O' and 'I know that I know that I know O', and so on.

That is a problem that even recursively trained neural networks don't reach. The problem is that artificial intelligence is nothing but artificial cognition (thinking), an attempt (if self-awareness is the goal of artificial intelligence) destined to fail because four causes are reduced to efficient cause. Algorithms (like those in computers) are nowhere to be found in our brains and this fact is not just a minor technical detail, but rather a part of the very reason why artificial machines will never be conscious. Even if we assume that artificial neural networks can exhibit morphodynamics similar to our brains, how are we supposed to introduce teleodynamics?

While talking about intentions and subsequent actions and a single neural detail at the lower level, Juarrero (1999) says "The higher level is metastable despite multiple realizability at the lower level. As we saw in the case of Benard cells, it does not matter whether the cells are made of water or other viscous materials."

In this example we are talking neither about top-down nor bottom-up causation. Deacon does acknowledge that constraints simplify reality (reduced degrees of freedom in order to have coherent and goal-directed behaviour) rather than make it more complex, but teleodynamics in his work seems to be introduced simply because our minds are teleodynamic. Acknowledging that dynamical architecture brings intentional properties is a good direction, but how to move forward if we persist that there is nothing to add to the physics of mind? If Newtonian dynamics (seeing everything as one big machine) really is such a dead end, why stick to it? In Juarrero's (1999) words:

In contrast to covering-law accounts, hermeneutic explanations of phase change transformations must therefore make note of and emphasize the particular case's concrete and temporal details even more than when they explain behavior issuing from established dynamics.

Though Juarrero suggests hermeneutic explanations of dynamics within a self-aware entity, it is still uncertain how this approach allows free will, anticipation, and phase changes to be possible. There is a difference between being too complex to explain and being impossible to explain and predict. Goal-driven phase changes in a reality where time flows in only one direction would be left to constrained, but still random events. It's not just explanations that need to be hermeneutic – the underlying physics also needs to be hermeneutic (see also Montero and Appendix B (Emergence and the Problem of Downward Causation) in Thompson (2007), especially the part on what it means to be physical). Hermeneutics as interpretations of mind is compatible with Jungian psychotherapy, especially its mythical/alchemical part (individuation, alchemy, the hero journey (Campbell, 2004)), and it allows an unconventional take on the physics of consciousness (Jung, 1996).

Let's suppose that instead of sentence (1) oscillating between "true" and "false", we are dealing with a whole book describing someone's life story. Can paying attention to synchronicity in your life story allow you to read your life story in advance? "Refusing to call hermeneutical, genealogical interpretations "explanation" begs the question in favor of the Humean model," says Juarrero (1999). The idea that hermeneutical interpretations are relevant is applicable when prophecies, dreams, and visions are included in a decision-making process. If we insist that time (at least in physics sufficient for consciousness to emerge) has only one direction, such an approach just claims that the Humean model has a very limited explanatory power, but that it is still sufficient (no matter how confusing and boring – inclusion of every atom of a bicycle into an explanation of its trajectory would be ridiculous, but a bicycle is still made of interacting atoms and without free will) for the world as we know it to exist.

Perhaps this chapter is already too full of bold speculations. But, if synchronicity really exists and considering that Rosen (2012) wanted to implement his ideas about anticipation in a broader scale of society containing self-aware and self-reflective beings (how to be collectively even more anticipatory and self-aware), it makes sense here to speculate for awhile in this direction. Synchronicity beyond the individual level is for instance already elaborated by Baets (2012), Hardy (2004), and Jargodzki (2009). What would happen if people around us were massively expecting and experiencing synchronicity in this increasingly interconnected world? Could the Internet be a "Global Brain" (Heylighen, 2011; Turchin, 1977) combined with the media and collective expectations of meaningful coincidences on a daily basis boost our psychic abilities (more frequent synchronicity and more successful anticipation)? Is it possible to create an idea space (Ogle, 2007) for new ideas to emerge and be applied by humans aided by a "sixth sense"?

I-Thou Interpretation of Quantum Mechanics

Interpretations of quantum mechanics can fall into six categories (Penrose, 2004b):

1. Copenhagen
2. Many worlds
3. Environmental decoherence
4. Consistent histories
5. Pilot wave
6. New theory with objective R.

The Copenhagen interpretation is loosely defined. It may either mean that the theory of quantum mechanics is a tool for scientists or that consciousness causes collapse of the wave function, something that does not take place (the superposition of the U process (before collapse of the wave function) remains intact) on distant planets where life and consciousness don't have any access to quantum phenomena. Since such uncertainty would manifest on macroscopic phenomena such as weather, Penrose calls this idea (the second take on the Copenhagen interpretation) absurd. We shall later discuss this absurdity.

The many worlds interpretation claims that in quantum measurement something strange happens to a scientist involved in the experiment: he splits into many parallel realities incapable to communicate between each other. It seems there is something special happening when a scientist from whichever planet does such an experiment for the first time, a similar kind of absurdity (but a different manifestation where human beings rather than clouds on some distant planet split into parallel realities) as the one mentioned in the previous paragraph.

The environmental decoherence approach sees the surroundings as important for a quantum experiment and claims that a measurement process cannot be taken in isolation.

The consistent histories approach is a generalization of different approaches. It allows any explanation as long as the history is consistent (something similar to the "I-Thou" interpretation described later in this text). In the pilot wave case there are two levels of reality: the firmer (the actual behaviour of the particle) and the other (the wave function as a mathematical formalism). Under the "new theory with objective R" (R means reduction or collapse of the wave function) we shall mention Penrose's approach in which gravitation causes collapse of the wave function. Through elaboration of the uncertainty principle of energy Penrose (2004b) explains how an objective collapse might take place as gravitation (the amount of matter and mass) goes beyond a threshold which divides quantum phenomena from our macroscopic realm where classical physics defines reality. The theory of everything (one theory connecting theory of relativity and quantum mechanics) is still an unresolved mystery for scientists, but it does have a name upon which many scientists agree: quantum gravity. There is a lot of theoretical and experimental knowledge about the other three types of physical interactions (electromagnetic, strong, and weak) on the quantum level, but gravitation (one of the reasons is that it's the weakest interaction, insignificant for subatomic particles) is still a mystery.

So, what would be the I-Thou interpretation? As it is mentioned earlier in this text, Buber (2000) was interested in relationships more than in objects, in interconnectedness more than in parts. What if interconnectedness is at least as fundamental as division into parts? It doesn't mean just the same air we all breathe or some poetical and spiritual perception of wholeness, not even entanglement and the Grandfather Paradox (Edwards, 2013). Perhaps nature is always a step ahead of us and the question whether or not there is a superposition of clouds on some distant planet is the real absurdity. Perhaps there is out there a physical equivalent of Gödel's theorem manifesting itself, totally independent of what we think about it. On the other hand, perhaps in this part of the universe accessible to us there is some isomorphism in consciousness and gravitation that causes collapse of the wave function. Also, perhaps different interpretations of quantum mechanics can take over and become the proper reality (maybe even many worlds for macroscopic lifeless and unconscious objects) within a specific situation in a way similar to the wave-particle complementarity (Walborn et al., 2002).

Our sense of what is absurd and what looks real doesn't mean that reality should somehow align to our wishful thinking. But, more often than not we tend to be entrapped in our belief (regardless of scientific discipline) and call it facts and even reality. There is nothing in known science that may disapprove the idea that more than one interpretation of quantum mechanics can be true and that relations are at least as basic components of reality as parts. It is very difficult to express in words, but we are talking here about something more holistic (Naranjo, 2011) than quantum entanglement (it is difficult to even properly ask whether consciousness and life have the origin in classical or quantum physics (Abbott, Davies, & Pati, 2008)), a realm in which entanglement plays an important role and which is akin to Rosen's (2012) notion that physics isn't the most fundamental science. Zen Buddhism ("What is the sound of one hand clapping?", "Show me your real face before your parents were born", and "Stop a galloping horse" (collected from various sources and used here in illustration rather than as verbatim quotations) are *koans* that Zen monks deal with on their way towards satori or enlightenment) is perhaps the best approach to the described above.

Considering the subchapter "In Search for the Most Fundamental Scientific Discipline", let's quote Penrose (2004b; OR means "objective reduction"):

A standard position is that of computational functionalism, according to which it is merely computational activity (of some suitable but yet unspecified nature) that gives rise to conscious mentality. I have argued strongly against this view (partly using reasoning based on Gödel's theorem and the notion of Turing computability—see §16.6), and I have indeed suggested that consciousness actually depends upon the missing (gravitational) OR theory. My arguments demand that this missing theory must be a non-computational theory (i.e. its actions lie outside the scope of Turing machine simulation, §16.6). Theoretical ideas for producing an OR model of this type are in a very preliminary stage, at present, but possibly there are some clues here.

CONCLUSION

This chapter is at the same time an attempt to explain reality by combining different scientific disciplines and to make a statement that the world where consciousness, life, and quantum effects exist isn't just a big deterministic machine. First we encounter tangled hierarchies as we are looking for the most fundamental scientific discipline. Then we introduce four causes as they appear "out of nowhere" (as a strange loop should appear, without axioms and first assumptions) in Jung's work and earlier in alchemy and Aristotle's metaphysics. The schematic pattern that is also a tangled hierarchy or strange loop is identified in (all of them appearing in four elements) Aristotle's causes (final cause similar to Rosen's concept of anticipation), Jung and Pauli's principles, psychological functions as defined by Jung, and physical interactions. If this model is genuine, reality described in this way makes artificial consciousness impossible, but it is open for altered states of consciousness and perception. This is exactly Buber's idea of reality where the real I and Thou encounter never happens, but it's worth trying to get closer to it. Even if the world isn't a machine, perhaps interconnected machines might allow us to better understand the mysteries that are out there somewhere waiting to be revealed, imagined, and anticipated.

ACKNOWLEDGMENT

The author is grateful to many people who through e-mail communication indirectly contributed to this paper. If you are one of them (if you are alive and active, perhaps your name is in the references) and are reading this, thank you. The main reason why this text exists in this shape and under this title (older but never before published ideas updated and combined with Rosen and Aristotle's thoughts) is Kineman's (2012) contribution to the second edition of Rosen's book *Anticipatory Systems*. During the earliest stage in 2002, Professor Dejan Raković was important with his approach to biophysics (Raković, 1995), as well as later in 2014 Kent Palmer, a member of Depth Psychology Alliance. Still, any conceptual mistake is strictly the author's.

REFERENCES

Abbott, D., Davies, P., & Pati, A. (Eds.). (2008). *Quantum Aspects of Life*. London, UK: Imperial College Press.

Allen, T., Tainter, J., & Hoekstra, T. (1999). Supply-Side Sustainability. *Systems Research and Behavioral Science, Syst. Res, 16*(5), 403-427. Retrieved from http://www.buildftw.org/sites/buildftw.org/files/shared_assets/Allen, Tainter, Hoekstra - 1999 - Supply-side sustainability.pdf

Aquinas, T. (1961). *Commentary on the Metaphysics*. Chicago, IL. Retrieved from http://dhspriory.org/thomas/Metaphysics.htm

Aristotle. *Metaphysics*. The Internet Classics Archive. Retrieved from http://classics.mit.edu//Aristotle/metaphysics.html

Baets, W. (2012). Complexity, consciousness and a-causality: A new organizational paradigm. Graduate School of Business, University of Cape Town. Retrieved from http://blogs.sun.ac.za/complexityforum/files/2012/05/BAETS-Forum-Keynote-Slides.pdf

von Bertalanffy, L. (1950). An Outline of General System Theory. *The British Journal for the Philosophy of Science, 1*(2), 134–165. http://www.isnature.org/Events/2009/Summer/r/Bertalanffy1950-GST_Outline_SELECT.pdf doi:10.1093/bjps/I.2.134

Bhattacharya, S. (2003). Stupidity should be cured, says DNA discoverer. *NewScientist*. Retrieved from http://www.newscientist.com/article/dn3451-stupidity-should-be-cured-says-dna-discoverer.html#.U67DdihtxxU

Bohm, D. (1996). *On Dialogue*. London, New York: Routledge. doi:10.4324/9780203180372

Bohm, D. (2005). *Wholeness and the Implicate Order*. London, New York: Routledge.

Bright, B. (2009). The Shamanic Perspective: Where Jungian Thought and Archetypal Shamanism Converge. *Shamanswell.org*. Retrieved from https://www.academia.edu/1020632/The_Shamanic_Perspective_Where_Jungian_Thought_and_Archetypal_Shamanism_Converge

Buber, M. (2000). *Ja i Ti [I and Thou]*. Belgrade, Serbia: Rad.

Campbell, J. (2004). *The Hero with a Thousand Faces*. Princeton, Oxford: Princeton University Press.

Campbell, T. (2005). *My Big TOE: Awakening, Discovery, Inner Workings*. USA: Lightning Strike Books LLC.

Di Corpo, U., & Vannini, A. (2012). Syntropy, Cosmology and Life. *Syntropy*, (1), 90-103. Retrieved from http://www.sintropia.it/english/2012-eng-1-6.pdf

Cramer, J. (1986). The Transactional Interpretation of Quantum Mechanics. *Reviews of Modern Physics, 58*(3), 647–688. doi:10.1103/RevModPhys.58.647

Deacon, T. (2012). *Incomplete Nature: How Mind Emerged from Matter*. New York, London: W.W. Norton & Company.

Descartes, R. (n.d.). *Principles of Philosophy*. Retrieved from http://www.ahshistory.com/wp-content/uploads/2012/07/descprin.pdf

Dodig-Crnkovic, G. (2012). Physical Computation as Dynamics of Form that Glues Everything Together. *Information, 3*(4), 204–218. doi:10.3390/info3020204

Doyle, J., Francis, B., & Tannenbaum, A. (1990). Feedback Control Theory. London, UK: Macmillan Publishing Co. Retrieved from www.control.utoronto.ca/people/profs/francis/dft.pdf

Edwards, A. (2013). Time Travel and Newcomb's Problem. Champaign, IL: University of Illinois at Urbana. Retrieved from http://static.squarespace.com/static/50c0f505e4b0633592d3cf29/t/517aad57e4b0f0be01c32027/1366994263878/presentation_6.pdf

Fredkin, E. (2003). An Introduction to Digital Philosophy. *International Journal of Theoretical Physics, 42*(2), 189–247. doi:10.1023/A:1024443232206

Friendshuh, L., & Troncale, L. (2012). SoSPT I.: Identifying Fundamental Systems Processes for a General Theory of Systems. In *Proceedings of the 56th Annual Conference*. San Jose, California: International Society for the Systems Sciences (ISSS). Retrieved from http://journals.isss.org/index.php/proceedings56th/article/viewFile/2145/676

Gödel, K. (1931). Über formal unentscheidbare Sätze der Principia Mathematica und verwandter Systeme, I. *Monatshefte für Mathematik und Physik, 38*(38), 173–198. doi:10.1007/BF01700692

Gökmenoğlu, T., Eret, E., & Kiraz, E. (2010). Crises, Reforms, and Scientific Improvements: Behaviorism in the Last Two Centuries. *Elementary Education Online, 9*(1), 292-300. Retrieved from http://ilkogretim-online.org.tr/vol9say1/v9s1m22.pdf

Hardy, C. (2004). Synchronicity: Interconnection through a Semantic Dimension. Curitiba, Brazil: Faculdades Integradas. Retrieved from http://hardy.christine.free.fr/39-Synchronicity.doc

Hari, S. D. (2012). A Few Questions About Consciousness Suggested By Comparing the Brain and the Computer. *NeuroQuantology, 10*(2), 286–301. doi:10.14704/nq.2012.10.2.407

Heidegger, M. (1977). The Question Concerning Technology. Retrieved from http://simondon.ocular-witness.com/wp-content/uploads/2008/05/question_concerning_technology.pdf

Hesse, H. (1987). *Demijan (Demian)*. Belgrade, Serbia: Beogradski izdavačko-grafički zavod (BIGZ).

Heylighen, F. (2011). Conceptions of a Global Brain: an historical review. In L. Grinin, R. Carneiro, A. Korotayev, & F. Spier (Eds.), Evolution: Cosmic, Biological, Social (pp. 274–289). Volgograd, Russia: Uchitel Publishing House. Retrieved from http://pespmc1.vub.ac.be/Papers/GBconceptions.pdf

Hofstadter, D. (2002). *Gedel, Ešer, Bah: Jedna beskrajna zlatna nit [Gödel, Escher, Bach: An Eternal Golden Braid]*. Belgrade, Serbia: Prosveta.

Huggett, N., Vistarini, T., & Wüthrich, C. (2013). Time in Quantum Gravity. In A. Bardon & H. Dyke (Eds.), Blackwell Companion to the Philosophy of Time (pp. 242–261). Hoboken, NJ: Wiley-Blackwell. Retrieved from http://www.academia.edu/2046778/Time_in_Quantum_Gravity doi:10.1002/9781118522097.ch15

Jargodzki, C. (2009). From Stephen Hawking's Flexiverse to Synchronicity: Intimations of Our Trans-human Future. In *Metanexus Institute Conference*. Retrieved from http://www.metanexus.net/archive/conference2009/abstract/default-id=10819.aspx.html

Juarrero, A. (1999). *Dynamics in Action: Intentional Behavior as a Complex System*. Cambridge and London: The MIT Press. Retrieved from http://aliciajuarrerodotcom1.files.wordpress.com/2012/02/dynamics-in-action-pdf1.pdf

Juarrero, A. (2000). Dynamics in Action: Intentional Behavior as a Complex System. *Emergence*, *2*(2), 24–57. http://intersci.ss.uci.edu/wiki/pub/Juarrero(2000)Dynmcs_Action(ECO).pdf doi:10.1207/S15327000EM0202_03

Jung, C. G. (1978a). Sinhronicitet kao princip akauzalnih veza [Synchronicity: An Acausal Connecting Principle]. In C.G. Jung, (1978) Duh i život [Spirit and Life] (pp. 119-197). Novi Sad, Serbia: Matica srpska.

Jung, C.G. (1978b). *Psihološki tipovi* [Psychological Types]. Novi Sad, Serbia: Matica srpska.

Jung, C. G. (1996). Aion. Belgrade, Serbia: Atos. Kari, J. Cellular Automata: Tutorial. Turku, Finland: University of Turku. Retrieved from http://users.utu.fi/jkari/ca/CAintro.pdf

Kineman, J. (2012). Relational Science: Towards a Unified Theory of Nature. In R. Rosen (Ed.), *Anticipatory Systems: Philosophical, Mathematical, and Methodological Foundations, IFSR International Series on Systems Science and Engineering 1* (pp. 399–419). New York, NY: Springer.

King, C. (2011). The Central Enigma of Consciousness. *Journal of Consciousness Exploration & Research*, *2*(1), 13–44. Retrieved from http://jcer.com/index.php/jcj/article/view/123/131

Koruga, Đ. (1996). Information physics: In search of a scientific basis of consciousness. In: D. Raković, & Đ. Koruga (Eds.), *Consciousness: Scientific Challenge of the 21st Century* (pp. 260-278). Belgrade, Serbia: United Nations University for Peace. Retrieved from http://www.dejanrakovicfund.org/knjige/1995-ecpd-consciousness.pdf

Lakoff, G. (2004). *Don't Think of an Elephant!: Know Your Values and Frame the Debate – The Essential Guide for Progressives*. White River Junction, Vermont: Chelsea Green Publishing.

Lanza, R., & Berman, D. (2009). *Biocentrism: How Life and Consciousness Are the Keys to Understanding the True Nature of the Universe*. Dallas, Texas: BenBella Books.

Lees, J., Poierau, V., & Tisserand, V. et al. (2012). Observation of Time-Reversal Violation in the B^0 Meson System. *Physical Review Letters*, *109*(21). Retrieved from https://physics.aps.org/featured-article-pdf/10.1103/PhysRevLett.109.211801 PMID:23215586

Lobach, E. (2008). *Presentiment Research: Past, Present, and Future*. Amsterdam, Netherlands: University of Amsterdam.

Lowenberg, A. (1990). Neoclassical Economics as a Theory of Politics and Institutions. *The Cato Journal*, *3*(9), 619–639. Retrieved from www.cato.org/cato-journal/winter-1990/neoclassical-economics-theory-politics-institutions

McNamara, C., & Troncale, L. (2012). SPT II.: How to Find & Map Linkage Propositions for a GTS from the Natural Sciences Literature. In *Proceedings of the 56ᵗʰ Annual Conference*. San Jose, California. ISSS. Retrieved from http://journals.isss.org/index.php/proceedings56th/article/viewFile/2153/679

Mikulecky, D. Robert Rosen. (n.d.). The Well Posed Question and Its Answer – Why Are Organisms Different from Machines? Richmond, VA: Medical Campus of Virginia Commonwealth University. Retrieved from http://www.people.vcu.edu/~mikuleck/PPRISS3.html

Miller, A. (2010). *137: Jung, Pauli, and the Pursuit of a Scientific Obsession*. New York, NY: W.W. Norton & Company.

Nadin, M. (2010). Anticipation and Dynamics: Rosen's Anticipation in the Perspective of Time. *International Journal of General Systems*, *39*(1), 3–33. http://www.nadin.ws/archives/966 doi:10.1080/03081070903453685

Naranjo, J. R. (2011). Bridging the Gap: Does Closure to Efficient Causation Entail Quantum-Like Attributes? *Axiomathes*, *21*(2), 315–330. http://link.springer.com/article/10.1007%2Fs10516-011-9146-z doi:10.1007/s10516-011-9146-z

Newton, I. (1846). *The Mathematical Principles of Natural Philosophy*. New York, NY: Daniel Adee.

Ogle, R. (2007). *Smart World: Breakthrough Creativity and the New Science of Ideas*. Boston, Massachusetts: Harvard Business School Press.

Palmer, K. (2000). *Reflexive Autopoietic Dissipative Special Systems Theory: An Approach to Emergent Meta-systems through Holonomics*. Retrieved from http://archonic.net/rastnopY.pdf

Peijnenburg, J. (2006). Shaping Your Own Life. *Metaphilosophy*, *37*(2), 240–253. doi:10.1111/j.1467-9973.2006.00424.x

Penrose, R. (2004a). *Carev novi um* [The Emperor's New Mind]. Belgrade, Serbia: Informatika.

Penrose, R. (2004b). *The Road to Reality: A Complete Guide to the Laws of the Universe*. London, UK: Jonathan Cape.

Poli, R. (2010). *The Complexity of Self-reference: A Critical Evaluation of Luhmann's Theory of Social Systems*. Trento, Italy: Dipartimento di Sociologia. Retrieved from http://web.unitn.it/files/quad50.pdf

Pražić, A. (2003). *Priroda i teleologija* [Nature and Teleology]. Belgrade, Serbia: Izdavačka kuća Plato.

Raković, D. (1995). *Osnovi biofizike* [Fundamentals of Biophysics]. Belgrade, Serbia: Grosknjiga.

Rickles, D. (2008). Quantum Gravity: A Primer for Philosophers. In D. Rickles (Ed.), The Ashgate Companion to Contemporary Philosophy of Physics. Farnham, UK: Ashgate. Retrieved from http://philsci-archive.pitt.edu/5387/1/Rickles_QG.pdf

Rosen, R. (2012). *Anticipatory Systems: Philosophical, Mathematical, and Methodological Foundations, IFSR International Series on Systems Science and Engineering 1*. New York, NY: Springer. doi:10.1007/978-1-4614-1269-4

Roth, R. (2002-2004). *The Return of the World Soul: Wolfgang Pauli, Carl Jung and the Challenge of the Unified Psychophysical Reality*. Zurich, Switzerland: Pro Litteris. Retrieved from http://paulijungunusmundus.eu/synw/pauli_fludd_flood_sync.htm

Schmidhuber, J. (1997). A Computer Scientist's View of Life, the Universe, and Everything. In C. Freksa (Ed.), Foundations of Computer Science: Potential – Theory – Cognition (pp. 201–208). New York, NY: Springer; Retrieved from http://arxiv.org/pdf/quant-ph/9904050

Soto-Andrade, J., Jaramillo, S., Gutiérrez, C., & Letelier, J.-C. (2011). Ouroboros avatars: A mathematical exploration of Self-reference and Metabolic Closure. *Conference: Advances in Artificial Life, ECAL*. Paris, France. Retrieved from http://mitpress.mit.edu/sites/default/files/titles/alife/0262297140chap115.pdf

Stenger, V. (2011). The Anthropic Principle. In T. Flynn (Ed.), The Encyclopedia of Nonbelief. New York, NY: Prometheus Books. Retrieved from http://www.colorado.edu/philosophy/vstenger/Cosmo/ant_encyc.pdf

Takagi, H. (1997). Introduction to Fuzzy Systems, Neural networks, and Genetic Algorithms. In D. Ruan (Ed.), Fuzzy Logic, Neural Networks, and Genetic Algorithms (pp. 1–33). Norwell, MA: Kluwer Academic Publishers. Retrieved from www.teleamerica.net/reference/Software/IntroToFuzzySystemsNuralNetsGeneticAlgorithms.pdf doi:10.1007/978-1-4615-6191-0_1

Taleb, N. N. (2007). *The Black Swan: The Impact of the Highly Improbable*. New York, NY: Random House.

Thompson, E. (2007). *Mind in Life: Biology, Phenomenology, and the Sciences of Mind*. Cambridge, London: The Belknap Press of Harvard University Press.

Troncale, L. (2013). Category Archives: SoSPT. Retrieved from http://lentroncale.com/?cat=10

Turchin, V. (1977). The Phenomenon of Science: a cybernetic approach to human evolution. New York, NY: Columbia University Press. Retrieved from http://pespmc1.vub.ac.be/POS/TurPOS-prev.pdf

Walborn, S., Terra Cunha, M., Pádua, S., & Monken, C. (2002). Double-slit quantum eraser. *Physical Review A., 65*(3), 033818. http://grad.physics.sunysb.edu/~amarch/Walborn.pdf doi:10.1103/PhysRevA.65.033818

Whitehead, A. N., & Russell, B. (1913). Principia Mathematica (three volumes). Cambridge, UK: Cambridge University Press. Retrieved from http://ia700402.us.archive.org/28/items/cu31924001575244/cu31924001575244.pdf

Wolf, F. A. (2000). *Mind into Matter: A New Alchemy of Science and Spirit*. Needham, MA: Moment Point Press.

Wolfram, S. (2002). *A New Kind of Science*. Champaign, IL: Wolfram Media.

Zeilinger, A. (1996). On the Interpretation and Philosophical Foundation of Quantum Mechanics. In U. Ketvel, et al. (Eds.), Vastakohtien todellisuus. Helsinki, Finland: Helsinki University Press; Retrieved from https://vcq.quantum.at/fileadmin/Publications/1996-03.pdf

KEY TERMS AND DEFINITIONS

Archetypes: Emotionally charged (overwhelming) manifestations of the collective unconscious appearing in dreams or as projections to other people (such as enemies, leaders, or when an individual falls in love).

Constraint: A shape and size of a container, spatial and functional relations between parts, joints of a body that allow some movements and forbid others (or reduce their likelihood).

Contragrade: Forced, pushed or pulled into a direction or shape.

Hermeneutic: Interpretational, like a story or myth.

Orthograde: Spontaneous, gradually approaching an equilibrium (stable state) or strange attractor (a dynamic equivalent to equilibrium, a pattern instead of randomness).

Strange Loop: Tangled hierarchy, circular logic.

Superposition: More elements simultaneously contributing to the overall reality.

Synchronicity: Meaningful coincidence, a connection between two or more events without any noticeable common cause.

Teleology: The philosophical discipline searching for existence and origin of purpose (and whether there is a purpose at all) of phenomena.

Wave Function: A function that figures in Schrödinger's equation (the most fundamental formula of quantum mechanics). Collapse of the wave function happens when a physical unknown is reduced to an actual value instead of probability.

Related References

To continue our tradition of advancing information science and technology research, we have compiled a list of recommended IGI Global readings. These references will provide additional information and guidance to further enrich your knowledge and assist you with your own research and future publications.

Aayeshah, W., & Bebawi, S. (2014). The Use of Facebook as a Pedagogical Platform for Developing Investigative Journalism Skills. In G. Mallia (Ed.), *The Social Classroom: Integrating Social Network Use in Education* (pp. 83–99). Hershey, PA: Information Science Reference; doi:10.4018/978-1-4666-4904-0.ch005

Adi, A., & Scotte, C. G. (2013). Barriers to Emerging Technology and Social Media Integration in Higher Education: Three Case Studies. In M. Pătruţ & B. Pătruţ (Eds.), *Social Media in Higher Education: Teaching in Web 2.0* (pp. 334–354). Hershey, PA: Information Science Reference; doi:10.4018/978-1-4666-2970-7.ch017

Agazzi, E. (2012). How Can the Problems of An Ethical Judgment on Science and Technology Be Correctly Approached? In R. Luppicini (Ed.), *Ethical Impact of Technological Advancements and Applications in Society* (pp. 30–38). Hershey, PA: Information Science Reference; doi:10.4018/978-1-4666-1773-5.ch003

Agina, A. M., Tennyson, R. D., & Kommers, P. (2013). Understanding Children's Private Speech and Self-Regulation Learning in Web 2.0: Updates of Vygotsky through Piaget and Future Recommendations. In P. Ordóñez de Pablos, H. Nigro, R. Tennyson, S. Gonzalez Cisaro, & W. Karwowski (Eds.), *Advancing Information Management through Semantic Web Concepts and Ontologies* (pp. 1–53). Hershey, PA: Information Science Reference; doi:10.4018/978-1-4666-2494-8.ch001

Ahrens, A., Bassus, O., & Zaščerinska, J. (2014). Enterprise 2.0 in Engineering Curriculum. In M. Cruz-Cunha, F. Moreira, & J. Varajão (Eds.), *Handbook of Research on Enterprise 2.0: Technological, Social, and Organizational Dimensions* (pp. 599–617). Hershey, PA: Business Science Reference; doi:10.4018/978-1-4666-4373-4.ch031

Akputu, O. K., Seng, K. P., & Lee, Y. L. (2014). Affect Recognition for Web 2.0 Intelligent E-Tutoring Systems: Exploration of Students' Emotional Feedback. In J. Pelet (Ed.), *E-Learning 2.0 Technologies and Web Applications in Higher Education* (pp. 188–215). Hershey, PA: Information Science Reference; doi:10.4018/978-1-4666-4876-0.ch010

Al-Hajri, S., & Tatnall, A. (2013). A Socio-Technical Study of the Adoption of Internet Technology in Banking, Re-Interpreted as an Innovation Using Innovation Translation. In A. Tatnall (Ed.), *Social and Professional Applications of Actor-Network Theory for Technology Development* (pp. 207–220). Hershey, PA: Information Science Reference; doi:10.4018/978-1-4666-2166-4.ch016

Al Hujran, O., Aloudat, A., & Altarawneh, I. (2013). Factors Influencing Citizen Adoption of E-Government in Developing Countries: The Case of Jordan. [IJTHI]. *International Journal of Technology and Human Interaction, 9*(2), 1–19. doi:10.4018/jthi.2013040101

Alavi, R., Islam, S., Jahankhani, H., & Al-Nemrat, A. (2013). Analyzing Human Factors for an Effective Information Security Management System. [IJSSE]. *International Journal of Secure Software Engineering, 4*(1), 50–74. doi:10.4018/jsse.2013010104

Altun, N. E., & Yildiz, S. (2013). Effects of Different Types of Tasks on Junior ELT Students' Use of Communication Strategies in Computer-Mediated Communication. [IJCALLT]. *International Journal of Computer-Assisted Language Learning and Teaching, 3*(2), 17–40. doi:10.4018/ijcallt.2013040102

Amaldi, P., & Smoker, A. (2013). An Organizational Study into the Concept of "Automation Policy" in a Safety Critical Socio-Technical System. [IJSKD]. *International Journal of Sociotechnology and Knowledge Development, 5*(2), 1–17. doi:10.4018/jskd.2013040101

An, I. S. (2013). Integrating Technology-Enhanced Student Self-Regulated Tasks into University Chinese Language Course. [IJCALLT]. *International Journal of Computer-Assisted Language Learning and Teaching, 3*(1), 1–15. doi:10.4018/ijcallt.2013010101

Andacht, F. (2013). The Tangible Lure of the Technoself in the Age of Reality Television. In R. Luppicini (Ed.), *Handbook of Research on Technoself: Identity in a Technological Society* (pp. 360–381). Hershey, PA: Information Science Reference; doi:10.4018/978-1-4666-2211-1.ch020

Anderson, A., & Petersen, A. (2012). Shaping the Ethics of an Emergent Field: Scientists' and Policymakers' Representations of Nanotechnologies. In R. Luppicini (Ed.), *Ethical Impact of Technological Advancements and Applications in Society* (pp. 219–231). Hershey, PA: Information Science Reference; doi:10.4018/978-1-4666-1773-5.ch017

Anderson, J. L. (2014). Games and the Development of Students' Civic Engagement and Ecological Stewardship. In J. Bishop (Ed.), *Gamification for Human Factors Integration: Social, Education, and Psychological Issues* (pp. 199–215). Hershey, PA: Information Science Reference; doi:10.4018/978-1-4666-5071-8.ch012

Ann, O. C., Lu, M. V., & Theng, L. B. (2014). A Face Based Real Time Communication for Physically and Speech Disabled People. In I. Management Association (Ed.), *Assistive Technologies: Concepts, Methodologies, Tools, and Applications* (pp. 1434-1460). Hershey, PA: Information Science Reference. doi:10.4018/978-1-4666-4422-9.ch075

Aricak, O. T., Tanrikulu, T., Siyahhan, S., & Kinay, H. (2013). Cyberbullying: The Bad and the Ugly Side of Information Age. In M. Pătruţ & B. Pătruţ (Eds.), *Social Media in Higher Education: Teaching in Web 2.0* (pp. 318–333). Hershey, PA: Information Science Reference; doi:10.4018/978-1-4666-2970-7.ch016

Ariely, G. (2011). Boundaries of Socio-Technical Systems and IT for Knowledge Development in Military Environments. [IJSKD]. *International Journal of Sociotechnology and Knowledge Development, 3*(3), 1–14. doi:10.4018/jskd.2011070101

Ariely, G. (2013). Boundaries of Socio-Technical Systems and IT for Knowledge Development in Military Environments. In J. Abdelnour-Nocera (Ed.), *Knowledge and Technological Development Effects on Organizational and Social Structures* (pp. 224–238). Hershey, PA: Information Science Reference; doi:10.4018/978-1-4666-2151-0.ch014

Arjunan, S., Kumar, D. K., Weghorn, H., & Naik, G. (2014). Facial Muscle Activity Patterns for Recognition of Utterances in Native and Foreign Language: Testing for its Reliability and Flexibility. In I. Management Association (Ed.), Assistive Technologies: Concepts, Methodologies, Tools, and Applications (pp. 1462-1480). Hershey, PA: Information Science Reference. doi:10.4018/978-1-4666-4422-9.ch076

Arling, P. A., Miech, E. J., & Arling, G. W. (2013). Comparing Electronic and Face-to-Face Communication in the Success of a Long-Term Care Quality Improvement Collaborative. [IJRQEH]. *International Journal of Reliable and Quality E-Healthcare, 2*(1), 1–10. doi:10.4018/ijrqeh.2013010101

Asghari-Oskoei, M., & Hu, H. (2014). Using Myoelectric Signals to Manipulate Assisting Robots and Rehabilitation Devices. In I. Management Association (Ed.), Assistive Technologies: Concepts, Methodologies, Tools, and Applications (pp. 970-990). Hershey, PA: Information Science Reference. doi:10.4018/978-1-4666-4422-9.ch049

Aspradaki, A. A. (2013). Deliberative Democracy and Nanotechnologies in Health. [IJT]. *International Journal of Technoethics, 4*(2), 1–14. doi:10.4018/jte.2013070101

Asselin, S. B. (2014). Assistive Technology in Higher Education. In I. Management Association (Ed.), Assistive Technologies: Concepts, Methodologies, Tools, and Applications (pp. 1196-1208). Hershey, PA: Information Science Reference. doi:10.4018/978-1-4666-4422-9.ch062

Auld, G., & Henderson, M. (2014). The Ethical Dilemmas of Social Networking Sites in Classroom Contexts. In G. Mallia (Ed.), *The Social Classroom: Integrating Social Network Use in Education* (pp. 192–207). Hershey, PA: Information Science Reference; doi:10.4018/978-1-4666-4904-0.ch010

Awwal, M. A. (2012). Influence of Age and Genders on the Relationship between Computer Self-Efficacy and Information Privacy Concerns. [IJTHI]. *International Journal of Technology and Human Interaction, 8*(1), 14–37. doi:10.4018/jthi.2012010102

Ballesté, F., & Torras, C. (2013). Effects of Human-Machine Integration on the Construction of Identity. In R. Luppicini (Ed.), *Handbook of Research on Technoself: Identity in a Technological Society* (pp. 574–591). Hershey, PA: Information Science Reference; doi:10.4018/978-1-4666-2211-1.ch030

Baporikar, N. (2014). Effective E-Learning Strategies for a Borderless World. In J. Pelet (Ed.), *E-Learning 2.0 Technologies and Web Applications in Higher Education* (pp. 22–44). Hershey, PA: Information Science Reference; doi:10.4018/978-1-4666-4876-0.ch002

Bardone, E. (2011). Unintended Affordances as Violent Mediators: Maladaptive Effects of Technologically Enriched Human Niches. [IJT]. *International Journal of Technoethics, 2*(4), 37–52. doi:10.4018/jte.2011100103

Basham, R. (2014). Surveilling the Elderly: Emerging Demographic Needs and Social Implications of RFID Chip Technology Use. In M. Michael & K. Michael (Eds.), *Uberveillance and the Social Implications of Microchip Implants: Emerging Technologies* (pp. 169–185). Hershey, PA: Information Science Reference; doi:10.4018/978-1-4666-4582-0.ch007

Bates, M. (2013). The Ur-Real Sonorous Envelope: Bridge between the Corporeal and the Online Technoself. In R. Luppicini (Ed.), *Handbook of Research on Technoself: Identity in a Technological Society* (pp. 272–292). Hershey, PA: Information Science Reference; doi:10.4018/978-1-4666-2211-1.ch015

Bauer, K. A. (2012). Transhumanism and Its Critics: Five Arguments against a Posthuman Future. In R. Luppicini (Ed.), *Ethical Impact of Technological Advancements and Applications in Society* (pp. 232–242). Hershey, PA: Information Science Reference; doi:10.4018/978-1-4666-1773-5.ch018

Bax, S. (2011). Normalisation Revisited: The Effective Use of Technology in Language Education. [IJCALLT]. *International Journal of Computer-Assisted Language Learning and Teaching, 1*(2), 1–15. doi:10.4018/ijcallt.2011040101

Baya'a, N., & Daher, W. (2014). Facebook as an Educational Environment for Mathematics Learning. In G. Mallia (Ed.), *The Social Classroom: Integrating Social Network Use in Education* (pp. 171–190). Hershey, PA: Information Science Reference; doi:10.4018/978-1-4666-4904-0.ch009

Bayerl, P. S., & Janneck, M. (2013). Professional Online Profiles: The Impact of Personalization and Visual Gender Cues on Online Impression Formation. [IJSKD]. *International Journal of Sociotechnology and Knowledge Development, 5*(3), 1–16. doi:10.4018/ijskd.2013070101

Bell, D., & Shirzad, S. R. (2013). Social Media Business Intelligence: A Pharmaceutical Domain Analysis Study. [IJSKD]. *International Journal of Sociotechnology and Knowledge Development, 5*(3), 51–73. doi:10.4018/ijskd.2013070104

Bergmann, N. W. (2014). Ubiquitous Computing for Independent Living. In I. Management Association (Ed.), Assistive Technologies: Concepts, Methodologies, Tools, and Applications (pp. 679-692). Hershey, PA: Information Science Reference. doi:10.4018/978-1-4666-4422-9.ch033

Bertolotti, T. (2011). Facebook Has It: The Irresistible Violence of Social Cognition in the Age of Social Networking. [IJT]. *International Journal of Technoethics, 2*(4), 71–83. doi:10.4018/jte.2011100105

Berzsenyi, C. (2014). Writing to Meet Your Match: Rhetoric and Self-Presentation for Four Online Daters. In H. Lim & F. Sudweeks (Eds.), *Innovative Methods and Technologies for Electronic Discourse Analysis* (pp. 210–234). Hershey, PA: Information Science Reference; doi:10.4018/978-1-4666-4426-7.ch010

Best, L. A., Buhay, D. N., McGuire, K., Gurholt, S., & Foley, S. (2014). The Use of Web 2.0 Technologies in Formal and Informal Learning Settings. In G. Mallia (Ed.), *The Social Classroom: Integrating Social Network Use in Education* (pp. 1–22). Hershey, PA: Information Science Reference; doi:10.4018/978-1-4666-4904-0.ch001

Bhattacharya, S. (2014). Model-Based Approaches for Scanning Keyboard Design: Present State and Future Directions. In I. Management Association (Ed.), Assistive Technologies: Concepts, Methodologies, Tools, and Applications (pp. 1497-1515). Hershey, PA: Information Science Reference. doi:10.4018/978-1-4666-4422-9.ch078

Bibby, S. (2011). Do Students Wish to 'Go Mobile'?: An Investigation into Student Use of PCs and Cell Phones. [IJCALLT]. *International Journal of Computer-Assisted Language Learning and Teaching, 1*(2), 43–54. doi:10.4018/ijcallt.2011040104

Bishop, J. (2014). The Psychology of Trolling and Lurking: The Role of Defriending and Gamification for Increasing Participation in Online Communities Using Seductive Narratives. In J. Bishop (Ed.), *Gamification for Human Factors Integration: Social, Education, and Psychological Issues* (pp. 162–179). Hershey, PA: Information Science Reference; doi:10.4018/978-1-4666-5071-8.ch010

Bishop, J., & Goode, M. M. (2014). Towards a Subjectively Devised Parametric User Model for Analysing and Influencing Behaviour Online Using Neuroeconomics. In J. Bishop (Ed.), *Gamification for Human Factors Integration: Social, Education, and Psychological Issues* (pp. 80–95). Hershey, PA: Information Science Reference; doi:10.4018/978-1-4666-5071-8.ch005

Biswas, P. (2014). A Brief Survey on User Modelling in Human Computer Interaction. In I. Management Association (Ed.), Assistive Technologies: Concepts, Methodologies, Tools, and Applications (pp. 102-119). Hershey, PA: Information Science Reference. doi:10.4018/978-1-4666-4422-9.ch006

Black, D. (2013). The Digital Soul. In R. Luppicini (Ed.), *Handbook of Research on Technoself: Identity in a Technological Society* (pp. 157–174). Hershey, PA: Information Science Reference; doi:10.4018/978-1-4666-2211-1.ch009

Blake, S., Winsor, D. L., Burkett, C., & Allen, L. (2014). iPods, Internet and Apps, Oh My: Age Appropriate Technology in Early Childhood Educational Environments. In I. Management Association (Ed.), K-12 Education: Concepts, Methodologies, Tools, and Applications (pp. 1650-1668). Hershey, PA: Information Science Reference. doi:10.4018/978-1-4666-4502-8.ch095

Boghian, I. (2013). Using Facebook in Teaching. In M. Pătruţ & B. Pătruţ (Eds.), *Social Media in Higher Education: Teaching in Web 2.0* (pp. 86–103). Hershey, PA: Information Science Reference; doi:10.4018/978-1-4666-2970-7.ch005

Boling, E. C., & Beatty, J. (2014). Overcoming the Tensions and Challenges of Technology Integration: How Can We Best Support our Teachers? In I. Management Association (Ed.), K-12 Education: Concepts, Methodologies, Tools, and Applications (pp. 1504-1524). Hershey, PA: Information Science Reference. doi:10.4018/978-1-4666-4502-8.ch087

Bonanno, P. (2014). Designing Learning in Social Online Learning Environments: A Process-Oriented Approach. In G. Mallia (Ed.), *The Social Classroom: Integrating Social Network Use in Education* (pp. 40–61). Hershey, PA: Information Science Reference; doi:10.4018/978-1-4666-4904-0.ch003

Bongers, B., & Smith, S. (2014). Interactivating Rehabilitation through Active Multimodal Feedback and Guidance. In I. Management Association (Ed.), Assistive Technologies: Concepts, Methodologies, Tools, and Applications (pp. 1650-1674). Hershey, PA: Information Science Reference. doi:10.4018/978-1-4666-4422-9.ch087

Bottino, R. M., Ott, M., & Tavella, M. (2014). Serious Gaming at School: Reflections on Students' Performance, Engagement and Motivation. [IJG-BL]. *International Journal of Game-Based Learning, 4*(1), 21–36. doi:10.4018/IJGBL.2014010102

Brad, S. (2014). Design for Quality of ICT-Aided Engineering Course Units. [IJQAETE]. *International Journal of Quality Assurance in Engineering and Technology Education, 3*(1), 52–80. doi:10.4018/ijqaete.2014010103

Braman, J., Thomas, U., Vincenti, G., Dudley, A., & Rodgers, K. (2014). Preparing Your Digital Legacy: Assessing Awareness of Digital Natives. In G. Mallia (Ed.), *The Social Classroom: Integrating Social Network Use in Education* (pp. 208–223). Hershey, PA: Information Science Reference; doi:10.4018/978-1-4666-4904-0.ch011

Bratitsis, T., & Demetriadis, S. (2013). Research Approaches in Computer-Supported Collaborative Learning. [IJeC]. *International Journal of e-Collaboration, 9*(1), 1–8. doi:10.4018/jec.2013010101

Brick, B. (2012). The Role of Social Networking Sites for Language Learning in UK Higher Education: The Views of Learners and Practitioners. [IJCALLT]. *International Journal of Computer-Assisted Language Learning and Teaching, 2*(3), 35–53. doi:10.4018/ijcallt.2012070103

Burke, M. E., & Speed, C. (2014). Knowledge Recovery: Applications of Technology and Memory. In M. Michael & K. Michael (Eds.), *Uberveillance and the Social Implications of Microchip Implants: Emerging Technologies* (pp. 133–142). Hershey, PA: Information Science Reference; doi:10.4018/978-1-4666-4582-0.ch005

Burton, A. M., Liu, H., Battersby, S., Brown, D., Sherkat, N., Standen, P., & Walker, M. (2014). The Use of Motion Tracking Technologies in Serious Games to Enhance Rehabilitation in Stroke Patients. In J. Bishop (Ed.), *Gamification for Human Factors Integration: Social, Education, and Psychological Issues* (pp. 148–161). Hershey, PA: Information Science Reference; doi:10.4018/978-1-4666-5071-8.ch009

Burusic, J., & Karabegovic, M. (2014). The Role of Students' Personality Traits in the Effective Use of Social Networking Sites in the Educational Context. In G. Mallia (Ed.), *The Social Classroom: Integrating Social Network Use in Education* (pp. 224–243). Hershey, PA: Information Science Reference; doi:10.4018/978-1-4666-4904-0.ch012

Busch, C. D., Lorenzo, A. M., Sánchez, I. M., González, B. G., García, T. P., Riveiro, L. N., & Loureiro, J. P. (2014). In-TIC for Mobile Devices: Support System for Communication with Mobile Devices for the Disabled. In I. Management Association (Ed.), Assistive Technologies: Concepts, Methodologies, Tools, and Applications (pp. 345-356). Hershey, PA: Information Science Reference. doi:10.4018/978-1-4666-4422-9.ch017

Bute, S. J. (2013). Integrating Social Media and Traditional Media within the Academic Environment. In M. Pătruţ & B. Pătruţ (Eds.), *Social Media in Higher Education: Teaching in Web 2.0* (pp. 75–85). Hershey, PA: Information Science Reference; doi:10.4018/978-1-4666-2970-7.ch004

Butler-Pascoe, M. E. (2011). The History of CALL: The Intertwining Paths of Technology and Second/Foreign Language Teaching. [IJCALLT]. *International Journal of Computer-Assisted Language Learning and Teaching, 1*(1), 16–32. doi:10.4018/ijcallt.2011010102

Cabrera, L. (2012). Human Implants: A Suggested Framework to Set Priorities. In R. Luppicini (Ed.), *Ethical Impact of Technological Advancements and Applications in Society* (pp. 243–253). Hershey, PA: Information Science Reference; doi:10.4018/978-1-4666-1773-5.ch019

Cacho-Elizondo, S., Shahidi, N., & Tossan, V. (2013). Intention to Adopt a Text Message-based Mobile Coaching Service to Help Stop Smoking: Which Explanatory Variables? [IJTHI]. *International Journal of Technology and Human Interaction*, 9(4), 1–19. doi:10.4018/ijthi.2013100101

Caldelli, R., Becarelli, R., Filippini, F., Picchioni, F., & Giorgetti, R. (2014). Electronic Voting by Means of Digital Terrestrial Television: The Infrastructure, Security Issues and a Real Test-Bed. In I. Management Association (Ed.), *Assistive Technologies: Concepts, Methodologies, Tools, and Applications* (pp. 905-915). Hershey, PA: Information Science Reference. doi:10.4018/978-1-4666-4422-9.ch045

Camacho, M. (2013). Making the Most of Informal and Situated Learning Opportunities through Mobile Learning. In M. Pătruţ & B. Pătruţ (Eds.), *Social Media in Higher Education: Teaching in Web 2.0* (pp. 355–370). Hershey, PA: Information Science Reference; doi:10.4018/978-1-4666-2970-7.ch018

Camilleri, V., Busuttil, L., & Montebello, M. (2014). MOOCs: Exploiting Networks for the Education of the Masses or Just a Trend? In G. Mallia (Ed.), *The Social Classroom: Integrating Social Network Use in Education* (pp. 348–366). Hershey, PA: Information Science Reference; doi:10.4018/978-1-4666-4904-0.ch018

Campos, P., Noronha, H., & Lopes, A. (2013). Work Analysis Methods in Practice: The Context of Collaborative Review of CAD Models. [IJSKD]. *International Journal of Sociotechnology and Knowledge Development*, 5(2), 34–44. doi:10.4018/jskd.2013040103

Cao, G. (2013). A Paradox Between Technological Autonomy and Ethical Heteronomy of Philosophy of Technology: Social Control System. [IJT]. *International Journal of Technoethics*, 4(1), 52–66. doi:10.4018/jte.2013010105

Carofiglio, V., & Abbattista, F. (2013). BCI-Based User-Centered Design for Emotionally-Driven User Experience. In M. Garcia-Ruiz (Ed.), *Cases on Usability Engineering: Design and Development of Digital Products* (pp. 299–320). Hershey, PA: Information Science Reference; doi:10.4018/978-1-4666-4046-7.ch013

Carpenter, J. (2013). Just Doesn't Look Right: Exploring the Impact of Humanoid Robot Integration into Explosive Ordnance Disposal Teams. In R. Luppicini (Ed.), *Handbook of Research on Technoself: Identity in a Technological Society* (pp. 609–636). Hershey, PA: Information Science Reference; doi:10.4018/978-1-4666-2211-1.ch032

Carroll, J. L. (2014). Wheelchairs as Assistive Technology: What a Special Educator Should Know. In I. Management Association (Ed.), *Assistive Technologies: Concepts, Methodologies, Tools, and Applications* (pp. 623-633). Hershey, PA: Information Science Reference. doi:10.4018/978-1-4666-4422-9.ch030

Casey, L. B., & Williamson, R. L. (2014). A Parent's Guide to Support Technologies for Preschool Students with Disabilities. In I. Management Association (Ed.), *Assistive Technologies: Concepts, Methodologies, Tools, and Applications* (pp. 1340-1356). Hershey, PA: Information Science Reference. doi:10.4018/978-1-4666-4422-9.ch071

Caviglione, L., Coccoli, M., & Merlo, A. (2013). On Social Network Engineering for Secure Web Data and Services. In L. Caviglione, M. Coccoli, & A. Merlo (Eds.), *Social Network Engineering for Secure Web Data and Services* (pp. 1–4). Hershey, PA: Information Science Reference; doi:10.4018/978-1-4666-3926-3.ch001

Chadwick, D. D., Fullwood, C., & Wesson, C. J. (2014). Intellectual Disability, Identity, and the Internet. In I. Management Association (Ed.), *Assistive Technologies: Concepts, Methodologies, Tools, and Applications* (pp. 198-223). Hershey, PA: Information Science Reference. doi:10.4018/978-1-4666-4422-9.ch011

Chao, L., Wen, Y., Chen, P., Lin, C., Lin, S., Guo, C., & Wang, W. (2012). The Development and Learning Effectiveness of a Teaching Module for the Algal Fuel Cell: A Renewable and Sustainable Battery. [IJTHI]. *International Journal of Technology and Human Interaction, 8*(4), 1–15. doi:10.4018/jthi.2012100101

Charnkit, P., & Tatnall, A. (2013). Knowledge Conversion Processes in Thai Public Organisations Seen as an Innovation: The Re-Analysis of a TAM Study Using Innovation Translation. In A. Tatnall (Ed.), *Social and Professional Applications of Actor-Network Theory for Technology Development* (pp. 88–102). Hershey, PA: Information Science Reference; doi:10.4018/978-1-4666-2166-4.ch008

Chen, E. T. (2014). Challenge and Complexity of Virtual Team Management. In E. Nikoi & K. Boateng (Eds.), *Collaborative Communication Processes and Decision Making in Organizations* (pp. 109–120). Hershey, PA: Business Science Reference; doi:10.4018/978-1-4666-4478-6.ch006

Chen, R., Xie, T., Lin, T., & Chen, Y. (2013). Adaptive Windows Layout Based on Evolutionary Multi-Objective Optimization. [IJTHI]. *International Journal of Technology and Human Interaction, 9*(3), 63–72. doi:10.4018/jthi.2013070105

Chen, W., Juang, Y., Chang, S., & Wang, P. (2012). Informal Education of Energy Conservation: Theory, Promotion, and Policy Implication. [IJTHI]. *International Journal of Technology and Human Interaction, 8*(4), 16–44. doi:10.4018/jthi.2012100102

Chino, T., Torii, K., Uchihira, N., & Hirabayashi, Y. (2013). Speech Interaction Analysis on Collaborative Work at an Elderly Care Facility. [IJSKD]. *International Journal of Sociotechnology and Knowledge Development, 5*(2), 18–33. doi:10.4018/jskd.2013040102

Chiu, M. (2013). Gaps Between Valuing and Purchasing Green-Technology Products: Product and Gender Differences. [IJTHI]. *International Journal of Technology and Human Interaction, 8*(3), 54–68. doi:10.4018/jthi.2012070106

Chivukula, V., & Shur, M. (2014). Web-Based Experimentation for Students with Learning Disabilities. In I. Management Association (Ed.), *Assistive Technologies: Concepts, Methodologies, Tools, and Applications* (pp. 1156-1172). Hershey, PA: Information Science Reference. doi:10.4018/978-1-4666-4422-9.ch060

Coakes, E., Bryant, A., Land, F., & Phippen, A. (2011). The Dark Side of Technology: Some Sociotechnical Reflections. [IJSKD]. *International Journal of Sociotechnology and Knowledge Development, 3*(4), 40–51. doi:10.4018/ijskd.2011100104

Cole, I. J. (2013). Usability of Online Virtual Learning Environments: Key Issues for Instructors and Learners. In C. Gonzalez (Ed.), *Student Usability in Educational Software and Games: Improving Experiences* (pp. 41–58). Hershey, PA: Information Science Reference; doi:10.4018/978-1-4666-1987-6.ch002

Colombo, B., Antonietti, A., Sala, R., & Caravita, S. C. (2013). Blog Content and Structure, Cognitive Style and Metacognition. [IJTHI]. *International Journal of Technology and Human Interaction, 9*(3), 1–17. doi:10.4018/jthi.2013070101

Constantinides, M. (2011). Integrating Technology on Initial Training Courses: A Survey Amongst CELTA Tutors. [IJCALLT]. *International Journal of Computer-Assisted Language Learning and Teaching, 1*(2), 55–71. doi:10.4018/ijcallt.2011040105

Cook, R. G., & Crawford, C. M. (2013). Addressing Online Student Learning Environments and Socialization Through Developmental Research. In M. Khosrow-Pour (Ed.), *Cases on Assessment and Evaluation in Education* (pp. 504–536). Hershey, PA: Information Science Reference; doi:10.4018/978-1-4666-2621-8.ch021

Corritore, C. L., Wiedenbeck, S., Kracher, B., & Marble, R. P. (2012). Online Trust and Health Information Websites. [IJTHI]. *International Journal of Technology and Human Interaction, 8*(4), 92–115. doi:10.4018/jthi.2012100106

Covarrubias, M., Bordegoni, M., Cugini, U., & Gatti, E. (2014). Supporting Unskilled People in Manual Tasks through Haptic-Based Guidance. In I. Management Association (Ed.), *Assistive Technologies: Concepts, Methodologies, Tools, and Applications* (pp. 947-969). Hershey, PA: Information Science Reference. doi:10.4018/978-1-4666-4422-9.ch048

Coverdale, T. S., & Wilbon, A. D. (2013). The Impact of In-Group Membership on e-Loyalty of Women Online Shoppers: An Application of the Social Identity Approach to Website Design. [IJEA]. *International Journal of E-Adoption, 5*(1), 17–36. doi:10.4018/jea.2013010102

Crabb, P. B., & Stern, S. E. (2012). Technology Traps: Who Is Responsible? In R. Luppicini (Ed.), *Ethical Impact of Technological Advancements and Applications in Society* (pp. 39–46). Hershey, PA: Information Science Reference; doi:10.4018/978-1-4666-1773-5.ch004

Crespo, R. G., Martíne, O. S., Lovelle, J. M., García-Bustelo, B. C., Díaz, V. G., & Ordoñez de Pablos, P. (2014). Improving Cognitive Load on Students with Disabilities through Software Aids. In I. Management Association (Ed.), *Assistive Technologies: Concepts, Methodologies, Tools, and Applications* (pp. 1255-1268). Hershey, PA: Information Science Reference. doi:10.4018/978-1-4666-4422-9.ch066

Croasdaile, S., Jones, S., Ligon, K., Oggel, L., & Pruett, M. (2014). Supports for and Barriers to Implementing Assistive Technology in Schools. In I. Management Association (Ed.), *Assistive Technologies: Concepts, Methodologies, Tools, and Applications* (pp. 1118-1130). Hershey, PA: Information Science Reference. doi:10.4018/978-1-4666-4422-9.ch058

Cucchiarini, C., & Strik, H. (2014). Second Language Learners' Spoken Discourse: Practice and Corrective Feedback through Automatic Speech Recognition. In H. Lim & F. Sudweeks (Eds.), *Innovative Methods and Technologies for Electronic Discourse Analysis* (pp. 169–189). Hershey, PA: Information Science Reference; doi:10.4018/978-1-4666-4426-7.ch008

Dafoulas, G. A., & Saleeb, N. (2014). 3D Assistive Technologies and Advantageous Themes for Collaboration and Blended Learning of Users with Disabilities. In I. Management Association (Ed.), *Assistive Technologies: Concepts, Methodologies, Tools, and Applications* (pp. 421-453). Hershey, PA: Information Science Reference. doi:10.4018/978-1-4666-4422-9.ch021

Dai, Z., & Paasch, K. (2013). A Web-Based Interactive Questionnaire for PV Application. [IJSKD]. *International Journal of Sociotechnology and Knowledge Development*, 5(2), 82–93. doi:10.4018/jskd.2013040106

Daradoumis, T., & Lafuente, M. M. (2014). Studying the Suitability of Discourse Analysis Methods for Emotion Detection and Interpretation in Computer-Mediated Educational Discourse. In H. Lim & F. Sudweeks (Eds.), *Innovative Methods and Technologies for Electronic Discourse Analysis* (pp. 119–143). Hershey, PA: Information Science Reference; doi:10.4018/978-1-4666-4426-7.ch006

Davis, B., & Mason, P. (2014). Positioning Goes to Work: Computer-Aided Identification of Stance Shifts and Semantic Themes in Electronic Discourse Analysis. In H. Lim & F. Sudweeks (Eds.), *Innovative Methods and Technologies for Electronic Discourse Analysis* (pp. 394–413). Hershey, PA: Information Science Reference; doi:10.4018/978-1-4666-4426-7.ch018

Dogoriti, E., & Pange, J. (2014). Considerations for Online English Language Learning: The Use of Facebook in Formal and Informal Settings in Higher Education. In G. Mallia (Ed.), *The Social Classroom: Integrating Social Network Use in Education* (pp. 147–170). Hershey, PA: Information Science Reference; doi:10.4018/978-1-4666-4904-0.ch008

Donegan, M. (2014). Features of Gaze Control Systems. In I. Management Association (Ed.), Assistive Technologies: Concepts, Methodologies, Tools, and Applications (pp. 1055-1061). Hershey, PA: Information Science Reference. doi:10.4018/978-1-4666-4422-9.ch054

Douglas, G., Morton, H., & Jack, M. (2012). Remote Channel Customer Contact Strategies for Complaint Update Messages. [IJTHI]. *International Journal of Technology and Human Interaction*, 8(2), 43–55. doi:10.4018/jthi.2012040103

Drake, J. R., & Byrd, T. A. (2013). Searching for Alternatives: Does Your Disposition Matter? [IJTHI]. *International Journal of Technology and Human Interaction*, 9(1), 18–36. doi:10.4018/jthi.2013010102

Driouchi, A. (2013). ICTs and Socioeconomic Performance with Focus on ICTs and Health. In ICTs for Health, Education, and Socioeconomic Policies: Regional Cases (pp. 104-125). Hershey, PA: Information Science Reference. doi:10.4018/978-1-4666-3643-9.ch005

Driouchi, A. (2013). Social Deficits, Social Cohesion, and Prospects from ICTs. In ICTs for Health, Education, and Socioeconomic Policies: Regional Cases (pp. 230-251). Hershey, PA: Information Science Reference. doi:10.4018/978-1-4666-3643-9.ch011

Driouchi, A. (2013). Socioeconomic Reforms, Human Development, and the Millennium Development Goals with ICTs for Coordination. In ICTs for Health, Education, and Socioeconomic Policies: Regional Cases (pp. 211-229). Hershey, PA: Information Science Reference. doi:10.4018/978-1-4666-3643-9.ch010

Drula, G. (2013). Media and Communication Research Facing Social Media. In M. Pătruţ & B. Pătruţ (Eds.), *Social Media in Higher Education: Teaching in Web 2.0* (pp. 371–392). Hershey, PA: Information Science Reference; doi:10.4018/978-1-4666-2970-7.ch019

Druzhinina, O., Hvannberg, E. T., & Halldorsdottir, G. (2013). Feedback Fidelities in Three Different Types of Crisis Management Training Environments. [IJSKD]. *International Journal of Sociotechnology and Knowledge Development*, 5(2), 45–62. doi:10.4018/jskd.2013040104

Eason, K., Waterson, P., & Davda, P. (2013). The Sociotechnical Challenge of Integrating Telehealth and Telecare into Health and Social Care for the Elderly. [IJSKD]. *International Journal of Sociotechnology and Knowledge Development*, 5(4), 14–26. doi:10.4018/ijskd.2013100102

Edenius, M., & Rämö, H. (2011). An Office on the Go: Professional Workers, Smartphones and the Return of Place. [IJTHI]. *International Journal of Technology and Human Interaction*, 7(1), 37–55. doi:10.4018/jthi.2011010103

Eke, D. O. (2011). ICT Integration in Nigeria: The Socio-Cultural Constraints. [IJTHI]. *International Journal of Technology and Human Interaction*, 7(2), 21–27. doi:10.4018/jthi.2011040103

Evett, L., Ridley, A., Keating, L., Merritt, P., Shopland, N., & Brown, D. (2014). Designing Serious Games for People with Disabilities: Game, Set, and Match to the Wii. In J. Bishop (Ed.), *Gamification for Human Factors Integration: Social, Education, and Psychological Issues* (pp. 97–105). Hershey, PA: Information Science Reference; doi:10.4018/978-1-4666-5071-8.ch006

Evmenova, A. S., & Behrmann, M. M. (2014). Communication Technology Integration in the Content Areas for Students with High-Incidence Disabilities: A Case Study of One School System. In I. Management Association (Ed.), Assistive Technologies: Concepts, Methodologies, Tools, and Applications (pp. 26-53). Hershey, PA: Information Science Reference. doi:10.4018/978-1-4666-4422-9.ch003

Evmenova, A. S., & King-Sears, M. E. (2014). Technology and Literacy for Students with Disabilities. In I. Management Association (Ed.), Assistive Technologies: Concepts, Methodologies, Tools, and Applications (pp. 1269-1291). Hershey, PA: Information Science Reference. doi:10.4018/978-1-4666-4422-9.ch067

Ewais, A., & De Troyer, O. (2013). Usability Evaluation of an Adaptive 3D Virtual Learning Environment. [IJVPLE]. *International Journal of Virtual and Personal Learning Environments*, 4(1), 16–31. doi:10.4018/jvple.2013010102

Farrell, H. J. (2014). The Student with Complex Education Needs: Assistive and Augmentative Information and Communication Technology in a Ten-Week Music Program. In I. Management Association (Ed.), K-12 Education: Concepts, Methodologies, Tools, and Applications (pp. 1436-1472). Hershey, PA: Information Science Reference. doi:10.4018/978-1-4666-4502-8.ch084

Fathulla, K. (2012). Rethinking Human and Society's Relationship with Technology. [IJSKD]. *International Journal of Sociotechnology and Knowledge Development*, 4(2), 21–28. doi:10.4018/jskd.2012040103

Fidler, C. S., Kanaan, R. K., & Rogerson, S. (2011). Barriers to e-Government Implementation in Jordan: The Role of Wasta. [IJTHI]. *International Journal of Technology and Human Interaction*, 7(2), 9–20. doi:10.4018/jthi.2011040102

Fischer, G., & Herrmann, T. (2013). Socio-Technical Systems: A Meta-Design Perspective. In J. Abdelnour-Nocera (Ed.), *Knowledge and Technological Development Effects on Organizational and Social Structures* (pp. 1–36). Hershey, PA: Information Science Reference; doi:10.4018/978-1-4666-2151-0.ch001

Foreman, J., & Borkman, T. (2014). Learning Sociology in a Massively Multi-Student Online Learning Environment. In J. Bishop (Ed.), *Gamification for Human Factors Integration: Social, Education, and Psychological Issues* (pp. 216–224). Hershey, PA: Information Science Reference; doi:10.4018/978-1-4666-5071-8.ch013

Fornaciari, F. (2013). The Language of Technoself: Storytelling, Symbolic Interactionism, and Online Identity. In R. Luppicini (Ed.), *Handbook of Research on Technoself: Identity in a Technological Society* (pp. 64–83). Hershey, PA: Information Science Reference; doi:10.4018/978-1-4666-2211-1.ch004

Fox, J., & Ahn, S. J. (2013). Avatars: Portraying, Exploring, and Changing Online and Offline Identities. In R. Luppicini (Ed.), *Handbook of Research on Technoself: Identity in a Technological Society* (pp. 255–271). Hershey, PA: Information Science Reference; doi:10.4018/978-1-4666-2211-1.ch014

Fox, W. P., Binstock, J., & Minutas, M. (2013). Modeling and Methodology for Incorporating Existing Technologies to Produce Higher Probabilities of Detecting Suicide Bombers. [IJORIS]. *International Journal of Operations Research and Information Systems*, 4(3), 1–18. doi:10.4018/joris.2013070101

Franchi, E., & Tomaiuolo, M. (2013). Distributed Social Platforms for Confidentiality and Resilience. In L. Caviglione, M. Coccoli, & A. Merlo (Eds.), *Social Network Engineering for Secure Web Data and Services* (pp. 114–136). Hershey, PA: Information Science Reference; doi:10.4018/978-1-4666-3926-3.ch006

Frigo, C. A., & Pavan, E. E. (2014). Prosthetic and Orthotic Devices. In I. Management Association (Ed.), *Assistive Technologies: Concepts, Methodologies, Tools, and Applications* (pp. 549-613). Hershey, PA: Information Science Reference. doi:10.4018/978-1-4666-4422-9.ch028

Fuhrer, C., & Cucchi, A. (2012). Relations Between Social Capital and Use of ICT: A Social Network Analysis Approach. [IJTHI]. *International Journal of Technology and Human Interaction*, 8(2), 15–42. doi:10.4018/jthi.2012040102

Galinski, C., & Beckmann, H. (2014). Concepts for Enhancing Content Quality and eAccessibility: In General and in the Field of eProcurement. In I. Management Association (Ed.), *Assistive Technologies: Concepts, Methodologies, Tools, and Applications* (pp. 180-197). Hershey, PA: Information Science Reference. doi:10.4018/978-1-4666-4422-9.ch010

Galván, J. M., & Luppicini, R. (2012). The Humanity of the Human Body: Is Homo Cybersapien a New Species? [IJT]. *International Journal of Technoethics*, 3(2), 1–8. doi:10.4018/jte.2012040101

García-Gómez, A. (2013). Technoself-Presentation on Social Networks: A Gender-Based Approach. In R. Luppicini (Ed.), *Handbook of Research on Technoself: Identity in a Technological Society* (pp. 382–398). Hershey, PA: Information Science Reference; doi:10.4018/978-1-4666-2211-1.ch021

Gill, L., Hathway, E. A., Lange, E., Morgan, E., & Romano, D. (2013). Coupling Real-Time 3D Landscape Models with Microclimate Simulations. [IJEPR]. *International Journal of E-Planning Research*, 2(1), 1–19. doi:10.4018/ijepr.2013010101

Godé, C., & Lebraty, J. (2013). Improving Decision Making in Extreme Situations: The Case of a Military Decision Support System. [IJTHI]. *International Journal of Technology and Human Interaction*, 9(1), 1–17. doi:10.4018/jthi.2013010101

Griol, D., Callejas, Z., & López-Cózar, R. (2014). Conversational Metabots for Educational Applications in Virtual Worlds. In I. Management Association (Ed.), Assistive Technologies: Concepts, Methodologies, Tools, and Applications (pp. 1405-1433). Hershey, PA: Information Science Reference. doi:10.4018/978-1-4666-4422-9.ch074

Griol Barres, D., Callejas Carrión, Z., Molina López, J. M., & Sanchis de Miguel, A. (2014). Towards the Use of Dialog Systems to Facilitate Inclusive Education. In I. Management Association (Ed.), Assistive Technologies: Concepts, Methodologies, Tools, and Applications (pp. 1292-1312). Hershey, PA: Information Science Reference. doi:10.4018/978-1-4666-4422-9.ch068

Groba, B., Pousada, T., & Nieto, L. (2014). Assistive Technologies, Tools and Resources for the Access and Use of Information and Communication Technologies by People with Disabilities. In I. Management Association (Ed.), Assistive Technologies: Concepts, Methodologies, Tools, and Applications (pp. 246-260). Hershey, PA: Information Science Reference. doi:10.4018/978-1-4666-4422-9.ch013

Groß, M. (2013). Personal Knowledge Management and Social Media: What Students Need to Learn for Business Life. In M. Pătruţ & B. Pătruţ (Eds.), *Social Media in Higher Education: Teaching in Web 2.0* (pp. 124–143). Hershey, PA: Information Science Reference; doi:10.4018/978-1-4666-2970-7.ch007

Gu, L., Aiken, M., Wang, J., & Wibowo, K. (2011). The Influence of Information Control upon Online Shopping Behavior. [IJTHI]. *International Journal of Technology and Human Interaction*, 7(1), 56–66. doi:10.4018/jthi.2011010104

Hainz, T. (2012). Value Lexicality and Human Enhancement. [IJT]. *International Journal of Technoethics*, 3(4), 54–65. doi:10.4018/jte.2012100105

Harnesk, D., & Lindström, J. (2014). Exploring Socio-Technical Design of Crisis Management Information Systems. In I. Management Association (Ed.), Crisis Management: Concepts, Methodologies, Tools and Applications (pp. 514-530). Hershey, PA: Information Science Reference. doi:10.4018/978-1-4666-4707-7.ch023

Hicks, D. (2014). Ethics in the Age of Technological Change and its Impact on the Professional Identity of Librarians. In *Technology and Professional Identity of Librarians: The Making of the Cybrarian* (pp. 168–187). Hershey, PA: Information Science Reference; doi:10.4018/978-1-4666-4735-0.ch009

Hicks, D. (2014). Technology, Profession, Identity. In *Technology and Professional Identity of Librarians: The Making of the Cybrarian* (pp. 1–20). Hershey, PA: Information Science Reference; doi:10.4018/978-1-4666-4735-0.ch001

Hirata, M., Yanagisawa, T., Matsushita, K., Sugata, H., Kamitani, Y., Suzuki, T., . . . Yoshimine, T. (2014). Brain-Machine Interface Using Brain Surface Electrodes: Real-Time Robotic Control and a Fully Implantable Wireless System. In I. Management Association (Ed.), *Assistive Technologies: Concepts, Methodologies, Tools, and Applications* (pp. 1535-1548). Hershey, PA: Information Science Reference. doi:10.4018/978-1-4666-4422-9.ch080

Hodge, B. (2014). Critical Electronic Discourse Analysis: Social and Cultural Research in the Electronic Age. In H. Lim & F. Sudweeks (Eds.), *Innovative Methods and Technologies for Electronic Discourse Analysis* (pp. 191–209). Hershey, PA: Information Science Reference; doi:10.4018/978-1-4666-4426-7.ch009

Hoey, J., Poupart, P., Boutilier, C., & Mihailidis, A. (2014). POMDP Models for Assistive Technology. In I. Management Association (Ed.), *Assistive Technologies: Concepts, Methodologies, Tools, and Applications* (pp. 120-140). Hershey, PA: Information Science Reference. doi:10.4018/978-1-4666-4422-9.ch007

Hogg, S. (2014). An Informal Use of Facebook to Encourage Student Collaboration and Motivation for Off Campus Activities. In G. Mallia (Ed.), *The Social Classroom: Integrating Social Network Use in Education* (pp. 23–39). Hershey, PA: Information Science Reference; doi:10.4018/978-1-4666-4904-0.ch002

Holmqvist, E., & Buchholz, M. (2014). A Model for Gaze Control Assessments and Evaluation. In I. Management Association (Ed.), *Assistive Technologies: Concepts, Methodologies, Tools, and Applications* (pp. 332-343). Hershey, PA: Information Science Reference. doi:10.4018/978-1-4666-4422-9.ch016

Hsiao, S., Chen, D., Yang, C., Huang, H., Lu, Y., Huang, H., & Lin, Y. et al. (2013). Chemical-Free and Reusable Cellular Analysis: Electrochemical Impedance Spectroscopy with a Transparent ITO Culture Chip. [IJTHI]. *International Journal of Technology and Human Interaction, 8*(3), 1–9. doi:10.4018/jthi.2012070101

Hsu, M., Yang, C., Wang, C., & Lin, Y. (2013). Simulation-Aided Optimal Microfluidic Sorting for Monodispersed Microparticles. [IJTHI]. *International Journal of Technology and Human Interaction, 8*(3), 10–18. doi:10.4018/jthi.2012070102

Huang, W. D., & Tettegah, S. Y. (2014). Cognitive Load and Empathy in Serious Games: A Conceptual Framework. In J. Bishop (Ed.), *Gamification for Human Factors Integration: Social, Education, and Psychological Issues* (pp. 17–30). Hershey, PA: Information Science Reference; doi:10.4018/978-1-4666-5071-8.ch002

Huseyinov, I. N. (2014). Fuzzy Linguistic Modelling in Multi Modal Human Computer Interaction: Adaptation to Cognitive Styles using Multi Level Fuzzy Granulation Method. In I. Management Association (Ed.), *Assistive Technologies: Concepts, Methodologies, Tools, and Applications* (pp. 1481-1496). Hershey, PA: Information Science Reference. doi:10.4018/978-1-4666-4422-9.ch077

Hwa, S. P., Weei, P. S., & Len, L. H. (2012). The Effects of Blended Learning Approach through an Interactive Multimedia E-Book on Students' Achievement in Learning Chinese as a Second Language at Tertiary Level. [IJCALLT]. *International Journal of Computer-Assisted Language Learning and Teaching, 2*(1), 35–50. doi:10.4018/ijcallt.2012010104

Iglesias, A., Ruiz-Mezcua, B., López, J. F., & Figueroa, D. C. (2014). New Communication Technologies for Inclusive Education in and outside the Classroom. In I. Management Association (Ed.), *Assistive Technologies: Concepts, Methodologies, Tools, and Applications* (pp. 1675-1689). Hershey, PA: Information Science Reference. doi:10.4018/978-1-4666-4422-9.ch088

Inghilterra, X., & Ravatua-Smith, W. S. (2014). Online Learning Communities: Use of Micro Blogging for Knowledge Construction. In J. Pelet (Ed.), *E-Learning 2.0 Technologies and Web Applications in Higher Education* (pp. 107–128). Hershey, PA: Information Science Reference; doi:10.4018/978-1-4666-4876-0.ch006

Ionescu, A. (2013). Cyber Identity: Our Alter-Ego? In R. Luppicini (Ed.), *Handbook of Research on Technoself: Identity in a Technological Society* (pp. 189–203). Hershey, PA: Information Science Reference; doi:10.4018/978-1-4666-2211-1.ch011

Jan, Y., Lin, M., Shiao, K., Wei, C., Huang, L., & Sung, Q. (2013). Development of an Evaluation Instrument for Green Building Literacy among College Students in Taiwan. [IJTHI]. *International Journal of Technology and Human Interaction*, *8*(3), 31–45. doi:10.4018/jthi.2012070104

Jawadi, N. (2013). E-Leadership and Trust Management: Exploring the Moderating Effects of Team Virtuality. [IJTHI]. *International Journal of Technology and Human Interaction*, *9*(3), 18–35. doi:10.4018/jthi.2013070102

Jiménez-Castillo, D., & Fernández, R. S. (2014). The Impact of Combining Video Podcasting and Lectures on Students' Assimilation of Additional Knowledge: An Empirical Examination. In J. Pelet (Ed.), *E-Learning 2.0 Technologies and Web Applications in Higher Education* (pp. 65–87). Hershey, PA: Information Science Reference; doi:10.4018/978-1-4666-4876-0.ch004

Jin, L. (2013). A New Trend in Education: Technoself Enhanced Social Learning. In R. Luppicini (Ed.), *Handbook of Research on Technoself: Identity in a Technological Society* (pp. 456–473). Hershey, PA: Information Science Reference; doi:10.4018/978-1-4666-2211-1.ch025

Johansson, L. (2012). The Functional Morality of Robots. In R. Luppicini (Ed.), *Ethical Impact of Technological Advancements and Applications in Society* (pp. 254–262). Hershey, PA: Information Science Reference; doi:10.4018/978-1-4666-1773-5.ch020

Johansson, L. (2013). Robots and the Ethics of Care. [IJT]. *International Journal of Technoethics*, *4*(1), 67–82. doi:10.4018/jte.2013010106

Johri, A., Dufour, M., Lo, J., & Shanahan, D. (2013). Adwiki: Socio-Technical Design for Mananging Advising Knowledge in a Higher Education Context. [IJSKD]. *International Journal of Sociotechnology and Knowledge Development*, *5*(1), 37–59. doi:10.4018/jskd.2013010104

Jones, M. G., Schwilk, C. L., & Bateman, D. F. (2014). Reading by Listening: Access to Books in Audio Format for College Students with Print Disabilities. In I. Management Association (Ed.), *Assistive Technologies: Concepts, Methodologies, Tools, and Applications* (pp. 454-477). Hershey, PA: Information Science Reference. doi:10.4018/978-1-4666-4422-9.ch022

Kaba, B., & Osei-Bryson, K. (2012). An Empirical Investigation of External Factors Influencing Mobile Technology Use in Canada: A Preliminary Study. [IJTHI]. *International Journal of Technology and Human Interaction*, *8*(2), 1–14. doi:10.4018/jthi.2012040101

Kampf, C. E. (2012). Revealing the Socio-Technical Design of Global E-Businesses: A Case of Digital Artists Engaging in Radical Transparency. [IJSKD]. *International Journal of Sociotechnology and Knowledge Development*, *4*(4), 18–31. doi:10.4018/jskd.2012100102

Kandroudi, M., & Bratitsis, T. (2014). Classifying Facebook Usage in the Classroom or Around It. In G. Mallia (Ed.), *The Social Classroom: Integrating Social Network Use in Education* (pp. 62–81). Hershey, PA: Information Science Reference; doi:10.4018/978-1-4666-4904-0.ch004

Kidd, P. T. (2014). Social Networking Technologies as a Strategic Tool for the Development of Sustainable Production and Consumption: Applications to Foster the Agility Needed to Adapt Business Models in Response to the Challenges Posed by Climate Change. In I. Management Association (Ed.), Sustainable Practices: Concepts, Methodologies, Tools and Applications (pp. 974-987). Hershey, PA: Information Science Reference. doi:10.4018/978-1-4666-4852-4.ch054

Kirby, S. D., & Sellers, D. M. (2014). The Live-Ability House: A Collaborative Adventure in Discovery Learning. In I. Management Association (Ed.), Assistive Technologies: Concepts, Methodologies, Tools, and Applications (pp. 1626-1649). Hershey, PA: Information Science Reference. doi:10.4018/978-1-4666-4422-9.ch086

Kitchenham, A., & Bowes, D. (2014). Voice/Speech Recognition Software: A Discussion of the Promise for Success and Practical Suggestions for Implementation. In I. Management Association (Ed.), Assistive Technologies: Concepts, Methodologies, Tools, and Applications (pp. 1005-1011). Hershey, PA: Information Science Reference. doi:10.4018/978-1-4666-4422-9.ch051

Konrath, S. (2013). The Empathy Paradox: Increasing Disconnection in the Age of Increasing Connection. In R. Luppicini (Ed.), *Handbook of Research on Technoself: Identity in a Technological Society* (pp. 204–228). Hershey, PA: Information Science Reference; doi:10.4018/978-1-4666-2211-1.ch012

Koutsabasis, P., & Istikopoulou, T. G. (2013). Perceived Website Aesthetics by Users and Designers: Implications for Evaluation Practice. [IJTHI]. *International Journal of Technology and Human Interaction*, 9(2), 39–52. doi:10.4018/jthi.2013040103

Kraft, E., & Wang, J. (2012). An Exploratory Study of the Cyberbullying and Cyberstalking Experiences and Factors Related to Victimization of Students at a Public Liberal Arts College. In R. Luppicini (Ed.), *Ethical Impact of Technological Advancements and Applications in Society* (pp. 113–131). Hershey, PA: Information Science Reference; doi:10.4018/978-1-4666-1773-5.ch009

Kulman, R., Stoner, G., Ruffolo, L., Marshall, S., Slater, J., Dyl, A., & Cheng, A. (2014). Teaching Executive Functions, Self-Management, and Ethical Decision-Making through Popular Videogame Play. In I. Management Association (Ed.), Assistive Technologies: Concepts, Methodologies, Tools, and Applications (pp. 771-785). Hershey, PA: Information Science Reference. doi:10.4018/978-1-4666-4422-9.ch039

Kunc, L., Míkovec, Z., & Slavík, P. (2013). Avatar and Dialog Turn-Yielding Phenomena. [IJTHI]. *International Journal of Technology and Human Interaction*, 9(2), 66–88. doi:10.4018/jthi.2013040105

Kuo, N., & Dai, Y. (2012). Applying the Theory of Planned Behavior to Predict Low-Carbon Tourism Behavior: A Modified Model from Taiwan. [IJTHI]. *International Journal of Technology and Human Interaction*, 8(4), 45–62. doi:10.4018/jthi.2012100103

Kurt, S. (2014). Accessibility Issues of Educational Web Sites. In I. Management Association (Ed.), Assistive Technologies: Concepts, Methodologies, Tools, and Applications (pp. 54-62). Hershey, PA: Information Science Reference. doi:10.4018/978-1-4666-4422-9.ch004

Kuzma, J. (2013). Empirical Study of Cyber Harassment among Social Networks. [IJTHI]. *International Journal of Technology and Human Interaction*, 9(2), 53–65. doi:10.4018/jthi.2013040104

Kyriakaki, G., & Matsatsinis, N. (2014). Pedagogical Evaluation of E-Learning Websites with Cognitive Objectives. In D. Yannacopoulos, P. Manolitzas, N. Matsatsinis, & E. Grigoroudis (Eds.), *Evaluating Websites and Web Services: Interdisciplinary Perspectives on User Satisfaction* (pp. 224–240). Hershey, PA: Information Science Reference; doi:10.4018/978-1-4666-5129-6.ch013

Lee, H., & Baek, E. (2012). Facilitating Deep Learning in a Learning Community. [IJTHI]. *International Journal of Technology and Human Interaction*, 8(1), 1–13. doi:10.4018/jthi.2012010101

Lee, W., Wu, T., Cheng, Y., Chuang, Y., & Sheu, S. (2013). Using the Kalman Filter for Auto Bit-rate H.264 Streaming Based on Human Interaction. [IJTHI]. *International Journal of Technology and Human Interaction*, 9(4), 58–74. doi:10.4018/ijthi.2013100104

Li, Y., Guo, N. Y., & Ranieri, M. (2014). Designing an Online Interactive Learning Program to Improve Chinese Migrant Children's Internet Skills: A Case Study at Hangzhou Minzhu Experimental School. In Z. Yang, H. Yang, D. Wu, & S. Liu (Eds.), *Transforming K-12 Classrooms with Digital Technology* (pp. 249–265). Hershey, PA: Information Science Reference; doi:10.4018/978-1-4666-4538-7.ch013

Lin, C., Chu, L., & Hsu, H. (2013). Study on the Performance and Exhaust Emissions of Motorcycle Engine Fuelled with Hydrogen-Gasoline Compound Fuel. [IJTHI]. *International Journal of Technology and Human Interaction*, 8(3), 69–81. doi:10.4018/jthi.2012070107

Lin, L. (2013). Multiple Dimensions of Multitasking Phenomenon. [IJTHI]. *International Journal of Technology and Human Interaction*, 9(1), 37–49. doi:10.4018/jthi.2013010103

Lin, T., Li, X., Wu, Z., & Tang, N. (2013). Automatic Cognitive Load Classification Using High-Frequency Interaction Events: An Exploratory Study. [IJTHI]. *International Journal of Technology and Human Interaction*, 9(3), 73–88. doi:10.4018/jthi.2013070106

Lin, T., Wu, Z., Tang, N., & Wu, S. (2013). Exploring the Effects of Display Characteristics on Presence and Emotional Responses of Game Players. [IJTHI]. *International Journal of Technology and Human Interaction*, 9(1), 50–63. doi:10.4018/jthi.2013010104

Lin, T., Xie, T., Mou, Y., & Tang, N. (2013). Markov Chain Models for Menu Item Prediction. [IJTHI]. *International Journal of Technology and Human Interaction*, 9(4), 75–94. doi:10.4018/ijthi.2013100105

Lin, X., & Luppicini, R. (2011). Socio-Technical Influences of Cyber Espionage: A Case Study of the GhostNet System. [IJT]. *International Journal of Technoethics*, 2(2), 65–77. doi:10.4018/jte.2011040105

Linek, S. B., Marte, B., & Albert, D. (2014). Background Music in Educational Games: Motivational Appeal and Cognitive Impact. In J. Bishop (Ed.), *Gamification for Human Factors Integration: Social, Education, and Psychological Issues* (pp. 259–271). Hershey, PA: Information Science Reference; doi:10.4018/978-1-4666-5071-8.ch016

Lipschutz, R. D., & Hester, R. J. (2014). We Are the Borg! Human Assimilation into Cellular Society. In M. Michael & K. Michael (Eds.), *Uberveillance and the Social Implications of Microchip Implants: Emerging Technologies* (pp. 366–407). Hershey, PA: Information Science Reference; doi:10.4018/978-1-4666-4582-0.ch016

Liu, C., Zhong, Y., Ozercan, S., & Zhu, Q. (2013). Facilitating 3D Virtual World Learning Environments Creation by Non-Technical End Users through Template-Based Virtual World Instantiation. [IJVPLE]. *International Journal of Virtual and Personal Learning Environments*, *4*(1), 32–48. doi:10.4018/jvple.2013010103

Liu, F., Lo, H., Su, C., Lou, D., & Lee, W. (2013). High Performance Reversible Data Hiding for Mobile Applications and Human Interaction. [IJTHI]. *International Journal of Technology and Human Interaction*, *9*(4), 41–57. doi:10.4018/ijthi.2013100103

Liu, H. (2012). From Cold War Island to Low Carbon Island: A Study of Kinmen Island. [IJTHI]. *International Journal of Technology and Human Interaction*, *8*(4), 63–74. doi:10.4018/jthi.2012100104

Lixun, Z., Dapeng, B., & Lei, Y. (2014). Design of and Experimentation with a Walking Assistance Robot. In I. Management Association (Ed.), Assistive Technologies: Concepts, Methodologies, Tools, and Applications (pp. 1600-1605). Hershey, PA: Information Science Reference. doi:10.4018/978-1-4666-4422-9.ch084

Low, R., Jin, P., & Sweller, J. (2014). Instructional Design in Digital Environments and Availability of Mental Resources for the Aged Subpopulation. In I. Management Association (Ed.), Assistive Technologies: Concepts, Methodologies, Tools, and Applications (pp. 1131-1154). Hershey, PA: Information Science Reference. doi:10.4018/978-1-4666-4422-9.ch059

Luczak, H., Schlick, C. M., Jochems, N., Vetter, S., & Kausch, B. (2014). Touch Screens for the Elderly: Some Models and Methods, Prototypical Development and Experimental Evaluation of Human-Computer Interaction Concepts for the Elderly. In I. Management Association (Ed.), Assistive Technologies: Concepts, Methodologies, Tools, and Applications (pp. 377-396). Hershey, PA: Information Science Reference. doi:10.4018/978-1-4666-4422-9.ch019

Luor, T., Lu, H., Johanson, R. E., & Yu, H. (2012). Minding the Gap Between First and Continued Usage of a Corporate E-Learning English-language Program. [IJTHI]. *International Journal of Technology and Human Interaction*, *8*(1), 55–74. doi:10.4018/jthi.2012010104

Luppicini, R. (2013). The Emerging Field of Technoself Studies (TSS). In R. Luppicini (Ed.), *Handbook of Research on Technoself: Identity in a Technological Society* (pp. 1–25). Hershey, PA: Information Science Reference; doi:10.4018/978-1-4666-2211-1.ch001

Magnani, L. (2012). Material Cultures and Moral Mediators in Human Hybridization. In R. Luppicini (Ed.), *Ethical Impact of Technological Advancements and Applications in Society* (pp. 1–20). Hershey, PA: Information Science Reference; doi:10.4018/978-1-4666-1773-5.ch001

Maher, D. (2014). Learning in the Primary School Classroom using the Interactive Whiteboard. In I. Management Association (Ed.), K-12 Education: Concepts, Methodologies, Tools, and Applications (pp. 526-538). Hershey, PA: Information Science Reference. doi:10.4018/978-1-4666-4502-8.ch031

Manolache, M., & Patrut, M. (2013). The Use of New Web-Based Technologies in Strategies of Teaching Gender Studies. In M. Pătruţ & B. Pătruţ (Eds.), *Social Media in Higher Education: Teaching in Web 2.0* (pp. 45–74). Hershey, PA: Information Science Reference; doi:10.4018/978-1-4666-2970-7.ch003

Manthiou, A., & Chiang, L., & Liang (Rebecca) Tang. (2013). Identifying and Responding to Customer Needs on Facebook Fan Pages. [IJTHI]. *International Journal of Technology and Human Interaction*, 9(3), 36–52. doi:10.4018/jthi.2013070103

Marengo, A., Pagano, A., & Barbone, A. (2013). An Assessment of Customer's Preferences and Improve Brand Awareness Implementation of Social CRM in an Automotive Company. [IJTD]. *International Journal of Technology Diffusion*, 4(1), 1–15. doi:10.4018/jtd.2013010101

Martin, I., Kear, K., Simpkins, N., & Busvine, J. (2013). Social Negotiations in Web Usability Engineering. In M. Garcia-Ruiz (Ed.), *Cases on Usability Engineering: Design and Development of Digital Products* (pp. 26–56). Hershey, PA: Information Science Reference; doi:10.4018/978-1-4666-4046-7.ch002

Martins, T., Carvalho, V., & Soares, F. (2014). An Overview on the Use of Serious Games in Physical Therapy and Rehabilitation. In I. Management Association (Ed.), Assistive Technologies: Concepts, Methodologies, Tools, and Applications (pp. 758-770). Hershey, PA: Information Science Reference. doi:10.4018/978-1-4666-4422-9.ch038

Mathew, D. (2013). Online Anxiety: Implications for Educational Design in a Web 2.0 World. In M. Pătruţ & B. Pătruţ (Eds.), *Social Media in Higher Education: Teaching in Web 2.0* (pp. 305–317). Hershey, PA: Information Science Reference; doi:10.4018/978-1-4666-2970-7.ch015

Mazzanti, I., Maolo, A., & Antonicelli, R. (2014). E-Health and Telemedicine in the Elderly: State of the Art. In I. Management Association (Ed.), Assistive Technologies: Concepts, Methodologies, Tools, and Applications (pp. 693-704). Hershey, PA: Information Science Reference. doi:10.4018/978-1-4666-4422-9.ch034

Mazzara, M., Biselli, L., Greco, P. P., Dragoni, N., Marraffa, A., Qamar, N., & de Nicola, S. (2013). Social Networks and Collective Intelligence: A Return to the Agora. In L. Caviglione, M. Coccoli, & A. Merlo (Eds.), *Social Network Engineering for Secure Web Data and Services* (pp. 88–113). Hershey, PA: Information Science Reference; doi:10.4018/978-1-4666-3926-3.ch005

McColl, D., & Nejat, G. (2013). A Human Affect Recognition System for Socially Interactive Robots. In R. Luppicini (Ed.), *Handbook of Research on Technoself: Identity in a Technological Society* (pp. 554–573). Hershey, PA: Information Science Reference; doi:10.4018/978-1-4666-2211-1.ch029

McDonald, A., & Helmer, S. (2011). A Comparative Case Study of Indonesian and UK Organisational Culture Differences in IS Project Management. [IJTHI]. *International Journal of Technology and Human Interaction*, 7(2), 28–37. doi:10.4018/jthi.2011040104

McGee, E. M. (2014). Neuroethics and Implanted Brain Machine Interfaces. In M. Michael & K. Michael (Eds.), *Uberveillance and the Social Implications of Microchip Implants: Emerging Technologies* (pp. 351–365). Hershey, PA: Information Science Reference; doi:10.4018/978-1-4666-4582-0.ch015

McGrath, E., Lowes, S., McKay, M., Sayres, J., & Lin, P. (2014). Robots Underwater! Learning Science, Engineering and 21st Century Skills: The Evolution of Curricula, Professional Development and Research in Formal and Informal Contexts. In I. Management Association (Ed.), *K-12 Education: Concepts, Methodologies, Tools, and Applications* (pp. 1041-1067). Hershey, PA: Information Science Reference. doi:10.4018/978-1-4666-4502-8.ch062

Meissonierm, R., Bourdon, I., Amabile, S., & Boudrandi, S. (2012). Toward an Enacted Approach to Understanding OSS Developer's Motivations. [IJTHI]. *International Journal of Technology and Human Interaction*, *8*(1), 38–54. doi:10.4018/jthi.2012010103

Melius, J. (2014). The Role of Social Constructivist Instructional Approaches in Facilitating Cross-Cultural Online Learning in Higher Education. In J. Keengwe, G. Schnellert, & K. Kungu (Eds.), *Cross-Cultural Online Learning in Higher Education and Corporate Training* (pp. 253–270). Hershey, PA: Information Science Reference; doi:10.4018/978-1-4666-5023-7.ch015

Melson, G. F. (2013). Building a Technoself: Children's Ideas about and Behavior toward Robotic Pets. In R. Luppicini (Ed.), *Handbook of Research on Technoself: Identity in a Technological Society* (pp. 592–608). Hershey, PA: Information Science Reference; doi:10.4018/978-1-4666-2211-1.ch031

Mena, R. J. (2014). The Quest for a Massively Multiplayer Online Game that Teaches Physics. In T. Connolly, T. Hainey, E. Boyle, G. Baxter, & P. Moreno-Ger (Eds.), *Psychology, Pedagogy, and Assessment in Serious Games* (pp. 292–316). Hershey, PA: Information Science Reference; doi:10.4018/978-1-4666-4773-2.ch014

Meredith, J., & Potter, J. (2014). Conversation Analysis and Electronic Interactions: Methodological, Analytic and Technical Considerations. In H. Lim & F. Sudweeks (Eds.), *Innovative Methods and Technologies for Electronic Discourse Analysis* (pp. 370–393). Hershey, PA: Information Science Reference; doi:10.4018/978-1-4666-4426-7.ch017

Millán-Calenti, J. C., & Maseda, A. (2014). Telegerontology®: A New Technological Resource for Elderly Support. In I. Management Association (Ed.), Assistive Technologies: Concepts, Methodologies, Tools, and Applications (pp. 705-719). Hershey, PA: Information Science Reference. doi:10.4018/978-1-4666-4422-9.ch035

Miscione, G. (2011). Telemedicine and Development: Situating Information Technologies in the Amazon. [IJSKD]. *International Journal of Sociotechnology and Knowledge Development*, *3*(4), 15–26. doi:10.4018/jskd.2011100102

Miwa, N., & Wang, Y. (2011). Online Interaction Between On-Campus and Distance Students: Learners' Perspectives. [IJCALLT]. *International Journal of Computer-Assisted Language Learning and Teaching*, *1*(3), 54–69. doi:10.4018/ijcallt.2011070104

Moore, M. J., Nakano, T., Suda, T., & Enomoto, A. (2013). Social Interactions and Automated Detection Tools in Cyberbullying. In L. Caviglione, M. Coccoli, & A. Merlo (Eds.), *Social Network Engineering for Secure Web Data and Services* (pp. 67–87). Hershey, PA: Information Science Reference; doi:10.4018/978-1-4666-3926-3.ch004

Morueta, R. T., Gómez, J. I., & Gómez, Á. H. (2012). B-Learning at Universities in Andalusia (Spain): From Traditional to Student-Centred Learning. [IJTHI]. *International Journal of Technology and Human Interaction*, 8(2), 56–76. doi:10.4018/jthi.2012040104

Mosindi, O., & Sice, P. (2011). An Exploratory Theoretical Framework for Understanding Information Behaviour. [IJTHI]. *International Journal of Technology and Human Interaction*, 7(2), 1–8. doi:10.4018/jthi.2011040101

Mott, M. S., & Williams-Black, T. H. (2014). Media-Enhanced Writing Instruction and Assessment. In J. Keengwe, G. Onchwari, & D. Hucks (Eds.), *Literacy Enrichment and Technology Integration in Pre-Service Teacher Education* (pp. 1–16). Hershey, PA: Information Science Reference; doi:10.4018/978-1-4666-4924-8.ch001

Mulvey, F., & Heubner, M. (2014). Eye Movements and Attention. In I. Management Association (Ed.), Assistive Technologies: Concepts, Methodologies, Tools, and Applications (pp. 1030-1054). Hershey, PA: Information Science Reference. doi:10.4018/978-1-4666-4422-9.ch053

Muro, B. F., & Delgado, E. C. (2014). RACEM Game for PC for Use as Rehabilitation Therapy for Children with Psychomotor Disability and Results of its Application. In I. Management Association (Ed.), Assistive Technologies: Concepts, Methodologies, Tools, and Applications (pp. 740-757). Hershey, PA: Information Science Reference. doi:10.4018/978-1-4666-4422-9.ch037

Muwanguzi, S., & Lin, L. (2014). Coping with Accessibility and Usability Challenges of Online Technologies by Blind Students in Higher Education. In I. Management Association (Ed.), Assistive Technologies: Concepts, Methodologies, Tools, and Applications (pp. 1227-1244). Hershey, PA: Information Science Reference. doi:10.4018/978-1-4666-4422-9.ch064

Najjar, M., Courtemanche, F., Hamam, H., Dion, A., Bauchet, J., & Mayers, A. (2014). DeepKøver: An Adaptive Intelligent Assistance System for Monitoring Impaired People in Smart Homes. In I. Management Association (Ed.), Assistive Technologies: Concepts, Methodologies, Tools, and Applications (pp. 634-661). Hershey, PA: Information Science Reference. doi:10.4018/978-1-4666-4422-9.ch031

Nap, H. H., & Diaz-Orueta, U. (2014). Rehabilitation Gaming. In J. Bishop (Ed.), *Gamification for Human Factors Integration: Social, Education, and Psychological Issues* (pp. 122–147). Hershey, PA: Information Science Reference; doi:10.4018/978-1-4666-5071-8.ch008

Neves, J., & Pinheiro, L. D. (2012). Cyberbullying: A Sociological Approach. In R. Luppicini (Ed.), *Ethical Impact of Technological Advancements and Applications in Society* (pp. 132–142). Hershey, PA: Information Science Reference; doi:10.4018/978-1-4666-1773-5.ch010

Nguyen, P. T. (2012). Peer Feedback on Second Language Writing through Blogs: The Case of a Vietnamese EFL Classroom. [IJCALLT]. *International Journal of Computer-Assisted Language Learning and Teaching*, 2(1), 13–23. doi:10.4018/ijcallt.2012010102

Ninaus, M., Witte, M., Kober, S. E., Friedrich, E. V., Kurzmann, J., Hartsuiker, E., & Wood, G. et al. (2014). Neurofeedback and Serious Games. In T. Connolly, T. Hainey, E. Boyle, G. Baxter, & P. Moreno-Ger (Eds.), *Psychology, Pedagogy, and Assessment in Serious Games* (pp. 82–110). Hershey, PA: Information Science Reference; doi:10.4018/978-1-4666-4773-2.ch005

Olla, V. (2014). An Enquiry into the use of Technology and Student Voice in Citizenship Education in the K-12 Classroom. In I. Management Association (Ed.), *K-12 Education: Concepts, Methodologies, Tools, and Applications* (pp. 892-913). Hershey, PA: Information Science Reference. doi:10.4018/978-1-4666-4502-8.ch053

Orange, E. (2013). Understanding the Human-Machine Interface in a Time of Change. In R. Luppicini (Ed.), *Handbook of Research on Technoself: Identity in a Technological Society* (pp. 703–719). Hershey, PA: Information Science Reference; doi:10.4018/978-1-4666-2211-1.ch036

Palmer, D., Warren, I., & Miller, P. (2014). ID Scanners and Überveillance in the Night-Time Economy: Crime Prevention or Invasion of Privacy? In M. Michael & K. Michael (Eds.), *Überveillance and the Social Implications of Microchip Implants: Emerging Technologies* (pp. 208–225). Hershey, PA: Information Science Reference; doi:10.4018/978-1-4666-4582-0.ch009

Papadopoulos, F., Dautenhahn, K., & Ho, W. C. (2013). Behavioral Analysis of Human-Human Remote Social Interaction Mediated by an Interactive Robot in a Cooperative Game Scenario. In R. Luppicini (Ed.), *Handbook of Research on Technoself: Identity in a Technological Society* (pp. 637–665). Hershey, PA: Information Science Reference; doi:10.4018/978-1-4666-2211-1.ch033

Patel, K. K., & Vij, S. K. (2014). Unconstrained Walking Plane to Virtual Environment for Non-Visual Spatial Learning. In I. Management Association (Ed.), *Assistive Technologies: Concepts, Methodologies, Tools, and Applications* (pp. 1580-1599). Hershey, PA: Information Science Reference. doi:10.4018/978-1-4666-4422-9.ch083

Patrone, T. (2013). In Defense of the 'Human Prejudice'. [IJT]. *International Journal of Technoethics*, *4*(1), 26–38. doi:10.4018/jte.2013010103

Peevers, G., Williams, R., Douglas, G., & Jack, M. A. (2013). Usability Study of Fingerprint and Palmvein Biometric Technologies at the ATM. [IJTHI]. *International Journal of Technology and Human Interaction*, *9*(1), 78–95. doi:10.4018/jthi.2013010106

Pellas, N. (2014). Theoretical Foundations of a CSCL Script in Persistent Virtual Worlds According to the Contemporary Learning Theories and Models. In E. Nikoi & K. Boateng (Eds.), *Collaborative Communication Processes and Decision Making in Organizations* (pp. 72–107). Hershey, PA: Business Science Reference; doi:10.4018/978-1-4666-4478-6.ch005

Perakslis, C. (2014). Willingness to Adopt RFID Implants: Do Personality Factors Play a Role in the Acceptance of Überveillance? In M. Michael & K. Michael (Eds.), *Überveillance and the Social Implications of Microchip Implants: Emerging Technologies* (pp. 144–168). Hershey, PA: Information Science Reference; doi:10.4018/978-1-4666-4582-0.ch006

Pereira, G., Brisson, A., Dias, J., Carvalho, A., Dimas, J., Mascarenhas, S., & Paiva, A. et al. (2014). Non-Player Characters and Artificial Intelligence. In T. Connolly, T. Hainey, E. Boyle, G. Baxter, & P. Moreno-Ger (Eds.), *Psychology, Pedagogy, and Assessment in Serious Games* (pp. 127–152). Hershey, PA: Information Science Reference; doi:10.4018/978-1-4666-4773-2.ch007

Pérez Pérez, A., Callejas Carrión, Z., López-Cózar Delgado, R., & Griol Barres, D. (2014). On the Use of Speech Technologies to Achieve Inclusive Education for People with Intellectual Disabilities. In I. Management Association (Ed.), Assistive Technologies: Concepts, Methodologies, Tools, and Applications (pp. 1106-1117). Hershey, PA: Information Science Reference. doi:10.4018/978-1-4666-4422-9.ch057

Peschl, M. F., & Fundneider, T. (2014). Theory U and Emergent Innovation: Presencing as a Method of Bringing Forth Profoundly New Knowledge and Realities. In O. Gunnlaugson, C. Baron, & M. Cayer (Eds.), *Perspectives on Theory U: Insights from the Field* (pp. 207–233). Hershey, PA: Business Science Reference; doi:10.4018/978-1-4666-4793-0.ch014

Petrovic, N., Jeremic, V., Petrovic, D., & Cirovic, M. (2014). Modeling the Use of Facebook in Environmental Higher Education. In G. Mallia (Ed.), *The Social Classroom: Integrating Social Network Use in Education* (pp. 100–119). Hershey, PA: Information Science Reference; doi:10.4018/978-1-4666-4904-0.ch006

Phua, C., Roy, P. C., Aloulou, H., Biswas, J., Tolstikov, A., Foo, V. S., . . . Xu, D. (2014). State-of-the-Art Assistive Technology for People with Dementia. In I. Management Association (Ed.), Assistive Technologies: Concepts, Methodologies, Tools, and Applications (pp. 1606-1625). Hershey, PA: Information Science Reference. doi:10.4018/978-1-4666-4422-9.ch085

Potts, L. (2011). Balancing McLuhan With Williams: A Sociotechnical View of Technological Determinism. [IJSKD]. *International Journal of Sociotechnology and Knowledge Development*, 3(2), 53–57. doi:10.4018/jskd.2011040105

Potts, L. (2013). Balancing McLuhan With Williams: A Sociotechnical View of Technological Determinism. In J. Abdelnour-Nocera (Ed.), *Knowledge and Technological Development Effects on Organizational and Social Structures* (pp. 109–114). Hershey, PA: Information Science Reference; doi:10.4018/978-1-4666-2151-0.ch007

Potts, L. (2014). Sociotechnical Uses of Social Web Tools during Disasters. In I. Management Association (Ed.), Crisis Management: Concepts, Methodologies, Tools and Applications (pp. 531-541). Hershey, PA: Information Science Reference. doi:10.4018/978-1-4666-4707-7.ch024

Proença, R., Guerra, A., & Campos, P. (2013). A Gestural Recognition Interface for Intelligent Wheelchair Users. [IJSKD]. *International Journal of Sociotechnology and Knowledge Development*, 5(2), 63–81. doi:10.4018/jskd.2013040105

Quilici-Gonzalez, J. A., Kobayashi, G., Broens, M. C., & Gonzalez, M. E. (2012). Ubiquitous Computing: Any Ethical Implications? In R. Luppicini (Ed.), *Ethical Impact of Technological Advancements and Applications in Society* (pp. 47–59). Hershey, PA: Information Science Reference; doi:10.4018/978-1-4666-1773-5.ch005

Rambaree, K. (2014). Computer-Aided Deductive Critical Discourse Analysis of a Case Study from Mauritius with ATLAS-ti 6.2. In H. Lim & F. Sudweeks (Eds.), *Innovative Methods and Technologies for Electronic Discourse Analysis* (pp. 346–368). Hershey, PA: Information Science Reference; doi:10.4018/978-1-4666-4426-7.ch016

Ratan, R. (2013). Self-Presence, Explicated: Body, Emotion, and Identity Extension into the Virtual Self. In R. Luppicini (Ed.), *Handbook of Research on Technoself: Identity in a Technological Society* (pp. 322–336). Hershey, PA: Information Science Reference; doi:10.4018/978-1-4666-2211-1.ch018

Rechy-Ramirez, E. J., & Hu, H. (2014). A Flexible Bio-Signal Based HMI for Hands-Free Control of an Electric Powered Wheelchair. [IJALR]. *International Journal of Artificial Life Research, 4*(1), 59–76. doi:10.4018/ijalr.2014010105

Reiners, T., Wood, L. C., & Dron, J. (2014). From Chaos Towards Sense: A Learner-Centric Narrative Virtual Learning Space. In J. Bishop (Ed.), *Gamification for Human Factors Integration: Social, Education, and Psychological Issues* (pp. 242–258). Hershey, PA: Information Science Reference; doi:10.4018/978-1-4666-5071-8.ch015

Reinhardt, J., & Ryu, J. (2013). Using Social Network-Mediated Bridging Activities to Develop Socio-Pragmatic Awareness in Elementary Korean. [IJCALLT]. *International Journal of Computer-Assisted Language Learning and Teaching, 3*(3), 18–33. doi:10.4018/ijcallt.2013070102

Revuelta, P., Jiménez, J., Sánchez, J. M., & Ruiz, B. (2014). Automatic Speech Recognition to Enhance Learning for Disabled Students. In I. Management Association (Ed.), Assistive Technologies: Concepts, Methodologies, Tools, and Applications (pp. 478-493). Hershey, PA: Information Science Reference. doi:10.4018/978-1-4666-4422-9.ch023

Ribeiro, J. C., & Silva, T. (2013). Self, Self-Presentation, and the Use of Social Applications in Digital Environments. In R. Luppicini (Ed.), *Handbook of Research on Technoself: Identity in a Technological Society* (pp. 439–455). Hershey, PA: Information Science Reference; doi:10.4018/978-1-4666-2211-1.ch024

Richet, J. (2013). From Young Hackers to Crackers. [IJTHI]. *International Journal of Technology and Human Interaction, 9*(3), 53–62. doi:10.4018/jthi.2013070104

Rigas, D., & Almutairi, B. (2013). An Empirical Investigation into the Role of Avatars in Multimodal E-government Interfaces. [IJSKD]. *International Journal of Sociotechnology and Knowledge Development, 5*(1), 14–22. doi:10.4018/jskd.2013010102

Rodríguez, W. R., Saz, O., & Lleida, E. (2014). Experiences Using a Free Tool for Voice Therapy based on Speech Technologies. In I. Management Association (Ed.), Assistive Technologies: Concepts, Methodologies, Tools, and Applications (pp. 508-523). Hershey, PA: Information Science Reference. doi:10.4018/978-1-4666-4422-9.ch025

Rothblatt, M. (2013). Mindclone Technoselves: Multi-Substrate Legal Identities, Cyber-Psychology, and Biocyberethics. In R. Luppicini (Ed.), *Handbook of Research on Technoself: Identity in a Technological Society* (pp. 105–122). Hershey, PA: Information Science Reference; doi:10.4018/978-1-4666-2211-1.ch006

Rowe, N. C. (2012). The Ethics of Cyberweapons in Warfare. In R. Luppicini (Ed.), *Ethical Impact of Technological Advancements and Applications in Society* (pp. 195–207). Hershey, PA: Information Science Reference; doi:10.4018/978-1-4666-1773-5.ch015

Russo, M. R. (2014). Emergency Management Professional Development: Linking Information Communication Technology and Social Communication Skills to Enhance a Sense of Community and Social Justice in the 21st Century. In I. Management Association (Ed.), Crisis Management: Concepts, Methodologies, Tools and Applications (pp. 651-665). Hershey, PA: Information Science Reference. doi:10.4018/978-1-4666-4707-7.ch031

Sajeva, S. (2011). Towards a Conceptual Knowledge Management System Based on Systems Thinking and Sociotechnical Thinking. [IJSKD]. *International Journal of Sociotechnology and Knowledge Development*, *3*(3), 40–55. doi:10.4018/jskd.2011070103

Sajeva, S. (2013). Towards a Conceptual Knowledge Management System Based on Systems Thinking and Sociotechnical Thinking. In J. Abdelnour-Nocera (Ed.), *Knowledge and Technological Development Effects on Organizational and Social Structures* (pp. 115–130). Hershey, PA: Information Science Reference; doi:10.4018/978-1-4666-2151-0.ch008

Saleeb, N., & Dafoulas, G. A. (2014). Assistive Technologies and Environmental Design Concepts for Blended Learning and Teaching for Disabilities within 3D Virtual Worlds and Learning Environments. In I. Management Association (Ed.), Assistive Technologies: Concepts, Methodologies, Tools, and Applications (pp. 1382-1404). Hershey, PA: Information Science Reference. doi:10.4018/978-1-4666-4422-9.ch073

Salvini, P. (2012). Presence, Reciprocity and Robotic Mediations: The Case of Autonomous Social Robots. [IJT]. *International Journal of Technoethics*, *3*(2), 9–16. doi:10.4018/jte.2012040102

Samanta, I. (2013). The Impact of Virtual Community (Web 2.0) in the Economic, Social, and Political Environment of Traditional Society. In S. Saeed, M. Khan, & R. Ahmad (Eds.), *Business Strategies and Approaches for Effective Engineering Management* (pp. 262–274). Hershey, PA: Business Science Reference; doi:10.4018/978-1-4666-3658-3.ch016

Samanta, S. K., Woods, J., & Ghanbari, M. (2011). Automatic Language Translation: An Enhancement to the Mobile Messaging Services. [IJTHI]. *International Journal of Technology and Human Interaction*, *7*(1), 1–18. doi:10.4018/jthi.2011010101

Sarkar, N. I., Kuang, A. X., Nisar, K., & Amphawan, A. (2014). Hospital Environment Scenarios using WLAN over OPNET Simulation Tool. [IJICTHD]. *International Journal of Information Communication Technologies and Human Development*, *6*(1), 69–90. doi:10.4018/ijicthd.2014010104

Sarré, C. (2013). Technology-Mediated Tasks in English for Specific Purposes (ESP): Design, Implementation and Learner Perception. [IJCALLT]. *International Journal of Computer-Assisted Language Learning and Teaching*, *3*(2), 1–16. doi:10.4018/ijcallt.2013040101

Saykili, A., & Kumtepe, E. G. (2014). Facebook's Hidden Potential: Facebook as an Educational Support Tool in Foreign Language Education. In G. Mallia (Ed.), *The Social Classroom: Integrating Social Network Use in Education* (pp. 120–146). Hershey, PA: Information Science Reference; doi:10.4018/978-1-4666-4904-0.ch007

Sayoud, H. (2011). Biometrics: An Overview on New Technologies and Ethic Problems. [IJT]. *International Journal of Technoethics*, *2*(1), 19–34. doi:10.4018/jte.2011010102

Scott, C. R., & Timmerman, C. E. (2014). Communicative Changes Associated with Repeated Use of Electronic Meeting Systems for Decision-Making Tasks. In E. Nikoi & K. Boateng (Eds.), *Collaborative Communication Processes and Decision Making in Organizations* (pp. 1–24). Hershey, PA: Business Science Reference; doi:10.4018/978-1-4666-4478-6.ch001

Scott, K. (2013). The Human-Robot Continuum of Self: Where the Other Ends and Another Begins. In R. Luppicini (Ed.), *Handbook of Research on Technoself: Identity in a Technological Society* (pp. 666–679). Hershey, PA: Information Science Reference; doi:10.4018/978-1-4666-2211-1.ch034

Shasek, J. (2014). ExerLearning®: Movement, Fitness, Technology, and Learning. In J. Bishop (Ed.), *Gamification for Human Factors Integration: Social, Education, and Psychological Issues* (pp. 106–121). Hershey, PA: Information Science Reference; doi:10.4018/978-1-4666-5071-8.ch007

Shen, J., & Eder, L. B. (2011). An Examination of Factors Associated with User Acceptance of Social Shopping Websites. [IJTHI]. *International Journal of Technology and Human Interaction*, *7*(1), 19–36. doi:10.4018/jthi.2011010102

Shrestha, P. (2012). Teacher Professional Development Using Mobile Technologies in a Large-Scale Project: Lessons Learned from Bangladesh. [IJCALLT]. *International Journal of Computer-Assisted Language Learning and Teaching*, *2*(4), 34–49. doi:10.4018/ijcallt.2012100103

Silvana de Rosa, A., Fino, E., & Bocci, E. (2014). Addressing Healthcare On-Line Demand and Supply Relating to Mental Illness: Knowledge Sharing About Psychiatry and Psychoanalysis Through Social Networks in Italy and France. In A. Kapoor & C. Kulshrestha (Eds.), *Dynamics of Competitive Advantage and Consumer Perception in Social Marketing* (pp. 16–55). Hershey, PA: Business Science Reference; doi:10.4018/978-1-4666-4430-4.ch002

Smith, M., & Murray, J. (2014). Augmentative and Alternative Communication Devices: The Voices of Adult Users. In I. Management Association (Ed.), Assistive Technologies: Concepts, Methodologies, Tools, and Applications (pp. 991-1004). Hershey, PA: Information Science Reference. doi:10.4018/978-1-4666-4422-9.ch050

Smith, P. A. (2013). Strengthening and Enriching Audit Practice: The Socio-Technical Relevance of "Decision Leaders". In J. Abdelnour-Nocera (Ed.), *Knowledge and Technological Development Effects on Organizational and Social Structures* (pp. 97–108). Hershey, PA: Information Science Reference; doi:10.4018/978-1-4666-2151-0.ch006

So, J. C., & Lam, S. Y. (2014). Using Social Networks Communication Platform for Promoting Student-Initiated Holistic Development Among Students. [IJISSS]. *International Journal of Information Systems in the Service Sector*, *6*(1), 1–23. doi:10.4018/ijisss.2014010101

Söderström, S. (2014). Assistive ICT and Young Disabled Persons: Opportunities and Obstacles in Identity Negotiations. In I. Management Association (Ed.), Assistive Technologies: Concepts, Methodologies, Tools, and Applications (pp. 1084-1105). Hershey, PA: Information Science Reference. doi:10.4018/978-1-4666-4422-9.ch056

Son, J., & Rossade, K. (2013). Finding Gems in Computer-Assisted Language Learning: Clues from GLoCALL 2011 and 2012 Papers. [IJCALLT]. *International Journal of Computer-Assisted Language Learning and Teaching*, *3*(4), 1–8. doi:10.4018/ijcallt.2013100101

Sone, Y. (2013). Robot Double: Hiroshi Ishiguro's Reflexive Machines. In R. Luppicini (Ed.), *Handbook of Research on Technoself: Identity in a Technological Society* (pp. 680–702). Hershey, PA: Information Science Reference; doi:10.4018/978-1-4666-2211-1.ch035

Spillane, M. (2014). Assistive Technology: A Tool for Inclusion. In I. Management Association (Ed.), Assistive Technologies: Concepts, Methodologies, Tools, and Applications (pp. 1-11). Hershey, PA: Information Science Reference. doi:10.4018/978-1-4666-4422-9.ch001

Stahl, B. C., Heersmink, R., Goujon, P., Flick, C., van den Hoven, J., Wakunuma, K., & Rader, M. et al. (2012). Identifying the Ethics of Emerging Information and Communication Technologies: An Essay on Issues, Concepts and Method. In R. Luppicini (Ed.), *Ethical Impact of Technological Advancements and Applications in Society* (pp. 61–79). Hershey, PA: Information Science Reference; doi:10.4018/978-1-4666-1773-5.ch006

Stern, S. E., & Grounds, B. E. (2011). Cellular Telephones and Social Interactions: Evidence of Interpersonal Surveillance. [IJT]. *International Journal of Technoethics*, 2(1), 43–49. doi:10.4018/jte.2011010104

Stinson, J., & Gill, N. (2014). Internet-Based Chronic Disease Self-Management for Youth. In I. Management Association (Ed.), Assistive Technologies: Concepts, Methodologies, Tools, and Applications (pp. 224-245). Hershey, PA: Information Science Reference. doi:10.4018/978-1-4666-4422-9.ch012

Stockwell, G. (2011). Online Approaches to Learning Vocabulary: Teacher-Centred or Learner-Centred? [IJCALLT]. *International Journal of Computer-Assisted Language Learning and Teaching*, 1(1), 33–44. doi:10.4018/ijcallt.2011010103

Stradella, E. (2012). Personal Liability and Human Free Will in the Background of Emerging Neuroethical Issues: Some Remarks Arising From Recent Case Law. [IJT]. *International Journal of Technoethics*, 3(2), 30–41. doi:10.4018/jte.2012040104

Stubbs, K., Casper, J., & Yanco, H. A. (2014). Designing Evaluations for K-12 Robotics Education Programs. In I. Management Association (Ed.), K-12 Education: Concepts, Methodologies, Tools, and Applications (pp. 1342-1364). Hershey, PA: Information Science Reference. doi:10.4018/978-1-4666-4502-8.ch078

Suki, N. M., Ramayah, T., Ming, M. K., & Suki, N. M. (2011). Factors Enhancing Employed Job Seekers Intentions to Use Social Networking Sites as a Job Search Tool. [IJTHI]. *International Journal of Technology and Human Interaction*, 7(2), 38–54. doi:10.4018/jthi.2011040105

Sweeney, P., & Moore, C. (2012). Mobile Apps for Learning Vocabulary: Categories, Evaluation and Design Criteria for Teachers and Developers. [IJCALLT]. *International Journal of Computer-Assisted Language Learning and Teaching*, 2(4), 1–16. doi:10.4018/ijcallt.2012100101

Szeto, A. Y. (2014). Assistive Technology and Rehabilitation Engineering. In I. Management Association (Ed.), Assistive Technologies: Concepts, Methodologies, Tools, and Applications (pp. 277-331). Hershey, PA: Information Science Reference. doi:10.4018/978-1-4666-4422-9.ch015

Tamim, R. (2014). Technology Integration in UAE Schools: Current Status and Way Forward. In I. Management Association (Ed.), K-12 Education: Concepts, Methodologies, Tools, and Applications (pp. 41-57). Hershey, PA: Information Science Reference. doi:10.4018/978-1-4666-4502-8.ch004

Tan, R., Wang, S., Jiang, Y., Ishida, K., & Fujie, M. G. (2014). Motion Control of an Omni-Directional Walker for Walking Support. In I. Management Association (Ed.), Assistive Technologies: Concepts, Methodologies, Tools, and Applications (pp. 614-622). Hershey, PA: Information Science Reference. doi:10.4018/978-1-4666-4422-9.ch029

Tankari, M. (2014). Cultural Orientation Differences and their Implications for Online Learning Satisfaction. In J. Keengwe, G. Schnellert, & K. Kungu (Eds.), *Cross-Cultural Online Learning in Higher Education and Corporate Training* (pp. 20–61). Hershey, PA: Information Science Reference; doi:10.4018/978-1-4666-5023-7.ch002

Tchangani, A. P. (2014). Bipolarity in Decision Analysis: A Way to Cope with Human Judgment. In A. Masegosa, P. Villacorta, C. Cruz-Corona, M. García-Cascales, M. Lamata, & J. Verdegay (Eds.), *Exploring Innovative and Successful Applications of Soft Computing* (pp. 216–244). Hershey, PA: Information Science Reference; doi:10.4018/978-1-4666-4785-5.ch012

Tennyson, R. D. (2014). Computer Interventions for Children with Disabilities: Review of Research and Practice. In I. Management Association (Ed.), Assistive Technologies: Concepts, Methodologies, Tools, and Applications (pp. 841-864). Hershey, PA: Information Science Reference. doi:10.4018/978-1-4666-4422-9.ch042

Terrell, S. S. (2011). Integrating Online Tools to Motivate Young English Language Learners to Practice English Outside the Classroom. [IJCALLT]. *International Journal of Computer-Assisted Language Learning and Teaching, 1*(2), 16–24. doi:10.4018/ijcallt.2011040102

Tiwary, U. S., & Siddiqui, T. J. (2014). Working Together with Computers: Towards a General Framework for Collaborative Human Computer Interaction. In I. Management Association (Ed.), Assistive Technologies: Concepts, Methodologies, Tools, and Applications (pp. 141-162). Hershey, PA: Information Science Reference. doi:10.4018/978-1-4666-4422-9.ch008

Tomas, J., Lloret, J., Bri, D., & Sendra, S. (2014). Sensors and their Application for Disabled and Elderly People. In I. Management Association (Ed.), Assistive Technologies: Concepts, Methodologies, Tools, and Applications (pp. 357-376). Hershey, PA: Information Science Reference. doi:10.4018/978-1-4666-4422-9.ch018

Tomasi, A. (2013). A Run for your [Techno]Self. In R. Luppicini (Ed.), Handbook of Research on Technoself: Identity in a Technological Society (pp. 123-136). Hershey, PA: Information Science Reference. doi:10.4018/978-1-4666-2211-1.ch007

Tootell, H., & Freeman, A. (2014). The Applicability of Gaming Elements to Early Childhood Education. In J. Bishop (Ed.), *Gamification for Human Factors Integration: Social, Education, and Psychological Issues* (pp. 225–241). Hershey, PA: Information Science Reference; doi:10.4018/978-1-4666-5071-8.ch014

Tsai, C. (2011). How Much Can Computers and Internet Help?: A Long-Term Study of Web-Mediated Problem-Based Learning and Self-Regulated Learning. [IJTHI]. *International Journal of Technology and Human Interaction, 7*(1), 67–81. doi:10.4018/jthi.2011010105

Tsai, W. (2013). An Investigation on Undergraduate's Bio-Energy Engineering Education Program at the Taiwan Technical University. [IJTHI]. *International Journal of Technology and Human Interaction, 8*(3), 46–53. doi:10.4018/jthi.2012070105

Tsiakis, T. (2013). Using Social Media as a Concept and Tool for Teaching Marketing Information Systems. In M. Pătruţ & B. Pătruţ (Eds.), *Social Media in Higher Education: Teaching in Web 2.0* (pp. 24–44). Hershey, PA: Information Science Reference; doi:10.4018/978-1-4666-2970-7.ch002

Tu, C., McIsaac, M. S., Sujo-Montes, L. E., & Armfield, S. (2014). Building Mobile Social Presence for U-Learning. In F. Neto (Ed.), *Technology Platform Innovations and Forthcoming Trends in Ubiquitous Learning* (pp. 77–93). Hershey, PA: Information Science Reference; doi:10.4018/978-1-4666-4542-4.ch005

Valeria, N., Lu, M. V., & Theng, L. B. (2014). Collaborative Virtual Learning for Assisting Children with Cerebral Palsy. In I. Management Association (Ed.), Assistive Technologies: Concepts, Methodologies, Tools, and Applications (pp. 786-810). Hershey, PA: Information Science Reference. doi:10.4018/978-1-4666-4422-9.ch040

Van Leuven, N., Newton, D., Leuenberger, D. Z., & Esteves, T. (2014). Reaching Citizen 2.0: How Government Uses Social Media to Send Public Messages during Times of Calm and Times of Crisis. In I. Management Association (Ed.), Crisis Management: Concepts, Methodologies, Tools and Applications (pp. 839-857). Hershey, PA: Information Science Reference. doi:10.4018/978-1-4666-4707-7.ch041

Vargas-Hernández, J. G. (2013). International Student Collaboration and Experiential Exercise Projects as a Professional, Inter-Personal and Inter-Institutional Networking Platform. [IJTEM]. *International Journal of Technology and Educational Marketing*, 3(1), 28–47. doi:10.4018/ijtem.2013010103

Velicu, A., & Marinescu, V. (2013). Usage of Social Media by Children and Teenagers: Results of EU KIDS Online II. In M. Pătruţ & B. Pătruţ (Eds.), *Social Media in Higher Education: Teaching in Web 2.0* (pp. 144–178). Hershey, PA: Information Science Reference; doi:10.4018/978-1-4666-2970-7.ch008

Vidaurre, C., Kübler, A., Tangermann, M., Müller, K., & Millán, J. D. (2014). Brain-Computer Interfaces and Visual Activity. In I. Management Association (Ed.), Assistive Technologies: Concepts, Methodologies, Tools, and Applications (pp. 1549-1570). Hershey, PA: Information Science Reference. doi:10.4018/978-1-4666-4422-9.ch081

Viswanathan, R. (2012). Augmenting the Use of Mobile Devices in Language Classrooms. [IJCALLT]. *International Journal of Computer-Assisted Language Learning and Teaching*, 2(2), 45–60. doi:10.4018/ijcallt.2012040104

Wallgren, L. G., & Hanse, J. J. (2012). A Two-Wave Study of the Impact of Job Characteristics and Motivators on Perceived Stress among Information Technology (IT) Consultants. [IJTHI]. *International Journal of Technology and Human Interaction*, 8(4), 75–91. doi:10.4018/jthi.2012100105

Wang, H. (2014). A Guide to Assistive Technology for Teachers in Special Education. In I. Management Association (Ed.), Assistive Technologies: Concepts, Methodologies, Tools, and Applications (pp. 12-25). Hershey, PA: Information Science Reference. doi:10.4018/978-1-4666-4422-9.ch002

Wang, S., Ku, C., & Chu, C. (2013). Sustainable Campus Project: Potential for Energy Conservation and Carbon Reduction Education in Taiwan. [IJTHI]. *International Journal of Technology and Human Interaction*, 8(3), 19–30. doi:10.4018/jthi.2012070103

Wang, Y., & Tian, J. (2013). Negotiation of Meaning in Multimodal Tandem Learning via Desktop Videoconferencing. [IJCALLT]. *International Journal of Computer-Assisted Language Learning and Teaching*, 3(2), 41–55. doi:10.4018/ijcallt.2013040103

Wareham, C. (2011). On the Moral Equality of Artificial Agents. [IJT]. *International Journal of Technoethics*, 2(1), 35–42. doi:10.4018/jte.2011010103

Warwick, K., & Gasson, M. N. (2014). Practical Experimentation with Human Implants. In M. Michael & K. Michael (Eds.), *Uberveillance and the Social Implications of Microchip Implants: Emerging Technologies* (pp. 64–132). Hershey, PA: Information Science Reference; doi:10.4018/978-1-4666-4582-0.ch004

Welch, K. C., Lahiri, U., Sarkar, N., Warren, Z., Stone, W., & Liu, C. (2014). Affect-Sensitive Computing and Autism. In I. Management Association (Ed.), Assistive Technologies: Concepts, Methodologies, Tools, and Applications (pp. 865-883). Hershey, PA: Information Science Reference. doi:10.4018/978-1-4666-4422-9.ch043

Wessels, B., Dittrich, Y., Ekelin, A., & Eriksén, S. (2014). Creating Synergies between Participatory Design of E-Services and Collaborative Planning. In I. Management Association (Ed.), Assistive Technologies: Concepts, Methodologies, Tools, and Applications (pp. 163-179). Hershey, PA: Information Science Reference. doi:10.4018/978-1-4666-4422-9.ch009

White, E. L. (2014). Technology-Based Literacy Approach for English Language Learners. In I. Management Association (Ed.), K-12 Education: Concepts, Methodologies, Tools, and Applications (pp. 723-740). Hershey, PA: Information Science Reference. doi:10.4018/978-1-4666-4502-8.ch042

Whyte, K. P., List, M., Stone, J. V., Grooms, D., Gasteyer, S., Thompson, P. B., & Bouri, H. et al. (2014). Uberveillance, Standards, and Anticipation: A Case Study on Nanobiosensors in U.S. Cattle. In M. Michael & K. Michael (Eds.), *Uberveillance and the Social Implications of Microchip Implants: Emerging Technologies* (pp. 260–279). Hershey, PA: Information Science Reference; doi:10.4018/978-1-4666-4582-0.ch012

Wilson, S., & Haslam, N. (2013). Reasoning about Human Enhancement: Towards a Folk Psychological Model of Human Nature and Human Identity. In R. Luppicini (Ed.), *Handbook of Research on Technoself: Identity in a Technological Society* (pp. 175–188). Hershey, PA: Information Science Reference; doi:10.4018/978-1-4666-2211-1.ch010

Woodhead, R. (2012). What is Technology? [IJSKD]. *International Journal of Sociotechnology and Knowledge Development*, 4(2), 1–13. doi:10.4018/jskd.2012040101

Woodley, C., & Dorrington, P. (2014). Facebook and the Societal Aspects of Formal Learning: Optional, Peripheral, or Essential. In G. Mallia (Ed.), *The Social Classroom: Integrating Social Network Use in Education* (pp. 269–291). Hershey, PA: Information Science Reference; doi:10.4018/978-1-4666-4904-0.ch014

Yamazaki, T. (2014). Assistive Technologies in Smart Homes. In I. Management Association (Ed.), Assistive Technologies: Concepts, Methodologies, Tools, and Applications (pp. 663-678). Hershey, PA: Information Science Reference. doi:10.4018/978-1-4666-4422-9.ch032

Yan, Z., Chen, Q., & Yu, C. (2013). The Science of Cell Phone Use: Its Past, Present, and Future. [IJCBPL]. *International Journal of Cyber Behavior, Psychology and Learning*, 3(1), 7–18. doi:10.4018/ijcbpl.2013010102

Yang, Y., Wang, X., & Li, L. (2013). Use Mobile Devices to Wirelessly Operate Computers. [IJTHI]. *International Journal of Technology and Human Interaction*, 9(1), 64–77. doi:10.4018/jthi.2013010105

Yartey, F. N., & Ha, L. (2013). Like, Share, Recommend: Smartphones as a Self-Broadcast and Self-Promotion Medium of College Students. [IJTHI]. *International Journal of Technology and Human Interaction*, 9(4), 20–40. doi:10.4018/ijthi.2013100102

Yaseen, S. G., & Al Omoush, K. S. (2013). Investigating the Engage in Electronic Societies via Facebook in the Arab World. [IJTHI]. *International Journal of Technology and Human Interaction*, 9(2), 20–38. doi:10.4018/jthi.2013040102

Yeo, B. (2012). Sustainable Economic Development and the Influence of Information Technologies: Dynamics of Knowledge Society Transformation. [IJSKD]. *International Journal of Sociotechnology and Knowledge Development*, 4(3), 54–55. doi:10.4018/jskd.2012070105

Yu, L., & Ureña, C. (2014). A Review of Current Approaches of Brain Computer Interfaces. In I. Management Association (Ed.), *Assistive Technologies: Concepts, Methodologies, Tools, and Applications* (pp. 1516-1534). Hershey, PA: Information Science Reference. doi:10.4018/978-1-4666-4422-9.ch079

Zelenkauskaite, A. (2014). Analyzing Blending Social and Mass Media Audiences through the Lens of Computer-Mediated Discourse. In H. Lim & F. Sudweeks (Eds.), *Innovative Methods and Technologies for Electronic Discourse Analysis* (pp. 304–326). Hershey, PA: Information Science Reference; doi:10.4018/978-1-4666-4426-7.ch014

Compilation of References

The Silicon Valley Letter.(2013). The Economist, 9. Retrieved from http://www.economist.com/blogs/babbage/2013/12/tech-firms-and-spies

Abbott, D., Davies, P., & Pati, A. (Eds.). (2008). *Quantum Aspects of Life*. London, UK: Imperial College Press.

Abeler, J., Calaki, J., Andree, K., & Basek, C. (2010). The power of apology. *Economics Letters*, *107*(2), 233–235. doi:10.1016/j.econlet.2010.01.033

Ackerman, E. (2014, January 22) U.S. Army Considers Replacing Thousands of Soldiers With Robots. *IEEE Spectrum*.

Ahmed, A. S. (2013) *The Thistle and the Drone: How America's War on Terror Became a Global War on Tribal Islam*. Harrisonburg: R.R. Donnelley.

Ahmed, N. (2013, Dec 23). Former BP geologist: peak oil is here and it will 'break economies'. *The Guardian*. Retrieved from http://www.theguardian.com/environment/earth-insight/2013/dec/23/british-petroleum-geologist-peak-oil-break-economy-recession

Alferes, J. J., Pereira, L. M., & Swift, T. (2004). Abduction in well-founded semantics and generalized stable models via tabled dual programs. *Theory and Practice of Logic Programming*, *4*(4), 383–428. doi:10.1017/S1471068403001960

Ali, S. M. (2002). The end of the Dreyfus affair: (Post) Heideggererian meditations on man, machine and meaning. *International Journal of Cognitive Technology*, *1*(1), 85–96. doi:10.1075/ijct.1.1.06ali

Allen, T., Tainter, J., & Hoekstra, T. (1999). Supply-Side Sustainability. *Systems Research and Behavioral Science, Syst. Res, 16*(5), 403-427. Retrieved from http://www.buildftw.org/sites/buildftw.org/files/shared_assets/Allen,Tainter, Hoekstra - 1999 - Supply-side sustainability.pdf

Allen, C., Smit, I., & Wallach, W. (2005). Artificial morality: Top-down, bottom-up, and hybrid approaches. *Ethics and Information Technology*, *7*(3), 149–155. doi:10.1007/s10676-006-0004-4

Allen, C., Varner, G., & Zinser, J. (2000). Prolegomena to any future artificial moral agent. *Journal of Experimental & Theoretical Artificial Intelligence*, *12*(3), 251–261. doi:10.1080/09528130050111428

Allen, C., Wallach, W., & Smit, I. (2006). Why machine ethics? *IEEE Intelligent Systems*, *21*(4), 12–17. doi:10.1109/MIS.2006.83

Allhoff, F. (2005). Germ-line genetic enhancement and rawlsian primary goods. *Kennedy Institute of Ethics Journal*, *15*(1), 43–60. doi:10.1353/ken.2005.0007 PMID:15881795

Allhoff, F., Lin, P., Moor, J., & Weckert, J. (2009). *Ethics of human enhancement: 25 questions & answers*. U.S. National Science Foundation.

Allhoff, F., Lin, P., & Steinberg, J. (2011). Ethics of human enhancement: An executive summary. *Science and Engineering Ethics*, *17*(2), 201–212. doi:10.1007/s11948-009-9191-9 PMID:20094921

Al-Muslimi, F. (2013, April 23). Drone Wars: The Constitutional and Counterterrorism Implications of Targeted Killing [Statement]. *United States Senate Judiciary Committee Subcommittee on the Constitution, Civil Rights and Human Rights*. Retrieved from http://www.judiciary.senate.gov/imo/media/doc/04-23-13Al-MuslimiTestimony.pdf

Al-Smadi, M., & Gütl, C. (2008). Past, present and future of e-assessment: Towards a flexible e-assessment system. *Conference ICL*.

Altbach, P. G. (2013, December 4). MOOCs as neo-colonialism: Who controls knowledge? *The Chronicle of Higher Education*. Retrieved from http://chronicle.com/blogs/worldwise/moocs-as-neocolonialism-who-controls-knowledge/33431

Anderson, M., & Anderson, S. L. (2007). Machine ethics: Creating an ethical intelligent agent. *AI Magazine*, *28*(4), 15–26.

Anderson, M., & Anderson, S. L. (2008). EthEl: Toward a principled ethical eldercare robot. In *AAAI Fall Symposium Technical Report on AI in Eldercare*. Palo Alto, CA: AAAI Press.

Anderson, M., & Anderson, S. L. (2010). Robot be good: A call for ethical autonomous machines. *Scientific American*, *303*(4), 54–59. doi:10.1038/scientificamerican1010-72 PMID:20923132

Anderson, M., & Anderson, S. L. (2014a, April). Toward Ethical Intelligent Autonomous Healthcare Agents: A Case-Supported, Principle-Based Behavior Paradigm. *Proceedings of the 50th Annual Convention of the Society for the Study of Artificial Intelligence and the Simulation of Behaviour (AISB-50) Symposium on Machine Ethics in the Context of Medical and Care Agents*, London, UK.

Anderson, M., & Anderson, S. L. (2014b, July 27-31). GenEth: A General Ethical Dilemma Analyzer. *Proceedings of the Twenty-Eighth AAAI Conference on Artificial Intelligence*, Quebec City, Quebec, Canada, (pp. 253-261).

Anderson, M., & Anderson, S. L. (Eds.). (2011). *Machine ethics*. Cambridge: Cambridge University Press. doi:10.1017/CBO9780511978036

Anderson, M., Anderson, S. L., & Armen, C. (2005). Towards machine ethics: Implementing two action-based ethical theories. In *AAAI Fall Symposium Technical Report on Machine Ethics*. Palo Alto, CA: AAAI Press.

Anderson, M., Anderson, S. L., & Armen, C. (2006). MedEthEx: a prototype medical ethics advisor. In *Proceedings of the Eighteenth Conference on Innovative Applications of Artifical Intelligence (IAAI'06)*. Palo Alto, CA: AAAI Press.

Andrade, H. G. (2001, April17). The effects of instructional rubrics on learning to write. *Current Issues in Education*, *4*(4), 1–28.

Anglin, L., Anglin, K., Schumann, P. L., & Kaliski, J. A. (2008, January). Improving the efficiency and effectiveness of grading through the use of computer-assisted grading rubrics. *Decision Sciences Journal of Innovative Education*, *6*(1), 51–73. doi:10.1111/j.1540-4609.2007.00153.x

Anscombe, G. E. (1958). Modern moral philosophy. *Philosophy (London, England)*, *33*(124), 1–19. doi:10.1017/S0031819100037943

Ansell-Pearson, K. (2002). *Philosophy and the Adventure of the Virtual: Bergson and the Time of Life*. London, UK: Routledge.

Aoun, J. E. (2012, November 17). A shakeup of higher education. *The Boston Globe*. Retrieved from http://www.northeastern.edu/masterplan/wp-content/uploads/2012/11/TheShakeupofHigherEducation_Globe-op-ed.pdf

Aquinas, T. (1961). *Commentary on the Metaphysics*. Chicago, IL. Retrieved from http://dhspriory.org/thomas/Metaphysics.htm

Arendt, H. (1963). On Revolution. New York: Viking Press.

Arendt, H. (2005). *The Promise of Politics* (J. Kohn, Ed.). New York, NY: Schocken Books.

Aristotle. *Metaphysics*. The Internet Classics Archive. Retrieved from http://classics.mit.edu//Aristotle/metaphysics.html

Arkin, R. (2009). *Governing lethal behavior in autonomous robots*. Boca Raton: CRC Press. doi:10.1201/9781420085952

Arpaly, N. (2004). *Unprincipled virtue: An inquiry into moral agency*. Oxford: Oxford University Press.

Asada, M., Nagai, Y., & Ishihara, H. (2012). Why not artificial sympathy? In ShuzhiSam Ge, Oussama Khatib, John-John Cabibihan, Reid Simmons, and Mary-Anne Williams, (Eds.), Social Robotics, 7621, (pp. 278–287). doi:10.1007/978-3-642-34103-8_28

Ashford, E., & Mulgan, T. (2007). Contractualism. In E. N. Zalta (Ed.), *The Stanford Encyclopedia of Philosophy* (Fall 2012 Edition). Retrieved from http://plato.stanford.edu/entries/contractualism/

Asimov, I. (1950). I, Robot. New York, NY: Doubleday & Company.

Augustine of Hippo. (426). De Civitate Dei Contra Paganos [The City of God Against the Pagans]. In G.C. Walsh, S.J. Demetrius, B. Zema, S.J. Grace, O.S.U. Monahan, & D.J. Hogan (Eds.), The City of God. Image Books/Doubleday.

Austin, A. A. (2013). Where will all the waste go?: Utilizing extended producer responsibility framework laws to achieve zero waste. *Golden Gate University Environmental Law Journal, 6(2)*, 220-257. Retrieved from http://digitalcommons.law.ggu.edu/cgi/viewcontent.cgi?article=1101&context=gguelj

Axelrod, R. (1984). *The Evolution of Cooperation*. New York: Basic Books.

Axelrod, R. (1986). An evolutionary approach to norms. *The American Political Science Review, 80*(4), 1095–1111. doi:10.2307/1960858

Baets, W. (2012). Complexity, consciousness and a-causality: A new organizational paradigm. Graduate School of Business, University of Cape Town. Retrieved from http://blogs.sun.ac.za/complexityforum/files/2012/05/BAETS-Forum-Keynote-Slides.pdf

Bailey, R. (2005). *Liberation biology: The scientific and moral case for biotech revolution*. Amherst, NY: Promrtheus Books.

Bamford, J. (2012, March 13). The NSA Is Building the Country's Biggest Spy Center (Watch What You Say). Retrieved from http://www.wired.com.

Bamford, J. (2009). *The shadow factory: The NSA from 9/11 to the eavesdropping on America*. New York: Anchor.

Baral, C., Gelfond, M., & Rushton, N. (2009). Probabilistic reasoning with answer sets. *Theory and Practice of Logic Programming, 9*(1), 57–144. doi:10.1017/S1471068408003645

Barandiaran, X. E., Di Paolo, E., & Rohde, M. (2009). Defining agency: Individuality, normativity, asymmetry, and spatio-temporality in action. *Adaptive Behavior, 17*(5), 367–386. doi:10.1177/1059712309343819

Barry, N. (2000). *Business ethics*. West Lafayett, IN: Purdue University Press.

Bateman, C. (2011). *Imaginary Games*. Winchester, Washington: Zero Books.

Bateman, C. (2012). *The Mythology of Evolution*. Winchester, Washington: Zero Books.

Bateman, C. (2014). *Chaos Ethics*. Winchester and Chicago, IL: Zero Books.

Baumard, N. (2010). *Comment nous sommes devenus moraux: Une histoire naturelle du bien et du mal*. Paris: Odile Jacob.

Belin, M.-Å., & Tillgren, P. (2013). Vision Zero. How a Policy Innovation is Dashed by Interest Conflicts, but May Prevail in the End. *Scandinavian Journal of Public Administration, 16*(3), 83–102.

Benhabib, S. (1992). *Situating the self: Gender, community, and postmodernism in contemporary ethics*. New York: Routledge.

Bentham, J. (1789). *An Introduction to the Principles and Morals of Legislation*. London: T. Payne. doi:10.1093/oseo/instance.00077240

Bentham, J. (1890). *Utilitarianism*. London: Progressive Publishing Company.

Bergson, H. (1957). *Time and Free Will*. London, UK: Unwin.

Bergson, H. (1988). *Matter and Memory*. Brooklyn, NY: Zone Books.

Bergson, H. (1999). *Duration and Simultaneity*. Manchester, UK: Clinamen Press Ltd.

Bhattacharya, S. (2003). Stupidity should be cured, says DNA discoverer. *NewScientist*. Retrieved from http://www.newscientist.com/article/dn3451-stupidity-should-be-cured-says-dna-discoverer.html#.U67DdihtxxU

Boden, M. A. (1998). Autonomy and artificiality. *Cognitive Architectures in Artificial Intelligence: The Evolution of Research Programs, 2*, 300–312.

Boden, M. A. (2008). Autonomy: What is it? *Bio Systems, 91*(2), 305–308. doi:10.1016/j.biosystems.2007.07.003 PMID:17996363

Boehm, F. (2013). Nanomedical Device and Systems Design: Challenges, Possibilities, Visions. New York, NY: CRC Press, especially Chapter 17: Nanomedicine in Regenerative Biosystems, Human Augmentation, and Longevity. (pp. 654-722). doi:10.1201/b15626

Boehm, C. (1999). *Hierarchy in the Forest: The Evolution of Egalitarian Behavior*. Cambridge, MA: Harvard University Press.

Boehm, C. (2012). *Moral Origins: The Evolution of Virtue, Altruism, and Shame*. New York: Basic Books.

Bohm, D. (1996). *On Dialogue*. London, New York: Routledge. doi:10.4324/9780203180372

Bohm, D. (2005). *Wholeness and the Implicate Order*. London, New York: Routledge.

Bonabeau, E., Dorigo, M., & Theraulaz, G. (1999). *Swarm Intelligence: From Natural to Artificial Systems*. New York: Oxford University Press.

BonJour. L. (2013). Epistemological Problems of Perception. In E.N. Zalta (Ed.), *The Stanford Encyclopedia of Philosophy*. Retrieved from http://plato.stanford.edu/archives/spr2013/entries/perception-episprob/

Boren, Z. D. (2014, Oct 7). There are officially more mobile devices than people in the world. *The Independent*. Retrieved from http://www.independent.co.uk/life-style/gadgets-and-tech/news/there-are-officially-more-mobile-devices-than-people-in-the-world-9780518.html

Börgers, T., & Sarin, R. (1997). Learning Through Reinforcement and Replicator Dynamics. *Journal of Economic Theory, 77*(1), 1–14. doi:10.1006/jeth.1997.2319

Borgmann, A. (1984). *Technology and the character of contemporary life*. Chicago, IL: University of Chicago Press.

Bostrom, N. (2003). Are You Living in a Computer Simulation? *Philosophical Quarterly 53*(211). 243-55.

Bostrom, N. (2014). Superintelligence: Paths, dangers, strategies. Oxford: Oxford University Press.

Bostrom, N., & Sandberg, A. (2006). *Cognitive enhancement: Methods, ethics, regulatory challenges*. Retrieved from http://www.nickbostrom.com/cognitive.pdf

Bostrom, N. (2005). A history of transhumanist thought. *Journal of Evolution & Technology, 14*(1), 1–25.

Bostrom, N., & Roache, R. (2008). Ethical issues in human enhancement. In J. Ryberg, T. Petersen, & C. Wolf (Eds.), *New waves in applied ethics* (pp. 120–152). Pelgrave MacMillan.

Bostrom, N., & Savulescu, J. (2008). Human enhancement ethics: The state of the debate. In J. Savulescu & N. Bostrom (Eds.), *Human enhancement* (pp. 1–22). Oxford University Press.

Boudreau, T. E. (2008). *Packing Inferno: The Unmaking of a Marine*. Port Townsend, WA: Feral House.

Bowles, S., & Gintis, H. (2011). *A Cooperative Species: Human Reciprocity and Its Evolution*. Princeton: Princeton University Press.

Boyd, R., & Richerson, P. (1992). Punishment allows the evolution of cooperation (or anything else) in sizable groups. *Ethology and Sociobiology, 13*(3), 171–195. doi:10.1016/0162-3095(92)90032-Y

Boysen, E. (2014). Nanotechnology in Medicine – Nanomedicine. UnderstandingNano.com. Retrieved from http://www.understandingnano.com/medicine.html

Bratman, M. E. (1987). *Intention, Plans and Practical Reasoning*. Cambridge, MA: Harvard University Press.

Breslow, L., Pritchard, D. E., DeBoer, J., Stump, G. S., Ho, A. D., & Seaton, D. T. (2013). Studying learning in the worldwide classroom: Research into edX's first MOOC. *Research & Practice in Assessment, 8*(1), 13–25.

Brey, P. (2000). Technology and Embodiment in Ihde and Merleau-Ponty. In C. Mitcham (Ed.), Metaphysics, Epistemology, and Technology: Research in Philosophy and Technology. Retrieved from http://www.utwente.nl/bms/wijsb/organization/brey/Publicaties_Brey/Brey_2000_Embodiment.pdf

Bright, B. (2009). The Shamanic Perspective: Where Jungian Thought and Archetypal Shamanism Converge. *Shamanswell.org*. Retrieved from https://www.academia.edu/1020632/The_Shamanic_Perspective_Where_Jungian_Thought_and_Archetypal_Shamanism_Converge

Bringsjord, S., Arkoudas, K., & Bello, P. (2006). Toward a general logicist methodology for engineering ethically correct robots. *IEEE Intelligent Systems, 21*(4), 38–44. doi:10.1109/MIS.2006.82

Bringsjord, S., Taylor, J., van Heuveln, B., Arkoudas, K., Clark, M., & Wojtowicz, R. (2011). Piagetian roboethics via category theory: Moving beyond mere formal operations to engineer robots whose decisions are guaranteed to be ethically correct. In M. Anderson & S. L. Anderson (Eds.), *Machine Ethics* (pp. 361–374). New York, NY: Cambridge University Press. doi:10.1017/CBO9780511978036.025

Brooks, D. (2011). *The Social Animal: The Hidden Sources of Love, Character, and Achievement*. Random House Publishing Group.

Brosnan, S. F., & De Waal, F. B. (2003). Monkeys reject unequal pay. *Nature, 425*(6955), 297–299. doi:10.1038/nature01963 PMID:13679918

Buber, M. (2000). *Ja i Ti [I and Thou]*. Belgrade, Serbia: Rad.

Calvo, R. A., & D'Mello, S. (2012). Frontiers of affect-aware learning technologies. *IEEE Intelligent Systems, 27*(6), 86–89. doi:10.1109/MIS.2012.110

Campbell, J. (1972). *Myths to Live By*. New York: Bantam.

Campbell, J. (2004). *The Hero with a Thousand Faces*. Princeton, Oxford: Princeton University Press.

Campbell, T. (2005). *My Big TOE: Awakening, Discovery, Inner Workings*. USA: Lightning Strike Books LLC.

Carnevale, A. P., Smith, N., & Melton, M. (2011). STEM. Georgetown University Center on Education and the Workforce. Retrieved from http://www9.georgetown.edu/grad/gppi/hpi/cew/pdfs/stem-complete

Carpenter, C. (2014). *Lost Causes: Agenda Vetting in Global Issue Networks and the Shaping of Human Security*. Ithaca: Cornell University Press.

Carver, L., & Harrison, L. M. (2013). MOOCs and democratic education. *Liberal Education, 99*(4).

Castells, M. (2012). *Networks of Outrage and Hope: Social Movements in the Internet Age*. Cambridge, UK: Polity.

Charniak, E., & Goldman, R. P. (1993). A Bayesian model of plan recognition. *Artificial Intelligence, 64*(1), 53–79. doi:10.1016/0004-3702(93)90060-O

Chatterjee, A. (2006). The promise and predicament of cosmetic neurology. *Journal of Medical Ethics, 32*(2), 110–113. doi:10.1136/jme.2005.013599 PMID:16446417

Cheney, D., & Seyfarth, R. (2007). *Baboon Metaphysics*. Chicago: Chicago University Press. doi:10.7208/chicago/9780226102429.001.0001

Childress, J. F. (1978). Just-War Theories: The Bases, Interrelations, Priorities, and Functions of Their Criteria. *Theological Studies, 39*(3), 427–445. doi:10.1177/004056397803900302

Chiu, C. Y., Hong, Y. Y., & Dweck, C. S. (1997). Lay dispositionism and implicit theories of personality. *Journal of Personality and Social Psychology, 73*(1), 19–30. doi:10.1037/0022-3514.73.1.19 PMID:9216077

Christensen, C. M., & Eyring, H. J. (2011). The innovative university: Changing the DNA of higher education from the inside out. John Wiley & Sons. Retrieved from https://net.educause.edu/ir/library/pdf/ff1207

Churchland, P. (2011). *Braintrust: What Neuroscience Tells Us about Morality*. Princeton: Princeton University Press. doi:10.1515/9781400838080

Clark, A. (1998). *Being There: Putting Brain, Body, and World Together Again*. London, UK: Bradford Books.

Clow, D. (2013). MOOCs and the funnel of participation.*Proceedings of the Third International Conference on Learning Analytics and Knowledge.* (pp. 85-189). doi:10.1145/2460296.2460332

Cohen, P. R., & Levesque, H. J. (1990). Intention is Choice with Commitment. *Artificial Intelligence, 42*(2-3), 213–261. doi:10.1016/0004-3702(90)90055-5

Coker, C. (2013). *Warrior Geeks: How 21st-century Technology Is Changing the Way We Fight and Think about War.* New York: Columbia University Press. doi:10.1093/acprof:oso/9780199327898.001.0001

Colebrook, C. (2002). *Understanding Deleuze.* Crows Nest, Australia: Allen & Unwin.

Comte, A. (1830). "Course of Positive Philosophy", reprinted. In G. Lenzer (Ed.), *Auguste Comte and Positivism: The Essential Writings* (pp. 71–86). New York, NY: Harper.

Conference of European Churches. (2010). *Human enhancement—A discussion document.* Conference of European Churches: Church & Society Commission. Retrieved from http://csc.ceceurope.org/fileadmin/filer/csc/Ethics_Biotechnology/Human_Enhancement_March_10.pdf

Conn, P. (2010, April 4). We need to acknowledge the realities of employment in the humanities. *The Chronicle of Higher Education, The Chronicle Review.* Retrieved from https://chronicle.com/article/We-Need-to-Acknowledge-the/64885/

Conrad, P., & Potter, D. (2004). Human growth hormone and the temptations of biomedical enhancement. *Sociology of Health & Illness, 26*(2), 184–215. doi:10.1111/j.1467-9566.2004.00386.x PMID:15027984

Cooper, M. (2014, Feb 20). Why the economics don't favor nuclear power in America. *Forbes.* Retrieved from http://www.forbes.com/sites/energysource/2014/02/20/why-the-economics-dont-favor-nuclear-power-in-america/

Cooper, D. E. (2005). Heidegger on nature. *Environmental Values, 14*(3), 339–351. doi:10.3197/096327105774434495

Cottee, S. (2014, November 17). ISIS and the Intimate Kill. *Atlantic (Boston, Mass.), Retrieved from* http://www.theatlantic.com/international/archive/2014/11/isis-and-the-intimate-kill-peter-kassig/382861/

Cowen, T. (2013). *Average is over: Powering America beyond the age of the great stagnation.* New York: Penguin Group.

Cramer, J. (1986). The Transactional Interpretation of Quantum Mechanics. *Reviews of Modern Physics, 58*(3), 647–688. doi:10.1103/RevModPhys.58.647

Crane, T. (2011). The Problem of Perception. In E.N. Zalta (Ed.), *The Stanford Encyclopedia of Philosophy.* Retrieved from http://plato.stanford.edu/archives/spr2011/entries/perception-problem/

Creveld, M. (2011). *The Age of Airpower.* New York: Public Affairs.

Cummings, M. L. (2004). Automation Bias in Intelligent Time Critical Decision Support Systems. Proceedings of *AIAA 1st Intelligent Systems Technical Conference,* Chicago. doi:10.2514/6.2004-6313

Curtis, J. W. (2014). The employment status of instructional staff members in higher education. *American Association of University Professors.* Retrieved from http://www.aaup.org/sites/default/files/files/AAUP-InstrStaff2011-April2014.pdf

Cushman, F., Young, L., & Greene, J. D. (2010). Multi-system moral psychology. In J. M. Doris (Ed.), *The Moral Psychology Handbook.* New York: Oxford University Press. doi:10.1093/acprof:oso/9780199582143.003.0003

D'Mello, S., & Graesser, A. (2012). AutoTutor and affective AutoTutor: Learning by talking with cognitively and emotionally intelligent computers that talk back.[TiiS]. *ACM Transactions on Interactive Intelligent Systems, 2*(4), 1–39. doi:10.1145/2395123.2395128

Dancy, J. (2004). *Ethics without principles.* Oxford: Oxford University Press. doi:10.1093/0199270023.001.0001

Daniels, N. (2000). Normal functioning and the treatment-enhancement distinction. *Cambridge Quarterly of Healthcare Ethics, 9*(3), 309–322. doi:10.1017/S0963180100903037 PMID:10858880

Danielson, P. (2010). Designing a machine to learn about the ethics of robotics: The N-reasons platform. *Ethics and Information Technology, 12*(3), 251–261. doi:10.1007/s10676-009-9214-x

Darwall, S., Gibbard, A., & Railton, P. (1997). *Moral discourse and practice*. New York: Oxford University Press.

de Gray, A. (2007). *Ending aging: The rejuvenation breakthroughs that could reserve human aging in our lifetime*. New York: Saint Martin's Press.

de Jongh, A., & Ten-Broeke, E. (2007). Treatment of specific phobia with EMDR: Conceptualization and strategies for selection of appropriate memories. *Journal of EMDR Practice and Research, 1*(1), 46–57. doi:10.1891/1933-3196.1.1.46

Deacon, T. (2012). *Incomplete Nature: How Mind Emerged from Matter*. New York, London: W.W. Norton & Company.

Deleuze, G. (1986). *Cinema 1: The-Movement-Image*. Minneapolis, MN: University of Minnesota Press.

Deleuze, G. (1989). *Cinema 2: The Time-Image*. Minneapolis, MN: University of Minnesota Press.

Deleuze, G., & Guatarri, F. (1987). *A Thousand Plateaus*. Minneapolis, MN: University of Minnesota Press.

Deleuze, G., & Guatarri, F. (1989). *Anti-Oedipus*. Minneapolis, MN: University of Minnesota Press.

Deleuze, G., & Guatarri, F. (1996). *What is Philosophy?* New York, NY: Columbia University Press.

DeLillo, D. (1997) Underworld. New York, NY: Scribner, 1997. (pp. 790).

Dell'Acqua, P., & Pereira, L. M. (2007). Preferential theory revision. *Journal of Applied Logic, 5*(4), 586–601. doi:10.1016/j.jal.2006.03.010

Dell'Acqua, P., Mattias Engberg, & Pereira, L. M. (2003). An Architecture for a Rational Reactive Agent In: Moura-Pires, F., & Abreu, S. (Eds.)., Proceedings of *11th Portuguese Intl.Conf. on Artificial Intelligence (EPIA'03)*, Beja, Portugal. (pp. 379-393). doi:10.1007/978-3-540-24580-3_44

Dell'Acqua, P., & Pereira, L. M. (2004). Common-sense reasoning as proto-scientific agent activity. *Journal of Applied Logic, 2*(4), 385–407. doi:10.1016/j.jal.2004.07.002

Dellarocas, C., & Van Alstyne, M. (2013). Money models for MOOCs. *Communications of the ACM, 56*(8), 25–28. doi:10.1145/2492007.2492017

Demenchonok, E. (2009). 10. The Universal Concept of Human Rights as a Regulative Principle: Freedom Versus Paternalism. *American Journal of Economics and Sociology, 68*(1), 273–301. doi:10.1111/j.1536-7150.2008.00624.x

Dennett, D. C. (1997). Consciousness in human and robot minds. In M. Io, Y. Miyashita, & E. T. Rolls (Eds.), *Cognition, Computation & Consciousness* (pp. 17–29). Oxford University Press.

Dennett, D. C. (2004). *Freedom evolves*. London: Penguin UK.

Dennett, D. D. (1973). Mechanism and Responsibility. In T. Honderich (Ed.), *Essays on Freedom of Action*. Boston: Routledge and Keegan Paul.

Dennett, D. D. (1997). When HAL Kills, Who's to Blame? Computer Ethics. In D. G. Stork (Ed.), *HAL's Legacy: 2001's Computer as a Dream and Reality*. Cambridge: MIT Press.

Denning, T., Matsuoka, Y., & Kohno, T. (2009). Neurosecurity: Security and privacy for neural devices. *Neurosurgical Focus, 27*(1), E7. doi:10.3171/2009.4.FOCUS0985 PMID:19569895

Descartes, R. (1637). *Dioptrics*. Retrieved from http://science.larouchepac.com/fermat/Descartes%20--%20Dioptrique.pdf

Descartes, R. (n.d.). *Principles of Philosophy*. Retrieved from http://www.ahshistory.com/wp-content/uploads/2012/07/descprin.pdf

Desjardins, J. (2013, May 21). What is the cost of mining gold? *Visual Capitalist*. Retrieved from http://www.visualcapitalist.com/what-is-the-cost-of-mining-gold/

Dewey, J. (1916). *Democracy and education*. New York: The Free Press.

Di Corpo, U., & Vannini, A. (2012). Syntropy, Cosmology and Life. *Syntropy*, (1), 90-103. Retrieved from http://www.sintropia.it/english/2012-eng-1-6.pdf

Diaz, J. (2013, Nov 16). US Army robots will outnumber human soldiers 10 to 1 by 2023. *Gizmodo*. Retrieved from http://sploid.gizmodo.com/us-army-robots-will-outnumber-human-soldiers-10-to-1-by-1465669535

Diederich, P.B., French, J.W., & Carlton, S.T. (August 1961). *Research Bulletin*. Princeton: Educational Testing Service.

Dodd, T. (2014, February 27). MOOC online courses about 'big data of learning' not just profit. *Financial Review*. Retrieved from http://www.afr.com/p/tech-gadgets/mooc_online_courses_about_big_data_f5kEJwBqz-2voWzpHH9EiEN

Dodig-Crnkovic, G. (2012). Physical Computation as Dynamics of Form that Glues Everything Together. *Information*, *3*(4), 204–218. doi:10.3390/info3020204

Doris, J. (2010). *The moral pshychology handbook*. Oxford: Oxford University Press. doi:10.1093/acprof:oso/9780199582143.001.0001

Dowd, A. W. (2013). Drone Wars: Risks and Warnings. *Parameters*, *43*, 7–16. Retrieved from http://www.strategicstudiesinstitute.army.mil/pubs/Parameters/

Doyle, J., Francis, B., & Tannenbaum, A. (1990). Feedback Control Theory. London, UK: Macmillan Publishing Co. Retrieved from www.control.utoronto.ca/people/profs/francis/dft.pdf

Dretske, F. I. (1988). *Explaining behavior: Reasons in a world of causes*. Cambridge, MA: MIT press.

Dreyfus, H. L., & Spinosa, C. (1997). *Highway bridges and feasts: Heidegger and Borgmann on how to affirm technology*. Retrieved from http://socrates.berkeley.edu/~hdreyfus/html/paper_highway.html

Dreyfus, H. L. (1991). *Being-in-the-world: A commentary on Heidegger's being and time (Division 1)*. Cambridge, MA: The MIT Press.

Duhigg, C. (2012, October 13). Campaigns Mine Personal Lives to Get Out Vote. *The New York Times*. Retrieved from http://www.nytimes.com/2012/10/14/us/politics/campaigns-mine-personal-lives-to-get-out-vote.html?pagewanted=all&_r=0

Dumouchel, P., & Damiano, L. (2011). Artificial empathy, imitation and mimesis. *Ars Vivendi Journal*, *1*, 18–31.

Dutton, K. (2012). *The Wisdom of Psychopaths: What Saints, Spies, and Serial Killers Can Teach Us about Success*. New York: Scientific American/Farrar, Straus and Giroux.

Dvorsky, G. (2009). All together now: Developmental and ethical considerations for biologically uplifting non-human animals. *Journal of Evolution and Technology*, *18*(1), 129–142.

Dworkin, G. (1988). *The Theory and Practice of Autonomy*. New York: Cambridge University Press. doi:10.1017/CBO9780511625206

Dyer, B. T. J., Noroozi, S., Sewell, P., & Redwood, S. (2010). The design of lower-limb sports prostheses: Fair inclusion in disability sport. *Disability & Society*, *25*(5), 593–602. doi:10.1080/09687599.2010.489309

Dyer, B. T. J., Noroozi, S., Sewell, P., & Redwood, S. (2011). The fair use of lower-limb running prostheses: A delphi study. *Adapted Physical Activity Quarterly; APAQ*, *28*(1), 16–26. PMID:21282845

Edwards, A. (2013). Time Travel and Newcomb's Problem. Champaign, IL: University of Illinois at Urbana. Retrieved from http://static.squarespace.com/static/50c0f505e4b0633592d3cf29/t/517aad57e4b0f0be01c32027/1366994263878/presentation_6.pdf

Eisenhower, D. D. (1953, Apr 16). *The Chance for Peace*. Speech to the American Society of Newspaper Editors.

Ellis, L. (2013, September 19). An adjunct's death becomes a rallying cry for many in academe. *The Chronicle of Higher Education*. Retrieved from: http://chronicle.com/article/An-Adjuncts-Death-Becomes-a/141709/

Elster, J. (1998). A plea for mechanisms. In P. Hedström & R. Swedberg (Eds.), *Social Mechanisms: An analytical approach to social theory* (pp. 45–73). Cambridge, NY: Cambridge University Press. doi:10.1017/CBO9780511663901.003

Emanuel, E. J. (2013). Online education: MOOCs taken by educated few. *Nature, 503*(7476), 342–342. doi:10.1038/503342a PMID:24256798

Environmental Protection Agency. (2012). *General information on e-waste*. Retrieved from http://www.epa.gov/epawaste/conserve/materials/ecycling/faq.htm

Epstude, K., & Roese, N. J. (2008). The functional theory of counterfactual thinking. *Personality and Social Psychology Review, 12*(2), 168–192. doi:10.1177/1088868308316091 PMID:18453477

Erdal, D., Whiten, A., Boehm, C., & Knauft, B. (1994). On human egalitarianism: An evolutionary product of machiavellian status escalation? *Current Anthropology, 35*(2), 175–183. doi:10.1086/204255

Fahlquist, J. N. (2008). Moral Responsibility for Environmental Problems—Individual or Institutional? *Journal of Agricultural & Environmental Ethics, 22*(2), 109–124. doi:10.1007/s10806-008-9134-5

Fallows, J. (2014, December 28). The Tragedy of the American Military. *Atlantic (Boston, Mass.), Retrieved from* http://www.theatlantic.com/features/archive/2014/12/the-tragedy-of-the-american-military/383516/

Farah, M. J. (2005). Neuroethics: The practical and the philosophical. *Trends in Cognitive Sciences, 9*(1), 34–40. doi:10.1016/j.tics.2004.12.001 PMID:15639439

Farah, M. J., Illes, J., Cook-Deegan, R., Gardner, H., Kandel, E., & King, P. et al. (2004). Neurocognitive enhancement: What we can do and what should we do. *Nature Reviews. Neuroscience, 5*(5), 421–425. doi:10.1038/nrn1390 PMID:15100724

Ferrari, A., Coenen, C., & Grunwald, A. (2012). Visions and ethics in current discourse on human enhancement. *NanoEthics, 6*(3), 215–229. doi:10.1007/s11569-012-0155-1

Fischbacher, U., & Utikal, V. (2013). On the acceptance of apologies. *Games and Economic Behavior, 82*, 592–608. doi:10.1016/j.geb.2013.09.003

Fischer, J. M., & Ravizza, M. (1998). *Responsibility and Control: A Theory of Moral Responsibility*. Cambridge: Cambridge University Press. doi:10.1017/CBO9780511814594

Fishman, C. (2011, Apr 29). The dangerously clean water used to make your iPhone. *Fast Company*. Retrieved from http://www.fastcompany.com/1750612/dangerously-clean-water-used-make-your-iphone

Floridi, L. (2009). Against Digital Ontology. Synthese. 151–178.

Floridi, L. (2011). The philosophy of information. Oxford. England: Oxford University Press.

Floridi, L. (2013, December 8). Enveloping the World How Reality Is Becoming AI Friendly - Keynote at *PT-AI 2013*. Retrieved from https://www.youtube.com/watch?v=D6lQ4Ko1Dbg

Floridi, L. (2007). A look into the future impact of ICT on our lives. *The Information Society, 23*(1), 59–64. doi:10.1080/01972240601059094

Floridi, L., & Sancers, J. (2004). The Foundationalist Debate in Computer Ethics. In R. Spinello & H. Tavani (Eds.), *Readings in CyberEthics* (pp. 81–95). Massachusetts: Jones and Bartlett.

Food and Agriculture Organization of the United Nations. (2012). *Coping with water scarcity: An action framework for agriculture and food security*. Retrieved from: http://www.fao.org/docrep/016/i3015e/i3015e.pdf

Foot, P. (1967). The problem of abortion and the doctrine of double effect. *Oxford Review, 5*, 5–15.

Forsyth, C., Butler, H., Graesser, A., Halpern, D, Millis, K., Cai, Z., & Wood, J. (2010). Higher contributions correlate with higher learning gains. *EDM*. 287-288.

Foucault, M. (1980). *Power/Knowledge*. New York, NY: Pantheon Books.

Fowler, R. B. (2002).

Frank, R. H. (2001). Cooperation through Emotional Commitment. In R. M. Nesse (Ed.), *Evolution and the capacity for commitment* (pp. 55–76). New York: Russell Sage.

Franssen, M., Lokhorst, G. J., & van de Poel, I. (2013). Philosophy of Technology. In E.N. Zalta (Ed.), *The Stanford Encyclopedia of Philosophy*. Retrieved from http://plato.stanford.edu/archives/win2013/entries/technology/

Fredkin, E. (2003). An Introduction to Digital Philosophy. *International Journal of Theoretical Physics*, 42(2), 189–247. doi:10.1023/A:1024443232206

Freitas, R. Jr. (2003). *Nanomedicine, Vol. IIA: Biocompatibility*. Austin, TX: Landes Bioscience.

Friedman, B. (1990). *Moral Responsibility and Computer Technology*. Paper presented at the Annual Meeting of the American Educational Research Association, Boston, MA.

Friedman, B. (1997). *Human values and the design of computer technology*. New York: Cambridge University Press.

Friedman, B., & Kahn, P. H. Jr. (2003). Human Values, ethics, and design. In J. A. Jacko & A. Sears (Eds.), *The human-computer interaction handbook* (pp. 1177–1201). Hillsdale, NJ: L. Erlbaum Associates Inc.

Friendshuh, L., & Troncale, L. (2012). SoSPT I.: Identifying Fundamental Systems Processes for a General Theory of Systems. In *Proceedings of the 56th Annual Conference*. San Jose, California: International Society for the Systems Sciences (ISSS). Retrieved from http://journals.isss.org/index.php/proceedings56th/article/viewFile/2145/676

Gallese, V.Gallese & Goldman. (1998). Mirror neurons and the simulation theory. *Trends in Cognitive Sciences*, 2(12), 493–501. doi:10.1016/S1364-6613(98)01262-5 PMID:21227300

Galliott, J. (Forthcoming). *Military Robots: Mapping the Moral Landscape*. Surrey: Ashgate.

Galliott, J. C. (2012). Uninhabited Systems and the Asymmetry Objection: A Response to Strawser. *Journal of Military Ethics*, 11(1), 58–66. doi:10.1080/15027570.2012.683703

Galliott, J. C. (2012/13). Closing with Completeness: The Asymmetric Drone Warfare Debate. *Journal of Military Ethics*, 11(4), 353–356. doi:10.1080/15027570.2012.760245

Ganascia, J.-G. (2012). An Agent-Based Formalization for Resolving Ethical Conflicts. In Proceedings of the *Workshop on Belief Change, Non-monotonic Reasoning, and Conflict Resolution (BNC@ECAI'12)*, Montpellier, France.

Ganascia, J.-G. (2007). Modelling ethical rules of lying with Answer Set Programming. *Ethics and Information Technology*, 9(1), 39–47. doi:10.1007/s10676-006-9134-y

Garis, H. (2005). The Artilect War: Cosmists vs. Terrans. Palm Springs, CA: ETC Publications.

Gartner. (2013, June 24). *Gartner says worldwide PC, tablet and mobile phone shipments to grow 5.9 percent in 2013 as anytime-anywhere-computing drives buyer behavior*. Retrieved from http://www.gartner.com/newsroom/id/2525515

Garvey, J. (2008). *The Ethics of Climate Change: Right and Wrong in a Warning World*. New York: Bloomsbury.

Gazzaniga, M. S. (2006). *The Ethical Brain: The Science of Our Moral Dilemmas*. New York: Harper Perennial.

Gelfond, M., & Lifschitz, V. (1988). The stable model semantics for logic programming. In *Proceedings of the Fifth International Conference on Logic Programming (ICLP)* (pp. 1070-1080). Cambridge, MA: MIT Press.

Gettleman, J. (2010, January 3). Americans' Role Seen in Uganda Anti-Gay Push. *The New York Times*.

Gibson, K. (1997). *Ethics and business. An introduction*. Cambridge University Press.

Gintis, H. (2001). Beyond selfishness in modeling human behavior. In R. M. Nesse (Ed.), *Evolution and the capacity for commitment*. New York: Russell Sage.

Glover, J. (1984). *What sort of people should there be?* Penguin Books.

Gödel, K. (1931). Über formal unentscheidbare Sätze der Principia Mathematica und verwandter Systeme, I. *Monatshefte für Mathematik und Physik, 38*(38), 173–198. doi:10.1007/BF01700692

Godin, B. (2005). *Measurement and statistics on science and technology: 1920 to the present*. New York: Routledge.

Goffman, E. (1974). *Frame analysis: An essay on the organization of experience*. London: Harper and Row.

Gökmenoğlu, T., Eret, E., & Kiraz, E. (2010). Crises, Reforms, and Scientific Improvements: Behaviorism in the Last Two Centuries. *Elementary Education Online, 9*(1), 292-300. Retrieved from http://ilkogretim-online.org.tr/vol9say1/v9s1m22.pdf

Gotterbarn, D. (2001). Informatics and Professional Responsibility. *Science and Engineering Ethics, 7*(2), 221–230. doi:10.1007/s11948-001-0043-5 PMID:11349362

Gray, C. S. (1997). AI at War: The Aegis System in Combat. In D. Shculer (Ed.), *Directions and Implications of Advanced Computing.* (pp. 62–79). New York: Ablex.

Greely, H. T. (2005). Regulating human biological enhancements: Questions justifications and international complications. *The Mind, The Body, and The Law: University of Technology. The Sydney Law Review, 4*(2), 87–110.

Greely, H. T. (2006). Regulating human biological enhancements: Questions justifications and international complications. *Santa Clara Journal of International Law, 4*(2), 87–110.

Greene, J. (2013). *Moral Tribes: Emotion, Reason, and the Gap Between Us and Them.* New York: The Penguin Press HC.

Greene, J. D. (2013). *Moral Tribes: Emotion, Reason, and the Gap between Us and Them.* New York: Penguin Press.

Greene, J. D., Nystrom, L. E., Engell, A. D., Darley, J. M., & Cohen, J. D. (2004). The neural bases of cognitive conflict and control in moral judgment. *Neuron, 44*(2), 389–400. doi:10.1016/j.neuron.2004.09.027 PMID:15473975

Griffiths, A. J. F., Wessler, S. R., Lewontin, R. C., & Carroll, S. B. (9th Ed.). (2007). *Introduction to genetic analysis* W. H. Freeman and Company.

Grossman, D. (1995). *On killing: the psychological cost of learning to kill in war and society.* Boston: Little, Brown and Company.

Groves, T. (1973). Incentives in Teams. *Econometrica, 41*(4), 617–631. doi:10.2307/1914085

Guarini, M. (2006). Particularism and the Classification and Reclassification of Moral Cases. *IEEE Intelligent Systems, 21*(4), 22–28. doi:10.1109/MIS.2006.76

Guarini, M. (2011). Computational neural modeling and the philosophy of ethics: Reflections on the particularism-generalism debate. In M. Anderson & S. L. Anderson (Eds.), *Machine Ethics* (pp. 316–334). New York, NY: Cambridge University Press. doi:10.1017/CBO9780511978036.023

Guarini, M., & Bello, P. (2012). Robotic Warfare: Some Challenges in Moving from Non-civilian to Civilian Theaters. In P. Lin, K. Abney, & G. Bekey (Eds.), *Robot Ethics: The Ethical and Social Implications of Robotics* (pp. 129–145). Cambridge, MA: MIT Press.

Guattari, F. (2009). Chaosophy: Texts and Interviews 1972-1977. Los Angeles CA: Semiotext(e).

Guo, S., & Zhang, G. (2009). Robot rights. *Science, 323*(5916), 876. doi:10.1126/science.323.5916.876a PMID:19213895

Guston, D., Parsi, J., & Tosi, J. (2007). Anticipating the ethical and political challenges of human nanotechnologies. In F. Allhoff, P. Lin, J. Moor, J. Weckert, & M. C. Roco (Eds.), *Nanoethics: The ethical and social implications of nanotechnology* (pp. 185–198). Hoboken, NJ: John Wiley & Sons, Inc.

Guyer, P. (2003). Kant on the theory and practice of autonomy. *Social Philosophy & Policy, 20*(02), 70–98. doi:10.1017/S026505250320203X

Haidt, J. (2007). The new synthesis in moral psychology. *Science, 316*(5827), 998–1002. doi:10.1126/science.1137651 PMID:17510357

Haidt, J. (2012). *The righteous mind.* Pantheon.

Hall, J. S. (2007). *Beyond IA: Creating the conscience of the machine.* Amherst, NY: Promrtheus.

Han, T. A., & Pereira, L. M. (2011). Context-dependent incremental intention recognition through Bayesian network model construction. In A. Nicholson (Ed.), Proceedings of the Eighth UAI Bayesian Modeling Applications Workshop (Vol. 818, pp. 50–58). CEUR Workshop Proceedings; Retrieved from http://ceur-ws.org/Vol-818/paper7.pdf

Han, T. A., Pereira, L. M., & Lenaerts, T. (2014). Emergence of Commitments in Public Goods Game: Restricting vs. Avoiding Non-Committers (Submitted). Retrieved from http://centria.di.fct.unl.pt/~lmp/publications/online-papers/commitment_restriction.pdf

Han, T. A., Pereira, L. M., & Lenaerts, T. (2015). "Avoiding or Restricting Defectors in Public Goods Games?". *J. Royal Society Interface*, 12:2014. (pp. 1203).

Han, T. A., Pereira, L. M., & Santos, F. C. (2012b). The emergence of commitments and cooperation. In *Proceedings of the Eleventh International Conference on Autonomous Agents and Multiagent Systems* (pp. 559-566). International Foundation for Autonomous Agents and Multiagent Systems.

Hanson, V. D. (2001). *Carnage and Culture: Landmark Battles in the Rise of Western Power*. New York: Doubleday.

Han, T. A. (2013). *Intention Recognition, Commitments and Their Roles in the Evolution of Cooperation: From Artificial Intelligence Techniques to Evolutionary Game Theory Models. SAPERE series, 9*. Berlin: Springer-Verlag. doi:10.1007/978-3-642-37512-5

Han, T. A., & Pereira, L. M. (2013). Intention-based Decision Making via Intention Recognition and its Applications. In H. Guesgen & S. Marsland (Eds.), *Human Behavior Recognition Technologies: Intelligent Applications for Monitoring and Security* (pp. 174–211). Hershey: IGI Global. doi:10.4018/978-1-4666-3682-8.ch009

Han, T. A., Pereira, L. M., & Santos, F. C. (2011). Intention Recognition Promotes The Emergence of Cooperation. *Adaptive Behavior, 19*(3), 264–279.

Han, T. A., Pereira, L. M., & Santos, F. C. (2011a). Intention recognition promotes the emergence of cooperation. *Adaptive Behavior, 19*(3), 264–279.

Han, T. A., Pereira, L. M., & Santos, F. C. (2011b). The role of intention recognition in the evolution of cooperative behavior. In WalshT. (Ed.), *Proceedings of the 22nd International Joint Conference on Artificial Intelligence* (pp. 1684–1689). AAAI Press.

Han, T. A., Pereira, L. M., & Santos, F. C. (2012). Corpus-based Intention Recognition in Cooperation Dilemmas. *Artificial Life, 18*(4), 365–383. doi:10.1162/ARTL_a_00072 PMID:22938562

Han, T. A., Pereira, L. M., & Santos, F. C. (2012a). Corpus-based intention recognition in cooperation dilemmas. *Artificial Life, 18*(4), 365–383. PMID:22938562

Han, T. A., Pereira, L. M., & Santos, F. C. (2012c). Intention Recognition, Commitment, and The Evolution of Cooperation. In *Proceedings of IEEE Congress on Evolutionary Computation* (pp. 1–8). IEEE Press. doi:10.1109/CEC.2012.6256472

Han, T. A., Pereira, L. M., Santos, F. C., & Lenaerts, T. (2013). Good Agreements Make Good Friends. *Scientific Reports, 3*. doi:10.1038/srep02695 PMID:24045873

Han, T. A., Pereira, L. M., Santos, F. C., & Lenaerts, T. (2013b). Why is it so hard to say sorry: The evolution of apology with commitments in the iterated Prisoner's Dilemma. In *Proceedings of the Twenty-Third International Joint Conference on Artificial Intelligence* (pp. 177–183). Palo Alto: AAAI Press.

Han, T. A., Pereira, L. M., Santos, F. C., & Lenaerts, T. (in press). Emergence of Cooperation via Intention Recognition, Commitment, and Apology -- A Research Summary. *AI Communications*.

Han, T. A., Saptawijaya, A., & Pereira, L. M. (2012). Moral reasoning under uncertainty. In BjørnerN.VoronkovA. (Eds.), *Proceedings of the Eighteenth International Conference on Logic for Programming Artificial Intelligence and Reasoning (LNCS)* (Vol. 7180, pp. 212-227). Berlin:Springer-Verlag. doi:10.1007/978-3-642-28717-6_18

Harasim, L. (2000). Shift happens online education as a new paradigm in learning. *The Internet and Higher Education, 3*(1-2), 41–61. doi:10.1016/S1096-7516(00)00032-4

Hardin, G. (1968). The tragedy of the commons. *Science, 162*(3859), 1243–1248. doi:10.1126/science.162.3859.1243 PMID:5699198

Hardy, C. (2004). Synchronicity: Interconnection through a Semantic Dimension. Curitiba, Brazil: Faculdades Integradas. Retrieved from http://hardy.christine.free.fr/39-Synchronicity.doc

Hari, S. D. (2012). A Few Questions About Consciousness Suggested By Comparing the Brain and the Computer. *NeuroQuantology*, *10*(2), 286–301. doi:10.14704/nq.2012.10.2.407

Harris, J. (2007). *Enhancing evolution: The ethical case for making ethical people.* Princeton: Princeton University Press.

Hauser, M. D. (2006). *Moral Minds: The Nature of Right and Wrong.* New York: Harper Perennial.

Hauser, M., Cushman, F., Young, L., Jin, R. K., & Mikhail, J. (2007). A dissociation between moral judgments and justifications. *Mind & Language*, *22*(1), 1–21. doi:10.1111/j.1468-0017.2006.00297.x

Healy, P. (2009, November 11) The Anguish of War for Today's Soldiers, Explored by Sophocles. *The New York Times.* Retrieved from http://www.nytimes.com

Heidegger, M. (1977). The question concerning technology. In W. Lovitt (Ed.), The question concerning technology and other essays (trans.) (pp. 3-35). New York: Harper & Row.

Heidegger, M. (1982). The Question Concerning Technology. In W. Lovitt, (Ed.), The Question Concerning Technology and Other Essays New York, NY: Harper and Row.

Heinze, C. (2003). *Modeling Intention Recognition for Intelligent Agent Systems* (Doctoral Dissertation). The University of Melbourne, Australia.

Henrich, J., & Boyd, R. (2001). Why people punish defectors: Weak conformist transmission can stabilize costly enforcement of norms in cooperative dilemmas. *Journal of Theoretical Biology*, *208*(1), 79–89. doi:10.1006/jtbi.2000.2202 PMID:11162054

Hesse, H. (1987). *Demijan (Demian).* Belgrade, Serbia: Beogradski izdavačko-grafički zavod (BIGZ).

Hess, U., & Thibault, P. (2009). Darwin and Emotion Expression". *The American Psychologist*, *64*(2), 120–128. doi:10.1037/a0013386 PMID:19203144

Heussner, K. (2013). A new Blackboard? 4 ways the ed tech giant's new CEO hopes to win back market share. Retrieved from http://gigaom.com

Heylighen, F. (2011). Conceptions of a Global Brain: an historical review. In L. Grinin, R. Carneiro, A. Korotayev, & F. Spier (Eds.), Evolution: Cosmic, Biological, Social (pp. 274–289). Volgograd, Russia: Uchitel Publishing House. Retrieved from http://pespmc1.vub.ac.be/Papers/GBconceptions.pdf

Hickok, G. (2009). Eight problems for the mirror neuron theory of action understanding in monkeys and humans. *Journal of Cognitive Neuroscience*, *21*(7), 1229–1243. doi:10.1162/jocn.2009.21189 PMID:19199415

Higuchi, S., Rzepka, R., & Araki, K. (2008). A Casual Conversation System Using Modality and Word Associations Retrieved from the Web.*Proceedings of the 2008 Conference on Empirical Methods in Natural Language Processing*, Honolulu, USA, (pp. 382-390). doi:10.3115/1613715.1613765

Hill, S. E. (2006). *Dissatisfied by design: The evolution of discontent.* Dissertation. University of Texas, Austin, TX.

Hodge, N. (2012) In the Afghan War, a Little Robot Can Be a Soldier's Best Friend. *The Wall Street Journal.* Retrieved from http://www.wsj.com

Hodge, J. (1995). *Heidegger and ethics.* London: Routledge.

Hofbauer, J., & Sigmund, K. (1998). *Evolutionary Games and Population Dynamics.* New York, NY: Cambridge University Press. doi:10.1017/CBO9781139173179

Hoffman, R. (1975). Scientific research and moral rectitude. *Philosophy (London, England)*, *50*(194), 475–477. doi:10.1017/S0031819100025675

Hofstadter, D. (2002). *Gedel, Ešer, Bah: Jedna beskrajna zlatna nit [Godel, Escher, Bach: An Eternal Golden Braid].* Belgrade, Serbia: Prosveta.

Holert, T. (2012). A live monster that is fruitful and multiplies: Capitalism as Poisoned Rat?. *e-flux, 36.* Retrieved from http://www.e-flux.com/journal/%E2%80%9Ca-live-monster-that-is-fruitful-and-multiplies%E2%80%9D-capitalism-as-poisoned-rat/

Horton, R. (2004). Rediscovering human dignity. *Lancet*, *364*(9439), 1081–1085. doi:10.1016/S0140-6736(04)17065-7 PMID:15380969

Hu, C. M., Fang, R. H., Copp, J., Luk, B. T., & Zhang, L. (2013). A biomimetic nanosponge that absorbs pore-forming toxins. *Nature Nanotechnology*, *8*(5), 336–340. doi:10.1038/nnano.2013.54 PMID:23584215

Huggett, N., Vistarini, T., & Wüthrich, C. (2013). Time in Quantum Gravity. In A. Bardon & H. Dyke (Eds.), Blackwell Companion to the Philosophy of Time (pp. 242–261). Hoboken, NJ: Wiley-Blackwell. Retrieved from http://www.academia.edu/2046778/Time_in_Quantum_Gravity doi:10.1002/9781118522097.ch15

Humphreys, P. (2004). *Extending ourselves: Computational science, empiricism, and scientific method.* New York: Oxford University Press. doi:10.1093/0195158709.001.0001

Humphries, M. (2012, June 8). Rare earth elements: The global supply chain. *Congressional Research Service*. Retrieved from http://www.relooney.info/0_New_14118.pdf

Ihde, D. (2001). Bodies. In *Technology (Electronic Mediations)*. Minneapolis, MN: University of Minnesota Press.

Ihde, D. (2010). A phenomenology of technics. In C. Hanks (Ed.), *Technology and Values: Essential Readings* (pp. 134–155). New York, NY: Wiley-Blackwell.

Illich, I. (1974). *Energy and Equity*. London, UK: Harper and Row.

Inhelder, B., & Piaget, J. (1958). *The Growth of Logical Thinking from Childhood to Adolescence*. New York, NY: Basic Books. doi:10.1037/10034-000

International Federation of Robotics. (2013). *Service robot statistics*. Retrieved October 7, 2014, from www.ifr.org/service-robots/statistics

International Federation of Robotics. (2014). *IFR: All-time-high for industrial robots in 2013*. Retrieved from http://www.ifr.org/news/ifr-press-release/ifr-all-time-high-for-industrial-robots-in-2013-601/

Jackson, M. O. (2000). Mechanism theory. In U. Derigs (Ed.), *Optimization and Operations Research*. Paris: EOLSS Publishers.

Jacobsen, P. L. (2003). Safety in numbers: More walkers and bicyclists, safer walking and bicycling. *Injury Prevention*, *9*(9), 205–209. doi:10.1136/ip.9.3.205 PMID:12966006

Jargodzki, C. (2009). From Stephen Hawking's Flexiverse to Synchronicity: Intimations of Our Transhuman Future. In *Metanexus Institute Conference*. Retrieved from http://www.metanexus.net/archive/conference2009/abstract/default-id=10819.aspx.html

Jebari, K. (2013). Brain machine interface and human enhancement—An ethical review. *Neuroethics*, *6*(3), 617–625. doi:10.1007/s12152-012-9176-2

Johnson, S. (2012). *Future Perfect: The Case for Progress in a Networked Age*. New York: Riverhead Books.

Jones, J. N. (2011, November 11). Six Questions for Slavoj Žižek. *Harper's Blog*. Retrieved from harpers.org/blog/2011/11/six-questions-for-slavoj-zizek/

Jong, D. (2014, January 26). Have MOOCs replaced the classroom? *Minding the Campus: Reforming Our Universities*. Retrieved from http://www.mindingthecampus.com/originals/2014/01/have_moocs_replaced_the_classr.html

Jónsdóttir, B. (2013, August 21). Bradley Manning's Sentence: 35 Years for Exposing Us to the Truth. The Guardian. Retrieved from http://www.theguardian.com

Jonsen, A. R., & Toulmin, S. (1988). *The Abuse of Casuistry: A History of Moral Reasoning*. Oakland, CA: University of California Press.

Juarrero, A. (1999). *Dynamics in Action: Intentional Behavior as a Complex System*. Cambridge and London: The MIT Press. Retrieved from http://aliciajuarrerodotcom1.files.wordpress.com/2012/02/dynamics-in-action-pdf1.pdf

Juarrero, A. (2000). Dynamics in Action: Intentional Behavior as a Complex System. *Emergence*, *2*(2), 24–57. http://intersci.ss.uci.edu/wiki/pub/Juarrero(2000)Dynmcs_Action(ECO).pdf doi:10.1207/S15327000EM0202_03

Juengst, E. (1997). Can enhancement be distinguished from prevention in genetic medicine? *The Journal of Medicine and Philosophy*, *22*(2), 125–142. doi:10.1093/jmp/22.2.125 PMID:9186925

Jung, C. G. (1978a). Sinhronicitet kao princip akauzalnih veza [Synchronicity: An Acausal Connecting Principle]. In C.G. Jung, (1978) Duh i život [Spirit and Life] (pp. 119-197). Novi Sad, Serbia: Matica srpska.

Jung, C. G. (1996). Aion. Belgrade, Serbia: Atos. Kari, J. Cellular Automata: Tutorial. Turku, Finland: University of Turku. Retrieved from http://users.utu.fi/jkari/ca/CAintro.pdf

Jung, C.G. (1978b). *Psihološki tipovi* [Psychological Types]. Novi Sad, Serbia: Matica srpska.

Jünger, E., & Hofmann, M. (2004) Storms of Steel. (pp. 234).New York: Penguin Books.

Kahneman, D. (2002). Nobel prize lecture: Maps of Bounded Rationality: a perspective on intuitive judgment and choice. In T. Frangsmyr (Ed.), *Nobel Prizes 2002: Nobel Prizes, Presentations, Biographies, & Lectures* (pp. 416–499). Stockholm: Almqvist & Wiksell Int.

Kahneman, D. (2003). A perspective on judgment and choice. *The American Psychologist*, *58*(9), 697–720. doi:10.1037/0003-066X.58.9.697 PMID:14584987

Kahneman, D. (2013). *Thinking, Fast and Slow*. New York, NY: Farrar, Straus and Giroux.

Kahn, P. H. Jr. (1992). Children's obligatory and discretionary moral judgments. *Child Development*, *63*(2), 416–430. doi:10.2307/1131489 PMID:1611944

Kahn, P. H. Jr. (1999). *The human relationship with nature: Development and culture*. Cambridge, MA: MIT Press.

Kaiman, J. (2014, Mar 20). Rare earth mining in China: The bleak social and environmental costs. *The Guardian*. Retrieved from: http://www.theguardian.com/sustainable-business/rare-earth-mining-china-social-environmental-costs

Kaku, M. (2004). *Einstein's cosmos: How Albert Einstein's vision transformed our understanding of space and time*. New York: Atlas Books.

Kamm, F. M. (2006). *Intricate Ethics: Rights, Responsibilities, and Permissible Harm*. New York, NY: Oxford University Press.

Kant, I. (1781). Kritik der reinen Vernunft. Trans. P. Guyer & A. Wood (Eds.), Critique of Pure Reason (1998). Cambridge: Cambridge University Press. doi:10.1017/CBO9780511804649

Kant, I. (1784). Beantwortung der Frage: Was ist Aufklärung? [An Answer to the Question: What is Enlightenment?] In M. J. Gregor (Ed.), Practical Philosophy. (1996). (pp. 17–22). Cambridge: Cambridge University Press.

Kant, I. (1785). Grundlegung zur Metaphysik der Sitten. Trans. A. W. Wood (Ed.), Groundwork for the Metaphysics of Morals (2002). New Haven, CT: Yale University Press.

Kant, I. (1795). Zum ewigen Frieden. Ein philosophischer Entwurf [Toward Perpetual Peace: A Philosophical Sketch]. In P. Kleingeld & D. L. Colclasure (Eds.), Toward Perpetual Peace and Other Writings on Politics, Peace, and History (pp. 67–109). New Haven, CT: Yale University Press.

Kant, I. (2002). *Groundwork for the Metaphysics of Morals*. New Haven: Yale University Press.

Karoliszyn, H. (2014, September 3). Do We Want Minority Report Policing? *Aeon Magazine*. Retrieved from http://aeon.co/magazine/technology/do-we-want-minority-report-policing/

Karpin, I., & Mykitiuk, R. (2008). Going out on a limb: Prosthetics, normalcy and disputing the therapy/enhancement distinction. *Medical Law Review*, *16*(3), 413–436. doi:10.1093/medlaw/fwn018 PMID:18635592

Kateb, B., & Heiss, J. D. (Eds.). (2013). *The Textbook of Nanoneuroscience and Nanoneurosurgery*. New York, NY: CRC Press. doi:10.1201/b15274

Keane, J. (2009). The Life and Death of Democracy. New York: W.W. Norton.

Keeley, L. H. (1996). *War before Civilization* (p. 144). New York: Oxford University Press.

Kelly, K. (1995). Out of Control: The New Biology of Machines, Social Systems, and the Economic World (pp. 22). Reading, Mass.: Addison-Wesley.

Kelly, K. (2014). Conversation: The Technium. *Edge*. Retrieved from http://edge.org/memberbio/kevin_kelly

Khadaroo, S. (2014). Data breach at Indiana University: Are colleges being targeted? *The Christian Science Monitor*. Retrieved from http://www.csmonitor.com

Kilcullen, D. (2013). *Out of the Mountains: The Coming Age of the Urban Guerrilla* (p. 174). New York: Oxford University Press.

Kilgannon, C. (2014, March 27). Without tenure or a home. *The New York Times*. Retrieved from http://www.nytimes.com/2014/03/30/nyregion/without-tenure-or-a-home.html?_r=3

Kineman, J. (2012). Relational Science: Towards a Unified Theory of Nature. In R. Rosen (Ed.), *Anticipatory Systems: Philosophical, Mathematical, and Methodological Foundations, IFSR International Series on Systems Science and Engineering 1* (pp. 399–419). New York, NY: Springer.

King, C. (2011). The Central Enigma of Consciousness. *Journal of Consciousness Exploration & Research*, 2(1), 13–44. Retrieved from http://jcer.com/index.php/jcj/article/view/123/131

King, M. (2001). *A guide to Heidegger's being and time*. State University of New York.

Klapoetke, N. C., Murata, Y., Kim, S. S., Pulver, S. R., Birdsey-Benson, A., & Cho, Y. K. et al. (2014). Independent Optical Excitation of Distinct Neural Populations. *Nature Methods*, 11(3), 338–346. doi:10.1038/nmeth.2836 PMID:24509633

Koepsell, D. (2007). *The ethics of genetic engineering: A position paper from the center for inquiry office of public policy*. Washington, DC: Center for Inquiry.

Kohlberg, L. (1981). *The Philosophy of Moral Development*. Harper and Row.

Kolowich, S. (2013, July 8). A university's offer of credit for a MOOC gets no takers. The Chronicle of Higher Education. Retrieved from http://www.fulbright.de/fileadmin/files/tousa/stipendien/ees/Educational_Experts_Seminar_2013/A_University_s_Offer_of_Credit_for_a_MOOC_Gets_No_Takers_-_Technology_-_The_Chronicle_of_Higher_Education.pdf

Koruga, Đ. (1996). Information physics: In search of a scientific basis of consciousness. In: D. Raković, & Đ. Koruga (Eds.), *Consciousness: Scientific Challenge of the 21st Century* (pp. 260-278). Belgrade, Serbia: United Nations University for Peace. Retrieved from http://www.dejanrakovicfund.org/knjige/1995-ecpd-consciousness.pdf

Koutropoulos, A., Gallagher, M. S., Abajian, S. C., de Waard, I., Hogue, R. J., Keskin, N. O., & Rodriguez, C. O. (2012). Emotive Vocabulary in MOOCs: Context & Participant Retention. *European Journal of Open, Distance and E-Learning*.

Kowalski, R. (2011). *Computational logic and human thinking: how to be artificially intelligent*. Cambridge: Cambridge University Press. doi:10.1017/CBO9780511984747

Krausz, M. (2011). Varieties of relativism and the reach of reasons. In *S. D. Hales, A companion to relativism.*. Oxford, UK: Wiley-Blackwell. doi:10.1002/9781444392494.ch4

Krebs, D. L. (2011). *The Origins of Morality: An Evolutionary Account*. New York: Oxford University Press. doi:10.1093/acprof:oso/9780199778232.001.0001

Kshetri, N., & Dholakia, N. (2009). *Global digital divide*. Retrieved from http://ebooks.narotama.ac.id/files/Encyclopedia%20of%20Information%20Science%20and%20Technology%20%282nd%20Edition%29/Global%20Digital%20Divide.pdf

Kudo, T. (2005). *MeCab: Yet Another Part-of-Speech and Morphological Analyzer*. http://mecab.sourceforge.net/

Kurzweil, R. (2005). *The singularity is near: When humans transcend biology*. New York: Viking Penguin.

Lackey, D. P. (1994). Military Funds, Moral Demand: Personal Responsibilities of the Individual Scientist. In E. Sherwin, S. Gendlin, & L. Keliman (Eds.), *Ethical Issues in Scientific Research: An Anthology* (pp. 397–409). New York: Garland.

Lakoff, G. (2004). *Don't Think of an Elephant!: Know Your Values and Frame the Debate – The Essential Guide for Progressives*. White River Junction, Vermont: Chelsea Green Publishing.

Lanier, J. (2010). You Are Not a Gadget: A Manifesto. (pp. 134). New York: Alfred A. Knopf.

Lanier, J. (2013). Who Owns the Future? New York: Simon and Schuster.

Lanier, J. (2014, November 14). The Myth Of AI. *Edge.org*. Retrieved from. http://edge.org/conversation/the-myth-of-ai

Lanier, J. (2013). *Who Owns the Future?* New York, NY: Simon & Schuster.

Lanza, R., & Berman, D. (2009). *Biocentrism: How Life and Consciousness Are the Keys to Understanding the True Nature of the Universe.* Dallas, Texas: BenBella Books.

Laplace, P. (1951). Theorie analytique des probabilities. In F.W. Truscott & F.L. Emory. (Eds.), A Philosophical Essay on Probabilities. (6th Ed). New York: Dover Publications. (pp. 4).

Laplante, P. A. (2013). Courses for the masses? *IT Professional, 15*(2), 57–59. doi:10.1109/MITP.2013.27

Latour, B. (1993). *We Have Never Been Modern* (C. Porter, Trans.). Cambridge, MA: Harvard University Press.

Latour, B. (1994). On Technical Mediation. *Common Knowledge, 3*(2), 29–64.

Latour, B. (2004). *Politics of Nature: How to Bring the Sciences into Democracy* (C. Porter, Trans.). Cambridge, MA: Harvard University Press.

Latour, B., & Venn, C. (2002). Morality and Technology The End of the Means. *Theory, Culture & Society, 19*(5/6), 247–260. doi:10.1177/026327602761899246

Lawrence, S., & Sharma, U. (2002). Commodification of education and academic labour-using the balanced scorecard in a university setting. *Critical Perspectives on Accounting, 13*(5), 661–677. doi:10.1006/cpac.2002.0562

Lea, R. D. (2009). Ethical considerations of biotechnologies used for performance enhancement. *The Journal of Bone and Joint Surgery, 91*(8), 2048–2054. doi:10.2106/JBJS.I.00023 PMID:19651979

Lebedev, M. A., & Nicolelis, M. A. L. (2006). Brain machine interfaces: Past, present and future. *Trends in Neurosciences, 29*(9), 536–546. doi:10.1016/j.tins.2006.07.004 PMID:16859758

Lee, P., & George, R. P. (2008). The nature and basis of human dignity. *Ratio Juris, 21*(2), 173–193. doi:10.1111/j.1467-9337.2008.00386.x

Lees, J., Poierau, V., & Tisserand, V. et al. (2012). Observation of Time-Reversal Violation in the B^0 Meson System. *Physical Review Letters, 109*(21). Retrieved from https://physics.aps.org/featured-article-pdf/10.1103/PhysRevLett.109.211801 PMID:23215586

Lesh, N. (1998). *Scalable and Adaptive Goal Recognition* (Doctoral Dissertation). University of Washington.

Leveson, N. G. (1991). Software safety in embedded computer systems. *Communications of the ACM, 34*(2), 34–46. doi:10.1145/102792.102799

Lewin, T. (2013, January 6). Students rush to web classes, but profits may be much later. *The New York Times*. Retrieved from http://www.nytimes.com/2013/01/07/education/massive-open-online-courses-prove-popular-if-not-lucrative-yet.html?pagewanted=all&_r=0

Lichocki, P., Kahn, P., & Billard, A. (2011). The ethical landscape in robotics. *IEEE Robotics & Automation Magazine, 18*(1), 39–50. doi:10.1109/MRA.2011.940275

Lin, P. (2009, June 22). The ethical war machine. *Forbes*. Retrieved from http://www.forbes.com/2009/06/18/military-robots-ethics-opinions-contributors-artificial-intelligence-09-patrick-lin.html

Lin, P. (2011, December 15). Drone-Ethics Briefing: What a Leading Robot Expert Told the CIA. Atlantic (Boston, Mass.). Retrieved from http://www.theatlantic.com

Lin, P., Abney, K., & Bekey, G. (2011). Robot ethics: Mapping the issues for a mechanized world. *Artificial Intelligence, 175*(5/6), 942–949. doi:10.1016/j.artint.2010.11.026

Lin, P., Abney, K., & Bekey, G. A. (2011). *Robot ethics: the ethical and social implications of robotics.* Cambridge: MIT Press.

Lin, P., & Allhoff, F. (2008). Untangling the debate: The ethics of human enhancement. *NanoEthics, 2*(3), 251–264. doi:10.1007/s11569-008-0046-7

Littlejohn, A. (2013). *Understanding massive open online courses*. CEMCA EdTechnotes. Retrieved from http://cemca.org.in/ckfinder/userfiles/files/EdTech%20 Notes%202_Littlejohn_final_1June2013.pdf

Liu, H., & Singh, P. (2004). ConceptNet: A Practical Commonsense Reasoning Toolkit. *BT Technology Journal, 22*(4), 211–226. doi:10.1023/B:BTTJ.0000047600.45421.6d

Lobach, E. (2008). *Presentiment Research: Past, Present, and Future*. Amsterdam, Netherlands: University of Amsterdam.

Lokhorst, G.-J., & van den Hoven, J. (2012). Responsibility for military robots. In P. Lin, K. Abney, & G. Bekey (Eds.), *Robot Ethics: The Ethical and Social Implications of Robotics*. (pp. 145–156). Cambridge: MIT Press.

Lopes, G., & Pereira, L. M. (2006). Prospective Programming with ACORDA, In *Empirically Successful Computerized Reasoning (ESCoR'06) workshop at The 3rd International Joint Conference on Automated Reasoning (IJCAR'06)*, Seattle, USA.

Lopes, G., & Pereira, L. M. (2006). Prospective programming with ACORDA. In *Proceedings of the FLoC'06 Workshop on Empirically Successful Computerized Reasoning (ESCoR'06)*, Seattle, USA.

Lopes, G., & Pereira, L. M. (2010). Prospective storytelling agents. In Carro M. Peña R. (Eds.), *Proceedings of the Twelfth International Symposium on Practical Aspects of Declarative Languages (LNCS)*. (pp. 294-296). doi:10.1007/978-3-642-11503-5_24

Losing Humanity. (2012, November 19). *Human Rights Watch*. Retrieved from http://www.hrw.org/reports/2012/11/19/losing-humanity

Lovelock, J. (2004, May 24). Nuclear power is the only green solution. *The Independent*. Retrieved from http://www.independent.co.uk/voices/commentators/james-lovelock-nuclear-power-is-the-only-green-solution-6169341.html

Lowenberg, A. (1990). Neoclassical Economics as a Theory of Politics and Institutions. *The Cato Journal, 3*(9), 619–639. Retrieved from www.cato.org/cato-journal/winter-1990/neoclassical-economics-theory-politics-institutions

MacIntyre, A. (2nd Ed.). (1984). *After Virtue: A Study in Moral Theory* Notre Dame, IN: University of Notre Dame Press.

Mackness, J., Mak, S., & Williams, R. (2010). The ideals and reality of participating in a MOOC. In: Dirckinck-Holmfeld L. Hodgson V., C. Jones, M. De Laat, D. McConnell and T. Ryberg, (Eds.). *Proceedings of the 7th International Conference on Networked Learning 2010*, Lancaster. (pp. 266-275).

Madrigal, A. (2014, July 23). Smart Things in a Not-Smart World. The Atlantic (Boston, Mass.). Retrieved from http://www.theatlantic.com/technology/archive/2014/07/there-are-only-12-quiet-places-left-in-america/374885/

Manders-Huits, N. (2006). Moral responsibility and IT for human enhancement. Proceedings of *Association for Computing Machinery Symposium on Applied Computing*, Dijon. doi:10.1145/1141277.1141340

Marcini, P. (2014, October 1). How to Upgrade Democracy for the Internet Era. *TED*.

Markman, K. D., Gavanski, I., Sherman, S. J., & McMullen, M. N. (1993). The mental simulation of better and worse possible worlds. *Journal of Experimental Social Psychology, 29*(1), 87–109. doi:10.1006/jesp.1993.1005

Markoff, J. (2013, April 4). Essay-Grading software offers professors a break. *The New York Times*.

Markoff, J. (2014, November 11) Fearing Bombs That Can Pick Whom to Kill. *The New York Times*. Retrieved from http://www.nytimes.com/2014/11/12/science/weapons-directed-by-robots-not-humans-raise-ethical-questions

Marx, K. (1867). Das Kapital, Bd. 1. [Capital, Volume 1]. In S. Moore & E. Aveling, (Eds.) *Capital, Volume One* (1887). Retrieved from http://www.marxists.org/archive/marx/works/1867-c1/index.htm

Matthias, A. (2004). The Responsibility Gap: Ascribing Responsibility for the Actions of Learning Automata. *Ethics and Information Technology, 6*(3), 175–183. doi:10.1007/s10676-004-3422-1

Mavroidis, C. (2014). *Nano-Robotics in Medical Applications: From Science Fiction to Reality*. Northeastern University. Retrieved from http://www.albany.edu/self-organization/presentations/2-mavroidis.pdf

Mazoue, J. G. (2013). The MOOC model: Challenging traditional education. *EDUCAUSE Review Online*. Retrieved from http://er.dut.ac.za/bitstream/handle/123456789/71/Mazoue_2013_The_MOOC_Model_Challenging_Traditional_Education.pdf?sequence=1

McAfee, R. P. (1993). Mechanism Design by Competing Sellers. *Econometrica*, *61*(6), 1281–1312. doi:10.2307/2951643

McCabe, M. J., & Snyder, C. M. (2005, May). Open access and academic journal quality. *The American Economic Review*, *95*(2), 453–458. doi:10.1257/000282805774670112

McCloy, R., & Byrne, R. M. J. (2000). Counterfactual thinking about controllable events. *Memory & Cognition*, *28*(6), 1071–1078. doi:10.3758/BF03209355 PMID:11105533

McDermott, D. (2008). Why ethics is a high hurdle for AI. Paper presented at the *North American Conference on Computers and Philosophy*, Bloomington, IN.

McDonough, J. (2003). Descartes' "Dioptrics" and "Optics.". In L. Nolan (Ed.), *The Cambridge Descartes Lexicon*. Cambridge: Cambridge University Press.

McDougall, W. (1923). *Outline of psychology*. London.

McIntyre, A. (2004). Doctrine of double effect. In E. N. Zalta (Ed.), The Stanford Encyclopedia of Philosophy (Fall 2011 edition). Retrieved from http://plato.stanford.edu/entries/double-effect/

McLaren, B. M. (2003). Extensionally Defining Principles and Cases in Ethics: An AI Model. *Artificial Intelligence Journal*, *150*(Nov.), 145–181. doi:10.1016/S0004-3702(03)00135-8

McLaren, B. M. (2006). Computational models of ethical reasoning: Challenges, initial steps, and future directions. *IEEE Intelligent Systems*, *21*(4), 29–37. doi:10.1109/MIS.2006.67

McMahan, J. (2009). *Killing in War*. Oxford: Oxford University Press. doi:10.1093/acprof:oso/9780199548668.001.0001

McNamara, C., & Troncale, L. (2012). SPT II.: How to Find & Map Linkage Propositions for a GTS from the Natural Sciences Literature. In *Proceedings of the 56th Annual Conference*. San Jose, California. ISSS. Retrieved from http://journals.isss.org/index.php/proceedings56th/article/viewFile/2153/679

Meltzoff, A. N. (2005). Imitation and other minds: the "like me" hypothesis. In *Perspectives On Imitation: From Neuroscience to Social Science. Imitation, Human Development, and Culture* (pp. 55–77). Cambridge, MA: MIT Press.

Melville, C. (2009). The City & the City. New York: Del Rey Ballantine Books.

Merrit, T. (2012). *A Chronology of Tech History* [E-book].

Meyer, J. P., & Zhu, S. (2013). Fair and equitable measurement of student learning in MOOCs: An introduction to item response theory, scale linking, and score equating. *Research & Practice in Assessment*, *8*(1), 26–39.

Miah, A. (2001). Genetic technologies and sport: The new ethical issue. *Journal of the Philosophy of Sport*, *28*(1), 32–52. doi:10.1080/00948705.2001.9714599

Miah, A. (2011). Ethical issues raised by human enhancement. In F. Gonzalez (Ed.), *Values and ethics for the 21st century* (pp. 199–231). Spain: Fundacion BBVA.

Midgley, M. (2003). *The Myths We Live By*. London, New York: Routledge.

Migliore, S., Curcio, G., Mancini, F., & Cappa, S. F. (2014). Counterfactual thinking in moral judgment: An experimental study. *Frontiers in Psychology*, *5*, 451. doi:10.3389/fpsyg.2014.00451 PMID:24904468

Mikhail, J. (2011). *Elements of moral cognition: Rawls' linguistic analogy and the cognitive science of moral and legal judgment*. Cambridge: Cambridge University Press. doi:10.1017/CBO9780511780578

Mikulecky, D. Robert Rosen. (n.d.). The Well Posed Question and Its Answer – Why Are Organisms Different from Machines? Richmond, VA: Medical Campus of Virginia Commonwealth University. Retrieved from http://www.people.vcu.edu/~mikuleck/PPRISS3.html

Millar, J. (2014). Technology as Moral Proxy: Autonomy and Paternalism by Design, *Proceedings of IEEE Ethics in Engineering, Science and Technology Conference*. Retrieved from https://ethicstechnologyandsociety.files.wordpress.com/2014/06/millar-technology-as-moral-proxy-autonomy-and-paternalism-by-design.pdf

Millar, J., & Kerr, I. (2012). Delegation, Relinquishment and Responsiibility: The Prospect of Expert Robots. Proceedings of *We Robot*, Coral Gables.

Miller, R. (2012, Aug 14). Data center water use moves to the forefront. *Datacenter Knowledge*. Retrieved from http://www.datacenterknowledge.com/archives/2012/08/14/data-center-water-use-moves-to-center-stage/

Miller, A. (2010). *137: Jung, Pauli, and the Pursuit of a Scientific Obsession*. New York, NY: W.W. Norton & Company.

Miller, G. (1995). WordNet: A Lexical Database for English. *Communications of the ACM, 38*(11), 39–41. doi:10.1145/219717.219748

Miller, S. (2008). Collective Responsibility and Information and Communication Technology. In J. van den Hoven & J. Weckert (Eds.), *Information Technology and Moral Philosophy*. (pp. 226–250). Cambridge: Cambridge University Press.

Milligan, C., Littlejohn, A., & Margaryan, A. (2013). Patterns of engagement in connectivist MOOCs. *MERLOT Journal of Online Learning and Teaching, 9*(2), 149–159.

Mitchell, C., & Sackney, L. (2011). *Profound improvement: Building capacity for a learning community*. New York: Routledge.

Moore, A. D. (1998). Intangible property: Privacy, power, and information control. *American Philosophical Quarterly, 35*(4), 365–378.

Moore, G. E. (1903). *Principia Ethica*. Cambridge, UK: Cambridge University Press.

Moore, G. E. (1965). Cramming more components onto integrated circuits. *Electronics Magazine, 38*(8), 114–117.

Moor, J. H. (2006). The nature, importance, and difficulty of machine ethics. *IEEE Intelligent Systems, 21*(4), 18–21. doi:10.1109/MIS.2006.80

Morozov, E. (2011). The Net Delusion: The Dark Side of Internet Freedom. New York, NY: Public Affairs.

Morozov, E. (2013, January 1). The Meme Hustler. *The Baffler*. 22. Retrieved from http://www.thebaffler.com/articles/the-meme-hustler

Moss, G. (2014, February 26). MOOCs remain on Carolina's drawing board – Dr. Jeff Pomerantz one of the first to teach MOOCs for UNC at Chapel Hill. UNC School of Information and Library Science. Retrieved from http://sils.unc.edu/news/2014/moocs-pomerantz

Mouffe, C. (2000). The Democratic Paradox. London: Verso.

Murakami, Y. (2004). Utilitarian Deontic Logic. In *Proceedings of the Fifth International Conference on Advances in Modal Logic (AiML'04)*. London: King's College Publications.

Myers, A. (2014, November 24). Competency-based accelerated training. *EDUCAUSE Review Online*. Retrieved from https://www.educause.edu/ero/article/competency-based-acceleratedtraining?utm_source=Informz&utm_medium=Email+marketing&utm_campaign=EDUCAUSE

Myerson, R. (1979). Incentive compatibility and the bargaining problem. *Econometrica, 47*(1), 61–73. doi:10.2307/1912346

Myskaja, B. K. (2006). The moral difference between intragenic and transgenic modification of plants. *Journal of Agricultural & Environmental Ethics, 19*(3), 225–238. doi:10.1007/s10806-005-6164-0 PMID:17061380

Naam, R. (2005). *More than human*. New York: Broadway Books.

Nabi, S. (2012). 7 Blackboard competitors with online learning solutions. Retrieved from educationdive.com

Nadin, M. (2010). Anticipation and Dynamics: Rosen's Anticipation in the Perspective of Time. *International Journal of General Systems, 39*(1), 3–33. http://www.nadin.ws/archives/966 doi:10.1080/03081070903453685

Naím, M. (2014). The End of Power From Boardrooms to Battlefields and Churches to States. New York: Basic Books.

Nakamura, A. (1993). *Kanjo hyogen jiten* [Dictionary of Emotive Expressions]. Tokyodo Publishing.

Naor, M., Pinkas, B., & Sumner, R. (1999). Privacy preserving auctions and mechanism design. In *Proceedings of the 1st ACM Conference on Electronic Commerce* (pp. 129–139). ACM. doi:10.1145/336992.337028

Naranjo, J. R. (2011). Bridging the Gap: Does Closure to Efficient Causation Entail Quantum-Like Attributes? *Axiomathes*, *21*(2), 315–330. http://link.springer.com/article/10.1007%2Fs10516-011-9146-z doi:10.1007/s10516-011-9146-z

Nesse, R. M. (2001a). Natural selection and the capacity for subjective commitment. In R. M. Nesse (Ed.), *Evolution and the Capacity for Commitment* (pp. 1–44). New York: Russell Sage.

Nesse, R. M. (2001b). *Evolution and the Capacity for Commitment*. New York: Russell Sage.

Newton, I. (1846). *The Mathematical Principles of Natural Philosophy*. New York, NY: Daniel Adee.

NHTSA. (2009). Geospatial Analysis of rural Motor Vehicle Traffic Fatalities. Retrieved from http://www-nrd.nhtsa.dot.gov/Pubs/811196.pdf

Nicolelis, M. (2011). *Beyond Boundaries: The New Neuroscience of Connecting Brains with Machines--and How It Will Change Our Lives*. New York: Times Books/Henry Holt and Co.

Nisan, N., & Ronen, A. (1999). Algorithmic mechanism design. In *Proceedings of the Thirty-First Annual ACM Symposium on Theory of Computing* (pp. 129–140). ACM. doi:10.1145/301250.301287

Noble, D. (1998). Digital diploma mills: The automation of higher education. *Science as Culture*, *7*(3), 355–368. doi:10.1080/09505439809526510

Noorman, M. (2012). Computing and Moral Responsibility. *Stanford Encyclopedia of Responsibility*. Retrieved from http://plato.stanford.edu/archives/fall2012/entries/computing-responsibility/

Nordmann, A. (2014). Responsible innovation, the art and craft of anticipation. *Journal of Responsible Innovation.*, *1*(1), 87–98. doi:10.1080/23299460.2014.882064

Nowak, M. A. (2006a). *Evolutionary Dynamics: Exploring the Equations of Life*. Cambridge, MA: Harvard University Press.

Nowak, M. A. (2006b). Five rules for the evolution of cooperation. *Science*, *314*(5805), 1560–1563. doi:10.1126/science.1133755 PMID:17158317

Nowak, M. A., & Sigmund, K. (1992). Tit for tat in heterogeneous populations. *Nature*, *355*(6357), 250–253. doi:10.1038/355250a0

Nowak, M. A., & Sigmund, K. (2005). Evolution of indirect reciprocity. *Nature*, *437*(7063), 1291–1298. doi:10.1038/nature04131 PMID:16251955

Nozick, R. (1974). *Anarchy, state, and utopia*. New York: Basic Books.

Nuclear Energy Institute. (2014). *On-site storage of nuclear waste*. Retrieved from: http://www.nei.org/Knowledge-Center/Nuclear-Statistics/On-Site-Storage-of-Nuclear-Waste

Nummenmaa, L., Glerean, E., Hari, R., & Hietanen, J. K. (2014). Bodily maps of emotions. *Proceedings of the National Academy of Sciences of the United States of America*, *111*(2), 646–651. doi:10.1073/pnas.1321664111 PMID:24379370

O'Brien, M. (2011). The future of humanity: Heidegger, personhood and technology. *Comparative Philosophy*, *2*(2), 23–49.

O'Mathuna, D. P. (2013). Human dignity and the ethics of human enhancement. *Trans-Humanities*, *6*(1), 99–120.

Ogle, R. (2007). *Smart World: Breakthrough Creativity and the New Science of Ideas*. Boston, Massachusetts: Harvard Business School Press.

Ohtsubo, Y., & Watanabe, E. (2009). Do sincere apologies need to be costly? Test of a costly signaling model of apology. *Evolution and Human Behavior*, *30*(2), 114–123. doi:10.1016/j.evolhumbehav.2008.09.004

Olson, P. (2012). We Are Anonymous: Inside the Hacker World of Lulzsec, Anonymous, and the Global Cyber Insurgency. New York: Little, Brown and Company.

Ostrom, E. (1990). *Governing the commons: The evolution of institutions for collective action*. Cambridge, MA: Cambridge University Press. doi:10.1017/CBO9780511807763

Pacheco, J. M., Santos, F. C., & Chalub, F. A. C. (2006). Stern-judging: A simple, successful norm which promotes cooperation under indirect reciprocity. *PLoS Computational Biology*, 2(12), e178. doi:10.1371/journal.pcbi.0020178 PMID:17196034

Pacific Northwest Pollution Prevention Resource Center. (2009). *Semiconductor manufacturing*. Retrieved from: http://www.pprc.org/hubs/printfriendly.cfm?hub=1004&subsec=14&nav=1

Paine, L. P. (2013). *The Sea and Civilization: A Maritime History of the World*. Alfred A. Knopf.

Palloff, R., & Pratt, K. (2005). *Collaborating online: Learning together in community*. San Francisco: John Wiley & Sons, Inc.

Palmer, K. (2000). *Reflexive Autopoietic Dissipative Special Systems Theory: An Approach to Emergent Meta-systems through Holonomics*. Retrieved from http://archonic.net/rastnopY.pdf

Pappano, L. (2012, November 2). The year of the MOOC. The New York Times. Retrieved from http://edinaschools.org/cms/lib07/MN01909547/Centricity/Domain/272/The%20Year%20of%20the%20MOOC%20NY%20Times.pdf

Pardo, A., & Siemens, G. (2014). Ethical and privacy principles for learning analytics. *British Journal of Educational Technology*, 45(3), 1–13. doi:10.1111/bjet.12152

Parfit, D. (1984). *Reasons and Persons*. Oxford: Clarendon Press.

Parfit, D. (1986). *Reasons and persons*. New York: Oxford University Press. doi:10.1093/019824908X.001.0001

Parfit, D. (2011). *On What Matters* (Vol. 1 and 2). Oxford, UK: Oxford University Press.

Pariser, E. (2011). The Filter Bubble: What the Internet Is Hiding from You. New York: Penguin Press.

Parr, C. (2013, April 18). How was it? The UK's first Coursera MOOCS assessed. Times Higher Education. Retrieved from http://www.timeshighereducation.co.uk/news/how-was-it-the-uks-first-coursera-moocs-assessed/2003218.fullarticle

Patten, N. (2012). *The egranary digital library*. Educause Review Online.

Patterson, S. (2010). The Quants: How a Small Band of Math Wizards Took over Wall St. and Nearly Destroyed It. New York: Crown.

Pearl, J. (2009). *Causality: Models, Reasoning and Inference*. New York, NY: Cambridge University Press. doi:10.1017/CBO9780511803161

Peckham, M. (2012, May 1). The collapse of Moore's law: Physicist says it's already happening. *Time*. Retrieved from http://techland.time.com/2012/05/01/the-collapse-of-moores-law-physicist-says-its-already-happening/

Peijnenburg, J. (2006). Shaping Your Own Life. *Metaphilosophy*, 37(2), 240–253. doi:10.1111/j.1467-9973.2006.00424.x

Pellegrino, G., Fadiga, L., Fogassi, L., Gallese, V., & Rizzolatti, G. (1992). Understanding motor events: A neurophysiological study. *Experimental Brain Research*, 91(1), 176–180. doi:10.1007/BF00230027 PMID:1301372

Penrose, R. (2004a). *Carev novi um* [The Emperor's New Mind]. Belgrade, Serbia: Informatika.

Penrose, R. (2004b). *The Road to Reality: A Complete Guide to the Laws of the Universe*. London, UK: Jonathan Cape.

Pereira, L. M., & Lopes, G. (2007). Prospective Logic Agents, In: J. M. Neves, M. F. Santos, & J. M. Machado (Eds.), Progress in Artificial Intelligence. Proceedings of 13th Portuguese Intl. Conf. on Artificial Intelligence (EPIA'07), (pp.73-86).

Pereira, L. M., & Saptawijaya, A. (2007a). Moral Decision Making with ACORDA. In *Local Proceedings of the Fourteenth International Conference on Logic for Programming Artificial Intelligence and Reasoning (LPAR'07)*, Yerevan, Armenia.

Pereira, L. M., & Saptawijaya, A. (2014). *Counterfactuals in Logic Programming with Applications to Agent Morality* (Submitted). Retrieved from http://centria.di.fct. unl.pt/~lmp/publications/online-papers/moral_counterfactuals.pdf

Pereira, L. M., Han, T. A., & Santos, F. C. (2014). Complex Systems of Mindful Entities -- on Intention Recognition and Commitment. In: Magnani, L. 2014 (Ed.), Model-Based Reasoning in Science and Technology: Theoretical and Cognitive Issues. (pp. 499-525). Berlin, Springer-Verlag. doi:10.1007/978-3-642-37428-9_28

Pereira, L. M. (2012). Evolutionary Tolerance. In L. Magnani & L. Ping (Eds.), *Philosophy and Cognitive Science—Western & Eastern Studies (SAPERE)* , 2. (pp. 263–287). Berlin: Springer-Verlag. doi:10.1007/978-3-642-29928-5_14

Pereira, L. M. (2012b). Turing is Among Us. *Journal of Logic and Computation*, 22(6), 1257–1277. doi:10.1093/logcom/exs035

Pereira, L. M. (2014). Can we not Copy the Human Brain in the Computer? In *Brain.org* (pp. 118–126). Lisbon: Fundação Calouste Gulbenkian.

Pereira, L. M., Dell'Acqua, P., Pinto, A. M., & Lopes, G. (2013). Inspecting and preferring abductive models. In K. Nakamatsu & L. C. Jain (Eds.), *The Handbook on Reasoning-Based Intelligent Systems* (pp. 243–274). World Scientific Publishers. doi:10.1142/9789814329484_0010

Pereira, L. M., & Han, T. A. (2009a). Evolution Prospection. In NakamatsuK.Phillips-WrenG.JainL. C.HowlettR. J. (Eds.), *Proceedings of the First KES International Symposium IDT (New Advances in Intelligent Decision Technologies)* (Vol. 199, pp. 51-63). Berlin: Springer-Verlag. doi:10.1007/978-3-642-00909-9_6

Pereira, L. M., & Han, T. A. (2009b). Intention recognition via causal Bayes networks plus plan generation. In *Proceedings of 14th Portuguese International Conference on Artificial Intelligence (LNCS)* (Vol. 5816, pp. 138–149). Berlin: Springer-Verlag. doi:10.1007/978-3-642-04686-5_12

Pereira, L. M., & Han, T. A. (2011). Intention recognition with evolution prospection and causal Bayesian networks. In A. Madureira, J. Ferreira, & Z. Vale (Eds.), *Computational Intelligence for Engineering Systems: Emergent Applications* (pp. 1–33). Berlin: Springer-Verlag. doi:10.1007/978-94-007-0093-2_1

Pereira, L. M., & Saptawijaya, A. (2007). Modelling morality with prospective logic.*Proceedings of the 13th Portuguese International Conference on Artificial Intelligence (EPIA'07)*. (pp. 1-28).

Pereira, L. M., & Saptawijaya, A. (2007). Moral Decision Making with ACORDA. In *Local Proceedings of the Fourteenth International Conference on Logic for Programming Artificial Intelligence and Reasoning (LPAR'07)*, Yerevan, Armenia.

Pereira, L. M., & Saptawijaya, A. (2007b). Modelling Morality with Prospective Logic. In NevesJ. M.SantosM. F.MachadoJ. M. (Eds.), *Proceedings of the Thirteenth Portuguese Conference on Artificial Intelligence (LNCS)* (Vol. 4874, pp. 99-111). Berlin: Springer-Verlag.

Pereira, L. M., & Saptawijaya, A. (2009). Modelling Morality with Prospective Logic. *International Journal of Reasoning-based Intelligent Systems*, 1(3/4), 209–221. doi:10.1504/IJRIS.2009.028020

Pereira, L. M., & Saptawijaya, A. (2011). Modelling Morality with Prospective Logic. In M. Anderson & S. L. Anderson (Eds.), *Machine Ethics* (pp. 398–421). New York, NY: Cambridge University Press. doi:10.1017/CBO9780511978036.027

Perry, D. (2014). Faculty members are not cashiers. *The Chronicle of Higher Education*.

Pesce, M. (1997, January 1). Ignition (A Ritual For the Festival of Brigit). *Hyper-real*. Retrieved from http://hyperreal.org/~mpesce/Ignition.html

Petersen, A. C. (2012). *Simulating nature: a philosophical study of computer-simulation uncertainties and their role in climate science and policy advice*. Boca Raton: CRC Press. doi:10.1201/b11914

Peters, T. (2007). Are we playing god with nanoenhancement? In F. Allhoff, P. Lin, J. Moore, & J. Weckert (Eds.), *Nanoethics: The ethical and social implications of nanotechnology*. Hoboken, NJ: John Wiley & Sons.

Petitt, P. (2007). Responsibility Incorporated. *Ethics, 117*(2), 171–201. doi:10.1086/510695

Phelps, S., McBurney, P., & Parsons, S. (2010). Evolutionary mechanism design: A review. *Autonomous Agents and Multi-Agent Systems, 21*(2), 237–264. doi:10.1007/s10458-009-9108-7

Picard, R. W., & Klein, J. (2002). Computers that recognise and respond to user emotion: Theoretical and practical implications. *Interacting with Computers, 14*(2), 141–169. doi:10.1016/S0953-5438(01)00055-8

Pierce, M. A., & Henry, J. W. (1996). Computer ethics: The role of personal, informal, and formal codes. *Journal of Business Ethics, 14*(4), 425–437. doi:10.1007/BF00380363

Pinheiro, F. L., Pacheco, J. M., & Santos, F. C. (2012). From Local to Global Dilemmas in Social Networks. *PLoS ONE, 7*(2), e32114. doi:10.1371/journal.pone.0032114 PMID:22363804

Pinker, S. (2008). *The stupidity of dignity*. The New Republic. Retrieved from http://www.newrepublic.com/article/the-stupidity-dignity#

Pinker, S. (2011). *The Better Angels of Our Nature: Why Violence Has Declined*. Penguin Group.

Plus, P. C. (2012, July 22). The weird and wonderful materials that make up your PC. *Techrader*. Retrieved from http://www.techradar.com/us/news/computing/pc/the-weird-and-wonderful-materials-that-make-up-your-pc-1089510

Poell, T. (2004). Movement and Time in Cinema, Discernements: Deleuzian Aesthetics. In J. Bloois (Ed.), *Rodopi* (pp. 1–21).

Poli, R. (2010). *The Complexity of Self-reference: A Critical Evaluation of Luhmann's Theory of Social Systems*. Trento, Italy: Dipartimento di Sociologia. Retrieved from http://web.unitn.it/files/quad50.pdf

Pols, A. J. K. (2012). How Artefacts Influence Our Actions. *Ethical Theory and Moral Practice*. Retrieved from http://link.springer.com/content/pdf/10.1007%2Fs10677-012-9377-0

Pontier, M. A., & Hoorn, J. F. (2012). *Toward Machines that Behave Ethically Better than Humans Do*. Proceedings of the *34th International Annual Conference of the Cognitive Science Society, CogSci*, Sapporo, Japan.

Powers, T. M. (2006). Prospects for a Kantian machine. *IEEE Intelligent Systems, 21*(4), 46–51. doi:10.1109/MIS.2006.77

Pražić, A. (2003). *Priroda i teleologija* [Nature and Teleology]. Belgrade, Serbia: Izdavačka kuća Plato.

President's Council on Bioethics. (2003). *Beyond therapy: Biotechnology and the pursuit of happiness*. Washington, DC: Government Printing Office.

Preston, S., & de Waal, F. (2002). Empathy: Its ultimate and proximate bases. *Behavioral and Brain Sciences, 25*, 1–72. PMID:12625087

Priest, D., & Arkin, W. M. (2011). Top Secret America: The Rise of the New American Security State. New York: Little, Brown and Company.

Provenzale, J. M., & Mohs, A. M. (2010). Nanotechnology in Neurology: Current Status and Future Possibilities. *US Neurology., 6*(1), 12–17.

Ptaszynski, M., Rzepka, R., Araki, K., & Momouchi, Y. (2012). Annotating Syntactic Information on 5 Billion Word Corpus of Japanese Blogs. *Proceedings of The Eighteenth Annual Meeting of The Association for Natural Language Processing (NLP-2012)*, pp. 14-16.

Rahwan, I., & Simari, G. (Eds.). (2009). *Argumentation in Artificial Intelligence*. Berlin: Springer-Verlag.

Raković, D. (1995). *Osnovi biofizike* [Fundamentals of Biophysics]. Belgrade, Serbia: Grosknjiga.

Rand, D. G., Fudenberg, D., & Dreber, A. (2013). It's the thought that counts: The role of intentions in noisy repeated games. *Social Science Research Network*. Retrieved from http://ssrn.com/abstract=2259407

Rawls, J. (1971). *A Theory of Justice*. Cambridge, MA: Belknap Press of Harvard University Press.

Regan, T. (1986). *The Case for Animal Rights*. Berkeley: University of California Press.

Rescher, N. (1980). The canons of distributive justice. In J. P. Sterba (Ed.), *Justice: Alternative political perspectives*. Belmont, CA: Wadsworth Publishing Company.

Rickles, D. (2008). Quantum Gravity: A Primer for Philosophers. In D. Rickles (Ed.), The Ashgate Companion to Contemporary Philosophy of Physics. Farnham, UK: Ashgate. Retrieved from http://philsci-archive.pitt.edu/5387/1/Rickles_QG.pdf

Rigby, A. (2005). Forgiveness and Reconciliation in Just Post Bellum. In M. Evans (Ed.), *Just War Theory A Reappraisal* (pp. 177–200). New York: Palgrave Macmillan. doi:10.3366/edinburgh/9780748620746.003.0009

Ripley, A. (2012). College is dead. Long live college. *Time Magazine, 180*(18), 33-41.

Rivard, R. (2013a, March 15). Humans fight over robo-readers. *Inside Higher Education*. Retrieved from http://www.insidehighered.com

Rivard, R. (2013b, March 8). Measuring the MOOC dropout rate. Inside Higher Education. Retrieved from http://www.immagic.com/eLibrary/ARCHIVES/GENERAL/GENPRESS/I130308R.pdf

roadmap. Washington DC: Department of Defense.

Robertson, S. L. (2014). Untangling theories and hegemonic projects in researching education and the knowledge economy. In A.D. Reid, E.P. Hart, M.A. Peters (eds.) A Companion to Research in Education. Dordrecht: Springer Science+Business Media. doi:10.1007/978-94-007-6809-3_35

Rodenburg, D. (2010). Resistance is futile—Confronting the ethics of the "enhanced human" athlete. Retrieved from http://www.ischool.utoronto.ca/system/files/pages/docs/itable/RodenburgResistance.pdf

Rodriguez, C. O. (2012). MOOCs and the AI-Stanford like courses: Two successful and distinct course formats for massive open online courses. *European Journal of Open, Distance and E-Learning*.

Rogers, W., & Rogers, S. (1992). *Storm Center: The USS Vincennes and Iran Air Flight 655*. Annapolis: Naval Institute Press.

Rosenblum, P. (2014). The target data breach is becoming a nightmare. *Forbes*. Retrieved from http://www.forbes.com

Rosen, R. (2012). *Anticipatory Systems: Philosophical, Mathematical, and Methodological Foundations, IFSR International Series on Systems Science and Engineering 1*. New York, NY: Springer. doi:10.1007/978-1-4614-1269-4

Rose, S. P. R. (2002). Smart drugs: Do they work? Are they ethical? Will they be legal? *Nature Reviews. Neuroscience, 3*(12), 975–979. doi:10.1038/nrn984 PMID:12461554

Ross, D. (2005). *Economic theory and cognitive science: Microexplanation*. Cambridge, MA: MIT press.

Ross, L., & Nisbett, R. E. (2011). *The Person and the Situation: Perspectives of Social Psychology*. London, UK: Pinter & Martin Ltd.

Ross, W. D. (1930). *The Right and the Good*. Oxford: Oxford University Press.

Roth, R. (2002-2004). *The Return of the World Soul: Wolfgang Pauli, Carl Jung and the Challenge of the Unified Psychophysical Reality*. Zurich, Switzerland: Pro Litteris. Retrieved from http://paulijungunusmundus.eu/synw/pauli_fludd_flood_sync.htm

Roy, O. (2009). *Thinking before Acting: Intentions, Logic, Rational Choice* (Doctoral Dissertation). ILLC Dissertation Series DS-2008-03, Amsterdam.

Roy, P., Bouchard, B., Bouzouane, A., & Giroux, S. (2007). A hybrid plan recognition model for alzheimer's patients: interleaved-erroneous dilemma. In *Proceedings of IEEE/WIC/ACM International Conference on Intelligent Agent Technology* (pp. 131–137).

Rushton, J. P. (1975). Generosity in children: Immediate and long-term effects of modeling, preaching, and moral judgment. *Journal of Personality and Social Psychology, 31*(3), 459–466. doi:10.1037/h0076466

Ruvinsky, A. I. (2007). Computational ethics. In M. Quigley (Ed.), *Encyclopedia of information ethics and security* (pp. 73–76). Hersey, PA: IGI Global. doi:10.4018/978-1-59140-987-8.ch012

Ryberg, J. (2003). Ethics and Military Research: on the Moral Responsibility of Scientists. In B. Booss-Bavnbek & J. Høyrup (Eds.), *Mathematics and War* (pp. 352–366). Berlin: Birkhäuser Verlag. doi:10.1007/978-3-0348-8093-0_19

Rzepka, R. & Araki, K. (2012). Polarization of consequence expressions for an automatic ethical judgment based on moral stages theory. *IPSJ SIG Notes 2012-NL-207(14)*. (pp. 1-4).

Rzepka, R., & Araki, K. (2005). What Statistics Could Do for Ethics? - The Idea of Common Sense Processing Based Safety Valve. *AAAI Fall Symposium on Machine Ethics, FS-05-06*.

Rzepka, R., & Araki, K. (2013a). Web-based five senses input simulation – ten years later. In Technical Reports of Japanese Society of AI SIG-LSE B301, 5, pp. 25–33.

Rzepka, R., & Araki, K. (2013b). Possible Usage of Sentiment Analysis for Calculating Vectors of Felicific Calculus, *IEEE 13th International Conference on Data Mining Workshop "SENTIRE"*, Dallas, USA, (pp. 967-970).

Rzepka, R., & Araki, K. (2014b). ELIZA Fifty Years Later: An Automatic Therapist Using Bottom-Up and Top-Down Approaches. (To appear in) Intelligent Systems, Control and Automation: Science and Engineering, 74, van Rysewyk, Simon Peter, Pontier, Matthijs (Eds.)

Rzepka, R., Ge, Y., & Araki, K. (2005). Naturalness of an Utterance Based on the Automatically Retrieved Commonsense. Proceedings of *IJCAI 2005 - Nineteenth International Joint Conference on Artificial Intelligence*, Edinburgh, Scotland. (pp. 1696-1697.)

Rzepka, R., & Araki, K. (2014a). Experience of Crowds as a Guarantee for Safe Artificial Self. *AAAI Spring Symposium on Implementing Selves with Safe Motivational Systems & Self-Improvement*, Stanford, USA. (pp. 40-44).

Rzepka, R., Shibuki, H., Kimura, Y., Takamaru, K., Matsuhara, M., & Murakami, K. (2008). Judicial Precedents Processing Project for Supporting Japanese Lay Judge System. *Workshop on Semantic Processing of Legal Texts, LREC 2008*, Marrakech, Morocco. (pp.33-41).

Sadri, F. (2011). Logic-based approaches to intention recognition. In N.-Y. Chong & F. Mastrogiovanni (Eds.), *Handbook of Research on Ambient Intelligence: Trends and Perspectives* (pp. 346–375). Hershey, PA: IGI Global.

Sandeen, C. (2013). Assessment's place in the new MOOC world. *Research & Practice in Assessment*, 8(1), 5–12.

Sandeen, C. (2013). Integrating MOOCs into traditional higher education: The emerging "MOOC 3.0" era. *Change: The Magazine of Higher Learning.*, 45(6), 34–39. doi:10.1080/00091383.2013.842103

Sandel, M. (2007). *The case against perfection: Ethics in the age of genetic engineering*. Cambridge, MA: Belknap Press.

Sano, M. (2011). *Japanese dictionary of appraisal -attitude-* (JAppraisal Dictionary ver1.1.2). Tokyo: Gengo Shigen Kyokai. Retrieved from http://www.gsk.or.jp/catalog_e.html

Saptawijaya, A., & Pereira, L. M. (2013a). Tabled abduction in logic programs (Technical Communication of ICLP 2013). *Theory and Practice of Logic Programming, Online Supplement, 13(4-5)*. Retrieved from http://journals.cambridge.org/downloadsup.php?file=/tlp2013008.pdf

Saptawijaya, A., & Pereira, L. M. (2014). Joint tabling of logic program abductions and updates (Technical Communication of ICLP 2014). *Theory and Practice of Logic Programming, Online Supplement, 14(4-5)*. Retrieved from http://arxiv.org/abs/1405.2058

Saptawijaya, A., & Pereira, L. M. (2013b). Incremental tabling for query-driven propagation of logic program updates. In McMillan K. Middeldorp A. Voronkov A. (Eds.), *Proceedings of the Nineteenth International Conference on Logic for Programming Artificial Intelligence and Reasoning (LNCS)* (Vol. 8312, pp. 694-709). Berlin: Springer-Verlag. doi:10.1007/978-3-642-45221-5_46

Saptawijaya, A., & Pereira, L. M. (in press). The Potential of Logic Programming as a Computational Tool to Model Morality. In R. Trappl (Ed.), *A Construction Manual for Robots' Ethical Systems: Requirements, Methods, Implementations (Cognitive Technologies)*.

Sawyer, R. J. (2007). Robot ethics. *Science, 318*(5853), 1037. doi:10.1126/science.1151606 PMID:18006710

Scanlon, T. M. (1982). Contractualism and utilitarianism. In A. Sen & B. Williams (Eds.), *Utilitarianism and Beyond*. New York, NY: Cambridge University Press. doi:10.1017/CBO9780511611964.007

Scanlon, T. M. (1998). *What We Owe to Each Other*. Cambridge, MA: Harvard University Press.

Scanlon, T. M. (2008). *Moral Dimensions: Permissibility, Meaning, Blame*. Cambridge, MA: Harvard University Press.

Scanlon, T. M. (2014). *Being realistic about reasons*. Oxford: Oxford University Press. doi:10.1093/acprof:oso/9780199678488.001.0001

Scharre, P. (2014, July 29) How to Lose the Robotics Revolution. *War on the Rocks*. Retrieved from http://warontherocks.com/2014/07/how-to-lose-the-robotics-revolution/#_

Schenke, K., Tran, C., & Hickey, D. (2013, June 5). Design principles for motivating learning with digital badges. *HASTAC*. Retrieved from http://www.hastac.org/blogs/kschenke/2013/06/05/design-principles-motivating-learning-digital-badges

Schmidhuber, J. (1997). A Computer Scientist's View of Life, the Universe, and Everything. In C. Freksa (Ed.), Foundations of Computer Science: Potential – Theory – Cognition (pp. 201–208). New York, NY: Springer; Retrieved from http://arxiv.org/pdf/quant-ph/9904050

Schmidt, E., & Cohen, J. (2013). The New Digital Age: Reshaping the Future of People, Nations and Business (p. 174). New York: Random House.

Schneewind, J. B. (1998). *The invention of autonomy: A history of modern moral philosophy*. Cambridge: Cambridge University Press.

Schulz, M. J., Shanov, V. N., & Yun, Y. (Eds.). (2009). *Nanomedicine Design of Particles, Sensors, Motors, Implants, Robots, and Devices*. New York, NY: Artech House.

Searle, J. R. (1995). *The Construction of Social Reality*. New York: The Free Press.

Searle, J. R. (2010). *Making the Social World: The Structure of Human Civilization*. New York: Oxford University Press. doi:10.1093/acprof:osobl/9780195396171.001.0001

Segbroeck, S. V., Jong, S. D., Nowé, A., Santos, F. C., & Lenaerts, T. (2010). Learning to coordinate in complex networks. *Adaptive Behavior*, *18*(5), 416–427. doi:10.1177/1059712310384282

Seo, D., Carmena, J. M., Rabaey, J. M., Alon, E., & Maharbiz, M. M. (2013). Neural Dust: An Ultrasonic, Low Power Solution for Chronic Brain-Machine Interfaces. *arXiv*, 1307.2196 [q-bio.NC]. Retrieved from http://arxiv.org/abs/1307.2196

Seth, A. K. (2007). Measuring autonomy by multivariate autoregressive modelling. In *Proceedings of the 9th European conference on Advances in artificial life.* (pp. 475-484). doi:10.1007/978-3-540-74913-4_48

Seth, A. K. (2010). Measuring autonomy and emergence via Granger causality. *Artificial Life*, *16*(2), 179–196. doi:10.1162/artl.2010.16.2.16204 PMID:20067405

Sharkey, N. (2012) Killing Made Easy In P. Lin, K. Abney & G.A. Bekey (Eds.). Robot Ethics: The Ethical and Social Implications of Robotics. (pp. 111-128). Cambridge, MA: MIT Press.

Sharkey, N. (2008). The ethical frontiers of robotic. *Science*, *322*(5909), 1800–1801. doi:10.1126/science.1164582 PMID:19095930

Shin, P. C., Hallett, D., Chipman, M. L., Tator, C., & Granton, J. T. (2005). Unsafe driving in North American automobile commercials. *Journal of Public Health*, *27*(4), 318–325. doi:10.1093/pubmed/fdi049 PMID:16162638

Shirky, C. (2005, July 1). Institutions vs. Collaboration. *TED*.

Shirky, C. (2008). *Here Comes Everybody: The Power of Organizing without Organizations*. New York: Penguin Press.

Shue, H. (1988). Mediating Duties. *Ethics*, *98*(4), 687–704. doi:10.1086/292999

Shulman, C., Jonsson, H., & Tarleton, N. (2009). Which consequentialism? Machine ethics and moral divergence. In *AP-CAP 2009: The fifth Asia-Pacific Computing and Philosophy Conference*, University of Tokyo, Japan.

Siemens, G. (2005). Connectivism: A learning theory for the digital age. *International Journal of Instructional Technology and Distance Learning*, *2*(1), 3–10.

Siemens, G., & Long, P. (2011). Penetrating the fog: Analytics in learning and education. *EDUCAUSE Review*, *46*(5), 30–32.

Sigmund, K. (2010). *The Calculus of Selfishness*. Princeton, NJ: Princeton University Press. doi:10.1515/9781400832255

Simão, J., & Pereira, L. M. (2003, November). "Neuro-Psychological Social Theorizing and Simulation with the Computational Multi-Agent System Ethos", Invited paper in proceedings of *Congresso em Neurociências Cognitivas*, Évora, Portugal.

Singer, N. (2012, March 3). Mission Control, Built for Cities. *The New York Times*. Retrieved from http://www.nytimes.com/2012/03/04/business/ibm-takes-smarter-cities-concept-to-rio-de-janeiro.html?pagewanted=all&_r=0

Singer, P. (1981). *The expanding circle: Ethics and sociobiology*. New York: Farrar, Straus and Giroux.

Singer, P. (1993). *Practical ethics*. Cambridge: Cambridge University Press.

Singer, P. W. (2009). *Wired for War: The Robotics Revolution and Conflict in the 21st Century* (pp. 391–392). New York: Penguin Press.

Slade, S., & Prinsloo, P. (2013). Learning analytics: Ethical issues and dilemmas. *The American Behavioral Scientist*, *57*(10), 1510–1529. doi:10.1177/0002764213479366

Slavin, K. (2011, July 1). "How Algorithms Shape Our World. *TED*. Retrieved from http://www.ted.com/talks/kevin_slavin_how_algorithms_shape_our_world

Slote, M. (2010). *Essays on the history of ethics*. New York: Oxford University Press.

Smith, K. (2013). Making FERPA fit when we flip. Library Journal. Retrieved from http://lj.libraryjournal.com/2013/12/opinion/peer-to-peer-review/making-ferpa-fit-when-we-flip-peer-to-peer-review/#_

Smith, M., & Casserly, C. (2006). The promise of open educational resources. *Change: The Magazine of Higher Learning*.

Snead, A. (2012, May 3). A brief history of warnings about the demise of Moore's Law. *Slate*. Retrieved from http://www.slate.com/blogs/future_tense/2012/05/03/michio_kako_and_a_brief_history_of_warnings_about_the_end_of_moore_s_law_.html

Sober, E., & Wilson, D. (1998). *Unto Others: The Evolution and Psychology of Unselfish Behavior*. Cambridge, MA: Harvard University Press.

Soto-Andrade, J., Jaramillo, S., Gutiérrez, C., & Letelier, J.-C. (2011). Ouroboros avatars: A mathematical exploration of Self-reference and Metabolic Closure. *Conference: Advances in Artificial Life, ECAL*. Paris, France. Retrieved from http://mitpress.mit.edu/sites/default/files/titles/alife/0262297140chap115.pdf

Sparrow, R. (2007). Killer robots. *Journal of Applied Philosophy*, *24*(1), 62–77. doi:10.1111/j.1468-5930.2007.00346.x

Sperber, D. (1997). Individualisme méthodologique et cognitivisme. In R. Boudon, F. Chazel, & A. Bouvier (Eds.), *Cognition et sciences sociales* (pp. 123–136). Paris: Presses Universitaires de France.

Stanford International Human Rights and Conflict Resolution Clinic. (2012). Living Under Drones. Retrieved from http://www.livingunderdrones.org/living-under-drones/

Steiner, C. (2012). Automate This: How Algorithms Came to Rule Our World. New York: Portfolio/Penguin.

Stenger, V. (2011). The Anthropic Principle. In T. Flynn (Ed.), The Encyclopedia of Nonbelief. New York, NY: Prometheus Books. Retrieved from http://www.colorado.edu/philosophy/vstenger/Cosmo/ant_encyc.pdf

Stengers, I. (2003). Cosmopolitics II. trans. Bononno, R. [2011], Minneapolis, MN: University of Minnesota Press.

Stibel, J. M. (2009). Breakpoint: Why the Web Will Implode, Search Will Be Obsolete, and Everything Else You Need to Know about Technology Is in Your Brain. New York: Palgrave Macmillan, (pp. 93).

Stolberg, S. G., & Mouawad, J. (2008, May 17). Saudis rebuff Bush, politely, on pumping more oil. *The New York Times*. Retrieved from: http://www.nytimes.com/2008/05/17/world/middleeast/17prexy.html?_r=0

Strawser, B. J. (2010). Moral Predators: The Duty to Employ Uninhabited Aerial Vehicles. *Journal of Military Ethics*, *9*(4), 343–368. doi:10.1080/15027570.2010.536403

Strawson, G. (1994). The impossibility of moral responsibility. *Philosophical Studies*, *75*(1), 5–24. doi:10.1007/BF00989879

Strawson, P. F. (1974). *Freedom and Resentment Freedom and Resentment and Other Essays*. London: Methuen.

Stripling, J. (2011, May 15). Most presidents prefer no tenure for majority of faculty. *The Chronicle of Higher Education*.

Stromberg, J. (2014, August 20). Not a single person has died using bike share in the US. *Vox*, Retrieved from http://www.vox.com/2014/8/12/5994879/bike-share-citi-bike-deaths-safety

Strong, D., & Higgs, E. (2000). Borgmann's philosophy of technology. In E. Higgs, A. Light, & D. Strong (Eds.), *Technology and the good life?* (pp. 19–37). Chicago, London: The University of Chicago Press. doi:10.7208/chicago/9780226333885.003.0002

Strunk, V. A. (2012). Career college students' perceptions of rubrics orientation. *Dissertation Abstracts International*. (UMI 3542066)

Sullins, J. P. (2006). When is a Robot a Moral Agent. *International Review of Information Ethics*, *14*(2), 219–233.

Sun, R. (2013). Moral Judgment, Human Motivation, and Neural Networks. *Cognitive Computation*, *5*(4), 566–579. doi:10.1007/s12559-012-9181-0

Swan, M. (2014). Neural Data Privacy Rights: An Invitation For Progress In The Guise Of An Approaching Worry. In J. Brockman (Ed.), *What Should We Be Worried About?: Real Scenarios That Keep Scientists Up at Night*. New York, NY: Harper Perennial.

Swenson, J. (2014). Establishing an ethical literacy for learning analytics. *Proceedings from the Fourth International Conference on Learning Analytics and Knowledge*. ACM, 246-250. doi:10.1145/2567574.2567613

Swift, T., & Warren, D. S. (2012). XSB: Extending Prolog with tabled logic programming. *Theory and Practice of Logic Programming*, *12*(1-2), 157–187. doi:10.1017/S1471068411000500

Sydell, L. (2014, July 3). In A Battle For Web Traffic, Bad Bots Are Going After Grandma. National Public Radio. Retrieved from http://www.npr.org/blogs/alltechconsidered/2014/07/03/328196199/in-a-battle-for-web-traffic-bad-bots-are-going-after-grandma

Takagi, H. (1997). Introduction to Fuzzy Systems, Neural networks, and Genetic Algorithms. In D. Ruan (Ed.), Fuzzy Logic, Neural Networks, and Genetic Algorithms (pp. 1–33). Norwell, MA: Kluwer Academic Publishers. Retrieved from www.teleamerica.net/reference/Software/IntroToFuzzySystemsNuralNetsGeneticAlgorithms.pdf doi:10.1007/978-1-4615-6191-0_1

Takagi, K., Rzepka, R., & Araki, K. (2011). *Just Keep Tweeting, Dear: Web-Mining Methods for Helping a Social Robot Understand User Need*. Proceedings of Help Me Help You, Symposium of AAAI Spring 2011. (pp. 60-65).

Takamura, H., Inui, T., & Okumura, M. (2005). Extracting Semantic Orientations of Words using Spin Model. *Proceedings of the 43rd Annual Meeting of the Association for Computational Linguistics (ACL2005)*. (pp. 133-140). doi:10.3115/1219840.1219857

Takeuchi, K., Tsuchiyama, S., Moriya, M., & Moriyasu, Y. (2010). Construction of Argument Structure Analyzer toward Searching Same Situations and Actions. *IEICE Technical Report*, *109*(390), 1–6.

Taleb, N. N. (2007). *The Black Swan: The Impact of the Highly Improbable*. New York, NY: Random House.

Taylor, B. J., Cantwell, B., & Slaughter, S. (2013). Quasi-markets in U.S. higher education: The humanities and institutional revenues. *The Journal of Higher Education*, *84*(5), 675–707. doi:10.1353/jhe.2013.0030

Taylor, C. (1985). *Philosophy and the human sciences*. Cambridge: Cambridge University Press. doi:10.1017/CBO9781139173490

Tenbrunsel, A. E., & Messick, D. M. (2004). Ethical fading: The role of self deception in unethical behavior. *Social Justice Research*, *17*(2), 223–236. doi:10.1023/B:SORE.0000027411.35832.53

Thagard, P. (2007). I feel your pain: Mirror neurons, empathy, and moral motivation. *Journal of Cognitive Science*, *8*, 109–136.

Thaler, R. H., & Sunstein, C. (2008). Nudge: Improving Decisions about Health, Wealth, and Happiness. New Haven, Conn.: Yale University Press.

Thomas, J. (1975). The right to privacy. *Philosophy & Public Affairs*, *4*(4), 295–314.

Thompson, D. (1987). *Political Ethics and Public Office.* Cambridge: Harvard University Press.

Thompson, E. (2007). *Mind in Life: Biology, Phenomenology, and the Sciences of Mind.* Cambridge, London: The Belknap Press of Harvard University Press.

Thomson, J. J. (1971). A defense of abortion. *Philosophy & Public Affairs, 1*(1), 47–66.

Thomson, J. J. (1985). The trolley problem. *The Yale Law Journal, 279*(6), 1395–1415. doi:10.2307/796133

Tomasello, M. (2008). *Origins of Human Communication.* Cambridge, MA: MIT Press.

Tomasello, M. (2014). *A Natural History of Human Thinking.* Cambridge, MA: Harvard University Press.

Tomkin, J. H., & Charlevoix, D. (2014). Do professors matter?: Using an a/b test to evaluate the impact of instructor involvement on MOOC student outcomes. In *Proceedings of the First ACM Conference on Learning @ Scale conference.* ACM, 71-78. doi:10.1145/2556325.2566245

Tonkens, R. (2009). A challenge for machine ethics. *Minds and Machines, 19*(3), 421–438. doi:10.1007/s11023-009-9159-1

Townsend, A. M. (2014). Smart Cities: Big Data, Civic Hackers, and the Quest for a New Utopia. New York: W.W Norton & Company.

Tran, B. (2008a). *Expatriate selection and retention.* Doctoral dissertation, Alliant International University, San Francisco, CA.

Tran, B. (2008b). Paradigms in corporate ethics: The legality and values of corporate ethics. *A Special Issue of Social Responsibility Journal. Ethics and Morality in Business Practice, 4*(1/2), 158–171.

Tran, B. (2013). Industrial and organizational (I/O) psychology: The roles and purposes of I/O practitioners in global businesses. In B. Christiansen, E. Turkina, & N. Williams (Eds.), *Cultural and technological influences on global business* (pp. 175–219). Hersey, PA: Premier Reference Source/IGI Global. doi:10.4018/978-1-4666-3966-9.ch011

Tran, B. (2014a). The human element of the knowledge worker: Identifying, managing, and protecting the intellectual capital within knowledge management. In M. A. Chilton & J. M. Bloodgood (Eds.), *Knowledge management for competitive advantage: Issues and potential solutions* (pp. 281–303). Hersey, PA: Premier Reference Source/IGI Global. doi:10.4018/978-1-4666-4679-7.ch017

Tran, B. (2014b). Rhetoric of play: Utilizing the gamer factor in selecting and training employees. In T. M. Connolly, L. Boyle, T. Hainey, G. Baxter, & P. Moreno-Ger (Eds.), *Psychology, pedagogy and assessment in serious games* (pp. 175–203). Hersey, PA: Premier Reference Source/IGI Global. doi:10.4018/978-1-4666-4773-2.ch009

Tran, B. (2014c). Game theory versus business ethics: The game of ethics. In B. Christiansen & M. Basilgan (Eds.), *Economic behavior, game theory, and technology in emerging markets* (pp. 213–236). Hersey, PA: Premier Reference Source/IGI Global. doi:10.4018/978-1-4666-4745-9.ch012

Trevidi, A., Kar, D., & McNeil, H. (2003). *Automatic assignment management and peer evaluation.* Consortium for Computing in Small Colleges.

Troncale, L. (2013). Category Archives: SoSPT. Retrieved from http://lentroncale.com/?cat=10

Turchin, V. (1977). The Phenomenon of Science: a cybernetic approach to human evolution. New York, NY: Columbia University Press. Retrieved from http://pespmc1.vub.ac.be/POS/TurPOS-prev.pdf

Turiel, E. (1983). *The development of social knowledge.* Cambridge, England: Cambridge University Press.

Turing, A. M. (1937). On computable numbers, with an application to the Entscheidungsproblem. *Proceedings of the London Mathematical Society, 42*(1), 230–265. doi:10.1112/plms/s2-42.1.230

Turner, D. C., & Sahakian, B. J. (2006). Neuroethics of cognitive enhancement. *Biosocieties, 1*(1), 113–123. doi:10.1017/S1745855205040044

Tweed, K. (2013, Dec 17). Global e-waste will jump 33 percent in the next five years. *IEEE Spectrum.* Retrieved from http://spectrum.ieee.org/energywise/energy/environment/global-ewaste-will-jump-33-in-next-five-years

Tzeng, J.-Y. (2004). Toward a more civilized design: Studying the effects of computers that apologize. *International Journal of Human-Computer Studies*, *61*(3), 319–345. doi:10.1016/j.ijhcs.2004.01.002

United Nations Environment Program. (2010). *Assessing the environmental impacts of consumption and production: Priority products and materials*. Retrieved from http://www.unep.fr/shared/publications/pdf/DTIx1262xPA-PriorityProductsAndMaterials_Report.pdf

United Nations University. (2004). UN study shows environmental consequences from ongoing boom in personal computer sales. *Eurekalert*. Retrieved from http://www.eurekalert.org/pub_releases/2004-03/tca-uss030204.php

United States Census. (2014). *Census Data*. Retrieved from http://www.census.gov/popclock/

United States Department of Defense. (2009). *FY2009-2034 unmanned systems integrated*

United States Energy Information Administration. (2014). *Short-term energy outlook*. Retrieved from http://www.eia.gov/forecasts/steo/report/global_oil.cfm

United States Geologic Survey. (2014, Mar 19). *How much water is there on, in, and above the Earth?* Retrieved from: http://water.usgs.gov/edu/earthhowmuch.html

Utz, S., Matzat, U., & Snijders, C. (2009). On-line reputation systems: The effects of feedback comments and reactions on building and rebuilding trust in on-line auctions. *International Journal of Electronic Commerce*, *13*(3), 95–118. doi:10.2753/JEC1086-4415130304

van Barneveld, A., Arnold, K. E., & Campbell, J. P. (2012). *Analytics in higher education: Establishing a common language*. EDUCAUSE Learning Initiative.

Van Camp, N. (2012). Heidegger and the question concerning biotechnology. *Journal of Philosophy of Life*, *2*(1), 32–54.

van den Hoven, J., & Lokhorst, G.-J. (2002). Deontic logic and computer-supported computer ethics. *Metaphilosophy*, *33*(3), 376–386. doi:10.1111/1467-9973.00233

van Gelder, A., Ross, K. A., & Schlipf, J. S. (1991). The well-founded semantics for general logic programs. *Journal of the ACM*, *38*(3), 620–650. doi:10.1145/116825.116838

Vedder, A. H., & Klaming, L. (2010). Human enhancement for the common good: Using neurotechnologies to improve eyewitness memory. *American Journal of Bioethics Neuroscience*, *1*(3), 22–33.

Verbeek, P.-P. (2006). Materializing Morality: Design Ethics and Technological Mediation. *Science, Technology & Human Values*, *31*(3), 361–380. doi:10.1177/0162243905285847

Verbeek, P.-P. (2009). Cultivating Humanity: toward a non-humanist ethics of technology. In J. K. B. Olsen, E. Selinger, & S. Riis (Eds.), *New Waves in Philosophy of Technology* (pp. 241–263). Basingstoke, UK: Palgrave Macmillan.

Veruggio, G. (2010). Roboethics. *IEEE Robotics & Automation Magazine*, *17*(2), 105–109. doi:10.1109/MRA.2010.936959

Vitale, C. (2011). Guide to Reading Deleuze's The Movement-Image, Part I: The Deleuzian Notion of the Image, or Worldslicing as Cinema Beyond the Human. *networkologies*. Retrieved from http://networkologies.wordpress.com/2011/04/04/the-deleuzian-notion-of-the-image-a-slice-of-the-world-or-cinema-beyond-the-human/

von Bertalanffy, L. (1950). An Outline of General System Theory. *The British Journal for the Philosophy of Science*, *1*(2), 134–165. http://www.isnature.org/Events/2009/Summer/r/Bertalanffy1950-GST_Outline_SELECT.pdf doi:10.1093/bjps/I.2.134

Waelbers, K. (2009). Technological delegation: Responsibility for the unintended. *Science and Engineering Ethics*, *15*(1), 51–68. doi:10.1007/s11948-008-9098-x PMID:18937053

Walborn, S., Terra Cunha, M., Pádua, S., & Monken, C. (2002). Double-slit quantum eraser. *Physical Review A.*, *65*(3), 033818. http://grad.physics.sunysb.edu/~amarch/Walborn.pdf doi:10.1103/PhysRevA.65.033818

Wallace, W., Allen, C., & Smit, I. (2008). Machine morality: Bottoms-up and top-down approaches for modelling human moral faculties. *Ethics and Artificial Agents: Special Issue of AI & Society*, *22*(4), 565–582.

Wallach, W., & Allen, C. (2008). *Moral machines: Teaching robots right from wrong.* Oxford: Oxford University Press.

Wallach, W., & Allen, C. (2009). *Moral Machines: Teaching Robots Right from Wrong.* Oxford: Oxford University Press. doi:10.1093/acprof:oso/9780195374049.001.0001

Wallance, W., & Allen, C. (2006). EthicALife: A new field of inquiry. Paper presented at the *AnAlifeX workshop*, USA.

Walton, K. L. (1990). *Mimesis as Make-believe: On the Foundations of the Representational Arts.* Cambridge, MA: Harvard University Press.

Warwick, K. & Battistella, C. (2008). Four weddings and a funeral: Ethical issues surrounding the future of brain computer interfacing. *Rivista di filosofia fondata da Vittorio Sainati, 51(3)*, 176-195.

Warwick, K. (2004). Cyborg morals, cyborg values, cyborg ethics. *Ethics and Information Technology, 5*(3), 131–137. doi:10.1023/B:ETIN.0000006870.65865.cf

Warwick, K., & Ruiz, V. (2008). On linking human and machine brains. *Neurocomputing, 71*(13/15), 2619–2624. doi:10.1016/j.neucom.2007.06.017

Wertheim, M. (1999). The Pearly Gates of Cyberspace: A History of Space from Dante to the Internet. New York: W.W. Norton.

Wheeler, J. A. (1990). Information, physics, quantum: The search for links. In W. Zurek, Complexity, Entropy, and the Physics of Information. Redwood City, California: Addison-Wesley.

White, D. J. (2004, July). Danish wind: Too good to be true? *The Utilities Journal.* 37-39

Whitehead, A. N., & Russell, B. (1913). Principia Mathematica (three volumes). Cambridge, UK: Cambridge University Press. Retrieved from http://ia700402.us.archive.org/28/items/cu31924001575244/cu31924001575244.pdf

White, J. B. (2010). Understanding and augmenting human morality: An introduction to the ACTWith model of conscience. *Studies in Computational Intelligence, 314*, 607–621.

Whitten, L. S., Clarksville, T., Sanders, A. R., & Stewart, J. G. (2013). Degree Compass: The preferred choice approach. *Journal of Academic Administration in Higher Education, 9*(2), 39–43.

Wiegel, V. (2007). *SophoLab; Experimental Computational Philosophy* (Doctoral dissertation). Delft University of Technology, The Netherlands.

Williams, B. (1973). *Problems of the self.* Cambridge, UK: Cambridge University Press. doi:10.1017/CBO9780511621253

Williams, B. (1981). *Moral luck: philosophical papers 1973-1980.* Cambridge: Cambridge University Press. doi:10.1017/CBO9781139165860

Willis, III, J. E. & Pistilli, M. D. (2014, April 7). Ethical discourse: Guiding the future of learning analytics. *EDUCAUSE Review Online.*

Willis, III, J. E., Campbell, J. P., & Pistilli, M. D. (2013, May 6). Ethics, big data, and analytics: A model for application. *EDUCAUSE Review Online.*

Willis, J. E., III. (2013, July 5). MOOCs as a worldwide neocolonial force: A reflection on MIT's Learning International Networks Consortium (LINC) Conference. *Reflections on Teaching and Learning, Purdue University.* Retrieved from https://www.purdue.edu/learning/blog/?p=6258

Willis, E. M., & Raines, P. (2001). Technology in secondary education: Integration, implications, and ethics for the changing roles of teachers. *T.H.E. Journal, 29*(2), 54–64.

Winikoff, M. (2007). Implementing commitment-based interactions. In *Proceedings of the Sixth International Joint Conference on Autonomous Agents and Multiagent Systems* (pp. 868–875).

Wolf, F. A. (2000). *Mind into Matter: A New Alchemy of Science and Spirit.* Needham, MA: Moment Point Press.

Wolfram, S. (2002). A New Kind of Science. Champaign, IL: Wolfram Media.

Wolfram, S. (2002). *A New Kind of Science.* Champaign, IL: Wolfram Media.

Wolpe, P. R. (2002). Treatment, enhancement, and the ethics of neurotherapeutics. *Brain and Cognition, 50*(3), 387–395. doi:10.1016/S0278-2626(02)00534-1 PMID:12480485

Wong, W. W. S. (2013). *Emerging Military Technologies: A Guide to the Issues Praeger Security International.* Santa Barbara: Praeger.

Wood, A. (2011). Humanity as an End in Itself. In On What Matters, Volume 2. Oxford, UK: Oxford University Press, (pp. 58-82).

Woodall, J. (2007). Programmed dissatisfaction: Does one gene drive all progress in science and the arts? *Scientist (Philadelphia, Pa.), 2*(3), 251–264.

Wooldridge, M., & Jennings, N. R. (1999). The cooperative problem-solving process. *Journal of Logic and Computation, 9*(4), 563–592. doi:10.1093/logcom/9.4.563

World Health Organization. (2013). *Road traffic injuries*. Retrieved from http://www.who.int/mediacentre/factsheets/fs358/en/

Yampolskiy, R. V. (2013). Attempts to attribute moral agency to intelligent machines are misguided. Proceedings of *Annual Meeting of the International Association for Computing and Philosophy*, University of Maryland at College Park, MD.

Young, M., Daniels, H., Balarin, M., & Lowe, J. (Eds.). (2012). *Educating for the knowledge economy? Critical perspectives*. New York: Routledge.

Yuan, L., & Powell, S. (2013). MOOCs and open education: Implications for higher education. JISC CETIS: Centre for Educational Technology & Interoperability Standards, white paper, 1-21.

Yudkowsky, E. (2008). Aritifical intelligence as a positive and negative factor in global risk. In N. Bostrom & M. M. Cirkovic (Eds.), *Global catastrophic risks* (pp. 308–345). Oxford: Oxford University Press.

Zeilinger, A. (1996). On the Interpretation and Philosophical Foundation of Quantum Mechanics. In U. Ketvel, et al. (Eds.), Vastakohtien todellisuus. Helsinki, Finland: Helsinki University Press; Retrieved from https://vcq.quantum.at/fileadmin/Publications/1996-03.pdf

Zettler, P. J. (2009). Is it cheating to use cheetahs?: The implications of technologically innovative prostheses for sport values and rules. *Boston University International Law Journal, 27*(2), 367–409.

Zuboff, S. (1985). Automate/Informate: The Two Faces of Intelligent Technology. *Organizational Dynamics, 14*(2), 5–18. doi:10.1016/0090-2616(85)90033-6

About the Contributors

Jeffrey White received his Ph.D. in Philosophy from the University of Missouri-Columbia in 2006 with a dissertation titled: "Conscience: Toward the mechanism of morality". He also earned his MA in Philosophy and MS in Chemistry from Cleveland State University in 2001. Since 2010, Dr. White has served as a Lecturer at KAIST. His past experience includes Research/Teaching assistant at the University of Missouri-Columbia, Teaching/Graduate assistant at Cleveland State University, and Lab technician/assistant at Bowling Green State University. Dr. White has numerous publications and has presented and participated in various conferences throughout his professional career.

Rick Searle is an educator and freelance writer who explores the intersection of science, technology, philosophy and politics. He is an affiliate scholar with the Institute for the Ethics of Emerging Technology and is a frequent writer for the IEET website. He also blogs at utopiaordystopia.com.

***

Kenji Araki, born in 1959 in Otaru, Japan. He received B.E., M.E. and Ph.D. degrees in electronics engineering from Hokkaido University, Sapporo, Japan in 1982, 1985, and 1988, respectively. In April 1988, he joined Hokkai Gakuen University, Sapporo, Japan. He was a professor of Hokkai Gakuen University. He joined Hokkaido University in 1998 as an associate professor of the Division of Electronics and Information Engineering. He was a professor of the Division of Electronics and Information Engineering of Hokkaido University from 2002. Now he is a professor of the Division of Media and Network Technologies of Hokkaido University. His research interests include Natural Language Processing, Spoken Dialogue Processing, Machine Translation and Language Acquisition. He is a member of the AAAI, IEEE, JSAI, IPSJ, IEICE and JCSS.

Chris Bateman is a game designer, outsider philosopher, and author, who has worked on over forty game projects. In 2013 he became the first person to attain a doctorate in the aesthetics of play, via a PhD by Publication. He is currently pursuing research exploring phenomenological and neurobiological distinctions between different play styles and preferences, and recently completed a trilogy of books exploring the philosophy of imagination. The first book, *Imaginary Games* (published in 2011) examines imagination in games and art, asking if games can be art or whether all art is a kind of game. The second, *The Mythology of Evolution* (published the following year) explores the role of imagination in the sciences, asking if it possible to present the story of life without distorting it. The final book, *Chaos Ethics* (published in 2014), explores the role of imagination in morality, and defends a conception of moral chaos.

Fernando da Costa Cardoso is Posdoc at NOVA Laboratory for Computer Science and Informatics in the Universidade Nova de Lisboa with a grant from CNPQ/Brazil. He holds a Ph.D. in philosophy from UFRJ/Brazil and his main interests are in Ethical theory and Psychology and in Moral Machines and Artificial Morality. Currently he is working in a book about Moral Luck and in a Introduction to Artificial Morality.

Jai Galliott is a Researcher at Macquarie University in Sydney, Australia. His work focuses on the ethics of military robotics and, in particular, their effect on the laws of war. He is Lead Editor of Ashgate's Emerging Technologies, Ethics and International Affairs series and has published widely on the role of emerging technologies and their role in society. He is author of three forthcoming books, including Unmanned Systems: Mapping the Moral Landscape, Super Soldiers: The Ethical, Legal and Social Implications and Commercial Space Exploration: Ethics, Policy and Governance.

Jared Gassen holds a master's degree in Journalism from the University of Missouri-Columbia. He created JMG Advising to help students, authors, and small businesses with writing and editing. His website is www.jmgadvising.com.

Aleksandar Malečić is a graduate electrical engineer from Pančevo, Serbia. His profession after graduation is biomedical engineering. He is also a PhD student in Niš interested in renewable energy (wind and transition from non-renewable to renewable energy). Outside of engineering, he has a master degree in management. His curiosity about Carl Jung's approach to depth psychology does not belong to his formal education, but it affects his outlook and approach to work and writing. In a way all these aforementioned issues are about interactions (dynamics rather than parts) between humans and machines (human-human, machine-machine, or machine-machine) and their accompanying challenges (How can these interactions emerge and unfold?) and ethics.

Luís Moniz Pereira, born in 1947 in Lisbon, is Professor Emeritus of Computer Science and was Director of CENTRIA, the AI centre at Universidade Nova de Lisboa (1993- 2008) , being at present a researcher at at NOVA Laboratory for Computer Science. Doctor honoris causa by T.U. Dresden (2006), and elected ECCAI Fellow (2001), he launched and coordinated the Erasmus Mundus European MSc in Computational Logic at UNL (2004-2008), and belongs to both the Board of Trustees and to the Scientific Advisory Board of IMDEA – the Madrid Advanced Studies Institute (Software). His research interests centre on Knowledge Representation and Reasoning, Logic Programming, and the Cognitive Sciences. He was the founding president of the Portuguese AI association, and a founding member of the editorial boards of: J. Logic Programming, J. Automated Reasoning, New Generation Computing, Theory and Practice of Logic Programming, J. Universal Computer Science, J. Applied Logic, Electronic Transactions on AI, Computational Logic Newsletter, Intl. J. Reasoning-Based Intelligent Systems (Advisory-Editor), member of Logic Journal of the IGPL, and has been the Associate Editor for Artificial Intelligence of the ACM Computing Surveys. For more information see: http://centria.fct.unl.pt/~lmp/.

Rafal Rzepka, born in Szczecin, Poland, received M.A. from Adam Mickiewicz University in Poznan, Poland in 1999 and Ph.D. from Hokkaido University, Japan in 2004. Currently he is an assistant professor at the Graduate School of Information Science and Technology, Hokkaido University. His research interests are Common Sense Acquisition, Affective Processing and Machine Ethics. He is a member of AAAI, ACL, IPSJ, IEICE, JCSS and ANLP.

Ari Saptawijaya received his Master in Computer Science from Technische Universität Dresden in 2004. Since 2006 he has been a lecturer at the Faculty of Computer Science, Universitas Indonesia. He is currently a PhD student at NOVA Laboratory for Computer Science and Informatics (NOVA LINCS), Universidade Nova de Lisboa, Portugal. His research interests include knowledge representation and reasoning and computational logic.

Nak Young Seong is very interested in Physics and Chemistry and has studied in those fields for a long time. Seong believes that every science is based on common sense and that everyone can understand science very easily with common sense. So he works to increase others' understanding with common sense.

Viktoria Strunk earned her Ed.D. from Spalding University, specializing in Leadership Education. Her dissertation was a critical appraisal of the utility of rubrics in post-secondary writing courses. She has experience teaching writing courses, ethics, and sociology amongst other topics. Her research examines the state of educational delivery along with the ethical implications involved in teaching traditional, nontraditional, and ultra-nontraditional students.

Melanie Swan is a philosopher of information, technology, and science. She has an MBA from the Wharton School of the University of Pennsylvania, a BA from Georgetown University, and is currently a Contemporary Philosophy graduate student at Kingston University London and Université Paris 8. She is a faculty member at Singularity University, an Affiliate Scholar of the Institute for Ethics and Emerging Technology, an Advisor to the Foundational Questions Institute (FQXi), and an invited contributor to the Edge's Annual Essay Question. Ms. Swan founded the Institute for Blockchain Studies in 2014, and the citizen science organization DIYgenomics in 2010. Recent publications and research interests include an ethics of perception of nanocognition; the philosophy of big data; the ideology of the biocitizen and the quantified self; the future of personal identity; and the case for cognitive enhancement.

Ben Tran received his Doctor of Psychology (Psy.D) in Organizational Consulting/Organizational Psychology from California School of Professional Psychology at Alliant International University in San Francisco, California, United States of America. Dr. Tran's research interests include domestic and expatriate recruitment, selection, retention, evaluation, & training, CSR, business and organizational ethics, organizational/international organizational behavior, knowledge management, and minorities in multinational corporations. Dr. Tran has presented articles on topics of business and management ethics, expatriate, and gender and minorities in multinational corporations at the Academy of Management, Society for the Advancement of Management, and International Standing Conference on Organizational Symbolism. Dr. Tran has also published articles and book chapters with the Social Responsibility Journal, Journal of International Trade Law and Policy, Journal of Economics, Finance and Administrative Science, Financial Management Institute of Canada, and IGI Global. Dr. Tran can be reach at tranconsulting@gmail.com.

James E. Willis, III is a research associate in the Center for Research on Learning and Technology in the School of Education at Indiana University. He was previously an educational assessment specialist in the Office of Institutional Research, Assessment, and Effectiveness at Purdue University. James is responsible for evaluating the impact of educational technology like digital badges on student learning, assessing learning analytics, and critically examining pedagogical theories. His recent research and publications include work on the ethics of learning analytics, the intersection of automated technology and its potential ethical implications, and the future of educational technology. James has presented on the futurity of massive open online courses through the lens of Foucault's heterotopia at MIT, published in EDUCAUSE Review Online, and participated in various assessment projects within the CIC. His previous experience includes collegiate administration, teaching ethics and comparative religions in traditional and online modalities, and educational research in improving student outcomes. His previous research includes topics from several fields including Buddhist philosophy, French post-structuralism, medieval apophaticism, pedagogy in videoconferencing, and improving success rates for first-generation and low-income students through predictive analytics. Educated in theology, philosophy, and comparative religion, James holds a Ph.D. from King's College London, an M.Litt. from the University of St. Andrews in Scotland, and a B.A. from Roanoke College in Virginia.

Index

Information Resources Management Association

Become an IRMA Member

Members of the **Information Resources Management Association (IRMA)** understand the importance of community within their field of study. The Information Resources Management Association is an ideal venue through which professionals, students, and academicians can convene and share the latest industry innovations and scholarly research that is changing the field of information science and technology. Become a member today and enjoy the benefits of membership as well as the opportunity to collaborate and network with fellow experts in the field.

IRMA Membership Benefits:

- **One FREE Journal Subscription**

- **30% Off Additional Journal Subscriptions**

- **20% Off Book Purchases**

- Updates on the latest events and research on Information Resources Management through the IRMA-L listserv.

- Updates on new open access and downloadable content added to Research IRM.

- A copy of the Information Technology Management Newsletter twice a year.

- A certificate of membership.

IRMA Membership $195

Scan code to visit irma-international.org and begin by selecting your free journal subscription.

Membership is good for one full year.

Printed in the United States
By Bookmasters